5 APA, CMS, CSE, and CGOS Documentation

6 Designing and Presenting Information

7 Writing in Digital Spaces

8 Making Choices about Style

9 Understanding and Revising Sentences

10 Punctuating with Purpose

11 Understanding Mechanics

12 Grammar for Multilingual Writers

Writing: A Manual for the Digital Age, Brief Edition

David Blakesley
Purdue University

Jeffrey L. Hoogeveen
Lincoln University

Australia • Brazil • Japan • Korea • Mexico • Singapore • Spain • United Kingdom • United States

Writing: A Manual for the Digital Age, Brief Edition
David Blakesley/Jeffrey L. Hoogeveen

Editor in Chief: PJ Boardman

Publisher: Lyn Uhl

Acquisitions Editor: Star MacKenzie Burruto

Development Editor: Leslie Taggart

Managing Development Editor: Karen Judd

Assistant Editor: Cheryl Forman

Editorial Assistant: Megan Garvey

Senior Technology Project Manager: Joe Gallagher

Managing Marketing Manager: Mandee Eckersley

Senior Marketing Communications Manager: Stacey Purviance

Signing Representative: Ron Shelly

Senior Project Manager, Editorial Production: Samantha Ross, Lianne Ames

Senior Art Director: Cate Rickard Barr

Senior Print Buyer: Mary Beth Hennebury

Permissions Manager: Ron Montgomery

Text Permissions Researcher: Marcy Lunetta

Production Service: Lifland et al., Bookmakers

Text Designer: Linda Beaupré, Stone House Art

Photo Manager: Sheri Blaney

Photo Researcher: Francelle Carapetyan

Cover Designer: Bill Reuter, Reuter Design

Cover Printer: Phoenix Color

Compositor: Graphic World

Library of Congress Control Number: 2006937515

ISBN-13: 978-1-4282-9032-7 (paperbound) ISBN-10: 1-4282-9032-X (paperbound)
ISBN-13: 978-1-4282-9031-0 (casebound) ISBN-10: 1-4282-9031-1 (casebound)
ISBN-13: 978-0-4959-0065-8 (looseleaf) ISBN-10: 0-4959-0065-6 (looseleaf)

Wadsworth
20 Channel Center Street
Boston, MA 02210
USA

Cengage Learning is a leading provider of customized learning solutions with office locations around the globe, including Singapore, the United Kingdom, Australia, Mexico, Brazil, and Japan. Locate your local office at: **international.cengage.com/region**

Cengage Learning products are represented in Canada by Nelson Education, Ltd.

For your course and learning solutions, visit **academic.cengage.com**

Purchase any of our products at your local college store or at our preferred online store **www.ichapters.com**

Credits appear on pages C1–C4, which constitute a continuation of the copyright page.

Printed in the United States of America
1 2 3 4 5 6 7 12 11 10 09

Project Checklists

Project Checklists throughout the handbook are designed to help you to plan, write, organize, revise, and research your writing projects, whether they are in print, online, presented orally, or multimedia.

Technology Toolboxes throughout the handbook give specific step-by-step directions for using software to complete writing, research, design, and communication tasks.

Preface

At the heart of *Writing: A Manual for the Digital Age, Brief Edition* is our belief that rhetorical principles are flexible and powerful enough to teach writers how to write effectively in any context or medium. Contexts change from moment to moment, but the study of rhetorical principles helps students learn how to gauge situations and formulate effective responses to them by asking and answering questions about contexts, texts, purposes, and readers. The principles of rhetoric—as their endurance and appeal across time and place suggest—*are* transferable. They stick. They make as much sense today as they did a couple of thousand years ago. They expand a writer's capacity for responding to new situations with confidence and eloquence.

See page 3.

Writing in the Digital Age

Our digital age poses tremendous opportunities and problems for every writer and reader. We are excited by the rapid emergence in the past twenty years or so of new forms of electronic communication and literacy. One major goal of this handbook is to show students how to adapt the new tools of technology to support their writing across a broad range of situations in college and beyond. Throughout the book, Technology Toolboxes show students how to use software to accomplish rhetorical goals. We do much more than simply recommend that students "save a backup copy" or "add a visual to enhance a presentation." We show students how to accomplish such tasks and provide our explanations not as prescriptive rules, but as the result of the kind of rhetorical questioning that ought to guide any pragmatic or creative use of technology. You will find that, for us, writing and reading happen in print *and* online. It's no longer the case that printed text is the ur-form, the primary medium or interface for literate activity. This is not to say that it is secondary, either. Awareness of the multiple contexts for reading and writing is sifted finely with our discussions of rhetorical principles, with print and digital forms each playing their important roles.

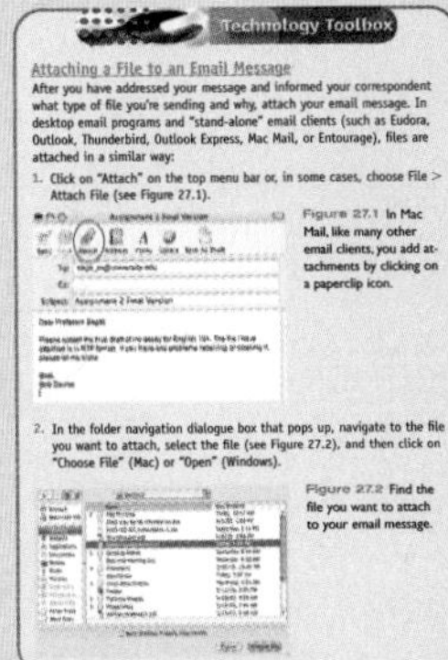

Technology Toolbox

Attaching a File to an Email Message

After you have addressed your message and informed your correspondent what type of file you're sending and why, attach your email message. In desktop email programs and "stand-alone" email clients (such as Eudora, Outlook, Thunderbird, Outlook Express, Mac Mail, or Entourage), files are attached in a similar way:

1. Click on "Attach" on the top menu bar or, in some cases, choose File > Attach File (see Figure 27.1).

Figure 27.1 In Mac Mail, like many other email clients, you add attachments by clicking on a paperclip icon.

2. In the folder navigation dialogue box that pops up, navigate to the file you want to attach, select the file (see Figure 27.2), and then click on "Choose File" (Mac) or "Open" (Windows).

Figure 27.2 Find the file you want to attach to your email message.

See page 338.

Information Architecture and Design

Reading habits have changed, partly as a response to the influx of information for the eyes to take in at a glance, in print and on screen. A writing handbook, especially, ought to take this change into account, and not simply for fashion's sake. *How* information is presented may be as important for learning as *what* is presented. Information architecture—the visual display of information to foster

See page 73.

Audience	General Purpose	Specific Purpose
People who hold views different from yours	To persuade people to change an attitude or behavior. Changing someone's attitude is possible only when knowledge is uncertain and there are multiple perspectives.	• To change people's minds and attitudes • To solve problems • To resolve conflict • To build consensus • To create community
People who share your view	To reinforce shared convictions. When people already agree, the purpose of argument may be to turn that agreement into action—for example, working to support a cause. In college classes, you typically won't argue issues on which your readers already agree. Instead, find the basis for disagreement on a subject, and build an argument from there.	• To reinforce belief • To move people toward commitment and action • To foster identification (see page 191)
People who wish to understand multiple views	To inquire into the shades of meaning in a subject so that you can open it up to reflection and reconsideration. It is often necessary to demonstrate that a subject lends itself to multiple perspectives. Help your audience understand that the subject is more complex than they had imagined.	• To open up a topic for discussion, debate, and further inquiry • To question common knowledge • To stimulate further research

See page 76.

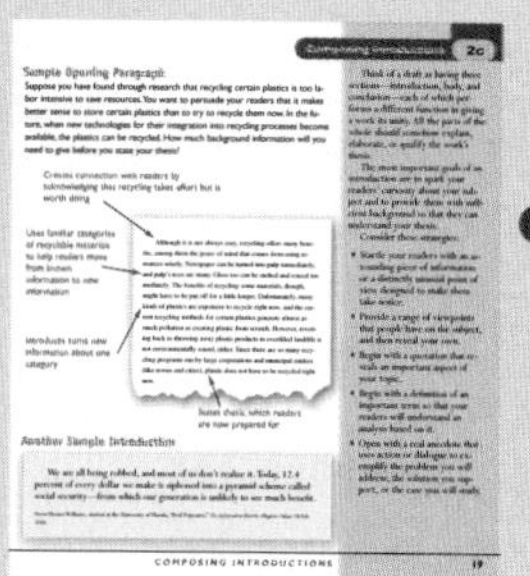

Composing Introductions 2c

Sample Opening Paragraph

Suppose you have found through research that recycling certain plastics is too labor intensive to save resources. You want to persuade your readers that it makes better sense to store certain plastics than to try to recycle them now. In the future, when new technologies for their integration into recycling processes become available, the plastics can be recycled. How much background information will you need to give before you state your thesis?

Another Sample Introduction

We are all being robbed, and most of us don't realize it. Today, 12.4 percent of every dollar we make is siphoned into a pyramid scheme called social security—from which our generation is unlikely to see much benefit.

Think of a draft as having three sections—introduction, body, and conclusion—each of which performs a different function in giving a work its unity.

Consider these strategies:

COMPOSING INTRODUCTIONS 19

See page 19.

learning—has been an overriding concern throughout the development of this book.

Handbooks especially need to communicate information efficiently, over time, and in a sufficiently interesting manner to encourage students to read, reread, and learn. The design of the book reflects these purposes. Visual content not only attracts the eye but also communicates information concisely and quickly. Readers remember challenging concepts more readily when they associate them with visual content, spatial location on the page, and even color. In classical terms, the visual display of information has mnemonic qualities, helping readers recall previous learning. So in the inner columns throughout the handbook, you will find a wide range of visual and verbal content, cast in ways that invite the attention, teaching core principles and providing concise guidelines for writing and reading. We also place real student writing in this spotlight because, in the end, it is students' work that matters most and that speaks most eloquently to other students.

At the same time, there are finer distinctions to be made, definitions to be learned, and a broader context to be considered. The verbal content in the outside margins throughout the book glosses and extends what you read and see in the inner columns. In many respects, the content of these outer columns is much like what you would find in any good handbook with rhetoric at its core. At the same time, we have composed that running narrative in concert with the content of the inner columns. The illustrations, for example, are not secondary, nor are they the whole story. Instead, the two columns work together on the page. In an age when much of our reading is, by necessity, composed of glosses, chunks, blocks, and images, this book's information architecture is coherent, organizing ideas in ways that make it easier for students to learn to write well and for instructors to show them how.

Visual Rhetoric

The information age, as we have suggested, has given way to a visual age. In introductory composition courses across the country, students still need to understand how to write effectively in traditional printed forms. Increasingly, they are also being asked to integrate their words into the flow of visual information that now surrounds all of us.

It is vitally important that writers appreciate the power of images to inform, persuade, and move. At the same time, as readers, they need to understand how images communicate meaning so that they can interpret them and, thus, respond critically.

As a field, rhetoric and composition has made good progress in explaining how to analyze images—including the display of visual information—in print and on the Web. We have struggled to find ways to teach writers how to create visual content, design it, and integrate it with their writing to create rich and persuasive texts.

Take inventory of your skills, experiences, and goals.
Find and analyze job ads. In your search, learn about and use various Web-based resources for job seekers, and ultimately select one job to pursue.
Write a resume suitable for such a position.
Compose a cover letter that identifies your reasons for applying and highlights your qualifications.

See page 88.

As we have mentioned, the visual design of the handbook stands as an example in its own right. We have included, as well, chapters on the use of visual content to inform and persuade, ways to interpret and write about visual content, and how to make documents for print and the Web that meet these rhetorical goals. We show how images function as arguments and even how graphic design can enhance and structure information so that it can be understood and believed.

Unique Features of *Writing: A Manual for the Digital Age, Brief Edition*

Writing instructors across a broad range of courses and college settings will find a wealth of features to help them achieve course outcomes; make the teaching of writing more effective, if not any easier; and instill in writers the rhetorical fluency that will serve them well in college and beyond.

Project Checklists

Most chapters contain clipboards with checklists that help writers ask detailed questions about the rhetorical situation or the aspect of writing or reading that is the focus of the chapter. The questions reinforce key principles as they provide students with additional means of inventing, elaborating, and evaluating content. See page v for a complete list of topics.

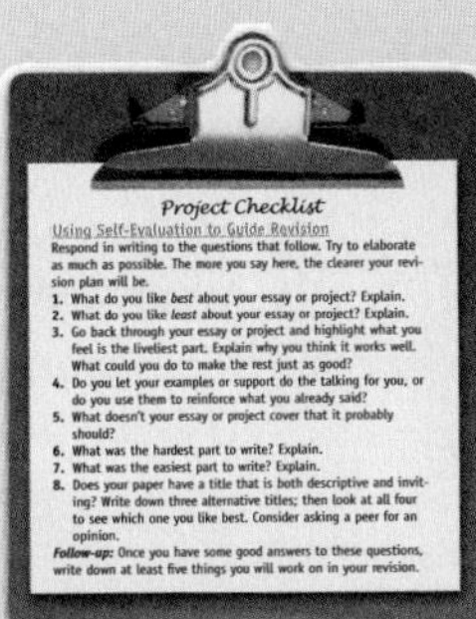

Project Checklist

Using Self-Evaluation to Guide Revision

Respond in writing to the questions that follow. Try to elaborate as much as possible. The more you say here, the clearer your revision plan will be.

1. What do you like *best* about your essay or project? Explain.
2. What do you like *least* about your essay or project? Explain.
3. Go back through your essay or project and highlight what you feel is the liveliest part. Explain why you think it works well. What could you do to make the rest just as good?
4. Do you let your examples or support do the talking for you, or do you use them to reinforce what you already said?
5. What doesn't your essay or project cover that it probably should?
6. What was the hardest part to write? Explain.
7. What was the easiest part to write? Explain.
8. Does your paper have a title that is both descriptive and inviting? Write down three alternative titles; then look at all four to see which one you like best. Consider asking a peer for an opinion.

Follow-up: Once you have some good answers to these questions, write down at least five things you will work on in your revision.

See page 31.

Technology Toolboxes

The overriding concern in the Technology Toolboxes has been to show students how to use software and hardware to accomplish their writing goals and how new tools can help them manage some of the challenges posed by computers, websites, and competing user interfaces across browsers, platforms, and software. We have created all of the screenshots ourselves and have run each through careful usability tests, conscious that people choose different operating systems and software to perform similar tasks, even down to the number of buttons they prefer on a mouse. We have also been careful to include suggestions for using nonproprietary and open source

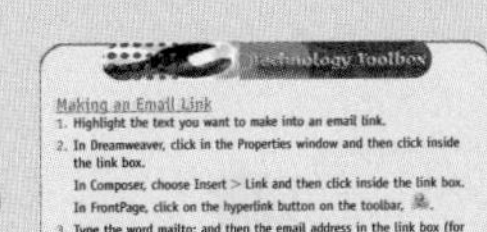

Technology Toolbox

Making an Email Link

1. Highlight the text you want to make into an email link.
2. In Dreamweaver, click in the Properties window and then click inside the link box.
   In Composer, choose Insert > Link and then click inside the link box.
   In FrontPage, click on the hyperlink button on the toolbar, .
3. Type the word mailto: and then the email address in the link box (for example, mailto:user@somewhere.edu).
4. Click OK.
5. Test the link in your browser.

See page 368.

software, some of which will perform writing and design tasks as well as or better than more expensive counterparts. See page vi for a complete list of topics.

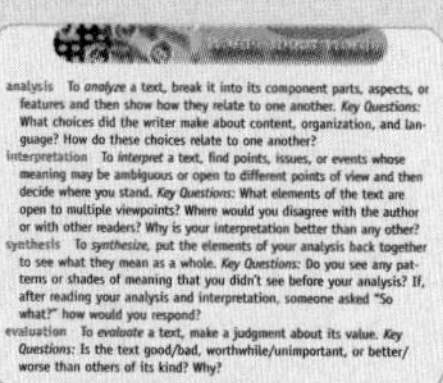
analysis To *analyze* a text, break it into its component parts, aspects, or features and then show how they relate to one another. *Key Questions:* What choices did the writer make about content, organization, and language? How do these choices relate to one another?
interpretation To *interpret* a text, find points, issues, or events whose meaning may be ambiguous or open to different points of view and then decide where you stand. *Key Questions:* What elements of the text are open to multiple viewpoints? Where would you disagree with the author or with other readers? Why is your interpretation better than any other?
synthesis To *synthesize*, put the elements of your analysis back together to see what they mean as a whole. *Key Questions:* Do you see any patterns or shades of meaning that you didn't see before your analysis? If, after reading your analysis and interpretation, someone asked "So what?" how would you respond?
evaluation To *evaluate* a text, make a judgment about its value. *Key Questions:* Is the text good/bad, worthwhile/unimportant, or better/worse than others of its kind? Why?

See page 53.

Words about Words

There are moments when we must pause to provide a nuanced explanation of how we are defining key terminology. For example, first-year students may not grasp the distinctions among analysis, interpretation, and evaluation. Multilingual writers may find the explicit definitions and comparisons in the Words about Words boxes particularly useful.

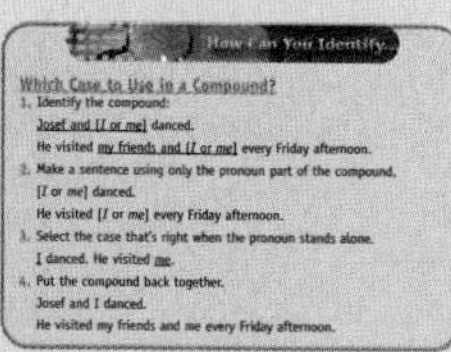
How Can You Identify...

Which Case to Use in a Compound?
1. Identify the compound:
   Josef and [*I* or *me*] danced.
   He visited my friends and [*I* or *me*] every Friday afternoon.
2. Make a sentence using only the pronoun part of the compound.
   [*I* or *me*] danced.
   He visited [*I* or *me*] every Friday afternoon.
3. Select the case that's right when the pronoun stands alone.
   I danced. He visited me.
4. Put the compound back together.
   Josef and I danced.
   He visited my friends and me every Friday afternoon.

See page 437.

How Can You Identify . . .

By pointing out such features as the parts of a URL, How Can You Identify . . . boxes help students with their research. How Can You Identify . . . boxes are also provided throughout the style and grammar chapters to help students locate certain sentence elements.

New Contexts for Writing: Civic Action

See page 332.

New Contexts for Writing

At the beginning of each part is a one-page presentation of a new context for writing. Our aim is to show students just a few of the new and interesting situations that may move them to write. Some of these contexts, such as weblogs and podcasts, are digital, but others suggest how writing functions in collaboration, civic action, volunteerism, gaming, and the creation of image-rich texts like comic books. Each part opener defines new terminology and suggests resources for additional inquiry.

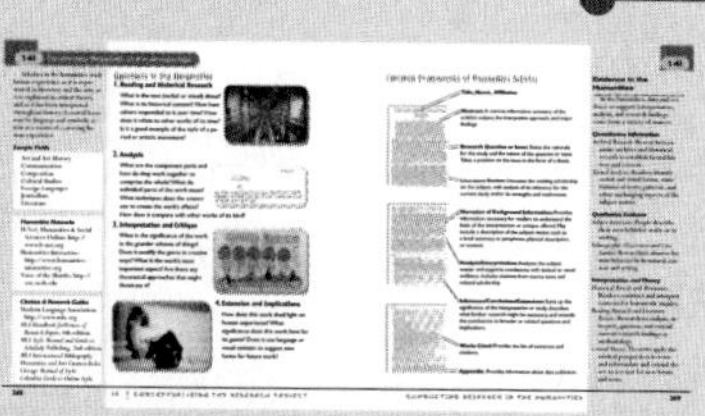

See pages 110–111.

Disciplinary Spreads

The disciplinary spreads in Chapter 9, Conceptualizing the Research Project, are two-page discussions and illustrations of key principles and methodologies in different fields of study. We start at the most general level, with one spread each on the humanities, the social sciences, and the sciences. Our goal is not to capture all the complexity of a discipline but to give students and instructors some insight into how specialists in a discipline think about their subject matter, what evidence they value, and what sorts of subjects they find interesting. An additional six example spreads—two in each of the broader disciplines—show students more specifically what writers and researchers do in the representative fields of film studies and history (the humanities), psychology and sociology (the social sciences), and biology and astronomy (the sciences). These snapshots help students understand that writing and rhetoric are not uniformly conceived and applied across fields. Instructors may find them helpful in introducing students to the broad range of intellectual life in college.

The Organization of *Writing: A Manual for the Digital Age, Brief Edition*

Context is the organizing principle that ties all of the parts together. As we move from the general to the particular through the parts, we show how rhetorical principles can help writers make good decisions sensitive to shifting contexts across the curriculum and into digital spaces. Our overriding concern has been to demonstrate that even though the territory may be new to many students—and may sometimes feel like an unexplored wilderness—they can learn to write effectively by always bearing in mind that diligent attention to the rhetorical situation can help them chart their course. Such attention will ensure they are habitually effective writers and aren't successful merely by chance or good luck.

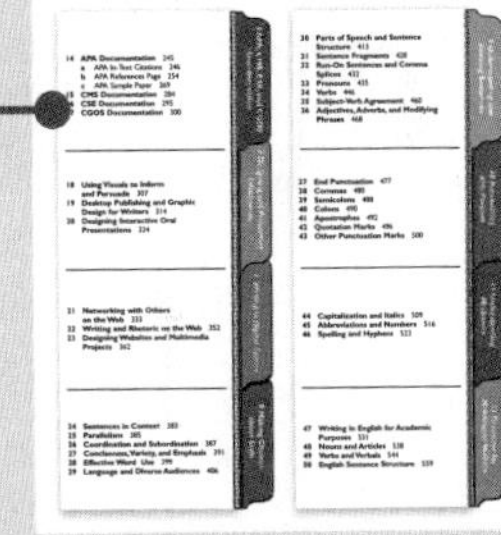

See inside front cover.

Teaching and Learning Resources

Instructor Flex-Files (1-4130-1202-7). Designed to give you maximum flexibility in planning and customizing your course, the Instructor Flex-Files provide an abundance of helpful materials, including sample syllabi, pedagogical questions and solutions, an ESL insert, and more. Part II provides a wealth of resources for instructors interested in incorporating technology into their composition course.

The Writing: A Manual for the Digital Age Workbook (1-4130-1179-9). This printed workbook combines exercises with clear examples and explanations of grammar, usage, and writing to supplement the information and exercises found in the handbook. It also covers technology in Part IV, Make Your Rhetoric Electric.

Technology Tools

You can learn more about these technology tools at **cengage.com/English/Blakesley**

CENGAGENOW™

CengageNOW™ for Blakesley and Hoogeveen's *Writing: A Manual for the Digital Age.* This powerful online teaching and learning tool features reliable solutions for delivering your course content and assignments, along with time-saving ways to grade and provide feedback. **CengageNOW** assists with the most common grading and reporting tasks that instructors perform every day. For students, **CengageNOW** provides an integrated ebook, diagnostic self-assessment, and Personalized Study that enables them to focus on what they need to learn and guides them in selecting activities that best match their learning styles. To package access to **CengageNOW** with every new copy of ***Writing: A Manual for the Digital Age, Brief Edition,*** contact your representative from Wadsworth, a part of Cengage Learning.

English21

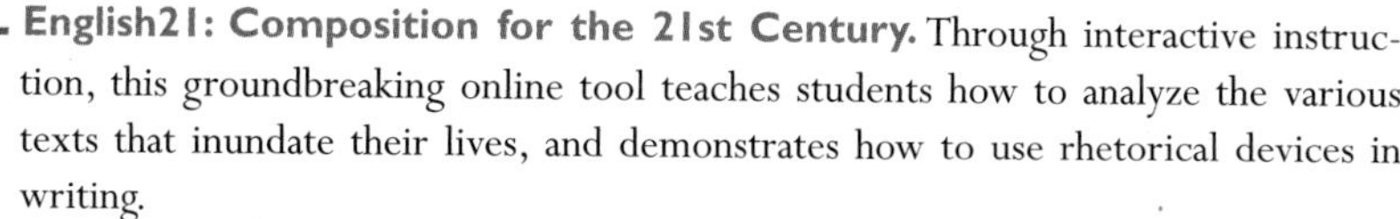

English21: Composition for the 21st Century. Through interactive instruction, this groundbreaking online tool teaches students how to analyze the various texts that inundate their lives, and demonstrates how to use rhetorical devices in writing.

Turnitin™. This proven online plagiarism-prevention software promotes fairness in the classroom by helping students learn to correctly cite sources and allowing instructors to check for originality before reading and grading papers.

Cengage Learning InSite for Writing and Research™. This multi-functional online writing and research tool includes electronic peer review, an originality checker, an assignment library, help with common errors, and access to InfoTrac College Edition. InfoTrac College Edition provides nearly instant access to more than 18 million reliable, full-text articles from 5,000 academic and popular journals.

WriteNote

WriteNote®. This Web-based research and writing tool helps students search for and organize references used in their academic papers, so that they can focus on the content of their research and the presentation of ideas.

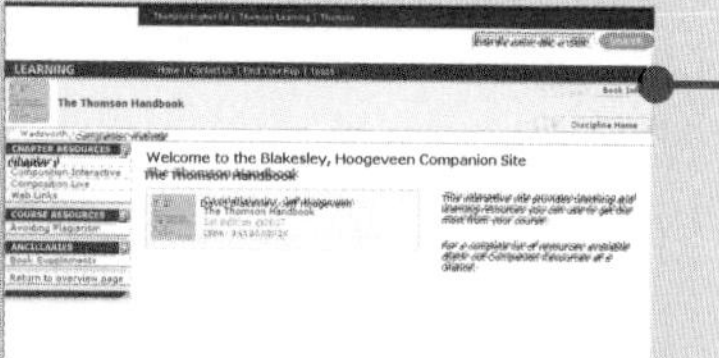

Book Companion Website. This site contains many interactive resources for students, including libraries that offer animated tutorials and information on diction, grammar, mechanics, punctuation, and research, as well as examples of student papers.

Acknowledgments

We have many people to thank for their help in making this book possible. Because it's a book that breaks the mold in many respects, all of them deserve credit for their vision and persistence. We would like to thank Leslie Taggart for her expert stewardship of this project from its inception. Leslie's eagerness to take risks, her willingness to experiment with new forms of presentation, and her patience and perseverance have always been inspiring. The finest qualities of this book are largely due to her expert guidance. We will take all the credit for every instance when it falls short of her high standards.

Michael Rosenberg, Publisher at Wadsworth, a part of Cengage Learning, has likewise supported our work enthusiastically. Dickson Musselwhite helped launch the project and remained an enthusiastic supporter of the project throughout. During production, Samantha Ross kept us on track as our production editor, overseeing all the details of writing, designing, and publishing a comprehensive and innovative handbook—no small feat. Sally Lifland, our project manager, oversaw all of the aspects of copyediting and proofing with the precision and talent that writers can only hope for in their editorial team. Linda Beaupré translated our ideas on information architecture into a beautiful book design, and Bill Reuter created the cover. The team at Graphic World carefully composed the pages and the extensive art program. Our researchers, Sheri Blaney, Francelle Carapetyan, Isabel Alves, and Marcy Lunetta, worked diligently and resourcefully to clear permissions. Karen Judd managed the process of creating a brief version of the handbook, which, because of the tight integration of verbal and visual content, posed considerable challenges. She is the editor of editors and—probably no thanks to us—has retained her great sense of humor. Star MacKenzie Burruto and Mandee Eckersley organized all of our focus groups and workshops, which helped us improve the book significantly.

The many reviewers and focus group participants who have had a hand in shaping this handbook deserve special recognition and thanks. The handbook benefited greatly from reviewers' responses to both the evolving manuscript and the design concept. We thank you for your patient reading and your insightful comments. In meetings with the development team in Miami, Houston, and Chicago, the focus group participants (whose names are indicated with an asterisk in the following list) provided many comments about the scope and sequence and the design of the handbook, which were helpful as we finished our work on this first edition. Thank you for your thoughtful collaboration.

Liz Ann Aguilar, *San Antonio College*
Preston Allen, *Miami Dade–North**
Sarah Arroyo, *University of Texas at Arlington*
Martha Bachman, *Camden Community College*
John Barber, *University of Texas at Dallas*
Bryan Bardine, *University of Dayton*
Papia Bawa, *Purdue University**
Kristina Beckman, *University of Arizona*
Michael Benton, *University of Kentucky*
Emily Biggs, *University of Kentucky*
Samantha Blackmon, *Purdue University*
Jennie Blankert, *Purdue University**
Bradley Bleck, *Spokane Falls Community College**
Anne Bliss, *University of Colorado at Boulder**
Beverley Braud, *Texas State University*
Anthony Campbell, *Eastern Kentucky University*
Geof Carter, *Purdue University**
Melvin Clarkheller, *South Texas Community College**
John Comeau, *Ivy Tech Community College of Indiana at South Bend*
Sean Conrey, *Purdue University**
Jennifer Consilio, *Lewis College**
Linda Coolen, *North Central Texas College**
Romana Cortese, *Montgomery College**
Emily Cosper, *Delgado Community College*
Nancy Cox, *Arkansas Tech University*
Paul Crawford, *Southeastern Louisiana University**
Linda Daigle, *Houston Community College, Central*
Dale Davis, *Northwest Mississippi Community College*
Marcia Dickson, *Ohio State University at Marion*
Carol Dillon, *University of Nebraska at Omaha*
Huiling Ding, *Purdue University**
Shannon Dobranski, *Georgia Institute of Technology*
Keith Dorwick, *University of Louisiana at Lafayette*
Marilyn Douglas-Jones, *Houston Community College*
Rebecca Duncan, *Meredith College*
Dawn Elmore-McCrary, *San Antonio College**
Joshua Everett, *Central Texas College**
James Fenton, *Delgado Community College*
Jane Focht-Hansen, *San Antonio College*
Murray Fortner, *Tarrant County Community College*
Judith Gardner, *University of Texas at San Antonio**
Dianna Gilroy, *Purdue University**
Mary Godwin, *Purdue University**
Anissa Graham, *University of North Alabama**
Andrew Green, *University of Miami**
Magnolia Hampton, *Hinds Community College*
Christopher Harris, *University of Louisiana–Monroe**
Carolyn Harrison, *Oakland Community College*

Betty Hart, *University of Southern Indiana*
Scott Hathaway, *Hudson Valley Community College*
Cynthia Haynes, *Clemson University*
Rebecca Hite, *Southeastern Louisiana University**
Carolyn Ho, *North Harris College*
Megan Hughes, *Purdue University**
Joanna Johnson, *University of Miami**
Rick Johnson-Sheehan, *Purdue University**
Rachel Jordan, *Hudson Valley Community College*
Paul Karpuk, *Central Connecticut State University*
Rick Kemp, *University of Maryland, University College*
Malcolm Kiniry, *Rutgers University*
Jessica Kohl, *Purdue University**
Cindy Konrad, *Purdue University**
Martina Kusi-Mensah, *Montgomery College**
Kathy Lattimore, *State University of New York at Cortland*
Mary Ann Lee, *Longview Community College*
Stephen Leone, *Westchester Community College*
Mia Leonin, *University of Miami*
Robert Leston, *University of Texas at Arlington*
Mike Lohre, *Ohio State University at Marion*
Charlie Lowe, *Grand Valley State University**
Clark Maddux, *Tennessee State University*
Gina Merys Mahaffery, *St. Louis University*
Carolyn Mann, *Morgan State University*
Gina Maranto, *University of Miami*
Rebecca Marez, *Del Mar College*
Mike Matthews, *Central Texas College**
Pat McMahon, *Tallahassee Community College*
Alisa Messer, *City College of San Francisco*
Susan Miller, *Mesa Community College*
Homer Mitchell, *State University of New York at Cortland*
Michael Mizell-Nelson, *Delgado Community College*
Kevin Moberly, *University of Louisiana at Lafayette*
Samantha Morgan-Curtis, *Tennessee State University*
Ed Moritz, *Indiana University–Purdue University at Ft. Wayne*
David Mulry, *Longview Community College**
Marshall Myers, *Eastern Kentucky University*
Mary Anne Nagler, *Oakland Community College*
Kathryn Naylor, *Purdue University**
Sally Nielsen, *Florida Community College at Jacksonville*
Matthew Novak, *California Polytechnic State University*
Carla Nyssen, *California State University at Long Beach*
Melinda Payne, *Houston Community College*

John Pekins, *Tallahassee Community College*
David Peterson, *University of Nebraska at Omaha*
Tim Poland, *Radford University*
Judie Rae, *American River College; Sierra College*
Kathryn Raign, *University of North Texas*
Colleen Reilly, *University of North Carolina*
Teresa Reynolds, *Indiana University–Southeast*
Melissa Richardson, *Central Texas College**
Thomas Rickert, *Purdue University*
Jared Riddle, *Ivy Tech State College–De La Garza*
Rochelle Rodrigo, *Mesa Community College*
Brooke Rollins, *University of South Carolina*
Linda Rosekrans, *State University of New York at Cortland*
Jill Terry Rudy, *Brigham Young University*
Kathy Sanchez, *Tomball College*
Joy Santee, *Purdue University**
John Schaffer, *Blinn College**
Susan Sens-Conant, *Johnson County Community College**
Annabel Servat, *Southeastern Louisiana University**
Barry Seyster, *Orange Coast College*
May Shih, *San Francisco State University*
Catherine Shuler, *Purdue University**
Susan Slavicz, *Florida Community College at Jacksonville*
Andrew Strycharski, *University of Miami*
Barbara Szubinska, *Eastern Kentucky University**
Chris Thaiss, *George Mason University*
Valerie Thomas, *University of New Mexico*
David Tietge, *Monmouth University*
Carla Todaro, *Walters State Community College*
Linda Toonen, *University of Wisconsin at Green Bay**
Alice Trupe, *Bridgewater College*
Sam Umland, *University of Nebraska*
Ralph Velazquez, *Rio Hondo College**
Kathryn Waltz-Freel, *Ivy Tech Community College of Indiana*
Colleen Weldele, *Palomar College*
Cornelia Wells, *William Patterson University*
Natasha Whitten, *Southeastern Louisiana University**
Sallie Wolf, *Arapahoe Community College**
Peggy Woods, *University of Massachusetts at Amherst*
Maria Zlateva, *Boston University**

In 2003, we conducted a survey of English instructors to find out what technology questions their students asked them so that we could develop our Technology Toolboxes to cover those topics students need help with. We thank you all for sharing that information with us.

James Allen, *College of DuPage*
Dana Anderson, *University of Indiana*
Kristina Beckman, *University of Arizona*
Anne Bliss, *University of Colorado at Boulder*
Vince Bruckert, *Wilbur Wright College*
Mattavia Burks, *Calhoun Community College*
Anthony Campbell, *Eastern Kentucky University*
Constance Chapman, *Clark Atlanta University*
Janice Clayton, *San Antonio College*
Taylor Emery, *Austin Peay State University*
Karen Gardiner, *The University of Alabama*
Baotong Gu, *Georgia State University*
Magnolia Hampton, *Hinds Community College*
Betty Hart, *University of Southern Indiana*
Scott Hathaway, *Hudson Valley Community College*
Matthew Higgs, *Northeastern University*
Klint Hull, *Spokane Community College*
Tim Lindgren, *Boston College*
Clark Maddux, *Tennessee State University*
Rebecca Marez, *Del Mar College*
Brett Millan, *South Texas Community College*
Susan Miller, *Mesa Community College*
Samantha Morgan-Curtis, *Tennessee State University*
Mary Anne Nagler, *Oakland Community College*
Troy Nordman, *Butler County Community College*
Matthew Novak, *California Polytechnic State University*
Ruth Oleson, *Illinois Central College*
John Pekins, *Tallahassee Community College*
Susan Sens-Conant, *Johnson County Community College*
Susan Slavicz, *Florida Community College at Jacksonville*
Monica Smith, *University of Georgia*
Peggy Woods, *University of Massachusetts at Amherst*

We also want to thank the students who filled out another version of the technology survey. Since several students expressed concerns about their privacy, we will not mention them by name, but instead offer a general thank-you for taking the time to complete the survey.

Additional Thanks from Jeff

I would like to first thank Dave, co-author extraordinaire, whose ideas, skills, friendship, and good humor made drafting this first edition a pleasure and a learning adventure. Ron Shelly, Cengage Learning sales rep, was incredibly generous with his time and resources as this idea became a manuscript over the last several years. Dr. Gladys Willis, who has been a mentor to me since I began at Lincoln and whose professional and collegial support have kept my ambitions harnessed to productive projects like this one, has my gratitude. Thanks to all my colleagues at Lincoln, who have supported my efforts since the project began, and to my students, who have listened, offered suggestions for examples, and provided writing for this book. Thanks to my wife, Kathy, who has offered numerous suggestions, listened and responded to drafts, and read the manuscript time and time again. Jean and Chet Hoogeveen, Diane Hallmann, and Neil and Marge O'Kane have always given me their unflagging support. I would also like to remember two generous friends and humble mentors who recently passed away: Scott Christianson of Radford University and Bill Mensel of the University of Rhode Island.

Additional Thanks from Dave

I would like to first thank the many students who contributed their fine writing, ideas, and suggestions to this book. My colleagues at Purdue have been graciously enthusiastic about all of my work, as have many outstanding graduate students. Charlie Lowe's deep knowledge of computers and writing pedagogy and the collaborative principles of open source has helped me appreciate even more the importance of reconceptualizing writing in our digital age and attention economy. Thanks also to Jill Jordan, who makes everything work better.

How does one properly thank a co-author? Jeff had the original idea for this book and invited me to join him, for which I am grateful. Colleen Brice brought her expertise on second language writing and linguistics to Part 12, composing each of those excellent chapters. Thanks to Erin Karper, who deserves enormous credit for writing the Flex-Files Instructor's Manual. While this book has been underway, my twins—Meagan and Matt—have grown from toddlers to tweeners, and even as I write this they wonder, "So when is the handbook coming?" Well, here it is! They are making their own books now, so maybe they think we're doing something interesting. My smart and beautiful wife, Julie, brought them into the world all at once, which makes the accomplishment of writing a handbook pale in comparison.

Writing: A Manual for the Digital Age, Brief Edition

Managing Your Writing

PART 1

New Contexts for Writing: Weblogs

Weblogs have spawned a new generation of writers, journalists, knowledge experts, and social networks. The millions of bloggers around the world have proven that the Internet is a hive of active and participatory culture, rather than the isolating cave that some commentators feared. Social relations and knowledge—the glue of our culture—develop and grow through weblogs. For these reasons, writers need to understand this new context for writing. The character of our culture depends on it.

You can think of a **weblog** as an online journal with accumulating content. The entries in a weblog, however, are not just written text; weblogs may include any kind of writing, photos, videos, software programs, or other multimedia projects. The term *weblog* is a fusion of *Web* (as in World Wide Web) and *log* (a record of activity). The term has been shortened further to *blog* (a noun), and the related verb is *to blog*. *To blog* something means to write about it in a weblog.

An **RSS feed** connects remote blogs together across the Internet. RSS stands for "Really Simple Syndication." (*To syndicate* means to distribute content for republication.) RSS feeds are collected by **aggregators,** which are a part of the blogging software that scours preselected blogs elsewhere for new posts and collects them for presentation at the local weblog.

The advantages of blogs are that bloggers can create content using a browser interface, don't have to worry about designing each new post, and can choose keywords to categorize content. All content is automatically archived. When you read a blog, you'll see the most recently posted entries first.

What a Powerful Web We Weave . . .

Perhaps the most important aspect of blogging is its connectior across time and space to the wider world of the Internet. With RS feeds and aggregation, bloggers network effortlessly with other around the globe, building the Internet from the inside with sharec content and richly linked information. Much like weblogs, new Wel browsers and even email programs will aggregate RSS feeds auto matically. Whereas the first generation of the Internet was connectec by hyperlinks to remote content, the next generation of the Internet sometimes called the *Semantic Web* or *Web 2.0*, is constructed on th fly, instantaneously and automatically, from bits and pieces of infor mation authored around the globe, giving the average person an im portant role in creating the Internet.

Anyone with an Internet connection can get started reading and writing weblogs Remember that the Internet—like a street corner, a mall, a bazaar, a cathedra or a carnival—may be filled with strange people and unfamiliar ideas. One goa of the "New Contexts for Writing" part openers is to teach you how to navi gate this world intelligently and enjoyably.

Weblog Services: Google these names to learn more: Blogger, Drupal, ELGG, Ex pressionEngine, Greymatter, LiveJournal, Moveable Type, MySpace, TypePac Wordpress, Xanga.

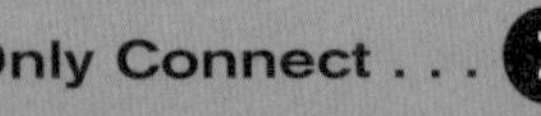

Syndicator: Technorati (http://www.technorati.com) tracks more than 26 millio weblogs and 1.9 billion links.

The Rhetorical Situation

At the start of any writing project, think through your writing in context, as a **rhetorical situation** involving your own ideas, the words and media that you will use to express them, and the ideas and expectations of your readers. The elements of context will shape your thinking at each node of this rhetorical triangle.

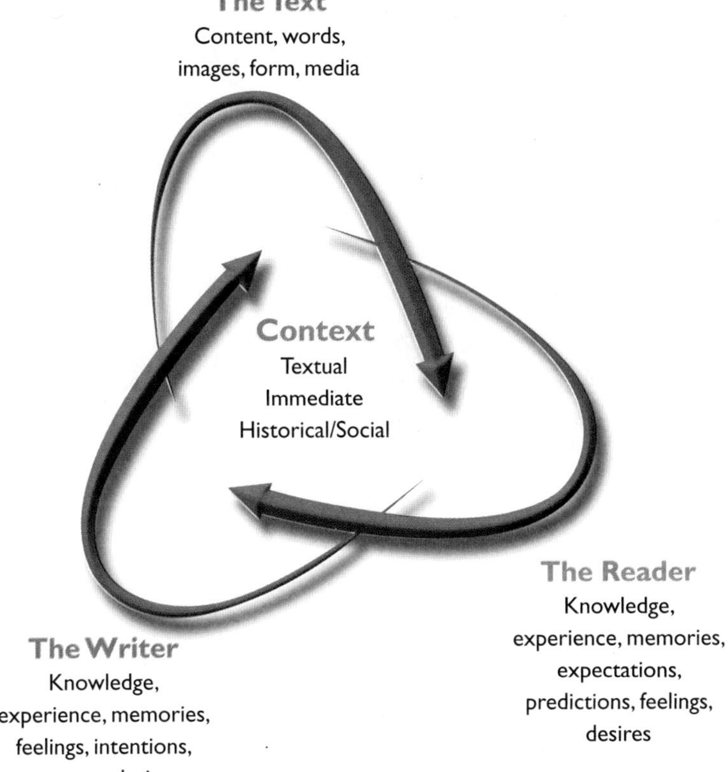

Each writing situation has contexts that should be considered carefully before you start writing and while you are writing and revising. When you consider contexts as a writer, you practice the art of rhetoric, which involves discovering ideas and using words and images designed to persuade, inform, or move readers.

Context refers to all the situational elements that might shape a writer's purpose. Context includes the situations of readers and writers, the historical and physical circumstances, other texts, and even the broader systems of meaning like ideology that "contain" the text. You can read books, films, TV shows, and cultures as texts that have contexts that shape meaning.

Bear in mind how these aspects of context might shape your purpose and meaning.

Suppose you want to ask a peer to give you feedback on a personal essay before you submit it to your instructor or to your campus literary magazine. The hard part about asking for a favor is not the gist of what you will say or write—"Would you please give me feedback on this essay?"—but figuring out *how* you will say or write it (the style, the words), what medium you should use (spoken words, a handwritten note, an email message, an instant message), under what circumstances your message will be read, and how the person will respond (yes, no, maybe, why? what?). You decide that you'll ask for help via email.

You also need to take into account your reader's context. Under what circumstances will he or she read your request for a favor? In the midst of a busy day, among lots of spam email? On a busy commute home on a wireless PDA? As a friend or mild acquaintance? What does your reader already know about you? Will he or she be inclined to respond? What might he or she expect in return?

The questions you ask and the rhetorical decisions you make should be governed by a sense of *kairos*. *Kairos*, a Greek concept meaning "timeliness" and "suiting the word to the occasion," is central to understanding rhetoric (and writing generally) as a method of discovering the available means of persuasion in any situation.

Scenes for writing and reading email

How would your message change if you knew it would be read in the contexts pictured here?

Project Checklist

Questioning the Writing Context

Use this list to guide you as you begin thinking about the ways that context can shape your project.

Textual Context

1. What is my purpose? To inform? Entertain? Persuade? Or something else?
2. What are the important terms and concepts associated with my topic?
3. What style and arrangement are best suited to my project?
4. What genre (or genres) will best represent my project? An essay, a Web page, a brochure, a letter?
5. What media will I use? Paper, website, poster display, oral presentation? Will my project be published or presented somewhere?

Immediate Context

6. What are the important facts about my topic?
7. Who will read what I write, and what do they already know about my subject? How do they feel about it?
8. What do these readers know about me or about my purpose for writing?
9. What will the situation be when readers respond to my work? How will the interface (paper, screen, event) affect what I write?
10. Should I expect my readers to respond to me directly or in some other way?

Social and Historical Context

11. Why is now a good time to write about this topic?
12. Have there been recent and relevant news reports or current events that make my timing good?
13. What have others written about my topic, recently and throughout history?
14. What other writers have successfully addressed this subject, and how did they pull it off?
15. What social or political issues does my project raise, and how do my readers feel about them?

Learning to draw on elements of the context in order to shape your purposes and your subject is a strategy you'll need in every situation that calls for you to communicate your ideas to others.

- The **textual context** consists of the words, images, or other symbols that contain or surround ideas. In the Declaration of Independence, phrases like "all men are created equal," "life, liberty, and the pursuit of happiness," and even the signatures themselves are part of the textual context.
- The **immediate context** is the situation to which the text responds. In a film review, it would include the reviewer, the review, the newspaper in which the review is published, the readers of the newspaper, and so on.
- The **social and historical context** is the broader context of attitudes and practices that have histories associated with them. For instance, a film review might be read in the context of conflicting cultural attitudes about violence.

About Project Checklists

When you are assigned a writing project or choose to take one on, consider the questions in the Project Checklists on pages 5, 6, and 7. For assistance with other aspects of writing, consult the list of Project Checklists on page v.

In college, your motives for writing either will arise naturally as a result of your interests or will result from assigned coursework. Even when you write because you've been assigned to do so, you can discover a personal motivation to make the enterprise more interesting—to express yourself, examine what you know, or "set the record straight," for example. Whatever the circumstances of your writing, one key to success is to approach any writing situation as an opportunity to learn, as well as to teach, persuade, or move others.

When your motivation is internal—when you have what psychologists call a "felt need" or there is some imbalance you need to respond to—you can still be systematic about the process you follow to produce good writing. For example, you may want to voice your opinion on a community problem in a letter to the editor of a newspaper, or you may want to post a review of a book you recently enjoyed on your reading blog at Blogger.com or Reger.com. Your reasons for writing may arise out of your own experiences and motives, but you will still need to examine the editorial policy of the newspaper or the blogging practices followed by others so that your writing will communicate effectively with readers. You will need to understand your writing in context.

Project Checklist

Understanding a Writing Assignment

1. **The prompt or topic.** What topic, question, or situation have you been asked to write about or respond to? How much freedom do you have to pick a specific subject or approach?
2. **The background information.** Assignments often discuss the prompt by explaining the context, providing more information about how to approach the topic or why the topic is important.
3. **Steps in the process.** Some assignments spell out what steps you need to follow to complete the writing project and even list due dates for completing intermediate steps, such as doing research, participating in peer review, and turning in rough drafts.
4. **The audience.** The assignment might identify a specific audience. For example, you might be asked to address your argumentative essay to readers who haven't yet made up their minds on a subject. Your sense of audience should help you guide your invention of subject matter and your methods of developing and organizing your content.
5. **Grading criteria.** To help you set your goals, assignments may provide you with specific criteria for measuring your success (called rubrics), or more general expectations regarding the form of your writing and its effectiveness in elaborating the subject, explaining information, or arguing a point.
   - ❑ Does your assignment discuss what kinds of evidence will be needed? Will details come from personal experience, talking with others, or conducting more formal research?
   - ❑ Does your assignment discuss what final form the project should take? For example, does it call for a five-page printed essay, a brochure, a Web page, or a lab report?
   - ❑ Is there a specific length requirement for the final project?
   - ❑ Are you required to cite or refer to a specific number of outside sources of information?
   - ❑ For projects that draw on outside sources, which documentation style should you use?

Project Checklist

Investigating the Rhetorical Situation

Take notes to identify the major aspects of the rhetorical situation to which you are responding.

Subject

- ❑ What do you already know about the subject?
- ❑ What have others said about it?
- ❑ What does your audience know about it?
- ❑ To develop your understanding of the subject, use the invention methods discussed in Chapter 2.

Purpose

- ❑ What are your purposes for writing this assignment? Will you analyze a trend, inform readers of a new policy, entertain them with a story, or persuade them to take action?
- ❑ What tone—your attitude expressed toward the subject—will best accomplish your purpose? Do you want to sound formal and distantly polite, informal but engaged with your subject, lively, reasoned, expert, or inexperienced but curious?
- ❑ What genre will best help you accomplish your purpose?

Audience

- ❑ Who is your **primary audience**—the people you want to influence most directly? Consider traits such as the age, gender, economic class, region, ethnicity/race, previous experiences, education, reading ability, and likely interests of your intended readers. Which of these (or other) traits of your audience is most important in this particular writing situation?
- ❑ Do you have a **secondary,** or **subsidiary, audience,** and if so, whom does it include? The subsidiary audience for your writing consists of readers who may read your work but who will do so with less investment than your primary audience. What audience expectations should you address in order to fulfill your purpose for writing? As your writing becomes more public—on the Web, for instance—you will find it increasingly important to consider how both primary and subsidiary audiences might respond to you.

Every call to write has a rhetorical situation. Analyzing it can help you make smart choices about how to approach your subject matter and present it to readers. In addition to considering the elements of context (discussed in section 1a), develop an understanding of the rhetorical situation—your subject, purpose, and audience—as you analyze your writing assignments.

Genre

A *genre* is a type of writing (or, more broadly, composition) used in a particular situation for a certain purpose and often with a conventional form, style, or subject. For example, there are genres and subgenres of nonfiction (such as biography and the personal essay), literature (poetry, fiction, drama), music (classical, country, punk, hip-hop, rap, rock), and art (still life, portrait, landscape, abstract).

Your understanding of genre will color many of your decisions throughout the planning, inventing, drafting, revising, and editing phases of your writing process. What expectations about your purpose, form, style, and subject matter will your audience bring to your work?

Genre becomes critically important as you write in classes across the curriculum: people learn to value a certain type of writing for certain purposes and in particular contexts. Readers bring expectations that help them decide how to read and respond to your writing. For example, the conventional form of an argumentative essay changes somewhat as you move from writing about literature to writing about science. A **thesis**—a statement to be proven—might organize your argument in an essay on literature, but in psychology, a **hypothesis** might organize a study whose results argue that the hypothesis itself is true or false (section 9k).

As you plan your writing projects, you should from the start try to learn the conventions of the genre so that you know what expectations your readers will bring to your work and how they are likely to respond to what you write.

The Academic Essay as a Genre

The genre of the academic essay has features that help readers distinguish it, for example, from a blog posting, a note between friends, a business letter, or a screenplay. Like any genre, it has conventions of form, style, and subject matter that distinguish it from personal narrative, fiction, poetry, or drama.

Genre Notes on the Academic Essay

A genre needs to be learned and practiced; no list of features can fully define it. The following guidelines are meant only as a starting point.

Form

- A *descriptive title* that suggests the subject and, if possible, the writer's perspective or position.
- *Introductory paragraphs* that invite readers into the subject by providing them with background information, context, and a thesis to be argued or a problem to be posed and explored.
- *Body paragraphs* that develop the reasons and evidence needed to support the thesis or elaborate the problem. Each body paragraph typically offers a full explanation of one major reason, idea, or example that supports the thesis statement or extends the inquiry.
- *Concluding paragraphs* that return to the thesis or problem, explain the implications of the argument or new ideas, or raise questions for further consideration.

Not all academic essays will be organized in this fashion, but if you are unsure how to organize your thoughts, these guidelines suggest a form that will be useful.

Style

- A *formal* or *semiformal* style in which the writer addresses a knowledgeable but unknown reader. Academic essays typically avoid slang and the colloquial language people use in everyday speech.
- *Specialized terms* that clarify or explain the subject. Be careful about your use of jargon, the field-specific words that people who share knowledge use to simplify their exchange of information. Good academic essays are not so jargon-laden that only a few people in the world can understand them. As academic essays have both primary and subsidiary audiences, you should define specialized terms so that all educated readers will understand your meaning.
- *Well-developed paragraphs and sentences* that help readers ponder meaning and follow a line of reasoning or explanation.

Subject

- *Subject matter* that people have conflicting opinions about, that is timely, that can help us solve or understand problems, or that inspires deeper understanding of the human condition.

- *Connections and circulation* with the ideas of others, whose work is cited. Academic essays join an ongoing conversation about the subject matter and so will typically acknowledge what others have written previously.
- *Citation style* appropriate to the given field of study.
- A *tone* of confidence in the writer's attitude toward the subject. Good academic essays show their writers to be careful, knowledgeable, and trustworthy. It is clear that the writer has thought carefully about the subject.

Global Contexts

Analyzing Genre Requirements and Learning Specialized Terms

When analyzing and completing assignments, writers using English as a second language sometimes face additional challenges, especially regarding genre.

- **Analyzing genre requirements.** If you have questions about what is expected of you when you are given an assignment, ask your instructor for help. If you can point to specific aspects of the assignment that you don't understand, write your questions down before you talk to your instructor. You can also ask to see examples of effective writing projects that were responses to similar assignments. Carefully examine the samples you are given and take notes on the features of the writing. Share the samples with peers in or out of class and discuss what they think is expected. After you look over the samples, go back to your instructor and share what you have learned about the assignment. Instructors will appreciate your early attempts to understand assignments and will help when they can.
- **Learning specialized terms.** Part of the difficulty of studying a new topic or a new academic discipline is learning the precise meanings of words or phrases that mean something different in general usage. For example, when you are asked to write a *critical analysis* in a composition course, that usually means more than criticizing something (as in finding fault with it). Critical analysis involves breaking a subject into its parts and explaining how and why these parts add up to something of value (or not). (See Key Terms for Understanding Exam Questions on page 86.) When you are dealing with complicated concepts and language, take the time to check your understanding of ideas and language with someone who knows your subject matter well, such as a tutor in the writing center.

Developing Content in Context: Understanding Ethos, Logos, and Pathos

Regardless of the genre in which you compose, three rhetorical concepts can help you decide how to develop your subject: ethos, logos, and pathos. In rhetoric, ethos, logos, and pathos describe the three kinds of proof, or rhetorical appeals, that a writer can draw on when deciding what to say about a subject and how to say it. Because they help writers make decisions about what to write and how to write it, ethos, logos, and pathos are considered aspects of **rhetorical invention.**

Ethos is the appeal to the character of the writer and his or her attitude toward the subject. Writers convey ethos with their depth of knowledge about a subject, tone or attitude toward the subject, awareness of alternative viewpoints, manner of addressing readers, and fairness and trustworthiness. **Logos** is the use of content as a form of proof or appeal and may include ideas, images, information, and evidence. **Pathos** is the appeal to the emotions of the audience. Writers use pathos to encourage readers to attach emotional responses to the content (logos) or writer (ethos) and thus to feel moved to action or belief.

1d Developing a Process for Writing

The writing process is the systematic craft of developing and presenting textual, visual, or other content to an audience in any rhetorical situation. The writing process is the agency—the means—with which you act in response to a call to write. Generally speaking, the process includes the acts of inventing, drafting, revising, and editing. They are not always performed in linear order, and each will occupy more or less attention, depending on your context and purpose.

Inventing

Inventing is figuring out what you and others know about the subject and what more there is to learn. An assignment may require research in the library or online. Or it may require fieldwork, such as conducting interviews.

Drafting

At some point, you need to assemble what you know and have learned about your subject into a composition—an organized set of elements—with a form that readers can understand and that helps you accomplish your purpose. Drafting may include informal and formal outlining, composing good sentences and paragraphs, storyboarding, and building a tentative argument.

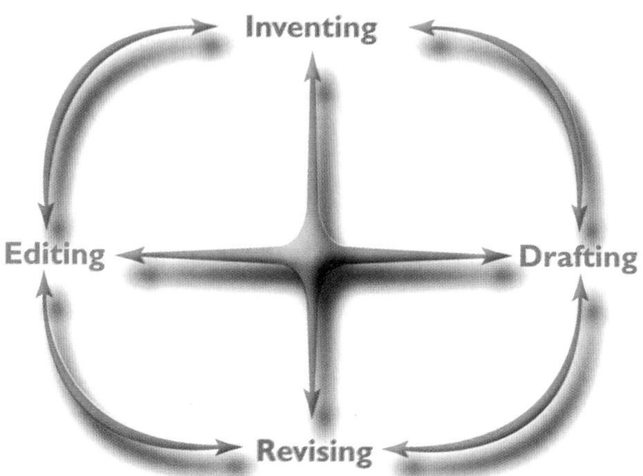

The writing process involves fluid movement among different kinds of activities. Although the activities of inventing, drafting, revising, and editing occur in different patterns depending on the writing project, the time you spend writing can become more productive if you have a rough idea of the tasks associated with each stage. For example, when you are brainstorming ideas in the invention stage, have a creative, even playful attitude. The more critical, evaluative attitude that's needed during the editing stage might slow down your production of new ideas.

Considering Technology Needs

If your assignment calls for the use of technology to research information, to record and transmit it, or to design it for readers, do you understand how to use the tools? When planning a project, you should consider well in advance any technology issues that are likely to come up as you develop and share your work.

Project Checklist

Questions to Ask about Your Technology Toolbox

Ask yourself the following questions when your assignment contains technology components:

1. Do you have access to the software and hardware you will need? If it is specialized software and you don't already have it on a public-access computer (in a lab or library, for instance) or on your own computer, how can you get access?
2. If the software or process is unfamiliar to you, what resources exist for help?
3. How will you balance the time needed to compose and shape your content with that needed to learn any unfamiliar technologies?

If you have been asked to submit your work electronically, will readers (your peers or instructor) be able to open the files you send them? (For text documents, RTF, or rich text format, is a universally readable format; see Chapter 23 for more on file management.) Be sure to follow up on electronic submissions to make sure your work has been received or posted.

Revising

For good writers, revising, or "re-seeing," is a critical step because it is when they develop their drafts into more precise compositions that reflect sharp awareness of the rhetorical situation—the subject matter, purpose, and audience. Revision may occur at any stage during the process. For example, sentences and paragraphs may be reworked as it becomes clearer to the writer how readers will receive them or what they will expect.

Editing

Many writers edit their work as they go, but they also spend concentrated time polishing their work. They clarify meaning and usage, punctuate and cite according to accepted guidelines, and double-check to make sure all components of an assignment have been addressed.

1e Contributing to Group Projects

The ability to work and write with others is one of the most important skills to develop if you want to participate successfully in academic, civic, and professional contexts. Group writing projects are often more complex than those assigned to individuals, so the group will need to analyze the assignment carefully and then decide how to proceed. Ultimately, everyone bears responsibility to contribute actively to the team, and you should volunteer if there's ever a feeling that you're not doing enough to help or to be evaluated fairly by your instructor.

Some teams elect group leaders, or they rotate the job of project leader. To stay organized, it's helpful to have a recorder for each group meeting to take notes on important decisions and then summarize them for the others. Rotate the role of recorder among group members as the project progresses.

Project responsibilities need to be defined and a schedule set up, with due dates for each important step toward the final draft. Plan to have a group meeting at least once before each major step or draft is supposed to be completed. Group meetings should be devoted to planning, not production. Take the time to discuss individual roles and tasks and manage other group activities. (See also the Project Checklist on page 379.)

Project Planning Software

Email programs, word processors, and weblogs often include tools that you can use to plan important steps in a project, keep the tasks of individual group members organized and on track, and take notes as you go. In Microsoft® Outlook®, for example, you can use the Task Manager and Calendar to schedule meetings and other steps in a project, even generating automatic reminders. You can also share these calendars and task lists with group members. You can create customized tables in your word processor to add notes, due dates, and other important project information. Learning to use tools like these early in your college career can be a great timesaver.

Month/Year						
Sunday	**Monday**	**Tuesday**	**Wednesday**	**Thursday**	**Friday**	**Saturday**
				Month and Day Assignment received and discussed in class.	Month and Day Review assignment and analyze it for task-related verbs.	Month and Day Create a list of 5 possible topics.
Month and Day	Month and Day Narrow list of topics to 1 and write a short paragraph explaining my reasoning.	Month and Day Submit topic proposal to instructor.	Month and Day Begin researching topic in 1) library; 2) online. Check any key terms in the *Oxford English Dictionary*.	Month and Day Get feedback in class from peers regarding choice of topic. Ask for advice about how to elaborate the topic. Also, what interests them about my topic?	Month and Day Categorize notes and begin planning draft 1.	Month and Day
Month and Day	Month and Day Complete draft 1.	Month and Day Peer review. Visit writing center to get feedback on draft.	Month and Day Revise draft and then save time for copyediting.	Month and Day Submit the project to the instructor. Check to make sure the format of the document is correct, that I include all required steps, and that it has submission notes (if required).	Month and Day	

This is a five-row, seven-column table created in a word processor for use as a three-week planning calendar. Once you have the table set up, you can save it as a document template for use in later projects. (Select Save As and then choose "template" (or the equivalent) in the Save as Type drop-down box.)

Project Checklist

Heuristics for a Narrative Essay

Asking questions is an effective way to start developing content for a piece of writing. The questions here could be used to get started on writing a narrative essay, for example, about a life-changing event or an influential person in your life. With some modification, they could also be used to develop a narration that acts as evidence for a larger point, within, for example, a persuasive essay.

Discover

1. What specific details do you remember?
2. What have others said or written about the event or person, in personal accounts, newspapers, blogs, or other forums?
3. How have other writers written about similar subjects?

Create

4. What made the event or person unique, unusual, or profound?
5. How did the event or person affect you? Why? Is there something unique in your experience that made the timing just right?

Elaborate

6. Can you make a point about the event and then find examples that will help readers appreciate its impact?
7. Why does this event or person stand out from all the rest? What difference has this event or person made for your life in the present? What can you point to in your life that shows this change?

Experienced writers follow some general principles that help them get from beginning to end more or less successfully and consistently, in a series of stages that have identifiable characteristics. There is, in other words, a writing process. Invention, drafting, and development are the major stages that are the subject of this chapter.

Invention involves discovering, creating, and elaborating ideas. It usually takes center stage early in the writing process and may also influence how content is shaped and revised later. Invention has three facets:

1. *Discovering* what you and others already know about a subject and how you and they feel about it.
2. *Creating* new ideas and describing new relationships among existing ideas.
3. *Elaborating* and developing what you and others know about a subject by connecting it with other subjects and finding examples that bring ideas to life.

When you need to discover what you know, generate new ideas and relationships, or decide on a way to frame your perspective on a general subject, you can use several methods for getting ideas down on paper or on screen.

Freewriting

Three general "rules" define freewriting:

1. Give your full attention, focus, and energy for the short amount of time you write (usually 5–15 minutes).
2. Write quickly without rushing.
3. Never stop for long to correct, think of the exact word, etc.

Focused Freewriting

Once you have gotten some thoughts on paper, you can go back and examine what you wrote to look for ideas to use as seeds for your next freewriting session.

1. Underline, circle, or highlight any interesting or surprising phrases or ideas.
2. Start a new freewriting that focuses on an idea, scene, or event that began to emerge in your first session.
3. After three or four of these sessions, perhaps spaced out over a day or two, freewrite a paragraph describing your writing process. (In thinking about this process, you make it familiar and habitual.)

Freewriting on the Computer

1. Open a new word processing document. Write your initial topic at the top, skip a space, and then position your cursor as if you were about to write as usual.
2. Turn off your monitor (not the computer itself) so that it doesn't display anything. Start your freewriting session.
3. After ten minutes or so, turn your monitor back on to read what you wrote.
4. Save your freewriting as a file if you want to keep it.

A Sample of Focused Freewriting

Session 1 Topic: Important Event

Write for 5 minutes she says. On an important event . . . (for me) . . . let's see. It's easy for me to remember how much fun I had playing games with my brother, Andy, when I was little. These were not one important event but a series of them over time that feel important now. He taught me how to play "by the rules" even if they were sometimes his rules. I just remember these being fun times . . .

Session 2: Why are games fun?

They just are. Well maybe not all of them are. I remember how awful it feels to lose, especially when someone rubs it in. I can understand losing ~~and can take it~~ as long as I can say I tried my best. It's fun to play video games with yourself when you can solve them without pulling your hair out. It didn't matter what game Andy and I played. So it was social. . .

Session 3: Games as social engagement

This is getting deeper but I had the thought that playing games taught me to enjoy dealing with other people and (hehe) even how to fake them out or trick them into thinking they knew better. There are "rules of engagement" that you can bend to your will, but you have to be careful that you don't bend them too far or else no one will play with you again and being social will be impossible, which gives me an idea for how to organize my essay around the title "Rules of Engagement." I think that's a phrase from a movie or something, so I will have to look it up.

social rules?

Could this be my thesis or main point?

A Sample of Group Brainstorming

Games and Gaming				
Rules	Competition	Strategies	Components	Types
suggestions	sports	cheating	playing pieces	card games
guidelines	fun	playing fair	money	gambling
laws	playing	jumping out to a fast start	people	board games
rights	losing		tokens	video games
practices		pacing yourself	cards	solo games
freedom			dice	handheld games

What would a game be like if there were no rules? What if the only way to win were to create your own pieces?

A Sample Cluster

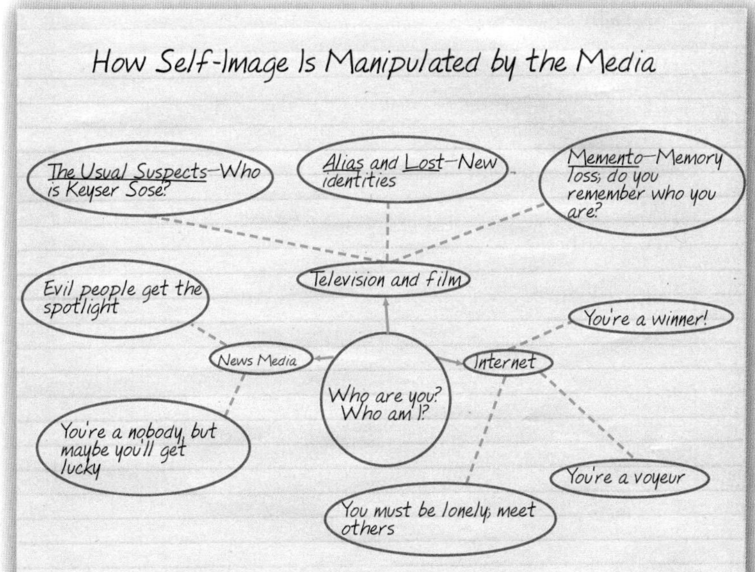

Brainstorming

When you brainstorm, the goal is to come up with as many ideas as possible in a short time. Use lists, words, images, drawings, or anything else related to your subject.

Group Brainstorming

Early in a collaborative project, it is helpful for all group members to contribute ideas without worrying about whether they will result in something useful.

1. Write your subject on a chalkboard. You may find it helpful to consider the subject as a noun—a "thing."
2. Break the subject into parts or features. Write these at the top.
3. Under each feature, list alternatives or examples that come to mind, as group members shout out possibilities.
4. Choose one word/feature in each column to circle, and then draw a line connecting the circles.
5. Discuss how the subject changes when you think of its key features in this way.

Clustering

Clustering is a method of developing a visual landscape of your ideas and how they break into categories and subcategories. To create a cluster, write your subject in the center of a sheet of paper, circle it, and then think of three or four subcategories of this larger subject. Write those in their own circles, with connecting lines to the center. Create as many layers of ideas as are helpful.

Topical Invention

Likely the oldest method of rhetorical invention, topical invention shows how ideas can relate to one another or to their context.

For the purposes of inventing and elaborating content, it is helpful to divide these topics into basic categories that arise when you ask what a subject means (definition), how it relates and compares with other subjects (comparison), what it results from or causes (cause, motive, or purpose), what people say about it (testimony), and where and when it has meaning (context or circumstances).

Under each category in the Project Checklist, you see questions that come to mind, with blanks inviting you to plug in your subject. If you answer these questions with a few sentences or more, you will have collected a broad range of information about your topic that could be used in an essay or project.

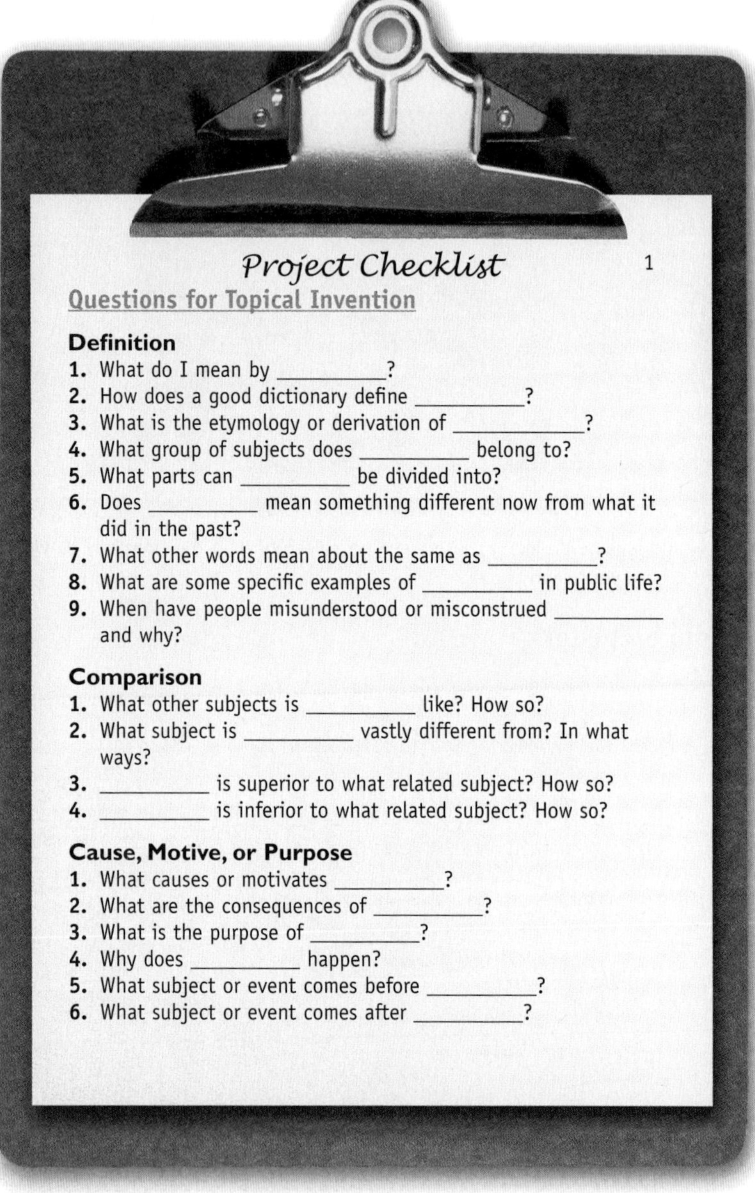

Project Checklist 1

Questions for Topical Invention

Definition

1. What do I mean by __________?
2. How does a good dictionary define __________?
3. What is the etymology or derivation of __________?
4. What group of subjects does __________ belong to?
5. What parts can __________ be divided into?
6. Does __________ mean something different now from what it did in the past?
7. What other words mean about the same as __________?
8. What are some specific examples of __________ in public life?
9. When have people misunderstood or misconstrued __________ and why?

Comparison

1. What other subjects is __________ like? How so?
2. What subject is __________ vastly different from? In what ways?
3. __________ is superior to what related subject? How so?
4. __________ is inferior to what related subject? How so?

Cause, Motive, or Purpose

1. What causes or motivates __________?
2. What are the consequences of __________?
3. What is the purpose of __________?
4. Why does __________ happen?
5. What subject or event comes before __________?
6. What subject or event comes after __________?

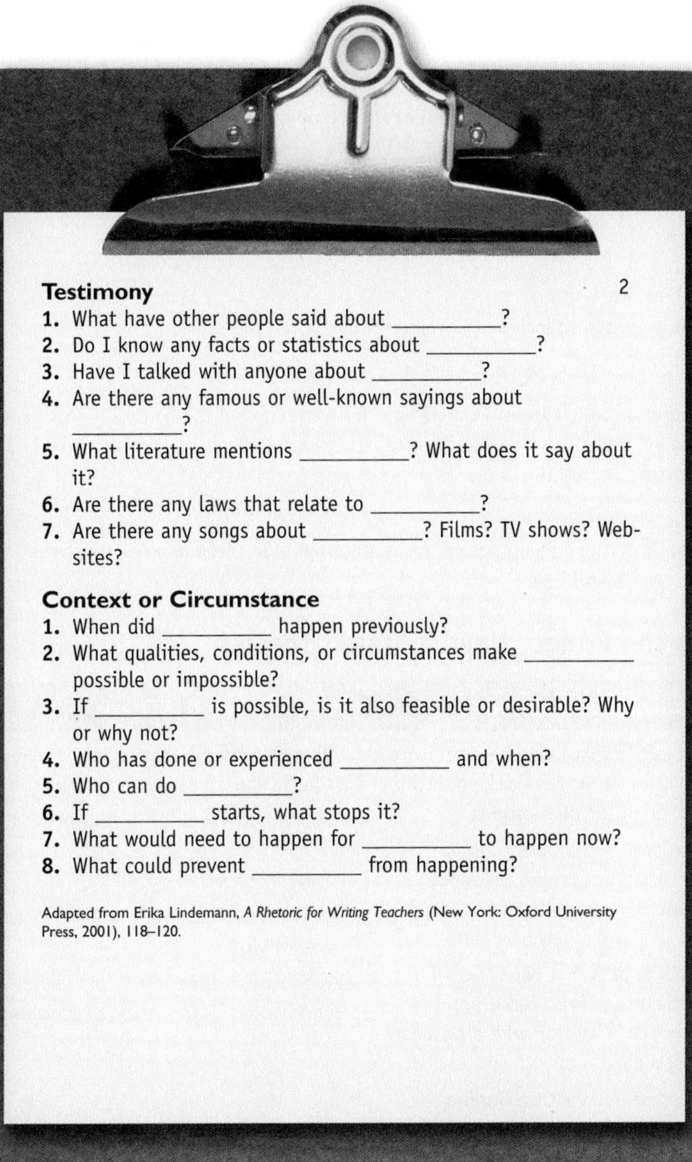

2

Testimony

1. What have other people said about __________?
2. Do I know any facts or statistics about __________?
3. Have I talked with anyone about __________?
4. Are there any famous or well-known sayings about __________?
5. What literature mentions __________? What does it say about it?
6. Are there any laws that relate to __________?
7. Are there any songs about __________? Films? TV shows? Websites?

Context or Circumstance

1. When did __________ happen previously?
2. What qualities, conditions, or circumstances make __________ possible or impossible?
3. If __________ is possible, is it also feasible or desirable? Why or why not?
4. Who has done or experienced __________ and when?
5. Who can do __________?
6. If __________ starts, what stops it?
7. What would need to happen for __________ to happen now?
8. What could prevent __________ from happening?

Adapted from Erika Lindemann, *A Rhetoric for Writing Teachers* (New York: Oxford University Press, 2001), 118–120.

Topical Invention for Narrowing a Subject

You can also use the questions for topical invention in reverse. Instead of using them to elaborate a subject, you can use them to narrow a subject that is too broad for the length of the project you are producing or the amount of time you have to write. Once you have explored your responses to some or all of the categories of questions, select one to consider in more detail. Responses to any one of the categories will supply plenty of options for narrower subjects.

Thesis statements are concise expressions of a writing project's central argument, including both the subject and the writer's approach toward or claim about the subject. Sometimes the thesis is called a *controlling idea* because it has a shaping influence on everything else.

- An effective thesis statement singles out some aspect of a subject for attention and clearly defines your approach to it. It says "Look at *this* rather than *that*" or "Think about *that* in *this* way."
- An effective thesis statement focuses on the subject, not on the act of writing itself.

Avoid phrases like these:
My firm belief is that . . .
It seems to me . . .
I want to show that . . .

- An effective thesis statement creates expectations. A good thesis statement arouses in readers expectations that help them predict what might come next.
- An effective thesis statement may sum up or interpret a personal insight in a broader context.

Most formal academic writing includes a thesis. In short interpretive or argumentative writing, the thesis often comes near the end of the first paragraph, where many readers will look for it by convention. Since short essays need to grab a reader's interest quickly, an early thesis statement is critical.

Sample Thesis Statement Revised

The following sentence just announces the subject of the essay without stating a position about it.

> *In the following essay, I discuss* the motives of language police.

Here it is revised to include the writer's claim about the subject:

> Language police are motivated by a desire to control the natural forces of change, which have always been resistant to organized or governmental control.

You can find more examples of thesis statements in the examples on pages 19, 27, 29, 30, 43, and 232.

Does the Project Need a Stated Thesis?

Probably Needs a Thesis	May Not Need a Thesis
Critical essays that interpret literature, film, art, social movements, political events, or other phenomena	*Informative essays* that cover a subject as fairly and as thoroughly as possible
Problem-posing or problem-solving essays that point to the presence of problems and/or means of solving them	*Reports* that record but do not interpret the results of fieldwork, lab research, or other studies
Research papers that report on a subject, cite sources, record and interpret data, and/or take a position on an issue	*Informal response writing* in a journal or on a weblog
Poster presentations that outline a perspective on an issue that lends itself to alternative viewpoints	*Websites* that function as portals or windows on a subject or organization
Narrative essays about a profound experience, important person, or social issue	

Sample Opening Paragraph

Suppose you have found through research that recycling certain plastics is too labor intensive to save resources. You want to persuade your readers that it makes better sense to store certain plastics than to try to recycle them now. In the future, when new technologies for their integration into recycling processes become available, the plastics can be recycled. How much background information will you need to give before you state your thesis?

Creates connection with readers by acknowledging that recycling takes effort but is worth doing

Uses familiar categories of recyclable materials to help readers move from known information to new information

Introduces some new information about one category

Although it is not always easy, recycling offers many benefits, among them the peace of mind that comes from using resources wisely. Newspaper can be turned into pulp immediately, and pulp's uses are many. Glass too can be melted and reused immediately. The benefits of recycling some materials, though, might have to be put off for a little longer. Unfortunately, many kinds of plastics are expensive to recycle right now, and the current recycling methods for certain plastics generate almost as much pollution as creating plastic from scratch. However, reverting back to throwing away plastic products in overfilled landfills is not environmentally sound, either. Since there are so many recycling programs run by large corporations and municipal entities (like towns and cities), plastic does not have to be recycled right now.

States thesis, which readers are now prepared for

Another Sample Introduction

We are all being robbed, and most of us don't realize it. Today, 12.4 percent of every dollar we make is siphoned into a pyramid scheme called social security—from which our generation is unlikely to see much benefit.

From Hunter Williams, student at the University of Florida, "Prof Potpourri," *The Independent Florida Alligator Online* 18 Feb. 2004.

Think of a draft as having three sections—introduction, body, and conclusion—each of which performs a different function in giving a work its unity. All the parts of the whole should somehow explain, elaborate, or qualify the work's thesis.

The most important goals of an introduction are to spark your readers' curiosity about your subject and to provide them with sufficient background so that they can understand your thesis.

Consider these strategies:

- Startle your readers with an astounding piece of information or a distinctly unusual point of view designed to make them take notice.
- Provide a range of viewpoints that people have on the subject, and then reveal your own.
- Begin with a quotation that reveals an important aspect of your topic.
- Begin with a definition of an important term so that your readers will understand an analysis based on it.
- Open with a real anecdote that uses action or dialogue to exemplify the problem you will address, the solution you support, or the case you will study.

Writers use paragraphs to organize their ideas. Each body paragraph performs a certain kind of work in the larger piece of writing—for example, to advance the argument, to provide illustrations and examples, to discuss the effects of a solution the writer is proposing. Paragraphs also have an internal logic; they focus attention on one idea at a time, along with a cluster of closely related sentences that explain, extend, or support that idea.

The form, length, style, and positioning of paragraphs will vary, depending on the nature and conventions of the medium (print or digital), the interface (size and type of paper, screen resolution and size), and the genre. For example, paragraphs in a work of creative nonfiction will likely include transitional words and sentence structures not often found in lab reports.

In an academic essay, the body paragraphs explain and develop the thesis. The longest section of the paper, the body offers a line of reasoning and a sufficient amount of information—evidence, facts, anecdotes, examples, statistics—to support, extend, or elaborate it.

Try T-R-I: Topic-Restriction-Illustration

In academic writing, many paragraphs include a topic sentence, one or more restrictive sentences, and illustrations. You can remember this pattern with the acronym T-R-I, or "try."

A **topic sentence** states the main subject or focus of the paragraph. A well-written topic sentence signals the reader about the focus of the paragraph, supports or extends the thesis, and unifies and summarizes the paragraph's content. Readers look for a topic sentence early in the paragraph to help them comprehend the significance of individual sentences.

Restrictive sentences explain or narrow the focus of the topic sentence by adding qualifying information. They take the more general assertion and channel it in a way that will make illustrative sentences the logical next step.

Illustrative sentences may provide examples that clarify the meaning of topic sentences and restrictive sentences, or they may show how the topic relates to a particular context or idea.

> Fear thrives best in the present tense. That is why experts rely on it; in a world that is increasingly impatient with long-term processes, fear is a potent short-term play. Imagine that you are a government official charged with procuring the funds to fight one of two proven killers: terrorist attacks and heart disease. Which cause do you think the members of Congress will open up the coffers for? The likelihood of any given person being killed in a terrorist attack is infinitesimally smaller than the likelihood that the same person will clog up his arteries with fatty food and die of heart disease. But a terrorist attack happens *now;* death by heart attack is some distant, quiet catastrophe. Terrorist acts lie beyond our control; french fries do not. Just as important as the control factor is what Peter Sandman calls the dread factor. Death by terrorist attack (or mad-cow disease) is considered wholly dreadful; death by heart disease is, for some reason, not.
>
> From Stephen D. Levitt and Stephen J. Dubner, *Freakonomics: A Rogue Economist Explores the Hidden Side of Everything* (New York: William Morrow, 2005), 151.

Although most paragraphs should have a topic sentence, some do not need one. You might be able to omit a topic sentence in a paragraph that narrates a series of events. Or you may not need a topic sentence when a paragraph continues developing an idea introduced (with a topic sentence) previously.

Keeping the Topic in the Forefront of the Reader's Mind

The topic—Hush Puppies—is introduced, defined

Topic shifts slightly, from type of shoes to brand of shoes

And from brand to sales of the brand

From sales of the shoes to the company that sells the shoes

And from the company to its executives

For Hush Puppies—the classic American brushed-suede shoes with the lightweight crepe sole—the Tipping Point came somewhere between late 1994 and early 1995. The brand had been all but dead until that point. Sales were down to 30,000 pairs a year, mostly to backwoods outlets and small-town family stores. Wolverine, the company that makes Hush Puppies, was thinking of phasing out the shoes that made them famous. But then something strange happened. At a fashion shoot, two Hush Puppies executives—Owen Baxter and Geoffrey Lewis—ran into a stylist from New York who told them that the classic Hush Puppies had suddenly become hip in the clubs and bars of downtown Manhattan. . . .

From Malcolm Gladwell, *The Tipping Point* (Boston: Little, Brown and Co., 2002), 3.

Coherence: Transitions, Pronouns, and Lexical Ties

Another characteristic of the creative person is that he is able to entertain and play with ideas that the average person might regard as silly, mistaken, or downright dangerous. All new ideas sound foolish at first, because they are new. (In the early days of the railroad, it was argued that speeds of twenty-five mph or over were impractical because people's brains would burst.) A person who is afraid of being laughed at or disapproved of for having "foolish" or "unsound" ideas will have the satisfaction of having everyone agree with him, but he will never be creative, because creativity means being willing to take a chance—to go out on a limb.

From S. I. Hayakawa, "What It Means to Be Creative," *Through the Communication Barrier* (New York: Harper & Row, 1979).

Transitions are marked in blue, lexical ties in green, and pronouns in red, to illustrate how the three coherence devices thread through the paragraph. Note that many people consider use of the pronoun *he* to mean "a person" sexist usage—see section 29a.

Coherence: The Networked Paragraph

Coherence in a paragraph is derived from the network of relationships between the topic, unifying idea, or theme and the other sentences, as well as the flow of information from one sentence to the next. Coherent paragraphs have sentences that flow easily and effectively, and the connections between the sentences and their ideas remain clear at all times.

- *Use pronouns to create ties to previous words and sentences.* Pronouns function like threads in a cloth, linking new information to old information. When you use a pronoun, you ask the reader to keep its antecedent in mind.
- *Use synonyms and repeat important words as necessary to create "lexical ties."* A lexical tie works like a pronoun, placing familiar words in new contexts or sentences where they take on added meaning.
- *Use parallel structures across sentences to create a framework.* Repeat grammatical patterns within and across sentences to create a consistent and familiar framework for reading your ideas. Using parallel structure—a kind of repetitive form—builds expectations in your readers so that, as they move forward, they catch the rhythm and swing along for the ride.

- *Use transitions and punctuation precisely. Transitions* are words or phrases that connect your ideas. Normally, when new information is given, a transition cues your reader how to interpret it. For example, the word *because* lets readers know that a cause is next; the word *however* that a contrast is coming. The phrases *the point is, the important thing to note,* and *what strikes me most is* all say "pay attention now."

  Punctuation performs similar functions but more quietly. A colon emphasizes important information, a semicolon shows that two ideas are closely related in content, and commas can show that a series of ideas are distinct yet similarly important.
- *Consider your readers' prior knowledge.* Effectively managing coherence involves more than just connecting ideas clearly, because clarity depends on prior knowledge. Thus, coherence depends on what your audience already knows about your controlling idea and what information you provide. Even if your topic is new to readers, they will accumulate information as they read your sentences.

Transitions

To give additional information or support:

Additionally, again, also, and, besides, equally important is, furthermore, in addition to, incidentally, in the first place, moreover, more so, next, otherwise, too

To provide examples:

Another example of this/that is, examples include, for example, for instance, in fact, in particular, one example of that/this is, specifically, that is, to illustrate this/the point

To compare and contrast:

Also, although, and, at the same time, but, despite (that), however, in a similar way, in contrast, in spite of this/that, likewise, nevertheless, on the contrary, on the other hand, similarly, still, though, yet

To indicate chronology or order:

After, afterward, and then, as, at last, before, during, earlier, finally, first/second/third, formerly, immediately, in the meantime, later, meanwhile, never, next, now, once, shortly, since, subsequently, then, thereafter, until, when, whence, while

To indicate placement or location:

Above, atop, below, beyond, close, farther, here, in, nearby, on, on top of that, opposite, over, south/north/east/west, there, to the right/left, underneath

To show logic:

Also, and, as a result, because, because of, but, consequently, for this reason, hence, however, if, otherwise, since, so, then, therefore, thus

To summarize:

Finally, in closing, in conclusion, in other words, in short, in summary, on the whole, so, that is, then, therefore, to close, to sum up, to summarize

Sample Description

Sets the scene

Dominant impression

Visual details

Anecdote that adds to impression of duration

Then Darlington, a town of portico and pediment, iron fences, big trees, and an old courthouse square that looked as though renovated by a German buzz bomb. But on the west side of the square stood the Deluxe Café. The times had left it be. The front window said AIR CONDITIONED in icy letters, above the door was neon, and inside hung an insurance agency calendar and another for an auto parts store. Also on the walls were the Gettysburg Address, Declaration of Independence, Pledge of Allegiance, a picture of a winged [J]esus ushering along two kids who belonged in a Little Rascals film, and the obligatory waterfall lithograph. The clincher: small, white hexagonal floor tiles. Two old men, carrying their arms folded behind, stopped to greet each other with a light, feminine touching of fingertips, a gesture showing the duration of their friendship. I went in happy.

From William Least Heat-Moon, *Blue Highways* (Boston: Houghton Mifflin Co., 1982), 67–68.

Sample Process Analysis

Names the process

Steps to prepare

Steps to eat

How to eat an avocado (you think you know how, but you don't). First of all, it must be a perfectly ripe Hass avocado (small, dark green, and with an alligator's crumply skin). Cut it in half and gently pop out the seed. Set each half, cut side up, in a shallow bowl. Now, in a separate dish, mix together (for every two halves) about a spoonful of olive oil, a good squeeze of fresh lime, a few drops of Tabasco, and a pinch of coarse salt. Mix this well and dribble a fair share into each avocado half. Now fall to, eating the avocado out of its skin with a teaspoon, catching a bit of the dressing with each bite. A little buttered bread is good with this; the oil and lime juice can be further enhanced, if you like, with a morsel of crushed garlic and, instead of the Tabasco, a sprinkle of powdered cayenne. God didn't make the avocado just for guacamole.

From John Thorne, with Matt Lewis Thorne, *Outlaw Cook* (New York: Farrar, Straus and Giroux, 1992), 20.

Development: Patterns and Purposes

Description

Writers use description to help readers see, hear, taste, smell, and feel the particulars of a scene or subject. Descriptive details are chosen to help readers form a dominant impression of the subject.

To craft evocative descriptions, ask

- What is the most interesting or important thing to convey about this subject, given the larger purpose for sharing the description?
- Which details will best convey this point?
- What does this subject look like? Sound like? Smell like? Taste like? How does it feel?

Process Analysis

A process is a series of events that can be replicated to produce a certain result. A process analysis often describes the sequence of events, the instructions, and any procedures to be followed, so the reader can successfully complete or understand the process.

To craft a useful process analysis, ask

- What is to be done, or what should happen?
- How long will it take?
- What will be needed?
- What are the steps required to complete the action?
- In what order do they occur?

Cause and Effect Analysis

A cause and effect paragraph answers the question "How did this come to be?" or "What happened because of this?" Be careful to base conclusions on adequate, reliable evidence from multiple sources. Avoid oversimplifying.

To discover causes and effects, ask

- What exactly happened, to whom, where, and when?
- How did the events unfold over time?
- What are the other possible causes or effects of this event?

Sample Cause and Effect Analysis

Provides necessary background information

Statement of the cause

Initial effects

Possible long-term effects

Soon after a baby was born, it was swaddled tightly into a basketry cradle. There were practical reasons for restraining a child: California had grizzly bears, rattlesnakes, scorpions, poisonous plants, rushing water, and numerous other dangers. Also, a swaddled baby seldom cried or fussed. Yet surely those early months packed into a basketry cradle must have greatly influenced personality. The severe restriction of movement curbed independence and a sense of experimentation. A child *watched* the world rather than acted upon it. Perhaps in the process the child developed an attitude of acceptance toward the world—an attitude that throughout a person's life would be amplified by other cultural experiences, until in the end *acceptance of the world* would become the very center of a complex system of belief and value.

From *The Way We Lived: California Indian Reminiscences, Stories, and Songs,* edited with commentary by Malcolm Margolin (Berkeley, CA: Heyday Books, 1981), 11.

Definition

Writers define terms to establish common ground with readers. If a reader accepts your definition of important terms, your chances of persuasion improve dramatically.

To craft a definition, ask

- What cluster of words is this term associated with? To what words is it closely related in meaning (e.g., *craft* and *skill, ideology* and *belief*)?
- What analogy, or comparison to another word, can be used to define this term?

Sample Definition

Paragraph begins with a clear and direct topic sentence

Illustration from experience

Restrictions of the topic sentence

Illustrations

Extension of the topic sentence explains significance

A central notion here is that perceptions are *hypotheses.* This is suggested by the fact that retinal images are open to an infinity of interpretations, and from the observed phenomena of ambiguity. The notion is that perceptions are like the predictive hypotheses of science. Hypotheses of perception and of science are risky, as they are predictive and they go beyond sensed evidence to hidden properties and to the future. For perception, as for science, both kinds of prediction are vitally important because the eye's images are almost useless for behaviour until they are read in terms of significant properties of objects, and because survival depends on behavior being appropriate to the immediate future, with no delay, although eye and brain take time to respond to the present. We behave to the present by anticipation of what is likely to happen, rather than from immediate stimuli.

From Richard L. Gregory, *Eye and Brain: The Psychology of Seeing,* 5th ed. (Princeton, NJ: Princeton University Press, 1997), 10.

Sample Contrast

First subject

Examples of first subject

Second subject

Examples of second subject

Recent discussions about the plight of African Americans—especially those at the bottom of the social ladder—tend to divide into two camps. On the one hand, there are those who highlight the *structural* constraints on the life chances of black people. Their viewpoint involves a subtle historical and sociological analysis of slavery, Jim Crowism, job and residential discrimination, skewed unemployment rates, inadequate health care, and poor education. On the other hand, there are those who stress the behavioral impediments on black upward mobility. They focus on the waning of the Protestant ethic—hard work, deferred gratification, frugality, and responsibility—in much of black America.

From Cornel West, *Race Matters* (New York: Vintage Books, 1994), 17–18.

Sample Problem-Solution Paragraph

States problem

Introduces the numerous solutions

It's hard enough to endure plunging temperatures if you can find shelter. Plants have evolved ingenious ways to survive winter. Many strategies will work, and here are just a few: Some plants hide out underground—as roots, bulbs, and tubers crammed with food—until it's safe to grow leaves again; many plants secrete alcohols and sugars as a kind of antifreeze to lower the temperature at which cell walls would burst; lichens dehydrate over the winter; some plants grow low to the ground to avoid windchill; others create their own microclimates underground; some flowering plants (like mountain laurel) grow hairs along their stems and fruit as insulation; arctic flowers often use large petals as sun traps; some just sink their roots deeper; plants that live in extreme cold (such as red algae, which can grow on top of ice) sometimes use a color like red to convert light into heat. The plants in my yard are luckier—I cover some with pink sheets for a short spell, then bundle them in parkas of canvas and pine needles and dry leaves. It's a symbiosis as dear as the one between dogs and humans. I nourish them and they nourish me.

From Diane Ackerman, *Cultivating Delight: A Natural History of My Garden* (New York: HarperCollins Publishers, 2001), 171.

Comparison and Contrast

The technique of comparison and contrast draws out the similarities and distinctions between two or more things. Two methods may be used to organize the comparison. The **subject-by-subject method** discusses each subject or particular features of the subject in its own section or paragraph. The **point-by-point method** features the points of comparison, with the comparison and contrast moving back and forth between subjects on each point.

To compare and contrast, ask

- How is A different from B?
- What do A and B have in common?
- What advantages are there to considering A in concert with B?
- Is A better than B, or not?

Problem and Solution

The questions posed are "What problems exist?" and "What will solve these problems?"

To pose problems, ask

- What problems are associated with the subject?
- Who is affected by the problem?
- What difference would solving the problem make?

To think of solutions, ask

- What is the fairest solution?
- Who will be most affected by the solution to the problem?
- How much will solutions cost?

Narration

A narrative is a story that makes a point. This message need not be a moral. Rather, a narrative essay can be used to evoke in readers a strong understanding of the events described in it and perhaps empathy with the people involved.

To create a narrative, ask

- What happened to make the story worth telling?
- Who was involved?
- When did it happen, and over how long a period of time did it happen?
- Why did the events happen?
- What is the scene?
- What can be learned from the experience or event?

Exemplification

Exemplification provides readers with examples to illustrate a larger point. Examples can be quotations, facts, narratives, statistics, details, analogies, opinions, or observations. Most generalizations you make need to be supported by plenty of examples.

To think of good examples, ask

- What does someone need to know to appreciate my point?
- What examples from my reading (or viewing) can I draw on to illustrate the point?
- What experiences do I have in common with my readers that might exemplify my point?

Sample Narration

Sets the scene

Narrates the conflict

Demonstrates cultural differences

Touch the Clouds, Crazy Horse's seven-foot Miniconjou friend, asked that Crazy Horse be allowed to die in an Indian lodge. Dr. McGillycuddy carried the request to General Bradley, adding that violence might result from putting Crazy Horse in the jail. Bradley said, "Please give my compliment to the officer of the day, and he is to carry out his original orders, and put Crazy Horse in the guard house." Dr. McGillycuddy relayed this to Kennington, who tried again. American Horse, who had recently conspired against Crazy Horse's life, protested that Crazy Horse was a chief, and could not be put in prison. Dr. McGillycuddy returned to Bradley and told him it would be death to try a third time. Bradley finally agreed to compromise and allow Crazy Horse to be taken to the adjutant's office, a small room with a desk, a kerosene lamp, and a cot. Several Indians carried him in a blanket and set him on the floor. He refused to lie on the cot.

From Ian Frazier, *Great Plains* (New York: Penguin Books, 1989), 112.

Sample Exemplification

In this example, Carl Sagan uses a narrative example to help readers imagine how people rationalize behavior by explaining away normally solid evidence.

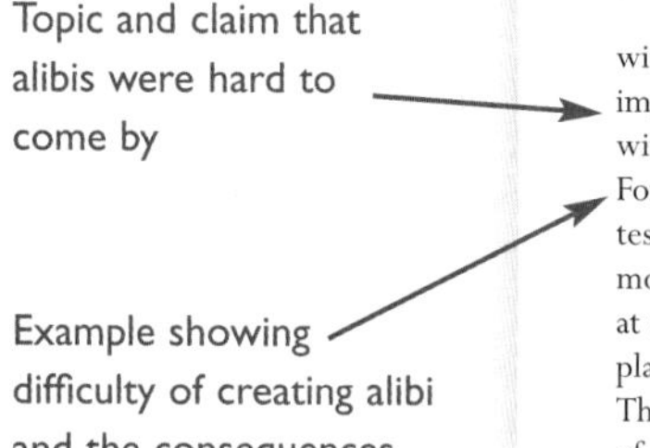

In the witch trials, mitigating evidence or defense witnesses were inadmissible. In any case, it was nearly impossible to provide compelling alibis for accused witches. The rule of evidence had a special character. For example, in more than one case a husband attested that his wife was asleep in his arms at the very moment she was accused of frolicking with the devil at a witch's Sabbath; but the archbishop patiently explained that a demon had taken the place of his wife. The husbands were not to imagine that their powers of perception could exceed Satan's powers of deception. The beautiful young women were perforce consigned to the flames.

From Carl Sagan, *The Demon-Haunted World: Science as a Candle in the Dark* (New York: Random House, 1996), 121.

Sample Classification and Division

Clear statement of topic

Describes historical context and previous types

Origin of the hybrid cycle-rickshaw

Division of cycle-rickshaws by type and according to geographical origin

The rickshaw designs are as widely variable as their riders. Hong Kong still has a handful of the old hand-pulled rickshaws and Calcutta is the only city on earth where they are still in use as everyday transport. In the other cities the rickshaw, a creation of the 1880s, gave birth to the cycle-rickshaw during the 1930s and 1940s but no standard pattern developed for this new-fangled device. In Manila, Rangoon and Singapore the cycle-rickshaws are standard bicycles with attached sidecars. The Manila versions with their mini-bikes and youthful riders look like a toytown model, while in Rangoon the passengers ride back-to-back. In Ara, Beijing, Dhaka and Macau the rider is out front and the passengers sit behind, as if the front part of a bicycle was mated with an old hand-pulled rickshaw. In Hanoi, Penang and Yogyakarta the meeting of bike and rickshaw produced precisely the opposite result, as if the back part of a bicycle had been joined to the old rickshaw seating; as a result the passengers sit, sometimes frighteningly, out front, watching oncoming traffic hurtling towards them.

From Tony Wheeler, *Chasing Rickshaws* (Melbourne: Lonely Planet Publications, 1998), 7.

Classification and Division

The method of classification and division involves dividing a subject into its parts and then grouping (classifying) them on the basis of similarities. Writers choose a principle of classification—the means of dividing the subject—and communicate that principle to readers.

To classify and divide a subject, ask

- What are the most important features of the subject?
- What do these features have in common with one another, and how do they differ?
- How have others classified and divided the subject?
- What features of your subject change over time? What features remain the same?

Threading the Thesis through the Paragraphs 2e

Using Key Terms to Keep Readers on Track

Thesis statement:

The **organic standards** that the Department of Agriculture recently tried to water down must be **maintained** to protect the **viability of small farms.**

Topic sentences and other sentences repeat the key terms:

These standards . . .
Organic crops provide . . .
Maintaining the standard . . .
In order to remain economically viable, small farms . . .

A thesis should function as the organizing principle or controlling idea for developing paragraphs in a project that argues a point or makes an interpretation. Key aspects of the thesis should be threaded through the paragraphs so that readers will understand how each part relates to the whole. To do this, use key terms in your thesis statement and then repeat them, with variations, throughout the work to keep readers on track.

An effective conclusion satisfies readers that they are finished reading, encourages them to reflect further on the issues, or urges them to act based on their new understanding. A conclusion usually does more than repeat the thesis or summarize what's already been written. In a shorter academic essay, a summation is not necessary; focus instead on extending the significance of the issue or even making a call to action that lets readers know what they might do (or think) next. In a very long essay or report or when the information is especially technical or complex, you should synthesize for your readers what they have just read and emphasize what is most important.

Don't offer entirely new material in the conclusion. If at the end of your draft you think of new material that seems important, then when you revise your first draft, move the point earlier and develop it in the body paragraphs.

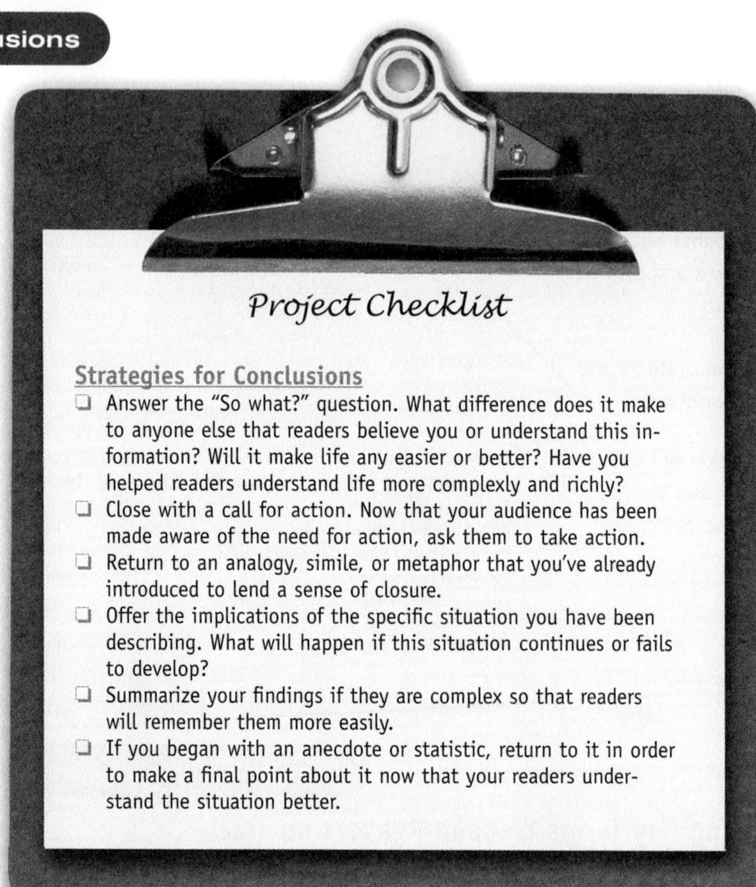

Project Checklist

Strategies for Conclusions

- ❑ Answer the "So what?" question. What difference does it make to anyone else that readers believe you or understand this information? Will it make life any easier or better? Have you helped readers understand life more complexly and richly?
- ❑ Close with a call for action. Now that your audience has been made aware of the need for action, ask them to take action.
- ❑ Return to an analogy, simile, or metaphor that you've already introduced to lend a sense of closure.
- ❑ Offer the implications of the specific situation you have been describing. What will happen if this situation continues or fails to develop?
- ❑ Summarize your findings if they are complex so that readers will remember them more easily.
- ❑ If you began with an anecdote or statistic, return to it in order to make a final point about it now that your readers understand the situation better.

A Conclusion Answering the "So What" Question

The introduction to the essay that this conclusion is drawn from is printed on page 19.

After everything they have done for us throughout the years, we owe it to our elderly to ensure their retirements are comfortable and secure. We need to make certain the system providing for them is strong and can endure until we retire, without passing on an unsustainable burden. Social security can be saved if it adapts. It is our responsibility as young people to encourage reform because, otherwise, the consequences will be ours to bear.

From Hunter Williams; see his introduction on page 52.

A Sample Working Outline

April Massiter, a second-year student, based her working outline on a tentative thesis statement.

Heart disease is on the rise in the United States because people are bombarded by advertising for fast, unhealthy food, making people associate being an American with being super-sized.

Intro:

—There has always been unhealthy food in abundance. Why should fast food chains be to blame? What is the difference between them and the typical supermarket? Or a classier restaurant?

—Mention the film Super-Size Me.

—Define fast food and give brief overview of history of fast food.

Body:

—Growth of fast food and franchise restaurants

—Fast food at school, prepared food at home, and thus, not much control over intake of fattening foods

—Rise of fad diets, especially Atkins, which encourage people to eat high-fat foods

—People seem to lack personal responsibility. They would rather sue fast food restaurants and cigarette manufacturers instead of watching what they put in their bodies. Be careful not to equate cigarettes—addictive—and French fries—delicious, but addictive?

—Diabetes, high blood pressure, lack of exercise, and cardiac problems

End:

Tell readers to pay attention to what they eat so that they can live healthy, long lives.

April noticed that her working outline suggested a historical progression and decided to try to arrange her ideas chronologically in her first draft.

Some writers like to organize their thoughts before drafting, and others prefer to write a draft first and then check the organization before writing another. When you need to check the organization of your writing project, an outline can be a helpful tool. Three kinds of outlines are the working outline, the topical outline, and the sentence outline. Your instructor may ask you to submit an outline with your project, so be sure to clarify which kind of outline is required.

Working Outlines

The **working outline** is a very rough guide to organization. Writers who want to get a quick handle on how they will organize (or how they have organized) their writing might jot down a working outline with just a few points.

Formal Outlines

Sentence outlines and **topical outlines** are more extensive than the working outline. In a sentence outline, each item is a complete sentence. The sentences at each level are written in parallel form. If you create a formal sentence outline, your first draft will be easy to write, since you can use sentences straight out of your outline in the draft. If your instructor requires that you submit a formal sentence outline with your project, double-check that the points in the outline and in the final project are arranged in exactly the same order.

The topical outline to the right was drafted by Brad Redrow, a first-year student at Camden County College, who was preparing an argument in response to the following assignment by Martha Bachman:

> Suppose someone argued that affirmative action is a necessary tactic to achieve more racial and cultural diversity on college campuses today. Referring to the essays by John Leo, Roger Wilkins, and Shelby Steele, how do you suppose they would respond to such an argument?

A Sample Topical Outline

Thesis: Although Roger Wilkins might argue that the advantages to society as a whole outweigh the disadvantages of using affirmative action to achieve more racial and cultural diversity on college campuses today, Shelby Steele and John Leo would vehemently argue that affirmative action should not be used for this purpose.

- I. Definition of affirmative action
  - A. Purpose of affirmative action
  - B. Actual uses of affirmative action, according to Steele and Leo
  - C. Use of affirmative action to promote diversity
- II. Wilkins
  - A. Disadvantages to white men
  - B. Benefits of affirmative action to society
    - 1. Increased opportunity for individuals
    - 2. Broader array of skills available in the American population utilized
- III. Steele
  - A. Detrimental effect on children who are not well off, but not "disadvantaged"
  - B. Unfair process of admissions
  - C. Misuse of affirmative action
- IV. Leo
  - A. Use of affirmative action to evade laws or court rulings against quotas
  - B. No racial and ethnic preferences allowed in the public sector in California
- V. Conclusion

REVISING, EDITING, AND PROOFREADING 3

Project Checklist

Using Self-Evaluation to Guide Revision

Respond in writing to the questions that follow. Try to elaborate as much as possible. The more you say here, the clearer your revision plan will be.

1. What do you like *best* about your essay or project? Explain.
2. What do you like *least* about your essay or project? Explain.
3. Go back through your essay or project and highlight what you feel is the liveliest part. Explain why you think it works well. What could you do to make the rest just as good?
4. Do you let your examples or support do the talking for you, or do you use them to reinforce what you already said?
5. What doesn't your essay or project cover that it probably should?
6. What was the hardest part to write? Explain.
7. What was the easiest part to write? Explain.
8. Does your paper have a title that is both descriptive and inviting? Write down three alternative titles; then look at all four to see which one you like best. Consider asking a peer for an opinion.

Follow-up: Once you have some good answers to these questions, write down at least five things you will work on in your revision.

When you revise your writing, you need to decide whether it achieves its purpose and rises to the level of quality that you envision for it. Eventually, you will learn to predict how your readers will react as well.

Revision focuses on content and form and usually involves adding, deleting, changing, and rearranging—all acts that require careful thought and even new research and writing. As you approach revision, you can ask yourself, "What do I want my writing to do?" "What have I done?" "What can I do now to meet my goals and reach my audience?"

Editing, in contrast, typically focuses on sentence-level and formatting issues at that point when a work has already undergone deep revisions.

Proofreading is a process of double- (or triple-) checking your writing systematically, looking for mistakes such as typos, unusual formatting, punctuation mistakes, spelling errors, and citation problems.

As you learn more about the subject in the act of writing, it becomes clearer how to shape this knowledge to suit the context, which consists of the audience, the purpose, and the rhetorical occasion, or *kairos.*

Revising for Audience

Step into the experience of at least one typical reader as you ask yourself how your draft would be read. For example, if you have written a first draft of a persuasive essay arguing that reality television actually does have some redeeming qualities, have you considered how people who have never seen these shows might respond?

Revising for Purpose

What is your purpose? As you reread your work, evaluate how close you have come to achieving it.

Revising for *Kairos*

Think carefully about your timing and the circumstances of the act of reading itself and what people are likely to know about your topic. How will these public circumstances affect responses to your work?

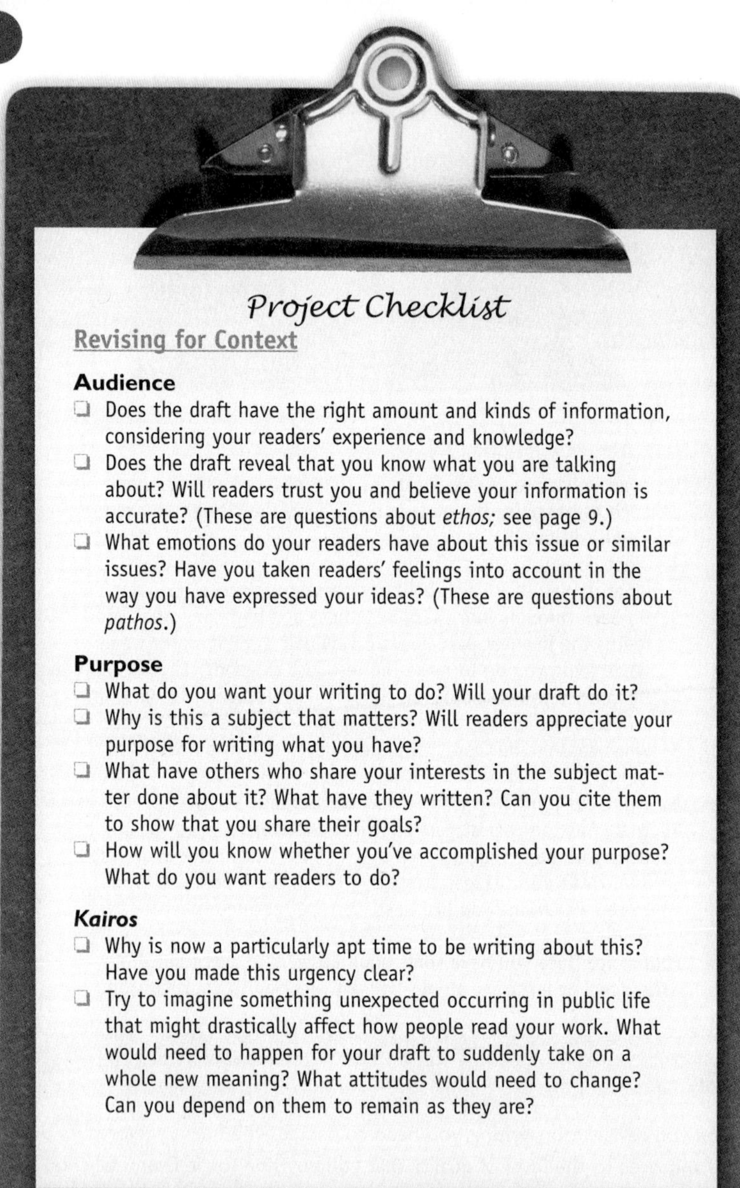

Project Checklist

Revising for Context

Audience

- ❑ Does the draft have the right amount and kinds of information, considering your readers' experience and knowledge?
- ❑ Does the draft reveal that you know what you are talking about? Will readers trust you and believe your information is accurate? (These are questions about *ethos;* see page 9.)
- ❑ What emotions do your readers have about this issue or similar issues? Have you taken readers' feelings into account in the way you have expressed your ideas? (These are questions about *pathos*.)

Purpose

- ❑ What do you want your writing to do? Will your draft do it?
- ❑ Why is this a subject that matters? Will readers appreciate your purpose for writing what you have?
- ❑ What have others who share your interests in the subject matter done about it? What have they written? Can you cite them to show that you share their goals?
- ❑ How will you know whether you've accomplished your purpose? What do you want readers to do?

Kairos

- ❑ Why is now a particularly apt time to be writing about this? Have you made this urgency clear?
- ❑ Try to imagine something unexpected occurring in public life that might drastically affect how people read your work. What would need to happen for your draft to suddenly take on a whole new meaning? What attitudes would need to change? Can you depend on them to remain as they are?

Wyatt's first draft starts very generally

Competition at Its Best

Most people have at least one very distinct quality about them that sets them apart from everybody else. Sometimes it is something as obvious as a physical condition: obesity, hair color, freckles, or glasses. But more often than not, it is something that you cannot see by just looking at the person. Perhaps it is something about their personality or something they like to do. Regardless of what the defining characteristic is, everybody has one, and for me it is competitiveness. Ever since I was a young boy, I loved to turn even the smallest of things into a competition. I would say to my brothers, "Hey, I'll race you to the end of the road," or "I'll bet I can beat you in a game of Monopoly." It didn't matter what the scenario was, but rather how can I turn it into a game? Through this portrait I hope to show that I am a competitive person.

Why this explanation of universality? I like the move from physical to personality, but I'm wondering why you make the case for all of us having that distinct quality. How else could you frame your competitiveness in this beginning?

Wyatt's second draft focuses on specific details

Competition at Its Best

Three broken collarbones, a torn ACL, a broken ankle, a separated shoulder, two torn hamstrings, a torn rotator cuff, and countless bumps, cuts, and bruises. It sounds like a list of injuries that you might see at a sports medicine clinic in a single day. These injuries, however, are a list of all of the things that have happened to my brothers and me over our football careers. The grand total for all of the expenses is estimated at around $85,000 (thank God for insurance). It sounds very painful and agonizing to many people, but if we were asked to do it all again knowing that we were going to have to go through all of these injuries the answer would be the same for all of us: "In a heart beat." So why would we do it all again? The enormous cost and wear and tear to your body would be enough to make most people hang it up. What was different about us? The answer is twofold: a deep love of football, but an even deeper love for the competition that it brings.

Sharpening the Focus

First drafts are often filled with generalities that represent several different approaches to the topic or even, on closer examination, completely different topics. If you find more general statements than details, you should focus your draft.

For example, Wyatt Roth, writing in a first-year composition course at Purdue University, revised his introductory paragraph radically based on feedback from his instructor, Colin Charlton. In the second draft, he introduced his essay with specific details about the injuries he and his brothers have sustained while playing sports. This approach gave Wyatt a dramatic way to emphasize his love of sports and competition.

Most of the time, a thesis statement is predictive of the overall form of a work. If the thesis statement is unclear, missing, tentative, or noncommittal, the draft will probably reflect that.

Adding Details and Evidence

Readers want to be shown the evidence on which you base your position. Knowing the details, they can then decide whether they agree with your central point in an argumentative essay or the gist and insights of a narrative. What kind of evidence or events you need to include depends on the point you are asking readers to accept or the feelings and thoughts you want them to keep in mind.

In many academic projects, evidence will emphasize the *why* and *how* of your thesis. If you write, "Even though it is not a poem, the film *Rabbit-Proof Fence* has many important qualities of an epic," then you will need to tell readers why you think so. How do several specific aspects of the film correspond to important qualities of an epic poem? The amount of supporting information you will need to support a given thesis will vary, too. If your readers hold a view contrary to yours, you will need more evidence than if they are likely to agree.

Project Checklist

Kinds of Evidence

If you find that your draft needs more details, evidence, scenes, or texture to draw out and elaborate its main points, consider these kinds of evidence, taking into account the rhetorical situation:

- ❑ *Sensory details*—visual details and contrasts, sounds, aromas, textures, and tastes—can all add atmosphere to a scene.
- ❑ *Facts* that go beyond common knowledge and that are properly cited show that you have done your research. (For more about common knowledge, see section 12f.)
- ❑ *Statistics* can appease readers who wonder whether your numbers really add up when you make generalizations about, for instance, how many people think this or that. In science and social science fields, statistical evidence can be especially important.
- ❑ *Voices of authority* and *expert opinion* can add credibility to your claims, improve your own ethos, and show that you know what others have already written about your topic. But don't let the voices of authority smother your voice. Be certain to cite direct and indirect uses of another's words and ideas.
- ❑ *Visual presentations*—graphs, charts, illustrations, tables, screenshots, and photographs—are useful ways to summarize data and show relationships across sets of data over time. Be sure that your visual information doesn't simply stand by itself but that you weave its meaning into your draft (▶ Chapter 18).
- ❑ *Experiential evidence* can be used when you have insider knowledge of an event, know how something works, or have acquired information over time. Draw from personal experience.

It is very likely that you will want to do additional research in order to find appropriate support for your thesis and details for your narratives. Conducting focused research at the stage of revision can be fun. You know what you need, and it's exciting to find it. (For advice on conducting research online, see Chapter 10; for library research, see Chapter 11.)

Writers working on a computer can experiment freely with revisions because word processing software allows for quick manipulation of text and images. Cut-and-paste makes it easy to move paragraphs and sentences around within a document and between documents if you need to adapt your writing to other contexts or media (such as a Web page).

Cut, copy, and paste also are useful for copying and moving text from email messages, browsers (URLs and page content, for example), and chat boxes. Although there may be some variation across programs, Windows® and Mac® operating systems generally use a standard set of keystrokes for the cut, copy, and paste functions.

Cutting, Copying, and Pasting Text and Images

1. Position your cursor where you want to begin cutting or copying.
2. To cut or copy, hold down the left mouse button (on a two-button mouse) or press the Command key (⌘) and click the mouse (on a Mac). Highlight the text or image by dragging the cursor over it. Then use the commands in the table below.
3. To paste, position the cursor at the insertion point and then key the paste command shown in the table.

Function	Windows Keystroke	Mac Keystroke
Cutting deletes the text or image and places it on the clipboard in your computer's memory for later pasting. Only the most recent cut is saved on the clipboard, so be careful!	Ctrl + X	Command (⌘) + X
Copying leaves the original text or image where it is but copies it to the clipboard for later pasting.	Ctrl + C	Command (⌘) + C
Pasting takes the content of the clipboard and inserts it at the location of the cursor.	Ctrl + V	Command (⌘) + V

Using the cut, copy, and paste keystrokes is the quickest method, but you may be more comfortable using a toolbar or menu to perform these functions. In Microsoft® Word® 2007, look for these functions on the Home ribbon: Paste Cut Copy Format Painter. In Microsoft® Word® Mac 2008, look under the Edit menu. Most word processors will also copy and paste the formatting styles of the source. Sometimes you will not want to preserve the original formatting in your new document, in which case you should use the Paste Special command (Alt + Ctrl + V in Word® 2007 or Edit > Paste Special in Mac Word® 2008), which allows you more control over exactly what gets pasted and how.

For instructions that apply to Microsoft® Word® 2003, visit the handbook's website: **cengage.com/english/blakesley**

3c Revising for Style

Sentences rarely come out finely tuned in a first draft, so experienced writers have learned to revise when their stylistic habits lead to unreadable or unnecessarily wordy prose.

The paramedic method was first devised by Richard Lanham in the 1970s. If you apply the paramedic method consistently to every one of your sentences, your writing will be clearer, more concise, and, most importantly, readable. You will also develop a sharper sense of what you have already written and thus clearer ideas about how to revise your writing so that it better accomplishes your purposes.

Using the Paramedic Method to Analyze and Revise Sentences

Using a double-spaced copy of your draft, do the following.

1. Underline the prepositional phrases (such as *of the night, for his work).*
2. Circle the "to be" verbs (*am, is, are, was, were, been*).
3. Find the action or state of being in the sentence. (Look for nominalizations, such as *description* rather than *describe,* since nominalizations often disguise the action in a sentence.)
4. Put this action in a simple (not compound) active verb.
5. Determine the agent of the action, and then compose the base clause.
6. Start fast—avoid long introductory phrases.
7. Try to keep the subject/agent of the sentence close to the action.
8. Vary the lengths of your sentences; go for rhythm and balance.
9. Read the passage aloud with emphasis and feeling. Revise sentences to improve rhythm and put stress on key ideas. (Information that comes last in a sentence is remembered most clearly.)

Use this method judiciously, depending on your rhetorical situation. Certain purposes require more linking verbs than others. Basic description, for example, often requires a simple verb, as in "The sky was blue." So does a sentence that defines a state of being, such as "The Fourth of July is a national holiday in the United States." In much expository prose, however, a ratio of no more than one "to be" verb to every five sentences is about right. In any event, be aware of your style and know that you have options.

3d Peer Review

Peer review of writing is a critical component of revision. Not only will your reading of another's work help the writer, but you will find yourself sharpening your critical reading ability in ways that help you evaluate and revise your own work. As a peer reviewer, you will also see options that you hadn't considered previously for approaching a topic.

As a writer, you will receive the valuable responses of real readers, who may be different from the ones you imagined while you were drafting. Reader feedback—when it is careful and reflective—almost always will help you improve your work.

Responding as a Reader: Pointing, Summarizing, Reflecting

It is sometimes helpful to respond to a draft as a reader, without the compulsion to offer specific suggestions for improving it. Writers find it valuable to know what their readers remember, what they felt as they read, and what they want to know more about. To give writers this kind of response, you can respond by pointing, summarizing, and reflecting.

- **Pointing.** What one idea or image really stands out? What is the most striking sentence? What do you remember most about it?

- **Summarizing.** What is the writing about? Give the most direct answer, and try to elaborate as much as possible. The idea is to give the writer a good sense of what readers remember about the work.
- **Reflecting.** If you have a chance to annotate the work, let the writer know what you are thinking as you read. For example, if you are lost, write "I am lost here." If you feel sad, write "This scene makes me feel sad." It's enough to reflect these kinds of responses back to writers. They may decide that you were lost because you weren't paying attention, or they may realize that they need to work a little harder to give you something that keeps your interest.

Project Checklist

Sample Peer Review Questions

Here is a general set of peer review guidelines you can use.

1. What is the main point or thesis? Is it clearly articulated in the draft?
2. Is the main point supported by the parts of the draft? Do the sections, panels, paragraphs, slides, Web pages, or other main units of thought offer support for the main point?
3. Does that support seem compelling? Why or why not?
4. For each part of the draft, are the general statements backed up by specific details?
5. Are there any areas that should be covered but are not? Is any necessary information missing?
6. What do you find interesting? What could be reworked to make it more interesting?
7. What is the best thing about the draft?
8. What is the major stumbling block in the draft?
9. What suggestions do you want to give the writer? What should be done to achieve the writer's purpose for the audience?

From the Reviewer's Perspective

As a reader helping a writer revise his or her work, you should keep some general principles in mind.

Find out about the context. Before you begin, ask the writer about the work's context. What is the assignment, or what is the writer trying to achieve? Who is the audience?

Read carefully and attentively. Give the writing your full attention. First, read through the whole work to get the gist. Then read it again more slowly, making notes as you go. If you are reading the work electronically, use the word processor's comment function (▶ page 38).

Make your comments constructive. It can be difficult to receive feedback, especially on a draft that took a lot of time and effort to write. Be supportive instead of negative, and offer suggestions as well as critical comments.

Be an interested reader, not an editor. At the drafting and revision stages, writers need feedback on the big issues: content, structure, flow, persuasiveness, examples, style, and so on. It's more important that you read as a reader than as an editor.

Provide specific suggestions for improvement. "I don't like this!" is not specific enough to be useful. Nor is "I liked your essay." Whether you do or don't like something, you should explain why and offer a suggestion for improvement.

From the Writer's Perspective

As a writer . . .

Don't preface the peer review with disclaimers. A disclaimer is a statement like "I only spent an hour on this draft" or "I didn't understand the assignment." The point of peer review is to give readers a chance to respond to what is actually written.

Elicit good responses. Ask readers to respond to aspects that trouble you or may need more attention.

Be receptive to feedback. Don't be dismissive about any reader's feedback. Sometimes people will read differently than we expect, but use that to your advantage.

Ask follow-up questions. Readers probably won't mind if you ask them questions about comments you don't understand or if you ask for a response to a particular part of your writing.

Revise with your reviewers' comments in mind. Keep the peer reviews next to you when revising. Read through them again as you plan your revision.

Commenting on a Document in a Word Processor

Most word processors allow writers and peer reviewers to comment on a text without changing the original text itself. In Microsoft Word, WordPerfect®, and OpenOffice.org Writer, the process works similarly. As different readers respond to a draft, their comments appear in different colors, and the initials of the respondent help writers identify who said what.

Balloon Commenting in Microsoft Word 2007

To make sure that your comments on a text appear as balloons, follow these steps:

1. Select the Review tab and then the down arrow on the Track Changes icon, which then allows you to choose "Change Tracking Options."
2. In the Options dialogue box, set "Use Balloons (Print and Web Layout)" to "Only for comments/formatting" in the drop-down menu.
3. Click OK.
4. Set your view to Print, Full Screen Reading, or Web Layout using the View ribbon: Choose View > Print Layout in most cases.

To insert balloon comments, follow these steps:

1. Choose the Review Tab.
2. Highlight the text you want to comment on.
3. On the Review ribbon, click on the New Comment button. (See Figure 3.1.)

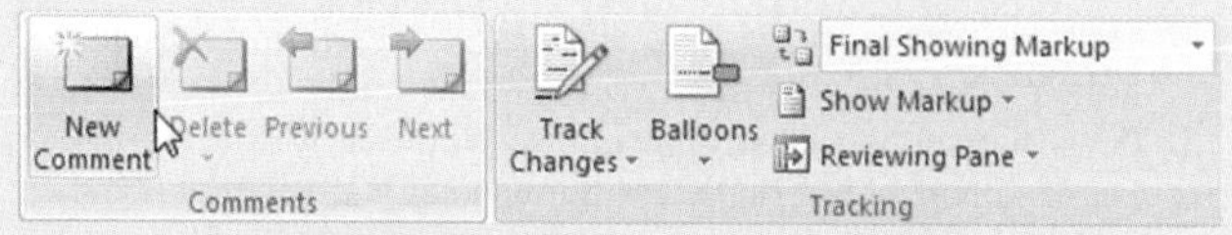

Figure 3.1 Inserting a Comment in Microsoft Word 2007

4. Type your comment in the balloon.
5. To insert another comment, repeat steps 2–4.

For instructions that apply to Microsoft® Word® 2003, visit the handbook's website: **cengage.com/english/blakesley**

Focal Points for Editing

Global Issues

If you have revised carefully, you may have already addressed most of the global issues that will affect the reception of your writing. However, at the editing stage, it is important to reconsider these issues as a final check. Use the Project Checklists on pages 32 and 34 to check global issues once again. Also take this opportunity to think about your title. Does it accurately reflect the work's content or purpose? Will it appeal to the intended audience? Check the title for spelling and grammatical mistakes.

Local Issues

- **Transitions.** Check to make sure that you use effective transitions across paragraphs. If transitions between sentences aren't necessary, eliminate them (◀ pages 21–22).
- **Metadiscourse.** Eliminate statements that merely announce your intentions, such as "In this paper, I will . . . ." These references to the act of writing itself—called metadiscourse—focus readers' attention on you rather than on the subject matter, where it belongs.
- **Coherence.** Read through your essay to see if you have good sentence-to-sentence coherence. Are there any abrupt leaps that need to be fixed?
- **Diction.** Make sure that you use terms that your audience will understand and that are appropriate to the subject matter and rhetorical situation (▶ Chapter 28).
- **Usage.** Check to see that you have followed usage guidelines for special or unusual terms, nonsexist language, spelling, and other conventions appropriate to the genre or discipline.

Software for Editors

If you do a lot of editing, you may find it useful to try out some software that makes routine editing tasks easier, especially when working with long and complex documents. One possibility is

Editor's ToolKit: **http://www.editorium.com**

(A free 45-day trial is available.)

Reading as an editor requires shifting the focus of your attention from that of writer to that of reader. When editing, you pay deliberate and systematic attention to the ways your work communicates with readers. How will they respond to your writing? You may find that a deep edit prompts you to return to revising in order to work out some of the problems that have surfaced. Like revision, editing may prompt rewriting.

Try these strategies.

Focus Your Editing

When you edit, focus on one feature at a time. When you look for something in particular—such as tone or your use of sources—you are much more likely to notice issues that need to be addressed.

Read Your Writing Aloud

When you read your work aloud, even by yourself, you will see and hear problems with the text. The act of translating the words to speech will help you notice awkward phrasings, repetition in word choice, problems with coherence, lapses in tone, and other stylistic problems that should be addressed. Read with pen in hand so that you can place a check mark next to sentences and sections that need further attention.

Edit on Paper and Screen

Edit on screen and then on paper, which will help you see your writing in two distinct ways. On screen, consider tracking the changes you make to your document so that you can read these changes as both a reader and an editor.

Read Line by Line

When you are editing at the sentence level, reducing the amount of text you see at any one time will help you focus your attention.

Make a List of the Words You Commonly Misspell

Keep a list of words you often misspell and refer to it as you edit and proofread. You can use your word processor's Find function (usually Ctrl + F on a PC or Apple + F on a Mac) to search for them. You can also add these words to your AutoCorrect dictionary if you are using Microsoft Word.

Keep Track of Your Most Common Errors

If you have learned that you have trouble with particular kinds of sentences, grammatical constructions, or comma rules, make a reference sheet to use while editing.

Style, Mechanics, and Spelling

- **Agent-action style.** Wherever possible, use an agent-action style. Use simple action verbs to add concreteness and liveliness to your writing (▶ Chapter 27).
- **Repetition.** Eliminate unnecessary repetition of words and ideas (▶ section 27a).
- **Parallel structure.** Use parallel structure with a series of items, phrases, or sentences when you want to establish a consistent pattern (▶ Chapter 25).
- **Sentence fragments.** Use complete sentences; if you use any fragments, make sure you have a rhetorically sound reason to do so (▶ Chapter 31).
- **Comma splices and run-ons.** Make sure that you don't use commas where periods or semicolons are needed (▶ Chapter 32).
- **Dangling modifiers.** Make sure that modifying phrases are next to the terms they modify (▶ section 36k).
- **Subject-verb agreement errors.** The verb should agree with the subject in every sentence. Double-check your sentences, especially when there is a prepositional phrase or modifier between the subject and the verb (▶ Chapter 35).
- **Pronoun reference and agreement.** All pronouns should have a clear antecedent and agree in number with that antecedent (▶ Chapter 33).
- **Clichés.** Eliminate clichés, as well as idiomatic phrases that some readers won't understand (▶ section 28f).
- **Homonyms.** Don't confuse homonyms, such as *cite, sight,* and *site* (▶ Glossary of Usage).
- **Missing words.** Make sure that you haven't left out any words needed to complete the meaning of a sentence (▶ Chapter 31).
- **Spelling.** Run your document through a spell checker *and* read through it one last time so that you catch the errors that spell checkers almost always miss, such as homonyms (▶ Chapter 46).
- **Citation style.** Check all the entries in your Works Cited, References, or Bibliography to make sure they include the required information, use the required form and style, and are listed in the required order (▶ Parts 4 and 5).
- **Punctuation.** Check punctuation throughout. Double-check the opening and closing sentences of all paragraphs (▶ Part 10).

Tracking Changes in Microsoft Word 2007

Note for Mac users: The Command key (⌘) on a Mac keyboard is the equivalent of the Ctrl key on a PC keyboard. To make the equivalent of a right click on a one-button mouse, hold down the Mac's Command key (⌘) while clicking; then select the function from the pop-up menu.

1. With your document open, choose the Review tab on the top menu bar.
2. Set your Track Changes options:
   a. Select the Review tab and then the down arrow on the Track Changes icon, which then allows you to choose "Change Tracking Options."
   b. Set the options for displaying the types of changes you make to your document, including the appearance of comments.
   c. Click OK when finished.
3. On the Review ribbon, you can adjust the location of balloon comments, which kind of markup to show (e.g., Insertions and Deletions, Formatting), whether you view Final Showing Markup, Final, Original Showing Markup, or Original. The Review ribbon also includes handy commands for using Track Changes, including icons for accepting and rejecting changes, new comments, and comparing two documents.
4. Click on the Track Changes icon on the Review ribbon or press and hold Ctrl + Shift + E to start tracking changes to the document.

As you add and delete text, move it around, or change its formatting, Word will record these changes. Turn to page 42 to see your options for viewing the changes.

For instructions that apply to Microsoft® Word® 2003, visit the handbook's website: **cengage.com/english/blakesley**

When you proofread, you examine your document carefully to make sure that you haven't left anything out, that the pages are formatted correctly, and that you haven't misspelled words or made any typos. Proofreading is the last step in polishing your work for readers, who will appreciate the extra care you have taken. Word processing programs include a variety of useful tools for checking your writing during this final stage.

Tracking Changes to a Document

Microsoft Word, WordPerfect, and OpenOffice.org Writer each allow users to track changes to a document and to compare documents so that the writer or the group members on a collaborative project can see what changes have been made. Tracking changes to a document can help you make sure that you haven't accidentally deleted important information from one draft to the next. You can also use the tracked changes to help you write submission notes, which instructors sometimes require with revisions.

Bookmarking Useful Reference Sites

In your Web browser, bookmark useful online reference sources so that you can access them easily as you check your facts and proofread. Here is a short list of writer's reference tools we find handy for this and many other purposes:

Merriam-Webster Online Dictionary:
http://m-w.com

Online Etymology Dictionary:
http://www.etymonline.com

RefDesk:
http://www.refdesk.com

Britannica Encyclopaedia:
http://www.britannica.com

Purdue's Online Writing Lab:
http://owl.english.purdue.edu

Spelling- and Grammar-Checking Resources Online

To find out how to use spelling and grammar checkers in your word processing program, visit cengage.com/English/Blakesley. You will also find lessons in

- how to customize your spelling and grammar checker
- how to add terms to your Auto-Correct dictionary in Word

Viewing the Changes

In Microsoft Word 2007, you have several options for adjusting your settings so that you can see the tracked changes properly.

1. With the document open, choose the Review tab to show the Review ribbon.
2. In the "Tracking" category, decide whether you would like to view the document in its final form with the proposed changes shown (Final Showing Markup), in its final form with the proposed changes applied (Final), or in its original form before changes were made (Original). We recommend editing your text using the setting Final Showing Markup (Figure 3.2).

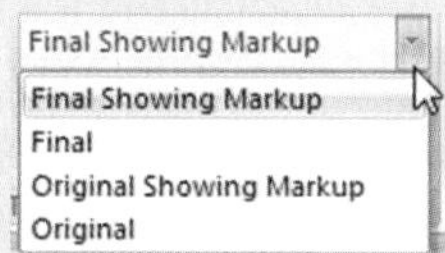

Figure 3.2 View options for tracked changes.

3. For ease of reading, you may want to hide all Formatting changes to the document. On the Review ribbon, click on the down arrow of the Show Markup icon, then make sure that "Formatting" is unchecked (Figure 3.3).

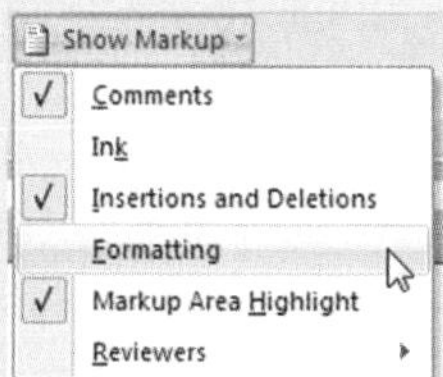

Figure 3.3 Show Markup options, here set to hide formatting changes.

For instructions that apply to Microsoft® Word® 2003, visit the handbook's website: **cengage.com/english/blakesley**

Garrison 1

Angela Garrison

Dr. Simpson

English 101

September 26, 2005

From Over There to Over Here:

War Blogs Get Up Close, Personal, and Profitable

Blog was the word looked up most often in the online *Merriam-Webster's Dictionary* in 2004 ("'Blog' Most Popular Word on Web Dictionary"). What's all this fuss? When you read someone else's personal blog, you find out what they like and don't like, what they're doing, and maybe other bits of gossip offered at random. You can read news blogs to find out what's going on lately, what other people think about it, and why it matters. You can keep your own blog to share your thoughts and feelings, to tell your friends and family what you're up to, and sometimes to capture the interest of someone you've never met. When you read and write blogs, you join, or even create, a community. Blogs are also an efficient way to break news, spread rumors, and glorify causes. In short, blogs help people do what they've always done as social beings, just more quickly now, and from almost anywhere on Earth. Soldiers on the ground fighting in Iraq are writing blogs from the front lines. But a review is now under way at the Pentagon to "better understand the overall implications of blogging and other Internet communications in combat zones," according to John Hockenberry in his *Wired* article "The Blogs of War." The benefits of blogs written by U.S. soldiers in Iraq far outweigh the hypothetical risks of revealing sensitive or strategic information. Those benefits, however, aren't as obvious as they might seem.

In spite of what the imagery of smart bombs and predator drones might lead television viewers to believe, wars are fought by people, not just technology. Most blogs start out as efforts to stay in touch with family and friends, but they quickly

Angela Garrison's class was asked to write a brief paper in response to an article by John Hockenberry called "The Blogs of War," which appeared online at *Wired* magazine. Although the assignment did not specifically require writers to consult other sources, she decided that to understand Hockenberry's article fully she should examine some of the blogs soldiers were posting online. She cites all her sources in the Works Cited list on the last page of her paper.

The opening provides background information about the popularity and uses of blogs.

Restricts the focus to war blogs

States the main focus of "The Blogs of War" article

The thesis statement makes a claim that the author will support in the rest of the response essay. The last sentence then functions as a transition that piques the readers' interest.

Topic sentence for the paragraph

These sentences restrict the topic by explaining how blogs humanize the war.

Example 1

Example 2

This sentence sums up the reasons for humanizing the war with milblogs.

This transitional sentence introduces a contrast, suggesting other motives for milblogs.

Topic sentence

The sentences that begin "If you visit . . . ," "Other milbloggers . . . ," and "Still others . . ." restrict the topic.

turn into a kind of citizen-on-the-street journalism. Blogs humanize soldiers by showing others what their lives are like on the front lines. One told the story of how "the braver [Iraqi] children will approach and try to practice their English skills, which usually revolves around the phrase 'Mr., Mr., Saddam is a dork'" (Bout). Naturally, the stories milbloggers (short for "military bloggers") tell are not always pretty, and many don't have happy endings or show people in their best light. One milblogger and doctor, Michael Cohen, wrote gripping accounts of the carnage following the suicide bombing of a mess tent and described the doctors' efforts to save the wounded (Hockenberry). Another milblogger, Neil Prakash, writes about how "the poetry of warfare is in the sounds of exploding weapons and the chaos of battle" (Hockenberry): "So far there hadn't been a single civilian in TF2-2's sector. We had been free to light up the insurgents as we saw them. And because of that freedom, we were able to use the main gun with less restriction" (Prakash). Danjel Bout, another milblogger, sums up the purpose of these front-line messages: "For people to really understand our day-to-day experience here, they need more than the highlights reel. They need to see the world through our eyes for a few minutes" (qtd. in Hockenberry).

The understanding Bout has in mind may be more than just appreciation for the tough and harrowing lives of the soldiers fighting for their country thousands of miles from home. Some milblogs exploit this realism for ulterior motives. If you visit these milblogs, you see that some of them have become vehicles for all kinds of propaganda on behalf of political views, serving both conservative and liberal agendas. Other milbloggers do everything they can to profit from their popularity--in the grand American tradition. Still others play up their role as unobstructed news from the front lines and become the examples used by Washington think-tanks to make their arguments, pro and con, for how the war is going. For example, "Blackfive," as he is known, kept his blog during his time as an intelligence officer in

Garrison 3

Iraq and has continued it now that he has become an IT officer for a high-tech firm (Hockenberry). Blackfive's blog is

> nearly as cluttered with ads as the Drudge Report, and the sales pitches mostly hawk "liberal-baiting merchandise." There are pictures of attractive women holding high-powered weapons, dozens of links to conservative books and films, and even the occasional big spender like Amazon.com. Blackfive also sells his own T-shirts to benefit military charities. (Hockenberry)

Right next to such ads, you can read the stories of distraught parents hearing the news that their son or daughter has been killed in action. The impression you get is not so much a sense of the human price of war, but the willingness of anyone to exploit and glorify pain and suffering to sell an idea or a t-shirt.

Because there are so many milbloggers and their messages range from personal stories to propaganda, it is unlikely that the enemy will monitor milblogs for clues about the American military's next move. The Department of Defense (DOD) realizes this, of course, so the milbloggers will no doubt continue their work to humanize the war, even as others profit from it. The DOD knows also that milblogs build the morale of the soldiers over there by giving them an outlet to express and share their fears with others, even opportunities to think about something other than what's around the next bend. The milblogs show us the heroes as well as the profiteers. Regardless of the purity of the motives of milbloggers, readers over here see a side of the war reported not by professional journalists but by the actors themselves. Although the function of these blogs has become much more than maintaining ties with friends and family, they still help all of us understand how our soldiers feel, how they respond to their situations, and how they confront and explain them. That insight can benefit everyone, especially those who instigate or prosecute war.

Extended example of how one person uses a milblog for profit.

Addresses the thesis statement and provides a reason that benefits outweigh security issues. This is also the topic sentence of the paragraph.

The sentences following the topic sentence restrict the focus of the topic to the DOD's position.

The concluding sentences "raise the stakes" by arguing that the benefits are more than just "staying in touch." Instead, milblogs offer insight into the day-to-day realities of war that may help us understand how to avoid it in the future.

The Works Cited section includes listings for all sources of outside information in the essay, including the citation for the term *blog*'s popularity, Hockenberry's article, and two milblogs that the writer tracked down through a Google search.

Garrison 4

Works Cited

"'Blog' Most Popular Word on Web Dictionary." *MSNBC.com.* MSNBC, 2 Dec. 2004. Web. 15 Sept. 2005.

Bout, Danjel. "Snapshots." *Frontline Blogs.* N.p., 21 Aug. 2005. Web. 15 Sept. 2005.

Hockenberry, John. "The Blogs of War." *Wired.com.* Wired, Aug. 2005. Web. 14 Sept. 2005.

Prakash, Neil. "11 November: Tank Mines." *Armor Geddon.* N.p., 23 Jan. 2005. Web. 15 Sept. 2005.

Reading and Writing Critically

PART 2

New Contexts for Writing: Collaboration in the Knowledge Universe

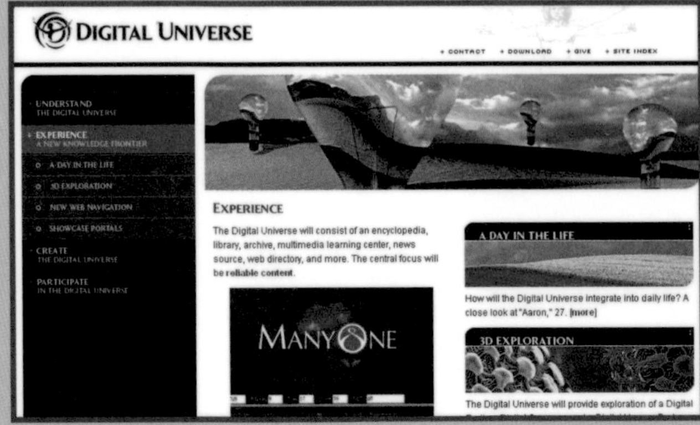

The Internet has the capacity to connect people with information and ideas, and search engines like Google and Yahoo! have made accessible more information than most people can handle. What's next? What is emerging as a way to manage information overload? We need readers who can evaluate information, and writers who can put it together in ways that make sense and that are accessible to everyone. In short, we need writers and "knowledge experts" who can create and synthesize content that is reliable, rich, and enduring.

The Digital Universe (http://www.digitaluniverse.net) is an initiative with high aspirations: to use an open collaboration system to build the world's largest and most reliable information resource on the Internet. In that respect, it competes with Wikipedia. By allowing users to contribute and edit content, Wikipedia has quickly built the world's largest encyclopedia. The Wikipedia model depends upon the integrity and knowledge of its contributors, so there are times when its information is not as reliable or as balanced as it could be. (Erroneous information tends to be weeded out quickly with the help of volunteer reviewers and editors.)

At the Digital Universe, the model is similar but with some additional features. The site will combine open collaboration with review by editors and "stewards," who are widely acknowledged experts in the subject matter. Stewards will map the direction of content areas and enlist writers to help create and improve it. Customized software will allow people to learn in visually rich ways. The public will play an important role in this collaborative effort.

Collaboration is the process of planning, creating, and writing with others to achieve a goal. It is, literally, a "working together." **Knowledge** is not simply a collection of facts or information, but a perspective on information, an attitude about how facts and information can be put to use to explain phenomena. A **knowledge network** is a system for relating ideas, usually facilitated by a **discourse community,** a group of people with shared interests and ideals who use a common language and set of perspectives, a kind of specialized literacy. A guiding principle of robust knowledge networks is the idea of **emergence,** a theory of knowledge production that says new knowledge and patterns of order can result from the uncoordinated but useful contributions of individuals, not unlike the emergent order in an ant colony.

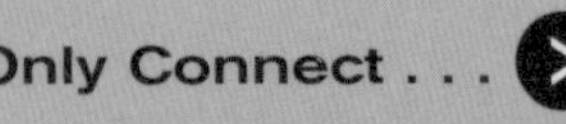

Collaborative Knowledge Networks

The Digital Universe | http://www.digitaluniverse.net
Internet Movie Database | http://www.imdb.com
EServer TC Library | http://tc.eserver.org
Wikipedia | http://www.wikipedia.org

An active reader asks questions

Read the text carefully several times to extend your understanding of what it says, what it means, why it's important (or not), and what use you can make of it.

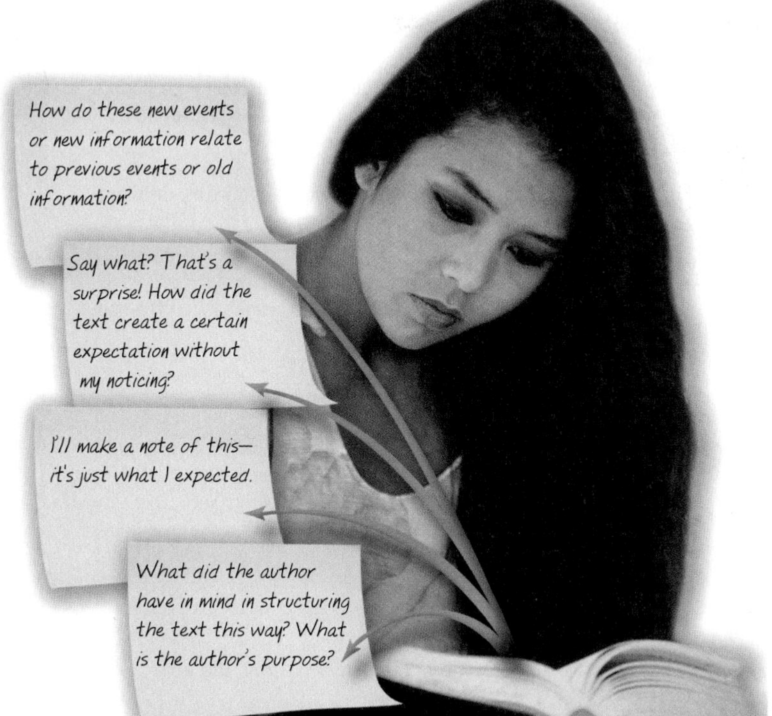

How do these new events or new information relate to previous events or old information?
Say what? That's a surprise! How did the text create a certain expectation without my noticing?
I'll make a note of this—it's just what I expected.
What did the author have in mind in structuring the text this way? What is the author's purpose?

Readers who have different purposes for reading attend to different aspects of a text in order to fulfill their needs. For example, you can focus on what a text meant historically or what it means now. You can read as a writer to see whether you can learn by example. You may simply read for pleasure.

Active Reading 4a

In college, read actively. Active reading begins with curiosity. By engaging your curiosity, you become alert to the possibilities of the text and your response to it. As you read, make predictions and see whether the text fulfills them in the way you anticipated. Argue with the author and ask questions about what you don't understand. Write down your thoughts and feelings about the text.

Making Predictions

You will find the text more engaging, and understand it more easily, if you spend a few minutes preparing to read by looking over key elements in order to make predictions about what is coming. Start by looking over the text from beginning to end, taking 5 or 10 minutes to gather information from its title, table of contents, abstract, section headers, jacket copy (or commentary), length, author biography, and any other features that frame or structure the text. If you are reading a text on a website, be sure you know where you are and who the author is—a person, a group, or a corporation, for example. Make note of any advertising.

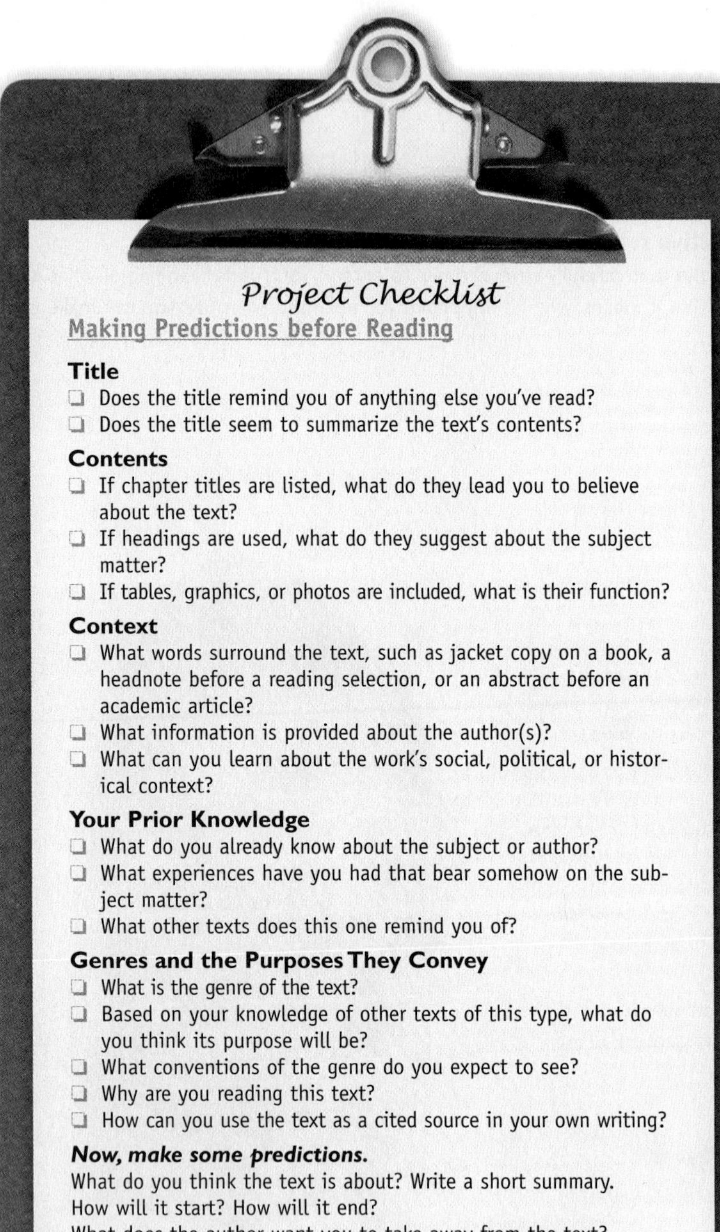

Project Checklist

Making Predictions before Reading

Title

- ❑ Does the title remind you of anything else you've read?
- ❑ Does the title seem to summarize the text's contents?

Contents

- ❑ If chapter titles are listed, what do they lead you to believe about the text?
- ❑ If headings are used, what do they suggest about the subject matter?
- ❑ If tables, graphics, or photos are included, what is their function?

Context

- ❑ What words surround the text, such as jacket copy on a book, a headnote before a reading selection, or an abstract before an academic article?
- ❑ What information is provided about the author(s)?
- ❑ What can you learn about the work's social, political, or historical context?

Your Prior Knowledge

- ❑ What do you already know about the subject or author?
- ❑ What experiences have you had that bear somehow on the subject matter?
- ❑ What other texts does this one remind you of?

Genres and the Purposes They Convey

- ❑ What is the genre of the text?
- ❑ Based on your knowledge of other texts of this type, what do you think its purpose will be?
- ❑ What conventions of the genre do you expect to see?
- ❑ Why are you reading this text?
- ❑ How can you use the text as a cited source in your own writing?

Now, make some predictions.

What do you think the text is about? Write a short summary.
How will it start? How will it end?
What does the author want you to take away from the text?

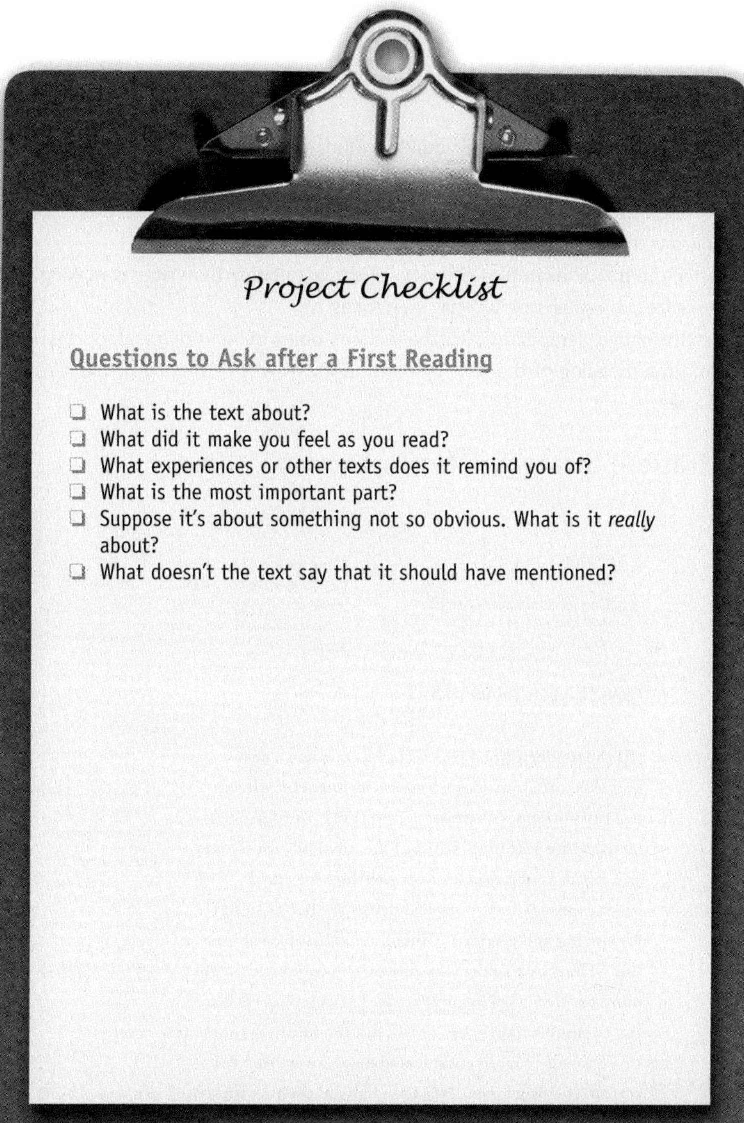

Project Checklist
Questions to Ask after a First Reading
❑ What is the text about?
❑ What did it make you feel as you read?
❑ What experiences or other texts does it remind you of?
❑ What is the most important part?
❑ Suppose it's about something not so obvious. What is it *really* about?
❑ What doesn't the text say that it should have mentioned?

Reading for the Gist

If your text is relatively short—something you can read in a half hour or so—then read the text straight through to get the gist, or central idea. Reading for the central idea will help you quickly find out more about the text's subject matter, purpose, and genre.

Rereading for Depth

After you've made predictions about a text and read it through once to get the gist, read more carefully and deeply, pausing to reflect on what the text says, what it reminds you of, how it connects to other texts, and what expectations it creates and satisfies.

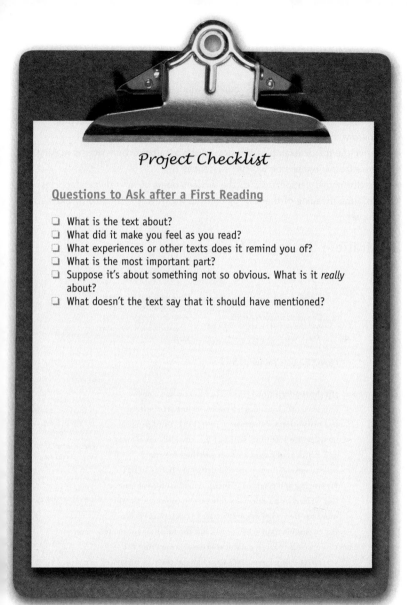

Annotating a Text

Active readers usually interact with the text by annotating it with a pencil, pen, highlighter, or sticky note as they read. They note agreements, disagreements, questions, connections they are making, and other reactions in the margins to help illuminate the text and to stay engaged.

Writing a Summary

To help you remember the content of a text, you can write a summary, reducing the text to its main points. Think of a summary as a set of topic sentences intended to jog your memory. Each sentence can be unpacked to reveal more details.

Writing a summary will ensure that you know the material well and can explain it. Even though it is written in your words, a summary does *not* include your interpretation of the text or your evaluation of its value. Since the ideas are not your own, note the complete publication information for the reading you are summarizing (▶ 9g).

For information on how to write a summary, see section 12a.

When you annotate while you read, you can . . .

- ask questions of the text
- connect the subject matter to your knowledge and experience
- make connections to other texts
- mark important or unfamiliar terms, look them up, and summarize their definitions in the margin
- number the major examples or parts of the argument the writer is making
- summarize paragraphs or difficult sentences
- offer alternative perspectives to the writer's point of view or assumptions
- extend the meaning of the text by considering how it relates to or explains big issues

Illustration: Strategies for Annotating a Text

Connection to other texts
We also read a selection from his book, Mind Wide Open.

Observation about genre
He's playing on the saying "Food for Thought," which suggests this is a reflective essay.

From "Tool for Thought" by Steven Johnson

Question
What did people used to think about word processors? It's hard to imagine being without them.

[I]f the modern word processor has become a near-universal tool for today's writers, its impact has been less revolutionary than you might think. Word processors let us create sentences without the unwieldy cross-outs and erasures of paper, and despite the occasional catastrophic failure, our hard drives are better suited for storing and retrieving documents than file cabinets. But writers don't normally rely on the computer for the more subtle arts of inspiration and association. We use the computer to process words, but the ideas that animate those words originate somewhere else, away from the screen. The word processor has changed the way we write, but it hasn't yet changed the way we think.

Summary
Weaknesses of word processors

Tell me about it!

Experience
This reminds me of invention and the idea that analogy is a way of making connections among ideas.

Summary
We only use word processors to get our ideas down, not to create them.

Extension to big ideas
Thesis. I'll bet he's going to show us a tool that might help change the way we think!

From Steven Johnson, "Tool for Thought," ***New York Times*** **30 Jan. 2005. Web. 8 Feb. 2005.**

analysis To *analyze* a text, break it into its component parts, aspects, or features and then show how they relate to one another. *Key Questions:* What choices did the writer make about content, organization, and language? How do these choices relate to one another?

interpretation To *interpret* a text, find points, issues, or events whose meaning may be ambiguous or open to different points of view and then decide where you stand. *Key Questions:* What elements of the text are open to multiple viewpoints? Where would you disagree with the author or with other readers? Why is your interpretation better than any other?

synthesis To *synthesize,* put the elements of your analysis back together to see what they mean as a whole. *Key Questions:* Do you see any patterns or shades of meaning that you didn't see before your analysis? If, after reading your analysis and interpretation, someone asked "So what?" how would you respond?

evaluation To *evaluate* a text, make a judgment about its value. *Key Questions:* Is the text good/bad, worthwhile/unimportant, or better/worse than others of its kind? Why?

Examples of Facts, Opinions, and Beliefs

A fact is a true statement that is specific and verifiable.

- On average, women tend to outlive men in the United States.
- In 2002, the life expectancy at birth for black women was 75.6 years; for white women, it was 80.3 years.
- For men, those figures were 68.8 (for black men) and 75.1 (for white men) years.

(Source: National Center for Health Statistics)

An opinion is based on facts, but also includes the writer's interpretation.

- The life expectancy for people in the United States has as much to do with social opportunity as with genetic factors.
- Men tend to live shorter lives than women in the United States because men's lives are more stressful.

(Note that to support either of these opinions adequately would require many facts not stated above.)

A belief is a deeply held conviction that cannot be proved or disproved.

- All people should have an equal opportunity to live a long and healthy life.

Critical reading is thinking while reading: questioning the author's intentions, line of argument, evidence, and choice of words, for example, and staying alert for what is going on below the surface. Do two parts of an argument seem contradictory? The critical reader will notice such instances and will try to figure out whether his or her interpretation is faulty or biased and, if it isn't, whether the author intended the contradiction or didn't realize there was one.

To investigate a text, you can use four interrelated thinking processes: analysis, interpretation, synthesis, and evaluation.

Critical reading involves carefully distinguishing fact, opinion, and belief; evaluating the evidence the writer puts forth; and evaluating the assumptions that underlie the writer's argument.

Distinguishing Fact, Opinion, and Belief

Facts are true statements that can be verified by multiple trusted sources. **Opinions** are interpretations of facts, and any set of facts may yield multiple interpretations. **Beliefs** are deeply held convictions. Beliefs can't be proved or disproved, no matter how many facts and reasons are piled up. Neither facts nor beliefs can act as the claim of an argument (▶ Chapter 7).

Evaluating Evidence

Facts are one kind of evidence that writers can present to support an opinion or claim. Other kinds of evidence are statistics (facts stated as numbers), specific examples, and expert opinion. (For a list of kinds of evidence, see page 34.)

For information on evaluating the sources of evidence, see sections 10h and 11f.

Evaluating Underlying Assumptions

When anyone makes a proposition about a subject—as in a thesis statement or an assertion of opinion—certain assumptions underlie their position.

For example, if I argue that humans should return to the moon to build agricultural stations and thus spare the Earth further ecological destruction, I make the underlying assumptions that (1) humans have visited the moon previously, (2) it is possible to build such a station without further depleting natural resources in the effort, and (3) the Earth is suffering ecological destruction. These assumptions may or may not be valid, but for the argument to work, writers and readers need to share them.

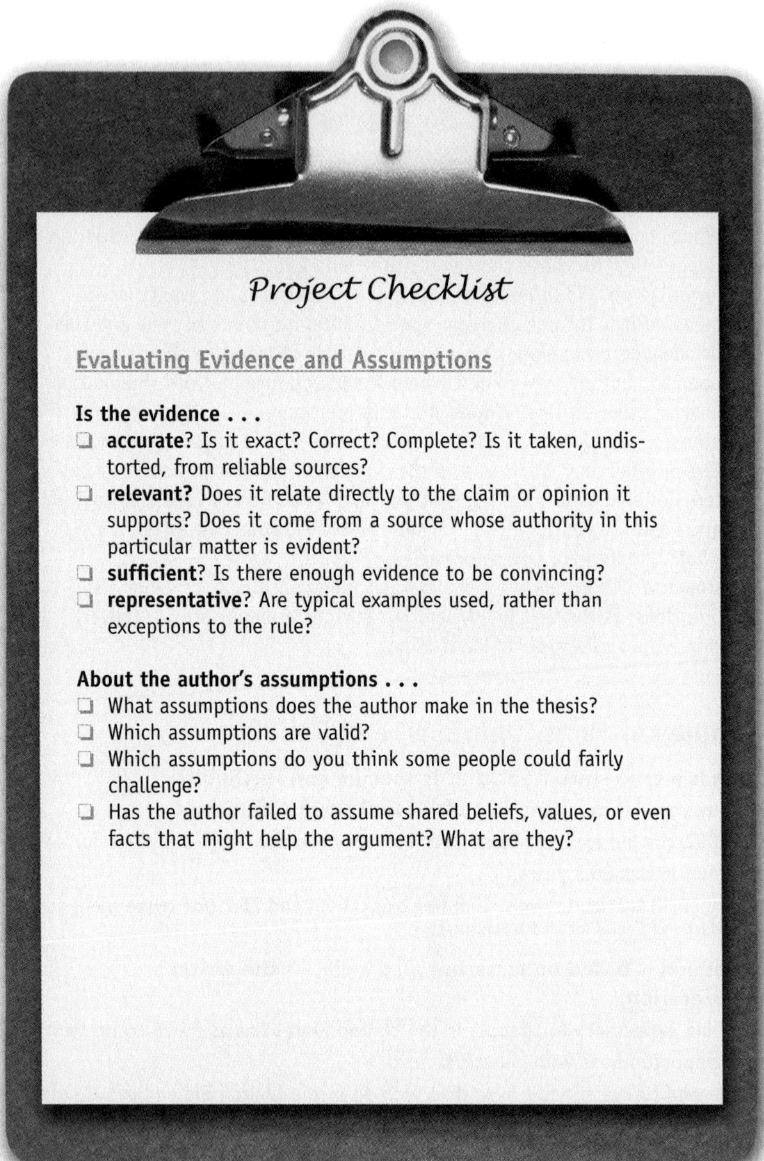

Project Checklist

Evaluating Evidence and Assumptions

Is the evidence . . .

- ❑ **accurate**? Is it exact? Correct? Complete? Is it taken, undistorted, from reliable sources?
- ❑ **relevant?** Does it relate directly to the claim or opinion it supports? Does it come from a source whose authority in this particular matter is evident?
- ❑ **sufficient**? Is there enough evidence to be convincing?
- ❑ **representative**? Are typical examples used, rather than exceptions to the rule?

About the author's assumptions . . .

- ❑ What assumptions does the author make in the thesis?
- ❑ Which assumptions are valid?
- ❑ Which assumptions do you think some people could fairly challenge?
- ❑ Has the author failed to assume shared beliefs, values, or even facts that might help the argument? What are they?

ethos The appeal to the character of the writer and his or her attitude toward the subject as a means of cultivating readers' trust. Ethos may be conveyed by tone (the writer's attitude toward the subject as expressed in the language), identification with readers, and even the writer's reputation (if the writer is known to the audience).

logos The use of content as a form of proof or appeal. Logos includes all of the content of a work—not only ideas, images, information, and evidence, but also diction, style and sentence structure, and arrangement of parts.

pathos The appeal to the emotions of the audience. These emotions are used to deepen an effect.

purpose The writer's aims, how others use or refer to the text, and its consequences.

context The rhetorical situation, consisting of the circumstances of the writer, the historical situation of the text, and the nature of the audience addressed.

Questions for a Rhetorical Reading

Who is the author, and what are his or her intentions?

- What are the author's purposes for writing? If there is more than one purpose, which one seems to predominate? How can you tell?
- How would you characterize the author's attitude toward the subject—the tone? Does the tone convey authority?
- What leads you to believe that the author is knowledgeable?
- How does the author establish that he or she is fair-minded and credible? Is the author trustworthy?
- Is the author's support of a position well considered and/or researched?
- Does the author treat opposing perspectives fairly and as thoroughly as necessary?

(continued)

Rhetorical analysis is a systematic method of analyzing the effects of a text and how the writer achieves them. The key question for a rhetorical analysis is "What effects does the writer achieve, and how exactly does the writer achieve them?"

Rhetorical analysis also examines purpose and context (the immediate social and historical circumstances of the text).

Reading Any Text as an Argument

When reading rhetorically and when writing a rhetorical analysis, think of the text as an argument that makes appeals to readers. Focus on logos. The text may be a straightforward argumentative essay that attempts to persuade readers to adopt a particular point of view. But a text that aims to inform or entertain can also be considered an argument because in singling out a subject for the reader's attention, it says, "Pay attention to *this*" and, by default, diverts attention from other subjects. Rhetorical analysis can help you appreciate the presence of influence and persuasion where it is not easy to spot.

Reading for the Use of Language

Writers choose words and adopt a style that helps them achieve their purposes and create effects in their readers. Word choice, or **diction,** has a major influence not just on meaning but on how a text is received. For example, it makes a great difference whether a change of government is labeled a "victory for the people" or a "disaster for freedom."

Diction conveys a writer's purpose and tone as well. Writers usually choose **formal diction** when the occasion for writing is a serious one (as in a research paper) or is part of a ritual (as in a speech to a graduating class). Writers use **informal diction** when they want to identify with their readers and cultivate trust and familiarity (▶ section 28b).

Style is the arrangement of words into sentences in a sequence and form. No one style is naturally better than any other; the use of each should be judged by how well it is suited to the circumstances.

What is the rhetorical context?

- What circumstances give rise to the text? When was the text written? What personal, historical, political, or social events might the author be responding to?
- Why do you think the author has written this text now? Is the text well-suited to its situation? Why or why not?
- Are there any distinctive values, opinions, or ideologies that help explain the text?
- How does this text fit into other conversations or texts about the subject?

Who are the intended readers, and how does the writer address them?

- Who is the author's intended audience?
- What knowledge and expectations do readers bring to the text?
- How are readers likely to feel about the subject matter or the author's presentation of it?
- What values do readers and the author seem to have in common? How does the writer appeal to these values?
- Does the writer have secondary (or subsidiary) audiences in mind?
- If the audience for the text is not obvious, who do you think the writer wants it to be?

What is the subject matter of the text, and how is it arranged?

- Does the author use examples or illustrations to prove points (argument), show events (in narrative), or explain methods (hypothesis testing)? (induction)
- Does the author build a case for his or her position by starting with widely accepted knowledge and then moving toward new insights or claims? (deduction)
- Does the author appeal to reason?
- Does the author use or invoke emotion to help make the point or show the story? (pathos)
- Does the author rely on his or her reputation or authority to garner the reader's interest or support? (ethos)
- Is the subject matter complemented by reference to outside sources, including other texts and voices?

How does the author present the text?

- How is the text structured?
- How would you characterize the text's genre?
- Is there anything unusual or particularly effective about the sentence style?
- What is the author's tone?
- Is there anything striking, original, or distinctive about the author's use of diction or specialized terminology?
- Does the visual design or layout affect the reception of the text?
- Does the presentation of the text, including its form, enhance the content?

Does the text succeed in accomplishing the author's purpose?

- Did the text persuade, teach, delight, or otherwise fulfill its purpose with you?
- Do you think it accomplishes its purpose with others?
- Is it likely to fail to accomplish its purpose with some readers? Who?
- Can you identify the responses of historical or contemporary audiences?

Reading for the Writer's Purposes

Your judgment about a writer's purposes can be formed by paying attention to the author's announcement of his or her **intention(s)** (if any are stated), by asking whether the readers' **expectations** are fulfilled (and thus anticipated by the writer), and by analyzing whether the **rhetorical context** provides any clues about what the writer might be trying to accomplish.

Reading for Rhetorical Context

Every text is part of some wider conversation that you can learn about and use to attribute motive to a writer and assign meaning to a text. A text is written at a unique time and place, usually for a specific purpose, and addressed to an audience.

Literature always has some context, a situation that accompanies the act of the writer and the reading of the work. Writers work hard to establish that context because it establishes verisimilitude, the appearance of truth that helps sustain the illusion of fiction. Readers likewise use context to give literature significance and meaning. When you read a work of literature, you consider within your own reading context whether the work is successful in achieving its apparent aims and the ways it goes about accomplishing them.

Noticing Your Responses

The key to developing an understanding of a work of literature is to be aware of what you think about and feel as you read, and then to try to discern later if the thoughts and feelings add up to a meaningful pattern. Very often, they will. You can start by exploring your responses in writing.

Making Predictions and Forming Expectations

When you read literature with the plan of writing about it later, you should be prepared to *analyze, interpret,* and *evaluate.* When you analyze a story, for example, you break it down into its components—such as

Exploring Your Responses in Writing

Writing in response to these questions one by one should give you plenty of ideas to build upon if your goal is to write an essay about a particular literary work.

- **Restatement.** What is the text about? Try to be as accurate as possible.
- **Affective response.** What did you feel as you read? Explain the reasons you felt as you did.
- **Associative response.** What does the text remind you of? Does it remind you of any personal experiences? Of anything else that you have read or seen?
- **Decisions about literary importance.** What do you think is the most important word, line, or scene in the text? People will naturally disagree about what is most important, so don't worry about making incorrect choices.
- **Imitation and parody.** Write about an event or person in your own experience as if you were this author. Imitate the author's style. Or exaggerate the author's style in a parody.
- **Extensions of your response.** Suppose that the text is not about what you said it was in your restatement above—that it's about something deeper, more complex, or less obvious. What is it *really* about?

You will find writing about literature more enjoyable, and even easier, once you understand that all of these types of responses add to our appreciation of literature's value. Especially when the work is fresh to you, see whether you can respond in multiple ways. More varied and rich responses will leave you more options for developing your initial responses into essays or other projects.

Critical Frameworks

Researchers and scholars in the humanities acknowledge that it is virtually impossible to approach a work of literature without some preconceptions about what is important in literature, what its role in personal and social life might be, and how it achieves its effects. When you write about literature, the terms and concepts you use act as filters that let new detail shine through. Your prior beliefs and values will also influence what meaning you derive from a text, as will its situation in history. *Literary theory* is an attempt to make such knowledge explicit *and* to use these insights to gain perspective when interpreting complex works.

- **Historical criticism** examines the work of literature in its place and time, with reference to the social, political, and historical contexts that influence the author and readers.
- **Cultural studies** takes a broad view of what counts as "literary" and so draws concepts from a variety of philosophical, theoretical, historical, and rhetorical perspectives to examine a wide range of texts from popular culture.
- **Marxist criticism** explores literature as a response to the negative effects of class division, which leads to alienation and oppression. Social and political circumstances (ideology) shape how people (and writers) think about and respond to the world.
- **Feminist criticism** studies cultural, political, and biological representations of women and men in literature. Feminist critics believe that gender and sexuality are central themes in literature.
- **Reader-response criticism** studies the literary work as an appeal to readers in a rhetorical situation. With its form and content, literature creates expectations in readers, and interpretation focuses on how the work creates and satisfies those expectations.
- **Formalist criticism** studies the literary work as an artifact that communicates meaningfully without the need for relating its meaning to historical, biographical, or social contexts.
- **Postmodernist criticism** studies literature as not merely an artifact but also a self-referential act that contests its own function and status as art. A novel or short story, for example, can also be said to be about the act of writing itself: how fiction communicates meaning (or not) and the techniques it uses to move the reader.
- **Deconstruction** studies the ways that a work of literature undermines itself in its reliance on binary oppositions. Deconstruction points out how these oppositions, which are embedded in language and culture, limit perspective, and it is the critic's job to build up the ignored term in the binary pair.

plot, point of view, and character—and consider how these features fit together in meaningful ways. When you interpret a story, you come to some conclusions about what the story means. When you evaluate a story, you consider its strengths and weaknesses. (See Words about Words on page 53.)

Spend a few moments thinking and even writing about the work before you start reading. *Anticipation* and *prediction* are two important steps in getting ready to read. Ponder the title of the work, recall what you know about the author or the author's works, read the "About the Author" note if one is present, and scan the work to see how long it is and whether it consists of chapters or other sections.

As you read, you can *form expectations* about, for example, what will happen next, how a character might change, or what problem a character faces. You can make predictions based on these expectations, as well. Good writers understand that readers form expectations, and they take advantage of those expectations to make the story more dramatic or meaningful or suspenseful, by using techniques such as *foreshadowing* (hints about later events). Paying attention to how your expectations take shape during your reading—even by jotting notes in the margins of a story—will help you focus your interpretation.

5a Terms for Understanding Fiction

When reading fiction, consider the terms and questions below.

Terms and Definitions	Questions to Ask about Fiction
PLOT The pattern of events of the story, with an emphasis on cause and effect.	What is the initial conflict in the story? How is it resolved?
CHARACTERS People, animals, aliens, or other beings who act on the world in the story.	Are the main characters in the story fully fleshed out ("round") or one-dimensional ("flat")? Static (unchanging) or dynamic (growing, changing)? What do you know about them? What role do the minor, or flat, characters play? Do you empathize with any of the characters? Do any make you feel angry or disappointed?
SETTING The place and time of the story.	Where and when does the story take place? What do you know about the social or historical circumstances of the story? How does the setting influence the plot?
IMAGERY Vivid language that helps readers imagine the visual or emotional qualities of objects, people, events, or places.	What are the most striking or memorable visual or emotional images in the story? How do these images comment on or develop the theme?
POINT OF VIEW The perspective or vantage point of the narrator.	How does the narrator's point of view give you insight into the characters or theme? Does the narrator use the first-person point of view ("I"), or does the narrator refer to characters in the third person ("he" and "she") and thus act as an outsider to the plot? Does the narrator seem all-knowing, or are certain characters or events outside of the narrator's range of knowledge? Is the narrator reliable or unreliable?
STYLE AND TONE *Style* refers to the overall flavor and texture created by the writer's word choices and sentence structures. *Tone* is an attitude toward the events of the story—humorous, ironic, cynical, and so on.	Does the author use a complex or straightforward style? How do you think the author feels about the story or particular characters in it? What word choices and sentence structures lead to that impression?
SYMBOLISM The use of one thing to stand for another, usually a larger or more abstract concept.	Does the author use any symbols that seem especially striking or memorable? Are the symbols woven into the story, or do they depend on your prior knowledge of their meaning (or both)?
THEME The central point(s) the work makes about some aspect of life or human values.	What theme or themes does the story confront? What do you think the central theme is? What elements of the plot or characterization support this central theme?

These terms will help you know what to look for when you read, analyze, and interpret poetry.

Terms and Definitions	Questions to Ask about Poetry
IMAGERY A pattern of images that creates meaning. For example, imagery with contrasting themes may suggest difference or disruption.	Is there a pattern of imagery in the poem? What is the most important or most emphasized image? How would you characterize the imagery in terms of tone?
SOUND How a poem sounds when read aloud. *Meter* is the poem's sound pattern, especially its sequence of stressed and unstressed syllables. *Rhyme* is the sound similarities across words or lines.	Does the poem have a regular pattern in its meter, rhyme, or sounds? What is the mood of the poem?
FORM A pattern of line length, rhyme, and meter. In open forms, the pattern varies across lines. Closed forms have regular patterns. Form in poetry may also be considered an appeal consisting of the arousal and fulfillment of the reader's or listener's desire.	Does the poem have an open or closed form? If it is open, are there any places where a pattern in line length, rhyme, or meter stands out? If it is closed, does the pattern depend on line length, rhyme, meter, or some combination of these? In this closed form, do any lines in particular have a special function?
DICTION AND SYNTAX *Diction* refers to word choice, which may be formal, informal, or varied in formality. Some words or phrases may be repeated several times, placing stress on their meaning and sound. The sequential patterns of the words are known as *syntax*.	What words in the poem seem most important or memorable? Are any words repeated? Is the diction formal or informal? If the poem is addressed to someone, does the speaker use everyday or elevated speech? Is there anything unusual about the poem's syntax or word order? Why does the poet vary the syntax?
RHETORICAL SITUATION Most poems can be considered events involving a speaker, an audience, a text, and a situation or context.	What is the rhetorical situation of the poem? What do you know about the speaker? Whom does the speaker address? What can you learn about the speaker's audience? What is the context of the poem? Is a conflict or crisis represented in the poem?

5c Terms for Understanding Drama

Reading a play is perhaps as common as watching one performed, but it is always important to remember that plays are written to be acted out on stage (dramatized).

Terms and Definitions	Questions to Ask about Drama
CHARACTERS Characters in plays may be flat or round, dynamic or static (◀ page 60). Usually, no narrator comments on characters' actions, so we have to infer their motives from what characters say and do and from how others respond to them.	Who are the most important characters in the play? Do any of them change significantly during the course of the play and, if so, how? What conflict do the important characters face? What roles do the minor characters play?
PLOT Like fiction, drama has plot (◀ page 60). Plays are divided into acts and scenes. Many plays are performed in five acts, each having a unified structure of its own (a conflict and crisis, for example).	What is the conflict in the play? What is the play's crisis? How is it resolved? Does the resolution turn out differently than you expected?
STAGING Playwrights usually include stage directions that indicate the characters' entrances and exits, physical gestures, and setting. Staging also includes costumes and scenery.	What stage directions does the playwright include? How much interpretation of the staging is left to the actors and the director (and, thus, the readers when the play is read)? How does the staging help draw out the theme(s) of the play?
THEME Like fiction (◀ page 60), plays have themes that are explored in the action. It can be helpful to think of a play as a question about a complex issue that lends itself to multiple responses. Characters act out possible responses on stage, and the audience is invited to decide which responses seem best.	What is the central theme of the play? What questions does the play ask? What answers, if any, to these questions are offered by the characters or in the resolution of the conflict?

Integrating and Documenting Source Material

Every source you quote, paraphrase, or summarize in your essay must be documented.

- **Quoting fiction.** In the parenthetical citation after a quotation, use page numbers to refer to the original. If the original includes quoted dialogue, use single quotation marks to represent that dialogue within your double quotation marks. See page 184 for treatment of quotations of four lines or more.

> At the end of "The Short Happy Life of Francis Macomber," Wilson accuses Margaret of deliberately shooting her husband: "'He would have left you, too'" (48).

- **Quoting poetry.** Use a forward slash with a space on each side to indicate line breaks in a poem. Use line numbers (not page numbers) in your parenthetical citation.

> Williams breaks compound nouns into separate words in "The Red Wheelbarrow" to show that it is in the particulars of experience that we find meaning. The red wheelbarrow is "glazed with rain / water / beside the white / chickens" (5–8). Rainwater and white chickens are single things, but here Williams divides them across line breaks to make his point.

- **Quoting drama.** Include the act, scene, and line numbers in your parenthetical citation. Use Arabic numerals.

> In Shakespeare's *As You Like It,* Jacques utters the famous lines that suggest life is like a play: "All the world's a stage, / And all the men and women merely players" (2.7.149–50). In its time, this well-known saying referred to two ideas. First, it was used as a metaphor to describe the dramatic nature of life itself. . . .

For writing strategies you can use to brainstorm ideas, organize, and draft your essay, refer to Chapters 1–3. Also consider the following aspects of writing about literature.

- *Use summary and paraphrase sparingly.* Avoid summarizing or paraphrasing large portions of the work for readers who are very familiar with the work.
- *Quote from the work.* Quote from the work to support and extend your analysis, interpretation, or evaluation. Be careful to explain to readers how the quotation contributes to your interpretation.
- *Use present tense verbs.* Use present tense verbs when discussing what happens in a literary work or when describing the author's act of writing it. Use the past tense when describing events surrounding the work—for example, the work's impact or reception in its time.
- *Don't mistake the narrator or speaker for the author.* Bear in mind that the narrator of a work of fiction or the speaker in a poem or play does not necessarily speak for the author's point of view.

5e Resources for Writing about Literature

An asterisk * indicates that the database resource is also available online.

CONDUCTING RESEARCH ON LITERATURE	Writing about Literature: A Guide to Research (University of Minnesota Libraries): **http://subject.lib.umn.edu/hum/writinglit.html** *MLA International Bibliography of Books and Articles on Modern Languages and Literatures** *Literary Research Guide* (Harner, MLA) *Characters in 20th Century Literature* (Harris) *Dictionary of Literary Biography** *Masterplots Cyclopedia of Literary Characters* (Magill) *Oxford English Dictionary** *The New Princeton Encyclopedia of Poetry and Poetics* *Book Review Index**
FINDING SOURCES IN JOURNALS	*Humanities Index** *British Humanities Index**
LITERARY TERMS AND PERIODS	*A Handbook to Literature* (Holman) *Oxford Companion to American Literature* *Oxford Companion to English Literature* *Cambridge Guide to Literature in English* Glossary of Literary Theory (Henderson and Brown): **http://www.library.utoronto.ca/utel/glossary/headerindex.html**
LITERARY AND CRITICAL THEORY	The Johns Hopkins Guide to Literary Theory and Criticism: **http://www.press.jhu.edu/books/hopkins_guide_to_literary_theory/** *Literary Theory: An Introduction,* 2nd ed. (Eagleton) Guide to Literary and Critical Theory: **http://www.cla.purdue.edu/academic/engl/theory/**
LINKS TO LITERARY RESOURCES ON THE WEB	Voice of the Shuttle: **http://vos.ucsb.edu/browse.asp?id=2718** Sarah Zupko's Cultural Studies Center: **http://www.popcultures.com**

In the film *Schindler's List,* director Steven Spielberg used color to show dominant contrast. The film was almost all in black and white, except for one scene of a little girl in a red coat being led away by Nazis.

Pictures, paintings, and other graphical representations may be examined critically as unique interpretations of visual experience. A photograph, for example, says, "Look at this." In leaving out the world beyond the edges of the photograph (and any movement that may be part of the picture's context), the photographer implicitly singles out the framed subject for our attention. It is important to learn to read such images critically because they are not simply unbiased representations of what's real. They are selections meant to reflect reality, but as reflections they are also deflections or (sometimes) distortions.

Reading inside the Frame: Composition 6a

In this still shot from Alfred Hitchcock's *Psycho,* Norman Bates is positioned on the right side of the frame and shot from a low angle, with a stuffed bird of prey hovering at the top of the frame. In the film, you also see more stuffed birds and two pieces of art depicting nudes in the center. Thus, Hitchcock invites the association between Norman and the birds, his sexual obsession, and possibly his own victimization by the voice of "Mother" inside his head. The low angle makes Norman look dominating even though most of his body is outside the frame.

The key concept for interpreting the visual content inside a frame is *composition*, the act of blending various elements into an artistic form.

- **Dominant contrast and intrinsic interest.** The subject matter in the frame draws attention because of its inherent interest or because of its placement in relation to other objects in the frame. The dominant contrast in a frame is what draws the eye first because of its visual appearance (it may be brightly colored, standing off by itself, or in some other way drawing the eye). Intrinsic interest refers to the visual appeal of an object because of what we already know about the subject matter.

- **Spatial relationships.** Visual elements appear near or far apart from one another, larger or smaller, closer to the viewer or farther away.
- **Placement in the frame.** Content is positioned to draw your attention to certain elements—in the center of the frame or near an edge, for instance.
- **Color, shapes, textures.** Color conveys mood, shows contrasts between elements, and creates visual appeal.

  Geometric shapes, such as lines in parallel, establish patterns and relationships among the subjects in a picture or graphic.

  Photographs depict objects with different textures to create patterns and contrasts. Painters use different kinds of paint and brushstrokes to add texture to the surface of the art.
- **Technique.** Photographers use filters to enhance or subtract detail and different lenses to draw aspects of the subject into relief. Graphic artists use a variety of software tools, which include layering, masking, or other filters, to create stylized images.

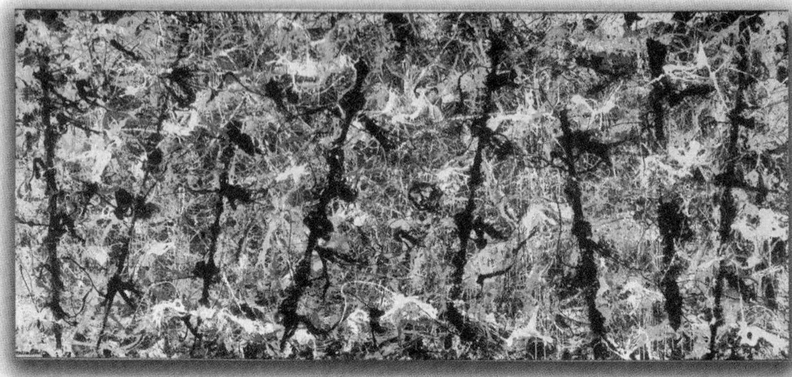

Jackson Pollock, *Blue Poles: Number 11, 1952*

American painter Jackson Pollock used a wide variety of colors, techniques, and brushes. He applied (or dripped) paint with sticks, with cooking basters, and even straight from the can. He also included glass, cigarette butts, and other objects to add more texture to show the energy of composition and the depth in his paintings.

Mt. Williamson, Sierra Nevada, from Manzanar, CA, 1945
Photograph by Ansel Adams

Adams uses an extreme closeup with a deep focus shot so that the rocks in the foreground and the majestic mountains in the background are in clear focus. The image contrasts the immediacy and familiarity of the rocks with the grandeur of the mountains shrouded in clouds and illuminated by the sun.

The Elements of Context

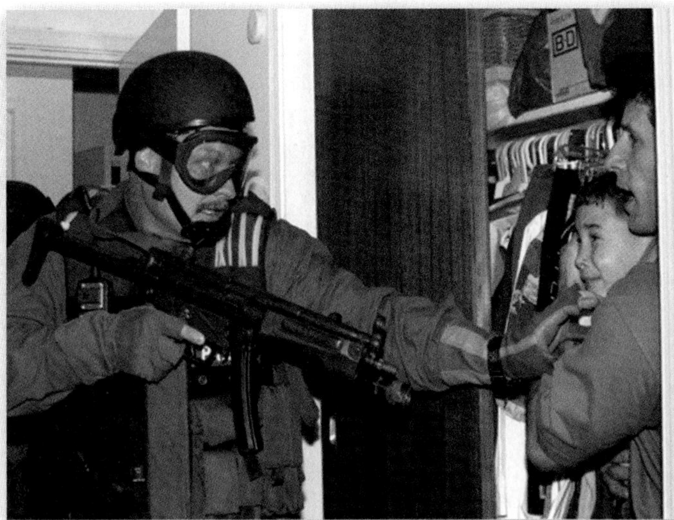

This photograph depicts one dramatic scene during the Elian Gonzalez case (April 22, 2000). In the original context, there was a custody battle over the young boy. Elian's father, a Cuban citizen, wanted Elian returned to Cuba after the boy's mother had drowned in her attempt to bring them both to the United States, but Elian's cousins insisted he stay in the United States. U.S. Attorney General Janet Reno ordered that the boy be taken forcibly from his cousins' home and returned to the custody of his father in Cuba. The political context included strained relations with Cuba, divisions among the Cuban-American community in Florida, and debates in Congress about granting Elian asylum in the United States.

This photograph depicts the actual armed seizure. So that you don't misunderstand what it means, you should consider the circumstances under which it was taken. It was shot by a professional photographer who had positioned himself in the room so that he would have a good angle to capture the moment. Elian was kept in the closet until the federal agents found him. How much of this event, and thus this image, was scripted in advance? It seems to document a spontaneous and frightening moment. But it may also be a scene manipulated for propaganda purposes. What else would you need to know to decide what this photograph shows? For further information, see "The Elian Gonzalez Case: An Online NewsHour Focus" (PBS), at **http://www.pbs.org/newshour/bb/law/elian/**.

What lies beyond the frame of an image is just as important in reading images critically as what is inside the frame. An image is part of a situation that shapes the intentions of the artist and its reception by viewers. To read images critically and to avoid limiting your interpretation to content within the frame, you can consider the ways the elements of context shape meaning.

Original Context

The original context refers to the personal and social situation in which the artist created the image. When was it created? What are the historical and social circumstances? Is there a particular style to the period? What shaped the artist's response? Under what conditions was the image produced?

Consider, for example, a photograph, which depicts a moment frozen in time. To understand its context, you can identify its subject matter, form, and style (the elements of composition in the frame). When and where was the photograph taken? How does its style fit with the artist's other work or the photographic style of the times? What has been happening in the world, and—especially in the case of documentary photographs (as in news photography)—what are the conditions under which the photograph was taken, including what might lie just beyond the frame?

Immediate Context

The immediate context refers to the conditions under which the image is viewed, including where it is viewed (on a Web page, in a museum, in a book), its surrounding context (other images and text), and the physical circumstances of the viewing (lighting, frames, the presence of other people).

Leonardo da Vinci's *Mona Lisa* is easily the most recognizable painting in the world. It has been viewed in the Louvre in Paris by millions of people. In its immediate context in the Louvre, the *Mona Lisa* rests behind bulletproof glass. There are almost always crowds, so people are lucky to get a good glimpse of the painting as other people rush by or stand on their toes in front of them. This context certainly affects our interpretation. In fact, while our appreciation of the painting itself might be diminished, its staging in the Louvre and its familiarity give the *Mona Lisa* another meaning as a cultural icon. To some it might symbolize the commodification of art; to others, the power of art to move millions.

Leonardo da Vinci's *Mona Lisa*

Museum visitors view the *Mona Lisa*.

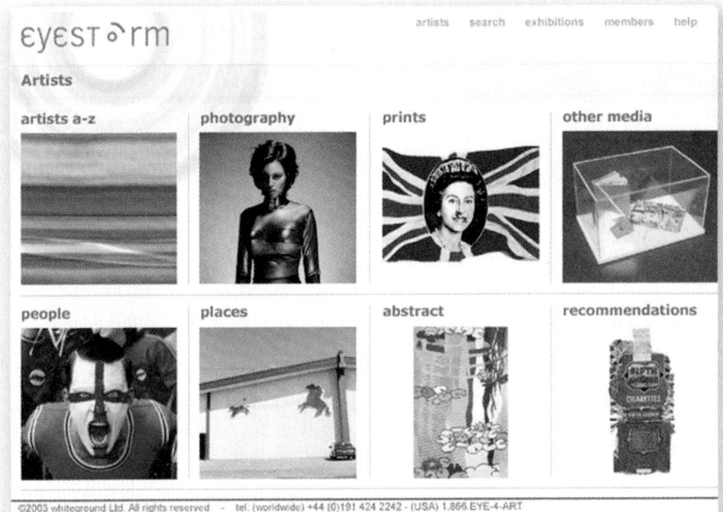

Here, words and images are linked by position, with the image itself creating visual interest and correspondence to the link (for example, "people" appears above a photograph of Robbie Williams as an excited soccer fan). From Eyestorm (Gallery of Artists): http://www.eyestorm.com/artists/.

Here the text takes the form of an image symbolizing a pip on a playing card. By graphic designer John Langdon: http://www.johnlangdon.net.

In this logo for San Diego State University Press's imprint Hyperbole Books, the word *hyperbole* (which means overstated comparison) is in the shape of an exclamation mark, which adds further emphasis! From http://www-rohan.sdsu.edu.

Images on websites add visual appeal, but they often have other uses that help Web authors create meaning.

1. As *navigational aids* (buttons and rollover images, arrows, menus, image maps, thumbnail images), images structure information so that it is accessible quickly to readers. Visual cues—in combination with text—train the reader's eye to make quick associations and thus help the reader learn to interact with the website.
2. As illustrations that complement the text or serve as examples (photographic essays, hypertext commentary, photo galleries, museum exhibits).
3. As primary material explained by the surrounding text (paintings on museum websites, for example).
4. As iconic symbols that have meaning in their own right and that make a point or convey an idea. (The *Mona Lisa* is often used to represent status, refinement, and artistic genius.) An *iconic symbol* is an image used as a direct representation of the thing it represents, or a modern hieroglyph, such as the image of a speaker on a radio's volume control.

Icons (such as a pointing finger) and logos (visual signs associated with an organization or company) may speak for themselves but may also represent some idea or feeling. Interestingly, over time, elements of our culture gain status as icons so that whenever we see them we have particular ideas. The images/icons represent not only the original object but also abstract ideas.

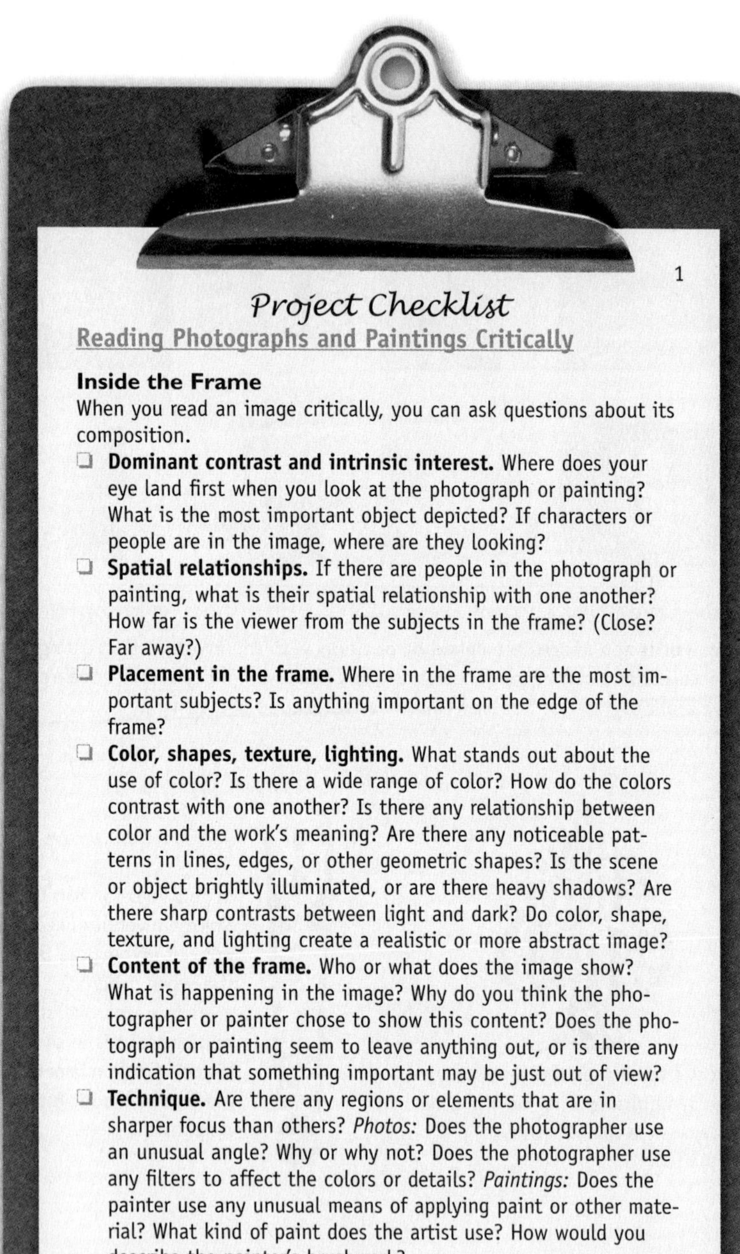

1

Project Checklist

Reading Photographs and Paintings Critically

Inside the Frame

When you read an image critically, you can ask questions about its composition.

- ❑ **Dominant contrast and intrinsic interest.** Where does your eye land first when you look at the photograph or painting? What is the most important object depicted? If characters or people are in the image, where are they looking?
- ❑ **Spatial relationships.** If there are people in the photograph or painting, what is their spatial relationship with one another? How far is the viewer from the subjects in the frame? (Close? Far away?)
- ❑ **Placement in the frame.** Where in the frame are the most important subjects? Is anything important on the edge of the frame?
- ❑ **Color, shapes, texture, lighting.** What stands out about the use of color? Is there a wide range of color? How do the colors contrast with one another? Is there any relationship between color and the work's meaning? Are there any noticeable patterns in lines, edges, or other geometric shapes? Is the scene or object brightly illuminated, or are there heavy shadows? Are there sharp contrasts between light and dark? Do color, shape, texture, and lighting create a realistic or more abstract image?
- ❑ **Content of the frame.** Who or what does the image show? What is happening in the image? Why do you think the photographer or painter chose to show this content? Does the photograph or painting seem to leave anything out, or is there any indication that something important may be just out of view?
- ❑ **Technique.** Are there any regions or elements that are in sharper focus than others? *Photos:* Does the photographer use an unusual angle? Why or why not? Does the photographer use any filters to affect the colors or details? *Paintings:* Does the painter use any unusual means of applying paint or other material? What kind of paint does the artist use? How would you describe the painter's brushwork?

2

Beyond the Frame

You can also ask questions about context.

- ❑ **Original context.** What can you learn about the photographer or painter? When and where was the photograph taken or the painting made? Are there any social, political, or other circumstances that "contain" the image in the photograph or painting?
- ❑ **Immediate context.** How is viewing a photograph or painting in a textbook different from viewing one in a museum? Would the photograph or painting have a different meaning if it were on the cover of *Life* magazine? *Cosmopolitan*? On display at a yard sale? Hanging in a Barnes and Noble coffee bar?

Questions to Ask about Images and Graphics on Websites

- ❑ Do the images and graphics help explain the verbal content, or are they the primary content of the website?
- ❑ Does the image have a clear purpose or meaning in relation to the verbal content of the site?
- ❑ Does the image overpower the rest of the content on the Web page, or is there a good balance between verbal and visual information?
- ❑ Does the image set the proper tone for the content?
- ❑ Does the graphical material complement the site's content?
- ❑ Do the images and graphics establish a consistent identity for the website?
- ❑ Are the images and graphics original, or do they appear to be borrowed from another source?
- ❑ Why is this graphic here? What is the motive or purpose for this graphic?
- ❑ Could the images and graphics be of better quality? How so?

When you write about an image, you probably will not have room to provide full answers to all of the questions in the checklist. Your aim should be to form a judgment about what a photograph or painting means or what it shows and why it is important. You then support your interpretation (your thesis) by drawing on your answers to these kinds of questions. If you believe that a work is significant and achieves its effects in interesting ways, you should be able to point specifically to the elements of composition and context that lead you to your interpretation. Very often you will find from a careful analysis that there's more in the image than you noticed at first glance.

Include the image with your writing or point your readers to it on the Web or in an easily accessible archive so that they can see what you are referring to.

List all citation information about the image's source. In educational contexts, it is acceptable to include the image in a printed document as long as the source information is also included (artist/photographer, title of work, date, copyright owner or museum, location, and—if found on the Web—the date of access).

7 WRITING ARGUMENTS

The process of writing to persuade begins the moment you, as a member of a community, feel an urge to set things straight or to make your position known.

7a Making Arguments in Academic Contexts

As a genre defined by social practice, arguments vary in form and content as you move across the curriculum and into new fields of practice. Conventions of form, for example, create expectations among readers in a given academic field that an argument—whether a report of research findings in the sciences or a literary interpretation in the humanities—will proceed in a certain way.

Conventional Forms

The conventional form of an argument within a discipline serves a purpose. For instance, a scientific research report includes certain sections because each one helps persuade other researchers that the hypothesis was a good one, the methods of testing it and studying the results were sound, and the analysis and conclusion are thus worth considering. A research report, when persuasive, will prompt other researchers to replicate the study or even to apply its conclusions to solve or explain other problems. Sections 7f and 7g detail two structures often used in arguments written in introductory composition.

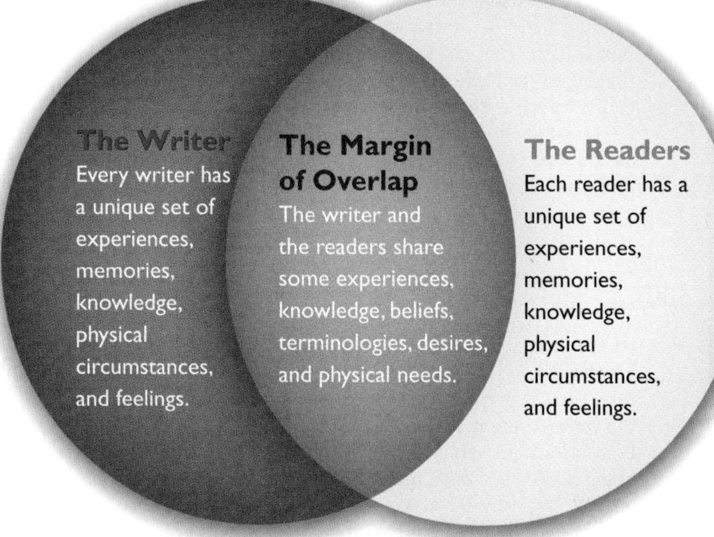

The Writer
Every writer has a unique set of experiences, memories, knowledge, physical circumstances, and feelings.
The Margin of Overlap
The writer and the readers share some experiences, knowledge, beliefs, terminologies, desires, and physical needs.
The Readers
Each reader has a unique set of experiences, memories, knowledge, physical circumstances, and feelings.

To persuade your readers, you look for common ground—points on which you agree or are likely to agree. Once you have established this connection, you can ease readers toward new insights or changes of attitude. The connection you have made shows readers they can trust you, and you can then widen the margin of overlap by providing authoritative information, good reasons, and vivid examples to support your position. This process makes it easier for readers to believe or learn what might have been beyond their experience previously.

Identifying Common Ground with Readers

What does your audience care about? See whether you can find a way to link your concerns, which they may not have thought about yet, to their existing concerns.

I want to show my friends that volunteering for Public Interest Research Group is worthwhile, but all they seem to be interested in is getting their careers started.

So how will volunteering help them in their careers? They might . . .

— develop research and presentation skills that they will be able to use on their jobs.

— be able to promote themselves as people who follow through to reach important goals.

— show potential employers they are willing to contribute toward the common good.

Maybe I should argue that they should each choose an organization to volunteer for, not just promote PIRG. Since my friends are going to be searching for different types of jobs, I'll bet they can each find an organization particularly suited to their interests.

7a Claim and Support

In the academic community, a successful argument includes a claim about a contested issue and support for the claim in the form of good reasons, examples, expert knowledge, and verbal and visual evidence. A claim is a position the writer stakes out in the thesis statement. Most issues that are considered worth writing arguments about are disputed; reasonable people disagree about them. When planning an argument, consider the many sides of a contested issue and then make smart and ethical decisions about what claims to put forth, how to support them, and how to persuade others that your point of view is warranted and desirable.

Choosing a Topic 7b

A good topic for an argument in a composition class has these important attributes:

- It is a contested issue. Reasonable people hold substantially different opinions about it.
- It is an issue you care about, feel invested in, or find intellectually stimulating.
- It is limited enough in terms of the amount of research you'll need to do and the number of pages it will take to cover the topic adequately.

The thesis statement in an argument is composed of (1) the topic and (2) your claim about the topic. The claim is the assertion that your paper will support with reasons and evidence. It's the opinion you develop about the topic as you think and conduct research.

As you start your project, developing a working thesis statement will help you learn more about your rhetorical situation and your topic. For instance, you might think, "Anger management classes should be required for people who display road rage." This idea is your working thesis. As you research the problem of road rage and some of the solutions that have been proposed, you may discover that several states already have anger management programs in place. In other states, community service is seen as a more effective way to treat those guilty of the crime. You may decide that community service shouldn't be associated with punishment. You decide that you will argue against community service as a "penalty" handed out by courts for a wide variety of minor offenses. You realize, however, that you will need to propose a way to encourage community service with a positive attitude—perhaps by letting road rage perpetrators choose among alternatives.

Conventional Forms for Argument Claims

Basic Form	Examples
Topic / Claim Something should (or shouldn't) be done.	Toxic waste disposal needs to be reconsidered because containers have a finite lifetime.
Something is good (or bad).	Hackers who expose security flaws in popular software protect consumers.
Something is true (or false).	Contrary to urban legend, alligators do not roam the New York City sewers.

Project Checklist

Do You Have an Effective Working Thesis Statement?

- ❑ Does it indicate that the issue is contestable? Consider which people or groups of people would not agree with your working thesis. Write down their objections. If you find at least a couple of substantial objections, the issue is contestable.
- ❑ Does it give a sharp focus to the topic? Does it provide a specific claim and possible reasons and evidence that support that claim?
- ❑ Does it have the potential to change as new information comes to light through research? If you can think of how and why it might change, then your thesis can be deliberated and debated.
- ❑ Does it help you map out the structure of your argument?
- ❑ Does it invite more information? Can you clearly see what you would need to include in order for it to be believable?

Identifying Other Perspectives

Think about your working thesis statement. Who *would agree* with it, who *might agree* with it, and who *would disagree* with it? Why? Divide the possible perspectives into at least two, and preferably more than two, camps. Set up a chart like the one below to help you keep track of them.

People who agree would think . . .	People who might agree would think . . .	People who disagree would think . . .

Then, using a key term on your topic, conduct an Internet search to find newspaper or online news source editorials that illustrate these positions. For example, if you wanted to survey the range of opinion on filesharing of music, you could try these steps:

1. Go to Google News: **http://news.google.com**.
2. Type "*filesharing*" (in quotation marks) in the search box at the top of the page, and then click on Search News. Your search results will include a long list of editorials on this topic from various news sources around the world. You can tell from the title of the page and the brief summary whether it's directly related to your topic. Even the first few search results for "filesharing" reveal a broad range of opinion, with headlines like "Filesharing is not the problem" and "Filesharing online: Good or bad for the local musician?"
3. Add to your chart a summary of each position or each editorial that looks helpful. (Be sure to include the citation information.)
4. Analyze an editorial on your topic from each camp, focusing on questions like these:
   - What position does the editorial take?
   - What evidence or reasons does the editorial provide?
   - What are the stakes of the argument?
   - Does the editorial address the views of the other side?
   - What doesn't the editorial say that it might have said in the interest of arguing its position more effectively?

To write an effective argument designed to persuade, you need to develop a keen understanding of the beliefs of the people opposed to your position, what arguments they make to one another, and which arguments on the other side (your side) they distrust. Consider that there may be moderate positions somewhere in the middle.

For example, suppose you believe that the death penalty is cruel and unusual punishment under any circumstances. If you want to persuade death penalty advocates of your point of view, research their views. Visit the *Weekly Standard* (http: //www.weeklystandard.com), the conservative, pro–death penalty journal, even if you prefer the position of the *New Republic* (http: //www.tnr.com). See whether you can identify positions that have qualifications. Research the positions of people who believe there should be a moratorium while we learn more about the issues, such as the North Carolina Commission for a Moratorium (http: //www.ncmoratorium.org/site/default.asp). Some people hold other views—for example, that the death penalty should not apply to juveniles or should be used only under extraordinary circumstances. Your best writing may emerge from using the evidence that others would use against you.

Writing arguments involves developing, shaping, and presenting content to an audience for a reason. When you *develop* an argument, you take your subject matter into account in great detail through a process of invention and inquiry. When you *shape* an argument, you consider audience and purpose to decide how much of that content is relevant or useful. When you *present* an argument, you consider how your content should be arranged and what style, diction, and tone best convey it to readers.

Effective writers shape and refine subject matter to suit circumstances, which include the opinions and attitudes of the audience and the purpose for writing. Your consideration of what your readers already know about the subject, how they feel about it, and what contrary opinions they hold toward it should guide every decision you make as you shape and present your argument. The aim of your argument—to change minds, rally supporters, foster sympathy, and so on—should likewise guide your selection, shaping, and presentation of subject matter.

A Comparison of the Audiences and Aims of Argument

Audience	General Purpose	Specific Purpose
 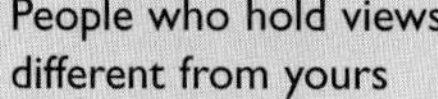 People who hold views different from yours	To persuade people to change an attitude or behavior. Changing someone's attitude is possible only when knowledge is uncertain and there are multiple perspectives.	▪ To change people's minds and attitudes ▪ To solve problems ▪ To resolve conflict ▪ To build consensus ▪ To create community
 People who share your view	To reinforce shared convictions. When people already agree, the purpose of argument may be to turn that agreement into action—for example, working to support a cause. In college classes, you typically won't argue issues on which your readers already agree. Instead, find the basis for disagreement on a subject, and build an argument from there.	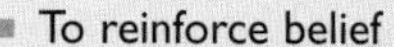 ▪ To reinforce belief ▪ To move people toward commitment and action ▪ To foster identification
 People who wish to understand multiple views	To inquire into the shades of meaning in a subject so that you can open it up to reflection and reconsideration. Help your audience understand that the subject is more complex than they had imagined.	▪ To open up a topic for discussion, debate, and further inquiry ▪ To question common knowledge ▪ To stimulate further research

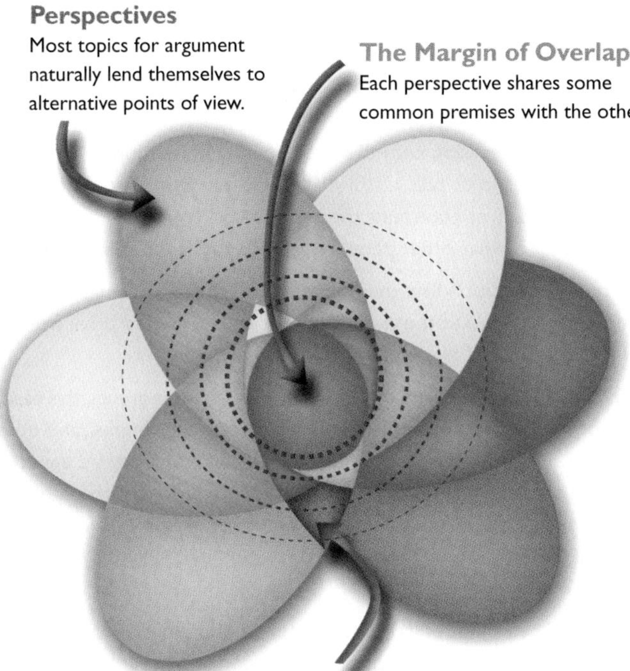

Perspectives
Most topics for argument naturally lend themselves to alternative points of view.
The Margin of Overlap
Each perspective shares some common premises with the others.
Rogerian Argument
The aim is to broaden the margin of overlap among positions by fairly representing multiple sides of an issue, creating the opportunity for finding common ground.

Rogerian argument acknowledges and accommodates alternative positions and perspectives. The purpose is not so much to settle an issue as to map the various positions that reasonable people might hold. Throughout a Rogerian argument, the writer emphasizes common ground, attempts to be objective and truthful about the alternative perspectives, and concedes the relevance of other points of view. The argument often provides background or context, in the hope that enlarging the frame of the argument will make it easier for the various disputants to find common ground. Rogerian argument is particularly useful when your audience is hostile.

Often an either/or argument not only presumes an issue has only two sides but also shows the amount of force holding people apart in the world. Sometimes people in ongoing debates and arguments become so defensive that they cannot even see the humanity of the people with whom they are arguing.

Arguing to inquire involves arguing ethically and intelligently in order to build grounds for consensus. One form of arguing to inquire is Rogerian argument, a method developed by Carl Rogers (1902–1987). The goal of Rogerian argument is to find as much common ground as possible so that parties in the debate or argument will see many aspects of the issue similarly. Believing that shared views of the world create more harmonious conditions, Rogers hoped that people would hold enough in common that they could be persuaded, through debate and dialogue, to allow differences to coexist peacefully. Rogerian argument seeks to resolve conflict by expanding the margin of overlap between people.

Aristotle described rhetoric as the art of finding the available means of persuasion in any particular case. This means, simply, that a speaker or writer needs to know what arguments to use and the best way to present them. Aristotle spent most of his time trying to identify how to invent arguments and how to determine their potential usefulness. Cicero, a Latin rhetorician, later described a generic form for the classical argument.

The classical form rests on the theory that we change our minds and come to believe in something new in a predictable pattern. First something needs to capture our attention. Then we need to learn more about it, analyze it, consider what others say about it, and interpret it.

The Classical Form of Argument

- **Introduction.** The introduction puts the reader in the right frame of mind and suggests, "Here comes something important." It might tell a story that illustrates the controversy or the need to resolve it.
- **Narration.** The narration provides background information necessary for understanding the issue or tells a story that makes a comparison, discredits opponents' views, or just entertains the audience. It often includes cited research and references to what other people have said about the topic in the past.
- **Partition.** The partition lists the points to be proven or divides the points into those agreed on and those in dispute. It is usually very brief, sometimes only a few sentences if the essay is short.
- **Confirmation.** The confirmation is the proof and thus argues the case, thesis, or main point of contention. It may include evidence, examples, and quotations from authoritative sources. Each premise or assumption may be unpacked, explained, and argued using deductive reasoning (arguing from accepted fact to implications) or inductive reasoning (arguing from examples). The confirmation takes up each of the points listed in the partition or implied in the thesis or controlling idea.
- **Refutation.** The refutation takes the other side or sides and shows why they don't hold. It may dispute the positions of opponents, using anticipated or actual arguments; cite claims of inadmissible premises, unwarranted conclusions, or invalid forms of argument; or cite stronger arguments that nevertheless apply only in unrealistic circumstances. The refutation should address the most likely counterarguments, treating them fairly and accurately so as not to arouse the indignation of the audience.
- **Conclusion.** The conclusion sums up or enumerates the points of the argument; it may appeal to the emotions of the readers, encouraging them to feel motivated to change attitudes and sometimes to feel resentful of opposing viewpoints or sympathetic to the writer's position. The conclusion should help people understand the significance of the issue and the importance of viewing it as the writer proposes. The conclusion may also rouse the audience to action or make a specific recommendation.

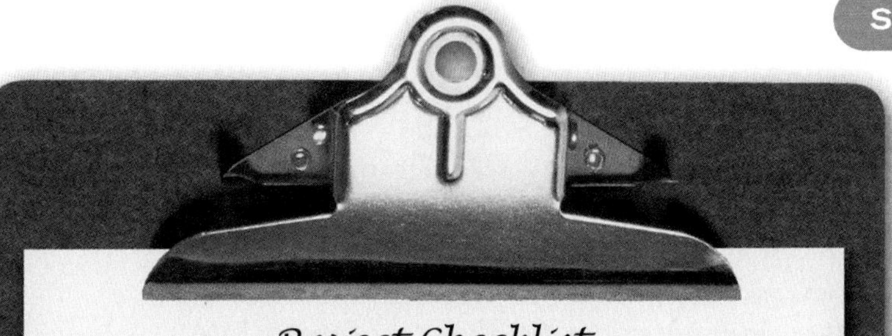

Project Checklist

Motivating Your Readers

How can you motivate your readers to identify with your position and change their actions or attitudes?

- ❑ **Consider the kinds of evidence that your audience will find persuasive.** Suppose you are against hunting animals for sport. Claiming that all animals should have the same rights as humans might not be persuasive with hunters, who might see their rights under the Constitution as superseding those of animals. Rather, you might suggest alternative sports that provide the same kind of satisfaction as hunting or demonstrate that, because of accidents and hunter-on-hunter violence, hunting is more dangerous to humans than to animals. You will need to include evidence that helps hunters see that it is in their best interest to try something else.
- ❑ **Treat your readers as intelligent and reasonable people, even if you think their positions are wrong.** Suppose you want to advance the cause of Students Against Drunk Driving. Saying that social drinkers are "incapable of knowing what is best for them" or calling them "future alcoholics" is likely to cause them to ignore the logic of your appeal.
- ❑ **Tell readers why they should consider your position, and be direct about what you want them to do or think.** What difference does it make if readers agree with you? What exactly should they take away from your argument? What do you want readers to do? How should they see the subject differently now?
- ❑ **Make the case for why the issue is important now.** Readers will want to feel some urgency. What difference does it make if they believe you now rather than later (or never)? What will happen if the situation is not resolved?

An effective argument includes reasons and evidence in support of the points you are asking readers to accept. Organized logically and presented persuasively, the reasons and evidence you provide make your case.

Research Your Topic

Find the background information and facts you can share with readers so that they will judge your argument as reasonable. It's smart to know more about your subject matter than your audience does so that you can shape their responses to it.

Define Terms to Establish Common Ground

Defining the terms you will use in your argument is crucial because it helps you establish common ground with your readers. You can use this consensus to develop definitions in a way that supports your point of view.

Use Evidence Effectively

Verifiable facts and widely accepted truths are almost always the most effective kinds of support.

Distinguish Fact from Opinion

When you gather evidence for your arguments, it is helpful to distinguish between fact and opinion. Facts will usually be more persuasive if your audience is fair-minded. The opinions of others don't prove an argument's claims, but they do show that others have come to similar conclusions, making your argument more believable.

Draw on Expert Testimony and Authoritative Sources

Cite the opinions of those who have expert knowledge of the subject matter because they have published books or articles on the subject, have studied it professionally, or have some other insight not shared by the general population. Knowledge that has been reviewed and edited by experts has an air of authority that can give added weight to a case.

Be Careful When Using Personal or Anecdotal Experience

A few personal experiences, no matter how poignant, are not enough support for an argument. You can certainly recount personal experiences, but base your argument mainly on statistics and other evidence.

Fact vs. Opinion

Prevention of Art Theft

The biggest art heist in history occurred in Boston in 1990, when thirteen pieces of art, including three Rembrandts, a Manet, a Vermeer, and five Degas drawings, were stolen from the Isabella Stewart Gardner Museum. ("The Gardner Heist," by Stephen Kurkjian, Boston Globe at boston.com, Globe Special Report, March 13, 2005, accessed March 13, 2005.)

A **fact** is a statement whose truth can be verified by observation, experimentation, or research.

Prevention of Art Theft

Museums should do their best to prevent art theft, but if they cannot prevent it, they should be financially prepared to replace stolen art with art of similarly high quality when necessary.

An **opinion** is an interpretation of evidence or experience.

Project Checklist

Questions to Ask about Your Reasoning

Ask these general questions about your reasoning. Refer to pages 142 and 151 for more information on evaluating research sources for comprehensiveness, reliability, and relevance.

- ❑ Have you supplied sufficient evidence to be convincing without boring your readers? Evidence is sufficient when it proves your argument but doesn't pile on unnecessary information that might distract readers from your point(s).
- ❑ Is the evidence you cite reliable and accurate? Can you confirm that the information is correct by finding it mentioned in other sources?
- ❑ Are the experts you cite in support of your argument knowledgeable, authoritative, and trustworthy?
- ❑ Are your examples relevant, sufficiently developed, and interesting?
- ❑ Does your argument proceed by sound logic? Have you avoided making logical fallacies (▶ page 84)?

If your argument is based on examples, also ask

- ❑ Do the examples show what you say they do?
- ❑ Are the examples familiar or obscure? Are they memorable? Why?
- ❑ Have you used a sufficient number of examples to make your point, but not so many that you bore or insult your reader?
- ❑ Do you explain clearly what your examples prove or illustrate?

If your argument moves from general to specific, also ask

- ❑ Will readers agree with your premises? If not, should you explain them?
- ❑ Is it clear how your conclusion follows from your premises?
- ❑ Are there any other conclusions to be drawn from your premises? Should you mention them?

When you write an argument, you can make three general kinds of appeals to readers.

- *Logos* is the appeal to reason.
- *Ethos* is the writer's presentation of herself or himself as fair-minded and trustworthy.
- *Pathos* is the appeal to the emotions of the audience.

Logos: The Appeal to Reason

Logos should be the focus of an academic argument.

Induction: Reasoning from Examples to Conclusions

Induction is the process of reasoning from experience, gaining insight from the signs and examples around us. Induction relies on examples to support or justify conclusions. The most important consideration with induction is to make sure that the examples support the conclusions—that they "exemplify" the case in the reader's mind. When the examples are valid and vivid, an inductive argument can be persuasive if you have properly gauged the rhetorical situation.

Deduction: Reasoning from General to Specific

In **deduction,** you argue from established premises, or truths about general cases, toward conclusions in more specific circumstances ("Given A, then B and C must follow"). A deductive pattern uses a syllogism or an enthymeme to draw a conclusion.

A **syllogism** is a form of logic that has a generalization (or major premise), a qualifier (or minor premise), and a conclusion. A syllogism starts with true statements from general cases and applies them to specific cases.

An **enthymeme,** which we have been calling a claim, suppresses one or more premises because the audience is likely to accept them.

Ethos: The Appeal of Being Trustworthy

Readers will look to see if the writer is someone they can trust. As a writer, you cultivate trust by showing readers that you know what you are talking about, have carefully considered the evidence and other perspectives on the issue, and have the audience's best interests at heart.

Pathos: The Appeal to Emotions

In most academic writing, you won't need to appeal to the emotions of your readers. However, emotion is naturally a factor when people are deciding whether to take action or change their attitudes.

Sample Syllogism

Generalization (major premise):	All curious people enjoy learning.
Qualifier (minor premise):	You are a curious person.
Conclusion:	Therefore, you will enjoy learning.

Sample Enthymemes

Minor premise — Conclusion

1. I'm a curious person, so I enjoy learning new things.

Major premise — Conclusion

2. Curious people enjoy learning, so I do, too.

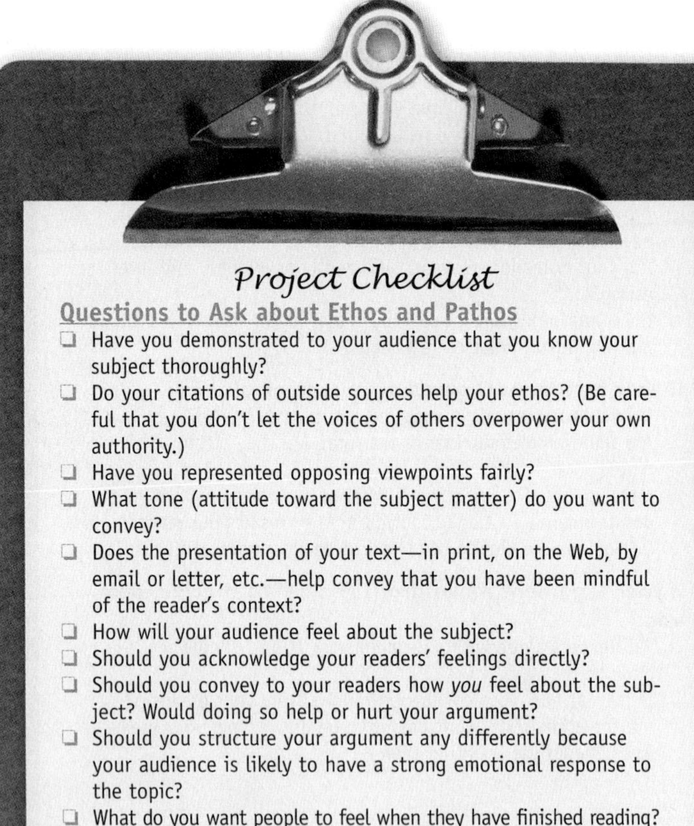

Project Checklist

Questions to Ask about Ethos and Pathos

- ❑ Have you demonstrated to your audience that you know your subject thoroughly?
- ❑ Do your citations of outside sources help your ethos? (Be careful that you don't let the voices of others overpower your own authority.)
- ❑ Have you represented opposing viewpoints fairly?
- ❑ What tone (attitude toward the subject matter) do you want to convey?
- ❑ Does the presentation of your text—in print, on the Web, by email or letter, etc.—help convey that you have been mindful of the reader's context?
- ❑ How will your audience feel about the subject?
- ❑ Should you acknowledge your readers' feelings directly?
- ❑ Should you convey to your readers how *you* feel about the subject? Would doing so help or hurt your argument?
- ❑ Should you structure your argument any differently because your audience is likely to have a strong emotional response to the topic?
- ❑ What do you want people to feel when they have finished reading?

Sample Toulmin Analysis

In your reading and research, you learn

> The U.S. government wants to spend billions of dollars to send people to the moon, once again, for the purposes of building a permanent colony there for scientific research and in preparation for sending astronauts to Mars. The government has also been slow to respond to the crisis of global warming. Data

So you claim

> NASA's inability to rectify the technical problems with the Space Shuttle after the Columbia disaster demonstrates that it is foolish to waste money on new ventures and divert taxpayer dollars from more pressing scientific problems like global warming. Claim

Then you ask: What are some of the warrants that support the claim?

> NASA has not fixed technical problems in the past.
> If you can't fix old problems, you shouldn't create new ones.
> Global warming is a more important issue than space exploration. Warrants

What are the less obvious warrants—ones that rest on value, belief, or ideology?

> Space exploration cannot help us solve problems like global warming.
> Discovery and adventure are overrated goals.
> Global warming is a problem that needs to and can be addressed effectively. Warrants

You may decide that you need backing for at least one of your warrants:

> Al Gore's film *An Inconvenient Truth* confronts global warming nay-sayers by showing indisputably that the phenomenon is already negatively affecting global agricultural production.
>
> California Governor Arnold Schwarzenegger and UK Prime Minister Tony Blair had to take the exceptional step of forming an alliance to address global warming because the U.S. government still refuses to accept its responsibility to act. Backing

And you must address a rebuttal that challenges one of your warrants, the belief that discovery and exploration always stimulate new knowledge and economic benefits:

> The pursuit of phlogiston showed that scientific exploration without clearly defined goals may siphon valuable money and attention from worthier pursuits. Rebuttal

Qualifier

The persuasiveness of your argument depends on a wide variety of factors: the willingness of your audience to assent and their motives for doing so, the common ground you establish, the effectiveness of your rhetorical appeals, and the context that defines all of these factors. Philosopher and rhetorician Stephen Toulmin recognized the importance of context in evaluating persuasion. He also developed a method for analyzing and mapping the structural basis and logic of persuasive arguments, what he called their *progression* (where an argument starts and how it unfolds). Writers can use the Toulmin method to analyze their own arguments or those of others.

Arguments proceed from **data** or **grounds** (facts, evidence, or reasons) that support a **claim** (a point of contention, a position on a controversial issue, a call to act, a thesis). Claims are based on **warrants,** the unstated premises that support a claim. Warrants require **backing** (support, additional data) when they are disputable. **Qualifiers** (terms like *some, most,* or *many*) may be used to soften the claim. **Rebuttals,** or challenges to the claim, focus on points that undermine the claim or invalidate the warrant.

A fallacy is an error in reasoning, whether deliberate or inadvertent. You can use your knowledge of fallacies to expose the problems in reading material, and you should check for fallacies in your own writing. *Fallacies of relevance* work by inviting readers to attach to a claim qualities that are not relevant to the subject. Fallacies of relevance bring unrelated evidence or information to bear on issues that are outside the scope of the subject matter or that have little or no bearing on our judgment of a case in its own right. *Fallacies of ambiguity* include ambiguous or unclear terms in the claim. Fallacies of ambiguity presume that something is certain or commonsensical when multiple viewpoints are possible.

For more on fallacies, visit The Writing Center of the University of North Carolina at Chapel Hill (http://www.unc.edu/depts/wcweb/handouts/fallacies.html).

Fallacies of Relevance

1. **Personal attack *(ad hominem)*.** Discrediting the person making the argument to avoid addressing the argument
2. **Jumping on the bandwagon (*ad populum*).** Arguing that something must be true or good because a lot of other people believe it
3. **Nothing suggests otherwise . . . (*ad ignorantiam*).** Claiming that something is true simply because there is no contrary evidence
4. **False authority (*ad vericundiam*).** Suggesting that a person has authority simply because of fame or notoriety
5. **Appeal to tradition.** Claiming that just because something has been so previously, it is justified or should remain unchanged
6. **The newer, the better (theory of the new premise).** Claiming that because the evidence is new, it is the best explanation

Fallacies of Ambiguity

7. **Hasty generalization.** Making a claim about a wide class of subjects based on limited evidence
8. **Begging the question.** Basing the conclusion on premises or claims that lack important information or qualification
9. **Guilt by association.** Claiming that the quality of one thing sticks to another by virtue of a loose association
10. **Circular argument.** Concluding from premises that are related to the conclusion
11. **"After this, therefore because of this" (*post hoc, ergo propter hoc*).** Assuming that because one thing followed another, the first caused the second
12. **Slippery slope.** Arguing that if one thing occurs, something worse and unrelated will follow by necessity (one stride up the slippery slope will take you two steps back)

Contending with Readers' Perspectives

Two methods exist for contending with readers with hostile or differing perspectives.

- You can demolish their arguments viciously (as many argument writers on unmoderated message boards do).
- You can anticipate their objections and refute them tactfully.

Where to Place Your Refutation

You should place your refutation at the spot in your argument where it will do the most good. If your readers are likely to have a refuting point in the forefront of their minds, then you need to address that opposing issue earlier rather than later. The longer you put off dealing directly with the likely objections of readers, the longer you postpone their possible agreement with your position. If there are important contrary views that your readers might not have made up their minds about, then your refutation will likely work best later in your essay. The important principle to remember is that effective writers raise issues (as in a refutation) at the opportune moment—just when readers expect them to be discussed.

When you *concede,* you give credence to an opposing or alternative perspective; you grant that some members of your audience might disagree with you and agree with another's point. When you *refute,* you examine an opposing or alternative point or perspective and demonstrate why it is incorrect or not the best response or solution.

If you address possible objections in a fair-minded but direct way, you increase the likelihood that the opposition will understand and be won over to your position. Fair-mindedness will also enhance your ethos with neutral readers, who will consider you a reliable and trustworthy source.

All responses to essay exam questions are arguments in the sense that you make a claim and then support it with relevant reasons, examples, and evidence. Your task is to persuade your instructor of the claim you are making, which in turn will demonstrate your grasp of the course content.

Your first step in writing a response is to plan your time carefully.

10:00–10:30 plan essay
10:30–11:45 write essay
11:45–11:50 proof essay

One-question tests: Allot one-quarter to one-third of your time for planning, including outlining your response, and leave two-thirds to three-quarters for writing the exam, paring off a smidgeon of that time for proofreading.

question 6	30 minutes	10:00–10:30
questions 4, 5	20 minutes each	10:30–11:10
questions 1, 2, 3	10 minutes each	11:10–11:45
proofing all	5 minutes	11:45–11:50

Multiple-question tests: Figure out how much time to allow for each question, based on how heavily each is weighted in your final score.

Understand the Question

Begin planning your essay by carefully evaluating the exam question. What precisely is the instructor asking for? Rewrite, underline, or highlight keywords as necessary. In some cases, the time you take to understand the question—and even to take issue with some of the terms it uses or the perspective it seems to present—can be the most critical step of the process because it helps you shape your approach carefully and thoughtfully, which leads to good writing.

Outline Your Response

Outlining your response and drafting a thesis statement are perhaps the most critical steps for keeping your essay on track. Make an informal outline that includes your thesis and the topic of each supportive paragraph, and then refer to it as you write your essay.

Key Terms for Understanding Exam Questions

Analyze: Divide a subject into its important parts, and examine each part separately and as it relates to the whole.

Argue: Take a position and support it with clearly articulated reasons and evidence.

Classify: Divide a large group into smaller groups based on shared characteristics.

Compare and contrast: Examine the similarities and differences between one thing and another.

Define: State the precise meaning of something and describe its essential properties. A definition is often followed by an example.

Describe: Systematically explain something, with attention to facts, details, and particulars. The term is often used to elicit a recounting or summarizing of course content.

Discuss: Present a close examination of something, considering as many important elements as you can. The term is often used to prompt an original argument and a demonstration of breadth of knowledge of a subject.

Evaluate, critique, assess: Give a reasoned, informed opinion, providing ample justification for your point of view.

Explain: Make a process, event, or idea clear and understandable. An explanation often breaks a subject into steps or categories, which are then appropriately amplified, illustrated, or supported by examples.

Explicate: Analyze a passage from a source text, explaining what lines or sentences mean in context, while also noting the ways in which the source text may be interpreted (or has been interpreted by others). An explication is sometimes referred to as a "close reading" of a text.

Illustrate, give examples: Develop, support, or clarify by providing examples.

Review: Provide a general survey (sometimes chronological, sometimes organized by other principles), critically evaluate, or reexamine. The term has different meanings depending on the context. Make sure you understand how it's being used before you answer the exam question.

Review the literature: Name and summarize the major sources of information and research on the subject. A review of the literature usually evaluates sources critically in light of their relevance and importance to the topic at hand.

Summarize: Present the substance of the material in a condensed form. Summaries are comprehensive but brief—often just a paragraph or sentence.

Excerpt from Successful Student Essay

First paragraph sets up the factors to be considered.

Although Lyme disease is carried by ticks, researchers have determined that major outbreaks of Lyme disease in oak-forest ecosystems in the northeastern United States result from complex interactions among oaks, ticks, and deer and rodents. These interactions can in turn affect gypsy moth, song bird, and predator populations. Balancing the effects of these interactions is a complex matter: While reducing the mouse population does reduce incidence of Lyme disease, it also increases incidence of gypsy moth outbreaks, which are especially devastating to oaks (oak leaves being one of the gypsy moth's favorite foods). While citizens want less Lyme disease, they also want healthy oaks and—oaks being the dominant species in the oak-forest system—healthy forests. Current research suggests that the best approach is to maintain both mice and gypsy moths at reasonable population levels by enhancing biodiversity.

Response is well organized, and transitional phrases and headings help the reader follow the train of thought.

Main assertion for the paragraph

Appropriately supported by evidence and detail

The Ecological Web of Lyme Disease

Oaks and Acorns. The ecological web of Lyme disease begins with the dominant species in the northeastern oak-forest system, the oak. One of the oak's strategies for escaping seed predation is masting: every so often oaks produce a bumper crop of acorns. Masting helps oaks reproduce successfully by outsmarting animals that feed on acorns. Take mice as an example. Mouse populations fluctuate in response to the availability of acorns. . . .

Present a Clear Argument

Begin with a strong thesis statement; advance your argument step by step logically; signal the progression of the argument clearly with appropriate transition phrases or other rhetorical strategies; support each point appropriately as you advance; finish with a strong conclusion that summarizes your points.

For the most part a timed essay is a place to demonstrate knowledge rather than a place to show what a great writer you are. Use clear, grammatical sentences and correct spelling and punctuation. Say what needs to be said in response to the question.

Sample Exam Question

What factors must be considered in managing outbreaks of Lyme disease in an oak-forest ecosystem in the northeastern United States? Describe the relevant ecological web and evaluate the pros and cons of various management strategies.

Proofread Your Work

Leave some time at the end to reread what you wrote, make simple insertions or changes, and correct grammar, spelling, and punctuation. Show changes as neatly and clearly as possible without recopying your work. Finally, if you must leave an essay or part of an essay unfinished, sketch a simple outline at the end so the instructor can see where your response might have headed.

8 WRITING FOR BUSINESS AND THE WORKPLACE

Learning to write effective cover letters and resumes is important because everyone will at some time apply for a new job, start a new career path, or move up the corporate ladder. To be successful, you need to let people know what you can do for them.

A **cover letter** is usually a one-page introduction (a "cover") to documents presented to readers, clients, or—in the case of a job search—a prospective employer. A specific type of cover letter is the job application letter, which does more than introduce the documents of an application. A job application letter also connects the applicant to the position, elaborates on relevant skills, and makes the case that the writer is the best person for the job.

A **resume** is a summary of your qualifications for employment and usually includes information about your education, work experience, accomplishments, and professional interests. As genres of writing, cover letters and resumes follow conventions in terms of format and content, but their form and content should also be responses to particular circumstances.

Reading and Writing in the Job Search

Take inventory of your skills, experiences, and goals.
Find and analyze job ads. In your search, learn about and use various Web-based resources for job seekers, and ultimately select one job to pursue.
Compose a cover letter that identifies your reasons for applying and highlights your qualifications.
Write a resume suitable for such a position.
Eugene Rhee

Taking Inventory of Your Skills, Experience, and Goals

To help you decide what kind of job you want and to generate ideas for your cover letter and resume, write down answers to the following questions.

Work Experience

1. What work experiences have you had? List them all, with the title of your position, the name and location of the company or organization, your supervisor's name, the dates of your employment, and the job's requirements.
2. Have you ever volunteered with a nonprofit organization? List the details, as in item 1.
3. Have you had any internship experiences? Describe them in detail.

Educational Experience

4. What courses, projects, and other activities have taught you valuable skills? Describe them in detail.
5. Have you received any scholarships or awards? Describe them in full.

Skills

6. What skills do you have that rise above the ordinary? What do you do especially well? Do you have any special talents (think broadly)? How do your skills and talents relate to the kind of job you seek?
7. Do you have skills in working with particular groups of people? Do you speak more than one language?
8. Do you have computer skills? What software programs do you know well?
9. Do you have skills working with particular kinds of equipment?

To generate more specific ideas about the skills you already possess, review the extensive list of terms that name these skills on the "Job Skills Checklist" at Purdue University's Online Writing Lab: **http://owl.english.purdue.edu/handouts/pw/p_skillinv.html**.

"Know thyself" was the common refrain of the Greek philosopher Socrates. If you want to have good content to work with when you portray yourself to others, you need to be sure that you have explored your talents fully. Who are you? What have you done and what can you do? Those are not always easy questions to answer, even though your field of research (the self) is as close to home as it can get. You may have some work-related experience to list. You will also have educational experience: courses, class projects, and other educational activities. Take inventory of your skills and experience.

Consider, too, what you want from a job, not to mention from your life. Are you looking for a position that will teach you new skills, such as an internship or apprenticeship? Are you looking for a position that will prepare you for higher-level work in your field? What do you enjoy doing most? Do you prefer working alone or with people? Where do you want to work?

You can find job listings in your local newspaper (online or offline) and in your college's employment or career center. In addition, you may find these Internet resources helpful. Once you have found an ad for a job that interests you and for which you are well qualified, you should spend some time analyzing the ad to make sure you understand the nature of the position and its requirements. You should also research the company itself. You will use information from this analysis as you tailor your cover letter and resume to the rhetorical situation.

Career Magazine:
http://www.careermag.com

CareerBuilder:
http://www.careerbuilder.com

Computerjobs:
http://www.computerjobs.com

InternWeb.Com:
http://www.internweb.com

Journalism Jobs:
http://journalismjobs.com

Manpower:
http://www.manpower.com

Monster.com:
http://www.monster.com

Net-Temps:
http://www.net-temps.com

Overseas Job Web:
http://www.overseasjobs.com

Yahoo! HotJobs:
http://hotjobs.yahoo.com

Excerpt from a Sample Job Ad

The ad asks for someone who excels at customer service.

WE'RE LOOKING FOR AMERICA'S BEST
The Best Eyecare ... Every Day

Job Title: Receptionist
Department: Retail Operations
Reporting Relationships:
Reports to Assistant Manager–Eyeglasses and Assistant Manager–Contact Lenses
Summary of Position:
Ensures telephones are answered promptly in accordance with company telephone protocol and that customers receive courteous service.
Essential Duties and Responsibilities:
- Schedule and confirm appointments, follow-up visits, and classes.
- Maintain permanent records.
- Ensure smooth flow of patients through store.
- Notify customers when orders are in or of any delays.
- Maintain neat and orderly front desk and waiting room.

Experience:
- Experience preferred, but not required.

They would like someone who has job-related experience, but other experience, such as volunteer work, may be acceptable as well.

The successful applicant will have good record-keeping skills, customer service experience, and phone skills.

Sample Response: Why Am I Interested? How Am I Qualified?

Jessica Hary, the student who found the job ad on page 90, wrote her answers to these questions in preparation for writing a cover letter.

America's Best Contacts and Eyeglasses

This is a position for a receptionist at America's Best Contacts and Eyeglasses. The responsibilities of this position are that you answer the phones in the appropriate business manner and that you be courteous to the patients. The duties and responsibilities of this position are very general. These duties include but are not limited to scheduling and confirming appointments with the patients, keeping up-to-date records for each and every patient, letting the patients know when their orders are in or if they are back ordered, and maintaining an organized desk.

I chose this position because of the fact that I want to be an optometrist. I have six years left before I am completely done with my schooling, so it is hard to find a job that fits my major. In this case, I would get some experience in the field of optometry. This would allow me to be able to converse with the doctor and ask questions and maybe even get to sit in on a checkup. This would also allow me to see what actually goes on in an optometrist's office, so in the future, when I am an optometrist, I will have some insight into what should take place in the office.

I believe that I am qualified for this position for many reasons. One reason is that I consider myself a people person, and I have several communication and people skills. I have worked at a grocery store for the past five years. This has allowed me to be able to communicate with different types of people and has taught me how to deal with certain situations. Another reason I consider myself qualified is because I have experience with answering phones. I worked in my high school main office for two years, answering phones and taking messages. I am also a very organized and neat person. I would not have a problem with keeping my work area organized and presentable.

Before you draft your cover letter, answer these questions:

- Why am I interested in this position?
- How am I qualified for it?

To prepare a cover letter, pay attention not only to the content of the ad but also to the circumstances of the company or organization. Think, too, about who might read your letter. What will they notice? What questions might they have?

In response to the ad she chose, Jessica Hary wrote the cover letter on page 92. Notice how she effectively addresses the two questions above, at least indirectly. In her first paragraph, she identifies her reasons for applying. She realizes that the employer might wonder why a student in optometry was applying for a job as a receptionist. She is careful in the following paragraphs to give details about her experience in customer service.

Parts of the Cover Letter

Heading. The various items in the heading should appear in this order: sender's name, address, and any other contact information; date; recipient's name or title and address; and greeting. Each chunk of information is separated by a blank line.

Greeting. Try to find the name of a person to address your cover letter to. If you can't find a name by doing research, use the person's exact title. "Dear" is the standard way to begin.

Opening. Let your reader know why she or he has received your letter, who you are, and which ad you are responding to.

Persuasion. In this section, which may be several paragraphs in length, you should explain in detail what you want your reader to remember about you or the material you are introducing (here, your resume and qualifications for the position).

Closing. "Sincerely" is an accepted closing. Vary from it only if you have a clear reason for doing so. For example, if you know the person well, you might instead choose to close with "Best regards." Sign your cover letter, and identify any accompanying documents in an "Enclosure" line.

Sample Job Application Cover Letter

Jessica Hary
123 Anywhere St.
West Lafayette, IN 47906
(555) 555-5555
nobody@purdue.edu

May 19, 2006

Human Resources Manager
America's Best Contacts and Eyeglasses
7255 Crescent Blvd.
Pennsauken, NJ 08110

Dear Human Resources Manager:

I am currently a student at Purdue University majoring in General Health Science with a focus on Pre-Optometry. I am applying for the position as a Receptionist at your Indianapolis store, advertised on Yahoo! HotJobs, and I have enclosed my resume in application for this position. I believe that my experiences in customer service and public relations would make me a valuable addition to your company. I am very interested in this position because I hope to be an optometrist someday and this would be a great starting place for me to learn about the everyday life of an optometrist.

For the past five years, I have been employed at a local grocery store, and I also volunteered answering phones in my high school's main office. I have gained considerable experience in these roles, which would benefit your company and would allow me to make an immediate contribution if I were successful in obtaining this position.

I am enthusiastic and hardworking and have excellent communication skills. Furthermore, I am a skilled user of Microsoft Word, Excel, and Money, as you can see from my resume. In addition, I know how to deal with difficult situations with customers in a polite and well-mannered way. These qualities have allowed me to build and maintain excellent relationships with customers and my fellow workers in my previous jobs. I would like to bring these experiences and skills to your company; I want to benefit your company and in the process learn from my experiences to further help me in the field of optometry. My salary requirements are $25,000.

Please contact me at (555) 555-5555 or by email at nobody@purdue.edu. I look forward to speaking with you. Thank you for your time and consideration.

Sincerely,
Jessica Hary

Enclosure: Resume

Sample Resume

Eugene Rhee

Campus Address
123 Somewhere Dorm
West Lafayette, IN 47906
(765) 555-1111

eugenerhee@purdue.edu

Permanent Address
456 Bonita Drive
Chula Vista, CA 91911
(619) 555-2222

Objective To obtain a position as a test engineer at Raytheon Company that utilizes my technical skills and knowledge to assure quality engineering and safety.

Education **Purdue University** West Lafayette, IN
Bachelor of Science, August 2004
Major: Electrical Engineering Minor: Management
Major GPA: 3.74/4.00 Grad GPA: 3.80/4.00 Minor GPA: 4.00/4.00

Engineering Coursework: Signals and Systems, Digital Signal Processing, Electromechanical Motion Devices, Electromagnetics, Optics, Feedback Systems

Management Coursework: Financial and Managerial Accounting, Finance, Marketing, Organizational Behavior

Skills
Operating Systems: Windows, Unix, Linux
Programming Languages: Matlab, C, HTML, ABEL, Basic
Applications: Excel, Matlab, Minitab, Microsoft Office
Testing Equipment: Spectrum Analyzer, Oscilloscope, Multimeter, Signal Generator, Power Meter, Analog Filter, Amplifier

Projects
Created a communications device to transmit and receive binary data and displayed data on seven-segment LEDs.
Assembled a video processor and captured the image on a computer screen.

Work Experience **Customer Service Representative** [Aug. 2003 - Present] Blockbuster Video, West Lafayette, IN
Ensured customer satisfaction.
Maintained organizational structure for effortless accessibility of company assets.
Collaborated with management to enhance a security system.

Office Assistant [June 2001 - Aug. 2001] Yongsan Military Base, Korea
Analyzed computer database program and made recommendations to change the software; changes were implemented shortly after internship.
Entered information in database of military housing records.
Organized and filed housing applications and other requests.

Activities **Korean American Students Association**
Joined to establish and maintain relations with Korean-American students.

Cornerstone Fellowship
Helped organize and participated in special events such as Goodwill Games and Graduation Night.
Helped cook for students living in the dormitories when cafeteria food was unavailable.

References Available on request.

A resume, like a cover letter, should be tailored to a specific rhetorical situation—as announced by a job ad, for instance—instead of being one size fits all. Many job seekers prepare multiple versions of their resume in order to respond to a range of positions.

Parts of a Typical Resume

Resumes typically contain contact information, career objectives, educational background, work experience, achievements, special skills, and a list of references or a statement that they are available. Precisely which headings you use to organize your resume will depend on the nature of the position you are applying for and the types of experience you have. If, for example, you are applying for a position that requires experience as a graphic designer, you might include a section called "Exhibitions and Portfolios." Or if you have substantial volunteer work experience, you might list that experience in its own section, "Volunteer Experience." The order of the sections will depend on which aspects of your qualifications you want to emphasize, with the most important aspects placed early in the resume.

Additional Headings That May Be Used in a Resume

The following headings are particularly useful for college students who don't yet have an extensive work history, homemakers returning to the paid workforce, and people changing careers:

Volunteer Service (or Volunteer Work)
Honors (or Achievements, Scholarships, Academic Recognition, Awards)
Technical Skills (or Software Skills, Equipment Skills, Certifications, Licenses)
Hobbies (or Interests and Activities, Extracurricular Activities)
Leadership Activities
Field Experience
Portfolios (or Exhibitions)
Languages

Designing the Resume

Resumes are challenging to design and present. They must include lots of information, presented logically in an aesthetically pleasing way, to readers who may not take more than a minute or two to read them. For these reasons, the design and layout of your resume are critically important.

Establish consistency among similar types or levels of information.

- All major section headings, such as "Education" and "Work Experience," should be in the same

1

Project Checklist

Evaluating Your Resume's Content

- ❑ **Contact information.** Your contact information should be listed prominently, usually near the top of the page, with no heading. Include your campus and/or permanent mailing address; your home and/or cell phone number; your email address (use a "professional" one); and, if appropriate, the URL for your home page or Web portfolio.
- ❑ **Objective** (sometimes listed as "Career Objective," "Objective Statement," "Career Goals," or "Philosophy Statement"). Resumes may include statements about career objectives, but in some occupations it is common practice not to include them, so find out whether others in your field do so. The objective should state clearly and concisely what you want to accomplish for yourself *and* for a company or organization. Remember: The reader wants to know what you can do for the company or the organization. Notice the difference.
  YES—What *you* can do for *them*
  Objective: To use my experience as a marketing strategist to help a fast-paced, creative ad agency in the fashion industry.
  NO—What *they* can do for *you*
  Objective: To obtain a high-paying position that will improve my skills as a marketing strategist in the fashion industry.
- ❑ **Education** ("Educational Experience"). Identify the level of education you have obtained and, if relevant, the degree you are working toward. If it is still early in your college career, list information about your high school diploma or equivalency; by the time you graduate, you probably won't need to include it. Some kinds of information are essential; others are optional, depending on how important they are to your case and to the specific rhetorical situation.
  Essential: Name and location of institution, inclusive dates of attendance, major, minor, degree obtained (or sought, with "date expected" listed)
  Optional: GPA, relevant courses taken, specializations, licenses and certificates obtained

2

- Work Experience ("Employment History" or "Employment"). Describe in detail any work experience that makes you a strong candidate and include all other experience relevant to the position. You needn't list every job you have ever had, but you do need to list all the recent ones. Employers will look for "gaps" in your employment history, so instead of leaving out recent jobs that seem irrelevant, list them briefly. A good "Work Experience" entry contains the position title, name and location of the company, dates of employment, and list of responsibilities.
- References ("List of References"). Employers expect you to provide references, either on request or on the resume itself. Be sure to talk to your references in advance, asking them if they can give you a good recommendation and letting them know what types of positions you plan to apply for. (If you are asking for letters of reference also, allow about 30 days for the letter-writing.)

Evaluating Your Resume's Design

Readers scanning a page tend to start in the top left corner and move down the page, left to right. Keep this in mind as you decide where to place information on your page and how to use typography and layout to draw the reader's eye.

- Is the contact information easy to find? Have you drawn the reader's eye to your name without overdoing it?
- Are columns of information aligned?
- Do section headings stand out clearly without taking too much space?
- Is each quarter of the page filled with about the same quantity of text?
- Have you used typography to draw attention to important information and to present detailed information legibly?
- Have you used white space (empty space) to help direct the reader's eye to important information? What will readers notice first?
- If readers had only 20 seconds to scan your resume, would they remember what you want them to remember?

typeface and font size, aligned consistently, and spaced the same distance from the text that comes before and after them.

- Group information to make it easier to grasp quickly. For example, consider using bulleted lists of your major responsibilities in your most relevant jobs to draw attention to each one.

Use contrast to show differences in the types or levels of information.

- The typefaces used for headings and body text should contrast with each other so that each type of information stands out. Sans serif typefaces such as Verdana, Geneva, Century Gothic, and Arial are good for headings in paper resumes, while serif faces like Times, Times New Roman, Garamond, and Palatino are easy enough to read to use as body text.
- Use indentations of various distances from the left margin to establish a visual hierarchy of information.

Make sure type is large enough to be legible. For serif fonts, use 11-point or larger type. You may be able to use 10-point sans serif fonts. For the body text, use a font no larger than 12 points. Do not try to squeeze in more information by reducing your font size.

Use white space to give readers' eyes a rest and to direct their attention. Your resume should have at least 1" margins all around, and within the text area there should be empty space around major headings so that they stand out from the rest of the words.

Maintain the right visual "attitude." For most applications, print your resume on a laser or high-quality inkjet printer, using only black ink on white or off-white paper. Most potential employers will not expect your resume to be flashy. In those rare cases when it is obvious that the employer does expect a flashy resume, your rhetorical situation has changed and you can likely take more chances with your design.

Polishing Your Resume

Be sure to spell-check and then proofread your resume—as you would any writing meant for an audience—so that you don't have any mistakes. On employment documents, typos and misspellings are often judged more harshly than they might be in other genres, so be extra careful.

Using Columns and Tables to Design a Resume

You can use your word processor's Table command to create perfectly aligned columns in your resume, rather than trying to use tabs or margin indentations. Once set in table columns, lists and other grouped information can be modified without much effort.

Suppose, for example, that you want to use two columns to list your relevant courses. In Microsoft Word 2007, you can do the following:

1. Place your cursor at the insertion point.
2. Select the Insert tab to show the Insert ribbon.
3. Select the down arrow beneath the Table icon.
4. Set the number of columns and rows; for a two-column list, you would choose two columns and one row. You can do this quickly by mousing over the boxes shown or by selecting "Insert Table," as shown to the right.
5. Leave "Fixed column width" set to Auto and readjust your column widths by placing your cursor over the table borders and dragging them to the desired width.

List of relevant courses formatted manually:

When you don't use a table, the long course title runs into the next column, forcing you to reformat all the lines.

English Composition Appreciation of Literature
Business Writing Critical Approaches to Film
Art History The Ideology of Religion
Oral Communication in the Workplace Senior Seminar in Sociology

List of relevant courses formatted as a table:

If you set the table border to 0, no border lines will show.

English Composition Business Writing Art History Oral Communication in the Workplace	Appreciation of Literature Critical Approaches to Film The Ideology of Religion Senior Seminar in Sociology

Here, the long course title is set with a hanging indentation. Other lines are not affected.

Adding or deleting list items will not upset the alignment of columns.

For instructions that apply to Microsoft® Word® 2003, visit the handbook's website: **cengage.com/english/blakesley**

Many employers like to scan resumes into a digital database that they can search using keywords. Thus, a computer, not a person, will read your words. A scannable resume presents the same content as a traditional resume, but has two key differences:

- To ensure that the resume includes keywords that employers might look for, nouns and noun phrases are used instead of verbs to describe jobs, skills, and responsibilities. Read job ads in your industry to see which keywords to use.
- Formatting is removed.

Rewriting Your Resume for Scannability

1. Turn important verb phrases that describe your jobs and skills into nouns. For example, the phrase "wrote advertising copy" would become "advertising copywriter."
2. Remove commas between the items in lists and periods after lists or phrases. Place spaces between the words.
3. Create a keyword summary that describes your major qualifications in terms your industry would use, and place it at the end of the resume. Check the spelling of all key terms several times.

Don't worry if the content of your scannable resume seems less coherent than that of your traditional resume. Employers will be looking at specific qualifications, not at your scannable resume as a whole.

Reformatting Your Resume for Scannability

1. Remove all tables, columns, and special text positioning.
2. Place each element (such as a line of an address, a phone number, or a skill) on its own line. Remove all bulleted lists. (Replace bullets with asterisks [*].) Left-justify all content.
3. Change all text to a 10- or 12-point serif font such as Times New Roman.
4. Remove italics, underlining, and boldface.

The scannable version of your resume may be longer than your traditional resume; this is perfectly acceptable.

Writing Effective Memos 8f

Memoranda—memos, for short—are documents circulated within an organization that convey important information or ask recipients to take some action. Memos keep the lines of communication open. They also provide a written historical archive of the activities of an organization and its people. In some well-known cases—the Enron case, for example—memos became the legal record of who knew what when during a company crisis.

Memos convey important information; for example, . . .

- they announce upcoming events.
- they announce policy changes.

Memos ask recipients to take some action, such as . . .

- to provide requested information
- to read an attached document

Purposes of Memos

Your purpose in a memo should be to convey information or request action clearly and concisely. Your readers will likely spend only a few moments reading your memo, so it needs to get across the important information quickly. Careful writers use memos judiciously to accomplish a specific purpose.

Primary and Secondary Audiences for Memos

The primary audience for a memo consists of the person or people who have the responsibility to address the memo or make note of the information it contains. The primary audience should be listed in the To: line. The secondary audience consists of people who need to be aware of the contents of the memo but who do not need to act on it. The secondary audience is not directly responsible for responding to the memo.

Sample Format for a Memorandum

Memorandum

To: List all primary recipients here, with full names, each separated by a comma
From: Author(s) of memo (Author should initial or sign here) RP
Author's title (if any and if customary in your organization)
Date: 23 February 2006
Subject: Concise but descriptive summary of memo's subject

Memoranda use a top-down structure, with the most important information listed first. In the introduction to your memo, you should state clearly what the memo is about. If you are writing an informative memo, you should give the most important information first. If you expect your readers to respond in some way, let them know what they need to do and, if relevant, the deadline they need to meet.

In your body paragraphs, provide further information or details regarding the subject of your memo, starting with the most important first. If you include dates, locations, or other information that you want people to access easily, you can use a list.

Event Title:
Time and Date:
Location:

You may have additional body paragraphs, but bear in mind that memos should generally be kept short so that readers can scan them quickly and access important information without misreading.

Close the memo with a short statement about how readers can request further information if any questions arise. You don't need to sign the memo at the bottom. However, you should identify any attached documents by title. If you are copying the memo to secondary recipients, you should identify them also.

Attachments: Planning Calendar

CC: John Jacob
Marisa Tomlinson

Conducting Research

PART 3

>

New Contexts for Writing: Hypertext and the Semantic Web

The Internet is evolving into a new digital ecosystem where everyone plays a part in writing, developing, sharing, and learning new content. The Semantic Web, also called Web 2.0, is a new vision of the Internet. Originally, the Internet was a collection of millions of pages on thousands of servers around the globe, connected only by hyperlinks. In the Semantic Web, writers, bloggers, and Web authors have their content (or data) networked—connected and refreshed automatically and quickly.

del.icio.us / dblakesley / by David Blakelsey
your bookmarks | inbox | for | post
popular | help
logged in as dblakesley | settings | logout
All your items (2)
search
« earlier | later » showing both items
National Holocaust Museum Survey on Propaganda
The museum has begun the process of developing a new exhibition on propaganda. This survey's questions show some of the limitations of perceiving propaganda as simply "the rhetoric of the bad guys" and not more complexly as a widespread method for shaping
to rhetoric holocaust, propaganda, surveys, museums ... on 2006-01-19 ... edit / delete
Steven Johnson on Web 2.0
Nice metaphor for a complex and important evolutionary step in Internet technologies
to web2.0 ... and 123 other people ... on 2006-01-19 ... edit / delete
« earlier | later » showing both items
tags holocaust, museums propaganda, rhetoric surveys, web2.0
options
› view as cloud | list
› sort by alpha | freq
› show | hide bundles
› arrange tags

This image of **del.icio.us,** a Web 2.0 free service for "social" (shared) bookmarking, shows tags and bundles in action. Users can track keywords as they appear in other sites in del.icio.us and on the Internet with just a few clicks.

Hypertext is text and information connected across Web pages and websites by **hyperlinks.** Hyperlinks, or **links,** are the directional pointers that, when clicked, tell a Web browser to retrieve new content from an Internet server. In **Web 1.0,** information was interconnected through these links, which function like signposts pointing the way.

In **Web 2.0,** or the **Semantic Web,** information is still linked, but sharing and republishing links is automated, allowing new content to be assembled, distributed, and linked on the fly by **RSS** ("Really Simple Syndication") feeds that scour the Web for new content, **aggregators** that assemble this new content, and **social networks,** where people connect with information and each other. Information is connected semantically using **keywords** and **metatags,** both of which function like terms in an index and help people locate shared interests and allow computers to create "bundles" of meaning.

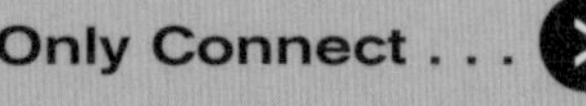

Information Flows

In the Web 2.0 model, we have thousands of services scrutinizing each new piece of information online, grabbing interesting bits, remixing them in new ways, and passing them along to other services. . . . Information in this new model is analyzed, repackaged, digested, and passed on down to the next link in the chain. It flows.

— Steven Johnson
"Web 2.0 Arrives"
Discover 26.10 (October 2005)
http://www.discover.com/issues/oct-05/departments/emerging-technology/

Link, Ping, and Tag Your Way to a Research Network

Share bookmarks and network with other researchers on your topic:
del.icio.us: http://del.icio.us

Tap some RSS feeds or feed some content yourself:
Technorati: http://www.technorati.com

Tag your digital images in a folksonomy:
FlickR: http://www.flickr.com

CONCEPTUALIZING THE RESEARCH PROJECT 9

Finding a Subject to Research

Get motivated by responding in writing to the following questions about possible research subjects.

1. What subjects are you passionate about or would you like to learn more about? (List at least three.) Why do you care about these subjects? How did you learn to care about them?
2. What subjects do you *need* to know more about? (List at least three.) How do you know you need to know more about these subjects?
3. Why would anyone want to learn about these subjects?
4. What would someone need or want to know about these subjects?

From your writings, choose three subjects to explore.

Research projects typically involve posing problems and answering questions about a subject that you want to learn about or that you think others should understand better. Learn to care about your subject by exercising your natural inclination to learn new things, right wrongs, uncover new truths, or discover complexity in the superficially obvious aspects of everyday life.

Planning Your Research Process 9a

Typical Tasks in the Research Process

Most research projects can be divided into the following tasks:

- finding, analyzing, and focusing a subject (sections 9b–9c)
- developing a research hypothesis (section 9d)
- finding background information (section 9e)
- determining which documentation style to use (Parts 4 and 5)
- using writing to track the results of your research (sections 9f–9g)
- doing focused research online, in the library, and in the field (Chapters 10 and 11)
- evaluating the sources and information you find (sections 10h and 11f)
- drafting, revising, editing, and proofreading the project (Chapters 2 and 3)

Create a schedule for your project using the list of tasks as a reference. See page 12 for software that can help.

When you are asked to write a dozen pages or write and design an informative website about an unfamiliar topic, the research process can seem daunting, even overwhelming. If, however, you plan ahead and immerse yourself in your subject early—right after you receive the assignment, for instance—you'll find managing the research project far less intimidating than it initially appears to be.

9b Analyzing Potential Research Subjects

Once you have chosen several potential subjects to research, consult the Project Checklists on pages 5, 6 and 7 as you ask questions about your subject, the assignment context (including its purpose), the broader social context of your writing, and your audience.

Exploring Your Subject

As you refine your subject, use these strategies to learn more about it.

1. Discuss possible topics with interested people.
2. If you know people who are knowledgeable about your subject, ask them whether they know of any hot issues that you could explore.
3. Do Web and/or library searches for popular news articles about your subject.
4. Using search engines such as Google, search for websites about your topic.
5. Look through Internet discussion groups such as Yahoo! Groups, located at **http://groups.yahoo.com**, or L-Soft's CataList, at **http://www.lsoft.com/catalist.html**, to see if there are any mailing lists that relate to your subject.
6. Use a search engine such as the Google Glossary™ to locate definitions of important terms or phrases. Go to **http://www.google.com**; then, in the search box, enter define:*yourterm*. Google will return a list of definitions drawn from reliable websites and provide links to those sites where you can learn more about the terms and phrases you're looking for.
7. Browse the library or a bookstore for magazines, newspapers, or books related to your topic.

9c Focusing Your Subject

Learn enough about your subject to be able to pose and respond to a problem. For instance, if your topic is national security, focus on the invasion of civil liberties or on how much privacy a person is entitled to in the face of threats to national security. Try to find a unique approach or problem. Perhaps you could focus on threats to the privacy of online communication. Can the government eavesdrop on people's email without their knowledge? You might want to conduct research to find out what countermeasures are being taken to protect email privacy. Has new technology been introduced that will increase the level of privacy?

Focusing Your Subject

As you think about your approach to your research topic, consider these questions, which will help you focus your subject.

- **Brainstorm.** What do people think about it? Why? How long has this topic been an issue in society? How does it affect people's lives?
- **Review texts that discuss your topic.** What has already been said? What solutions have been proposed to problems associated with your topic? Have any solutions been tried? Are people satisfied with the state of your issue/topic?
- **Consider the elements of your issue.** How long has it been an issue? Who is affected? Where and when does the problem occur? Does it primarily affect a certain group of people?
- **Compile ideas about problems and solutions.** What have you discovered so far about your issue? What new questions do you have in light of your recent discoveries about the topic?

Example: Developing a Hypothesis about Online Communities

Here's an example of one way to develop a hypothesis on the subject of online communities.

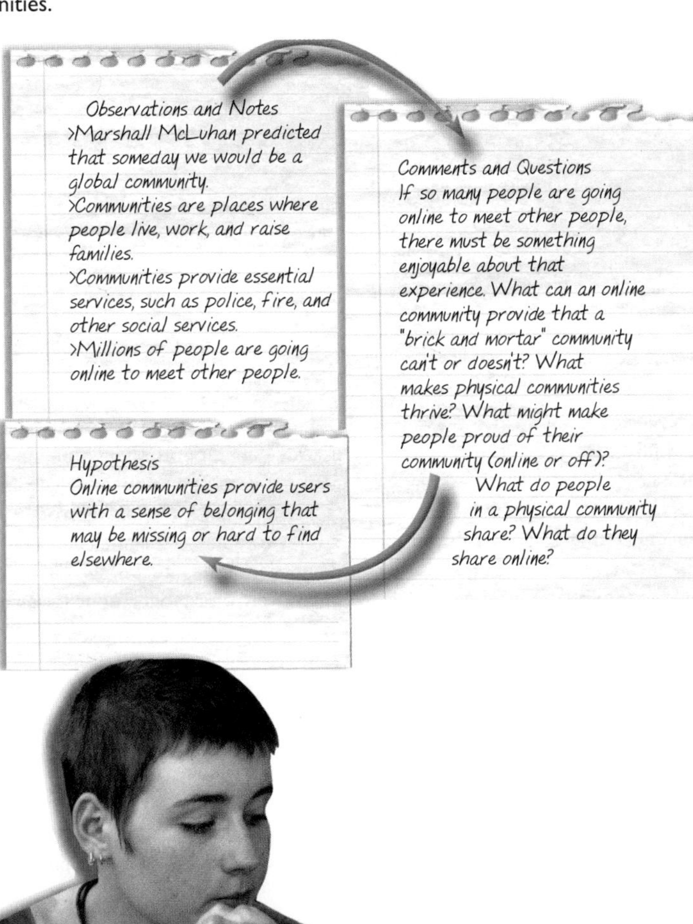

Observations and Notes
>Marshall McLuhan predicted that someday we would be a global community.
>Communities are places where people live, work, and raise families.
>Communities provide essential services, such as police, fire, and other social services.
>Millions of people are going online to meet other people.
Comments and Questions
If so many people are going online to meet other people, there must be something enjoyable about that experience. What can an online community provide that a "brick and mortar" community can't or doesn't? What makes physical communities thrive? What might make people proud of their community (online or off)? What do people in a physical community share? What do they share online?
Hypothesis
Online communities provide users with a sense of belonging that may be missing or hard to find elsewhere.

Once you have figured out what subject you want to research, begin considering the various elements or aspects of that subject. Look for new angles, trends, and ideas. It may help to consider what local perspectives there may be on your subject or how your subject affects you, your family, and/or your social group. Use the invention strategies in Chapter 2 as an aid. You may find the Project Checklist on pages 16 and 17 particularly helpful.

Once you have established your research question or problem, start gathering information. The following methods can help you establish a context for your hypothesis.

Begin with Overviews

Start with the most general ideas and move to the particular. Find broad overviews and definitions first and then look for recent, specific information in articles, in books, and on websites.

Track the Names of People Associated with Your Subject

Begin by noting, as you come across them, the names of people and texts that are cited in articles and stories about your topic. Some people or sources will emerge as authoritative after you've learned more about the subject.

Generate Keywords

Use keywords to look on the Web for information. **Keywords** are words or phrases, often nouns or noun phrases, that describe an element of your research question. Write down important words that appear in the hypothesis, important words from texts that you read as you do research, and synonyms for these terms.

Moving from General to Specific Ideas

This inverted pyramid shows how you can move from general to particular topics and ideas. Here, the top-level terms describe general notions of human community. Level 2 describes how that community takes shape and why. Level 3 shows some effects of community. Level 4 lists an important part of the process of building community. The bottom level comes to a more specific topic and thesis: the idea that weblogs build community only when they encourage dialogue among bloggers, not when they focus exclusively on reporting public (or even personal) news.

Using Keywords to Find Information

- Write down the definitions of your keyword so that you understand the range of the word's meaning and what other words it may be related to. Knowing this will help you guide further research.
- Plug your keywords into a search engine and look for basic definitions. Try entering a keyword, the Boolean operator AND, plus the word *definition*. The Google Glossary is an excellent resource.
- Talk like an insider: Use the terminology that people who know about your subject use to discuss it: If you are using one term and you find that other people tend to use a different one, switch to that term.

Looking Up Your Topic in Online Dictionaries and Encyclopedias

Look up your keywords online in the following resources:

1. An online dictionary such as Merriam-Webster (**http://www.m-w.com**), a set of dictionaries such as Dictionary.com (**http://www.dictionary.com**), or an online glossary such as Google (**http://www.google.com**; type: define: *yourterm*)
2. An online encyclopedia such as Britannica (**http://www.britannica.com**) or Wikipedia (**http://en.wikipedia.org**)
3. A hierarchical directory such as the Google Directory (**http://directory.google.com**) or the Yahoo! Directory (**http://dir.yahoo.com**)

Note the synonyms or specialized words or phrases that come up in your searches. Print out your results, or copy and paste interesting portions of your results into a separate file and print that out.

Locating Bibliographies

If you need help tracking down a research bibliography . . .

- ask a reference librarian for assistance.
- look on your library's website under categories like "Research Guides" or "Bibliographies."

After you've tracked down an article or two, you can also find good bibliographies in academic journals on your subject.

Locate Encyclopedias

Find an encyclopedia (online or in print) and use it to develop an expanded understanding of your subject, keywords, and important phrases. With its many links to online sources, Wikipedia (http://en.wikipedia.org) is an excellent place to launch your research. Like all encyclopedias, it is most useful as a stepping stone to more authoritative sources and not an end point for research.

Find Bibliographies

Bibliographies, which are lists of sources about a research subject, have probably already been compiled on your subject by others.

Annotated bibliographies, which are lists of sources with short descriptions, are an even more useful tool in the early stages of research. Online, you can get a head start by probing information portals (like Yahoo! or Google). To use Google, for example, go to http://directory.google.com/Top/Reference/Bibliography and enter your keywords in the search box.

Use a research journal to keep track of the places you have searched, the information and sources you have found (and how to find them again), and your thoughts about your research process. Record the ways your research process changes your understanding of your subject and your ideas about its key terms.

Your research journal may be in a word processing file, in a paper notebook, on a PDA, or even on one of several websites that help users keep track of research processes, such as Writenote® at http://www.writenote.com. Microsoft's Outlook has a useful Note function. On Macs, you'll find "Stickies." Post-it® Notes offers a free "Lite" version of "Post-it Software Notes" for PCs at http://www.3m.com/market/office/postit/com_prod/psnotes/index.html.

Above all, while you're conducting your research, take note of every interesting detail you can, even if it seems unimportant. If something captures your interest, unrelated or not, it might become useful later.

Always note precise publication information about each work that you examine (▶ section 9g).

Student Example: Excerpts from Alejandro Covas's Research Journal

JANUARY 2005						
						1
2	3	4	5	6	7	8
9	10	11	12	13	14	15
16	17	18	19	20	21	22
23/30	24/31	25	26	27	28	29

FEBRUARY 2005						
		1	2	3	4	5
6	7	8	9	10	11	12
13	14	15	16	17	18	19
20	21	22	23	24	25	26
27	28					

MARCH 2005						
		1	2	3	4	5
6	7	8	9	10	11	12
13	14	15	16	17	18	19
20	21	22	23	24	25	26
27	28	29	30	31		

January 5th
Since Music Education is my major I decided to find stuff on music therapy. This report is due March 10, 2005! . . .

January 27th
I have focused my research on a controversy about music therapy for children who have been traumatized. I have cut and pasted a bunch of articles from EBSCOhost and InfoTrac that are talking about how this school district in Texas has completely cut the music and other art curriculum, even the support things like music therapy. Turns out that they needed more money for their football team or something. Some parents sued the school district and all these music therapy experts testified in the case. I bet there are a dozen articles from these online sources that mention something about that lawsuit. . . . My research project is now about the value of music therapy in public schools when it comes time to cut school budgets.

February 2nd
Another lawsuit! This time in Pennsylvania. Some kid's parents think that the music therapy caused him to fight another kid and the kid's ear was bitten off. Now my whole research paper has to be rethought since someone is claiming not that music therapy is useless but that it causes anti-social behavior. I have decided to lead my paper off with this case and show how wrong the parents are and then move to how effective and useful music therapy really is.

Compile Information on Index Cards or in a Text File

Some people like to record their research on paper index cards, finding them easy to deal with at the library and easy to rearrange later in organizing their paper. If you work on your computer, you may prefer to set up a text file for tracking your sources.

Sample Book Entry in a Text File

Topic: Subtopic
Identity: National

Author | Title | Publication information

Kidder, Tracy. *Mountains Beyond Mountains*. New York: Random House, 2003. Print.

Summary

A book about Paul Farmer, a doctor who lives and works in Haiti several months out of every year (he volunteers)

Paraphrase of an event; quotations in quotation marks

Dr. Farmer talking with another doctor getting ready to leave Haiti. Farmer wondered if it would be difficult, but the other doctor couldn't wait to get back to America. He said, "I'm an American, and I'm going home." Farmer thought about this into the night: "What does that mean, 'I'm an American'? How do people classify themselves?" (page 80)

Reader's note to self, kept separate from summary

Compare with other accounts of Americans working abroad, such as those by Peace Corps volunteers: How much do they feel their "Americanness" and what impact does this have on how they view the people they work with?

Read 9/18/05 Call number: R154.F36 K53 2003

Always record the citation information for sources you find, including as much information as is available in the three main categories of all bibliographic references:

1. Authorship
2. Title information
3. Publication information

Even if the source you are reading doesn't seem to apply to your research project, take a moment to record the information on your source list. If your research focus changes (which is likely), having these other sources may prove valuable. In addition, at times you will need to let readers know what information you've considered and dismissed; this helps build your ethos.

Note the following kinds of information for each source:

- Quotations—enclosed in a pair of quotation marks so you will know later that they are another person's wording, rather than a paraphrase or summary of source material
- Complete bibliographical information, including the page number(s) of material you have quoted, paraphrased, or summarized
- The date you found the source (especially important for online sources)

You can record information on index cards or in a text file.

Here is some practical advice for using index cards:

- Use the same sized index cards and use only one side.
- Rewrite a card if it is overcrowded or illegible.
- Leave some free space on the card so you can add comments later.
- Use numbers or colors (with highlighters) to organize your index cards around subtopics.
- Alphabetize your index cards by author's last name within the subtopics.
- Read through your index cards often, and add comments and further questions.

Your index cards will be useful when it comes time to locate the most effective sources for your research project. Some people put their index cards in piles by subtopic to help them organize their drafts. Robert Pirsig, author of the interesting books *Zen and the Art of Motorcycle Maintenance* (1974) and *Lila* (1991), its sequel, used index cards (thousands of them) to organize his entire life, including the elaborate philosophy that he developed over a thirty-year period!

Sample Index Card for a Magazine Article

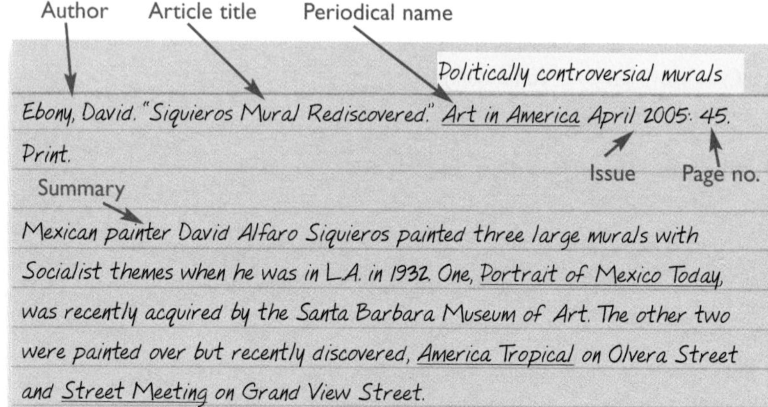

Sample Index Card for a Website

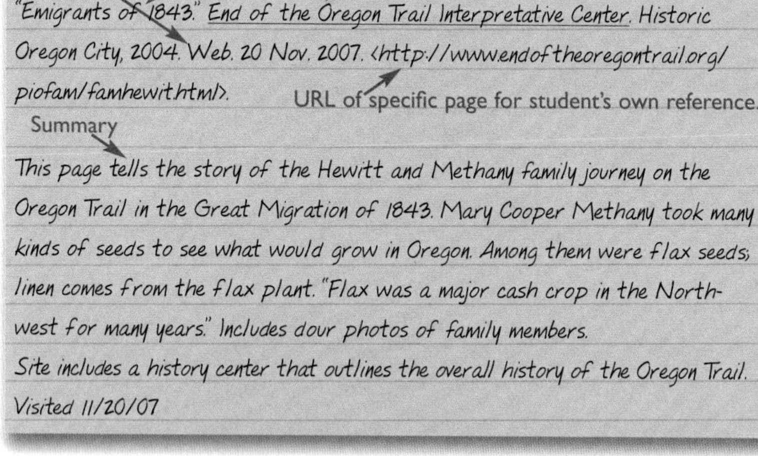

Student Example: An Entry in Juliette Ludeker's Working Annotated Bibliography (MLA)

Simpson, Philip L. "*Copycat*, Serial Murder, and the (De)Terministic Screen Narrative." *Terministic Screen: Rhetorical Perspectives on Film*. Ed. David Blakesley. Carbondale: Southern Illinois UP, 2003. 146-62. Print.

Simpson's essay is as much an exploration of the role society has in the formation of serial killers as it is a critique/exploration of the film *Copycat*. Using Kenneth Burke's notions of the terministic screen and of humans as symbol-using animals, Simpson posits, "Human beings (including serial killers) reconstruct reality into the narratives through which they make sense of the world" (147). Therefore, the tendency exists for humans to write themselves into a particular narrative they are experiencing. Film and visuals can cause a strong sense of identification in the viewer because they mimic (or might be understood as) "experiencing."

As you collect information from a variety of sources, recording all the bibliographic information as described on pages 107–108, one useful strategy is to incorporate a short summary of the work after the bibliographical information.

- Make your annotation descriptive. Information that might not seem relevant early on may become critical later.
- Provide an analysis of the quality of the source and its relevance to your research project.
- Don't focus on your emotional responses to the reading. However, do make the annotation serve your purposes.

Conducting Research in the Disciplines 9i

Scholars in the humanities, the social sciences, and the sciences approach research from different but not entirely dissimilar perspectives. All fields value ethical, rigorous, and interesting research, but each focuses on different aspects of experience, uses unique vocabularies to talk about the subject, and ranks some questions as more important than others. The next nine spreads offer a brief introduction to the questions asked across these broad fields of study and provide examples of how two specific disciplines in each broader field attempt to answer them.

This outside column identifies some of the fields, research networks, and citation guides used by researchers in the discipline.

This outside column identifies the nature of evidence that researchers use to support their findings and interpretation.

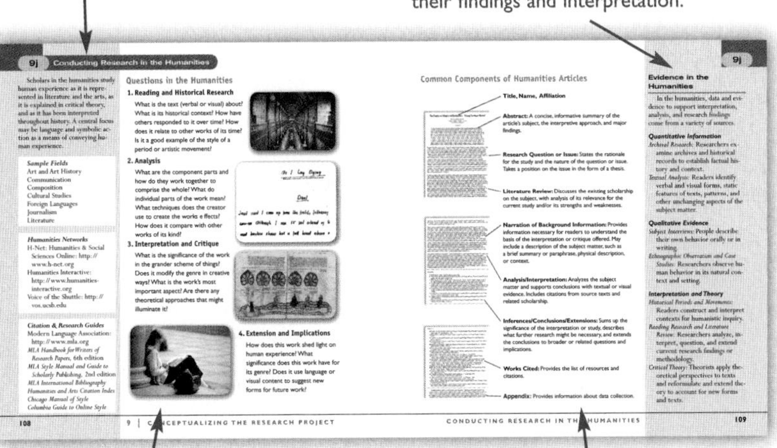

9j Conducting Research in the Humanities

Scholars in the humanities study human experience as it is represented in literature and the arts, as it is explained in critical theory, and as it has been interpreted throughout history. A central focus may be language and symbolic action as a means of conveying human experience.

Sample Fields
Art and Art History
Communication
Composition
Cultural Studies
Foreign Languages
Journalism
Literature

Humanities Networks
H-Net: Humanities & Social Sciences Online: http://www.h-net.org
Humanities Interactive: http://www.humanities-interactive.org
Voice of the Shuttle: http://vos.ucsb.edu

Citation & Research Guides
Modern Language Association: http://www.mla.org
MLA Handbook for Writers of Research Papers, 6th edition
MLA Style Manual and Guide to Scholarly Publishing, 2nd edition
MLA International Bibliography
Humanities and Arts Citation Index
Chicago Manual of Style
Columbia Guide to Online Style

Questions in the Humanities

1. Reading and Historical Research
What is the text (verbal or visual) about? What is its historical context? How have others responded to it over time? How does it relate to other works of its time? Is it a good example of the style of a period or artistic movement?

2. Analysis
What are the component parts and how do they work together to comprise the whole? What do individual parts of the work mean? What techniques does the creator use to create the works e ffects? How does it compare with other works of its kind?

3. Interpretation and Critique
What is the significance of the work in the grander scheme of things? Does it modify the genre in creative ways? What is the work's most important aspect? Are there any theoretical approaches that might illuminate it?

4. Extension and Implications
How does this work shed light on human experience? What significance does this work have for its genre? Does it use language or visual content to suggest new forms for future work?

108 9 | CONCEPTUALIZING THE RESEARCH PROJECT

Common Components of Humanities Articles

Title, Name, Affiliation

Abstract: A concise, informative summary of the article's subject, the interpretive approach, and major findings.

Research Question or Issue: States the rationale for the study and the nature of the question or issue. Takes a position on the issue in the form of a thesis.

Literature Review: Discusses the existing scholarship on the subject, with analysis of its relevance for the current study and/or its strengths and weaknesses.

Narration of Background Information: Provides information necessary for readers to understand the basis of the interpretation or critique offered. May include a description of the subject matter, such as a brief summary or paraphrase, physical description, or context.

Analysis/Interpretation: Analyzes the subject matter and supports conclusions with textual or visual evidence. Includes citations from source texts and related scholarship.

Inferences/Conclusions/Extensions: Sums up the significance of the interpretation or study, describes what further research might be necessary, and extends the conclusions to broader or related questions and implications.

Works Cited: Provides the list of resources and citations.

Appendix: Provides information about data collection.

9j

Evidence in the Humanities

In the humanities, data and evidence to support interpretation, analysis, and research findings come from a variety of sources.

Quantitative Information
Archival Research: Researchers examine archives and historical records to establish factual history and context.
Textual Analysis: Readers identify verbal and visual forms, static features of texts, patterns, and other unchanging aspects of the subject matter.

Qualitative Evidence
Subject Interviews: People describe their own behavior orally or in writing.
Ethnographic Observation and Case Studies: Researchers observe human behavior in its natural context and setting.

Interpretation and Theory
Historical Periods and Movements: Readers construct and interpret contexts for humanistic inquiry.
Reading Research and Literature Review: Researchers analyze, interpret, question, and extend current research findings or methodology.
Critical Theory: Theorists apply theoretical perspectives to texts and reformulate and extend theory to account for new forms and texts.

CONDUCTING RESEARCH IN THE HUMANITIES 109

This inside column tracks the typical research process in the discipline, from the formulation of research questions and methodology through analysis, interpretation, and significance.

This inside column describes the genre of published research, focusing on important structural elements of discipline-specific articles.

Scholars in the humanities study human experience as it is represented in literature and the arts, as it is explained in critical theory, and as it has been interpreted throughout history. A central focus may be language and symbolic action as a means of conveying human experience.

Sample Fields

Art and Art History
Communication
Composition
Cultural Studies
Foreign Languages
Journalism
Literature

Humanities Networks

H-Net: Humanities & Social Sciences Online: http://www.h-net.org
Humanities Interactive: http://www.humanities-interactive.org
Voice of the Shuttle: http://vos.ucsb.edu

Citation & Research Guides

Modern Language Association: http://www.mla.org
MLA Handbook for Writers of Research Papers, 7th edition
MLA Style Manual and Guide to Scholarly Publishing, 3rd edition
MLA International Bibliography
Humanities and Arts Citation Index
Chicago Manual of Style
Columbia Guide to Online Style, 2nd edition

Questions in the Humanities

1. Reading and Historical Research

What is the text (verbal or visual) about? What is its historical context? How have others responded to it over time? How does it relate to other works of its time? Is it a good example of the style of a period or artistic movement?

2. Analysis

As I Lay Dying

Darl

Jewel and I come up from the field, following ... although I am 15 feet ahead of h... and broken straw hat a full head above ...

What are the component parts and how do they work together to comprise the whole? What do individual parts of the work mean? What techniques does the creator use to create the work's effects? How does it compare with other works of its kind?

3. Interpretation and Critique

What is the significance of the work in the grander scheme of things? Does it modify the genre in creative ways? What is the work's most important aspect? Are there any theoretical approaches that might illuminate it?

4. Extension and Implications

How does this work shed light on human experience? What significance does this work have for its genre? Does it use language or visual content to suggest new forms for future work?

Common Components of Humanities Articles

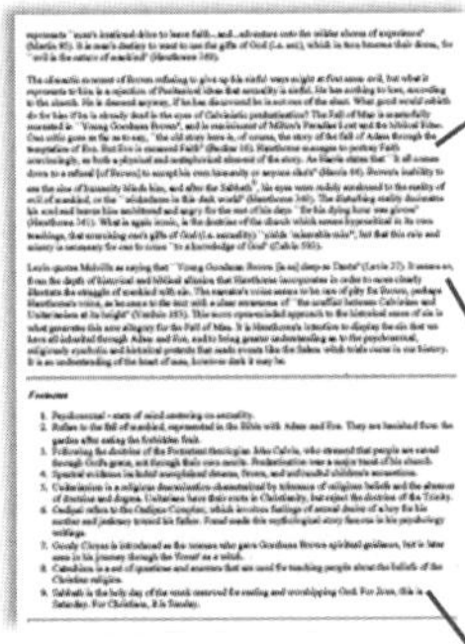

Title, Name, Affiliation

Abstract: A concise, informative summary of the article's subject, the interpretive approach, and major findings.

Research Question or Issue: States the rationale for the study and the nature of the question or issue. Takes a position on the issue in the form of a thesis.

Literature Review: Discusses the existing scholarship on the subject, with analysis of its relevance for the current study and/or its strengths and weaknesses.

Narration of Background Information: Provides information necessary for readers to understand the basis of the interpretation or critique offered. May include a description of the subject matter, such as a brief summary or paraphrase, physical description, or context.

Analysis/Interpretation: Analyzes the subject matter and supports conclusions with textual or visual evidence. Includes citations from source texts and related scholarship.

Inferences/Conclusions/Extensions: Sums up the significance of the interpretation or study, describes what further research might be necessary, and extends the conclusions to broader or related questions and implications.

Works Cited: Provides the list of resources and citations.

Appendix: Provides information about data collection.

Evidence in the Humanities

In the humanities, data and evidence to support interpretation, analysis, and research findings come from a variety of sources.

Quantitative Information

Archival Research: Researchers examine archives and historical records to establish factual history and context.

Textual Analysis: Readers identify verbal and visual forms, static features of texts, patterns, and other unchanging aspects of the subject matter.

Qualitative Evidence

Subject Interviews: People describe their own behavior orally or in writing.

Ethnographic Observation and Case Studies: Researchers observe human behavior in its natural context and setting.

Interpretation and Theory

Historical Periods and Movements: Readers construct and interpret contexts for humanistic inquiry.

Reading Research and Literature Review: Researchers analyze, interpret, question, and extend current research findings or methodology.

Critical Theory: Theorists apply theoretical perspectives to texts and reformulate and extend theory to account for new forms and texts.

Research in film studies focuses on how films achieve effects, how they reflect or challenge ideology, how they have progressed in technique or form, and how they contrast with other films in their genre. Researchers also are interested in how films function as cultural artifacts and as part of the larger industry of entertainment. Many films focus on the art of filmmaking or the act of viewing a film, inviting us to question the role of film as an art form that shares features with other art forms, like the novel, the short story, and various visual art forms.

Film Studies Networks

ScreenSite: http://www.screensite.org
Society for Cinema & Media Studies: http://www.cmstudies.org/scms_forums.html
American Film Institute: http://www.afi.com
Premiere Magazine: http://www.premieremag.com

Citation & Research Guides

Chicago Manual of Style Website: http://www.chicagomanualofstyle.org
Internet Movie Database: http://www.imdb.com
The New York Times Movies: http://movies.nytimes.com/pages/movies/index.html

The Art of Looking: Writing about Film as a Visual Medium

Opening credits, *Vertigo*, dir. Alfred Hitchcock

1. Working Thesis

Study a film or films and come to a provisional interpretation of their meaning and significance. *Sample Thesis: Many films portray the acts of watching and being watched to expose the power and danger of the gaze.* Why is this an important subject now? Are there also more innocent acts of watching? How can a person *being* watched wield power? How does this theme explain the pleasure of film viewing?

James Stewart as L. B. Jefferies in *Rear Window*, dir. Alfred Hitchcock

2. Approach to Gathering Evidence

To focus on film as a visual medium, you can draw from studies on visual rhetoric and the relationships among seeing, knowing, and power. Evidence can be gathered by using screen capture software (such as HyperSnap™) to take screenshots, carefully taking notes, and reading the script, if it's available.

3. Integration of Evidence

Build the argument by citing evidence from the film or films that illustrates the act of viewing and its function.

Guy Pearce as Leonard Shelby in *Memento*, dir. Christopher Nolan

4. Analysis, Inference, Extension

Break a film into its components and show how it "adds up." Does the film make a point about our "surveillance society"? Does it suggest that our ways of seeing are also ways of not seeing? Does it teach us how to read other films? Why is the thesis relevant to studies of visual culture?

Writing about Film Adaptations of Novels and Short Stories

In adapting a piece of fiction for the screen, directors, writers, and cinematographers face significant challenges, because film is primarily a visual medium while a novel or short story is purely verbal. Here are three approaches to film adaptation:

1. Fidelity: The film re-creates the plot as closely as possible, avoiding stylistic interpretation and divergence from the source text.
2. Interpretation: The film interprets the source text by stressing some aspects over others, exaggerating themes, or changing the plot and characters to make the film more dramatic or interesting for viewers.
3. Inspiration: The film draws thematic inspiration from its source but extends the themes to new contexts. A film may have fidelity to the source's themes while acting them out in completely new situations.

The excerpt below relates to the novel *Do Androids Dream of Electric Sheep?* (1968), by Philip K. Dick, and the films *Blade Runner* (1982) and *Blade Runner: The Director's Cut* (1992), directed by Ridley Scott.

> ...This novel's progression from print to screen is one of the better documented and most bitterly contested adaptations in film history. After producer Herb Jaffe's option to film Dick's novel ran out in 1978 (Dick thought the draft screenplay was "a bad joke"), the project was optioned to Hampton Fancher and Brian Kelly, then picked up by Universal. Fancher wrote increasingly variant screenplays of the novel, but when Ridley Scott, fresh off his success with *Alien*, was hired as the director, he began to convert the story into what Dick later called an "eat lead, robot!" screenplay, with Deckard as a "cliché-ridden Chandleresque figure" (Rickman).... Dick went public with his dissatisfaction, creating a nightmare for the film's publicist.... [E]ach of the collaborators had a distinct conception of what *Blade Runner* should be: Dick wanted the androids to be the catalysts for Deckard's and Isidore's moral and spiritual growth in facing evil; Fancher saw it as a love story about a man who discovers his conscience; Scott, a futuristic film noir set in a densely packed, garish cityscape (he wanted the final title to be Gotham City); Peoples, an exploration of the distinguishing qualities of humans and their replicants (Kolb). All four perspectives ultimately found their way into the film.... [I]n the end Dick believed that Peoples's revisions of the script made it a "beautiful, symmetrical reinforcement" of his novel's main theme. Ironically, Dick died suddenly of a stroke just a few months before the film's release....

Fidelity to the source

Interpretation of theme

Inspiration and extension

From David Blakesley, *Encyclopedia of Novel into Film*, 2nd ed., ed. John C. Tibbetts and James M. Welsh (New York: Facts on File, 2005).

Evidence in Film Studies

Evidence for analysis and interpretation, historical research, and film reviews comes from the films themselves and their context in the lives of artists and audiences. Films share qualities with other forms in terms of genre, style, and subject. You can draw on all these kinds of evidence.

Visual and Aural Evidence

Stills, Screenshots, Clips: Help explain complex descriptions of scenes. Clips (scene sequences) may be useful for multimedia essays.

Spoken Dialogue: Shows character or plot development and should be carefully transcribed.

Examples of Film Terminology

In addition to terms for literary analysis (◀ Chapter 5), film studies uses terms derived from film technique.

Editing: The way the sequences were put together.

Scene: A unified sequence of action.

Mise en scène: The arrangement of objects in the frame.

Contexts and Theory

Contexts and theory guide ways of reading by providing an interpretive lens. See the *Critical Dictionary of Film and Television Theory,* edited by Roberta E. Pearson and Philip Simpson (New York: Routledge, 2001).

9j Humanities Example: Research in History

Research in history focuses on documenting and interpreting the historical record of human social, political, and artistic life. Researchers use archival records and accounts to construct historical contexts, but they also draw on contemporary perspectives and values when selecting their subjects and when deciding on the relevance of historical research for our times. The work of historians both preserves and extends the record of human accomplishments—for good or ill—in the interest of divining the future by judging the past.

History Networks

Virtual Library History Central Catalogue: http://vlib.iue.it/history/index.html

Voice of the Shuttle: http://vos.ucsb.edu

PBS History: http://www.pbs.org/history/

Technology History: http://www.refstar.com/techhist/

Citation & Research Guides

Chicago Manual of Style Website: http://www.chicagomanualofstyle.org

Humanities Index

Historical Text Archive: http://historicaltextarchive.com

The Strange Uses of History: Was Albert Einstein Really a Bad Student?

1. Working Historical Question or Thesis

It's been said that Einstein was not always the best of students and that he failed math in high school. But by the age of 26 he had invented the general theory of relativity. Was he really a late-blooming student? What kind of student was he in high school and earlier? How did this experience lead him to become the greatest genius of his time? Where does this story come from, and why do people tell it?

2. Archival Research and Review of Primary and Secondary Sources

What have others said about this phenomenon? What do the primary sources say? Are there public records, personal memoirs and letters, or public accounts of Einstein's schooling? What do the formal histories say on this topic?

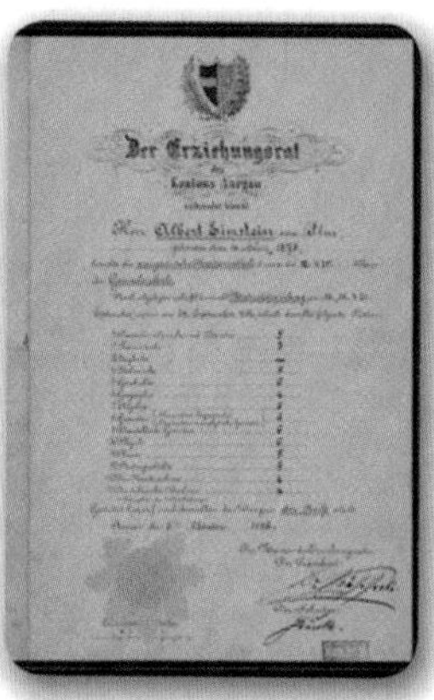

Der Erziehungsrat

Einstein's high school diploma shows sixes in math and physics, the highest score.

3. Evidence from Reliable Sources

Build the argument by citing evidence from Einstein's school records, his autobiography, and other biographies. Deal with evidence that may contradict your claim.

4. Analysis, Inference, Extension

How does the evidence about Einstein's early schooling contradict the mythology? Do people cite this story because they need to "bring him down to earth," as a kind of rationalization? What other figures have people explained in this way? Why is our construction of "fame" an important subject for history?

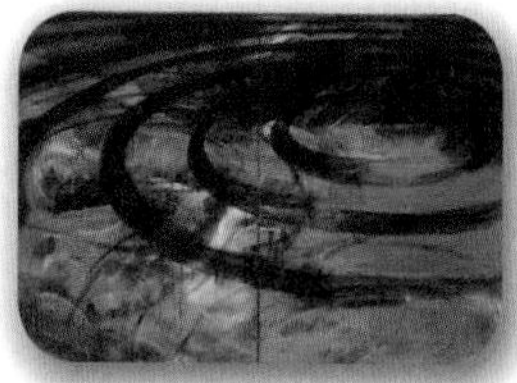

An interpretation, "Einstein's Dream Diptych" by Gerrit Greve

Deconstructing Urban Legends: *The Blair Witch Project*

Urban legends are stories that get passed among people but, when tested, prove to be based on unreliable historical evidence or unsubstantiated rumor. When questioning the truth of an urban legend, keep in mind the historian's need to depend on (1) reliable primary sources, (2) the factual historical record, and (3) secondary sources that have withstood the scrutiny of the scholarly community.

In some cases, people deliberately manufacture legends for entertainment, or even as hoaxes. One famous case concerns the film *The Blair Witch Project* and its supporting website, **http://www.blairwitch.com**. The legend is that a group of college students studying the history of the Blair Witch legend filmed their research but then disappeared. Their "found" film was shot as a documentary, lending realism to the legend. Haxan Films and distributor Artisan Entertainment built the legend by also creating a rich archive of primary sources, including images of the film reels that contained the original documentary evidence, diaries of the students completing the history project, and more. All of these elements drew their persuasive force from preconceived notions about what constitutes reliable historical evidence.

The excerpt that follows is from Redman Lucas Wells's *"The Blair Witch Project."*

> . . . it's quite surprising exactly how much of the Blair Witch story was fabricated by Haxan Films. Here's a quick introduction to some of the more basic facts behind the movie:
>
> - Yes, there is a real Burkittsville, Maryland (where the movie is set in the 'present day').
> - Burkittsville, however, was never known as Blair, Maryland.
> - In fact, there has never been a Blair, Maryland, past or present.
> - Burkittsville doesn't have a "real" Witch legend that bears even a remote resemblance to the tale unfolded in The Blair Witch Project.
> - The Witch legend, and all of the events associated with it in the movie, was manufactured entirely by the Haxan Film team. . . .
>
> So, unfortunately for those hunting for the "real" Blair Witch behind the hype of the movie treatment of the legend, there is no actual hidden substance to be found. The Blair Witch was entirely the product of the fertile minds of Haxan Films and may well go down as one of the most creatively marketed movies of the dying years of the 20th Century—if not of the history of cinema itself!

Factual record

This evidence relies on secondary sources that aren't mentioned

Analysis and implications of the evidence

Urban Legends Research Centre 1999, 6 Sept. 2004 <http://www.ulrc.com.au/html>.

Evidence in History

Evidence for history research comes from the historical record of facts, archival documents, images, and other artifacts. The chief task of the historian is to evaluate the integrity of the archival documents and to question previous interpretations.

Primary Sources

Archival Documents and Images: Libraries, museums, and other organizations keep original printed archives, which researchers may examine if prior approval has been granted.

Digital Archives: Online digital archives offer searchable databases of images of archival material.

Oral Histories: Sometimes, interviews can be or have been conducted with people involved in the events studied.

Secondary Sources

Original Secondary Sources: Use commentary and interpretation by others living at the time.

Subsidiary Contexts: People may have experienced the events secondhand or researched them.

Questions about Sources

Ask specific questions about the reliability and validity of your sources and the nature of their original contexts: What's the nature of the source? Is the source genuine? Who is the audience? Who is the author? When was the source produced?

Social scientists study society and the relationships and behavior of individuals within it. Research in the social sciences should be replicable, so the emphasis is on empirical methods, both quantitative and qualitative, that can be tested and improved.

Sample Fields
Anthropology
Archaeology
Economics
Environmental Science
Political Science
Urban Studies

Social Science Networks
Social Science Research Network: http://www.ssrn.com
Social Science Information Gateway: http://www.sosig.ac.uk
Social Sciences Virtual Library: http://www.clas.ufl.edu/users/gthursby/socsci/
Social Science at the Internet Public Library: http://www.ipl.org/div/aon/browse/soc00.00.00/

Citation & Research Guides
American Psychological Association: http://www.apa.org
Includes APA style helper, research and ethics guides, news, journals, books, and more. The official guide to APA style is the *Publication Manual of the American Psychological Association.*

Questions in the Social Sciences

1. Hypotheses

Based on experience, what do I expect to discover? How do behaviors or attitudes vary among subjects or across societies? What's wrong or inaccurate about historical accounts of this subject? How will people answer questions?

2. Research Method and Design

Should I use qualitative or quantitative methods or some combination of the two? What variables are there, and can they be isolated for study?

3. Data and Evidence

How will I collect the data and evidence? What practical challenges are there in conducting surveys, interviews, experimentation, testing, and research?

4. Analysis and Interpretation

What do the data and evidence show? How did subjects respond? What patterns are there? Do my hypotheses hold?

5. Conclusions

What type of report will best represent my findings? Can I contrast my results with other research?

Common Components of Research Reports in the Social Sciences

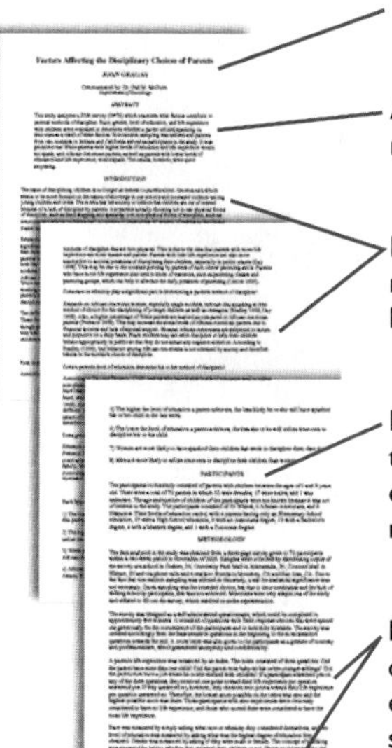

Title, Name, Affiliation

Abstract: A concise, informative summary of the report's hypotheses, methodology, and major findings.

Introduction/Hypotheses: Includes information necessary to understand the subject and working hypotheses, with reasons behind them.

Research Method/Design: Discusses in detail the methods used to collect data and/or gather evidence. Includes discussion of pros and cons of the methodology.

Data/Evidence: Provides the results of the qualitative or quantitative collection of data and evidence. Uses visuals such as charts and tables to show relationships in the data. Refers to appendix that shows the instrument of data collection.

Analysis/Interpretation: Analyzes the data and evidence collected. Explains what the visuals indicate. Discusses whether the data and evidence support hypotheses of the study.

Conclusions/Inferences: Sums up what the results indicate, describes what further research might be necessary, and extends the conclusions to broader or related questions.

Bibliography: Provides the list of resources and citations.

Appendix: Provides information about data collection.

Evidence in the Social Sciences

In the social sciences, data and evidence to support research hypotheses and findings come from a variety of sources.

Quantitative Data

Structured Observation: Researchers observe and measure social and individual behavior in controlled settings, where it can be isolated for study.

Experimentation: Researchers test hypotheses by creating artificial situations (scenarios) that can show the effects of variables on individual and social behavior, attitudes, and physiological responses.

Testing: Animal or human subjects are given behavioral tests whose results can be measured and compared under controlled conditions.

Qualitative Evidence

Subject Interviews, Self-Reports, Surveys: People describe their own behavior orally or in writing.

Naturalistic Observation: Researchers observe behavior in its natural context and setting.

Reading Research and Literature Review: Researchers analyze, interpret, question, and extend current research findings and methodology.

Psychologists study how human thought and action are affected by physiological and chemical processes, personality, and the environment. They study how the mind works and why, so that they can explain and influence behavior or improve mental health. Psychologists ask questions like these: How does trauma affect a person's personality? How do feelings of power affect altruistic behavior? How can depression affect learning? Why do sounds, such as music, evoke memories? How do people fall in love on the Internet?

Psychology Networks

Psychological Research on the Net: http://psych.hanover.edu/research/exponnet.html

PsychExperiments: http://psychexps.olemiss.edu/index.html

Citation & Research Guides

American Psychological Association: http://www.apa.org Includes APA style helper, research and ethics guides, news, journals, books, and more. The official guide to APA style is the *Publication Manual of the American Psychological Association*

Psychology at Science Direct: http://www.sciencedirect.com/science/home/psychology

The Psychology Tutor (Nicole Sage): http://www.psy.pdx.edu/PsyTutor/

Conducting Qualitative Research in Psychology: Subject Interviews

1. Create Hypotheses

What do I expect to discover from my interview subjects? What causes the behavior or attitude? How do behaviors or attitudes vary among subjects? How does a change in one of these variables affect the others?

2. Formulate Research Method and Design

What questions shall I ask to draw out the attitudes and behaviors of my subjects? In what sequence? What will be my methodology for analyzing the contents of the interviews? Do I need approval to conduct human subject research? From whom? What type of report will best represent my results—formal research report, poster session, oral presentation, or thesis?

3. Collect Evidence and Data

Should I record responses? Videotape them? How will I transcribe the interviews? Where will I conduct them?

4. Analyze, Infer, Extend

Do my hypotheses hold? How did my subjects respond? What patterns are there? What have I learned about their attitudes? About their behavior? What can others learn from my study? What inferences can I make about behavior? Can I contrast my results with other research?

Reading and Summarizing Research Reports

When you are reading research reports in the social sciences, you should keep your attention focused on these main questions, which will help you understand the report more quickly. You can also use them as an aid if you write a summary of the report.

1. What questions does this research address?
2. How did the researchers collect and analyze data?
3. What are the findings?

Neuron

The Neural Fate of Consciously Perceived and Missed Events in the Attentional Blink

Abstract

A glance at the February 5 issue of *Neuron*:

Seeing but not believing—or not noticing

Kellie Bartlett

You see more than you realize you do because two different parts of the brain are involved in recognizing scenes and consciously noticing them, according to a team of researchers led by René Marois, an assistant professor of psychology at Vanderbilt University.

In their study, members of Mr. Marois's team tried to determine what happens to visual information that a person is looking for, and sees, but does not report seeing. Researchers have noticed such "attentional blinks" in previous studies when people are focused on the first image they are looking for and miss the second, if it appears too quickly after the first.

Questions addressed by the research

Participants in the study were asked to look for two images, a face and a scene, among a series of scrambled scenes that were shown to them in quick succession. During that process, the participants were undergoing functional magnetic resonance imaging, which allowed the research team to see which parts of the participants' brains were activated during the test.

How the researchers collected data (methodology)

When participants reported seeing the face but missing the scene, seeing the scene "nonetheless activated regions of the medial temporal cortex involved in high-level scene representations, the parahippocampal place area," the researchers write. But "the frontal cortex was activated only when scenes were successfully reported," they say.

Analysis of data and findings

The article, "The Neural Fate of Consciously Perceived and Missed Events in the Attentional Blink," is available online to subscribers. Information about the journal is available at http://www.neuron.org

From "Magazine and Journal Reader," *Chronicle of Higher Education,* 10 Feb. 2004 <http://chronicle.com>.

Data and Evidence in Psychology

In psychology, evidence and data to support research hypotheses and findings come from a variety of sources.

Quantitative Data

Structured Observation: Researchers observe behavior in a controlled setting, where variables can be isolated for study.

Experimentation: Researchers test hypotheses by creating artificial situations that can show the effects of variables on behavior.

Testing: Animal or human subjects are given behavioral tests whose results can be measured and compared under controlled conditions.

Qualitative Evidence

Subject Interviews, Self-Reports, Surveys: People describe their own behavior orally or in writing.

Naturalistic Observation: Researchers observe behavior in its natural context and setting.

Reading Research and Literature Review: Researchers analyze, interpret, question, and extend current research findings and methodology.

Sociologists study group and social life, particular cultures and their history, and broader patterns in the development of society. Sociologists ask questions like these: How has the Internet affected social life? What is the relationship between violence and gender? How does socioeconomic class affect racial attitudes? How have conceptions of family changed? What is the role of culture in shaping attitudes toward aging?

Sociology Networks

Sociology Online: http://www.sociologyonline.co.uk

American Sociological Association Resources for Students: http://www.asanet.org/student/student.html

Citation & Research Guides

American Sociological Association: http://www.asanet.org

Electronic Journal of Sociology: http://www.sociology.org

Style Guide for the Electronic Journal of Sociology: http://www.sociology.org/styleguide.html

Sociological Data Resources: http://www.asanet.org/student/data.html

Pew Internet and American Life Project: http://www.pewinternet.org

Internet Globalization: Using Data Resources in Sociology Research

1. Create Hypotheses

The emergence of the Internet has negatively affected urban life and caused population decline in large cities. If this is so, what are the causes? If not, why might the availability of online meeting spaces lead to more clustering of populations offline? What variables are there with regard to access to the Internet? What will I contribute that isn't already present in the existing analysis of the data?

2. Formulate Research Method and Design

What questions shall I ask of the data resources? What will be my methodology for analyzing the data? Are there any methodological flaws in the design of the original study (or studies) that might compromise the data? How large was the sampling, and what is the margin of error? Shall I present my work as a formal research report, poster, oral presentation, or thesis?

3. Gather Data and Review Existing Research

What data resources are there for studying the effects of the Internet? Can I use multiple sources? What do the data show? Are there differences across socioeconomic class, gender, or age? What have others written about this topic?

4. Analyze, Infer, Extend

Does my hypothesis hold? Why has broadband Internet capability actually contributed to population growth in cities like New York, Boston, and San Francisco? What patterns are there in the data? Why did people think that the reverse would be the case? Can I contrast my results with other research?

Writing Informative Abstracts in Sociology

An abstract for a formal article or report on a sociological subject represents in compact form the context, purpose, methods, results, and conclusions of research. It typically runs no more than 250 words in length.

1. Objective: States the central issue, research topic, or purpose of the research.
2. Methods: Describes the population studied, how subjects were selected (sampling), and the design of the study.
3. Results: Summarizes the quantitative and/or qualitative results of the research.
4. Conclusion: Interprets the results in light of the hypotheses and suggests implications of the study for future research.

Collegiate Academic Dishonesty Revisited: What Have They Done, How Often Have They Done It, Who Does It, and Why Did They Do It?

Eric G. Lambert, Nancy Lynne Hogan, and Shannon M. Barton

Abstract

Academic dishonesty is a serious concern on most college campuses as it cuts to the heart of the purpose of higher education and the pursuit of knowledge. This study examined twenty different types of academic dishonesty as well as potential correlates of academic cheating by surveying 850 students at a four-year Midwestern university. While most past studies have used bivariate analysis, this study expands the literature by also including a multi-variate analysis to determine which correlates were most important in accounting for collegiate academic dishonesty. The results indicated that most of the bivariate associations were not observed in the Ordinary Least Squares analysis, suggesting that after controlling for shared effects, many variables have little overall effect on the summed measure of academic dishonesty. Specifically, only college level, membership in a fraternity or sorority, cheating to graduate, cheating to get a better grade, and past cheating in high school had a significant impact.

Objective: States the central issue

Methods: Names the population, sampling method, and methodology design

Results: Describes the research findings

Conclusion: Describes how the results support the hypothesis

From *Electronic Journal of Sociology* 7.4, 2003 <http://www.sociology.org/content/vol7.4/lambert_etal.html>.

Data and Evidence in Sociology

In sociology, evidence and data to support research hypotheses and deductions come from a variety of sources. The process may begin with **sampling,** a method of choosing an appropriate group of people for further study.

Quantitative Data

Analysis of Data Resources: Researchers study demographic and other statistical information gathered from a variety of sources: census data, statistical reports, and prior research.

Qualitative Evidence

Interviews, Self-Reports, Surveys, Questionnaires: People describe their own attitudes orally or in writing.

Ethnography: Researchers study cultures and subcultures in their natural context and setting from multiple perspectives, including those of participants and nonparticipants.

Reading Research and Literature Review: Researchers analyze, interpret, question, and extend current research findings (secondary data), theoretical positions, and methodology.

9l Conducting Research in the Sciences

The sciences study the processes and laws of the natural world to explain its origins, how it functions, and how it will change over time. Scientific research also predicts the behavior of the natural world based on mathematically expressed laws formulated from observation, testing, and analysis. Research in the sciences should be replicable, so the emphasis is on quantitative empirical methods that can be tested and improved.

Sample Fields

Chemistry	Medicine
Ecology	Physics
Genetics	Zoology

Science Networks

National Science Digital Library: http://www.nsdl.org
National Science Foundation: http://www.nfs.gov
Voice of the Shuttle: http://vos.ucsb.edu

Citation & Research Guides

Scientific Style and Format: *The CBE Style Manual for Authors, Editors, and Publishers:* http://www.councilscienceeditors.org/publications/style.cfm
AIP Style Manual (Astronomy, Physics): http://www.aip.org/pubservs/style/4thed/toc.html
The ACS Style Guide (Chemistry): http://pubs.acs.org/books/references.shtml

Questions in the Sciences

1. Hypotheses

Based on observation, what do I expect to discover? How has the phenomenon behaved previously, and what predictions does this help me make? What's wrong or inaccurate about prior research on this phenomenon?

2. Research Method/Materials/Design

What variables are there, and can they be isolated for research? Will the research involve measurement, observation, or testing? What protocols will be followed? What's the best way to study the phenomenon?

3. Data and Evidence

How will I collect the data and evidence? What instruments can I use to take measurements? What can I use as a control in order to measure the effect of variables on the processes I measure?

4. Analysis and Interpretation

What do the data and evidence show? What patterns are there? Do my hypotheses hold? Why is this research important?

5. Conclusions

What type of report will best represent my results? Can I contrast my findings with other research?

Common Components of Research Reports in the Sciences

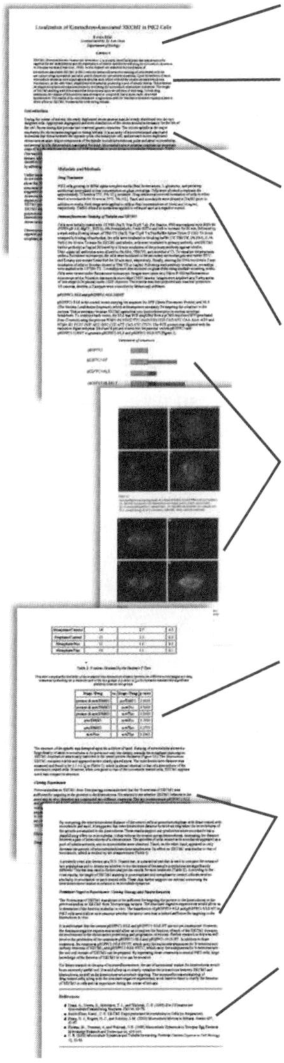

Title, Name, Affiliation

Abstract: Provides a concise, informative summary of the report's hypotheses, methodology, and major findings.

Introduction/Hypotheses/Review: Includes information necessary to understand the subject and working hypotheses, with reasons behind them. Reviews previous research.

Research Method/Materials/Design: Discusses in detail the methods used to collect data and/or gather evidence. Includes discussion of pros and cons of these methodologies.

Data/Evidence: Provides the results of the collection of data and evidence: observations, experiments, measurement, testing, and modeling. Uses visuals such as charts and tables to show relationships in the data. Refers to appendix that shows data instruments and models.

Analysis/Interpretation: Analyzes the data and evidence collected. Explains what the visuals indicate. Discusses whether the data and evidence support hypotheses of the research.

Conclusion/Inferences: Sums up what the results indicate, describes what further research might be necessary, and extends the conclusions to broader or related questions.

Bibliography: Provides the list of resources and citations.

Appendix: Provides information about data collection.

Data and Evidence in the Sciences

In the sciences, data and evidence to support research hypotheses and findings come from a variety of sources.

Quantitative Data

Measurement: Researchers measure change over time or the effects of introducing variables or materials.

Experimentation: Researchers test hypotheses by creating artificial situations that can show the effects of variables on natural processes.

Structured Observation: Researchers observe and measure phenomena in controlled settings, where they can be isolated for study.

Prediction, Modeling, Testing

Prediction: Drawing from research and extrapolating from mathematical principles, scientists predict the behavior of unexplained phenomena.

Modeling: Using extrapolations from mathematics and established scientific models, scientists test new models to measure and predict change and performance.

Testing: Animal or human subjects are given physiological tests whose results can be measured and compared under controlled conditions.

91 Science Example: Research in Biology

Biology research employs empirical methods to study living organisms in all of their forms and complexity. Researchers in biology conduct experiments that require attention to detail, as well as recording and interpreting data. They also synthesize the work of other researchers to address new questions. The experiments and methods of biologists need to be replicable so that other researchers can build on previous findings.

Biology Networks

BioTech Resources Web Project: http://biotech.icmb.utexas.edu
Human Genome Research Institute: http://www.nhgri.nih.gov
Voice of the Shuttle: http://vos.ucsb.edu
Science Direct: Digital Library of the Future: http://www.sciencedirect.com

Citation & Research Guides

Scientific Style and Format: The CBE Style Manual for Authors, Editors, and Publishers: http://www.councilscienceeditors.org/publications/style.cfm
Museum Stuff (Biology): http://www.museumstuff.com/links/science/biology.html

Conducting Research in Biology: The Behavior of Slime Molds

1. Hypotheses

Based on observation, what do I expect to discover? How have the biological processes of slime molds been measured previously, and what predictions can I make? Is there anything wrong or inaccurate about the idea that slime molds are complex, adaptive systems?

Researchers for the Human Genome Project are sequencing the genome of this type of slime mold.

2. Research Method/Materials/Design

What variables are there, and can they be isolated for research? Will the research involve measurement, observation, or testing? What protocols will be followed? What's the best way to study the process?

3. Data

How will I collect the data and evidence? What instruments can I use for the experiment? What can I use as a control in order to measure the effect of variables on the processes I measure?

4. Results

What do the data and evidence show? What patterns are there? Do my hypotheses hold? What do related studies show?

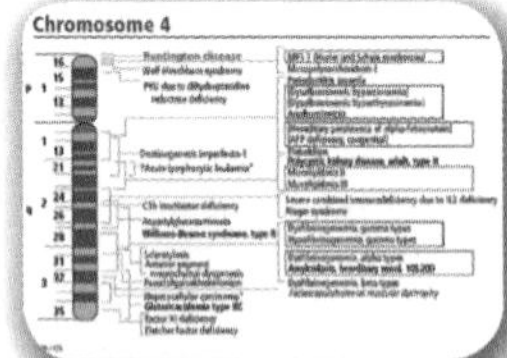

The slime mold genome may help us understand the human genome better.

5. Discussion

Interpret the data and make inferences about what the data show and why the results are important. Contrast the results with other research. Identify the ethical issues of the research.

Bioethics: Genetic Savings and Clone

Bioethics is a subdiscipline in biology dealing with the ethical implications of biological research and applications. Bioethicists examine implications of research whose methods and results may evolve faster than expected. Social and political systems need time to adapt as people grasp the full significance of their scientific discoveries. Bioethicists consider what's next in biology and how culture will be affected if the research proceeds and succeeds. Major laboratories and projects devote resources to studying the ethical implications of their research. It's their responsibility to communicate effectively with the public, which provides funding for efforts like the National Human Genome Research Institute. As a biologist, you need to represent your research accurately and consider its ethical and moral implications seriously.

Consider the following example of one company's effort to address issues of bioethics. Contrast it with what you find at the Human Genome Project: **http://www.nhgri.nih.gov/PolicyEthics/**

"CC" (short for "Carbon Copy") was the world's first cloned cat.

Ethics and Discussion
Genetic Savings & Clone, Inc.
The subject of cloning has long inspired writers and artists. Their work, in turn, has shaped popular myths and beliefs about cloning. Those myths and beliefs then affect public attitudes and expectations about the science. . . . Genetic Savings & Clone must routinely correct the misconception that a cloned pet will enter the world full-grown and equipped with the memories and precise personality of its genetic predecessor. It won't! The cloned pet will be a unique, newborn animal that will share genes and probably behavioral tendencies, but not memories, with its genetic predecessor.

GSC must also respond to the popular misconception that we'll increase the overpopulation of homeless cats and dogs, when in fact we'll reduce it . . . or the misconception that pet cloning will diminish canine and feline genetic diversity, when it will more likely preserve or expand that diversity.

GSC provides a link to its explanations, which come on a FAQ node.

But many people have legitimate concerns about cloning. Some clones produced to date — especially those created using pre-CT cloning methods — have had health problems that appear to be cloning-related. Yet some scientists are already attempting to clone humans. What are the implications of cloning for society? How can we ensure that the technology is not abused?

Cloning methods are explained on this node.

GSC welcomes questions and discussion on these and other issues. Feel free to explore this section of our web site and participate in our discussion forums.

The link to the discussion forums was dead in September 2004.

From http://savingsandclone.com/ethics/index.html.

Data and Evidence in Biology

In the sciences, data and evidence to support research hypotheses and findings come from a variety of sources.

Quantitative Data

Measurement: Researchers measure change over time or the effects of introducing variables or agents to which the organism reacts.

Experimentation: Researchers test hypotheses by creating artificial situations that can show the effects of variables on natural processes.

Prediction, Modeling, Testing

Prediction: Drawing from biology research and extrapolating from previous studies, biologists predict the behavior of unexplained processes.

Modeling: Using extrapolations from previous studies, the laws of biochemistry, and established scientific models, biologists create new models to measure effects and predict change.

Testing: Animal or human subjects are given physiological tests whose results can be measured and compared under controlled conditions.

Astronomers study the stars, planets, galaxies, and universe—including its current state, its motion and evolution, and its origins. Astronomy is the oldest of the empirical sciences, dating back thousands of years to early use of the stars for navigation and timekeeping. A branch of physics, which studies matter and energy, astronomy relies on observation, measurement, and mathematical proof to generate knowledge.

Astronomy Networks
NASA: http://www.nasa.gov
NASA's Jet Propulsion Laboratory: http://www.jpl.nasa.gov
Astronomy Magazine: http://www.astronomy.com
Space.com: http://www.space.com

Citation & Research Guides
AIP Style Manual (Astronomy, Physics): http://www.aip.org/pubservs/style/4thed/toc.html
Chicago Manual of Style
Columbia Guide to Online Style
"Writing about Science for General Audiences": http://www.stc.org/confproceed/2000/PDFs/00114.PDF

Seeing into the Past

1. Hypotheses

Based on prior observation and experience, what do I expect to discover? Would it still be possible to detect "light halos" from the supernova of 1054 C.E. that created the Crab Nebula in the constellation Taurus? Is the light from the blast only now illuminating distant objects, some 951 light-years distant?

2. Prediction

Calculations suggest that gaseous matter that comes into contact with light from the original Crab Nebula supernova will illuminate, even when the light source has dispersed so widely.

3. Research Method/Equipment/Design

Select for observation nebulous objects from the Crab supernova that are no greater than 951 light-years away. Schedule telescope viewing and data recording time. As a control, select an object more than 951 light-years away, with celestial coordinates similar to those of the target objects.

4. Evidence/Data

Record light data from target nebula. For comparison purposes, collect light data on target from 10 years prior to contact with light source.

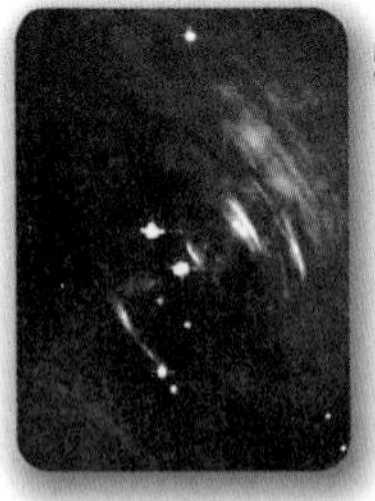

5. Analysis and Inference

The model predicts that light halos from the Crab supernova are detectable. Variations allow us to precisely chart the date and progression of the event. Contrast also with Hubble's recent measurement of the Crab pulsar's wave phenomenon.

Science Writing for General Audiences: SETI (The Search for Extraterrestrial Intelligence)

In translating specialized astronomical knowledge for general audiences, writers should be mindful to (1) establish context, (2) explain difficult concepts and specialized terminology, and (3) relate that knowledge to what readers will find familiar and interesting.

IT & SETI: The Role of Computer Technology in the Search for Extraterrestrial Intelligence
Kamil Z. Skawinski

SETI@Home is one unique undertaking that uses Internet-connected computers in the search for extraterrestrial intelligence. Launched on May 13, 1999, this best-known SETI endeavor consists of a special screensaver that computer users can readily download from the project's website setiathome.ssl.berkeley.edu. This special software, in turn, helps researchers at the University of California, Berkeley, efficiently evaluate the vast quantities of radio data received from the world's largest radio dish, the Arecibo Observatory in Puerto Rico. Faced with 50 terabytes of information to analyze, Berkeley's SETI team eventually turned to the public for help, which ultimately led to the launch of SETI@Home. . . .

> Explains the context of the SETI@Home project and provides necessary background information.

The distributed computing approach taken by SETI@Home, simply put, allows Berkeley's SETI researchers access to an enormous amount of essentially free computing power to evaluate the massive amount of data collected by the Arecibo dish. Every SETI@Home participant receives a "work unit" from the project's lab (consisting roughly of about 300 kilobytes of data), which is then processed by the PC whenever that user's machine is idle. Once the SETI@Home screensaver completes its analysis, the client then relays that processed information back to the lab at UC Berkeley. . . .

> Clarifies the concept of "distributed computing" and its significance.

Humans have been transmitting radio signals for a little over a century, and our high-powered signals have been generated only during the past 50 years—a blink of an eye in cosmic terms—and our radio emissions really have not traveled very far, astronomically speaking. Even if our broadcasts had encountered some civilized species some 50 or 60 light-years away, it will take any "reply" another 50 or 60 years to travel back to Earth. Therefore, patience and perseverance are musts in SETI research, for we simply do not know when we might discover that long-sought yet elusive signal from the stars.

> Connects SETI@Home to aspirations to make contact with intelligent life elsewhere in the universe.

From *California Computer News* 2 July 2002, 7 Sept. 2004 <http://www.ccnmag.com/index.php?sec=mag&id=156.0>.

Data and Evidence in Astronomy

In astronomy, data and evidence come from a variety of sources.

Quantitative Data

Observation: Astronomers use optical and radio telescopes to gather information about celestial bodies. Observations are recorded by computers and photographic equipment.

Measurement: Astronomers use equipment such as spectrometers to measure the results of observational data and to determine the distance, chemical composition, and rate of acceleration of objects.

Mathematical Proof: Astronomers use integral calculus, spherical trigonometry, and quantum mechanics to predict the behavior and motion of objects in space.

Information Processing: Relying on distributed computing power, researchers run complex calculations on data to produce usable results.

Modeling

Using extrapolations from mathematics and established physical models, astronomers create and test new models of the universe to explain observations and unexplained phenomena. Models guide observational methods and are verified or dismissed on the basis of further evidence.

10 ONLINE RESEARCH

Researching online can be convenient and fast.

See section 11d for information on searching indexes and databases.

10a Basic Online Research Strategies

Let's consider a sample search. Suppose you're interested in learning more about *family planning.* Before starting your search, you've narrowed your search to *prenatal care,* which is one aspect of family planning. Any of the larger search engines will look for those two words in that order; but the better search engines will also look for those two words in any order, and then for websites with either of those words. You can end up with thousands of results, many of which have little to do with prenatal care.

A Google search for *prenatal care,* without quotation marks around the phrase, turns up 2,990,000 results. That number is too high; you won't have time to look through screens and screens of results. You need to search more effectively. (See section 10h for more on judging the credibility of Internet sources.)

Yahoo! Web Portal

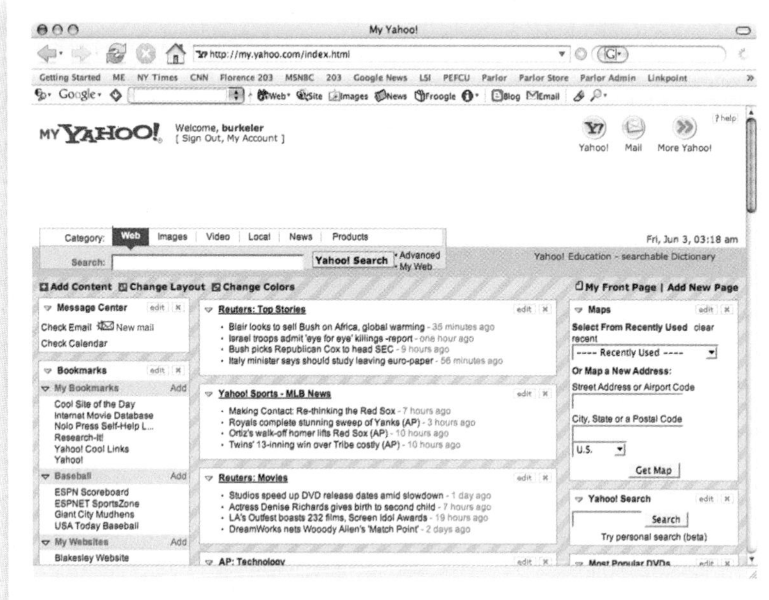

Perhaps the most commonly encountered search engine is one located on a Web portal. Many portals are designed to make money for the companies that offer them, so you need to judge the content in that context. It's not necessary to conduct searches through portals. For a list of helpful research portals, see page 139.

Google Results List

Web Images Groups News Froogle Local more »
Google "prenatal care" Search Advanced Search Preferences
Web Results 1 - 10 of about 891,000 for "prenatal care". (0.30 seconds)
Book results for "prenatal care"
Prenatal Care - edited by Sarah S. Brown - 268 pages
MedlinePlus: Prenatal Care
Prenatal Care. ... Also available in: Spanish; Prenatal Care (March of Dimes Birth Defects Foundation); Staying Healthy During Pregnancy (Nemours Foundation ...
www.nlm.nih.gov/medlineplus/prenatalcare.html - 36k - Cached - Similar pages
Pregnancy and prenatal care
pregnancy and prenatal care information regarding signs and symptoms of pregnancy, fetal development and early stimulation of babies.
www.makewayforbaby.com/prenatalcare.htm - 20k - Cached - Similar pages
Prenatal Care
Prenatal care means health care during your pregnancy before your baby is born. ... Getting regular prenatal care. Follow your health care provider's ...
www.4woman.gov/faq/prenatal.htm - 19k - 1 Jun 2005 - Cached - Similar pages
NCHS - FASTATS - Prenatal Care
Prenatal care for live births, according to detailed race and Hispanic origin of ... Early prenatal care according to race and Hispanic origin of mother, ...
www.cdc.gov/nchs/fastats/prenatal.htm - 32k - Cached - Similar pages
Prenatal Care
Trying to figure out whether to use a doctor or a midwife? Need to know your due date? What about ultrasounds, tests and other questions?
pregnancy.about.com/od/prenatalcare/ - 31k - Cached - Similar pages
Planned Parenthood Federation of America, Inc. - Having AHealthy ...
Arrange to have prenatal care as soon as you know you are pregnant. ... Your prenatal
Sponsored Links
Knoxville Gynecologists
Varied obstetrics and gynecology services and prenatal care.
www.realpagessites.com
Prenatal care
Interactive perinatal data resource developed by the March of Dimes.
www.marchofdimes.com/peristats
Downloadable Papers
Established site features papers on Prenatal care
http://www.1millionpapers.com
Qualified Pregnancy Help
All the pregnancy advice you need is here. just $4.95/mo -aff
whattoexpect.com

After you enter the terms for a Web search, you'll receive a results list, giving the websites that meet your search criteria. The search engine uses an algorithm to put the results into an ordered list, based on relevance to your search criteria and (on Google, for example) a particular site's popularity, measured by how many other sites link to it. A basic results list shows the Web page title and a link to the site. More complex results lists may also show a description of the Web page, its first few lines of text, the date it was last archived, its size, and a percentage ranking (or other indicator) of the page's relationship to your search criteria.

Some search engines allow advertisers to buy a higher ranking on a results list, so be wary. Avoid search engines that manipulate the results list in this way. Google's strategy is to place advertisers' links in a separate section to the right of the results list.

Search for Phrases When Possible

On Google, if you place *prenatal care* inside quotation marks, your search will return a results list of only sites with those two words together, in that order. Even using such a phrase search, however, you will still have too many results to sift through. Here, "*prenatal care*" returns 891,000 results. To get this number down to a manageable size, on Google you can search within results.

Search within Results

Scroll down to the bottom of the results list. At the bottom, you will find a "search within results" link. Suppose that you want information on increased federal funding for prenatal care. You can click on the "search within results" link and, in the next search box, type "*increased federal funding.*" Make sure that you consider whether you want to search for a phrase or to search for one word. We recommend using no more than one word or one phrase when searching within results, because you can always click on the back button on the toolbar and type in another word or phrase.

When we typed *"increased federal funding"* (with quotation marks) into the new search box and clicked Search, we received 79 items on the results list, which means that there are 79 sites with the terms *prenatal care* and *increased federal funding* on them. Five of the eight use both terms sequentially (i.e., in a row) and may be exactly what we are looking for. Four of the sites provide decent information for a paper arguing for the need for increased federal funding of prenatal care. Two of these are medical organizations that provide examples of why prenatal care is crucial for mothers and babies. One site is written by a political think-tank opposed to federal funding increases. This site may have some value for our research: it could provide statistics that we can check against other sources, for example. However, since the site has an overt political agenda, information might be one-sided (▶ section 10h).

Combine Phrases Initially

Once you gain experience at searching within results in this manner, you can shorten your work even further by entering two phrases in the general search box: *"prenatal care" "increased federal funding."* Your results list will include sites that use both of those phrases.

The Google Toolbar

Google, the most comprehensive search engine presently available, offers a free Google Toolbar that you can install as a browser plug-in for Firefox, Internet Explorer, Safari, or other browsers, enabling you to conduct Google searches no matter where you are on the Internet. (See **http://www.google.com/tools** for more information.) Google has become the preferred search engine of savvy Web researchers. It can be so effective when used smartly that some people have suggested that it may even eliminate the need for Web designers to create complex navigational schemes on their sites.

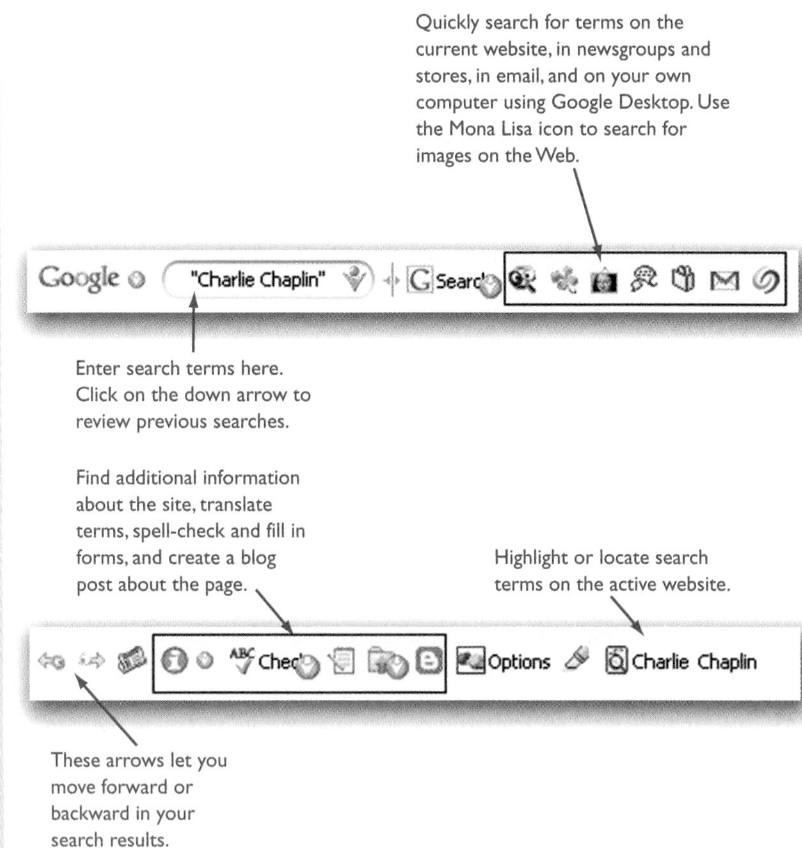

Quickly search for terms on the current website, in newsgroups and stores, in email, and on your own computer using Google Desktop. Use the Mona Lisa icon to search for images on the Web.
Google
"Charlie Chaplin"
Search
Enter search terms here. Click on the down arrow to review previous searches.
Find additional information about the site, translate terms, spell-check and fill in forms, and create a blog post about the page.
Highlight or locate search terms on the active website.
Check
Options
Charlie Chaplin
These arrows let you move forward or backward in your search results.

Boolean Operators

AND: Locates Web pages that contain all of the specified words or phrases. If you write *Music AND Videos,* then only Web pages with both words will be located.

AND NOT: Excludes Web pages that contain the specified word or phrase. If you write *Music AND NOT Videos,* then the search engine will return only those Web pages that contain the word *Music* and do not contain the word *Videos.* Make sure that you type in the two words *AND NOT,* rather than just typing in *NOT.*

NEAR and **W10:** Locates Web pages that contain both of the specified words or phrases within 10 words of each other. If you write *Music NEAR Videos,* then the search engine will return only those Web pages that have the word *Music* within 10 words of the word *Videos.* Using the W10 operator is another Boolean method of locating a word within 10 characters of another word on a Web page. You can also substitute other numbers for the 10. Both NEAR and W10 searches are called "proximity searches."

OR: Locates Web pages that contain at least one of the specified words or phrases. If you write *Music OR Videos,* then the search engine will return Web pages with either of those words.

Parentheses ( ): Allows use of two or more Boolean commands to locate Web pages. If you write *(Music AND Videos) AND (Eminem OR Rap),* then the search engine will return Web pages that contain either *Rap Music Videos* or *Eminem Music Videos.* If you changed the *OR* between *Eminem* and *Rap* to *AND,* then the search engine would return Web pages that contained *Rap Music Videos* and *Eminem Music Videos* and Web pages that contained *Eminem Rap Music Videos.*

Search engines offer helpful search features: Boolean searches, which establish particular relationships among your search terms; directory searches, which use preorganized categories of information; and advanced searches, which include special options.

Using Boolean Searches

Boolean searches rely on a programming system for making logical comparisons created by mathematician George Boole. When you use certain *Boolean operators* between search words, you tell the search engine to look for words in certain orders and arrangements and to exclude other words from your results list.

A Boolean search is assembled by joining your search words with combinations of the Boolean operators *AND, OR,* and *NOT.* Some search engines allow you to manually click on the Boolean operators you want applied to your search. Other search engines can handle the Boolean operators written among the search words, as search commands. Some search forms match pages on any of the terms (*OR*) and require the searcher to add a plus sign (+) to indicate that a particular term is required. *Because search engines vary widely in their acceptance of Boolean operators, refer to the "About" or "> more" pages on each search engine site to see which ones will work for you.*

Accessing Cached Results

Good search engines offer you the ability to examine *cached results* as one option for viewing your search results. When the search engine collects its database of sites on the Web, it collects (or caches) a copy of each page as it exists at that moment in time. Cached results can save you time on occasion. When you use cached results in Google, for instance, you can see your search terms highlighted on the page, which is handy for assessing quickly whether the current version of the Web page is a potentially good resource.

Conducting Directory Searches

Use a directory search when you are not certain about the specific words and phrases that you want your Web pages to contain. In directory searches, you rely on someone else's system of classifying information, which is fine for most purposes and will stimulate some connections for you. Instead of entering search words and phrases (which, in your search, are the smallest elements that you are looking for), you start with the largest category and search in increasingly narrower categories within it.

The Google Directory

Web Images Groups News Froogle Local **more »**

Preferences
Directory Help

Search Directory

The web organized by topic into categories.

Arts Movies, Music, Television,...	**Home** Consumers, Homeowners, Family,...	**Regional** Asia, Europe, North America,...
Business Industries, Finance, Jobs,...	**Kids and Teens** Computers, Entertainment, School,...	**Science** Biology, Psychology, Physics,...
Computers Hardware, Internet, Software,...	**News** Media, Newspapers, Current Events,...	**Shopping** Autos, Clothing, Gifts,...
Games Board, Roleplaying, Video,...	**Recreation** Food, Outdoors, Travel,...	**Society** Issues, People, Religion,...
Health Alternative, Fitness, Medicine,...	**Reference** Education, Libraries, Maps,...	**Sports** Basketball, Football, Soccer,...

World
Deutsch, Español, Français, Italiano, Japanese, Korean, Nederlands, Polska, Svenska, ...

In addition to using the directory at **http://www.google.com/dirhp** when you already know what your research question or hypothesis is, you can use the directory to generate ideas for topics. The section "Society – Issues" is particularly helpful for finding controversial subjects suitable for thesis-based research essays.

Sample Directory Search

Suppose you are doing research for a paper on contemporary female filmmakers. In a directory search, you would search smaller and smaller categories to find results:

Humanities → *Film* → *Filmmakers* → *Living filmmakers* → *Female filmmakers*

At this point, you could continue refining your search by selecting smaller and smaller categories, or you could begin viewing your results, which you see at each directory level. The results are usually alphabetized.

Advanced Search Options Typically Available

The advanced search feature of a search engine often includes the following options, though they may be configured differently on different engines.

- Search using "all of the words," "the exact phrase," "at least one of the words," and/or "none of the words," in any combination
- Search only pages updated within a certain time frame, with choices such as "anytime," "within the past three months," and "within the past six months"
- Search only pages written in certain languages
- Search only files saved in certain formats, such as those with .doc or .pdf at the end
- Search only certain domains, such as .edu, .com, or .gov
- Search only for search terms occurring in particular places, such as "in the URL," "in the title of the page," or "in the text of the page"

Conducting Advanced Searches

Some search engines have an advanced search feature. It may include options (generally separate search boxes) that allow you to search for words or phrases in the text of a website, in the URL, or in the titles of Web pages. We recommend using advanced search methods either at the very start or very early in your research process, once you know what you're looking for. You will soon be able to find exactly what you're looking for within seconds.

Understanding the Kinds of Searches You Can Conduct 10c

Natural language search
Example: Typing into the search box *How many college students in the U.S. are enrolled in a degree-granting program?*

Site search
Example: Searching the White House site (**http://www.whitehouse.gov**) for current information on presidential speeches

Wildcard search
Example: Typing *lab*r* into the search box in order to find "labor" and "labour"

Metasearch
Example: Using a metasearch engine such as Dogpile, Mamma, or Ixquick to search other search engines and return one results list

We've covered the basics of keyword and Boolean searches in sections 10a and 10b. This section discusses natural language searches, site searches, and wildcard searches. Metasearches are covered in section 10f.

Using Natural Language Searches

Natural language searches (and search engines) were invented so that people would not have to memorize Boolean operators; they could use simple *natural language* for their searches. The best-known natural language search engine is Ask. When you use a *natural language search,* you can type in, for example, "How many people read the news online every day?"

Using Site and Domain Searches

A site (or domain) search is one of the most effective methods of advanced searching. Site searches are handy when you know what sites should include information on your topic. For example, the CIA keeps track of vital statistics on every country in the world, so it's a good place to begin searching for country information.

The Parts of a URL?

A URL is the address for a site, file, or resource on the Web. A URL is made up of three main elements:

1. The protocol (that is, method of accessing the information), normally expressed as *http://* or, in some cases, *ftp://*.
2. The domain name, which is the main part of the address and can look like *purdue.edu* or *peta.org* or *creativecommons.org*. The domain name is the element of the name that most people remember.
3. The hierarchical name of the files on the site, such as *currentevents/listings.html,* in which the hierarchy is expressed with backslashes and the ending is often .html.

If you went to Yahoo.com (the domain), for example, and searched different protocols, such as *http://profiles,* you might find a specific place there where your friend's photo files were linked to her Yahoo! profile.

A URL identifies a folder structure targeting a particular file on a server. Sometimes that file is a static one (such as an .html file), and sometimes it is assembled from packets of information that depend on user input. Here's an example of a URL with the protocol, domain name, and folder structure indicated:

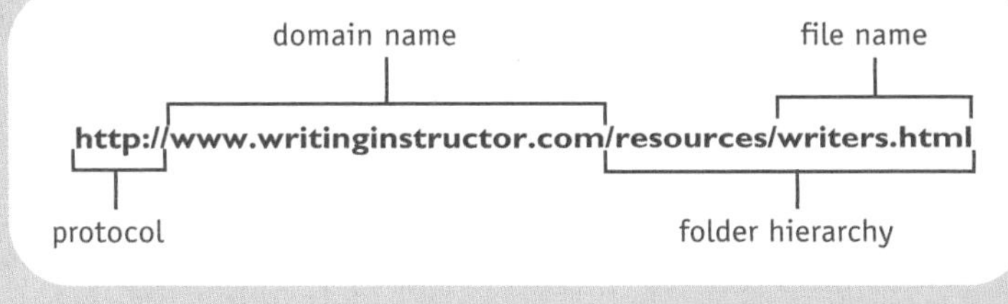

Search inside the Book

In October 2003, Amazon.com created a searchable digital library that enables users to "search inside the book." The library originally included 120,000 full, searchable books that publishers had made available to Amazon for scanning and uploading to the site (the number has significantly expanded with time). If you're looking for a particular phrase or trying to track down the source of a quotation, the "Search Inside the Book" service can be a great help. In this example from Amazon.com, the researcher was looking for the source of a quotation from the book *The Devil in the White City* by Erik Larson. At that book's page, she searched inside the book for the phrase "Ferris Wheel" by mousing over the book's image. She also noticed additional information about the book—including a concordance, "statistically improbable passages" (SIPs), capitalized phrases (CAPs), other books cited, and readability statistics. The results list returned 44 instances of "Ferris Wheel" in the book.

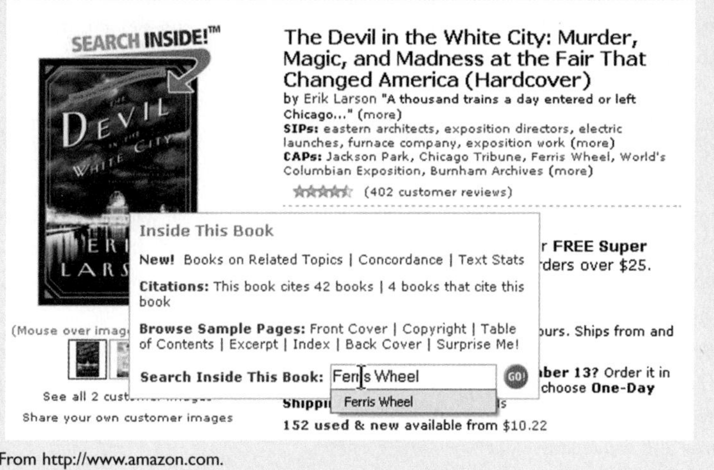

From http://www.amazon.com.

Using Wildcard Searches

A wildcard search uses an asterisk (*) to tell the search engine to look for a specific letter sequence plus any other letters. Wildcard searches are also referred to as *truncation* (when you search for any variation of the word's spelling) or *stemming* (when you use the stem of the word as a search term). The asterisk represents any letter or letters added onto your search words. Design* would cause the search engine to look for Web pages that contain *design, designer,* and *designing.* You should be thoughtful when using wildcard searches; in this example, the wildcard search would return a list of pages that contained *designation, designee, designator,* and other words that start with *design.*

Normally, you have to place three letters before the asterisk. You can put the asterisk anywhere inside the letters of your search word, which can help when you are uncertain about a search word's spelling or when another spelling can be used. For example, to cover both *theatre* and *theater,* you might type *theat**.

The search engines listed here are among the most effective now available.

Unless indicated, they automatically use the Boolean operator *AND* as a default when you write more than one search word. All of them also automatically use quotation mark phrase searches for proximity searching. All of them automatically sort your results by relevance or by a page's link frequency or popularity (how many other sites link to it). Some offer other ways of sorting the results list.

Search Engine Showdown

Search Engine Showdown is a website that ranks some but not all search engines. The site includes a chart organized by search engine, which can be found at http://www.searchengineshowdown.com/features/, and information organized by features (search capabilities), found at http://www.searchengineshowdown.com/features/byfeature.shtml.

Features of Popular Search Engines

Recommended Search Engines

Google: http://www.google.com
See also **http://www.google.com/intl/en/options/** for a list of special searches and tools that Google makes available, including the very useful Google Desktop Search™, which helps you quickly find files on your personal computer. (Apple makes a similar tool called Spotlight™ for OS 10.4 and higher.)

Google Scholar: http://scholar.google.com
Google Scholar™ enables you to "search specifically for scholarly literature, including peer-reviewed papers, theses, books, reprints, abstracts, and technical reports from all broad areas of research." If the work is published on the Internet, there's a strong chance Google Scholar will help you find it.

Google Images: http://images.google.com
Google Images™ enables Internet image-only searches.

Google Book Search: http://books.google.com
Google Book Search™ has begun digitizing the holdings of major libraries and publishers to allow full text searches of books, much like Amazon.com's "Search Inside the Book" feature.

Good Secondary Search Engines

Ask: http://www.ask.com
See **http://sp.ask.com/docs/about/tech_features.html** for a full list of features, including the new natural language question-asking tool, which analyzes search results for probable answers and categorizes them separately in your results list.

A9: http://a9.com
A9, developed by Amazon.com, is a good tool for researchers. Its integrative text and image search function allows users to sort results and add notes to them. See **http://a9.com/-/company/whatsCool.jsp** to learn more about A9's features and capabilities.

Clusty: http://clusty.com
Clusty groups the results list by topical categories. Clusty is a metasearch tool and so compiles results from MSN Search, Ask, Gigablast, Wisenut, and more. See **http://clusty.com/#** for a tour of Clusty's unique features.

Global Contexts

International Search Engines

Search Engine Colossus: International Directory of Search Engines: **http://www.searchenginecolossus.com**

Arnold Information Technology's List of International Search Engines: **http://www.arnoldit.com/lists/intlsearch.asp**

The search engines listed in this chapter include options for searching in a wide variety of languages. Be sure that your instructor permits the use of research materials in languages other than English. Also be careful to evaluate such resources just as you would those written in English (▶ section 10h).

Some of the major search engines have options for searching in French, Spanish, German, and Italian, and most will show only sites written in particular languages if you use the search engine's "preferences" settings. If you want to search in languages other than English, try the resources listed here, which include URLs to sites in English and other languages.

Good Secondary Search Engines

KartOO: http://www.kartoo.com
KartOO groups results in topical clusters and includes a visual map to show the relationships across clusters. For more information, see **http://www.kartoo.net/a/en/aide01.html**.

MSN Search: http://www.msn.com
MSN Search includes image, music, and news searches. MSN Search users can get a free pass to search the Encarta encyclopedia. Tour MSN Search's features at **http://www.imagine-msn.com/search/tour/moreprecise.aspx**.

Open Directory Project (ODP): http://dmoz.org
Search results are sorted in advance by people, who help make results more precise. See **http://dmoz.org/about.html** to learn more.

Yahoo! Search: http://www.yahoo.com
Yahoo!'s search engine is powered by Google. Sponsored results are listed at the top of the results page.

10f Metasearch Engines

Metasearches are handy when you are uncertain about which specific words and phrases you should use to begin your search. A **metasearch engine** conducts a search for results by sending your search words or phrases to other search engines, which then search for your words or phrases. The metasearch engine assembles all the results for you. The results from all of the searches are shown on the first metasearch results page.

A List of Metasearch Engines

Mamma: http://www.mamma.com

Search: http://www.search.com

Ixquick: http://www.ixquick.com

Dogpile: http://www.dogpile.com

10g Key Strategies for Effective Online Searches

Be Creative When You Search for Information

It is often simple to determine what terms to use to find information. You know what you want to write, and, to a certain extent, you know the terms used for your subject.

For instance, if you were against abortion and you wanted some information to support a paper explaining your position, then you would naturally search for websites using a term like *pro-life*. However, if you were for a woman's right to choose, you would just as naturally use a search term like *pro-choice*. Sometimes, when we occupy one position, we forget the terms and kinds of language used by people who hold other beliefs. By understanding the language and the terms that are used by people who have different opinions or beliefs, you can search more effectively.

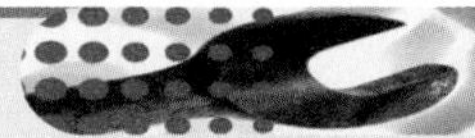

Technology Toolbox

Google Zeitgeist

Finding out what other people search for on the Internet can sometimes help you refine your own searches (or avoid advertisers, who often try to create sites that are based on popular search terms). Google's Zeitgeist™, at **http://www.google.com/intl/en/press/zeitgeist.html**, is a collection of data about how its users use the search engine, how terms come in and out of favor, and more.

As you can see, the most popular terms are tied to current events, so be as specific as possible with your terms. But remember that overly precise language may limit your results prematurely. Our advice is to make multiple searches, on different search engines, with different combinations of words and phrases.

Zeitgeist This Week

Top 15 Gaining Queries: Week Ending September 5, 2005

1. hurricane katrina	6. fema	11. hurricane katrina pictures
2. red cross	7. us open	12. tulane university
3. new orleans	8. kanye west	13. fats domino
4. gas prices	9. sania mirza	14. cheap gas
5. salvation army	10. cnn	15. gas shortage

Useful Research Portals

Research portals are sites that provide visitors with a collection of links and documents that are useful in research. Almost all of your research could start at **RefDesk** and you'd do well:
http://www.refdesk.com

Global Information (politics, culture, history, social sciences, humanities):
http://www.cia.gov/cia/publications/factbook/

Science Journals and Publications:
http://directory.google.com/Top/Science/Publications/Journals_and_Magazines/Free_Online_Journals/

Cultural and Social Issues:
http://directory.google.com/Top/Society/Issues/

Journal Archives:
You can search the EBSCOhost site either via the URL here or through your library's site if your college has a subscription to the service.
http://www.epnet.com/academic/default.asp

The Educational Resources Information Center (ERIC):
The national information system is designed to provide ready access to an extensive body of education-related research contributed by users.
http://www.eric.ed.gov

The Library of Congress:
Lists all books published in the United States and many published elsewhere.
http://www.loc.gov

Knowledge Network for Business, Technology, and Knowledge Management:
http://www.brint.com/interest.html

Refine Search Terms by Investigating Results

For your first couple of searches, reduce the results to fewer than 10,000 entries by searching within results or by changing your search words. Then use different terms in the Search within Results function to reduce the four-digit number down to no more than 30 or 40 results, when you can begin examining pages by opening them in new windows or tabs.

Quickly Find What You Need on a Web Page

Sometimes your search terms are buried within the website, in which case it may be handy to use the Find command. Put your cursor near the top of the Web page, click on Edit, and then select Find. When the Find window appears, type in your search term(s). The Find function will search the Web page either up or down, depending on where your cursor is.

Also consider using the metasearch engine Ixquick (http://ixquick.com). It offers results pages with the search terms highlighted and enlarged.

Try a URL Search

Using a search engine when you already have a sense of the URL (the website address) is likely to waste time. Before conducting a search, simply write the name, as you think it is spelled, in the address box, after the *http://*. You'll quickly find out whether you need to search further.

Evaluate the information you read online as carefully as possible.

Validate and Verify Your Information

Validate and verify your information by trying a new search, with different terms as starting points. For example, although we found thousands of results for *increased federal funding for family planning* and *prenatal care,* it would be a good idea to search again, using different terms or synonyms, such as *planned parenthood* or even *early pregnancy care*. You may find a wealth of new, supporting information. More importantly, you may discover an entirely new way of thinking about your subject, one that you have not yet considered.

Search for Domain-Level URLs

To make sure you don't miss a major source of information on your subject, run a domain-level search for sites on your topic. For example, you could try entering *www.plannedparenthood.org* (or *.com*) in your browser's address bar to see what turns up. In many cases, organizations with much information to offer on a subject also have rights to a domain name associated with it, so you can guess at what the URL might be.

Beware of Para-Sites

If you pay attention to purpose, you can determine rather easily that "The Beloved Community" is the authentic site of The King Center. The para-site that follows is affiliated with a hate group. With experience, you should be able to recognize quickly when a website (or any other source) is offering you dubious information.

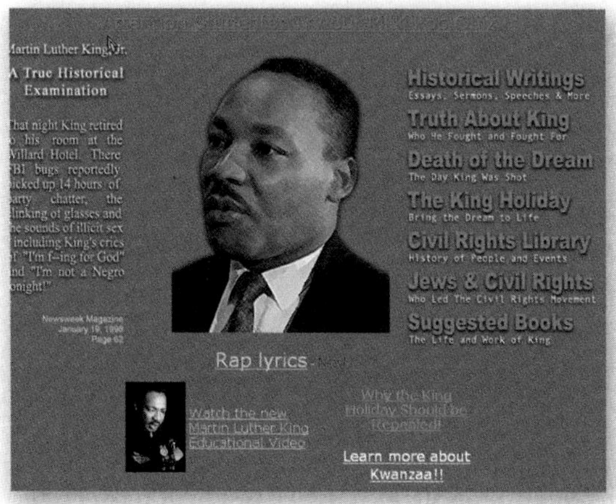

The para-site Martin Luther King Jr., which attempts to associate itself with the URL of the official voice of The King Center by using a similar URL: **http://www.martinlutherking.org**

The authentic site of The King Center: **http://www.martinlutherkingjr.com** or **http://www.thekingcenter.org/tkc/index.asp**

Primary Purposes of Websites

No website gains or loses credibility simply because it falls into one or another of these categories. For example, e-commerce sites can be terrific sources of reliable information. At major corporations' sites, you can find news releases about products, "white papers," and user documentation. Just be aware that the information is meant to support a product or service, not necessarily to present a well-rounded discussion of an issue.

- **Navigational:** information portals or pathways (like RefDesk, Yahoo!, MSN, AOL, or even *Arts and Letters Daily*)
- **Educational and academic:** sites of educational institutions (with the .edu suffix), encyclopedias, and professional journals and organizations
- **News media:** sites of newspapers, magazines, and TV networks (for example, CNN, MSNBC, *New York Times, US News and World Report,* and *The Chronicle of Higher Education*)
- **Government documentation:** sites of the Library of Congress, branches of government, the FBI, the CIA, and state governments
- **Public advocacy:** sites that advocate for a position on social issues
- **E-commerce:** sites that offer services or products to consumers and businesses
- **Personal:** home pages, weblogs, personal journals, and camsites

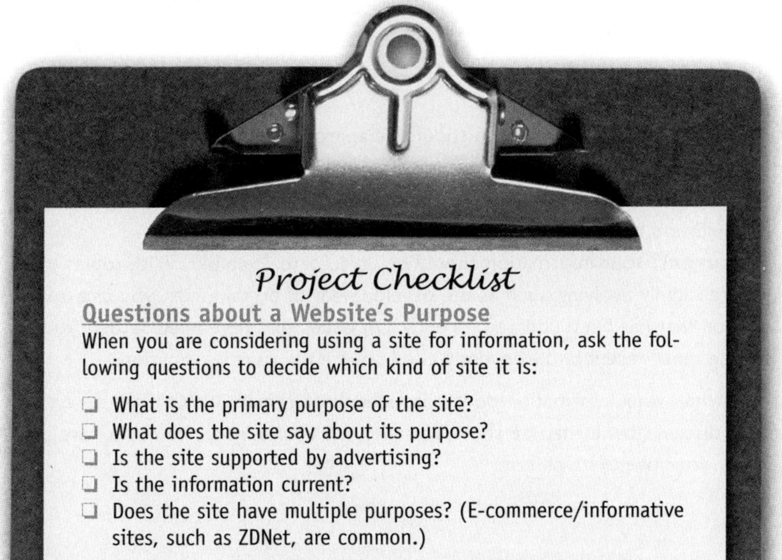

Project Checklist

Questions about a Website's Purpose

When you are considering using a site for information, ask the following questions to decide which kind of site it is:

- ❑ What is the primary purpose of the site?
- ❑ What does the site say about its purpose?
- ❑ Is the site supported by advertising?
- ❑ Is the information current?
- ❑ Does the site have multiple purposes? (E-commerce/informative sites, such as ZDNet, are common.)

Evaluate the Motives and Purpose of a Site

Information is always manipulated to achieve certain ends, and the facts that are important to one person may be irrelevant to another.

If you need information on gun control, for example, you should understand that while the National Rifle Association (NRA) website will offer you more information on that subject than most others, it will be information designed to support the NRA's position on gun control. You could say the same for the Million Mom March or Handgun Control, Inc. websites. Use information, but don't get used by it. You still need to verify figures and check facts with other sites. (For more on rhetorical analysis, see sections 4c and 10i.)

Evaluating Online Information by Purpose

Websites typically fall into one of seven categories, so you can begin your evaluation of a source's reliability by identifying its genre or primary purpose. When evaluating an online resource according to purpose, remember to consider all of its elements: text, graphics, advertising, layout, links, authorship, currency of information, domain name suffix, and any other aspects that will help you contextualize the information it provides.

Before citing information from online sources (or from print sources, for that matter), consider the likely reliability of those offering it. Typically, educational, government, and news media sites offer the most reliable information, but you should always try to find multiple sources to confirm a site's validity. Each research subject will have its own best kind of site(s) to use for support.

You can use information from personal or e-commerce sites, but make sure your reader understands the nature of the source and its reliability. Although the value of a particular site primarily depends on your subject and purpose for writing, the sites on page 141 are ordered according to their general acceptability to readers, from most acceptable to least. By describing the sources of information in your writing, you engender your reader's trust.

Criteria for Evaluating Information

Information is useful for research when it is valid, reliable, balanced, comprehensive, relevant, and current. It is the researcher's task to make sure that all information meets these criteria. Unfortunately, not all of it will. When it doesn't, you must either find better sources or use good judgment about how you frame the information in your research project.

Classifying Your Search Results

By now you should have a great many search results. Take a sample of five different sites from your search results, and evaluate them using the criteria presented in the Project Checklist on page 141. Answer the five questions, and then write a paragraph that describes each site's purpose for presenting information and puts the information in context.

Is the information . . .

- **valid?** Your information should be truthful. Example: If a website says that experiments with certain results were carried out at Columbia University in 1970, then, in fact, those experiments did take place and the results were as indicated.
- **reliable?** Your information should be consistent with that in other sources on the same subject. Example: You find the same facts in an encyclopedia and in a nonfiction book by a respected authority.
- **balanced?** Either your information should display no bias or its bias should be directly discussed as part of the presentation of the information. Example: You use information on the history of tobacco use in the United States, and the information serves neither to promote smoking nor to encourage smoking cessation.
- **comprehensive?** Your information should be essentially complete and not lack any valuable or integral elements. Example: In a critical review of popular diets in a nutrition course, you list all of the known drawbacks of each and don't let any escape notice.
- **relevant?** Your information should be appropriate to the situation. Example: You would cite a Shakespearean critic's analysis of Hamlet's character in a paper on the play *Hamlet,* but would probably avoid doing so in a paper on the children's book *Goodnight Moon.*
- **current?** Your information should be up to date. Example: With topics that are rapidly evolving, such as the development of digital media, you cite information that has been updated recently. On issues that have been settled, you use the most recent and frequently cited source for your information.

When your information does not meet these requirements, make sure that you discuss how it may fall short. This way, while your evidence might have problems, your use of it will not.

You can also evaluate your information resources by analyzing the rhetorical situation with respect to audience, authorship, and documents.

Project Checklist

Questions to Ask about Audience and Authorship

Questions about Audience

1. Who is the primary audience for the site? Is there any offensive or exclusionary language? (If so, consider using the information only to demonstrate how one person or group views your subject.)
2. What age/educational range does the site target? How valuable is the site for other ages/educational ranges?
3. Is the resource addressed to novices or experts on the subject?
4. Does the site provide a comment book or guest register? Does its content reveal anything about the audience?

Questions about Authorship

1. Who is the author or producer of the site? How does the author have the authority to provide this information? Has the author published anything else? Is the author cited by others?
2. Is the author associated with other individuals/groups? What do you find when you use the author's name as a search term?
3. What relevant professional, business, or political affiliations does the author have? Do any of these cast doubt on the author's objectivity, or do they add to the author's authority?
4. Who sponsors the site? Is the sponsor a nonprofit organization, a business, a government, or an educational institution? Does this sponsor's presence create bias?
5. Is the email address of a particular person provided, or is the person unnamed? (If there is no contact information, is this an anonymous site? If so, do not consider this source reliable.)
6. Who is the copyright owner of the site? If copyright is not listed, has the authorship of the information been clearly indicated otherwise? (If not, you shouldn't use it.)

Be among the 5%

Only about 5% of online researchers use any of the advanced search strategies we have discussed in this chapter. If you learn them well, you'll be able to conduct quick, focused, and productive searches through truly astonishing masses of information from around the world. If you then add rhetorical savvy by asking rigorous questions about the sources you find, you can be assured that your research projects will be based on accurate and reliable information.

Project Checklist

Questions to Ask about a Site's Documents

1. How accurate is the information provided on the site?
2. Are sources or citations given for any facts? (If not, be skeptical.)
3. What other kinds of information sources (i.e., books, journals) can you use to double-check the information?
4. Does this information appear only online or does it fit within an existing dialogue ongoing in other media?
5. Does the information appear too good to be true?
6. When was the document originally published? When was the site last updated? Can you find more up-to-date information elsewhere?
7. Are the links relevant and appropriate for the information? Are any links to sites that have moved? Are any of the linked sites out of date?
8. How well-rounded is the information on the site?
9. Is anything being sold at the page where you have found the information? Are there any connections between the information and the advertising that make the information seem dubious?
10. Does the site appear professional, or does it look hurriedly constructed?
11. Is the text grammatically and mechanically correct? Are there spelling errors?
12. Do the graphics relate to the site's content? Are any of the graphics simple clip art that doesn't serve an obvious purpose? Do the graphics complement the site's information well? Do they bias the information?
13. Is there an audio component? Does the audio produce any bias in relationship to the information? Does the audio interact appropriately with the site?
14. How convenient is the site to navigate?
15. Does the site have a search engine for internal elements on the site? Does it function properly? Or does the site use an external search engine?

LIBRARY AND FIELD RESEARCH 11

Survey library resources . . .

- Familiarize yourself with the library (or libraries) on your campus.
- Ask the librarians for help with questions large and small.
- Tour the library's website to discover the types of resources it has to offer.

The library in the digital age has a critical role to play not only as a repository and archive of the printed content in books and journals needed for research but also as a clearinghouse and filter for the best resources available. Every researcher can benefit from frequent trips to the library, online *and* off.

Starting with Subject-Area Research Guides 11a

An excellent way to begin your library research is to consult the research guide for your subject area, found on your library's website. This guide will point you toward specialized reference materials such as

- bibliographies and other kinds of specialized guides
- indexes and databases for finding articles and critical essays
- special indexes for finding primary sources, such as individual songs or paintings, in fields like music or art history
- links to websites considered to be appropriate to research in the field
- special library holdings

Examples of Subject-Area Research Guides

Introduction to Library Research in Anthropology
Using the Biological Literature: A Practical Guide
Literary Research Guide: A Guide to Reference Sources for the Study of Literature in English and Related Topics
Sources of Information in the Social Sciences: A Guide to the Literature
Psychology: A Guide to Reference and Information Sources
Sourcebook for Research in Music
Medieval Iconography: A Research Guide

Finding Subject-Area Guides for Your Research Project

Subject-area guides can be a useful resource when you're starting to explore an area of interest or beginning research for a paper.

1. Determine the subject area of your topic. For example, a paper about the dangers of overfishing would probably fit best in biology, marine biology, or environmental conservation.
2. Visit your library's website and locate its collection of subject-area guides. If your library's website does not have this resource, ask a librarian to help you locate a subject-area guide for your specific area.
3. Browse the subject-area guides and locate one that offers content relevant to your research.
4. Send an email to yourself and your instructor with the title and Web address of the guide.

Consulting reference works is a convenient way to get background information anytime you need a quick and clear overview of themes, questions, events, facts, or people. What they probably can't provide is the kind of in-depth information you'll need to adequately explain and support your research. Reference works have already synthesized a vast amount of content, and some of what's important to your project may have been left out.

General reference works address knowledge in all fields of inquiry. Specialized reference works are geared toward individual subject areas. Which reference works you choose will depend on your research area, your stage of research, the particular problem posed by your research, and your library's holdings. Many general and specialized references are also available online.

The Wide World of Reference Works

Reference Works	Examples
Almanacs, factbooks, news digests, and **yearbooks** provide country information and basic statistics. Facts and figures can also be found in **statistical abstracts** and **statistical indexes,** as well as in **books of historical statistics.**	*Statistical Abstract of the United States* *Facts on File: News Digest* *World Factbook* *World Almanac and Book of Facts* *Central Intelligence Agency Factbook on Intelligence* *ESPN Sports Almanac* *Fact Book on Higher Education*
Atlases are books of maps. Many also include statistical data. **Gazetteers** are geographical dictionaries.	*Dorling Kindersley World Reference Atlas* *Essential World Atlas* *Hammond Medallion World Atlas* *Maps for America* *Historical Atlas of South Asia* *Zondervan NIV Atlas of the Bible*
Bibliographic guides and **reference indexes** are indexed guides to available materials in individual subject areas.	*American Indian Studies: A Bibliographic Guide* *Guide to Reference Materials in Political Science: A Selective Bibliography* *Architecture: A Bibliographic Guide to Basic Reference Works, Histories, and Handbooks* *The Era of World War II: General Reference Works, Bibliography* *World Painting Index* *Popular Song Index* *Halliwell's Film and Video Guide*
Biographical reference works, often organized as either dictionaries or mini-encyclopedias, supply information about people.	*The Cambridge Biographical Encyclopedia* *Country Music: A Biographical Dictionary* *Who's Who in America* *International Women in Science: A Biographical Dictionary to 1950* *Distinguished Asian Americans: A Biographical Dictionary* *The Harvard Concise Dictionary of Music and Musicians* *Biographical Dictionary of Modern World Leaders, 1900–1991*

Reference Works	Examples
Concordances index every word in a particular book or body of work and show how each word is used contextually. For example, you could search a concordance of Shakespeare's work to find all uses of the word *dainty,* which could help you evaluate what the word meant in Renaissance England. (According to the Open Source Shakespeare concordance, the word appears 20 times, in 14 works.)	*Analytical Concordance to the New Revised Standard Version of the New Testament* *Harvard Concordance to Shakespeare* *Concordance to the Standard Edition of the Complete Psychological Works of Sigmund Freud* *Concordance to the Poetry of Robert Frost* *Concordance to the Correspondence of Voltaire* *Concordance to Beowulf*
Dictionaries define words and are arranged alphabetically. Dictionaries also provide guides to etymology, pronunciation, and usage. **Specialized dictionaries** define terms within a field of knowledge. Other language-usage reference works include **thesauruses,** which provide lists of synonyms.	*Oxford English Dictionary* *Random House Webster's Unabridged Dictionary* *American Heritage Dictionary of the English Language* *Dictionary of American History* *Dictionary of Archaeology* *Dictionary of Plant Sciences* *Oxford Dictionary of Philosophy*
Directories include guides to colleges, internships, organizations, foundations, and grant resources, as well as telephone and zip code directories.	*Directory of International Internships* *Directory of Recycling Programs: Recycle and Save* *Directory of Museums & Living Displays* *Directory of National Fellowships, Internships and Scholarships for Latino Youth*
Encyclopedias, companions, and **reader's guides** contain short topic-specific articles and are arranged alphabetically. They can be single- or multivolume. **Handbooks** provide a concise reference in an individual subject area.	*Encyclopaedia Britannica* *Encyclopedia of Bioethics* *Encyclopedia of Human Rights* *International Encyclopedia of Statistics* *Blackwell Handbook of Social Psychology* *World Hunger: A Reference Handbook* *Reader's Guide to Lesbian and Gay Studies*
Quotation books may be organized by author, by work, by keyword or subject area, or by chronology.	*Familiar Quotations* *Folger Book of Shakespeare Quotations* *Expanded Quotable Einstein* *The Words of Martin Luther King, Jr.*
Timelines and **chronologies** provide a historical overview in a table or other largely visual format.	*Chronology of World History* *Timelines of the Arts and Literature* *Chronology and Fact Book of the United Nations*

The library catalog is used for finding a wide variety of materials. The catalog lists the *names* of all the periodicals in the library's holdings, but it will not point you to individual articles. Only indexes and databases do that (▶ section 11d).

Author searches generally require that you enter the author's name, last name first, as in "dickens, charles."

Title searches generally require that you begin with the first word of the title (except articles, such as *a, an,* or *the*).

Keyword searches are the most flexible. Enter "charles dickens" in the keyword field and you'll find not only all catalog records in which "charles dickens" appears as an author, as a subject, or in a title, but also books of literary criticism of Dickens's works, biographies of Dickens's life, film versions of his novels, and sound recordings of *Oliver!* You'll find books on other subjects entirely but in which "charles dickens" is listed in the table of contents. You'll find Dickens's letters, reference works on Dickens's writing, and more.

Subject searches return all the library's entries in a given subject area. The five-volume, hardbound *LOC Subject Headings* is published annually and can be found in the reference section of your library. It's arranged alphabetically. Search the manual until you find the right subject category or cluster of categories for your research area.

Sample Title Record

This section provides essential publication information that you need to know for purposes of citation.

Clicking on "Drooker, Eric, 1958-" will lead you to other catalog listings where he is listed as the main author.

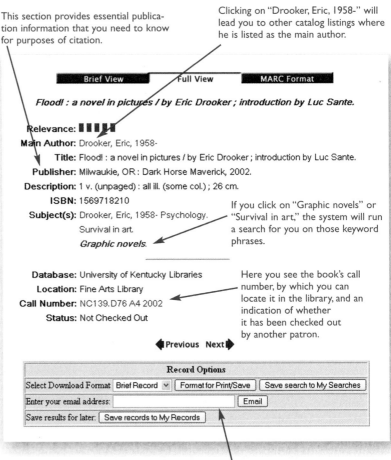

Brief View | Full View | MARC Format

Flood! : a novel in pictures / by Eric Drooker ; introduction by Luc Sante.

Relevance: ▮▮▮▮▮

Main Author: Drooker, Eric, 1958-

Title: Flood! : a novel in pictures / by Eric Drooker ; introduction by Luc Sante.

Publisher: Milwaukie, OR : Dark Horse Maverick, 2002.

Description: 1 v. (unpaged) : all ill. (some col.) ; 26 cm.

ISBN: 1569718210

Subject(s): Drooker, Eric, 1958- Psychology.
Survival in art.
Graphic novels.

If you click on "Graphic novels" or "Survival in art," the system will run a search for you on those keyword phrases.

Database: University of Kentucky Libraries

Location: Fine Arts Library

Call Number: NC139.D76 A4 2002

Status: Not Checked Out

Here you see the book's call number, by which you can locate it in the library, and an indication of whether it has been checked out by another patron.

◀ Previous Next ▶

Record Options

Select Download Format [Brief Record] [Format for Print/Save] [Save search to My Searches]

Enter your email address: [ ] [Email]

Save results for later: [Save records to My Records]

You can use the "Record Options" function to save the results of your search, print them immediately, save them as a file, or send them to yourself or someone else as an email message. We recommend (at least) sending yourself an email message so that you can recover the source information easily.

This is the full view of the record for *Flood! A Novel in Pictures* by Eric Drooker.
From InfoKat (University of Kentucky Libraries Online Catalog and Gateway), http://infokat.uky.edu.

General Indexes and Databases

Some Interdisciplinary Indexes

Academic Search Premier
AccuNet/Associated Press Multimedia Archive
Alternative Press Index
Biography Index
Book Review Digest (Print Only)
Book Review Index (Print and Restricted Online Only)
Consumer Index
Expanded Academic ASAP
FirstSearch
Ingenta
JSTOR
LexisNexis Academic Universe
LexisNexis Congressional Universe
LexisNexis Statistical Universe
PCI: Periodical Contents Index
Project Muse

News Indexes, Current and Archival

AccuNet/Associated Press Multimedia Archive
African American Newspapers: The 19th Century
The Civil War: A Newspaper Perspective
Ethnic News Watch
InfoTrac Custom Newspapers
Harper's Weekly
LexisNexis Academic Universe
New York Times Digital Full-text Edition
NewsBank
Pennsylvania Gazette, 1728–1800
World News Connection

Specialized Indexes and Databases

Education

ERIC

Fine and Performing Arts

Art Index
Art Index Retrospective
Arts and Humanities Citation Index
International Index to Music Periodicals
Music Index
RILM (Répertoire international de littérature musicale)
RIPM (Répertoire international de la presse musicale)

Humanities

AfricaBib
America: History and Life
American Bibliography of Slavic and East European Studies
Arts and Humanities Citation Index
ATLA—Religion Database
Bibliography of Asian Studies
Hispanic American Periodicals Abstract
International Medieval Bibliography
Iter: Gateway to the Middle Ages & Renaissance
MLA Bibliography
Philosopher's Index

To find articles in periodicals—newspapers, popular magazines, or scholarly journals—use indexes and databases. You'll see both "index" and "database" used on your library's website, often interchangeably, and they are closely allied. More precisely, a **database** is any electronically stored collection of information that can be retrieved and manipulated; a **periodicals index** is a listing of citations to journal, magazine, or newspaper articles.

Choosing Indexes and Databases

Determining which of the seemingly bewildering array of indexes and databases will best serve a particular research project is an advanced skill. **General-interest** or **interdisciplinary databases,** such as Academic Search Premier, Expanded Academic ASAP, FirstSearch, LexisNexis Academic Universe, and TDNet, index a wide variety of subject areas across the curriculum. **Specialized databases**, such as International Medieval Bibliography, CubaSource, or Oceanographic Literature Review, index particular subject areas. If you are unsure which databases to use for your research project, ask a reference librarian or your instructor, or consult the subject-area research guide on your library's website.

11d Searching Databases and Indexes

The easiest way to become adept at searching a particular database or index is to practice. Start with the basic search, then try the advanced. Familiarize yourself with the different search options that are available. Study the search tips. Another important way to enhance your skill is by mastering Boolean logic (◀ section 10b).

Visit cengage.com/English/Blakesley to find directions for accessing commonly used databases such as Academic Search Premier and Lexis Nexis.

Math, Science, Medicine, Technology

Agricola (FirstSearch version)
Applied Science & Technology
Biological & Agricultural Index
BIOSIS
Chemical Abstracts
General Science Abstracts
Geobase
Internet & Personal Computing Abstracts
MathSciNet
Medline
Oceanographic Literature Review
OSTI
PubMed
Web of Science

Social Sciences

CubaSource
EconLit
Hoover's Online
NotiCen
NotiSur
PAIS
PsycINFO
RePEc (Research Papers in Economics)
Social Sciences Citation Index
Sociological Abstracts
SourceMex

11e Working with Government Documents

The United States government is the world's largest publisher, producing thousands of books and reports each year. Federal documents of various types can be found in most libraries, and electronic resources now make government information available in a multiplicity of ways. Consult the federal documents specialist in your college or university library before you begin your research. Federal documents might be indexed in your library's online catalog. They can be found indexed and shelved according to their own separate system: the Superintendent of Documents number, which catalogs them according to issuing government agency.

Where to Find Government Documents

A variety of electronic resources provide access to government documents or provide indexing services for government documents:

FirstGov, the U.S. government's official Web portal: **http://www.firstgov.gov**
GPO Access: **http://www.gpoaccess.gov**
Thomas—Legislative Information on the Internet: **http://thomas.loc.gov**
Government Information Locator Service (GILS): **http://www.gils.net**
Google Uncle Sam: **http://www.google.com/unclesam**
GovEngine.com: **http://www.govengine.com**
Federal Web Locator, Villanova Center for Information Law and Policy: **http://www.lib.auburn.edu/madd/docs/fedloc.html**
Enhanced GPO Catalog (U.S. government publications, 1976–present)
LexisNexis Congressional Universe
FindLaw

For more information, see *Using Government Information Sources: Electronic and in Print* (Oryx Press, 2001), as well as Richard J. McKinney's "Internet and Online Sources of U.S. Legislative and Regulatory Information" (available through **http://www.library.cornell.edu/olinuris/ref/usdocs.html**).

Project Checklist

Evaluating Print Sources

For evaluating online sources, see section 10h.

- **Relevance.** Examine the title, table of contents, headings (if an article), index, and citations. What seems to be the slant on the general subject? Do any of your search terms appear in the index? Also, take care to differentiate general-interest works from scholarly works. Your own rhetorical situation will determine which is more appropriate for your project.
- **Timeliness.** Some projects require historical depth; others require current information. Most search vehicles let you screen by date.
- **Comprehensiveness.** A source that deliberately neglects significant information should be used with caution. However, you will often find a source that bears on only one aspect of your subject, and that's fine. Just be sure to use it within its own limits; don't overgeneralize any findings.
- **Balance.** There's nothing wrong with a biased source—as long as you know its flaws and can use it as an example of such. Authors who only present one side of an issue often haven't done their homework or have something to hide.
- **Reliability and validity.** Do you trust the information? Why or why not? Who is the author, and what are his or her credentials? Is the article from a scholarly journal? If it is from a popular magazine, what is the magazine's relation to its audience—does it inform, or is it mostly trying to stimulate consumption or amuse? Who is the publisher of the book? Is it a scholarly or university press, an alternative publisher, or a commercial publisher? Look also at a work's footnotes and bibliography. How extensive are they? Is the book well researched? Does the article's list of citations give you the impression that the author is steeped in the literature of his or her field?

At every stage of research, you must evaluate source materials—whether you're reviewing the results list from a search of an online catalog, index, or database; deciding which articles to scan briefly online, which to track down in bound periodicals, and which to read more closely; or examining a stack of books from the library shelves and choosing which to put back, which to take home, and which to read from cover to cover. You can evaluate material by analyzing it rhetorically in terms of authorship, audience, and purpose. Another way to evaluate material is to ask if it is valid, reliable, balanced, comprehensive, relevant, and current.

First Clarify Your Own Goals as a Writer

What is your purpose for writing? What do you want to say? What audience will you be addressing? What is the context? (If necessary, review the Project Checklist on page 5.)

Some research projects will require—or would benefit from—field research: an interview, observation, or survey. Many fields of study employ field research in their methodology. Take observation: Social sciences, life sciences, and fine and performing arts, as well as applied fields such as journalism and education, each have their own methodology (or methodologies) of observation. As a means of building a vocabulary of gesture and posture into a character, an actor might go to the zoo to observe how a particular animal moves. Someone interested in sports education might use CBAS, the coaching behavior assessment system, to observe and record how a particular coach employs positive and negative feedback in a practice session. A novelist might sit in a café and observe two lovers arguing.

1

Project Checklist

Conducting an Interview

Once you have clarified your purpose for conducting an interview, take the following steps to ensure that you find out what you want to know.

- ❑ **Plan ahead.** Know your subject matter and learn as much about your interviewee as you can before you conduct the interview. The purpose of an interview isn't to get basic information; it's to glean specifics from one person's knowledge or experience. The better prepared and informed you are, the better the quality of the information you'll derive from the interview.
- ❑ **Request the interview.** When you write to your prospective interviewee, take the time to introduce yourself and your research project. Be flexible about arranging a time at the interviewee's convenience. Let the person know how long you expect the interview to last, what questions you'd like to ask, and how you hope to use the interview results.
- ❑ **Construct questions carefully.** Brainstorm as many questions as you can. Set your timer to 5, 10, or 30 minutes and write down every question you can think of. Now go back and choose. Edit, select, and rearrange your questions so that the interview flows logically. Know which questions are the most essential. Avoid questions that can be answered with a simple yes or no.
- ❑ **Give and take.** Your carefully constructed series of interview questions provides an essential roadmap for the interview, but be prepared to adjust your questions to the flow of the conversation.
- ❑ **Consider the logistics.** Where will you interview the person? How will those surroundings affect the quality of the interview? Will you use a tape recorder? Will you be videotaping? If you'll be operating a tape recorder, are you sufficiently skilled? What's the condition of your equipment? Do you have the right kind of tapes on hand? Do you have pen and paper?

2

- **Hone listening and note-taking skills.** Listening is itself a skill. If you've never interviewed someone before, practice on a friend. Next practice listening and taking notes without losing track of the conversation or burying your face in your own papers. Add the tape recorder. Practice until you can juggle all three activities—listening, note-taking, and operating the tape recorder—at once, effortlessly.
- **Obtain appropriate permissions.** If the interview is to be videotaped, make sure the interviewee is well aware of this ahead of time and has agreed to it. If the interview is to be recorded, get the interviewee's written permission before you begin.
- **Observe interview decorum.** Dress appropriately. Be on time. Wear a watch and make sure that the interview goes only as long as scheduled. Thank the interviewee at the time and follow up with a written thank-you note.
- **Follow up promptly.** Go over your notes and write up what you want to use from the interview within 24 hours. Send your written thank-you note within two days, if not immediately. If you're transcribing the tape, listen to it right away to check for sound quality. It is ethical practice to send your results to the interviewee as well, particularly when you want to quote him or her directly. (Interviewees appreciate the opportunity to correct misstatements or other inaccuracies.)

Methods of field research vary with the subject area. Even the seemingly simplest method of field research can bring up complex questions about framing, assumptions, objectivity, and selectivity. If you plan to publish your research outside of the immediate context of your class, then you should also check with your instructor to make sure that you adhere to the college's guidelines for research involving human subjects.

Conducting Interviews

Perhaps you want to talk with someone who is an expert in the field, hear about an event from an eyewitness, or listen to two sides of a controversy from two individuals involved. Perhaps you know of someone who has a unique or colorful story to tell and you want to capture his or her voice. Have a purpose for conducting an interview.

Conducting Observations

Who or what are you observing and why? Five psychologists or educators might visit a preschool classroom but conduct five different observations. One might observe gender-based behavior. A second might observe overall language use. Another might observe positive and negative reinforcement in teachers' discipline.

How you conduct your observations depends on your purposes and the field of study in which you're conducting your observations.

Project Checklist

Conducting Observations

Once you have clarified your purpose and your methodology for conducting an observation, take the following steps to ensure that you find out what you want to know.

- ❑ **Obtain permissions as appropriate.** If your observation takes place in the campus lounge or a public park, you don't need permission. But if your site is one not open to the public—a classroom, a rehearsal, a labor-management contract negotiation session—obtain permission to observe and be prepared to take notes only. Audio or video taping usually requires the express written permission of all persons present.
- ❑ **Clarify context, using who, what, when, and where.** Label your observational context before you begin. Whom are you observing? What is the setting? Where are you? What time of day or season is it? The questions you want to address to clarify context will depend on your observation.
- ❑ **Be inconspicuous.** While observing, don't draw attention to yourself. Don't talk or engage with your subjects. If you have more detailed questions for someone in particular, set up a separate interview. If you find you need to survey a group of persons, conduct your survey at another time. Keep the process of observing distinct from other kinds of interactions.
- ❑ **Observe, don't interpret.** It sounds easy, but it's not. Study after study has shown how so-called observers' biases and preconceived ideas influence their research. When you construct your methodology, run it by your instructor for a bias check. Another easy technique is to set up your observation notebook in two columns: one for observations and one for questions, theories, and analysis.

Conducting Surveys

A survey is a means of sampling opinion in order to gather data representative of the larger group. You can conduct a survey by phone, by email, or by standing on the street corner. The two most important aspects of a survey are (1) whom you are asking and (2) what you are asking them. So consider carefully how you will make your sample reasonably representative of the group in question and how you will frame your questions so that your questionnaire most accurately reflects actual opinion. As in conducting an observation, perhaps the most difficult aspect of conducting a survey is designing a questionnaire free of your own biases and opinions.

Design your survey with a research hypothesis in mind. Ask yourself how the questionnaire will test your hypothesis and how your survey will advance your research.

Project Checklist

Conducting Surveys

Once you have clarified your hypothesis and your purpose for conducting a survey, take the following steps to ensure that you find out what you want to know.

- ❑ **Make the survey easy to take.** How long will it take someone to complete your questionnaire? The easier it is to take your survey, the more success you'll have in gathering a useful amount of data. If you can accomplish your research goal in a 10-question survey, don't ask 20 questions. Have all possible answers on the survey so that respondents can simply circle or check the correct answer. Try your questionnaire out on a small test group and get some feedback before launching the real thing.
- ❑ **Make it as easy as possible to tabulate,** given the kind of information you are searching for. Free-form comments are hard to tabulate. Fill-in-the-blank options are not. So design questions that have "yes" or "no" answers or a straightforward controlled range of responses, such as "strongly agree," "agree," "disagree," or "strongly disagree."
- ❑ **Make it fair and accurate.** Consider the range of opinions possible on the subject you are investigating. Design your survey to fairly and accurately accommodate opposite points of view (and all those in the middle). If you ask "Isn't the new parking policy unfair?" you've built your own bias right into the question. If you ask "Are you in favor of or against the new parking policy that assigns the closest spaces by lottery?" your survey will be more effective.
- ❑ **Make it representative.** If you think your survey might solicit different responses from different categories of people and if these differences are relevant to your research hypotheses, include checkable boxes for group identification. For example, is it important to your survey whether respondents are male or female? If so, include a checkbox for each group. Is income, class, or ethnicity important? Preserve anonymity when you gather demographic information.

12 USING SOURCES ETHICALLY

Every writer has an ethical responsibility to write truthfully, to represent the work of others fairly and accurately, and to give credit where it is due. To ensure that you use information responsibly, practice the guidelines for effective note-taking discussed in section 9g.

Three Methods of Integrating Souce Material

- Summary: a concise restatement of a source's main ideas, written in your own words
- Paraphrase: a detailed restatement of a source's idea, written in your own words
- Quotation: direct use of the source's words and punctuation

See section 12d on framing source material.

12a Using Summaries Effectively

A **summary** is a concise restatement of the main ideas of a source, written in your own words. A summary gives the gist of the source without using the source's words or sentence structure. A summary is considerably shorter than the original even though it still represents the original meaning as accurately as possible. Normally, when you summarize, you include only the main ideas or only the main ideas that are relevant to your needs. A summary of another person's ideas must be documented with information required by the citation style that you're using. (If you don't know which citation style to use, ask your instructor.)

When Should You Write a Summary?

- Summarize when a quotation or paraphrase would give unneeded detail or distracting minutiae.
- Summarize when several different kinds of information from the same source and author were provided over many pages in the original.

How Do You Write a Summary?

1. Read and reread the original until you are sure you understand it.
2. Identify the major ideas: the thesis statement, if there is one, and the topic sentences of paragraphs or sections. If the work is a narrative, write a very brief description of the major events in each section. If the work is very short, look for key ideas in repeated phrases.
3. Write one sentence that captures the main idea of the original. Then write any supporting sentences that are needed so that your readers will grasp the major idea. Rewrite them until you have a summary that someone unfamiliar with the work will understand.
4. Check the summary against the source to make sure you have used all your own words. If you need to use any phrases from the source because they are unique, enclose the phrases in a pair of quotation marks. Note the page number of the material you have quoted.
5. Check to be sure you have not included your own thoughts and opinions in the summary. The summary should include only the source's ideas, not yours. (Your ideas are relayed before and after the summary.)
6. Document your summary with the author's name, title of the work, and publishing information, including page numbers for print sources.

Sample Descriptive and Informative Summaries

Original

The Semantic Web will bring structure to the meaningful content of Web pages, creating an environment where software agents roaming from page to page can readily carry out sophisticated tasks for users. Such an agent coming to the clinic's Web page will know not just that the page has keywords such as "treatment, medicine, physical, therapy" (as might be encoded today) but also that Dr. Hartman works at this clinic on Mondays, Wednesdays, and Fridays and that the script takes a date range in yyyy-mm-dd format and returns appointment times. And it will "know" all this without needing artificial intelligence on the scale of *2001*'s Hal or *Star Wars*'s C-3PO. Instead these semantics were encoded into the Web page when the clinic's office manager (who never took Comp Sci 101) massaged it into shape using off-the-shelf software for writing Semantic Web pages along with resources listed on the Physical Therapy Association's site.

From Tim Berners-Lee et al., "The Semantic Web," *Scientific American,* May 17, 2001; also available at <http://www.scientificamerican.com>.

Descriptive Summary

Words that describe the act of the writers are highlighted.

In 2001, Tim Berners-Lee and his colleagues at W3C envisioned a new way to structure information on the Internet. They believed that content should be organized for users in terms of relations of meaning across databases.

Informative Summary

"The Semantic Web" is premised on the fact that users need to know how information is structured, not just where it is, and, crucially, how one bit of information is related to another, no matter where that information may be stored (Berners-Lee).

Descriptive vs. Informative Summary

There are two kinds of summaries: descriptive and informative. A *descriptive summary* explains the source from a reader's perspective, like a blow-by-blow description of what an author writes or what people do. It focuses on action. Descriptive summaries are most useful when the focus of your own writing is on something that has happened and the event (of reading, for example) is noteworthy in itself. For example, the sentence

> Faulkner begins his novel *Absalom, Absalom!* with a two-page-long sentence.

is a (very) short descriptive summary of how William Faulkner begins that novel.

An *informative summary,* by contrast, provides the content of a source in highly condensed form. So, for example, the descriptive summary above differs greatly from this short informative summary of the novel's beginning:

> Miss Coldfield knows from the very start why Quentin Compson has decided to go to Harvard.

Informative summaries are often useful when you need to provide a context for later analysis, such as a plot summary at the start of a film review that may be read by people who have not seen the film yet.

A **paraphrase** is a detailed restatement of a source, written in your own words. Unlike a summary, a paraphrase restates ideas in their entirety and reflects the source's order of ideas, emphasis, and tone. Because they include all the details and examples from the source, paraphrases are roughly the same length as or a bit longer than the original. It's critical that you remember that a paraphrase must be documented with information required by the citation style you're using (for example, MLA or APA).

See page 164 for information on introducing paraphrases.

When Should You Paraphrase?

- Paraphrase when you need to discuss details from the source.
- Paraphrase when the author's ideas and facts are more important than the language used to describe them or when a quotation might be distracting.
- Consider paraphrasing when the original text uses language that differs greatly in style, tone, or voice from your writing. Do paraphrase when the language of the original is technical, arcane, or complicated.

How Do You Paraphrase?

1. Read the part of the source you want to paraphrase several times, until you are sure you understand not only its ideas but also its tone and emphasis.
2. Find the key terms and think of synonyms you could use instead. If you must quote a key term, enclose the quotation in a pair of quotation marks and note the number of the page on which it appears.
3. Write the ideas in your own words, using a tone similar to the source's.
4. Check your draft against the source, and rewrite it as needed until it accurately represents the original. Be careful not to use the source's language.
5. Check to be sure you haven't included your own ideas or opinions.
6. Document the paraphrase with the author's name, the title of the work, and publishing information, including page numbers for print sources.

Original

In terms of subtle opposition, they used Christianity as an instrument of psychological and communal resistance, attempting to preserve both their individual and collective well being.

From Rupe Simms. "Slave Christianity." *The Western Journal of Black Studies* 22.1 (1998): 55.

Paraphrase

The slaves used the religion taught to them to create a sense of community and of individuality, both of which helped them maintain healthy personal and social attitudes (Simms 55).

See page 178 for another example of paraphrase.

When Should You Quote?

Before using a quotation, you should be certain that the source is reliable and that the author you're quoting is credible.

- Quote when the author's exact language will support your ideas better than a paraphrase or summary of the information.
- Quote language that is striking or highly nuanced, allowing for multiple interpretations that you need to demonstrate for your readers.
- Quote if you plan to spend time analyzing the quotation in your own text.
- Quote when you need to demonstrate what other people feel or think about a subject.
- Quote highly respected authorities whose words speak directly to one of your main points.

How Do You Quote?

1. Read the source carefully to understand the context of the words you are thinking of quoting.
2. Copy the quotation exactly, making sure to transfer the words, capitalization, punctuation, and even any errors in the source. If the source author has quoted someone else, enclose that quotation in a pair of single quotation marks (' '). Enclose the entire quotation you're using in a pair of double quotation marks (" ").
3. Check the quotation against the source word by word to make sure they match exactly.
4. Do not insert any other words into the quotation unless you enclose them in brackets (▶ page 163).
5. Document the quotation fully, including page numbers for print sources.

Quotation Explained

(The sentence of explanation is highlighted.)

> People these days seem to respond to reality as if it were a TV show, especially when they face momentous events in their lives. In a CNN story about a tornado in Utah, here's what one witness reported: "As I'm watching, I'm watching it just tear the roof off Anderson Lumber . . . . It was like a Discovery Channel special on tornadoes." In our media-saturated world, we sometimes act as mere witnesses to our own lives, finding it more comfortable or manageable to respond to our own experience as if it were a TV show, something we might see on the Discovery Channel.

A **quotation** is the direct use of a source's words and punctuation, exactly as they appear in the source. A quotation that directly demonstrates or elaborates an important point is one of the most powerful ways of conveying information. Many readers appreciate direct quotations of outside sources because quotations act as a sort of witness, testifying precisely to the validity or poignancy of your own writing. Quotations show readers that you have paid close attention to your subject and what others have said about it. When you use quotations ethically, they add another voice supporting or strengthening your ideas, which can improve your credibility and garner your reader's trust, two critical prerequisites of informative and persuasive writing.

Explain Every Quotation

When you use a quotation of a sentence or more, you should be careful to explain to your reader what the quotation means to you. Often, writers presume that there's only one way to interpret a quotation, but readers may interpret the quotation differently. Typically, you should provide at least one sentence of explanation for every sentence of quoted material.

Make Relationships Clear

Introduce quotations so that their relevance is clear and their tone is consistent with your own writing. Readers are easily distracted when the tone or coherence of writing is broken, which can happen if the content or tone of quotations has no obvious relationship to the surrounding text. For instance, in the first example to the right, Stuart Larkin doesn't show how the information about "industry irregularities" relates to the behavior of fish owners.

Don't Quote Too Much

To preserve coherence, use only the relevant parts of a quotation. Quotations shouldn't make your points; they should only validate or explain them. Another kind of coherence problem arises when a quotation includes information that moves the topic in a direction you don't intend to pursue. Quote only what is necessary for your purposes.

See pages 164–165 for information on introducing quotations.

Irrelevant Quotation

Many fish owners pride themselves on the environments they lovingly create for their fish, many of which are considered pets in the same way that another owner might love a dog or cat. "Ninety percent of all stock expires in transport due to customary industry irregularities" (Calolora 42). The level of affection shown toward their fish can come as a surprise to many non–fish owners.

The quotation isn't related to the paragraph's topic sentence, and its tone is different from Larkin's, which is slightly less formal and concerned with showing readers the relationship that fish owners have with their pets. In the revised paragraph below, a new topic sentence and a frame for the quotation help the quotation function more effectively as support for the paragraph's new main idea, which is that loving pet owners would be shocked to learn how their pets are handled before they get to the store.

Revised Paragraph (New material is highlighted.)

The importation of goldfish into the United States is often accompanied by a less noticed mortality rate for the goldfish that would horrify consumers. The level of affection shown toward their fish can come as a surprise to many non–fish owners. Many fish owners pride themselves on the environments they lovingly create for their fish, many of which are considered pets in the same way that another owner might love a dog or cat. Yet no cat or dog owner would tolerate the awful facts surrounding how many fish are brought into the United States just so that people can have a few in their tank. Philip Calolora, an expert in the fish importation industry, describes the incredibly high rate of mortality suffered: "Ninety percent of all stock expires in transport due to customary industry irregularities" (42). While Calolora's explanation is somewhat masked in industry jargon, the shocking truth is plain. Given fish owners' bond with their pets, outreach and education should cause the fish-owner community to address and correct the system of importation that supports their hobby.

You can see how the quotation blends in more effectively when it is subordinated to the author's ideas and language. The quotation is now introduced and woven into Larkin's sentence, not just dropped in with no explanation.

Punctuation with Quotations

Period after parenthetical citation at end of short, integrated quotation:

. . . zero in on what really matters" (33-34).

Period before parenthetical citation at end of long, indented quotation:

. . . the last word. (157)

Comma inside the closing quotation mark:

Jack Wilson writes that Bill Clinton "missed his father," especially when he was a young man.

Semicolon outside the closing quotation mark:

Wilson does not seem to respect Bill Clinton, calling him "[a]n outright liar"; it is obvious that Wilson is biased politically.

Above, the brackets indicate that a capital letter in the original was changed to lowercase.

Question mark inside the quotation mark only because it's part of the quotation:

Robert C. Allen, then the head of the honors program at University of North Carolina at Chapel Hill, describes a conversation he had with a venture capitalist. Allen asked Lucius Burch, "What made a difference to you when you were a student at Carolina?" only to find that Burch hadn't been a highly motivated student (B16).

Single quotation marks for a quotation that appeared in the original:

"Serious thinkers from both camps [liberals and conservatives] spoke against the principle of popular sovereignty," notes Lukacs, "and against what Tocqueville called 'the tyranny of the majority'" (15).

Above, brackets indicate material added by the writer to explain "both camps."

Slash with space on each side used to separate lines of poetry in a short quotation:

In "Ode on a Grecian Urn," John Keats describes the artist as one "who canst thus express / A flowery tale more sweetly than our rhyme" (3-4).

The numbers in parentheses are line numbers.

Punctuate Quotations Properly

Short quotations are set off from the rest of the sentence by a pair of quotation marks (section 42a). Put periods and commas inside the quotation marks, and leave any other punctuation marks outside the quotation marks unless they appear in the quoted original. (See the Project Checklist on page 499.) A sentence that includes a short quotation ends after the parenthetical citation, not right after the quotation. For punctuation of poetry in MLA style, see page 183.

Long quotations (in MLA style, more than four lines of prose or three of poetry) are set off by indenting them from the left margin. No quotation marks are used. If quotations appear in the original, use double, not single, quotation marks when reproducing them. To introduce long quotations, you may want to use a full sentence followed by a colon to help your readers move smoothly from your introduction into the quotation. Use a colon only if a full sentence introduces the quotation. If you use a phrase instead, you may or may not need a comma after it (section 38c). In a long quotation, the parenthetical citation comes *after* the closing period of the quotation (page 184).

Use an Ellipsis to Indicate an Omission

It is often advantageous to leave out words or sentences from quotations. For example, if an author refers to a portion of her work that you will not include in the quotation, readers wouldn't understand the reference.

Whenever you remove words from a quotation, you should insert an ellipsis: . . . ; if the original already includes an ellipsis, then your ellipsis should be placed inside brackets to distinguish the two, according to MLA style: [. . .]. (For more examples, see section 43d.)

Examples of Ellipses

Ellipsis to indicate omission of material:

In a 1999 interview with Jacob Sullum and Michael Lynch, editors at *Reason,* economist John Lott said, "I was shocked by how poorly done the existing research on guns and crime was. . . . By far the largest previous study on guns and crime had looked at just 170 cities within a single year, 1980."

A period ends the first sentence, and then the three spaced dots of the ellipsis are given.

Ellipsis at end to show a sentence has been truncated:

Accompanying Paul Farmer on a trip to Matrosskaya Tishina (Moscow's Central Prison), Kidder found it easy to imagine getting thrown in jail: "In Russia just now, a young man could get thrown in jail for stealing a loaf of bread or a bottle of vodka . . ." (226).

Note that the period follows the citation. See more examples in section 43d.

Where Not to Use Ellipses

- **Ellipses are *not* used** to indicate that there are sentences before or after your quotation. Experienced readers bring a commonsense approach to quotations: they understand that something was written before and after the quotation you are using. However, **do** use an ellipsis at the end of a quotation to indicate that you have omitted part of the last sentence.
- **Ellipses are *not* used** to make a quotation say what you need said in your writing. If your quotation does not suit your needs, do not think that you have the liberty to change someone else's words to fit your purposes. Qualify the quotation by indicating that it supports just a portion of your idea, and then do further research to find other material to support your point. Using a quotation out of context not only misrepresents the intention of the original author, but also may harm your relationship with your readers if they know the original context of the quotation.

Examples of Brackets

Brackets used to alter the quotation so it will fit the grammar of the sentence:

In an appendix to the Anchor edition of *Under the Banner of Heaven*, Jon Krakauer wrote that "[b]ecause the Mormon leadership [was] so obsessed with controlling how the Mormon past was interpreted and presented, histories sanctioned by the LDS [tended] to be extensively censored" (364).

We can surmise from the use of brackets that, in the original, Krakauer used verbs in the present tense.

[Sic] used because correct title is "Ode on a Grecian Urn":

"Keats's 'Ode to [sic] a Grecian Urn' is a poem about the timelessness of truth and beauty" (Schultz 19).

What to Do about Sexist Language in Quoted Material

At times the material you wish to cite may contain sexist or other discriminatory language, as described in Chapter 29. The general rule is not to change the source material by correcting such language—not to substitute nonsexist terms in brackets. Readers will understand that the language is that of the original source. When you do correct the sexist language in a source, you draw attention to it and may distract the reader from your main point in using the information in the first place. If necessary, you can use a note to explain to the reader that the sexist or other discriminatory language appears in the original.

Use Brackets When You Alter a Quotation

Do not change or add anything to a quotation unless you indicate the change with brackets. For instance, if you need to capitalize a letter to use a quotation to start your sentence, then indicate the change by placing brackets around the capitalized letter. (See the brackets in the punctuation examples on page 161.) You may also use brackets to change the tense or point of view in the quotation—if, for instance, the author writes in the first person and you use the quotation to describe her in the third person. (For more examples of brackets, see section 43c.)

Use *[sic]* to Indicate Errors in the Original

On occasion, you will discover an error in spelling or grammar in the material you want to quote. When that happens, you can indicate your awareness of the error by inserting *sic* in brackets next to it. That way your reader understands that you haven't accidentally made the error yourself. Don't be overzealous, however. Make sure that there is an error in the original before you use *[sic]*, and if there are several errors, consider not using the quotation at all. After all, how reliable is it if it contains so many errors?

Use Verbs to Frame Source Material

The verbs you use to introduce and comment on source material reveal your attitude toward the information itself, its author, or its importance. When possible, choose a verb that describes the nature of the original author's assertion. For example, if an author is *predicting* a future event, say "Jones *predicts,*" not "Jones *says.*" Each verb lends a different emphasis or tone. Saying that an author "insists" on a point suggests that you do not agree or that the author's tone is aggressive; "suggests" reveals a more tentative stance on the part of the author.

Use Signal Phrases to Integrate Source Material

Signal phrases—such as "Susan Orleans writes that" and "Glazier disputed her interpretation by noting"—introduce and integrate source material into writing. It's usually more graceful to cite the author of a quotation in a signal phrase than to name him or her afterward in parentheses.

Verbs That Can Be Used to Frame Source Material

argues
asserts
believes
claims
concludes
considers
disagrees
discusses
emphasizes
explains
imagines
implies
indicates
notes
observes
offers
predicts
proposes
questions
reasons
refutes
remarks
reports
responds
says
shows
states
thinks
wonders

Examples of Sentences That Frame Source Material

Dr. M. Monica Sweeney asserts that "the health of the world depends on condoms" (Brody).

Bill Bryson observes that "[e]ven a long human life adds up to only about 650,000 hours" (2).

Jared Diamond defines *collapse* as a "a drastic decrease in human population size and/or political/economic/social complexity, over a considerable area, for an extended time" (3). He cautions that there is an "arbitrary" distinction inherent in using the word *drastic* in that definition (3).

Where to Name the Author: Two Variations

Smith-Johnson writes, "Being older is being in a situation where access to wisdom is granted more often" (35). MLA (see also page 182)

Aging has its benefits: "Being older is being in a situation where access to wisdom is granted more often" (Smith-Johnson 2005, p. 35). APA (see also page 245)

How to Identify the Author: Credentials

When you quote experts with distinguished credentials that might add to their credibility, provide the reader with a phrase that identifies their expertise:

Michael Hudson, Distinguished Professor of Economics at the University of Missouri, . . .

Lynne Truss, author of three novels and book reviewer for *The Sunday Times,* . . .

Wangari Maathai, noted environmentalist and winner of the Nobel Peace Prize, . . .

Including Signal Phrases to Make Prose Read Smoothly

(Signal phrases are highlighted.)

Malcolm Gladwell describes his idea as "the theory of thin slices" (23). By using very small amounts of information, experts in various fields are able to make remarkably accurate predictions about people's behavior. They throw out the irrelevant material that might overwhelm the lay person, says Gladwell, in order to focus on the thinner slice of what really matters. For example, psychologist John Gottman focuses on what he calls "the Four Horsemen" of emotions in order to decide whether a couple is likely to stay together or divorce—"defensiveness, stonewalling, criticism, and contempt" (qtd. in Gladwell 32). But he can slice thinner than that, saying that if he knows whether the partners show contempt for each other he can tell if their marriage is in trouble. Through the use of numerous case studies, Gladwell demonstrates why he believes in the power of the unconscious to "[sift] through the situation . . . [and] zero in on what really matters" (33-34).

Consider whether you should provide a phrase that gives the quoted person's credentials as a way of improving ethos. The opinion of an expert in the field you are discussing will carry more weight with readers than that of a person whose credentials are unidentified.

Introductions to long, indented quotations are often whole sentences punctuated at the end with a colon. For an example, see the indented quotation on page 184.

Vary the position of signal phrases in different sentences to aid readability.

In most contexts, plagiarism is understood to be a writer's deliberate misrepresentation of another's writing or ideas as his or her own. The principles and practices of academic integrity in your local environment will define plagiarism more precisely. As the contexts for your writing change and you communicate across fields with different groups of readers, the community's definition of sound research practice may change slightly. This can be true even at a college or university, where ethical standards for using information (or "intellectual property") may vary across different fields.

It's your responsibility as a writer to be aware of these issues and to ask questions when you're uncertain about the rules that define ethical academic conduct. You should review your own college's policies on plagiarism and academic honesty, which are usually published in the college catalog and on its website.

Take Care to Avoid Plagiarism

1. Read carefully.

Ideas precede our understanding of facts, although the overabundance of facts tends to obscure this. A fact can be comprehended only within the context of an idea. And ideas are irrevocably subjective, which makes facts just as subjective.

2. Take notes carefully.

Wurman states that "[a] fact can be comprehended only within the context of an idea" (31).

Wurman, Richard Saul. Information Anxiety 2. Indianapolis: Que, 2001.

Examples of Plagiarism

1. Reproducing another person's words, published or unpublished, as one's own;
2. Permitting another person to alter substantially one's written work;
3. Failing to acknowledge the ideas or words of another person, including verbatim use of another's words without proper documentation or paraphrasing of another's words without proper documentation;
4. Using material from the World Wide Web, Internet, videos, encyclopedias, books, magazines, newspapers, and student papers without indicating where the material was found.

From Southern State Community College, "Academics," at www.sscc.edu/Academics/academic_misconduct.htm.

3. Use source information carefully.

Richard Saul Wurman notes that facts are subjective because they are always understood "within the context of an idea"; and ideas are always subjective (31).

OR

Each person screens reality through his or her own perceptions and beliefs. In the context of information delivery, Richard Saul Wurman agrees, stating that "[a] fact can be comprehended only within the context of an idea" (31).

Global Contexts

Many students who have lived in different parts of the world find the idea of common knowledge confusing because information that is common knowledge in one part of the world may not be common knowledge in another. Common knowledge, as a concept, refers to the shared knowledge of your intended audience rather than just any group of people outside of a particular context. A group of people somewhere might know, for instance, all the procedures for currency devaluation by the World Bank, but if you're writing to an audience who doesn't, then you need to cite the sources of your information. In cases where you offer evidence and support but do not cite the source of your information, be certain that the information is common knowledge for your audience.

In many definitions of plagiarism, the concept of *common knowledge* is used to determine what source information needs to be cited; if an idea is "common knowledge," then it doesn't need to be cited. But it's not always easy to determine what material falls in the domain of common knowledge. Here's how we define the concept:

> Knowledge is "common knowledge" when it's widely shared and known among a group of people and is a matter of the historical or factual record that no one would contest.

As researchers, we often communicate to diverse audiences that may not share the same body of common knowledge, hence the challenge of deciding what information needs to be attributed to a source and what information we can assume is widely known. Furthermore, if what you know with certainty is not common knowledge, then according to our definition of plagiarism, you still need to attribute it to a source (even when that source is your own experience). Sometimes information that is new to you falls within the scope of common knowledge, in which case citing it would be inappropriate.

If you understand why we don't cite common knowledge, you'll find it easier to judge for yourself whether information needs to be attributed to a source. In research writing, we cite sources to show how our own ideas are consistent with or contrast with those of other researchers—the place of our research in the larger conversation on knowledge. We also cite sources to express verifiability, which is one criterion for evaluating whether statements have validity. We want to show how new knowledge is constructed on existing knowledge. To ensure the assent of the community of readers, we want to establish that we're using information that others also deem to be credible.

When information falls in the realm of common knowledge, there's no need to reassert its credibility because people already believe it to be true. Common knowledge is often *uncontestable,* in other words. Since readers already presume common knowledge to be true, attributing common-knowledge

What Is Common Knowledge?

Here are some categories of information usually considered to be common knowledge, even though in some cases the information seems rather esoteric.

Dates of events in history

July 20, 1969

Well-known phrases

"All men are created e

Definitions of nonspecialize

philosophy

Greek *philos* (loving) + *sophia* (

The etymology of *philosop*

Geographical information

Lake Tahoe straddles Nevada and California.

Names of people

Mahatma Gandhi

Genealogies

Princess Margaret
1930–2002
m. Anthony, Earl of Snowdon

David, Viscount Linley b. 1961	Lady Sarah Armstrong-Jones b. 1964

English royal lineage

Information gathered through the senses

The moon appears red during a lunar eclipse.

material to a source (such as an encyclopedia or dictionary) actually harms the author's ethos; it implicitly suggests that the author and readers don't already share such knowledge, or that it can be contested in the first place. Citing common knowledge has the rhetorical effects of boring readers and inviting them to question the author's level of awareness regarding what the community already knows to be true. Furthermore, we don't cite common knowledge in academic writing because doing so would make the task of sharing new information impossibly complex.

As you can tell, there will still be instances when it's difficult to decide whether factual information falls in the realm of common knowledge. When you're uncertain about the information you are drawing from a source, you should cite the source. Over time, you will gain experience judging what information is common knowledge; early in the process, it's better to be safe than sorry.

12g Plagiarism and Academic Integrity in Context

The following table answers common questions that may arise in different contexts. As a rule, if you are unsure whether to cite a source, go ahead and cite it.

Writing Context and Possible Questions	How to Avoid Plagiarism
COLLABORATIVE PROJECTS How much help can I accept? What kind of help can I accept? How much credit should I give when someone gives me an idea? When someone does some writing?	■ Follow your instructor's guidelines for tracking and reporting individuals' contributions. ■ If yours is the only author name, this means that you have done all the writing, even though you may have benefited from advice, written feedback, and pointed questions from friends or writing center tutors. ■ If others have written part of the project, they need to be listed as co-authors. ■ If others have contributed ideas but not writing, they need to be cited as research sources. (But see "Ideas a Friend Gives You" on page 171 for help.) ■ If you need extra collaboration or help in an area that chronically troubles you, ask your instructor for assistance.
SOMEONE ELSE'S EXACT LANGUAGE You have cut and pasted information from the Internet or email, or you have copied quotations into your notes from sources at the library. Do I have to cite the sources? What kinds of publication information must I note? How can I keep my sources' ideas and my own ideas distinct?	■ You must cite all quotations. See pages 176–177 for examples of cited and uncited quotations. ■ Include all source information in your notes: author, title, and publication information—location, publisher, date, page numbers (if applicable), and URL and date of access (if applicable). ■ Put all the text you cut and paste inside quotation marks. ■ Every time you integrate a quotation into your own writing, put the author's last name and the page number in parentheses at the end of the quotation. If you are using more than one work by the same author, include a short title. If you have two authors with the same last name, add their initials so you'll remember which author a quotation is from.

Writing Context and Possible Questions	How to Avoid Plagiarism
CHANGING "JUST ENOUGH" How much do I have to change to make the material my own, to avoid citing it? Where in my work do I cite a source?	▪ It is plagiarism to alter a source's phrasing slightly and then integrate the material into your work without citation. Any deliberate attempt to blur the distinction between your ideas and those of your source is plagiarism. You should consider quoting if the source's language is so memorable that you want it in your essay. ▪ The placement of your parenthetical citation is crucially important. Every sentence that includes a quotation must have at least a page number in parentheses before the sentence ends; if the author's name hasn't appeared recently, the last name should be in parentheses there, too. Every summary and paraphrase must be documented. ▪ When you place a parenthetical citation, you are signaling to your reader that this point is the end of another person's ideas and the resumption of your thinking. Don't make the mistake of placing the citation too early, making it appear that later ideas in your work originated with you when in fact they are another author's. To avoid this kind of plagiarism, compare the original idea to your use of the source, word for word, to ensure that your ideas grow out of the other person's ideas but are not repetitions of them.
IDEAS A FRIEND GIVES YOU Suppose you are working on a position paper concerning diesel emissions and air pollution. A friend tells you that she read something on how types of respiratory distress (such as asthma) might develop around urban areas where diesel engines are used the most. Should I cite my friend? Is that good enough?	▪ We strongly encourage you to discuss your projects with others; academic writing almost always emerges from discussion, consideration, and revision. You'll often get good ideas from discussions you have, and that is fine. ▪ If you believe that the idea about a connection among diesel fumes, urban areas, and respiratory distress is worth including, then you need to cite the author of the original research, which means you have to find it. This might seem like a lot of trouble, but if the idea is a good one, it will be worth the effort. ▪ You do not need to cite the person who suggested the idea to you, but if the idea is critical to your project, it wouldn't be a bad practice to thank the person for the input in a footnote or endnote, as often happens in published academic articles and in the acknowledgments section in a book.

Writing Context and Possible Questions	How to Avoid Plagiarism
IDEAS SIMILAR TO THE IDEA YOU HAD If I have an idea, but then I find someone else has had a very similar idea, do I need to cite the outside source? Why?	▪ It is certainly conceivable that your good ideas have been thought by someone else previously. ▪ Even if you've never read anything about your subject, it's your obligation as an academic writer to research ideas and review existing information when you are in a situation where you need to develop theories of your own or analyze the ideas of others. If you find information that is similar to what you have developed, then cite it. ▪ By citing similar ideas, you are indicating that the idea is so worthy of consideration that other people have published research about it also.
NUMERICAL AND STATISTICAL DATA How do I cite research that I conducted? How do I cite other people's research? Do I need to cite another person's research when I just duplicated it and got the same results?	▪ If you write, "Seventy percent of my friends have tried junk food but have not become addicted," you are reporting data entirely attributable to you because you conducted the research. There is no need to cite this category of data unless you previously published the research. ▪ If you write, "Seventy percent of adults from 18 to 25 have tried junk food without becoming addicted," clearly someone else has done the research and needs to be cited in your writing. ▪ If you know of existing research on the effects of eating junk food and then conduct your own survey, you should cite the original research. If you know that another study proved exactly or even essentially what you are attempting to prove and you have used this research as a foundation or starting point for your own, cite the original. Doing so will add credence to your findings.

Writing Context and Possible Questions	How to Avoid Plagiarism
DUPLICATE SUBMISSION If I wrote an assignment for another class, can I turn it in again for a different class? Can I rewrite it and turn it in?	■ If you write an assignment for one class and then submit it as new work for another class without the prior approval of your instructor, that's a form of academic dishonesty. However, you may pursue the same ideas in different disciplines, looking, for instance, at the ramifications of gender inequity in society in different classes as you progress through your studies. You may even develop a specialization if you pursue ideas with that level of rigor and enthusiasm, and your specialization may become something that your school, family, and friends take pride in. ■ Sometimes teachers will allow you to revise or modify work produced previously or elsewhere, but in every case you should be absolutely clear about the origins of your work. ■ The following tips will help you to avoid misrepresenting your work and to make existing ideas fresh once again: ***Reexamine familiar secondary sources.*** Even if you feel that you know the secondary source by heart or if you find yourself relying on the same quotation again and again as evidence, reread your sources. You are likely to find some aspect that is especially relevant to your current work. ***Keep up with publications in your area of interest.*** Staying current with scholarship in your area of interest will give you the opportunity to connect the theories you are learning about with the theories you encountered in earlier classes. ***Never cut and paste anything from a previous assignment,*** even if it would be convenient. Revisit your sources instead and rewrite the evidence and the bibliographies. Your writing will likely come out much better the second time around. ***Ask your instructor.*** Don't ask the instructor whether you can simply write the same paper for different classes, which would be insulting. Instead, mention that you completed a research project in another course that you now want to pursue further. Ask the instructor how you can tailor that research interest in ways that will meet the goals of your current course.

Writing Context and Possible Questions	How to Avoid Plagiarism
CITATION INFORMATION ISN'T AVAILABLE What if I can't find the publication information that I am supposed to include?	■ Consider not using the source at all. If it can't be attributed to an author or organization or if there's no telling when it was published, then it may be unreliable information. Unconfirmed sources are never very persuasive, as you know if you've read tabloids. ■ There are occasions when some aspects of information are simply unavailable. For instance, some websites fail to provide information about date of publication, authorship, or copyright. But suppose you still want to use the source? Ultimately, you just may not find the information you need in order to construct a proper citation. All the citation styles have a procedure for indicating that some source information is unavailable. (See section 13b for MLA and 14b for APA.) If you have confirmed that the information you need doesn't exist, then consult the appropriate style manual (in print or on the Web), ask your instructor, or consult with a writing tutor. ■ **Don't** attempt either of these ad hoc solutions, which are violations of basic academic integrity: ***Do not insert false information.*** Clearly, researchers do a disservice to readers and violate their ethical responsibilities as citizens in a social process of inquiry if they falsify information. For professionals, the penalties for doing so can be severe. Student writers will find that if citation information appears obviously wrong to their readers, their credibility (ethos) will be seriously compromised. ***Do not fail to take the time to track down citation information.*** If you create false citation information or claim that the information is unavailable because you do not have time to prepare an accurate bibliography, your readers will judge your writing harshly. ■ Many readers of academic writing thumb immediately to the bibliography as a method of assessing the quality of the research as a whole. The bibliography for a research project should never be an afterthought, but its foundation.

Writing Context and Possible Questions	How to Avoid Plagiarism
AIDING IN THE MISUSE OF INFORMATION What do I do if a friend wants to copy my work? How can I protect my documents on a publicly accessible computer?	■ In college or high school, where the pressure to succeed is high and time is often short, you may have heard sob stories from desperate friends with deadlines to meet and no way of meeting them. Allowing another person to copy your work or aiding in the misuse of information is just as unethical as copying or misusing it yourself. It may not be plagiarism, but it will certainly be considered a violation of academic honesty policies. ■ Be careful to protect your own documents. If you write a paper on someone else's computer or a publicly accessible computer, don't leave the file on the computer—or, at the very least, protect the file with a password. Most word processing programs allow authors to protect documents in this way. ■ If you find you have been put in a tough situation by a peer, consider responding in one of the following ways: ***Encourage the person to discuss the problem with the instructor to see if a solution can be negotiated.*** In most cases, discussion with the instructor will yield a painless solution. Most writing instructors are eager to assist students when they're in tight spots. ***Provide some tutoring or refer the writer to a writing center.*** It's okay to tutor a friend, but one of the cardinal rules of tutoring is that you shouldn't do the work for the person, which prevents learning and thus does a disservice in the end.

As you can see from the list of questions researchers have about using source material, there are well-defined rules for using sources ethically. It may take some time to absorb all the rules; do your best to learn them thoroughly. Talk to your instructor or a writing center tutor any time you aren't clear on how to proceed.

Here is an excerpt from a *New York Times* article on Web logs. Read it and then study the examples of misuses and effective uses of this source.

New York Times,
October 23, 2003

Blog Bog and an Email Pony Express

Pamela LiCalzi O'Connell

Are Web logs more fizzle than sizzle? A recent study by Perseus Development, a research firm and maker of software for surveys, finds that fully 66 percent of the 4.12 million blogs, or online journals, created on eight leading blog-hosting services have been "abandoned"—that is, not updated for at least two months. And 1.09 million of those were one-day wonders.

The study went on to puncture other bits of common wisdom about blogs, like the frequency with which they are updated. Fewer than 50,000 of the sites in the study were updated every day. As for the notion that most blogs comment on the news, only 9.9 percent had a main-page posting that linked to a traditional news site. Perhaps most biting, the study

Proper Citation of Source

Reference to publisher

Title of article

A recent *New York Times* article, "Blog Bog and an Email Pony Express," cites a study by Perseus Development showing that 1.09 million of the current blogs now published on the Internet were created and then abandoned after only one day (O'Connell).

Information drawn from article (and not common knowledge)

Parenthetical citation of author of the article (MLA style). Note that there is no page number listed because the source is online. The URL will be listed in the Works Cited under the entry for "O'Connell."

Failure to Cite Source

Of the current blogs now published on the Internet, 1.09 million were created and then abandoned after only one day.

This information clearly comes from the source and needs to be cited. Readers know that information like this stems from formal research.

Changing the Information Slightly and Failing to Cite the Source

Of the current blogs now published on the Internet, a million were created and then abandoned after only one day.

This information clearly comes from the source and needs to be cited. Readers know that information like this stems from formal research and needs to be cited.

Misleading Citation Information

Of the current blogs now published on the Internet, 1.09 million were created and then abandoned after only one day (Perseus Development).

This citation is misleading. It suggests that the Perseus research was cited directly, when actually O'Connell cited the research in her article.

Properly Cited Indirect Source

Original source of the statement is named

Even though many blogs are abandoned after just one day, the story, according to Jeffrey Henning, is "how many people are trying blogs, not how many are giving up" (qtd. in O'Connell).

Use indirect citations sparingly, but when you do, MLA recommends this format.

This is an indirect quotation because O'Connell cited it in her article.

Using Quotation Marks without Documenting the Source

Even though many blogs are abandoned after just one day, the story is "how many people are trying blogs, not how many are giving up."

Clearly, someone has been quoted here and should be cited.

Inaccurate Attribution of Source to Another Person

Even though many blogs are abandoned after one day, the story is "how many people are trying blogs, not how many are giving up" (O'Connell).

This citation is inaccurate because it implies that O'Connell made the statement when Henning actually did.

found that the typical blog is written by a teenage girl who uses it twice a month to update her friends. Are blogs just that old friend from the 90's, the Web diary, dressed up in new tools?

The answer is yes and no. Perseus itself offers some significant caveats to its study. For one, only blogs on blog-hosting services like LiveJournal were studied. Blogs maintained by individuals on their own servers were not included, and one could argue that the most influential blogs fall in that category.

"This study is like a Rorschach test," said Jeffrey Henning, chief operating officer of Perseus. "Some people see it as dismissive of blogs. I look at it and see an incredibly accessible technology. The story is how many people are trying blogs, not how many are giving up."

From Pamela LiCalzi O'Connell, Online Diary, "Blog Bog and an Email Pony Express," *New York Times,* 23 Oct. 2003, 12 Sept. 2005 <http://www.nytimes.com/>.

New York Times,
October 23, 2003

Blog Bog and an Email Pony Express

Pamela LiCalzi O'Connell

Are Web logs more fizzle than sizzle? A recent study by Perseus Development, a research firm and maker of software for surveys, finds that fully 66 percent of the 4.12 million blogs, or online journals, created on eight leading blog-hosting services have been "abandoned"—that is, not updated for at least two months. And 1.09 million of those were one-day wonders.

Effective Paraphrase of First Paragraph

The expressive "fizzle" and "sizzle" have been paraphrased.

The verb "ask" reveals that O'Connell began with a question.

Pamela LiCalzi O'Connell asks in a *New York Times* article whether Web logs fail more often than they succeed. Perseus Development just completed a survey that revealed that 66 percent of the 4.12 million blogs that were posted on the eight most popular blog-hosting services had not been revised for a minimum of two months. Of that 66 percent, 1.09 million were forgotten by their authors after a single day ("Blog Bog").

The writer keeps the percentage exactly as in the original (66 percent) to avoid misrepresenting data. The writer could do the math to figure out how many million 66 percent of 4.12 million would equal (2.72 million) if a number would be more appropriate. There is no logical way to paraphrase an exact number such as 4.12 million. If precision were not important, the whole phrase could be paraphrased more vaguely as "well over 60 percent of the four million."

The citation gives only a short title since the article was posted online and thus does not have a page number. The author is named in the first sentence.

Ineffective Paraphrase That Fails to Cite Quotations from the Source

This phrase needs to be enclosed in quotation marks to show that it is a direct quotation.

Pamela LiCalzi O'Connell asks in a *New York Times* article whether Web logs are more fizzle than sizzle. A recent survey by Perseus Development, a research firm and software maker for surveys, notes that a full 66 percent of blogs, that is, online journals, posted on eight leading blog-hosting services, have been abandoned. They hadn't been updated for at least two months. And 1.09 million were "one-day wonders."

Some words here come directly from the source or are recast only slightly and need to be enclosed in quotation marks. Compare with the original. The sentence also includes source information that may not be critical, such as that about Perseus Development.

MLA Documentation

PART 4

>

New Contexts for Writing: Podcasting Music, Film, and Video Game Reviews

You may soon be listening to podcasts of course lectures or producing and broadcasting your own audio content—and you won't need expensive equipment or complicated software to do it. If you like to review new music, movies, or video games, now you can share your reviews with others, just as you would if you hosted your own radio show. Your reviews—if they're engaging and thoughtful—might be heard by more people than watch the nightly news on television.

Podcasting, which first became popular in 2004, refers to the process of recording audio programs—music, lectures, readings, radio shows, interviews, and more—and then preparing them for distribution on the Internet. Podcasting involves recording an **MP3** file using a digital audio recorder or a computer with a microphone and sound editing software like Audacity (audacity.sourceforge.net) or Apple GarageBand™. The MP3 file (a common file format for audio) can then be uploaded to a free hosting service like Ourmedia.org.

Podcast files are distributed through syndicators like Podcast.net and services like Apple's iTunes® and can be easily accessed with podcast aggregator software (called **podcatchers**) like iPodder, Ziepod, or iTunes. Using an iPod® or another MP3 player, users can subscribe to **feeds** that will automatically update the list of available podcasts as they are published elsewhere.

With the emergence of Apple's video-playing iPod, podcasting may now include the syndication of video content also.

Writing Good Reviews

When you write, speak, or publish content for a public audience, you need to consider and define your audience, develop content that will be interesting, and bear in mind that your words and images have consequences for others.

Good reviews of music, film, and video games do more than summarize and analyze. They situate the subject of the review in its historical context (its predecessors), relate it to other familiar works, analyze its strengths and weaknesses, and take a position on whether it's worth listening to, watching, or playing. Script your podcast reviews as carefully as you would any other public document.

Podcast Clearinghouses

Podcast.net
http://podcast.net

IGN Entertainment (music, movies, and video games)
http://www.ign.com/index/podcasts.html

Only Connect . . .

The Link between the In-Text Citation and the Work Cited Entry

In-text citation of a work:

> Jones 3
>
> Hosseini has his protagonist, Amir, describe finding out how the Hazaras had been mistreated by the Pashtuns: "my people had killed the Hazaras, driven them from their lands, . . . and sold their women" (9).

Notice in the in-text citation:

- Both the author's last name and the page number of the quotation are given.
- The quotation is placed inside a pair of quotation marks.
- The page number is placed inside parentheses.
- The sentence ends after the in-text citation. The period follows the last parenthesis.

Also consult . . .
Chapter 9 on thinking about the research project
Chapters 10 and 11 on finding and evaluating information
Chapter 12 on integrating sources and avoiding plagiarism

Work Cited entry:

> Jones 6
>
> Work Cited
>
> Hosseini, Khaled. *The Kite Runner*. New York: Riverhead, 2003. Print.

Notice in the Work Cited entry:

- The author's last name is used to alphabetize the entry. A comma separates the author's last name from the first name. A period follows.
- The book title is italicized. A period follows.
- The publication information includes the city of publication, followed by a colon; the name of the publisher, followed by a comma; the year of publication, followed by a period; and the medium of publication. A period follows to end the entry.
- The first line of an entry starts at the left margin, but the second and subsequent lines are indented 1/2" from the left margin. (This is called a *hanging indentation.*)

The citation style recommended by the Modern Language Association (MLA) is used to cite sources in the fields of English, rhetoric and composition, foreign languages, and literature. If you major in one of these fields, you may want to examine a copy of the *MLA Handbook for Writers of Research Papers,* 7th edition (New York: MLA, 2009).

The MLA style includes two basic components: (1) citations of summaries, paraphrases, and quotations given inside parentheses in the body of the text and (2) an alphabetically organized Works Cited page at the end of the text, which provides the author, title, and publication details for each source used. The two components work hand in hand. The information that appears in your in-text citation leads readers to the corresponding entry in the Works Cited list. Typically, the author's last name is the link.

MLA INDEXES

Parenthetical in-text citations should include the minimum amount of information—usually the author's last name and the relevant page number(s). That information helps the reader locate the source in the Works Cited list and then track down the precise location of the quoted material in the original source.

You have two choices about how to identify the source of the quotation (or paraphrase or summary):

- Use the author's name in your introduction to the quotation, in which case you place just the page number of the source in the parenthetical citation.
- Introduce the quotation without the author's name and then, before the sentence ends, place the author's last name and the page number of the source in parentheses.

Two Ways to Identify the Source in the Text

Author's name in introduction:

King 5

In her remarkable autobiography, Harriet Jacobs writes that slavery was "demeaning to everyone involved in its vile operation" (124).

- The first time the author's name is used in an introduction to source material, the first and last names are often included.
- Be sure to include page numbers when taking notes from a source.

Author's name in parentheses:

King 5

Slavery was described by a former slave as "demeaning to everyone involved in its vile operation" (Jacobs 124).

- Even though the author's last name is not used in the introduction, the writer has included a phrase that identifies the author of the quotation: "a former slave." This phrase gives the quotation added impact, since its author was a participant in the subject she is evaluating.
- No comma is used between the author's name and the page number within the parentheses.
- If the author of the work you are citing is anonymous or if you are using more than one work by the same author, include an abbreviated version of the title. (See citation model 7 on page 187.)

Short Quotations

When you use a prose quotation of four or fewer of your lines (or a quotation of poetry that includes three or fewer lines of the poem), incorporate it as seamlessly as possible into your own sentence. Use quotation marks before the first word and after the last word of the quoted material to separate it from your text. Place the citation as close as possible to the material being quoted, either at a natural break in the sentence or at the end of it.

Remember that the sentence ends *after* the parenthetical information, so the period goes after the closing parenthesis, not within the last quotation mark. The exception to this rule is when your quotation ends with an exclamation point or a question mark. In this case, the punctuation mark stays within the quotation marks, and then you add the parenthetical citation followed by a period.

If you are quoting two or three lines of poetry, use a slash with a space on either side after each line to show the reader where the lines of poetry break. The citation gives the line numbers you are citing.

End punctuation after citation in short quotation:

Cervantes 2

Michael J. Fox describes his experiences with Parkinson's disease as "a situation of daily life that can seem both tragic and humorous at once" (196).

? or ! within the quotation:

Maclin 3

Most music reviewers have the same question about Vanilla Ice, the 1980s rapper with no street credibility: "Did he appropriate another culture's traditions when he began using the call and response rhythm of hip hop?" (Oakwood 101).

Slashes with spaces to indicate where lines of poetry break:

Hall 4

Coleridge's "Kubla Khan" demonstrates the use of inverted sentence structure: "In Xanadu did Kubla Khan / A stately pleasure dome decree" (1-2).

Long Quotations

When a quotation takes five or more of your lines, omit the quotation marks, indent the entire quotation 1" (or 10 typewriter spaces) from the left margin, and double-space the lines just as you have in the rest of the paper. Often, an entire sentence, followed by a colon, is used to introduce a long quotation. The parenthetical citation is given after the last punctuation mark of the block quotation, with one space between them.

Whenever you use a block quotation, a careful explanation of its purpose or meaning is called for. While you should explain the significance of all uses of source material, a block quotation in particular requires ample discussion so readers understand why you found the material important enough to quote at length.

If you are quoting from a single paragraph, do not indent the first line even if it is the first line of the source's paragraph. If more than one paragraph is quoted, indent each paragraph an additional 1/4" (or 3 typed spaces) from the indented left margin.

Hackman 7

McRobbie describes the punk rock phenomenon as mainly a consumer event:

> Punk was, first and foremost, cultural. Its self-expressions existed at the level of music, graphic design, visual images, style and the written word. It was therefore engaging with and making itself heard within the terrain of the arts and the mass media. . . . In the realm of style, the same do-it-yourself ethic prevailed and the obvious place to start was the local flea market. (198)

McRobbie's sense of the consumer ethic of punk differs from many cultural critiques of newer art and music movements. While purchasing the right kinds of clothing was essential for the punk fan, the main concept of consumerism was ironically ignored as punk's visionaries clothed themselves in used and vintage fashions.

Many writers use block quotations when a brief paraphrase or summary would achieve the same goal. Some mistakenly use block quotations simply to meet length requirements. Extensive use of block quotations may indicate that a writer is not using sources economically (that is, using brief examples from them to illustrate key points) or that the writer doesn't have much to say. If you are wondering about whether to use a long quotation, ask the following questions:

- Can you summarize the essential points instead of quoting them directly (◀ section 12a)?
- Can you use ellipses to cut out parts of the quotation that are not absolutely essential (◀ section 12c)?
- Can you integrate the source's ideas more smoothly into your prose while also clearly citing the source (◀ section 12d)?

MLA In-Text Citation Models

1. Author named in your text

> Marsh tells us that the term "'Hooligan' derives from the name 'Houlihan,' a noticeably anti-social Irish family in nineteenth-century east London" (335).

The first time you use an author's name in your text, it's customary to use the first and last name. Then in subsequent references, such as the one above, you would use just the last name.

Notice that the original source included quotation marks already. Since the writer had to put all the source material in quotation marks, the ones from the original are changed to single quotation marks to distinguish them.

2. Author not named in your text

> The term "'Hooligan' derives from the name 'Houlihan,' a noticeably anti-social Irish family in nineteenth-century east London" (Marsh 335).

Readers will see the author's last name in parentheses, which cues them to the entry in the Works Cited list.

3. No author's or editor's name

Sometimes you may use a source that has no author or editor. Refer to it by title in the body of your text, or shorten the title to one or more words in a parenthetical citation, but make sure the first word is the same one you use when you alphabetize the title in your Works Cited list.

> In the article "Running and Health," a daily workout is described as "a mundane activity that generates health" (21).

MLA In-Text Citations Index

Or you could write

> A daily workout is described as "a mundane activity that generates health" ("Running and Health" 21).

Notice that no comma is used between the title and the page number.

4. Two or three authors

Write the authors' names in the order in which they appear in the source. For the first reference in your text to two authors, use their first and last names; if there are more than two, you may want to use just last names. With two names, use the conjunction *and* between the authors' names:

> Trent Collins and Andrea Junkins describe the academic experience as a form of "systematic hazing" (31).

When there are three or more authors, punctuate the names like a series, with a comma after each name and the conjunction *and* between the last two names:

> Hollis, Johnson, and Ruotolo note that "binge drinking has emerged as the number one concern of university administrators" (111).

5. Four or more authors

When your source has four or more authors, you can either list them all as they appear in the source or use the first author's name followed by *et al.* (an abbreviation for the Latin term *et alii,* meaning "and others"). Note that there is no period after *et,* but there is a period after *al.*

> Some writers express discomfort at the label "poor" (Blinn et al. 119), preferring instead the expression "economically challenged" (Blinn et al. 120).

6. Two or more authors with the same last name

When you use two or more authors with the same last name as sources, use their first initials in your parenthetical citations to identify which one you are referring to. In the unlikely situation where the first initials are the same, use their middle initials also or the full name if no middle initial is available.

> Open houses were used to keep English language tutors motivated (J. Scott 1). As is pointed out in "Volunteer Motivation," it's crucial for refugees to build a network of reliable support, and one way to help achieve this goal is to ensure that volunteers serving a particular family continue volunteering (M. Scott 14).

7. More than one source by the same author

When you cite more than one source by the same author or authors, you should place a comma after the author's last name, shorten the title of the source, and insert that shortened title after the last name and before the page number or numbers—without a comma between the last two items.

> (Foucault, *Discipline* 198-202)
> (Foucault, *History* 32)

If you use the name of the author in the in-text citation, simply place the shortened title and page number or numbers in the parenthetical citation—with no comma between the two items.

> Foucault writes, "The Panopticon is a machine for dissociating the see/being seen dyad" (*Discipline* 201-02).

If you use the author's name and the shortened or full title in the introduction to your quotation, then use only the page number or numbers in the parenthetical citation.

MLA In-Text Citations Index

MLA In-Text Citations Index

8. Corporate author or government publication

When you cite a source with a corporate author or one written by a governmental entity, use the standard conventions. Treat the entity that wrote or sponsored the creation of the source as the author, and name it either in the parenthetical citation or in the introduction.

> The Federal Emergency Management Agency describes most toxic waste situations as "controllable and not a major problem to the nearby corporations" (22).

9. Two or more sources in the same citation

If you need to cite several sources in your parenthetical reference, include the author's last name and the page number or numbers for each, with a semicolon dividing the citations:

> (Highsmith 212; Hockley 23-45; McGrath 110-11)

Your readers might find this kind of in-text citation disruptive, so consider using an endnote. Don't forget to include the entries for these citations, as you would the entry for any other in-text citation, on your Works Cited page.

10. The entire work

To cite a complete work, use the author or other creator's name in the text rather than in parentheses:

> Allison's *Bastard Out of Carolina* provoked horrified tears and feelings of betrayal.

A work that does not have any page numbers can be referred to in this manner as well.

11. Multivolume work

If your source is from a work that includes multiple volumes, then your citation needs to direct readers to the correct volume. Between the author's last name and the page number or numbers, insert the volume number (as a numeral) with a colon after it—dividing it from the page number(s).

> "Truth is a fickle creature" (Wellman 2: 134).

Alternatively, you could write

> Wellman writes, "Truth is a fickle creature" (2: 134).

12. Source from an anthology or other collection

When your source is a text in an anthology or other collection compiled by an editor, use the author's name and the title in the text and the editor and the page number in the parenthetical reference:

> Walker's ode to womanism, "In Our Mothers' Gardens," fully elaborates upon her beliefs that gender and race create more new conditions of identity than previously realized (Moon 47).

(For correct citation in the Works Cited list, see citation model 9 on page 198.)

13. Literary source such as play, novel, or poem

When you cite literary sources, realize that they often come in several editions, so it is considerate to provide more information than just the author and page number to make sure readers can locate the information. Start by giving the page number, followed by a semicolon. Then you might include the chapter number or, in a poem, the stanza number. Use abbreviations for these parts of the text:

pt. for part	bk. for book	sc. for scene
ch. for chapter	sec. for section	st. for stanza

MLA In-Text Citations Index

MLA In-Text Citations Index

> Modern poets such as e.e. cummings always enjoyed what he called "the fortunate situation literature and poetry occupy in this culture" (22; st. 2, line 4).

Certain conventions and abbreviations are used for classic works. For example, the plays of Shakespeare each have a standard abbreviation; the one below refers to *Hamlet*. The act, scene, and line numbers are given, with periods in between.

> Shakespeare writes, "To be or not to be—that is the question" (*Ham.* 3.1.64).

14. Sacred book

When you cite a sacred book like the Bible, the Talmud, the Vedas, or the Koran, do not italicize the title. Provide the specific part of the book from which the quotation comes.

> According to the Bible, "Any . . . foreigner among you who blasphemes the Lord's name will surely die" (Lev. 24.16).

When you create the Works Cited entry, provide as much detailed information about the specific edition as possible.

15. Indirect source

Try to avoid using indirect sources. Instead, using information from the indirect source's Works Cited page or bibliography, locate the original source, verify the quotation, and then cite the original source. However, if you must include indirect sources, insert *qtd. in* in the parenthetical citation immediately before the author's last name—the author, that is, of the indirect source.

> The Dalai Lama says, "Holiness is a state of grace equivalent to any other kind of acting; it is a charade" (qtd. in Perry 244).

16. Electronic source with an author, title, and page numbers

When you cite electronic sources that have the standard author, title, and page numbers, follow the same conventions as you would for an equivalent printed text:

> In his online book *Modern Mystics*, Smith describes alchemy as "a modern science with ancient roots" (22).

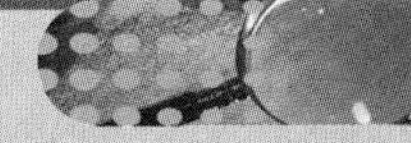

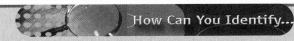

How Can You Identify...

The Author of a Web Page?

Inexperienced researchers may think that a Web page does not have an author if the author's name is not readily available. To locate an author's name, look for a "contact us" or "about us" link in the site navigation or at the bottom of the home page.

If you want to cite a single page inside a larger site, return to the home page by erasing the last parts of the URL in your browser's address bar. For instance, if you are at a page whose URL is http://mybandaids.tripod.com/bandaid_index.htm, you might "back up" to http://mybandaids.tripod.com to find more information about the site.

Don't include a URL in your parenthetical documentation unless your text is electronic and you are creating a hyperlink.

17. Electronic source with numbered paragraphs

Some electronic sources use numbered paragraphs, which can be a great convenience for anyone who wants to locate the information on a lengthy Web page, for instance. In this case, cite the paragraph number in the parenthetical citation, preceded by *par.*:

> Octavia Deft, in her comprehensive website on modern dance, calls ballet "just so much courtesy and manners on sets of well-clad feet" (par. 17).

MLA In-Text Citations Index

MLA In-Text Citations Index

18. Electronic source without page or paragraph numbers

At times, the only information you will be able to glean from an electronic source such as a website will be the author's name and the work's title. Never use the URL as an in-text or parenthetical citation unless you want to create a hyperlink in an electronic document. Instead, use the information you have, beginning with the author's name and then the title.

> Sensenbrenner expresses doubt about "the road ahead for politics as usual, given the damage partisanship has already caused" (*Political Roundtable*).

We strongly caution you about sources for which you can't obtain basic information. Do everything you can to find out who has posted the material and what level of credibility or expertise that person has in your subject area.

19. Painting, sculpture, photograph, drawing, map, chart, or graph

In-text citation for images is handled in a caption printed below the image. Each image in your project is labeled *Fig.* (for *Figure*) and given a figure number; these run consecutively throughout the paper. A typical caption then lists the author's name (in regular order); the title of the work; the date of composition; the medium of composition; the source information, which may be the name of the museum, including the city, that holds the work; book information if the image was published in that format, or website information if the image was published online. (For information on positioning images in a document, see page 228.)

> Fig. 1. Leonardo da Vinci, *Mona Lisa*, c. 1503-05, oil on panel, Louvre Museum, Paris.
>
> Fig. 2. Michelangelo, *The Last Judgment*, 1536-1541, oil on wall, Vatican City, Vatican Palace, Sistine Chapel, from Roberto Salvini, Michelangelo (Danbury: MasterWorks, 1976; print; 125).

Sample Works Cited Page

McClure 16

Works Cited

1"

Bacon-Smith, Camille. *Enterprising Women: Television Fandom and the Creation of Popular Myth*. Philadelphia: U of Pennsylvania P, 1992. Print.

Chonin, Neva. "Love between Men Is a Powerful Thing in *Lord of the Rings*." *SFGate.com*. Hearst Communications, 15 Jan. 2002. Web. 11 Aug. 2002.

Green, Shoshanna, Cynthia Jenkins, and Henry Jenkins. "Normal Female Interest in Men Bonking: Selections from *The Terra Nostra Underground* and *Strange Bedfellows*." *Theorizing Fandom: Fans, Subculture and Identity*. Ed. Cheryl Harris. Cresskill: Hampton, 1998. 9-38. Print.

Irena. "For the Good of Gondor." *Fanfiction.net*. Xing Li, 21 June 2003. Web. 10 Dec. 2003.

Jackson, Peter, dir. *The Two Towers*. Special extended edition. New Line Cinema/WingNut Films, 2002. DVD.

Jenkins, Henry. *Textual Poachers: Television Fans and Participatory Culture*. New York: Routledge, 1992. Print.

LeGuin, Ursula. "Is Gender Necessary? Redux." *Dancing at the Edge of the World*. New York: Grove, 1989. Print.

Rose, Alix. "Slash Universe." *Soapbox Girls*. Lauren Bacon and Emira Mears, Mar. 2002. Web. 10 Nov. 2003.

1"

1/2"

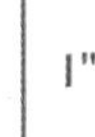

The MLA Works Cited page offers readers a uniform system for locating the sources cited in your text. The Works Cited page follows the text, notes, appendix, bibliography, charts, and any other end matter except an index (if there is one). It should contain only the sources you have used for summaries, paraphrases, and direct quotations in your paper. (If your instructor asks for a complete list of works you have consulted, title it Works Consulted or Bibliography.) If you are citing only one source, your page will be titled Work Cited.

Format of an MLA Works Cited Page

Start your Works Cited list on the first new page immediately after the last page of your text, and continue the same page numbering system, with your last name and the page number in the upper right corner. Center the title Works Cited 1" from the top of the page. Each entry starts at the left margin. When an entry takes more than one line, indent the second and subsequent lines 1/2" (or five typewriter spaces) so readers see only the alphabetized last names as they scan down the list. Double-space between entries and within each individual entry. (See section 13c for specifics on how to format your essay using Microsoft Word.)

An important feature of the MLA Works Cited page is that entries are organized alphabetically by authors' last names. If there is no author, use the first word in the title (but not *A*, *An*, or *The*). This arrangement allows readers to easily thumb from a quotation, for instance, to the Works Cited page and find the full name of the author, the title of the publication, and its source so they can locate the original work.

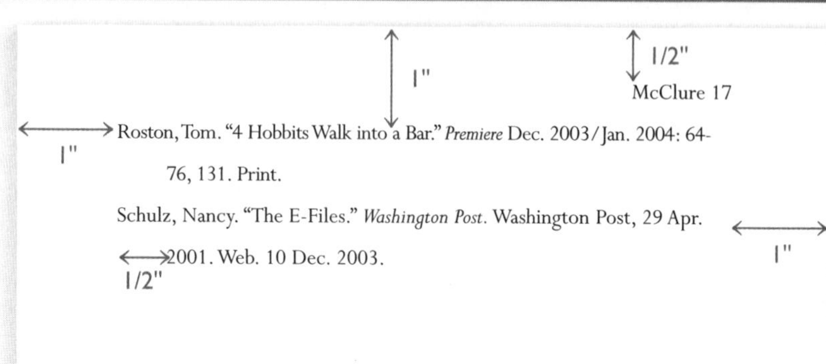

Citing Books: General Information

Following are general guidelines. For models of specific kinds of book citations, see the index that begins on page 196.

Author's Name

Put the last name of the first or only author first, followed by a comma, and then the first and middle names or initials as they appear on the title page of the source. List multiple authors in the order in which they appear on the title page, and write the names of all the authors, reversing the name of the first author only. Use a comma after each author's full name, and use *and* before the final name, which is followed by a period.

Title of Book or Part of Book

Capitalize all significant words in a title, including the first and last words of the title and the subtitle.

Note: *Medium of publication.* Publications come in many forms. Note the medium of the entries on the Works Cited page (above) and those indicated with the entries that follow in this chapter. The medium consulted could be print, Web, LP, audiocassette, CD-ROM, DVD, and so on.

Basic Format for Authors of Books

One author	Allison, Dorothy.
Two authors	Levitt, Steven D., and Stephen J. Dubner.
Three or more authors	Yassin, Omar, George Goldberg, and Sunny Taylor.
Corporate author	Vermont Refugee Resettlement Program.

- Do not include an author's title or degrees.
- Do not abbreviate names to initials unless that is how the names appear on the book's title page.

Basic Format for Titles

Book	*Freakonomics: A Rogue Economist Explores the Hidden Side of Everything.*
Article	"Death of a Mountain: Radical Strip Mining and the Leveling of Appalachia."

Look for Publication Information on the Title and Copyright Pages

- **The city in which the work was published.** If several cities are listed, use only the first one. If the city is outside the United States and not well known, include an abbreviation for the country.
- **The publisher of the work.** Shorten the name of the publisher but make sure it will be easily recognizable to readers (e.g., *Random* for *Random House, Inc.* or *Simon* for *Simon and Schuster, Inc.*). Omit articles (*A, An, The*), business abbreviations (*Inc., Corp., Ltd.*), and words such as *Books, Publishers,* and *Press.* For university presses, use the capital letters *U* and *P* (without periods). If no publisher is named, use the abbreviation *n.p.*
- **The date of publication.** Write the date numerically (e.g., 2004). If no publication date is provided, use the abbreviation *n.d.*

When Publication Information Is Unknown

When you cannot locate elements of the publication information, use the following abbreviations:

n.p. for either no place of publication or no publisher
n.d. for no date
n. pag. for no pagination

Foster, Thomas C. *How to Read Literature like a Professor: A Lively and Entertaining Guide to Reading between the Lines*. N.p.: Harper, 2003. Print.

When you are able to locate some of the information from some other source, include that information in brackets to indicate that the publication information came from somewhere other than the source you are using.

Foster, Thomas C. *How to Read Literature like a Professor: A Lively and Entertaining Guide to Reading between the Lines*. [New York]: Harper, 2003. Print.

Significant words are all the nouns, pronouns, verbs, adjectives, adverbs, and subordinate conjunctions. The following kinds of words should **not** begin with capital letters:

- the coordinating conjunctions *and, but, or, nor, for, so, yet*
- the word *to* when it is part of a verb, as in *Born to Die*
- the articles *a, an,* and *the*
- prepositions such as *between, near, from, to, under, over*

But even these words should be capitalized when they appear first or last in the title or subtitle: *On the Run* or *The World Is Flat: A Brief History of the Twenty-first Century.*

Italicize the titles of longer works, such as books or journals, and use quotation marks around the titles of shorter pieces, such as poems, articles, or short stories. For detailed lists of works whose titles should be in quotation marks or italicized, see sections 42d and 44g.

Publication Information

You can usually find the publication information on the title page of a book or on the copyright page on the reverse of the title page. In your listing, you should include information about the city of publication, the publisher, the year of publication, and the medium of publication.

MLA Works Cited Index: Books and Other Print Nonperiodicals

1. Book by a single author
2. Book by two or three authors
3. Book by four or more authors
4. Two or more books by the same author
5. Book by an unknown author
6. Book with a corporate or group author
7. Book with an author and editor
8. Anthology or book with an editor
9. One selection from an anthology
10. Two or more selections from the same anthology
11. Translated book
12. Sacred book
13. Book in second or subsequent edition
14. Reprinted book
15. Book in more than one volume
16. Book in a series
17. Introduction, preface, foreword, or afterword
18. Article in a reference work (encyclopedia, dictionary)
19. Government publication
20. Published or unpublished dissertation
21. Published proceedings of a conference
22. Booklet or pamphlet

MLA Works Cited Models

1. Book by a single author

List the author's last name first, followed by a comma, the first and middle names or initials, and then a period. Italicize the book title but not the period that follows the title. Next give the name of the city of publication, followed by a colon; the name of the publisher, followed by a comma; the year of publication, followed by a period; and the medium of publication, which ends with a period.

McCourt, Frank. *Teacher Man: A Memoir*. New York: Scribner's, 2005. Print.

Note: The seventh edition of the *MLA Handbook for Writers of Research Papers* now recommends using italics in place of underline.

2. Book by two or three authors

For books with two or three authors, list the names in the order in which they appear on the title page of the text, followed by a period. Only reverse the name of the first author; then list the other name or names, separating each using a comma and placing *and* before the last name.

Stevens, Mark, and Annalyn Swan. *De Kooning: An American Master*. New York: Knopf, 2004. Print.

3. Book by four or more authors

You can either list all the authors' names that appear on the title page, reversing only the first one, or write the first name followed by the abbreviation *et al.*

Bazerman, Charles, Joseph Little, Lisa Bethel, Teri Chavkin, Danielle Fouquette, and Janet Garufis. *Reference Guide to Writing across the Curriculum*. West Lafayette: Parlor, 2005. Print.

Bazerman, Charles, et al. *Reference Guide to Writing across the Curriculum*. West Lafayette: Parlor, 2005. Print.

4. Two or more books by the same author

List each source as a separate entry and alphabetize the entries according to the first major word of the second element of the entry (normally, the title of the text). List the author's full name only in the first entry. For subsequent entries, substitute three hyphens for the author's name, followed by a period (the three hyphens stand for exactly the same name given in the preceding entry). If the person edited or compiled the book, place a comma after the last hyphen and add the appropriate abbreviation (*ed.* for editor or *comp.* for compiler).

> Diamond, Jared. *Collapse: How Societies Choose to Fail or Succeed*. New York: Viking, 2004. Print.
>
> ---. *Guns, Germs, and Steel: The Fates of Human Societies*. New York: Norton, 1999. Print.
>
> ---. *Why Is Sex Fun? The Evolution of Human Sexuality*. Science Masters Series. New York: Basic, 1997. Print.

Note: If any of the books are co-authored, both authors' names have to be given in full, unless all of the authors are the same.

5. Book by an unknown author

If you cannot find the name of the book's author or the author is anonymous, alphabetize your entry using the first major word of the title, ignoring *A, An,* or *The*. Do not write *Anon.* or *Anonymous*.

> *Staying Clean: Living without Drugs*. N.p.: Hazelden, 1987. Print.

6. Book with a corporate or group author

Often books written by businesses and other kinds of organizations have no single author because many different people worked on them. In this case, list the institution, organization, or business as the author.

> American Association of Retired Persons. *Guide to Social Security Changes Enacted by the Congress in 2004*. Washington: AARP, 2004. Print.

MLA Works Cited Index: Books and Other Print Nonperiodicals

MLA Works Cited Index: Books and Other Print Nonperiodicals

7. Book with an author and editor

List the author (last name first) and then the title. Use the abbreviation *Ed.* (short for *edited by*) and then the editor's name, in the usual first and last name order, followed by a period. Follow with any additional contributors.

> Lorde, Audre. *Marvelous Arithmetics of Distance: Poems, 1987-1992*. Ed. Daryl Cumber Dance. Nikki Giovanni. New York: Norton, 1998. Print.

8. Anthology or book with an editor

Use the name of the editor as you would the name of an author, followed by a comma, and then write the abbreviation *ed.* for editor. If there is more than one editor, use the abbreviation *eds.* after the last name in the list.

> Garcia, Cristina, ed. *¡Cubanísimo! The Vintage Book of Contemporary Cuban Literature*. New York: Vintage, 2003. Print.

9. One selection from an anthology

When you cite a selection from an anthology or other collection, start your entry with the name of the author (in reverse order) who wrote the part you are citing from, followed by a period. Then write the title of the selection you are citing from (for example, a short story, poem, or reprinted article), followed by a period and enclosed in quotation marks. Next, provide the title of the anthology or collection, italicized and followed by a period. Write *Ed.* (short for *edited by*) after the title, followed by the name of the editor (in normal order), the publication information, the page numbers of the entire selection you are citing, and the medium of publication. (Do not use the abbreviation *pp.*)

> Connors, Brian R. "Principles of Legal Necessity." *Introduction to the Law*. Ed. Wendy Karlson. Chicago: Lighthouse, 2004. 22-28. Print.

Note: If the selection you are citing was originally published as an independent work, you should italicize its title.

10. Two or more selections from the same anthology

When you cite two or more anthologized pieces from the same text, you might wish to set up a separate entry for each source and then have each entry refer to an entry that cites the anthology. This saves space and avoids repetition. For instance, consider the anthology referred to in citation model 9. If you cited two articles from the same anthology, you would set up the entries like this:

> Connors, Brian R. "Principles of Legal Necessity." Karlson 22-28.
>
> Karlson, Wendy, ed. *Introduction to the Law*. Chicago: Lighthouse, 2004. Print.
>
> Somers, Renee. "Purchasing a Home and Your Legal Rights." Karlson 29-36.

The second entry is for the anthology itself, and the other two entries are for the individual selections from it. Notice that no punctuation is inserted between the cross-referenced editor's name and the inclusive pages for each piece.

11. Translated book

Place *Trans.* and the translator's name (or names) after the title.

> Djebar, Assia. *Women of Algiers in Their Apartment*. Trans. Marjolijn De Jager. Charlottesville: UP of Virginia, 1992. Print.

12. Sacred book

The titles of sacred books such as the Bible, the Koran, the Talmud, and the Upanishads are *not* italicized. When citing a standard version of the Bible, you do not need to include the version or publication information. However, if you are citing individual published editions of a sacred work, you should treat them as you would any other published book, italicizing as appropriate.

> *The New Oxford Annotated NRSV Bible with the Apocrypha*. Ed. Michael D. Coogan, Marc Z. Brettler, Carol A. Newsom, and Pheme Perkins. 3rd ed. Oxford: Oxford UP, 2001. Print.
>
> Upanishads. Trans. Eknath Easwaran. Tomales: Nilgiri, 1987. Print.

MLA Works Cited Index: Books and Other Print Nonperiodicals

MLA Works Cited Index: Books and Other Print Nonperiodicals

13. Book in second or subsequent edition

Indicate which edition you are using so your readers can locate information from your citations. Set up the entry as you would for any other book, and insert *2nd ed., 3rd ed.*, or whatever is appropriate after the title and preceding the publication information.

> Whitman, Walt. *Leaves of Grass*. Ed. Malcolm Cowley. 4th ed. New York: Penguin, 1976. Print.

14. Reprinted book

When your book is a reprint of an original printing, include the normal book entry information, and insert the original publication year, followed by a period, after the title of the book and before the reprint edition's publication information.

> Bradfield, Scott. *The History of Luminous Motion*. 1989. New York: Penguin Classics, 2001. Print.

15. Book in more than one volume

If you use information from only one volume of a multivolume set, write the capitalized abbreviation *Vol.* and the number of the appropriate volume right before the publication information in your entry.

> Dorfman, Rachelle A., ed. *Paradigms of Clinical Social Work*. Vol. 3. New York: Brunner-Routledge, 1988. Print.

Although it is not required, you can add the total number of volumes at the end of your entry.

If you are using material from more than one volume, cite the total number of volumes in the work immediately after the title (or after the editor's name or information about the specific edition), followed by the abbreviation *vols.*

> Guanzhong, Luo. *Three Kingdoms: Chinese Classics*. Trans. Moss Roberts. 4 vols. N.p.: Foreign Languages, 2001. Print.

If the volumes you cite were published over a period of years, give the inclusive dates at the end of the citation.

> Copelston, Frederick. *A History of Philosophy*. 9 vols. Garden City: Doubleday, 1946-75. Print.

If the volumes are part of an ongoing series, write the words *to date* after the number of volumes and leave a space after the hyphen when you write the publication date.

Note: Specific information about the volume you are referring to, including relevant page numbers, should be included in your in-text citation (see citation model 11 on page 189).

16. Book in a series

If you are citing information from a book that is one of a series (check the title page at the front of the book), insert the series name and the book number, if any, immediately after the medium of publication, at the end of the entry.

> Hay, Samuel. *African American Theater: A Historical and Critical Analysis*. Cambridge: Harvard UP, 1994. Print. The Harvard Series on American Culture 12.

MLA Works Cited Index: Books and Other Print Nonperiodicals

MLA Works Cited Index: Books and Other Print Nonperiodicals

17. Introduction, preface, foreword, or afterword

Start with the name of the author who wrote the specific part of the book. If the part has a title, put it in quotation marks and place it immediately before the name of the part. Give the name of the part you are citing (such as *Introduction, Preface, Foreword,* or *Afterword*), capitalized, followed by a period. If the author of the part is *not* the author of the entire book, cite the name of the author of the work after the title, in normal order and preceded by the word *By*. If the author of the part you are citing is the same person who wrote the entire book, repeat the last name only, preceded by the word *By*. Provide the full publication information as outlined in the first citation model on page 196; end with the inclusive page numbers, followed by a period, and the medium of publication, ending with a period.

McCourt, Frank. Foreword. *Eats, Shoots & Leaves: The Zero Tolerance Approach to Punctuation*. By Lynne Truss. New York: Gotham, 2004. xi-xiv. Print.

18. Article in a reference work (encyclopedia, dictionary)

When citing an article in an encyclopedia or an entry in a dictionary, follow the format outlined in citation model 9 (page 198) for listing a selection in an anthology, but omit the name of the editor. If the article is signed, alphabetize the entry using the last name of the author. If it is unsigned, give the title first. If entries in the work you are citing are arranged alphabetically, you do not have to cite page and volume numbers. If the reference work is frequently revised, do not provide full publication information; just list the edition and year published.

Chamberlain, Daniel. "Maurice Merleau-Ponty." *Encyclopedia of Contemporary Literary Theory: Approaches, Scholars, Terms*. Toronto: U of Toronto P, 1993. Print.

19. Government publication

Since there are so many different governments (municipal, local, state, federal) and agencies of government, citing the author of a government publication can be tricky. When you do not have a specific author, you should list the government and then the agency that produced the publication. For instance, you might cite the author like any of these:

Atlanta. City Commission on Historic Locations.
Minnesota. Dept. of Agriculture.
United States. Dept. of Homeland Security.

After you have cited the author, italicize the title of the publication (using *H* or *HR* for the House of Representatives and *S* for the Senate when citing congressional documents—for instance, *HR Bill 32.45*), and then write the publisher of the source. In the United States, most federal publications are produced by the GPO, the Government Printing Office, in Washington.

United States. Commerce Dept. Census Bureau. *Statistical Abstract of the United States, 2005: The National Data Book*. Washington: GPO, 2006. Print.

20. Published or unpublished dissertation

If you are citing from a published dissertation, treat the entry like that for a book, but insert pertinent information about the dissertation before the publication information. If the dissertation was published by University Microfilms International (UMI) in Ann Arbor, then you can include the reference number after the publication information; the medium follows the reference number at the end of the entry.

Lavagnino, John. *Nabokov's Realism*. Diss. Brandeis U, 1998. Ann Arbor: UMI, 1999. AAT 9829823. Print.

MLA Works Cited Index: Books and Other Print Nonperiodicals

MLA Works Cited Index: Books and Other Print Nonperiodicals

1. Book by a single author
2. Book by two or three authors
3. Book by four or more authors
4. Two or more books by the same author
5. Book by an unknown author
6. Book with a corporate or group author
7. Book with an author and editor
8. Anthology or book with an editor
9. One selection from an anthology
10. Two or more selections from the same anthology
11. Translated book
12. Sacred book
13. Book in second or subsequent edition
14. Reprinted book
15. Book in more than one volume
16. Book in a series
17. Introduction, preface, foreword, or afterword
18. Article in a reference work (encyclopedia, dictionary)
19. Government publication
20. Published or unpublished dissertation
21. Published proceedings of a conference
22. Booklet or pamphlet

If the dissertation has not been published, then enclose the title of the dissertation in a pair of quotation marks (do not italicize), write *Diss.* after the title, and write the name of the school that granted the degree and the year it was granted.

> Schindler, Richard A. "Art to Enchant: A Critical Study of Early Victorian Fairy Painting and Illustration." Diss. Brown U, 1988. Print.

21. Published proceedings of a conference

For conference proceedings, create entries in the same way you would for a book. The only difference is that you include information about the conference, unless it is included in the title of the work.

> Cozolino, Louis. *The Neuroscience of Psychotherapy: The Building and Rebuilding of the Human Brain*. Proc. of the 2002 Conf. on Neurology and the Future of Surgical Invasions. New York: Norton, 2003. Print.

22. Booklet or pamphlet

Treat pamphlets, even short ones, as you would a book. Include the author's name, the title of the pamphlet (italicized), and the publication information.

> United States Copyright Office. *Copyright Basics*. Washington: GPO, 2004. Print.

When there is no author, put the title first.

Basic Format for Scholarly Journal Articles

Author's last name, first name. "Article title: Subtitle." *Journal name* Volume number.Issue number (Year of publication): Inclusive page numbers. Medium of publication.

Basic Format for Magazine Articles

Author's last name, first name. "Article title: Subtitle." *Magazine name* Date: Inclusive page numbers. Medium of publication.

Basic Format for Newspaper Articles

Author's last name, first name. "Article title." *Name of newspaper* Date, edition name: Inclusive page numbers. Medium of publication.

Citing Periodicals: General Information

When you cite journal, magazine, or newspaper articles, note the following general considerations.

Author information. See citation models 1 through 8 (pages 196–198).

Article title. Capitalize all important words, including the first word of the subtitle.

Periodical name. Write out journal and magazine names in full. For newspapers, omit the initial *A, An,* or *The: New York Times.*

Volume and issue information. Provide this information only in citations to scholarly journals.

Date. The information you provide depends on how often a periodical is published; see individual citation models. Use abbreviations for all months except May, June, and July. September is abbreviated *Sept.*; other abbreviations consist of the first three letters of the name of the month. Follow an abbreviation with a period.

Inclusive page numbers. For numbers from 1 through 99, write both numerals out in full. For larger numbers, give only the last two digits of the second numeral, unless more are needed for accuracy or clarity: *367-73,* but *367-401*. When page numbers are not consecutive, write the first page number followed by a + sign: *52+*.

Medium of publication. See Note on page 194 for an explanation.

MLA Works Cited Index: Periodicals and Print Correspondence

MLA Works Cited Models

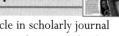

23. Article in scholarly journal with continuous pagination throughout annual volume

Most scholarly journals paginate consecutively from issue to issue throughout the course of a year. The year's issues make up one volume, which can be bound, and referred to, as a single entity. When citing an article from a continuously paginated journal, start your entry with the author's name, reversed and followed by a period, and then give the name of the article in quotation marks. Next write the name of the journal, italicized, and follow it with a single space. Add the volume number (do not use the abbreviation *vol.*) followed by a period and, when available, the issue number. Write the year in parentheses followed by a colon. End the entry with one more space, the inclusive page numbers for the entire article cited followed by a period, and the medium consulted and concluding period. (If page numbers are not continuous, give the number of the first page immediately followed by a plus sign.)

Walichinsy, Eileen. "Linguistic and Empathetic Understanding." *Distance Studies in Language* 16.1 (2002): 444-67. Print.

24. Article in scholarly journal that pages each issue separately

Some journals number the pages of each issue separately, starting each issue on page 1. For these journals, an issue number will almost certainly be available for you to include with the volume number.

Lassitor, Jules. "Cutting Short Communication When It's Painful." *Washington Regional Journal of Communication Studies* 21.3 (2004): 12-27. Print.

Note: Some journals number only the issues, not the annual volumes; when citing them, use the issue number as if it were a volume number.

25. Article in monthly or bimonthly magazine

If a magazine is published on a monthly or bimonthly schedule, use the format in citation model 24, but provide the month or months (abbreviated, except for May, June, and July) and year after the title, followed by a colon and the inclusive page numbers of the article. Do not include the volume or issue number.

> Stix, Gary. "Owning the Stuff of Life." *Scientific American* Feb. 2006: 76-83. Print.

26. Article in weekly or biweekly magazine

For magazines published every week or biweekly, provide the full date of the issue after the title. Begin with the day, abbreviate the month (except for May, June, and July), and give the year. Follow this information with a colon and the inclusive page numbers of the article. Do not include the volume or issue number.

> Wilkinson, Alec. "The Open Man." *Rolling Stone* 26 Jan. 2006: 31+. Print.

27. Article in daily newspaper

When citing a newspaper, give its name as it appears on the first page, omitting any introductory article (*A, An,* or *The*). Some newspapers do not include their home city in their titles. For these papers, put the home city in square brackets, after the title of the newspaper and before the period: *Journal Record* [Oklahoma City]. (This is not necessary for nationally published newspapers like the *Wall Street Journal.*) You do not have to include a volume number, an issue number, or a publication code. However, it is important to mention the edition (i.e., national edition, late edition, etc.) if it is listed at the top of the first page. Also, if the newspaper is divided into lettered sections and includes these designations before the page numbers, you need to do the same.

> Gonzalez, Juliet. "Scores for Sports." *Atlanta Constitution* 14 Apr. 2004, natl. ed.: C3-5. Print.

MLA Works Cited Index: Periodicals and Print Correspondence

MLA Works Cited Index: Periodicals and Print Correspondence

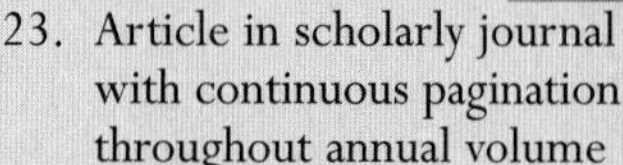

You would write *C3+* if the pages were not consecutive pages. If a paper is divided into numbered sections, provide the number of the section before the colon—for example, *sec. 4: 7-8.*

28. Anonymous article

When no author's name is given, use the title of the article. When you alphabetize, ignore *A, An,* or *The.*

> "Primary Care Reforms Are Urged." *Wall Street Journal* 31 Jan. 2006: D4. Print.

29. Editorial or letter to the editor

Use the letter writer's name, if available, and then the title of the letter in quotation marks. Next provide a description of the work, such as *Editorial* or *Letter.* Then insert the appropriate information from the newspaper or magazine and conclude with the medium consulted.

> Bennett, Jana M. "Doubting Thomas." Letter. *Harper's* Feb. 2006: 4-5. Print.

30. Review

Use the reviewer's name and then the title of the review, if any. After the title of the review, write *Rev. of* and then name the work that was reviewed (if it was another article, use quotation marks; if it was a book, italicize the title). Also include the name of the author of the reviewed work, preceded by a comma and the word *by.* Finish with the publication information.

> Pearson, Allison. "The Untalented Mr. Ripple." Rev. of *It's All Right Now*, by Charles Chadwick. *New York Times Book Review* 26 June 2005: 16. Print.
>
> "Revelation without Reflection." Rev. of *The Duff Cooper Diaries*, ed. John Julius Norwich. *Economist* 1 Oct. 2005: 80. Print.

31. Abstract of dissertation or article

When you create an entry for an abstract, start the entry with the author's name and the work's title, and include the publication information for the original work (the one the abstract summarizes). Finally, include the publication information for the abstract.

Pender, Kelly. "Annotated Bibliography: Questions and Answers about the Pentad." *College Composition and Communication* 29 (1978): 330-35. Abstract. *Invention in Rhetoric and Composition*. West Lafayette: Parlor Press, 2004. Print.

32. Published or unpublished letter

Treat letters differently depending on whether they are published or unpublished. For unpublished letters—for instance, correspondence you received from another writer—cite the author and insert the words *Letter to* and the recipient, followed by the date and medium consulted. Use *TS* to indicate Typescript and *MS* to indicate Manuscript.

Heckerling, Amy. Letter to the author. 23 May 2006. TS.

If the letter has been published, handle the letter as if it were an article, including the original date and then the publication in which the letter is now collected.

Thomas, Edward. "Thomas to Frost." 1914. Letter 14 of *Elected Friends: Robert Frost and Edward Thomas to One Another*. Ed. Matthew Spencer. New York: Handsel-Other, 2003. 29-30. Print.

MLA Works Cited Index: Periodicals and Print Correspondence

Citing Digital Sources: General Information

Some digital sources are published on CD-ROM and other portable media, such as diskettes and magnetic tape. For instance, databases are often provided in libraries on CD-ROM. Other digital sources are online: websites; various kinds of documents on websites; online magazines, newspapers, and journals; ebooks; message board postings; and so on. For almost all digital entries, you will need to cite

- the author's name(s)
- the title of the publication
- information about print publication (if applicable)
- information about electronic publication
- access information, including medium consulted, access date, and URL, if needed (For more information on URLs, see Note on right.)

Basic Format for Digital Sources

See book models 1–8 for author information

Use quotation marks unless you are citing an entire site or ebook.

Consult the models for books and periodicals to find the right citation style.

Author's last, first name. "Title of work: Subtitle." Print publication information, if any. *Title of digital source*. Date of publication or update. Medium of publication. Access date <URL>.

Do this because e-sources can change quickly.

Do not add a hyphen when you break a URL at the end of a line.

Italicize the title of a website; give the date of e-publication or the date of latest update (use the abbreviation *n.d.* if not available); and name the organization that sponsors the site, if any (if none, use the abbreviation *N.p.*).

See citation model 33 on page 211 for general information about CD-ROM publications. See model 36 on page 212 for general information about online sources.

Note: Current MLA guidelines recommend including electronic addresses (URLs) as supplementary information only when the source would be difficult to find without one. If the URL takes up more than one line, it should be broken right after a slash. For examples of Web citations that include the URL, see citation models 53-55 on page 219.

MLA Works Cited Models

33. CD-ROM, DVD, or portable database

When you cite information from portable databases, CD-ROMs, and DVDs, provide the following information:

Author's last name, first name. Original publication data if the article was once a printed source (that is, "Title." *Name of periodical* (Date): Inclusive pages). Medium of publication (e.g., CD-ROM, DVD, portable database). *Title of database.* Name of computer service. Publication date.

"Windhover." The Oxford English Dictionary. 2nd ed. Oxford: Oxford UP, 2001. DVD-ROM.

Jackson, Peter. "Bullish on This Market." *Wall Street Journal* 12 Mar. 2003: 21-24. CD-ROM. *Wall Street Press.* SIRS. June 2004.

34. Source on nonperiodical database (CD-ROM, DVD, diskette, magnetic tape)

Cite a nonperiodical publication on CD-ROM, DVD, etc., the same way you would cite a book, but include the appropriate medium of publication.

Content Guide to Accompany NBC News Archive, Sociology Lecture Launcher, Collection 1.0. New York: McGraw-Hill, 2008. DVD-ROM.

Note: For more information on citing visual media such as film, videotape, and DVD, see citation model 56 on page 220.

35. Source on periodical CD-ROM database

If the CD-ROM is part of a periodical database, provide the author's name, the publication information from the printed source (including title and date of publication), the medium, the title of the database (italicized), the name of the vendor of the database, and the electronic publication date.

MLA Works Cited Index: Digital Sources, Online and Offline

WriteOnline

MLA Works Cited Index: Digital Sources, Online and Offline

Hickoks, Helen. "Recovering Sociological Foundations." *Sociology Quarterly* 23.5 (2001): 123-32. CD-ROM. *InfoTrac: Magazine Index Plus.* Information Access. Jan. 2002.

36. Online source, in general

Online sources are found by downloading information through a computer service, rather than inserting a CD-ROM, diskette, or other portable medium. Because the sources in an online database are revised frequently, their Works Cited entries must include the date of access (the date when you found, read, printed, or used the source) as well as the date of publication or the most recent revision.

37. Entire website (scholarly, professional, personal)

When you cite an entire website, your entry should include the following information.

Author's last name, first name. *Title of site*. Name of the editor of the site (if provided), preceded by the abbreviation *Ed.* Version number, if it is pertinent and not included in the site's title (e.g., Vers. 3.5). Date of publication or of most recent update (day, abbreviated month, and year), if available. Use the abbreviation *n.d.* if no date is given. Name of the organization that sponsors the site, if available (if not available, use the abbreviation *N.p.* for No publisher.) Medium of publication. Date you accessed the site.

Lowe, Charlie. *Cyberdash*. N.p., 11 Apr. 2004. Web. 28 Oct. 2005.

You may not be able to find all of the above information for your entries. Trying to find an author's name can sometimes be extremely frustrating. However, it is worth taking the time to follow hyperlinks and to closely examine the entire website in order to find the author's name. If you cannot find the author's name or, as may happen in some cases, a title or date of creation for the page, then you do not have to include this information in your citation. However, if the website has no authorship or other identifying information (called *provenance*), then you should strongly consider not using the source at all.

38. Short work from online site

Let's say you are using just one part or page of a larger website, and it has a different title from the main site. As you would for a collection of essays, put the part title in quotation marks and follow it with the title of the main page, italicized. Your complete entry would include the following information:

Author's last name, first name. "Title of page." *Title of site*. Sponsor, Date the page was created or last updated (day month year). Medium of publication. Date (in the same format) that you last visited the page.

> Drudge, Bob. "Dictionaries and Language Resources." *Refdesk.com*. Refdesk, 2005. Web. 5 Nov. 2005.

39. Source from online service that your library subscribes to

When you use information from a service that your library subscribes to, follow the guidelines for citing articles in print periodicals, leaving out the medium of original publication (Print). Then provide the service title, medium consulted, and, finally, the date of access.

> Hesten, Phillip. "Oscillations and the Global Weather." *Meteorology* 21 Mar. 2000: 122-28. *UNI-Information*. Web. 12 June 2002.

40. Source from online service that you subscribe to

When you use information from a source that you subscribe to (for instance, AOL), the major difference between this and other online source entries is the information you include about keywords, so that your reader can go back and find your information using your search method.

MLA Works Cited Index: Digital Sources, Online and Offline

MLA Works Cited Index: Digital Sources, Online and Offline

"18th Century Occidental Exploitation of Asian Resources." *Merriam Webster's Online Encyclopedia*. Merriam Webster, 2000. *America Online*. Web. 26 Sept. 2002. Keywords: Asian Resources and 18th Century.

41. Source from home page (academic department, course, personal)

When you cite information from an online personal or professional site, provide the name of the author (i.e., the person who created the site), if available; the title of the work (in quotation marks); and the title of the site (italicized) or, if there is no title, a description (Home page, Dept. home page, etc.). Provide the name of any organization associated with the page or site, the date of the last update, the publication medium, the date of your access, and the URL (if needed).

Barlow, John Perry. "Is Spalding Gray Finally Swimming to Cambodia?" *BarlowFriendz*. N.p., 16 Jan. 2004. Web. 22 Apr. 2004.

42. Online book

How you cite an online book depends on whether you used part of the book or the complete book. For complete online books, cite the author's or editor's name (last, first); the title (italicized); the name of the editor, translator, or compiler, if any; publication information, including version; medium of publication; and date of access.

Wynants, Marleen, and Jan Cornelis, eds. *How Open Is the Future? Economic, Social & Cultural Scenarios Inspired by Free and Open-Source Software*. Brussels: Brussels UP, 2005. Web. 6 Nov. 2005.

For parts of a book, insert the title of the part (if it is a chapter, use quotation marks; if it is an introduction, preface, or afterword, simply write that) after the name and before the title of the complete book.

Rushkoff, Douglas. Introduction. *Open Source Democracy*. Project Gutenberg, 2003. Web. 6 Nov. 2005.

43. Article in online journal

Provide the following information when citing an article from an online journal:

Author's last name, first name. "Title of article." *Title of online periodical* Volume number.Issue number (Date of publication): Page (if not provided, write *n. pag.*) Medium of publication. Date of your most recent access.

Weber, Brenda R. "Beauty, Desire, and Anxiety: The Economy of Sameness in ABC's *Extreme Makeover*." *Genders* 41 (2005): n. pag. Web. 6 Nov. 2005.

44. Article in online magazine

Provide the following information when citing an article from an online magazine:

Author's last name, first name. "Title of article." *Title of online magazine.* Sponsor of site, Date of publication: Page, paragraph, or reference numbers (if provided). Medium of publication. Date of your most recent access.

Saletan, William. "The Brontosaurus: Monty Python's Flying Creationism." *Slate.* Slate Magazine, 27 Oct. 2005. Web. 6 Nov. 2005.

MLA Works Cited Index: Digital Sources, Online and Offline

MLA Works Cited Index: Digital Sources, Online and Offline

45. Article in online newspaper or on online newswire

Provide the following information when citing an article from an online newspaper:

Author's last name, first name. "Title of article." *Title of newspaper.* Date of publication: Medium of publication. Date of your most recent access.

McNerthney, Casey. "Seattle Landmark Set for Restoration." *Seattlepi.com.* Hearst Newspapers, 27 Mar. 2009. Web. 27 Mar. 2009.

Note: When citing a newswire article, substitute the title of the online wire service for the newspaper title.

46. Article from online government publication

When you create an entry for an online government publication, use the same information as you would for the printed government publication, and then insert the medium of publication and the date of access.

United States. NASA. "Expedition 9 in Command of Station." 6 June 2004. Web. 6 Nov. 2005.

47. Online abstract

When you cite an online abstract, provide the author's name, the title of the work, the name of the publication, any volume and issue numbers, the date, and the inclusive page numbers (if none are given, use the abbreviation *n. pag.*) for the document the abstract summarizes. Then add the word *Abstract,* the medium of publication, and the date of access.

Vandenberg, Kathleen M. "Sociological Propaganda: A Burkean and Girardian Analysis of Twentieth-Century American Advertising." *KB Journal* 2.1 (2004): n. pag. Abstract. Web. 6 Nov. 2005.

48. Online review

When you cite an online review, provide the reviewer's name; the title of the review (if any); the words *Rev. of* and the title of the work being reviewed; the word *by* and the author of the work; the name, any volume and issue numbers, and the date of the publication in which the review was originally published; the medium of publication; and the date of your access.

Longaker, Mark Garrett. Rev. of *Rhetorical Landscapes in America*, by Gregory Clark. *KB Journal* 1.2 (2004): n. pag. Web. 6 Nov. 2005.

49. Article in online database (dictionary, encyclopedia)

When you create an entry for an online dictionary, encyclopedia, or other reference work, cite the entry title (e.g., "Digestion"); the name and version, if appropriate, of the online database; the sponsor of the site (if none is given, use the abbreviation *N.p.*); the date of the last update; the medium of publication; and the date of access.

"Digestion." *Wikipedia*. Wikipedia, 12 Mar. 2003. Web. 4 Nov. 2005.

50. Email

Provide the following information when citing an email communication:

Email author's last name, first name. "Title of email from subject line." Brief description of message (including the recipient). Use the word *Message* (e.g., "Message to the author"). Day abbreviated month year the message was sent. Medium of delivery.

Jacobson, Jack. "Re: Harassment in the Textiles Department." Message to the author. 18 Apr. 2003. Email.

Note: The seventh edition of the *MLA Handbook for Writers of Research Papers* (published in 2009) shows the word *email* with a hyphen.

MLA Works Cited Index: Digital Sources, Online and Offline

MLA Works Cited Index: Digital Sources, Online and Offline

51. Online posting/message board

Provide the following information when citing an online posting to a discussion list. If possible, cite an archival version of the posting to make it easier for your readers to find.

Author of posting's last name, first name. "Title of posting as given in subject line." Description of type of message (i.e., Online posting). Day abbreviated month year of posting. Name of message board/posting site. Medium of publication. Date of access.

Greer, Michael Gordon. "Rhetoric Requires Magic." Online posting. 5 Nov. 2005. Kairosnews. Web. 6 Nov. 2005.

If you do not know the author's name, use the email address or screen name.

AriAorta. "Oh, the Monorail." Online posting. 4 Nov. 2005. Music for America. Web. 6 Nov. 2005.

Note: If the name of the Internet site is unknown, give the email address of the moderator or list supervisor.

52. Posting to newsgroup or Web forum

When you cite a posting to a newsgroup or a Web forum, you need to create an entry that begins with the poster's name (or email or screen name, if the poster's name is not available). Then include the title, the words *Online posting,* the date of the posting, the site sponsoring the posting or news group, the medium of publication, the date of access, and the URL (if needed).

Cypher. "Is Art Dead?" Online posting. 25 Oct. 2005. Art. Google Group. Web. 6 Nov. 2005.

53. Synchronous communication (chat)

Provide the following information when citing an online synchronous communication:

Author of posting's last name, first name. Description of event. Day abbreviated month year of posting. Forum for the communication (e.g., MUD, MOO). Medium of delivery. Date of access. <URL with prefix *telnet://*>.

Note: If the full name is not available, use the screen name.

> JaniceW. Editor's Mtg-2/12. 12 Feb. 2001. LinguaMOO. Web. 6 Nov. 2005. <telnet://lingua.utdallas.edu:7000/9879/>.

54. Computer software

When you cite information from a particular piece of downloaded software, include the name of the software or program (italicized), any appropriate information about versions, the medium consulted, the date you accessed the software, and the URL where you found the software.

> *TK3 Author*. Vers. 1.1. Web. 22 Mar. 2006. <http://www.nightkitchen.com/download/index.phtml>.

55. Online video, graphic, or audio source

When you cite information from an online film clip, picture or graphic file, or audio clip, include the author's name (if any), the title of the digital source (italicized if considered a long work, such as a film or computer game; within quotation marks if considered a short work, such as a song; see 52d and 56a), the title of the website (italicized), any appropriate information about versions, the site's sponsor (if not available, use "N.p."), the date of the digital source (if not available, use "n.d."), the kind of digital medium, the medium consulted (Web), the date you accessed it, and the URL where you found the source, if your reader would have difficulty locating it.

> *The Gundertaker.* Machinima video. *Machinima.com.* Web. 29 Mar. 2009. <http://www.machinima.com/film/view&id=1357>.

MLA Works Cited Index: Digital Sources, Online and Offline

Citing Visual and Performance Media and Other Sources

Some sources of information do not easily fit into one of the preceding categories. Nevertheless, you have the same basic responsibility when using them as sources in your writing: you need to make it possible for your readers to locate and verify your sources.

MLA Works Cited Index: Visual and Performance Media and Other Sources

MLA Works Cited Models

56. Film, videotape, or DVD

Title of film. Director's first name and last name, preceded by *Dir*. Main performers' first names and last names (usually no more than three or four), preceded by *Perf*. Name of distributor, year of distribution. Medium.

You can include other information you consider important, such as the name of the writer or producer, between the title and the distributor.

> *Pulp Fiction*. Dir. Quentin Tarantino. Perf. Samuel L. Jackson and John Travolta. Miramax, 1996. Film.

If you are citing one person's contribution, begin the entry with the person's name (last name, first name), followed by a description of the person's role (e.g., *Dir.* for director or *Perf.* for performer).

Note: Other visual media such as DVDs, videocassettes, laser discs, slide shows, and filmstrips are cited in the same way, only you need to include the original release date (if relevant) and state the medium before the name of the distributor.

57. Sound recording

Last name, first name of the individual you are citing (this could be the composer, conductor, or performer, depending on the emphasis of your paper). "Title of song" (if you are citing a song or song lyrics). *Title of CD* (you do not italicize the titles of musical works identified just by form, number, or key). Performer(s) or conductor (if relevant). Manufacturer's name, year of CD's release. Medium.

To cite lyrics from the song "Milquetoast," from Helmet's album *Betty,* you would create the following Works Cited entry:

> Helmet. "Milquetoast." *Betty*. Interscope, 1994. LP.

Note: If you are not citing a CD (see above), you should indicate the medium the work appears in (e.g., Audiocassette or LP) after the date of release, *not* in quotation marks or italicized.

58. Live performance

Williams, Dar. *Dar Williams in Concert.* Scottish Rite Auditorium, Collingswood, NJ. 14 June 2004. Performance.

59. Television show or radio program

"Title of episode, show, or segment." *Title of program.* Title of series (if any). Name of network. Call letters, City of the local station (if any). Broadcast date. Medium of reception.

Other information, such as the names of the producer, director, and performers, can be included as relevant.

"Backwards Episode." *Seinfeld.* Prod. Larry David. Perf. Jerry Seinfeld. WNBC, Baltimore. 10 Dec. 2003. Television.

If you are citing one person's contribution, begin the entry with the person's name (last name, first name), followed by a description of the person's role (e.g., *Narr.* for narrator or *Dir.* for director).

60. Painting, sculpture, or photograph

Provide the artist's name (last, first), the title of the work of art (italicized), the date of composition, the medium of composition, and the place where the work resides (the institution and the city, if the city is not a part of the institution's name). If you are citing a reproduction of a work of art, add the author of the book, the title of the book, and the usual publication data, ending with the medium (Print). If the work is cited on the Web, add the medium (Web), the date of access, and the URL (if needed).

Nauman, Bruce. *Clown Torture.* 1987. Video (multimedia). Art Institute of Chicago. Web. 12. Apr. 2004.

MLA Works Cited Index: Visual and Performance Media and Other Sources

61. Lecture or speech

Speaker's last name, first name. "Title of speech." Title of meeting. Name of sponsoring organization. Place of speech. Date of speech. Form of delivery.

Cone, James. "Black Theology/Black Pride." Larry Neal Lecture Series. Lincoln University School of Humanities. Mary Dod Brown Memorial Chapel, Lincoln University. 12 Mar. 2003. Lecture.

If the speech has no title, provide a concise description of it. Do not use quotation marks around your description.

62. Published or unpublished interview

Provide the following information for an unpublished interview you conducted:

Interviewee's last name, first name. Type of interview (e.g., Personal interview, Telephone interview, Email interview). Date of interview.

Soto, Dan. Personal interview. 21 Feb. 2006.

Published interviews are treated the same as other print sources. Broadcast or taped interviews are treated as broadcast programs. For both, provide the title of the interview if there is one, relevant source information, and the date the interview took place, if available.

Freedman, Jill. "Photographer." *Working: People Talk about What They Do All Day and How They Feel about What They Do*. By Studs Terkel. New York: Pantheon-Random, 1972. 153-54. Print.

63. Map, chart, or other illustration

When you cite a map, chart, or other illustration, include the name of the map, chart, or illustration; a description of the illustration (e.g., *Map, Chart, Illustration*); the title of the publication; the city of publication, publisher, year; the page numbers on which the illustration appears; and the medium of publication. If the work is online, write the appropriate medium (Web), the date of access, and the URL (if needed).

"Continental United States." Map. *Merriam Traveler's Guide*. Boston: Merriam, 2004. 22-23. Print.

64. Cartoon or comic strip

When you cite a cartoon or comic strip or include one in your work, create an entry that gives the artist's name and the title, if there is one, followed by the designation *Cartoon* or *Comic strip*. Then write the name of the publication in which it appears, along with the day month year of publication, page number, and medium of publication. Or write the appropriate medium (Web), the date of access, and the URL (if needed).

Trudeau, Gary. "Doonesbury: The Daily Dose." Comic strip. *New York Times* 6 Nov. 2005: C4. Print.

65. Advertisement

When you cite an advertisement or include one in your work, start with the product or institution being advertised and then the word *Advertisement.* Next write the name of the publication in which the advertisement appears, along with the date of publication, inclusive page number(s), and medium of publication. If the ad is online, provide the appropriate medium, the date of access, and the URL (if needed).

Palmolive Soap. Advertisement. *Ladies Home Journal* 1942. Digital Scriptorium. Web. 6. Nov. 2005.

MLA Works Cited Index: Visual and Performance Media and Other Sources

This section shows you how to format your work for submission in MLA style using the software program Microsoft Word.

How to Create 1" Margins and Double-Space Your Essay

MLA style requires margins of 1" on all four edges of the page. The entire text must be double-spaced. With your document open in Word, follow these steps:

1. Place your cursor anywhere in the body of the text.
2. Select the Page Layout tab to show the Page Layout ribbon.
3. Select the arrow on the lower-right corner of the "Page Setup" category.
4. In the Page Setup dialogue box, adjust your settings so that they match those in Figure 13.1. Top, Bottom, Left, and Right all show 1". Orientation should be "Portrait." Pages should show "Normal," and Preview > Apply to: should list "Whole document."
5. Click on OK.

For instructions that apply to Microsoft® Word® 2003, visit the handbook's website: **cengage.com/english/blakesley**

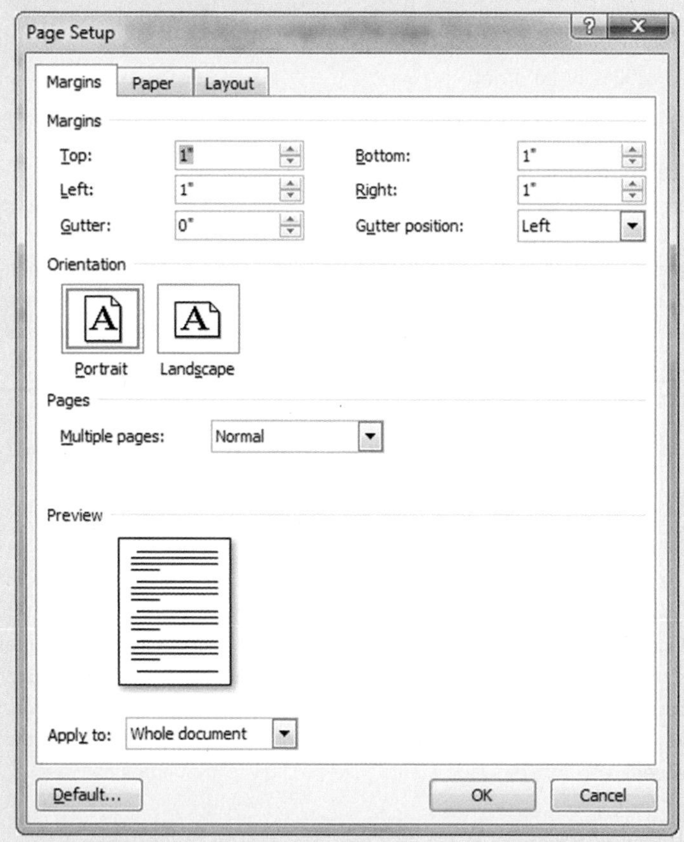

Figure 13.1 Setting Up Page Layout in Word according to MLA Style

How to Create Running Headers with Your Last Name and Page Number

MLA requires that each page of your essay include in the upper right corner a running header that gives your last name and the page number. With your essay open in Word, follow these steps:

1. Place your cursor anywhere in the body of the text.
2. On the top menu bar, choose the Insert tab to show the Insert ribbon.
3. In the Header & Footer category, click on the Page Number icon, and then choose Top of Page and select "Plain Number 3" (in the visual display of options), which will place the number in the upper-right corner of the page, as shown in Figure 13.2.
4. If needed, you can change the page numbering format by clicking on Page Numbers in the Design Ribbon in the Header & Footer category, as shown in Figure 13.3.
5. You now need to add your last name and also remove the header from the first page of your document. Double-click anywhere in the header region near the page number, which will reveal the Design ribbon automatically.

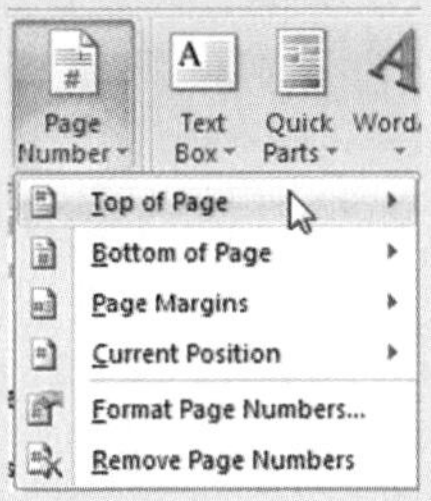

Figure 13.2 Insert Page Numbers in a Document

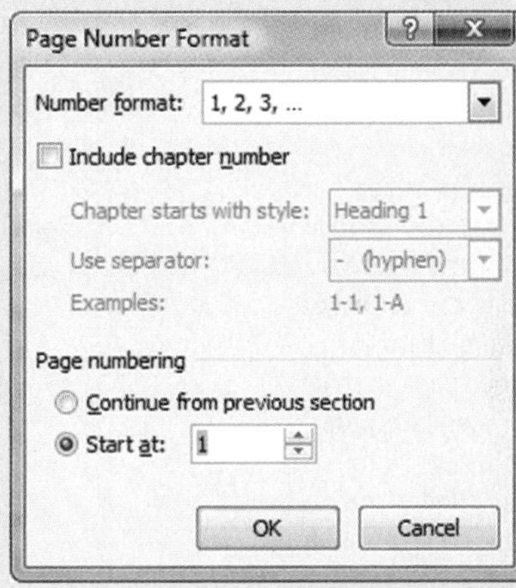

Figure 13.3 Adjusting Page Number Format in a Document according to MLA Style

(continued)

6. In the Options category, check the box next to "Different First Page" to hide the page number and header on page 1 of your document. (You can also adjust this setting using the Page Setup dialogue box shown in Figure 13.5 (see Step 9).
7. To add your last name as the running header next to the page number, double-click in the header region, type your name as you would like it to appear, select "Insert Alignment Tab" in the Position category and select Right to position your name on the right side of the page to the left of the page number. Insert an extra space after your name to separate it from the number, as shown in Figure 13.4.
8. With the cursor still in the header region, you can change the font and style as needed. Choose the Home tab to make routing formatting changes.
9. Confirm that your page numbers and running headers are properly positioned by checking your Page Setup. Under the Page Layout tab, choose the arrow on the Page Setup category label. Your settings should look like those shown in Figure 13.5.

For instructions that apply to Microsoft® Word® 2003, visit the handbook's website: **cengage.com/english/blakesley**

Figure 13.4 Adding and Positioning Your Last Name in the Running Header

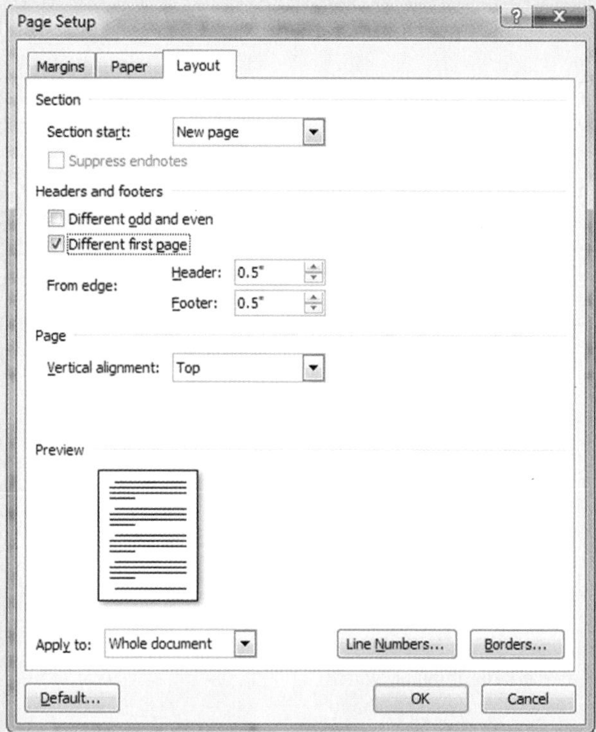

Figure 13.5 Setting the Header's Distance from the Top Edge

How to Create Block Quotations

MLA style calls for all prose quotations longer than four of your lines to be inset an additional 1" from the left margin. (The right margin remains at 1".)

1. Insert a return before and after your quotation so that it stands as its own paragraph. There should not be any extra line spaces above or below the quotation.
2. Place your cursor anywhere in the quotation paragraph.
3. On the Home ribbon in Word 2007, click twice on the Increase Indent button: ⇥. The quotation will be indented an additional 1" from the left margin.

moving on may involve retracing our steps, returning to that alembic center, the molten mass

Left Indent

where all distinctions converge and of which he spoke in *A Grammar of Motives*:

Distinctions, we might say, arise out of a great central moltenness, where all is merged. They have been thrown from a liquid center to the surface, where they have congealed. Let one of these crusted distinctions return to its source, and in

Figure 13.6 Formatting a Block Quotation

First Line Indent

acc... did see Julia again," he notes, "although by then no one, not even her own family back in Davenport, Iowa, could have been expected to recognize her." [. . .]

The book is no less vivid about its more solid citizens, the ones responsible for bringing the World's Columbian Exposition Company into being. Over the kind of menu that featured green turtle consommé and woodcock on toast, they laid glorious plans.

By citing Maslin as I have, I don't mean to suggest that anyone but Holmes is the devil referred to in the book's title. But I do think it's interesting to notice how the parallel themes in these two

Figure 13.7 Adding a Paragraph Indent Using the Margin Guide

Alternatively, on the top ruler bar, position your cursor over the small square box and then drag both arrows to the 1" mark. Since the page margin should already be set at 1", your indented block quotation will now be offset 2". See Figure 13.6. If you need to indent the first line of a paragraph in your block quotation, place the cursor anywhere in the paragraph you want to indent and then drag the top arrow of the margin guide .25" to the right, as shown in Figure 13.7. Note that you do not need to indent the first sentence of a paragraph if you are quoting from a single paragraph. If you are quoting from two or more paragraphs, indent those sentences that begin each paragraph in the source.

For instructions that apply to Microsoft® Word® 2003, visit the handbook's website: **cengage.com/english/blakesley**

How to Place an Image and Add a Caption

1. In Word 2007, place your cursor in your text where you would like to place the image.
2. Choose the Insert tab to show the Insert ribbon. Click on the Insert Picture icon. (If you want to include clip art, shapes, SmartArt, charts, Word art, or other images, you can choose to do so on the Insert ribbon.)
3. Navigate to the image, select it, and click OK. Your image will be placed in the text.
4. To adjust the precise placement and look of your image with a two-button mouse, click once on the image so that it's selected. The Format ribbon will appear. You can then adjust the alignment, position, text wrapping, and more. Figure 13.8 illustrates how to adjust the position. To add fills, lines, and other special effects, as well as adjust brightness, contrast, and more, right click on the image and select "Format Picture."
5. To add a caption, select the image with your mouse, right-click and choose Insert Caption. In the Caption dialogue box, enter the content of the caption in the "Caption:" box and adjust any other settings. See Figure 13.9. Then click OK. Once your caption has been placed, you can edit it just as you would any other text in your document. Word will keep track of the numbering sequence automatically.

For instructions that apply to Microsoft® Word® 2003, visit the handbook's website: **cengage.com/english/blakesley**

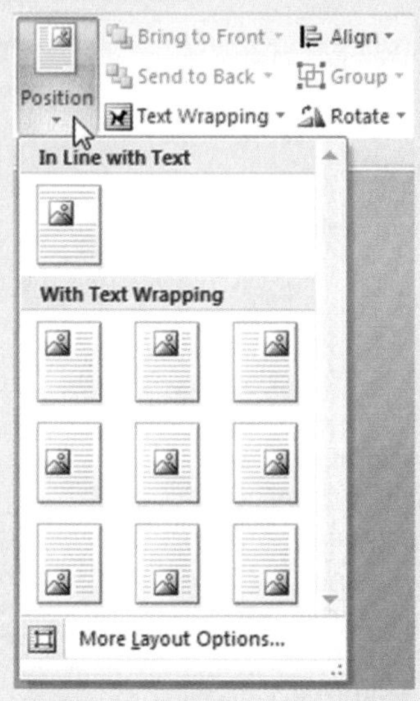

Figure 13.8 Position an Image In Line or with Text Wrapping

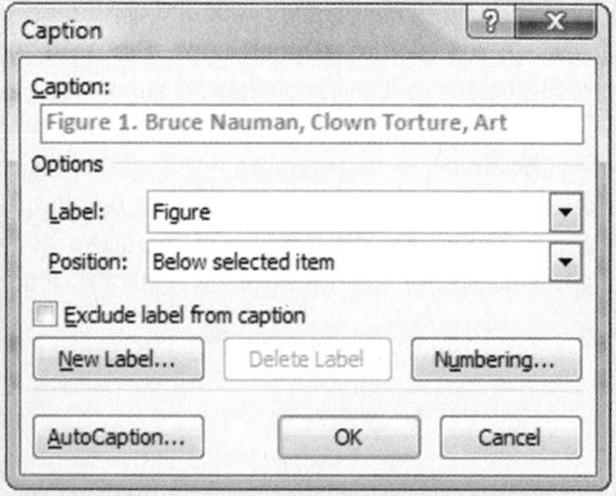

Figure 13.9 Adjusting the settings in the Caption Dialogue Box

How to Turn Off Automatic Hyperlink or Remove a Hyperlink

Microsoft Word comes with a default setting to automatically format any URL or e-mail address into a blue hyperlink. You should disable this function unless your document is online. You may also find that you need to remove formatted hyperlinks that already appear in your document.

Remove Hyperlink Formatting
On a PC, right-click on the hyperlink and choose "Remove Hyperlink" from the pop-up menu. On a Mac with a one-button mouse, hold down the Ctrl key and choose Hyperlink > Edit Hyperlink and then click on "Remove Hyperlink" in the Edit Hyperlink dialogue box.

Prevent Automatic Hyperlink Formatting

1. Choose the Office button and then Word Options.
2. Under Proofing, choose the "AutoCorrect Options button.
3. Unselect the box next to "Internet and network paths with hyperlinks" under the AutoFormat tab and the AutoFormat As You Type" tab.
4. You can also turn off this automatic formatting function by clicking on the Office button and selecting Word Options > Proofing > AutoCorrect Options. Under the AutoFormat tab, uncheck the box as shown in Figure 13.10.
5. Click OK.

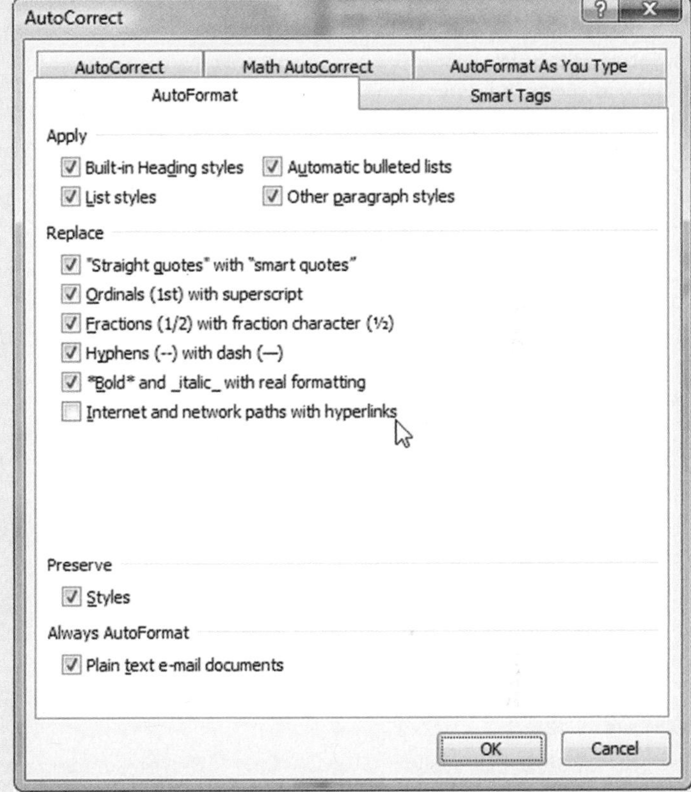

Figure 13.10 Removing the Automatic Hyperlink Insertion in Microsoft Word

For instructions that apply to Microsoft® Word® 2003, visit the handbook's website: **cengage.com/english/blakesley**

How to Format a Works Cited Page with Hanging Indentations

MLA style requires that entries in the Works Cited section be formatted with hanging indentations, as shown in Figure 13.11.

1. Starting with your Works Cited entries in double-spaced, flush-left format, select all entries by placing your cursor before the first entry, holding down the left mouse button (or the only button on a one-button mouse), to select all the entries.
2. To use the default keyboard shortcut, press Ctrl + T (or Command + T on a Mac keyboard) and you will see the hanging indentation applied. Alternatively, drag the bottom arrow of the ruler guide .5" to the right so that it looks like what is shown in Figure 13.12.

For instructions that apply to Microsoft® Word® 2003, visit the handbook's website: **cengage.com/english/blakesley**

Hanging Indent

Garrison 4

Works Cited

"'Blog' Most Popular Word on Web Dictionary." *MSNBC.com*. MSNBC, 2 Dec. 2004. Web. 15 Sept. 2005.

Bout, Danjel. "Snapshots." *Frontline Blogs*. N.p., 21 Aug. 2005. Web. 15 Sept. 2005.

Hockenberry, John. "The Blogs of War." *Wired.com*. Wired, Aug. 2005. Web. 14 Sept. 2005.

Prakash, Neil. "11 November: Tank Mines." *Armor Geddon*. N.p., 23 Jan. 2005. Web. 15 Sept. 2005.

Figure 13.11 A Works Cited Page with Hanging Indentations for Each Entry

Hanging Indent

Bout, Danjel. "Snapshots."

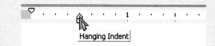

Figure 13.12 Dragging the Bottom Arrow of the Margin Guide to Create Hanging Indentations

McClure 1

Molly McClure

Dr. Shaun Hughes

English 130

May 15, 2006

"Get a Life!"

Misconceptions about the Tolkien Fan Fiction Culture

Fan fiction is a genre whose writers use existing stories, characters, plots, themes, and scenes as the starting point for extensions or retellings of the original. Fan fiction writers fill in gaps in the original story, track characters past the boundaries of the original work, or even create entirely new versions of stories. The modern genre has its origins in retellings and reworkings of science fiction and fantasy story lines, but today fan fiction encompasses creative responses to television series, movies, comic books, and books in many subgenres. Recently, a large body of fan fiction has grown up around J. R. R. Tolkien's *The Lord of the Rings* series, partly due to the popularity of the recent movies.

While some authors ridicule the efforts of fan fiction writers, often as a smokescreen for protecting their copyright interests, to say that fan fiction writers have overactive imaginations and too much time on their hands is to say the same about J. R. R. Tolkien himself.[1] Tolkien spent years of his life dreaming up every little detail about Middle Earth, including genealogies, maps, and languages; fan fiction writers borrow and expand on his inventions with creative and sometimes critical elaborations. In method, but not degree, perhaps their efforts are not so different from Tolkien's. Tolkien based his work on existing sources, great works of mythology and Anglo-Saxon literature such as *Beowulf*, as Christopher Tolkien (the author's son) has shown in *The History of* The Lord

Molly McClure's essay presents an argument using research from outside sources to build the case for correcting misperceptions about fan fiction, a wildly popular form of writing on the Internet. The title is an allusion to a famous *Saturday Night Live* skit in which William Shatner spoke to *Star Trek* fans at a convention and told them to "get a life."

The first paragraph provides some useful background information for understanding the basis of the argument, such as the definition of fan fiction.

This raised (superscript) number indicates that a note related to the sentence can be found at the end of the paper, after the main text and before the Works Cited page.

This general reference to an entire work includes the author's name and the title of the work, but not page numbers, which if included would indicate a more specific use of source material. Note, too, that the title of this work includes another book's title. The title within the title is not underlined or italicized.

This thesis statement follows a series of points about some misperceptions of fan fiction. It makes an argument that can be debated and also emphasizes the importance of overcoming these misperceptions for important subjects like literacy and literary appreciation.

McClure 2

of the Rings. To say that fan fiction is a passing fad would also be a mistake because its roots go back thousands of years, long before Tolkien inspired so many new authors. To say that fan fiction is not serious is to slight those who do take it seriously and to ignore that fan fiction may be one of the most popular and accessible forms of literary criticism in our culture. Like "remixing" and "sampling"—two popular forms of appreciating and extending music—good fan fiction requires practice, creativity, patience, and technical skill. Misperceptions about fan fiction writers, fan culture in general, and Tolkien fandom in particular prevent us from seeing its value as a form of critical literacy and a healthy form of literary appreciation.

The stereotypical—but by no means typical—fan fiction writer or reader is a heterosexual (predominantly but not exclusively) unmarried (sometimes) woman (usually true) with more time than she knows what to do with (definitely *not* true). Fan fiction writers and readers are women *and* men in every age group, every social class, every marital status, and every sexual orientation. These are not people with too much time on their hands; these are people who must make time to take part in their hobby. Reading and writing fan fiction are activities that require hours of thought and effort. Readers and writers of fan fiction cannot be dismissed as geeks, perverts, or sloths; to do so is to ignore the merit and worthiness of all types of fan fiction and to slight the value of literary appreciation itself.[2]

In literary history, Shakespeare and even his followers rewrote well-known plays to suit their present circumstances.[3] The impulse to reshape existing plots has an even longer history, however. Fan fiction writers are participating in a line of literary appreciation and intertextuality that extends back thousands of years, to times when stories and myths were preserved through successive retellings and elaborations. More so than people who simply read books or watch movies, fan

McClure 3

fiction writers are active creators who deserve recognition, not ridicule, for their efforts. Henry Jenkins begins his well-known book on fan culture, *Textual Poachers*, by saying it "documents a group insistent on making meaning from materials others have characterized as trivial and worthless" (3). Jenkins goes on to say, "I want to participate in the process of redefining the public identity of fandom . . . and to encourage a greater awareness of the richness of fan culture" (7). Fan culture is indeed rich, and richly diverse. Some of the biggest and longest-lasting fandoms are in science fiction/fantasy: *Star Trek, Star Wars, The X-Files, Harry Potter, The Lord of the Rings, Buffy the Vampire Slayer, X-Men*. Fandoms have now sprouted around just about every TV show imaginable: *ER, The West Wing, MASH, Alias, Smallville, NYPD Blue, Gilmore Girls, JAG,* and *Xena: Warrior Princess*. The same goes for books and authors: *The Baby-Sitters Club*, the Bible, Charles Dickens, *The Diary of Anne Frank*, the *Hardy Boys*, Jane Austen, *Les Misérables, Lord of the Flies*, Shakespeare, *To Kill a Mockingbird*, and *Sherlock Holmes*. Still other fandoms are based on movies: *Nightmare on Elm Street, The Breakfast Club, Bring It On, Chicken Run, Rocky Horror Picture Show, Pirates of the Caribbean, Moulin Rouge!, Men in Black, The Magnificent Seven, The Fast and the Furious*. Fandom is not the realm of a few geeks; it is a widespread culture of literary appreciation whose writers find value in what some others might find "worthless" (Jenkins 3).

Fan fiction became hugely popular with the emergence of the Internet as a new venue for gathering information about books and movies and sharing writing related to them. The Internet has made information about such films, TV shows, and literature easily accessible to anyone. Email, instant messaging, weblogs, discussion forums, newsgroups, online journals and ezines, mailing

The first time a source is cited, it's common practice to include the author's full name and the title of the work. Since the author's name is given in the text, only the page number needs to be included in parentheses at the end of the sentence.

An ellipsis (three spaced dots) shows readers that some words from the source have not been reprinted in the paper. See section 43d for a discussion of using ellipses.

Molly lists the wide variety of sources for fan fiction to help make her point in the last sentence of the paragraph: fan fiction "is a widespread culture of literary appreciation." Simply saying so would not be enough, so she gives direct evidence. Lists like these are common knowledge (and available widely), so the information doesn't need citation.

The name of a website is sometimes the same as the site's URL (without the *http://www.*). Molly shows the title the way it is shown on the website, with each significant word capitalized. (Remember that current MLA guidelines no longer require a URL for Web sources unless it is needed for the reader to find the source or your instructor requires one.) If Molly had to use the actual URL (in this case, http://www.fanfiction.net), it would appear only in the Works Cited entry.

The quotation from Nancy Schulz illustrates effective use of an external source to help provide background information that is not common knowledge. The parenthetical citation doesn't include a page number because the entire article appeared on a single page. The page number is included in the corresponding Works Cited entry.

Molly gathered this information herself from *FanFiction.Net*. Since it's an observable fact (and therefore common knowledge), no citation is required.

McClure 4

lists, and message boards now facilitate the kind of communication among fans that builds community and in turn nourishes fan fiction into existence. It's not surprising that fan fiction has evolved beyond its early focus on science fiction.

Today, one of the most popular and easily accessible websites for finding fan fiction is *FanFiction.Net*, which as early as April 2001, according to Nancy Schulz, already had "more than 41,000 stories in all, the work of 13,000 authors" ("The E-Files"). Those numbers have grown substantially in the last five years. One of the largest categories of stories at *FanFiction.Net* is based on *The Lord of the Rings (LOTR)*, partly because of the recent movies, which have made the *LOTR* trilogy more popular than ever. Although *LOTR* has been around much longer than many of the works common in fandom, there has not been much research into its particular nature, perhaps because until recent years the fandom was much quieter than others, with only the books to rely on. With the release of the movies, however, more and more people are reading and watching *LOTR* and becoming interested in the complex relationships among its characters. *The Silmarillion* category at *FanFiction.Net* has almost 1,000 stories, whereas *The Lord of the Rings* category is one of the biggest on the site: more than 36,000 stories are now posted.

Some of the popularity of writing about Tolkien's work has to do with the attractive actors in the films: there are more stories about Legolas than any other *LOTR* character at *FanFiction.Net*, due in no small part to Orlando Bloom's good looks. Many of these stories are "Mary Sues" written by "fangirls"; that is, the authors are girls and women who desire Bloom, so they write stories about Legolas in which he falls in love with original female characters who bear a striking resemblance to the story's author, sometimes even with the same name. These stories are some of the most despised in fandom, as the whole plot of the

McClure 5

story is for Legolas to fall madly in love with the perfect woman, marry her, father her children, and live happily ever after. Not all original characters are so stigmatized, but original love interests, especially Legolas's, are always looked on with suspicion lest Mary Sue/Marty Stu characteristics develop. Jenkins labels this writing technique "personalization":

> Fan writers . . . work to efface the gap that separates the realm of their own experience and the fictional space of their favorite programs. "Mary Sue" stories . . . constitute one of the most disputed subgenres of fan fiction. So strong is the fan taboo against such crude personalizations that original female characters are often scrutinized for any signs of autobiographical intent. (171-73)

Mary Sue stories are not the only kind of story popular with fan fiction writers. In addition to personalization, Jenkins explains some other strategies of writing fan fiction. He labels one popular subgenre "recontextualization," saying that "fans often write short vignettes ('missing scenes') which fill in the gaps in the original and provide additional explanations for the character's conduct; these stories focus on off-screen actions and discussion that motivated perplexing on-screen behavior" (162). In *The Lord of the Rings* fandom, stories detail scenes like the Fellowship's stay in Lothlorien, Aragorn's trip along the Paths of the Dead and up the Anduin, and the discovery of Pippin on the battlefield in front of the Black Gate. In *The Silmarillion*, popular topics include Feanor's sons' reaction to Fingon bringing Maedhros back to them. Jenkins also explains that "expanding the series timeline" is a common technique because "the primary texts often provide hints or suggestions about the characters' backgrounds not fully explored within the episodes" (163). It is common for writers to take these tidbits as starting points for writing prologues or counter

Molly uses a complete sentence followed by a colon to introduce a block quotation. See page 184 for a discussion of block quotations.

At the end of a block quotation, a period ends the final sentence before the parenthetical citation is provided. This is one difference between citing a quotation that is run into your own sentence and one that is blocked off. See pages 183–184.

In this paragraph, Molly continues the strategy of defining strategies of fan fiction, using the Jenkins source, a recognized authority, to help guide the discussion and carefully citing it along the way. Examples are drawn from the Tolkien fandom.

The brackets around "of narrative crisis" indicate that Molly added words that did not come from the original source in order to make sure readers would understand the quotation in the context of her research paper. See page 503.

McClure 6

narratives. In *The Lord of the Rings* fandom, writers detail Legolas's life in Mirkwood before becoming a part of the Fellowship, or any of the characters' early lives: Boromir and Faramir as brothers in Minas Tirith, Gimli at the Lonely Mountain, and so on. Topics also include what happens next: What adventures do Aragorn, Gimli, and Legolas have as rulers of their own lands? Do Eomer and Faramir join them on these journeys? What happens once Frodo reaches Valinor? If Gimli really sails West with Legolas, how is he received? Alternate universe stories (AUs) fall within this category as well. For example, a story may posit that Elrond stays in Rivendell to see his grandchildren before sailing West. Frodo may live with Sam and Rosie and help them raise their children instead of leaving them at Bag End.

Another popular subgenre in fan fiction is "hurt/comfort," which falls under Jenkins's heading "emotional intensification" and "centers almost entirely upon such moments [of narrative crisis], sometimes building on a crisis represented within the series proper . . . other times inventing situations where the characters experience vulnerability" (174). A near brush with death or a serious revelation will allow two (normally male) characters to become closer to one another. Jenkins argues that the drives behind such stories "cut to the heart of our culture's patriarchal conception of the hero as a man of emotional constraint and personal autonomy, a man in control of all situations" (175). Hurt/comfort stories also reveal the natural and human weaknesses in larger-than-life heroes, which makes their recovery from near tragedy inspiring and all the more amazing. One favorite subject of hurt/comfort stories (commonly abbreviated as h/c) in the *LOTR* realm is Legolas, prompting fan fiction writers to invent the phrase "elf torture" as another name for stories in which he is in physical or mental distress. The character who seems to comfort Legolas the

McClure 7

most is Aragorn, followed closely by Gimli. The popularity of this subgenre is also clear in the *X-Files* fandom, where there is an archive called "Mulder Torture Anonymous" that is filled with thousands of h/c stories.

How men and women might approach fan fiction differently has been the subject of interesting debates, reminiscent of those that have also focused on how women and men might read differently. Jenkins explores this subject by discussing studies done by David Bleich and Elizabeth Segel on the differences between male and female readers of literary texts. He claims that David Bleich's 1986 study found that "female readers entered directly into the fictional world, focusing less on the extratextual process of its writing than on the relationships and events" (108). In contrast, male readers "acknowledged and respected the author's authority, while women saw themselves as engaged in a 'conversation' within which they could participate as active contributors" (108). Male readers also "tended to maintain the narrative focus on a central protagonist, while female readers eagerly explored a broader range of social relationships" (Jenkins 109). Female readers, Bleich argued, sought to "retell the story more in terms of interpersonal motives, allegiances, and conflicts" (qtd. in Jenkins 109). Jenkins uses Elizabeth Segel's 1986 study of gender and reading to make the point that young girls are typically encouraged to "make sense" of male-centered narratives. Young boys, the study suggests, can't be coaxed into experimenting with female characters in their narratives, so their responses to fiction often focus on the weaknesses of female-centered stories (Jenkins 114). This certainly rings true when looking at *The Lord of the Rings*, in which there is a dearth of strong female characters. Women must interpret from the book what they can because there are hardly any women in the story to do it for them.

It's better to cite a source directly, rather than citing it as you saw it reprinted in another source. But sometimes you simply don't have access to the original source. In this case, you can note that you found the first source "quoted in" another. Notice in this paragraph how careful Molly is to distinguish the words of Henry Jenkins discussing David Bleich's study and the words of Bleich himself.

This sentence and the discussion below raise the point that fan fiction tackles important social issues.

McClure 8

Anna Smol argues in "'Oh . . . Oh . . . Frodo!' Readings of Male Intimacy in *The Lord of the Rings*" that Tolkien fandom has intensified interest in exploring male relationships in ways that traditional criticism could not, adding to *LOTR*'s intertextuality (969). Fan fiction stories known as "slash," which focus on same-sex couples, also raise important social questions about gender identity. Jenkins explains his interest in slash in part by saying, "Slash . . . posits an explicit critique of traditional masculinity, trying to establish an homosocial-homoerotic continuum as an alternative to repressive and hierarchical male sexuality. Both partners retain equality *and* autonomy while moving into a more satisfying and committed relationship" (219). Slash may even have greater worth and value than "gen" (general, non-romance) or "het" (heterosexual romance) fan fiction. Certainly the reasons people write it and the questions it raises are just as interesting as, if not more interesting than, regular fan fiction. Whether slash fiction is considered perverted or not, often the politics behind slash fiction is fascinating. Neva Chonin wrote an article for *SFGate.com* in which she says a certain passage between Sam and Frodo in *The Two Towers* "illustrates one of the most basic and overlooked aspects of Tolkien's trilogy. Beneath its mythic layers of good and evil, wizards and kings and tyrants, . . . it's a tribute to love between men." It is not a great leap, then, for some writers to imagine physical expressions of two characters' love for each other. Camille Bacon-Smith says in *Enterprising Women* that "Many women perceive a deep and loving relationship between characters . . . because series creators put it there. The homosocial partnership has been a staple of Western romance tradition for at least two thousand years" (234). Strong relationships and bonds among men have been around for millennia, then, so perhaps it is understandable that women are writing about them in such large numbers.

McClure 9

Works of fan fiction—like the stories on which they are based—ask us to imagine alternative universes so that we can gain perspective on our own. In the end, the reason people write fan fiction is simple, no different from the reason J. R. R. Tolkien wrote his epic novels. On the special extended DVD edition of *The Two Towers*, Brian Sibley (also author of *The Lord of the Rings: The Making of the Movie Trilogy*) shares this story:

> There was a conversation that took place between Tolkien and C. S. Lewis . . . in which they were talking about the fact that they felt a frustration that they couldn't pick up and read the kind of books and stories that they liked to read. And they both came to this conclusion that in the end maybe they had to write the books they wanted to read. (qtd. in Jackson)

Writers of fan fiction, whether they are writing gen, slash, het, h/c, or another subgenre, have come to the same conclusion, and they are no more worthy of scorn than Tolkien himself.

The first sentence of the conclusion explains how fan fiction worlds have social and personal value. It addresses the "so what?" question that readers sometimes expect to find answered by the end of an essay.

Molly uses a long quotation at the end of her essay to emphasize once again a point she made at the beginning: the same creative impulse drives fan fiction writers and the more famous authors whose work inspires them.

Notes serve two functions in MLA style: (1) they provide information relevant to the argument but not relevant enough to put in the body of the paper, and (2) they provide citations that would clutter the main text if placed there.

Here, note 1 adds information about critics of fan fiction that might have sidetracked Molly's main argument if it had been put in the body of the paper. Notes 2 and 3 also provide qualifying information and point to two websites.

The first line of each note is indented, and the note number appears in superscript (raised) style. A space follows the superscript number.

McClure 10

Notes

[1] Anne Rice, author of *Interview with the Vampire*, initially supported fan fiction based on her work, but when characters were developed in ways she disliked, she launched a "cease and desist" campaign that resulted in the removal of that novel as a source at *FanFiction.Net* and other sites. The forums at the website *Godawful Fan Fiction* include criticism of fan fiction in general and single out particularly bad examples for ridicule.

[2] Perhaps the best way to break down stereotypes is with knowledge. Although it should only be considered a starting point for further research and, like any such article, may contain inaccuracies, the Wikipedia article on fan fiction provides a lengthy and detailed overview of its major features, history, types, and devotees: http://en.wikipedia.org/wiki/Fan_fiction.

[3] See, for example, Nahum Tate's famous adaptation of *King Lear*, which has an alternative ending in which everyone survives, both happy and smarter, unlike in Shakespeare's original: http://andromeda.rutgers.edu/~jlynch/Texts/tatelear.html.

McClure 11

Works Cited

Bacon-Smith, Camille. *Enterprising Women: Television Fandom and the Creation of Popular Myth*. Philadelphia: U of Pennsylvania P, 1992. Print.

Chonin, Neva. “Love between Men Is a Powerful Thing in *Lord of the Rings*.” *SFGate.com*. Hearst Communications. 15 Jan. 2002. Web. 11 Aug. 2002.

FanFiction.Net. 2006. Web. 17 Feb. 2006.

Godawful Fan Fiction. 2006. Web. 17 Feb. 2006.

Jackson, Peter, dir. *The Two Towers*. Special Extended Edition. New Line Cinema/WingNut Films, 2004. DVD.

Jenkins, Henry. *Textual Poachers: Television Fans and Participatory Culture*. New York: Routledge, 1992. Print.

Rice, Anne. “Important Message from Anne on ‘Fan Fiction.’” *AnneRice.com*. 2000. Web. 17 Feb. 2006.

Schulz, Nancy. “The E-Files.” *Washington Post* 29 Apr. 2001: G1. Print.

Smol, Anna. “‘Oh . . . Oh . . . Frodo!’ Readings of Male Intimacy in *The Lord of the Rings*.” *Modern Fiction Studies* 50.4 (2004): 949-79. Print.

Tolkien, Christopher. *The History of* The Lord of the Rings. 5 vols. New York: Houghton, 2000. Print.

The Works Cited list includes all sources quoted, summarized, or paraphrased.

A book by one author

An article published in an online newspaper

Even though this source was discussed only in a note, it must be included in the Works Cited.

The title of this article from a scholarly journal includes a quotation enclosed in a pair of single quotation marks, as well as the title of the work being discussed, which is italicized because it is a book. The whole article title is then enclosed in double quotation marks. It’s important to get these details right when preparing a Works Cited list.

APA, CMS, CSE, and CGOS Documentation

PART 5

New Contexts for Writing: Social Networks

Social networks link people with common interests on public or semi-public Internet sites, where they can share facts (or fabrications), photos, stories, calendars, notes, friends, and more. Social networking technologies interlink the data, making it possible for people to form groups around almost any interest or attitude imaginable. Effective self-representation, always a challenge for a writer, becomes critical, since how you identify yourself—your ethos—will shape the character of your relations with others in the present and, very likely, for many years to come.

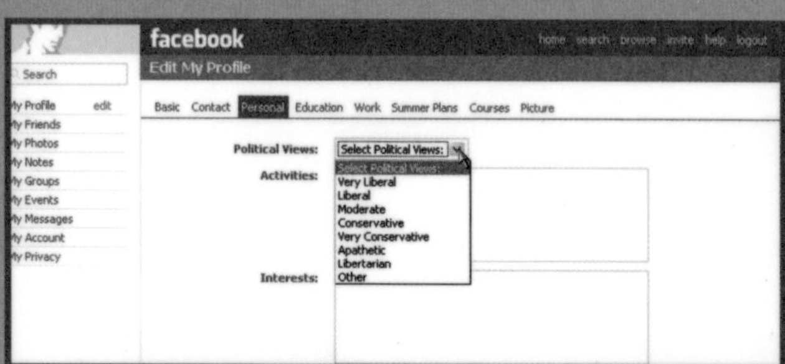

Facebook (http://www.facebook.com) is one of the most popular social networking services for college students. Anyone with an email address from a "supported high school, college, or company" can create a profile, which becomes the basis for creating a network of people, lists of shared interests, and more. Other popular sites include MySpace (http://www.myspace.com) and Orkut (http://www.orkut.com).

Social networking services make it easier for people to act together, in whatever ways they decide are worthwhile, for good or ill. That's why they are so popular. They also can have unanticipated side-effects. Because social networks are public spaces and may be archived and mined for data, information that gets posted may remain available for a long time, may be read by more than a circle of friends (such as future employers), and may present an image people regret later. Some users create false identities and use them to manipulate others.

A **network** is an online system of links connecting information and people. Social networking sites can offer free services either because they are supported by ads or because they compile and sell information about users and their interests through a process called **data mining.** Data mining helps companies make decisions about how to develop products and services and how to market them. **Privacy policies** at such sites should identify what control you have over the information you provide and how it may be used by others. Typically, users are able to adjust some privacy settings in their system **profile,** which includes personal information.

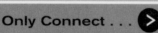

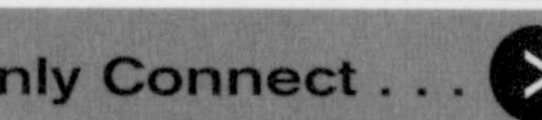

To learn more about the rhetoric of social networking, read . . .

"How Will Your Online Profile Affect Potential Job Offers?" (JobWeb)
http://www.jobweb.com/resources/library/Interviews/How_Will_Your_O_302_1.htm

"Thoughts on Facebook" (Tracy Mitrano, Cornell University IT Policy Office)
http://www.cit.cornell.edu/policy/memos/facebook.html

or watch . . .

Parodies of MySpace and Facebook at YouTube.com. (Search using the name of each site for a list of hilarious movies about MySpace and Facebook from an insider's point of view.)

The Link between the In-Text Citation and the Reference

In-text citation of a book:

> Cultural Tasks 2
>
> Woodman (1992) suggests that a main task in our culture is to learn to relate to archetypes without identifying with them (p. 13).

Reference entry:

> Cultural Tasks 7
>
> Reference
>
> Woodman, M. (1992). *Leaving my father's house: A journey to conscious femininity.* Boston: Shambhala.

Notice in the in-text citation:

- The author's last name, the publication date, and the page number are all provided.
- The publication date is given in parentheses—often as you see it here, directly after the author's last name.
- The page number is given within parentheses, with the abbreviation *p.* used for "page" (and *pp.* used for "pages").
- The sentence ends after the in-text citation.
- An alternative is to place the author's last name, the publication date, and the page number all within parentheses: (Woodman, 1992, p. 13).

Notice in the Reference entry:

- The author's last name is used to alphabetize the entry. The author's first name is reduced to an initial. A comma and space separate the two.
- The publication date is given in parentheses. A period follows.
- The book title is given in italics. Only the first word of the main title, the first word of the subtitle, and any proper nouns (none here) are capitalized. A period follows.
- The publication information includes the city of publication, followed by a colon, and the name of the publisher, followed by a period.
- The first line starts at the left margin, but the second and subsequent lines are indented from the left margin.

The citation style recommended by the American Psychological Association (APA) is used to cite sources in the social sciences—psychology, education, management, anthropology, political science, sociology, and economics. If you major in one of these fields, you may want to examine a copy of the *Publication Manual of the American Psychological Association,* 5th edition.

The APA style has two basic components: (1) citations of summaries, paraphrases, and quotations given inside parentheses in the body of the research paper and (2) an alphabetically organized References page at the end of the text, which provides the publication information. In the social sciences, new research results frequently correct previous knowledge. To establish the research timeline, the APA system includes the date of publication in the in-text citation. The author's last name and the publication date link the in-text citation to the References entry.

APA INDEXES

Models of in-text citations begin on page 248.

Treat short quotations and long quotations according to APA guidelines.

Short Quotations

Quotations of fewer than 40 words should be incorporated into the body of your text and enclosed in double quotation marks (" "). Place the citation as close as possible to the material being quoted, either immediately after the quotation if it will not distract the reader or at the end of the sentence. Page numbers are required, as are the author's name and the publication year.

The period goes after the closing parenthesis at the end of the sentence, not within the last quotation mark. However, when your quotation ends with an exclamation point or question mark, the punctuation mark stays within the quotation marks, and then you add the parenthetical citation followed by a period.

If the source you are quoting includes quoted sources or dialogue, change the quotation marks around the original quotation to single marks.

End punctuation after citation in short quotation:

> Genetic Basis 4
>
> Turner (2003) suggests that habitual behavior is often the "genius of genetic coding carried to an infinite degree of hereditary variables" (pp. 32–33).

? or ! within the quotation:

> Varied Intelligences 2
>
> Gardner (1983) asks, "What if one were to let one's imagination wander freely, to consider the wider range of performances that are in fact valued throughout the world?" (p. 4).

Original source material with quotation marks, from *Family Therapy in Clinical Practice,* by Murray Bowen, M.D. (1985), page 348:

> The team-group meetings are commonly used for "training" inexperienced professional people who learn by participation in the team meetings, and who can rather quickly gain the status of "family therapist."

Text citation, with double quotation marks changed to singles:

> Family Therapy 3
>
> Bowen (1985) describes one type of problem-focused family therapy: "The team-group meetings are commonly used for 'training' inexperienced professional people who learn by participation in the team meetings, and who can rather quickly gain the status of 'family therapist'" (p. 348).

Parenthetical citation after a long quotation:

Adoptive Family 9

Oxengale and Ferris (1999) cite disturbing trends in adoption:

> Unfortunately, the various entities of the states' DSS units often cull children from neglectful or absent parents, whose main offense seems to be more a medical one . . . than a criminal or DSS-related issue. During these periods of heavy growth in children taken into the custody of the states, foster parents are often even more difficult to locate. This causes systematic breakdown and overcrowding of wards best kept open for criminal-related individuals. (pp. 322–323)

Original source material from *The Developing Person through the Life Span,* 5th ed., by Kathleen Stassen Berger (2001), page 423:

> Provocative international data from European nations show a negative correlation between hours of employment after school and learning in school (Kelly, 1998). Such correlations do not prove causation, but it is curious that U.S. fourth-graders, who obviously do not have jobs, score much closer to their European peers on standardized tests than U.S. twelfth-graders do.

Text citation, with ellipsis points:

Teenage Employment 5

Berger (2001) summarizes Kelly's (1998) European data and then cautiously notes that "such correlations do not prove causation, but . . . U.S. fourth-graders . . . score much closer to their European peers on standardized tests than U.S. twelfth-graders do" (p. 423).

Long Quotations

Quotations of 40 or more words should be set out in block format, *without* quotation marks. Block quotations should be started on a new line, indented 1/2" (five spaces) from the left margin, and double-spaced throughout. If the quotation is more than one paragraph, indent the first line of the second and any additional paragraphs in the quotation an additional 1/2" (a total of ten typewriter spaces). The parenthetical citation is given after the last punctuation mark of the block quotation, separated by one space.

Any quotation marks in the original can remain double, since the overall quotation is indicated by indentation, not by quotation marks.

Making Changes to Quotations

If you make any changes to quotations, you need to let readers know that you have done so.

Taking Words Out

Use an ellipsis (three spaced dots) to show that you have omitted material from a quotation. If you omit material from the beginning of a sentence that follows the end of another, use four dots—one for the period and three for the ellipsis. (See section 12c.)

Adding Words or Explanations

Use brackets to indicate additions or explanations. (See section 12c.)

APA In-Text Citations Index

APA In-Text Citation Models

1. Author named in your text

Hillman (2004) says that we cannot understand war until we "understand the madness of its love" (p. 1).

Place the citation either at a natural break in a sentence or at the end of it. Always provide a specific page number immediately after a direct quotation.

2. Author not named in your text

Fascism is said to be "absolute politics for people with absolute agendas" (Hoskins, 2001, p. 21).

3. No author's or editor's name or anonymous source

Use an abbreviated form of the title, dropping *The, A,* or *An* from the beginning. Use quotation marks to enclose an article or chapter title; put the title of a book, periodical, or report in italics. Then in the References list, use the full title in place of the author's name.

Binge drinking is cited as the most common form of teenage substance abuse ("Alcohol linked," 2002, p. 34).

Note: Although you do not use quotation marks around article titles in the References list, you *do* use them around article titles in your text.

If a source lists the author as "Anonymous," use that word as the author, along with the date:

(Anonymous, 2004).

4. Two authors

Include both last names in your text each time you refer to the source. For in-text introductions, use the word *and* to join the names:

> Hollis and Ware (1994) felt confident that "hatred leads to aggression" (p. 11).

In parenthetical citations, use an ampersand (&) to join the names:

> Some reports suggest that "hatred leads to aggression" (Hollis & Ware, 1994, p. 11).

5. Three to five authors

Write all the authors' last names the first time you refer to the source, followed by the date of publication in parentheses. After that, include only the first author's last name in the text, followed by the abbreviation *et al.* (an abbreviation for the Latin term *et alii,* meaning "and others"), and provide the date only if you are citing the source for the first time in a paragraph.

> Hockney, Allison, Fielding, Johnson, and Glade (2003) indicate that "politics have been corrupted by wealthy individuals creating foundations with overly partisan agendas" (p. 12).

> Hockney et al. (2003) express their disdain in agreeing that "openness and candor are missing from some foundation sources this election cycle" (p. 33).

Note: If you use two sources published the same year and the last names of the first authors are also the same, cite the last names of as many of the other authors as needed to distinguish the sources from each other.

APA In-Text Citations Index

APA In-Text Citations Index

6. Six or more authors

For both introductory and parenthetical citations, use the first author listed and then the phrase *et al.*

> Ruotolo et al. (1985) lament the loss of "job and social stability when personnel depart the military" (p. 33).

In the References list, give the last names and first initials of the first six authors and then write *et al.*

7. Chapter in an edited book or anthology

Use the standard APA in-text citation format, giving the name of the author of the specific article or chapter you are referencing.

> Rogers (2004) noted . . . (p. 222).
>
> or
>
> (Rogers, 2004, p. 222).

8. Two or more primary authors with the same last name

The primary author is the first one listed for a particular source. Even if the publication dates of two works by primary authors with the same last name would distinguish the sources, use their initials each time you mention them in the text to avoid confusion.

> P. L. Knox and Allen (2004) found . . .
>
> A. J. Knox and Henry (2001) studied . . .

9. More than one source by the same author

If you are citing works by the same author(s) published in different years, including the dates in parentheses is enough to allow readers to identify the sources in your References. If the sources were published in the same year, alphabetize them in the References list according to title and then, in that order, assign each one a letter suffix (*a*, *b*, *c*, and so on) after the date.

> Surely, Smith (2001a) cannot be correct when she writes, "David Harris and other occupational therapists have violated their field's norms" (pp. 23–24).

Corresponding references list:

> Smith, J. D. (2001a). Occupational therapy and magnetic resonance . . .
> Smith, J. D. (2001b). Treating blood disorders . . .
> Smith, J. D. (2001c). Verification of patient responsibilities . . .

10. Corporate or other group author

Use the full name of the group or entity that created the source each time, unless the name is very long or unless an acronym for the group is well known—for instance, *CIA*. In this case, spell out the name the first time, along with the acronym, and use the acronym the second and subsequent times.

> The National Security Agency (NSA, 2004) identifies terrorism as "the major weapon of disempowered groups throughout the world" (p. 233).

Subsequent references:

> . . . (NSA, 2004).

APA In-Text Citations Index

APA In-Text Citations Index

11. Two or more sources by different authors in the same citation

In parentheses immediately following the use of the information (which often is not quoted but summarized), list the sources alphabetically by first author's last name and include the year of publication. Separate the information for each source with a semicolon. Include page numbers if they are known.

> Many researchers (Holtzbringer, 2001; Mallory, 2003, p. 99; Vickenstein, 2001, p. 76) have described rehabilitation as a painful, long, and grueling process. Holtzbringer (2001) has provided four criteria to use in judging how long rehabilitation is likely to take.

12. Two or more sources by the same author in the same citation

Write the author's name or authors' names only once, and then list the sources by year of publication, starting with the oldest. In-press publications are listed last. (These are works that aren't yet published but have been accepted for publication.)

> (MacKnight & Lovington, 1999, 2002, in press)

If two or more sources are by the same author(s) and have the same publication year, use suffixes (*a, b, c,* and so on) and repeat the year each time. (See citation model 9 on page 251.)

> Three surveys (Wangera, 2004a, 2004b, 2004c) . . .

13. Indirect source

When you cite an indirect source, provide the secondary source in the reference list. For your in-text citation, name the original source and then provide a separate citation for the secondary source.

For instance, if Cronenberg's quotation is found in an article written by Harding and Fields and you cannot locate the original Cronenberg source, list Harding and Fields in the in-text citation:

> David Cronenberg stated that "the future of Cinema is only limited by the dark imaginations of those involved in the production of filmic texts, while technology's role is overstated enthusiastically by those people with limited capacities for understanding the work of film in society" (cited in Harding & Fields, 2003, p. 34).

14. Electronic source

Include the author's last name and the publication date as you would for a printed source. If you directly quote material from an electronic document that numbers paragraphs rather than pages, use the abbreviation *para.* or the symbol ¶ before the number in your parenthetical citation.

> Horatio and Holder (2004) describe alternative treatments for sickle cell disease (Method section, para. 7).

Note: Because another researcher would not be able to locate the information later, informal electronic communications, such as personal email and posts to unarchived discussion groups, are only cited in the text and not listed in the References. Check with your instructor to be sure using such sources is acceptable.

15. Personal communication

When you cite personal communications (telephone conversations, personal interviews, emails, letters, and so on), write *personal communication* after the author's or speaker's name, followed by the full date of the communication.

> He describes *basic methods* as "facile and easily imitated versus more professional and less likely to be deviated from" (T. L. Scholder, personal communication, October 23, 2004).

Note: APA style calls for personal communications not to be listed in the References. However, your instructor may want you to list them anyway, so be sure to ask.

APA In-Text Citations Index

14a

APA In-Text Citations Index

16. Photograph or figure

Copyright information for photos and figures is given at the end of the image's caption. (The caption explains the image and is placed after it.) Your entry will start a new line after the rest of the caption.

Format if the image is from a book:

> *Note.* From *The Visual Turn and the Transformation of the Textbook* (p. 17), by J. A. Laspina, 1998, Mahwah, NJ: Lawrence Erlbaum Associates. Copyright 1998 by Lawrence Erlbaum Associates, Inc. Reprinted with permission.

Format if the image is from an article:

> *Note.* From "Article Title," by initials and last name of author, year, *Name of Journal, volume number,* page number(s). Copyright year by the copyright holder's name. Reprinted with permission.

If you make any changes to the image, write *Adapted* instead of *Reprinted.*

For information on how to place an image and add a caption using Microsoft Word, see page 228.

14b APA References Page

The APA References page includes only information on sources that are summarized, paraphrased, or quoted in your paper. The reference list starts on a separate page at the end of your text and is paginated consecutively in the same style as the rest of the work. See page 280 for an example. If you cite only one source, call the list *Reference*.

Common APA Abbreviations Used in References Entries

chap.: chapter
ed.: edition
Ed. (Eds.): Editor (Editors)
No.: Number
n.d.: no date
p. (pp.) (include a space after the period): page (pages)
para: paragraph
Pt.: Part
Rev. ed.: Revised edition
2nd ed., 3rd ed.: second edition, third edition
Trans.: Translator(s)
Vol. (Vols.): Volume (Volumes)

APA References Models

1. Book by a single author

List the author's last name first, followed by a comma and the initials of the first and any middle names. Then provide the year of publication in parentheses, followed by a period. Italicize the title, capitalizing only the first word of the title and the subtitle and any proper nouns, followed by a period. Then give the city of publication, followed by a colon and the shortened form of the publisher's name.

> Bazerman, C. (2002). *The languages of Edison's light.* Cambridge, MA: MIT Press.

2. Book by two to six authors

Separate the names by commas, and use an ampersand (&) immediately before the last author's name.

> Burawoy, M., Burton, A., Ferguson, A. A., & Fox, K. J. (1991). *Ethnography unbound: Power and resistance in the modern metropolis.* Berkeley: University of California Press.

3. Book by seven or more authors

Write the first six names and then *et al.,* followed by the year in parentheses.

> Delay, F., Deville, P., Echenoz, J., Greenlee, S., Mathews, H., Polizzotti, M., et al. (1997). *S: A novel.* Cambridge, MA: Brookline Books.

4. Book by an unknown or anonymous author

Start with the title, followed by any edition information.

> *Rhetoric to Herennius.* (1964). H. Caplan (Trans.). Cambridge, MA: Harvard University Press.

APA References Index: Books and Other Nonperiodicals

1. Book by a single author
2. Book by two to six authors
3. Book by seven or more authors
4. Book by an unknown or anonymous author
5. Book with a corporate or group author
6. Book with an editor
7. Book with a translator
8. Chapter in an edited book or anthology
9. Two or more books by the same author published in the same year
10. Book in a second or subsequent edition
11. Work in more than one volume
12. Government publication
13. Report from a private organization
14. Report available from ERIC
15. Brochure

APA References Index: Books and Other Nonperiodicals

5. Book with a corporate or group author

Use as the author the name of the group or organization that created the document. When the publisher and the author are the same, use *Author* instead of repeating the group's name.

> American Psychiatric Association. (1994). *Diagnostic and statistical manual of mental disorders* (4th ed.). Washington, DC: Author.

6. Book with an editor

Use names of editors as you would those of authors. Identify them as editors by putting *Ed.* or *Eds.* in parentheses after the name(s). **Note:** Use a period after the abbreviation *and* after the parenthesis.

> Johnson, M. H. (Ed.). (1993). *Brain development and cognition: A reader.* Cambridge, MA: Blackwell.

7. Book with a translator

Write the name of the translator after the title, in parentheses, followed by a comma and the abbreviation *Trans.* Place a period after the parenthesis. **Note:** Use first and middle initials and then the last name.

> Bertolucci, A. (2005). *Winter journey* (N. Benson, Trans.). West Lafayette, IN: Parlor Press.

8. Chapter in an edited book or anthology

Start the entry with the name(s) of the author(s) of the chapter and the date on which the *entire* work was published. Next, write the title of the chapter and follow with a period. Then write the word *In* followed by the name(s) of the editor(s) of the text, including first and any middle initials and giving the names in normal order. Continue with the abbreviation *Ed.* or *Eds.* in parentheses, a comma, the book or anthology title, page number(s) of the chapter in parentheses, and a period. Close with the publication information.

LeBon, G. (1997). The crowd: A study of the popular mind. In C. D. Ellis (Ed.), *The investor's anthology: Original ideas from the industry's greatest minds* (pp. 6–12). New York: Wiley.

9. Two or more books by the same author published in the same year

When you use two or more books or other sources by the same author that were published in the same year, use lowercase letters—starting with *a, b,* and *c*—to differentiate them. The letter follows the year. Organize the works alphabetically by title, ignoring any initial article (*A, The, An*). Double-check your in-text citations to make sure you have labeled each source properly.

Tufte, E. R. (1997a). *The visual display of quantitative information* (2nd ed.). Cheshire, CT: Graphics Press.

Tufte, E. R. (1997b). *Visual explanations: Images and quantities, evidence and narrative.* Cheshire, CT: Graphics Press.

10. Book in a second or subsequent edition

For books in a second or later edition, provide the edition number and *ed.* in parentheses after the title, followed by a period. Use the abbreviation *Rev. ed.* for *Revised edition.*

Patton, M. Q. (2002). *Qualitative research and evaluation methods* (3rd ed.). Thousand Oaks, CA: Sage.

11. Work in more than one volume

When you use only one volume from a multivolume work, cite the one volume.

Trumbach, R. (1998). *Sex and the gender revolution* (Vol. 1). Chicago: University of Chicago Press.

APA References Index: Books and Other Nonperiodicals

APA References Index: Books and Other Nonperiodicals

When you use more than one volume, cite all of the volumes you use.

Pelikan, J. (1975–1991). *The Christian tradition: A history of the development of doctrine* (Vols. 1–5). Chicago: University of Chicago Press.

12. Government publication

If no author is named for a government report, use the name of the sponsoring agency to start your entry. Include the publication number in parentheses after the title of the pamphlet or report, and show the U.S. Government Printing Office (GPO) as the publisher if the document is available from the GPO:

Office of Native American Programs. (1995). *Our home: Achieving the Native American dream of homeownership* (HH 1.6/3: H75/12). Washington, DC: GPO.

13. Report from a private organization

Use the standard book format. Use the author's name when available; otherwise, use the corporate name as the author. If there is a report or edition number, include it in parentheses immediately after the title:

National Urban League. (2005). *The state of black America: Prescriptions for change.* New York: Author.

Nierenberg, D. (2005). *Happier meals: Rethinking the global meat industry* (Worldwatch Paper #171). Washington, DC: Worldwatch Institute.

14. Report available from ERIC

Use the standard book format if the report did not originally appear in a journal. Add the ERIC reference number in parentheses.

> Hassel, B., Ziebarth, T., & Steiner, L. (2005). *A state policymaker's guide to alternative authorizers of charter schools* (ECS Issue Brief). Denver: Education Commission of the States. (ERIC Document Reproduction Service No. ED489327)

15. Brochure

After the title of the work, include information on the form of the work in brackets.

> University of South Carolina Office of Student Orientation and Testing Services. (2005). *Parent information 2005* [Brochure]. Columbia: Author.

16. Article in journal with continuous pagination throughout annual volume

Start with the author's last name and then initials, followed by the publication date in parentheses. Titles of articles are never underlined or italicized; capitalize only the first word of the title and the subtitle and any proper nouns. Each important word in the journal name is capitalized, and the journal name *is* italicized, as is the volume number that follows it. Do not use the abbreviation *p.* or *pp.* before the page numbers. The title, volume number, and pages are separated by commas and end with a period. When an article is from a journal that numbers issues consecutively over the course of a year, you do not include the issue number.

> Towler, A. J., & Schneider, D. J. (2005). Distinctions among stigmatized groups. *Journal of Applied Social Psychology, 35,* 1–14.

For author variations, see citation models 1 through 5 (pages 255–256) and 9 (page 257).

APA References Index: Books and Other Nonperiodicals

Periodicals

APA References Index: Periodicals

17. Article in journal that pages each issue separately

When an article is in a journal that paginates each issue separately (each issue starts with page 1), you need to include the issue number. Put it in parentheses immediately after the volume number (do not put a space between them), and do not italicize it.

> Miles, L. (2000). Constructing composition: Reproduction and WPA agency in textbook publishing. *Writing Program Administration, 24*(1–2), 27–51.

18. Abstract of journal article

Write the author's name, the date (typically only the year), and the title of the article; then identify it with *[Abstract]*. Give the journal name in italics, and add the page number(s).

> Nespor, M., & Sandler, W. (1999). Prosody in Israeli sign language [Abstract]. *Language and Speech, 42,* 143.

19. Article in magazine

Start with the author's name and the date. If it's a monthy magazine, put the year, a comma, and the month. If it's a weekly or daily publication, put the year, a comma, the month, and the day. Then write the title of the article (without quotation marks or italics) and the magazine name (in italics). Write the volume number. Finish with the page number(s).

> Rosenwald, M. (2006, January). The flu hunter. *Smithsonian, 36*, 36–46.

20. Article in newspaper

Write the author's name, the date (year, month, and day), the title of the article, the newspaper's name (in italics), and the page number(s), preceded by the abbreviation *p.* or *pp.*

Farrell, E. F. (2005, April 1). Starving for attention. *The Chronicle of Higher Education,* pp. A45–A46.

If no author's name appears, alphabetize by the first word of the title, excluding *A, An,* or *The*. If the page numbers aren't consecutive, give all page numbers, separated by commas: "pp. A2, A5, A7–A8."

21. Letter to the editor

Write the author's name, the date of publication (in parentheses), the title of the letter (if there is one), and *[Letter to the editor]*. Give the name of the journal or newspaper that printed the letter and the page number(s).

Masterson, G. (2006, February 25). Coyote hunting I [Letter to the editor]. *The Addison Eagle,* p. 4.

22. Review

After the title of the review, in brackets add the words *Review of* and then give the kind of work reviewed—such as book, article, film, or CD—and the title of the work reviewed. Name the publication that printed the review, the volume number (if applicable), and the page number(s).

Mondragon, T. (2004, March 29). Exposing the myth of the Matrix [Review of the motion picture *The Matrix Reloaded*]. *Contemporary Cinema, 13,* 32–57.

APA References Index: Periodicals

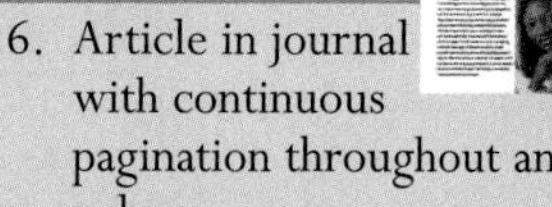

APA References Index: Digital Sources

23. Entire website
24. Journal article that appears in print and electronic formats
25. Article in online journal only
26. Journal article retrieved from electronic database
27. Article in online newspaper
28. Article from university or government website
29. Part of an online document
30. Retrievable online posting (discussion group, online forum, electronic mailing list)
31. Email or nonretrievable online posting
32. Computer software
33. Information service

About URLs

Preferably, provide the URL that links directly to the relevant document and not simply to a home page. If the URL is too long to include on one line, break it before a period or after a slash. Do *not* add any hyphens to URLs. To ensure that your URL is correct, use the copy-and-paste function to move the URL from your browser's address bar to your document. No period follows a URL in a reference entry.

23. Entire website

Albrecht, K. (2005). *Consumers against supermarket privacy invasion and numbering.* Retrieved April 22, 2005, from http://www.nocards.org

Unless you are referring generally to an entire website, make every effort to provide a URL that links directly to the specific content you are referencing.

If no author is listed (but see the box on page 191), start the entry with the name of the company, organization, or entity that supports the site's content. Or start with the site name if such information cannot be found. Include the date on which the page was written or last updated. Give the date on which you retrieved the material and the URL.

International Council for Caring Communities. (2005). Retrieved April 22, 2005, from http://www.international-iccc.org

24. Journal article that appears in print and electronic formats

When the online version is the same as the print version, use the same format as you would for an article in a journal. (See citation model 16 on page 259.) The only difference is that you place the words *Electronic version* in brackets after the title of the article.

Kensinger, E. A., Krendl, A. C., & Corkin, S. (2005). Memories of an emotional and a nonemotional event: Effects of aging and delay interval [Electronic version]. *Experimental Aging Research, 32,* 23–45.

If the online article is different from the print version—for example, the format is not the same—then you need to add the date on which you accessed the article and its URL.

Viano, M. (1999). *Life Is Beautiful:* Reception, allegory, and Holocaust laughter. *Jewish Social Studies, 5*(3), 47–66. Retrieved February 28, 2006, from http://muse.jhu.edu/demo/jewish_social_studies/v005/5.3viano.html

25. Article in online journal only

For articles published only in online journals, use the same format as in the example above.

Moss, S. A., & Ngu, S. (2006). The relationship between personality and leadership preferences. *Current Research in Social Psychology, 11*(6), 70–91. Retrieved February 28, 2006, from http://www.uiowa.edu/~grpproc/crisp/crisp11_6.pdf

26. Journal article retrieved from electronic database

Many articles are available in electronic databases. They can be accessed through a college library website or other websites and are sometimes in CD-ROM format. When citing these articles, provide the name of the database you used and the date you accessed it.

McArt, E., Shulman, D., & Gajary, E. (1999). Developing an educational workshop on teen depression and suicide: A proactive community intervention. *Child Welfare, 78*(6), 793–806. Retrieved January 3, 2006, from PsycINFO database.

APA References Index: Digital Sources

WriteOnline

APA References Index: Digital Sources

23. Entire website
24. Journal article that appears in print and electronic formats
25. Article in online journal only
26. Journal article retrieved from electronic database
27. Article in online newspaper
28. Article from university or government website
29. Part of an online document
30. Retrievable online posting (discussion group, online forum, electronic mailing list)
31. Email or nonretrievable online posting
32. Computer software
33. Information service

27. Article in online newspaper

For an online version of a newspaper, follow the directions for a print version (see citation model 20 on page 261), and then add the date on which you retrieved it and the full URL.

> Vedantam, S. (2006, March 1). Veterans report mental distress. *The Washington Post.* Retrieved March 1, 2006, from http://www.washingtonpost.com/wp-dyn/content/article/2006/02/28/AR2006022801712.html

28. Article from university or government website

For texts on university websites, write the host's name and the university program or department after the date of retrieval and before the URL. Place a colon between the host information and the URL.

> Felluga, D. (2003). *Introductory guide to critical theory.* Retrieved March 1, 2006, from Purdue University, College of Liberal Arts Website: http://www.cla.purdue.edu/academic/engl/theory/index.html

When you cite a text found on a government-sponsored website, make sure the URL you provide links directly to the search screen for the database.

> Federal Emergency Management Agency. (2003). *A citizen guide to disaster preparedness.* Retrieved March 1, 2006, from http://www.pueblo.gsa.gov/cic_text/family/disaster-guide/disasterguide.htm

29. Part of an online document

Your goal is to help your readers locate your sources, so provide the author's name, the date, and the title of the source and note the header, subheader, or section. Then write the title of the sponsoring organization, entity, or company, if available. Then write *Retrieved* and the date, followed by the full URL.

Hübler, M. (2005). The drama of technological society: Using Kenneth Burke to symbolically explore the technological worldview discovered by Jacques Ellul (header 2). *KB Journal 1*(2). Retrieved January 29, 2006, from http://kbjournal.org/node/60

30. Retrievable online posting (discussion group, online forum, electronic mailing list)

Be careful that any material you take from newsgroups, discussion groups, or online forums has academic value; articles from these sources have usually not been peer reviewed. Also, they must be archived if other researchers are to be able to access them. Many such sources are not archived for long periods of time.

If you are unable to locate the author's name, use the writer's screen name. Cite the exact date of the posting and the subject line of the discussion.

Downs, D. (2002, January 18). Re: inventing FYC. Message posted to WPA-L electronic mailing list, archived at http://lists.asu.edu/cgi-bin/wa?A2=ind0201&L=wpa-l&D=1&O=D&F=&S=&P=26473

31. Email or nonretrievable online posting

APA does not recommend listing personal communications or nonretrievable postings in the References, since readers will be unable to locate them. If your instructor asks you to list them anyway, indicate that such an entry was a private communication (such as email) or unrecorded or nonarchived chat. If you do not have the author's name, use the person's screen name.

Wellman, M. (2006, February 13). Tele-intern. Email to the author.

APA References Index: Digital Sources

32. Computer software

When you cite information from computer software, provide the name of the author (if you can find it), the date (in parentheses), the name of the software (including the version number, if any), a description of the software (in square brackets), and the location and publisher of the software.

> The Movies [PC video game]. (2005). Surrey, UK: Lionhead.

33. Information service

Write the name of the author or editor, if applicable, and the name of the service. Follow with the date in parentheses. Give the place of publication, followed by a colon, and the name of the publisher. Provide the date you retrieved the information, and end with a description of the medium or the URL.

> *SchoolMatters.* (2005). New York: Standard & Poor's. Retrieved January 2, 2006, from http://www.schoolmatters.com

34. Film, videotape, or DVD

For movies, write the producer's and director's names (each followed by that designation in parentheses), the year of release (in parentheses), and the title, in italics. Follow with *[Motion picture]* in brackets, the country of origin, and the studio or production company that made the film.

> Eszterhas, J. (Producer), & Verhoeven, P. (Director). (1995). *Showgirls* [Motion picture]. United States: Universal Pictures.

35. Television show, series, or episode

When you cite a television show, consider whether you are citing a show, an ongoing series, or a particular episode.

A show:

Shaffer, D. (Director). (2006, March 11). *Best friends: The power of sisterhood* [Television broadcast]. Alexandria, VA: PBS.

A series:

Chase, D. (Producer). (2004). *The Sopranos* [Television series]. Hollywood, CA: HBO Productions.

An episode from an ongoing series:

Weiner, M. (Writer), & Bogdanovich, P. (Director). (2004). Sentimental education [Television series episode]. In D. Chase (Producer), *The Sopranos* (Ep. 28). Hollywood, CA: HBO Productions.

36. Sound recording

Music:

Keenan, M. J., Jones, A., Carey, D., & Chancellor, J. (2001). The grudge [Recorded by Tool]. On *Lateralus* [CD]. San Diego, CA: Volcano Entertainment.

Other audio:

Wells, J., & House, J. (Speakers). (n.d.). *Sounds of the international phonetic alphabet* [Recorded by the Dept. of Phonetics and Linguistics, University College London]. London: International Phonetic Association.

APA References Index: Visual and Performance Media and Other Sources

APA References Index: Visual and Performance Media and Other Sources

37. Photograph or figure

Copyright information for photographs and figures you reprint is given in the caption to the figure or photo rather than in the reference list. See in-text citation model 16 on page 254.

38. Unpublished paper presented at meeting or symposium

When you cite an unpublished paper presented at a meeting, symposium, or conference, write the name of the author, the year and month of the gathering at which the paper was presented, the title of the presentation, and the name of the conference. Finally, indicate the location (city and state) of the conference.

Langtree, L., & Briscoe, C. (2001, December). *Calibrating the frontal trajectory of handgun entry wounds.* Paper presented at the meeting of the American Medical Association's 2001 Conference on Adolescent Health, San Francisco, CA.

39. Unpublished interview

When you cite an unpublished interview, you do *not* place an entry in the reference list, unless your instructor wants you to. Instead, insert a parenthetical in-text reference that includes the interviewee's name in regular order, the fact that it was a personal communication, and the precise date of the interview.

(O. de la Hoya, personal communication, September 22, 2005).

Parental Risk Factors 1

Running head: CONSTELLATIONS OF PARENTAL RISK FACTORS

A separate running head on the title page is required if you submit your paper for publication. It should be no longer than 50 characters, including punctuation and spaces.

A shortened version of the title is used as a page header on every page, along with the page number.

Constellations of Parental Risk Factors

Associated with Child Maltreatment

Jenny Chow, Mira Zaharopoulos,

Nancy Huynh, and Xin Xin Wu

University of California, Los Angeles

Advisor: Alexander Tymchuk, Ph.D.

The title and your name are typed, double-spaced, in the upper half of the page.

Note that the information provided in section 13c can be used to format your APA paper using Microsoft Word. You will need to make the following changes to the MLA information to set up your paper in APA style:

1. The amount of space you indent a block quotation from the left margin is 1/2", or five spaces. If any new paragraphs begin in your block quotation, indent the first line an additional 1/2".
2. The page header includes a short version of your paper's title (two or three words), followed by five spaces and the page number.

Jenny Chow, Mira Zaharopoulos, Nancy Huynh, and Xin Xin Wu, psychology students at the University of California, Los Angeles, wrote the paper presented in this section as part of their participation in the Developmental Disabilities Immersion Program, a two-quarter program. Their paper was published in the *UCLA Undergraduate Psychology Journal*.

Notice that the title of the research report is not printed on the Abstract page. The page does include the page header, with the page number 2, however.

The APA abstract accurately summarizes the content of the research report. Note that the abstract cannot be used to comment on the study; instead, it describes the research report.

The APA abstract must be concise: it should be no longer than 120 words. In this case, the students were following the guidelines of the journal to which they submitted their research report, the *UCLA Undergraduate Psychology Journal,* which requires that an abstract be fewer than 150 words.

The APA abstract must make sense on its own.

Parental Risk Factors 2

Abstract

Concern is widespread over the ability of parents with disabilities to care adequately for their children. The current study extends research previously conducted by Tymchuk, in the UCLA Parent/Child Health & Wellness Project. Data were collected on 261 cognitively impaired parents, with demographic characteristics included for determining health and safety knowledge and skills at the time of entry into the project. These data were analyzed in an attempt to identify parental characteristics that increase child risk for maltreatment. Cumulative risk indices within the three categories of family, parent, and child were correlated with performance variables relating to parents' medication usage, health and safety understanding, reading level, and the child's Alpern Boll score. The three cumulative risk indices were significantly correlated with low parental reading recognition and comprehension, which suggests that parents' reading abilities can be an important factor in providing adequate childcare.

Constellations of Parental Risk Factors

Associated with Child Maltreatment

Both laypersons and professionals have expressed concern that children of parents with cognitive disabilities may be more endangered than their counterparts without such disabled parents. Research has linked parental disability with heightened risk for child abuse and neglect (James, 2004). Because of this heightened risk, children of parents with disabilities frequently come to the attention of child protection services. However, research has also indicated it is not simply degree of intelligence that is a predictor of parental deficiency. It has been demonstrated that impoverished parents, and parents presumed to be mentally retarded, possess surprisingly similar—albeit limited—knowledge and skills concerning child healthcare and safety.

The best predictor for child safety is the adequacy of the parent's support system, regardless of parental knowledge and skill (Tymchuk, 1992). Further work has outlined risk factors that potentially increase probabilities of abuse and neglect. Such factors include (1) impoverished and chaotic living conditions, (2) the number of children in the household, (3) single parent status, and (4) the mother's history, such as foster home placement, reported sexual abuse, or status as a runaway (Ethier, Couture, & Lacharite, 2004).

These data suggest many factors affect parents' abilities in tending to the health and safety needs of their children across the development span. In an effort to reduce child maltreatment, various interventions have been implemented for enabling parents to provide more adequate care for their children. Recent empirical evidence has shown that tailoring educational intervention curricula to meet the needs of parents with cognitive disabilities can help these parents provide adequate health and safety care (Tymchuk, 1998).

The introduction to a research report in psychology (here, paragraphs 1 through 6) introduces the problem, summarizes any background needed to understand the problem, and ends with a brief description of how the report addresses the problem.

Reference to a 2004 work with three authors. If the three authors had been named in the writer's sentence rather than in the parentheses, the word *and* would have been written out: "Ethier, Couture, and Lacharite (2004)." See in-text citation model 5 on page 249.

To find the complete publication information, the reader will examine the References list on page 280 for the entry that starts with "Tymchuk." See in-text citation model 2 on page 248.

Randomized clinical trials involving persons with cognitive disabilities exercised two particular interventions. A number of parenting assessment instruments were developed and validated in conjunction with these interventions. The assessment instruments were created both to study possible differential effects of the interventions and to create a systematic parenting approach based on practicability of suggested and analyzed parenting techniques (Tymchuk, 1992). The UCLA Parent/Child Health & Wellness Project provided support and education to low-income parents with mild cognitive limitations. The Project's intent was to increase parental awareness of both parental and children's health and safety, thereby reducing risks of child neglect and abuse. People with special learning needs often have substantial problems in reading recognition and comprehension, and in recalling complex written and spoken information. Tymchuk (1998) has demonstrated that tailoring instruction materials to parents' reading and processing level can help remedy learning needs. Simplifying language and utilizing illustrations further facilitate understanding.

For works with two to five authors, cite all the authors' names on first mention. See in-text citation models 4 and 5 on page 249.

In earlier work, Tymchuk and Andron (1992) systematically developed and validated measures designed to determine levels of parental knowledge and skill. Tymchuk, Lang, Dolyniuk, Berney-Ficklin, and Spitz (1999) also developed and validated health and safety instructional packages containing curriculum and parent-use materials. Based on work in which the parents' reading recognition and comprehension grade levels and learning styles were determined, the contents of these packages were presented in ways that would optimize parental learning. This accessible presentation style consisted of using (1) a large font, (2) uncluttered pages presenting single concepts, (3) language geared toward 5th-grade reading level, and (4) colored illustrations.

The current study extends the earlier project's pursuit of certain associative characteristics—namely, those characteristics that correlate inadequate self and child healthcare with health and safety knowledge and skills. It was hypothesized that a constellation of risk factors would be significantly associated with inadequate healthcare knowledge. Specifically, it was hypothesized that parental economic impoverishment, fewer years of education than social norms, and limited opportunities for parents to participate in society would be associated with lower reading and comprehension levels and failure to recognize dangers in and around the home.

Methods

Participants

The UCLA Parent/Child Health & Wellness Project targeted parents from communities in Los Angeles and Ventura counties. These communities were notable for their high rates of economic impoverishment, reported crime, teen pregnancy, and physical injuries. Despite such conditions, families in these areas enjoyed few social services. Most parents were referred by community service agencies as being at high risk for child maltreatment and, as a result, for being declared unfit parents in danger of losing custody of their children. Such parents were primarily low-income, single Latina mothers, with a mean age of 19 years, who were assessed as having cognitive disabilities. Data analyzed in the present study derived from 261 such cognitively disabled parents who had children with average intelligence.

Materials

The present investigation utilized data obtained during pretesting in the Wellness Project. Investigative tools included those developed for the Wellness Project, as well as previously standardized techniques. Assessment approaches included (1) the Decoding Skills Test (DST), a standardized measure that was used to establish baseline reading recognition and comprehension levels of the parent (Richardson & DiBenedetto, 2004); (2) the Alpern Boll Developmental Profile,

The Methods section tells readers how the research was conducted so that they can evaluate the method and, in some cases, replicate the research. Typically, this section is divided into subsections with headings: "Participants" (or "Subjects"), "Methods" (or "Materials" or "Apparatus"), and "Procedure" (or "Design and Procedure").

used for determining children's developmental performance in relation to IQ equivalency with parents (Malhi & Singhi, 2003); (3) the UCLA Parenting Reading Recognition List, in which the parent was asked to pronounce words from a word list organized with varying levels of difficulty; (4) the UCLA Parenting Reading Comprehension List, in which the parent was asked to read a short passage and answer questions pertaining to the reading; (5) the Home Danger and Safety Precaution Observation Scale, in which a health educator utilized a checklist to record the presence of any situation that could endanger the child or parent and the presence of any behavior or procedure that could prevent the occurrence of an accident; and (6) the Illustrated Home Danger and Safety Precaution Checklist, in which parents identified illustrated dangers in six home areas and suggested suitable precautions for each specified danger. The health educator determined suitability of parents' responses based on a previously devised checklist of dangers and precautions. Materials used for instructional purposes were matched to the participants' level of reading comprehension and were presented in a large font with headings and paragraphs. Illustrations were shown along with text to facilitate understanding. An illustrated Home Safety/Danger scale depicted possible dangers found in six areas in and around the home.

Design and Procedure

The Wellness study administered a battery of tests designed to determine parental demographic and background information, IQ, reading recognition and comprehension, and health and safety knowledge and skills. This information provided the basis for determining teaching materials for meeting the parent's specific learning needs. Guided by the work of Carta et al. (2001), cumulative risk indices were created using the pretest data from the previous Wellness study, in order to identify parental risk factors for child mistreatment. In order to ensure uniform scoring across demographic variables, all demographic variables were

Reference to a 2001 work with six authors. Only the first author's name is given, followed by *et al.*, which means "and others." See in-text citation model 6 on page 250.

converted to values of 0 = no risk and 1 = risk. For instance, families with income levels below $19,000 were identified as at risk, and received a value of 1. Parents whose education level did not exceed high school were identified as at risk, and received a value of 1. Children who had never been sexually or physically abused were considered to be without risk, and received a value of 0. For the purpose of data reduction and analytical ease, composite variables were created from the original demographic variables. These composite variables were then grouped into three cumulative risk indices: (1) Cumulative Risk–Family—based on the composite family-level variables of parental income, number of children in the home, and living arrangements (single, married, living with guardian, etc.); (2) Cumulative Risk–Parent—based on the composite parent-level variables of parental abuse (the parents themselves were victims of abuse), parent education, parent health, parent daily activities (hobbies, exercise routine, social life, etc.), parent medical history, and prenatal risks (absence of prenatal healthcare); and (3) Cumulative Risk–Child—based on child disability and the composite child-level variables of child abuse (child is the victim of abuse) and child removal from the home (see Table 1). In addition, composite variables were also created from the original performance variables. In order to ensure uniform scoring across performance variables, all performance points were converted to scores ranging from 1 to 3. Points of 50 and below were assigned a score of 1. Points ranging from 51 to 75 received a score of 2. Points ranging from 76 to 100 received a score of 3. These performance composites included (1) parental medication usage (parent's understanding of prescription medication instructions and dosage), (2) reading recognition and comprehension, reading recognition total of Forms 1 and 2 (parent's identification of words from word lists Forms 1 and 2), DST total and grade equivalent, reading IQ of 85 or below, and (3) knowledge of illustrated home dangers and precautions (see Table 2). The three cumulative risk composites were

Every table and every figure (charts, graphs, diagrams, photos) used to provide additional information must be referred to in the report. In this report, the tables are all collected in an appendix after the References page. For papers not being submitted to journals, an instructor might prefer to have tables and figures placed closer to where they are referred to in the text.

The Results section provides the data and statistical analysis needed to support the conclusions. If tables or figures are used to display information, be sure to discuss the most important information they reveal in your text also; don't expect readers to interpret them entirely on their own.

correlated with the performance composites to test the hypothesis that greater cumulative risk in the above areas would be significantly associated with lower parental performance in reading and comprehension and inadequate healthcare knowledge. In order to determine the degree to which these risk indices were related to performance outcome, the Bonferroni correction for multiple correlations was employed, yielding calculated correlations between the data sets.

Results

Significant relationships were obtained between each of the cumulative risk indices and the performance composites. The relationships found are displayed in Table 3.

At the family level, greater cumulative risk is significantly associated with lower knowledge of proper medication usage ($r = -.212$, $p < .05$), lower parental reading scores ($r = -.201$, $p < .05$), and lower DST grade equivalent scores ($r = -.212$, $p < .05$).

At the parent level, greater cumulative risk is associated with lower levels of reading recognition and comprehension with respect to grade level ($r = .190$, $p < .05$), lower reading recognition with respect to age ($r = .278$, $p < .01$), lower reading comprehension ($r = -.260$, $p < .01$), lower Infant/Young Child Development scores ($r = -.242$, $p < .01$), lower reading recognition Forms 1 and 2 ($r = -.225$, $p < .01$), lower DST reading recognition and comprehension ($r = -.238$, $p < .01$), lower DST grade equivalent scores ($r = -.253$, $p < .01$), and reading recognition IQ of 85 or below ($r = .260$, $p < .05$).

At the child level, greater cumulative risk is associated with parental IQ of 70 or below ($r = .281$, $p < .05$). The child cumulative risk variable yielded surprising findings, indicating that greater child cumulative risk is associated with higher parental knowledge of illustrated dangers and precautions ($r = .307$, $p < .05$) and higher Child Alpern Boll IQ ($r = .268$, $p < .05$).

Of the three cumulative risk indices, parent-level risk factors were most often associated with poor performance on reading recognition and comprehension tasks.

Discussion

Our hypotheses were partially supported in the present study. The hypothesis that cumulative risk variables would be associated with lower parental reading and comprehension levels was supported. Parent and family cumulative risk variables were significantly associated with lower parental reading and comprehension levels. Our hypothesis that parent and family risk factors would be directly associated with parental knowledge of health and safety was not upheld. There were nonsignificant correlations between the family and parent cumulative risk indices and the Illustrated Dangers and Precautions Checklist. Thus, the current study failed to find evidence that the family and parent cumulative risk indices were related to home dangers and precautions. While it is surprising that family and parent risk factors were not directly associated with recognition of home dangers and precautions, this suggests there may be other moderating variables that link risk factors with knowledge of health and safety, an important finding that should be explored in future research.

Each of the patterns of findings within the cumulative risk indices has significant implications. At the family level, greater cumulative risk is significantly associated with lower knowledge of proper medication usage. The correlation obtained between inadequacy of medical knowledge and increased family-level risk indicates a relationship that should be further explored. It may be that designing and implementing interventions that enhance and maintain medical knowledge could help to reduce maltreatment risk.

At the parent level, greater cumulative risk is generally associated with lower reading and comprehension levels. Greater cumulative risk is associated with lower levels of reading recognition and comprehension with respect to grade level, lower

The Discussion section begins with a statement about whether the researchers' hypotheses were supported by the data analyzed. The Discussion should evaluate the research study and its results, and it should note any limitations of the study. This section can also refer to the larger issues at stake and further applications of the research.

reading recognition with respect to age, lower reading comprehension, lower DST reading recognition and comprehension, reading IQ of 85 or below, and lower Infant/Young Child Development scores. Although the correlation was not significant between parent-level risk and the safety knowledge variable, it is known that reading and comprehension are important factors in dispensing safety knowledge. Without such skills, the child becomes at increased risk of maltreatment. This finding suggests that adequate reading recognition and comprehension are thus crucial, because the printed word continues as the favored medium for providing information about medicines, drugs, and other products. Tailoring health and safety materials to meet the needs of parents with poor reading skills could help to address this problem in communication. In addition, intervention to foster better reading skills might in turn improve parental knowledge and understanding of health and safety. Reading recognition and comprehension skills would therefore appear to be of priority for setters of social policies.

At the child level, greater cumulative risk is associated with parental IQ of 70 or below. Contrary to expectations, it was found that lower risk in the Child Risk index was linked to lower parental knowledge of illustrated dangers and precautions, and lower IQ scores. This unusual finding could be related to an artifact of measurement error.

Discussion of the limitations of the study

Despite the significance of the present study, this study had several limitations. One limitation is related to the use of the original data set, which contained many variables. The large number of correlations examined can increase the probability of chance impacting findings. However, utilizing a Bonferroni correction for multiple correlations reduces this probability. A second possible limitation of the study is the correlational approach taken. This is because only relationships between the variables could be ascertained, without the possibility of inferring causation. Further work, using the posttest results obtained on the knowledge and skill measures, is underway so as to facilitate the ability to infer causation regarding the mechanisms that link parent and family risk factors to performance outcomes.

Despite limitations, the present study embodies some important strengths. This population has rarely been studied; given the dearth of data regarding this population, the present study addresses a gap in previous research. The present results highlight the importance of identifying risk factors associated with substandard health and safety knowledge for parents with cognitive difficulties. These results help illuminate areas for further understanding, thereby opening the door for future study. These findings also suggest significant clinical relevance. Establishing risk of parental maltreatment of children is a primary task for all child-protective agencies. Yet, there are few empirically derived risk indices in this field of study. The current investigation's data will therefore assist in such work. Developing cumulative risk indices and identifying child maltreatment risk factors supplement a curriculum for addressing the educational needs of parents with mild cognitive impairments. These findings may therefore aid in creating and maintaining parental assistance programs for improved childcare, thereby reducing risks of child abuse and neglect.

Discussion of the relevance and applications of the study results

The References list starts on a new page. It includes all sources quoted, paraphrased, and summarized.

Article from a journal with annual pagination. See citation model 16 on page 259.

Article from a journal with issue pagination. See citation model 17 on page 260.

Letter to the editor published in a journal. See citation model 21 on page 261 for a letter to the editor published in a newspaper.

Two entries by a single author are organized by date. The work that was published first is placed first in the references.

When several entries begin with the same author's name (as in the case of the articles by Tymchuk), those that are by that author alone precede any by the author and other writers. Entries that list the same first author but different additional authors are organized alphabetically by the second author's name (Andron before Lang).

Parental Risk Factors 12

References

Carta, J. J., Atwater, J. B., Greenwood, C. R., McConnell, S. R., McEvoy, M. A., & Williams, R. (2001). Effects of cumulative prenatal substance exposure and environmental risks on children's developmental trajectories. *Journal of Clinical Child Psychology, 30*, 327–337.

Ethier, L. S., Couture, G., & Lacharite, C. (2004). Risk factors associated with the chronicity of high potential for child abuse and neglect. *Journal of Family Violence, 19*(12), 13–24.

James, H. (2004). Promoting effective working with parents with learning disabilities. *Child Abuse Review, 13*, 31–41.

Malhi, P., & Singhi, P. (2003, May). Reply [Letter to the editor]. *Indian Pediatrics, 40,* 441–442.

Richardson, E., & DiBenedetto, B. (2004, January). (WPS-3) Decoding Skills Test. Retrieved May 25, 2005, from Slosson Educational Publications Website: http://www.slosson.com/item98689.ctlg

Tymchuk, A. J. (1992). Predicting adequacy of parenting by people with mental retardation. *Child Abuse and Neglect, 16,* 165–178.

Tymchuk, A. J. (1998). The importance of matching educational interventions to parent needs in child maltreatment: Issues, methods, and recommendations. In J. R. Lutzker (Ed.), *Handbook of child abuse research and treatment* (pp. 421–428). New York: Plenum Press.

Tymchuk, A. J., & Andron, L. (1992). Project parenting: Child interactional training with mothers who are mentally handicapped. *Mental Handicap Research, 5*(1), 5–32.

Tymchuk, A. J., Lang, C. M., Dolyniuk, C. A., Berney-Ficklin, K., & Spitz, R. (1999). The Home Inventory of Dangers and Safety Precautions—2: Addressing critical needs for prescriptive assessment devices in child maltreatment and in healthcare. *Child Abuse and Neglect, 23*, 1–14.

Appendix

Table 1

Cumulative Risk Indices: Family/Parent/Child

All composite variables listed below were derived from the original demographic variables in the UCLA Parent/Child Health & Wellness Project.

FAMILY (0=no risk, 1=risk)	PARENT (0=no risk, 1=risk)	CHILD (0=no risk, 1=risk)
Income: family yearly income, sources of income	**Education:** parent's highest level of education attained, parent ever had special education, parent's previous job activity, parent's primary language, parent born and raised in the US	**Removal from Home:** child ever been removed from home, length of time child was removed from home
Number of Children: number of children in the home, number of children belonging to the parent	**Activities:** parent participates in fun/relaxing activities, parent exercises, parent's current job activity, parent ever been incarcerated, parent makes decisions regarding the future	**Child Abuse:** child ever been sexually abused/physically abused
Living Arrangements: where parent lives, with whom, parent's happiness regarding living arrangement	**Health:** parent has disability (cognitive/physical), parent smokes, parent drinks alcohol, parent wears glasses, parent wears hearing aid, parent had/plans to have surgery, parent unfit, parent depressed, parent stressed, parent had any major illnesses	***Child Disability:** child has a cognitive/physical disability
	Parent Abuse: parent ever been sexually abused/physically abused	
	Medical History: parent has taken rx, parent has own doctor, parent has own health insurance, parent makes health decisions, parent takes medications	
	Prenatal Risk: parent's current age, parent's age when pregnant with index child, presence of prenatal care, location of prenatal care	

* Not a composite variable

Appendixes are used to provide detailed information that would be excessive in the body of the report. Here, the authors used an appendix to provide all the information they used to analyze the relationships between the cumulative risk indices (listed in Table 1) and the performance composite (Table 2). The results are shown in Table 3.

When there is a single appendix, it is labeled *Appendix.* If there are several appendixes, they are given letters to show the order in which they are mentioned in the paper: *Appendix A, Appendix B.* When an appendix includes only one table, the table doesn't need a separate title; it can be referred to by the appendix label. However, if several tables are in a single appendix, as in this paper, each table also needs to be numbered.

Table 2

Performance Composite

All composite variables listed below were derived from the original performance variables in the UCLA Parent/Child Health & Wellness Project.

PARENT	CHILD
Medication Usage: parent's demonstrated knowledge of prescription medication and safe medication usage	***Infant/Young Child Development Score:** child's performance on developmental tasks
Reading Total: parent's performance scores on reading recognition Forms 1 and 2	
Reading Recognition and Comprehension: performance scores indicate parent is 2 grade levels behind in reading recognition and comprehension	

Table 3

Cumulative Risk Indices Correlations (Risk Indices with Performance Composites)

Cumulative Risk Indices	Parents who are 2 grade levels below in reading recognition & comp	Parent age & reading recognition	Reading Comprehension	IQ 70	Child Alpern Boll IQ	Infant/Young Child Development
Family	0.103	0.142	−0.020	0.063	0.057	−0.155
Parent	0.190*	0.278**	−0.260**	0.203*	0.123	−0.242**
Child	0.106	0.216	−0.201	0.281*	0.268*	−0.164

*Correlations significant at .05 level

**Correlations significant at .01 level

Links between In-Text Citations, Notes, and Bibliography

In-text citation

> Hilary Siebert writes, "Short fiction as a genre is rapidly approaching the point at which its consumption is equal to its production."[1]

- A superscript (raised) number is placed immediately after the paraphrased, summarized, or quoted material you are citing.
- This number leads the reader to the relevant note.

Concise note

> 1. Siebert, "Be Careful What You Wish For," 213.

- The first line of the note is indented one tab key (five spaces).
- The relevant number, not raised and in the same font size as the rest of the note, begins the entry. It is followed by a period. The basic source information follows.
- The major elements are separated by commas, not periods.
- All major words in titles and journal names are capitalized.
- The author's last name is the usual link to the relevant bibliography entry.

Bibliography entry

> Siebert, Hilary. "Be Careful What You Wish For: Short Stories and Consumer Economics." *Studies in Short Fiction* 36 (2000): 213–17.

The bibliography entry provides complete publication information.

The Chicago Manual of Style (CMS), 15th edition, published by The University of Chicago Press, provides two documentation methods, one more suited to the humanities and the other more suited to the sciences. The sciences style is an author-date style similar to the APA style. If you are writing in the sciences, either use the APA style (◀ Chapter 14) or consult *The Chicago Manual of Style*. This chapter focuses on the CMS style more likely to be used in the arts, history, and literature.

In the CMS notes system, you can choose to use (1) concise footnotes or endnotes that relate to a complete bibliography of works cited in your paper or (2) detailed endnotes or footnotes that contain all the necessary bibliographic information, in which case a bibliography is optional.

CMS INDEXES

Concise or Detailed Notes

If you use concise notes and a bibliography, the first note to a particular source will look like Example 1.

If you use detailed notes, the first reference to a source must be complete like Example 3. If the information in a note is identical to that in the entry immediately preceding it or the same except for the page number, you can use the term *Ibid.*, which means "in the same place." If the page number differs from note to note, you add the page number after *Ibid*, as in Example 2.

Footnotes or Endnotes

You can place notes at the bottom (foot) of the page on which the source is cited (footnotes) or on a separate page at the end of the project (endnotes).

Footnotes may continue to the bottom of the next page if they are long. Double-space within and between footnotes.

Endnotes are placed on a separate page entitled *Notes*. Center the title, and list entries in numerical order. Indent each entry five spaces (one tab space), write the relevant number, followed by a period, and then give the bibliographic information. Each line after the first one in an entry starts at the left margin. Double-space the entire list.

Consecutive Concise Notes to a Book

Example 1 Concise note for a book

Author's last name only

Specific page number you are referring to

3. Larson, *Devil in the White City,* 34.

Shortened title that includes important words of the main title

Since this cites a book, the title is in italics. For an article title, use quotation marks instead.

Example 2 Note with *Ibid.*

The word *Ibid.* is in regular type.

4. Ibid., 35.

A period follows *Ibid.*

A comma separates *Ibid.* and the page number.

Detailed Notes

Example 3 Detailed note for a book

Author's name in regular order

Book title in italics

1. Erik Larson, *The Devil in the White City: Murder, Magic, and Madness at the Fair That Changed America* (New York: Random House, 2003), 12.

Place, publisher, and year of publication in parentheses

Page number after the comma, with no *p.* or *pp.* in front of the number

Example 4 Detailed note for a journal article

Author's name in regular order

Article title in quotation marks

2. Ellen Makowski, "Regarding the Health of Streams," *Local Environments* 14 (2004): 313.

Year of publication in parentheses

Page number

Journal name in italics, followed by volume number (or issue number, if given)

Format for CMS Bibliography

Authors

One author	Gore, Al.
Two to ten authors	Tucker, Robert W., and David C. Hendrickson.
More than ten authors	Jones, Kim, Ann Hertling, Scott C. Smith, Linda Conley, David Larson, Jim Karst, Pat Lynes, et al.
Same author as previous entry	———.

Titles

Book	*The Year of Magical Thinking*
Article	"Alternative Male Mating Strategies Are Intuitive to Women"

Publication information

New York: Harry N. Abrams

Lawrence: University Press of Kansas

Durham, NC: Duke University Press

For major cities and cities that wouldn't be confused with others, no state or country name is included. If the state is not part of a university press's name, include the abbreviation for the state after the name of the city.

Bibliography

Double-spaced

Bibliography ← Centered

Conklin, James. "The Theory of Sovereign Debt and Spain under Philip II." *Journal of Political Economy* 106 (June 1998): 483–513.

MacCaffrey, Wallace T. *Elizabeth I: War and Politics, 1588–1603.* Princeton, NJ: Princeton University Press, 1992.

Shakespeare, William. *Henry IV,* Part I, 1598/1599. *William Shakespeare Literature.* 2003. http://www.shakespeare-literature.com.

Author's Name
Entries are arranged alphabetically by the first author's last name, followed by the first name or initials. When there is no author name, start the entry with the name of the editor, translator, or compiler.

Title
Titles of books and journals are italicized; titles of articles, chapters, short stories, and other short works are put in quotation marks. Capitalize all the major words in the titles of books, articles, and journal names. Use the same format when citing electronic material.

Publication Information
Provide the name of the city where the book was published, the name of the publisher, and the date of publication. You can omit abbreviations such as *Inc., Ltd., Co.,* and *& Co.* Do not omit the word *Press* when citing university presses.

Page Numbers
Do *not* give page numbers for books or popular magazines. For scholarly journals, provide the page numbers for the entire article. For electronic sources, provide information such as a subhead that would help your reader locate your exact source.

Electronic Source Information
When citing Internet sources, provide the URL. For other electronic sources, indicate the type—for example, *DVD.*

The models illustrate the formats you would use for detailed footnotes or endnotes. If you use concise notes and a bibliography, see sections 15a–15b for examples.

CMS Books Index

CMS Citation Models

1. Book with one author or editor

1. Van Burnham, *Supercade: A Visual History of the Videogame Age, 1971–1984* (Cambridge, MA: MIT Press, 2001), 25.

2. Book with no (or an anonymous) author

2. *Jurisprudence and Individualism* (New York: Anchor Books, 1985), 63.

3. Book with two or three authors or editors

Do not use commas to separate the names of the authors in a note if there are only two of them; just use *and.*

3. Ellen Lupton and J. Abbott Miller, *Design | Writing | Research: Writing on Graphic Design* (New York: Princeton Architectural Press, 1996), 87.

4. Book with four to ten authors or editors

Rather than list all the editors or authors in the note, write *et al.* or *and others* after the first editor or author. When there are multiple editors, write *eds.* after the last editor.

4. Marla Hamburg Kennedy and others, eds., *Looking at Los Angeles* (New York: Metropolis Books, 2005), 22.

5. Book with a group or corporate author

5. National Geographic, *National Geographic Visual History of the World* (Hanover, PA: National Geographic Society, 2005), 16.

6. Book with a translator

6. Paulo Freire, *Pedagogy of the Oppressed,* 30th anniv. ed., trans. Myra Bergman Ramos (New York: Continuum Press, 2000), 381.

7. Second and subsequent editions

7. Jane Goodall, *My Life with the Chimpanzees,* rev. ed. (New York: Aladdin Books, 1996), 299.

8. Book in more than one volume

8. Sigmund Freud, *Collected Papers,* vol. 1, trans. Joan Riviere (London: Hogarth Press, 1950), 35.

9. Book in a series

9. Michael Carter, *Where Writing Begins: A Postmodern Reconstruction,* Rhetorical Philosophy and Theory Series (Carbondale: Southern Illinois University Press, 2003), 4.

CMS Books Index

CMS Books Index

10. Chapter from an edited book or anthology

10. Heidi Julavits, "The Miniaturists," in *McSweeney's Enchanted Chamber of Astonishing Stories,* ed. Michael Chabon, 129–53 (New York: Vintage Books, 2004), 144.

11. Article in a reference book

Citations to general encyclopedias and dictionaries are usually given in notes only. Include the title and edition number. If the work is organized alphabetically, provide the article title after the abbreviation *s.v.,* which means "under the word."

11. *World Book Encyclopedia,* 2006 ed., s.v. "Olympic Games."

For more specialized reference books, you may want to include full publication information and have a bibliography entry.

11. *The Oxford Companion to the English Language,* ed. Tom MacArthur (Oxford: Oxford University Press, 1992), s.v. "Idiom."

12. Sacred work

12. The Upanishads, trans. Eknath Easwaran (Tomales, CA: Blue Mountain Center of Meditation, 1987), 241.

13. Article in journal

13. Collin Gifford Brooke, "Forgetting to Be (Post)Human: Media and Memory in a Kairotic Age," *JAC* 20, no. 4 (Fall 2000): 779.

14. Article in monthly magazine

14. Michael Shermer, "Digits and Fidgets: Is the Universe Fine-Tuned for Life?" *Scientific American,* January 2003, 35.

15. Article in weekly magazine

15. Hugh Sidey, "Trying to Ensure an Epitaph," *Time,* August 19, 1974, 15B.

16. Newspaper article

In text: In CMS style, it is more common to cite newspapers in a note or in text than in a bibliography entry.

In the article "Social Control and Welfare Reform" (*Providence Journal,* August 12, 2003), Robert Ethier notes, "Welfare reform has brought with it characteristics of surveillance and control that are a combination of Foucauldian terror and Orwellian drama."

Periodicals: CMS Notes and Bibliography

When you cite a periodical, you should include some or all of the following information, as appropriate:

- the author's name or authors' names
- the article title
- the periodical name
- information about the issue (volume, issue number, date)
- page numbers

For online periodicals, see citation model 21 on page 291.

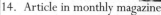

CMS Periodicals Index

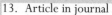

CMS Periodicals Index

CMS Index to Digital Sources

About URLs

Provide complete URLs for material you access via the Internet. Do *not* place angle brackets around URLs. Write them exactly as they are given on the site. If you have to break a URL at the end of a line, do so *immediately after* a single or double slash; *before* a tilde (~), period, comma, hyphen, underscore, question mark, number sign, or percent symbol; or *before or after* an equal sign or ampersand.

Note: A note for a newspaper article would be formatted like this:

> 16. Robert Ethier, "Social Control and Welfare Reform," *Providence Journal,* August 12, 2003, metro section.

17. Letter to the editor

> 17. Carolyn Kay, letter to the editor, *Washington Times,* June 21, 2004, national edition, sec. A.

18. Review

> 18. Daniel Aaron, "The Letter and the Spirit," review of *The Selected Correspondence of Kenneth Burke and Malcolm Cowley, 1915–1981,* ed. Paul Jay, *New Republic*, March 13, 1989, 34.

19. Website

When citing original content from a website (excluding online periodicals), include as much of the following information as you can locate: the name of the author, the title of the page, the name of the site, the date of publication, the URL, and the date of access (if time-sensitive). CMS recommends citing this information in a note.

> 19. Kathleen Fitzpatrick, "On the Future of Academic Publishing, Peer Review, and Tenure Requirements," *The Valve,* January 6, 2006, http://www.thevalve.org/go/valve/article/on_the_future_of_academic_publishing_peer_review_and_tenure_requirements_or/.

20. Online book

Use the same format as for printed books (see the citation models on page 286), and add the URL. If the material is time-sensitive, provide the date of access in parentheses at the end of the citation.

20. Kate Agena et al., eds., *Digital Publishing F5 | Refreshed,* 2nd ed. (West Lafayette, IN: Parlor Press, 2003), TK3 Reader ebook, http://www.parlorpress.com/digital.html.

Note: The fifteenth edition of *The Chicago Manual of Style,* published in 2003, shows the word *ebook* with a hyphen.

21. Online article

Use the same format as for printed articles, and add the URL. If the material is especially time sensitive, provide the last date of access in parentheses at the end of the citation. Include page numbers if they are available. Otherwise, if the article is long, include information such as a subhead or paragraph number that would enable your reader to find your exact source.

21. Moya Ball, "A Response to Andrew King's 'Disciplining the Master: Finding the Via Media for Kenneth Burke,'" *American Communication Journal* 4, no. 2 (Winter 2001), http://acjournal.org/holdings/vol4/iss2/special/Ball.htm.

22. Online government publication

22. Embassy of the United States, Islamabad, Pakistan, "212th Mobile Army Surgical Hospital Medical Outreach," press release, December 20, 2005, http://usembassy.state.gov/pakistan/h05122001.html (accessed January 3, 2006).

CMS Index to Digital Sources

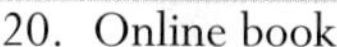

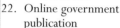

CMS Index to Digital Sources

CMS Index to Visual and Performance Media and Other Sources

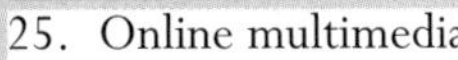

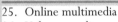

23. Information from database or subscription service

Use the same format as for a periodical article (see the index on pages 289–290), and then provide the URL to the main page of the service. If the material is time sensitive, include the last date you accessed the material in parentheses at the end of the entry.

> 23. Melanie Ann Rosen Brown, "Posthumanity's Manifest Destiny: NASA, Its Contradictory Image and Promises, and Popular Culture," PhD diss., University of Central Florida, 2004, UMI ProQuest: AAT 3134675, http://proquest.com/products_umi/dissertations/disexpress.shtml.

24. Email

CMS recommends citing emails in your text or as a note:

> 24. Claire Rocheston, email message to author, December 15, 2003.

If you are citing an email message that has been archived online, include the name of the list, the date the message was posted, and the URL. **Note:** The fifteenth edition of *The Chicago Manual of Style,* published in 2003, shows the word *email* with a hyphen.

25. Online multimedia

> 25. Martha Conway, *Girl, Birth, Water, Death,* 1995, http://ezone.org/ez/e2/articles/conway/jump1.html.

26. Video recording (movie, DVD)

Citations of recordings typically include some or all of the following information: the name of the person who created the content, such as a composer, writer, or performer; the title, in italics; the name of the recording company or publisher; the identifying number, if any; and the medium.

> 26. *Scream,* DVD, directed by Wes Craven (Burbank, CA: Dimension Films, 1996).

27. Audio recording

27. Jimi Hendrix, "Red House," MCA Records 11060, 1966, vinyl record.

Notice that "Red House" is a single song recorded on a 45 rpm record; thus it is considered a short work and its title is in quotation marks. For the titles of CDs and albums, which are considered long works, use italics instead.

28. Work of art

Copyright information about artwork is handled at the end of a caption to the piece of art, not in a note or bibliography entry.

Caption:

Figure 28. Matthew Barney, *Cremaster 2,* 1999. Photograph with Vaseline frame. New York, Guggenheim Collection. © 1999 by the Guggenheim Foundation. Reproduced by permission from the Guggenheim Foundation.

29. Lecture or public address

29. Virginia Anderson, "'The Perfect Enemy': Clinton, the Contradictions of Capitalism, and Slaying the Sin Within" (conference presentation, 1999 Triennial Conference of the Kenneth Burke Society, Iowa City, May 22, 1999).

Papers published as part of the proceedings of a conference can be cited like chapters from a book (citation model 10 on page 288). If the paper is published in a journal, use the format for a journal article (citation model 13 on page 289).

CMS Index to Visual and Performance Media and Other Sources

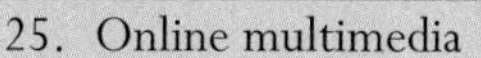

CMS Index to Visual and Performance Media and Other Sources

30. Published or broadcast interview

An interview that has been broadcast or published is cited in the same way as an article in a periodical.

> 30. Lawrence Lessig, "Remixing Culture: An Interview with Lawrence Lessig," interview by Richard Koman, *O'Reilly Network,* February 2, 2005, http://www.oreillynet.com/pub/a/policy/2005/02/24/lessig.html (accessed May 20, 2005).

If a live interview has not been published or broadcast, it is preferable to cite it in the text or as a note. You should include the names of the interviewer and interviewee, brief identifying information if necessary, the location and date of the interview, and, if a transcript or tape was made, where it can be located.

31. Personal communication (letter, phone call, memo)

Usually, refer to personal communications in your running text.

> Carburg wrote me a letter on October 12, 2004, suggesting we . . .

You may use a note also:

> 31. Daniel Carburg, letter to author, October 12, 2004.

The CSE style is used in the natural and applied sciences.

CSE's Three Methods 16a

Scientific Style and Format: The CSE Manual for Authors, Editors, and Publishers, 7th edition (published in 2006) is sponsored by the Council of Science Editors. The manual offers three methods for citing sources: name-year, citation-sequence, and citation-name.

The CSE name-year method of citation is similar to the name-year style used in APA documentation. The author's name and the year of publication are provided in text to refer readers to an alphabetized list of references.

In the citation-sequence method and the citation-name method, you place a superscript (raised) number immediately after the referenced material.

The references examples shown in the rest of the chapter can be used in the citation-sequence and the citation-name methods.

Citation-Sequence Method

Sources are numbered in the order in which they appear in your text, so the first referenced source is 1, the second is 2, and so on. Once you have used a number to identify a source, you continue to use the same number to refer to that source throughout the paper. These numbers correspond to a numbered list of references at the end of the work.

> No recent parenting books addressed more than half of the issues identified as critical by the American Medical Association[1]. Several studies[2–4,5,7,9,10] have confirmed this problem.

Superscript numbers are separated only by hyphens (or en-dashes) or commas; there are no spaces between the numbers.

> 2. Hunter W, Saluja G, Runyan C, Coyne-Beasley T. Injury prevention advice in top-selling parenting books. Pediatrics. 2005;116(5):1080–1088.

Citation-Name Method

You must first create the references list, arranging entries alphabetically by the authors' last names. Then number the list. Once you have numbers for the alphabetical references, go back to your text and use the assigned numbers for the relevant sources. Unlike in the citation-sequence method, the numbers will not be even approximately in sequence.

> Coronary heart disease may stem from impaired fetal growth[1].

> 1. Barker DJP. Fetal and infant origins of adult disease. London: BMJ Publishing; 1992. 343 p.

CSE References Index: Books

1. Book with one or more authors
2. Book with an editor
3. Selection from a book

About the Place of Publication
If there is any possibility of confusion about where the city of publication is located, you should include the state or country in parentheses after the city.

1. Book with one or more authors

1. Panno J. Animal cloning: the science of nuclear transfer. New York: Facts on File; 2005. 164 p.

If there are two or more authors, names are separated by commas, and you don't use *and* or an ampersand. If there are more than ten authors, list the first ten and then, after the final comma, add the phrase *et al.*

1. Freitas RA, Merkle RC. Kinematic self-replicating machines. Georgetown (TX): Landes Bioscience/Eurekah; 2004. 341 p.

2. Book with an editor

2. Thistlethwaite SB, editor. Adam, Eve, and the genome: the Human Genome Project and theology. Minneapolis: Fortress Pr; 2003. 200 p.

3. Selection from a book

Write the title of the cited selection after the author, followed by a period. Then write the word *In* (followed by a colon), the names of the editors (followed by the word *editors* and a period), and the title of the text (followed by a period). Add the publication information.

3. Hull DL. Scientific bandwagon or traveling medicine show? In: Gregory MS, Silvers A, Sutch D, editors. Sociobiology and human nature: an interdisciplinary critique and defense. San Francisco: Jossey-Bass; 1978. p. 50–59.

4. Journal article

4. Caldara R, Jermann F, Arango GL, Van der Linden M. Is the N400 category-specific? A face and language processing study. Neuroreport. 2004;15:2589–2594.

To cite an article in a journal that paginates each issue separately, include the issue number in parentheses after the volume number, with no space between them.

4. Jacyna S. Jean-Martin Charcot's mechanisms of language. Cortex. 2005;41(1):1–2.

5. Newspaper article

Include full date, section letter, and page and column number.

5. Stewart J. Physiological dilemmas in public education. Atlanta Journal-Constitution. 2005 Jul 21;Sect. C:9 (col. 2).

6. Editorial or letter to the editor

Include the title of the editorial or letter, the designation *editorial* or *letter to the editor* (in brackets and followed by a period), and then the publication information in newspaper or magazine format.

6. Smith K. Humanity at the crossroads [letter to the editor]. Sci Am. 2006 Jan:12.

CSE References Index: Periodicals

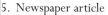

About the Authors

For journal articles with two or more authors, write the names in the order in which they appear, last names first followed by initials. Separate the names with commas. For organizational or corporate authors, use the full name of the entity in place of the author's name.

If the author of an article is not named, begin the entry with the title.

CSE References Index: Digital Sources

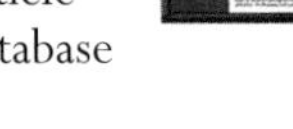

7. Online book
8. Online article
9. Online database
10. CD-ROM

About Citing Online Sources
When you cite Internet or other digital sources, include the standard information about author, title, place, publisher, and date that you would include in any reference. Then add the URL for the site, the date of any revisions, the date you cited the source, and the type of electronic medium involved.

7. Online book

At the end of the citation, write *Available from:* followed by the URL. Break URLs only after slashes.

7. Newton I. Observations upon the prophecies of Daniel, and the Apocalypse of St. John [Internet]. Project Gutenberg; 2005 [cited 2006 Jan 4]. Available from: http://www.gutenberg.org/etext/16878

8. Online article

8. Brown E. Revenge of the dotcom poster boy. Wired [Internet]. 2006 Jan [cited 2006 Jan 4];14(1). Available from: http://www.wired.com/wired/archive/14.01/blogger.html

9. Online database

9. Schelkunoff SA. Sailors, coconuts and monkeys. Sci Mon [Internet]. 1932 Sep [cited 2006 Jan 4];35(3):258–261. Available from: http://links.jstor.org/sici?sici=0096-3771%28193209%2935%3A3%3C258%3ASCAM%3E2.0.CO%3B2-E [Jstor]

10. CD-ROM

10. Feynman R. The Feynman lectures on physics, Volumes 1–2 [CD-ROM]. New York: Basic Books; 2003.

11. Recording (audio, video, film)

11. Wise R, director. The Andromeda strain [film]. Los Angeles: Universal Pictures; 1971.

12. Government publication

12. Metta G, Natale L, Rao S, Sandini G. Development of the "mirror system": a computational model. Genoa University, Italy; 2002. 1 p. Available from: NTIS, Springfield, VA; DABT-63-00-C-10102.

13. Technical report

13. Abad JL, Yacoub S. Ontology-based software development. 2005 Feb 1. Hewlett-Packard technical reports HPL-2005-13. 24 p. Available from: http://www.hpl.hp.com/techreports/2005/HPL-2005-13.html

14. Conference presentation

14. Zimmerman DE, Akerelrea CA, Smith JK, O'Keefe G. Assessing visualizations in public science presentations. STC 50th annual conference proceedings; 2003. 2 p. Available from: http://www.stc.org/ConfProceed/2003/PDFs/STC50-035.pdf

CSE References Index: Other Sources

17 CGOS DOCUMENTATION

The *Columbia Guide to Online Style* (CGOS), 2nd edition, by Janice R. Walker and Todd Taylor (New York: Columbia University Press, 2006), provides a citation system designed for digital documents. It allows you to cite electronic sources within the framework of the citation style you choose to use, such as MLA or APA.

17a CGOS In-Text Citations

Humanities (MLA)

See Chapter 13 for MLA guidelines for print sources. If a digital source does not have page numbers, provide only the author's name.

If other information would help readers locate specific text in a longer document (such as paragraph or section number), include it after the author's name, separated by a comma.

If the source does not list an author, use a shortened form of the title—page or document title or file name—in your citation.

Scientific (APA)

See Chapter 14 for APA guidelines for print sources. For electronic sources, provide only the last name and the year of publication. If no year is given, include the date you accessed the material: "11 Nov. 2006."

CGOS Humanities In-Text Citation Examples

> Hockey has been "among the most popular sports for the northern tier states for over three decades" (Hochberg).

> Associations can be a great source for locating "lists of members, rosters of committees, and other actionable information for marketing" (Sears, para. 4).

> The new Medicare Bill has been described as "a giveaway for the pharmaceutical industry" ("The Loyal Opposition?").

Note: Do not include the URL or electronic address in the text for sources you cite; this information goes in the References or Works Cited list.

CGOS Scientific In-Text Citation Examples

> Insurance regulation is "crippling the industry" (Smothers, 2003), say some members of the American Enterprise Institute.

> Whether or not you ask direct questions, Allan Sweetwater (2004) believes that the best survey instruments contain "at least two or three open-ended questions."

> Political donations are up this year, and "indications are that donations will be up again next year" (Holtry, 14 Jun. 2004). ← date of access

1. Website or Web page

Humanities (MLA): Start your entry with the author's name (last name, first name), if it is available. Then, in quotation marks, write the full title of the particular Web page you are citing, followed by a period. Follow this with the name of the entire website (if available) in italics, any version or file numbers, and the date of publication or the last update or revision (whichever is most recent) followed by a period. Finally, write the complete Web address (URL) preceded by the protocol (often *http://* but perhaps *gopher://* or *ftp://*). Conclude with the date you accessed the source (day, month, year) in parentheses and followed by a period.

> Duffy, W. Keith. "Digital Recording Technology in the Writing Classroom: Sampling as Citing." *The Writing Instructor.* 2004. http://www.writinginstructor.com/duffy (5 Jul. 2006).

Scientific (APA): If you can find it, begin your entry with the author's name (last name first, followed by initials). Then give the year of publication, if available, in parentheses, followed by a period. Write the full title of the source, capitalizing only the first word, the first word of any subtitle, and any proper nouns. Give the name of the complete website in italics, capitalizing only the first word and proper nouns. Provide any version or file numbers in parentheses. Finally, write the complete Web address preceded by the protocol (often *http://*), any paths or directories necessary to find the site, and the date you accessed it (day, month, year) in parentheses. Follow the closing parenthesis with a period.

> Duffy, W. K. (2004). Digital recording technology in the writing classroom: Sampling as citing. *The writing instructor.* http://www.writinginstructor.com/duffy (5 Jul. 2006).

CGOS Works Cited and References Index

About CGOS Format

- *Author's name.* If the author's name is difficult to locate or absent, CGOS allows you to use whatever name is provided, including aliases, handles, email addresses, and login names.
- *Date of publication.* On websites or blogs, the date of publication may be the "date last updated." Databases often list publication dates in their frontmatter.
- *Publication information.* For most online sources, the electronic address (the URL) is the most important publication information because it allows readers to find your sources for further research. An entry for a database may have a code or number assigned to it.

CGOS Works Cited or References Index

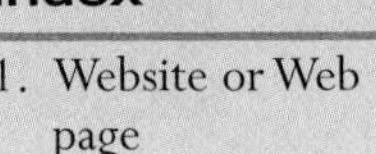
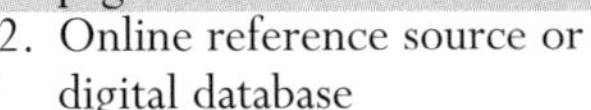

1. Website or Web page
2. Online reference source or digital database
3. Email, newsgroup, discussion list, forum, or blog
4. Chat or other synchronous communication transcript

About Formatting Entries

If you are using CGOS style to supplement MLA or APA style for print publication, use the MLA or APA guidelines for indenting the second and subsequent lines of each entry in your Works Cited or References list. However, if you will publish your work as a Web text for viewing in a browser, all lines of each entry should be flush left, with a blank line between each entry. (In HTML, you enclose each entry in the <p></p> tag.) You should not use hanging indentations because they may not display consistently across different browsers.

2. Online reference source or digital database

Humanities (MLA): Start with information related to a print version (if there is one), including the date. Next provide any publication information related to the online source, as well as the name of the online service you used (in italics) or the protocol, address, path, or directories needed to access the source. Finally, give the date you accessed the material (in parentheses).

> Golden, Leon. "Aristotle." *The Johns Hopkins Guide to Literary Theory and Criticism.* Ed. by Michael Groden and Martin Kreiswirth. 1997. http://www.press.jhu.edu/books/hopkins_guide_to_literary_theory/free/aristotle.html (5 Jul. 2005).

Scientific (APA): Write the author's name if you can find it, the date of publication (if it's not available, use the date you accessed the material), and the title of the article. Then write the word *In,* the names of the authors or editors, and the title of the work you are citing (in italics). Next provide any publication information relating to a print version, the number of the online edition (if any), and either the name of the database or online source service (in italics) or the protocol, address, path, or directories needed to access the source. Finally, if you have not already done so, give the date you accessed the material (in parentheses).

> Golden, L. (1997). Aristotle. In M. Groden & M. Kreiswirth (Eds.), *The Johns Hopkins guide to literary theory and criticism.* http://www.press.jhu.edu/books/hopkins_guide_to_literary_theory/free/aristotle.html (5 Jul. 2005).

3. Email, newsgroup, discussion list, forum, or blog

Humanities (MLA): When citing an email message sent to you or a discussion list, an online forum posting or RSS feed (see page 4), a message sent to a newsgroup, or an online posting in a blog or forum, start your entry with the author's name, if known (last name first). If the author's name is unavailable, use the handle, login name, alias, or email name (everything to the left of the @ sign).

CGOS Works Cited or References Index

1. Website or Web page
2. Online reference source or digital database
3. Email, newsgroup, discussion list, forum, or blog
4. Chat or other synchronous communication transcript

Follow by the subject line in quotation marks. Then write the date of the posting if it is different from the date on which you accessed it, the name of the listserv or discussion board (in italics), its address, and the date of access (in parentheses).

> Brooke, Collin. "Thinking Tools." 5 Dec. 2005. *Collin vs. Blog.* http://wrt-brooke.syr.edu/cgbvb/archives/2005/12/im_not_prone_to.html (4 Jan. 2006).

For an email message, write *Personal email.*

> Ethier, Robert. "SAT Scores and Your Admission." Personal email (20 Mar. 2002).

Scientific (APA): For listserv or discussion group entries, start with the author's name (last name first, followed by initials), if available. If it is not available, use the handle, login name, alias, or email name (everything to the left of the @ sign). Then, in parentheses, write the date of the posting if it is different from the date of access. Follow by the subject line (capitalizing only the first word and any proper nouns). Next write the name of the discussion group or listserv (again capitalizing only the first word and proper names) in italics. Finally, write the listserv or discussion group address and the date of access (in parentheses). For email, the term *Personal email,* in square brackets, is placed after the subject line and followed by a period.

> Brooke, C. (2005, Dec. 5). Thinking tools. *Collin vs. blog.* http://wrt-brooke.syr.edu/cgbvb/archives/2005/12/im_not_prone_to.html (4 Jan. 2006).

> Ethier, R. SAT scores and your admission [Personal email]. (20 Mar. 2002).

CGOS Works Cited or References Index

4. Chat or other synchronous communication transcript

Humanities (MLA): Write the author's name if you can find it (or alias), followed by the method of communication (e.g., Chat) or, if you are referring to a synchronous conference, its title in quotation marks. Next write the title of the website (if available) in italics, the protocol and address, relevant paths or directories, any necessary commands, and the date of the interaction.

> Gee, James Paul. "Video Games in the Classroom?" *Colloquy Live. Chronicle of Higher Education.* http://chronicle.com/colloquylive/2003/08/video/ (27 Aug. 2003).

Scientific (APA): Write the author's name or alias, followed by the method of communication (e.g., Chat) in brackets or, if you are referring to a synchronous conference, its title. Next write the title of the website (if available) in italics, the protocol and address, relevant paths or directories, any necessary commands, and the date of the interaction.

> Gee, J. P. Video games in the classroom? *Colloquy live. Chronicle of Higher Education.* http://chronicle.com/colloquylive/2003/08/video/ (27 Aug. 2003).

Designing and Presenting Information

PART 6

New Contexts for Writing: Comic Books and Graphic Novels

Comic books and graphic novels use images and words to tell stories. Writers now also use comic books to explain information and processes. In comic book format, for example, Scott McCloud, in *Understanding Comics*, explains how comics—with their tight integration of text, image, and iconography—create meaning. Descended from comic books, the graphic novel shares aims with the novel in its focus on character development and social critique.

You can create comic books and graphic novels on your own using software that makes the process manageable. Comic Life (Mac; **http://plasq.com**) and Comic Book Creator™ (Windows XP; **http://www.mycomicbookcreator.com**) are good examples. Using a technology autobiography, her own photographs, and remixed found images, Cas Riddle used Comic Life to tell the story of her life with technology, as shown in this page from her comic book.

While comic book software may help, it won't do the really hard work for you. *You* must create the meaningful and interesting narrative with images and words. Nevertheless, comic book software makes the technical challenge of design and layout simple enough that you can spend more of your time on composing effective stories and creating or repurposing images and artwork.

Writers use words, images, illustrations, and **iconography** (familiar symbols) to make comic books and graphic novels.

Comic books are often serialized, with stories told over several issues. They have a wide range of content but usually focus on superheroes and their adventures. The comic book format has also been used as an effective way to explain complex subjects, as in the popular *Beginner Books* series. With comic book software, writers also now create user documentation and newsletters.

Graphic novels are self-contained, full-length novels that reach beyond the traditional content of comic books (superheroes, for example), don't rely on serialization to keep an audience interested (they are self-contained), and display common features of the novel genre, such as complex character development and social commentary. **Manga** is the name given to Japanese comics, which have a distinct style (characters with large eyes, for example) and tell stories in the tradition of the epic and fantasy genres.

Only Connect . . .

Writing and Designing Comics
To create a comic book or graphic novel, you'll need to assemble images, drawings, icons, illustrations, and other visual content that you can then arrange to tell a story, explain a process, or communicate information. Textual content must work in concert with visual content.

Comic Life Gallery
http://plasq.com/comiclife/gallery/

Comic Book Resources
http://www.comicbookresources.com

Visual Content Serves Different Functions

How to Create/Locate It	What It Can Do
PHOTOGRAPHS ▪ Take photographs yourself that express the information or argument ▪ Search for photographs in image archives	▪ Convey information and content ▪ May (like illustrations) be touchstones for analysis in the text ▪ Help your reader see what you mean ▪ Allow you to focus on discussing the meaning and significance of a photograph's content rather than merely describing it
ILLUSTRATIONS ▪ Draw or paint original art, digitally or by hand ▪ Search for illustrations in image archives ▪ Use a map to show a route ▪ Create a timeline that shows key events graphically	▪ Act as visual interpretations of textual content ▪ Explain complex tasks, equipment, or objects ▪ Clarify concepts or processes ▪ Prove a point by showing an example as evidence ▪ Add aesthetic appeal
CHARTS AND GRAPHS ▪ Collect data through original research or at data repositories ▪ Use a spreadsheet program to create charts and graphs	▪ Represent data visually ▪ Show trends and relationships among variables ▪ Draw attention to the most important conclusions to be drawn from an analysis of data
DESIGN AND LAYOUT ELEMENTS ▪ Learn design conventions in the particular discipline, as described in style guides ▪ Study examples of effective design ▪ Use the layout and style features of a word-processing or desktop publishing program	▪ Direct the reader's eye to the most important information ▪ Express hierarchies of value and categories across information ▪ Convey tone and mood (professionalism, artistry, playfulness) ▪ Express form as visual content (patterns, lines, etc.) ▪ Add aesthetic appeal

Writers use **visual content,** such as photographs, illustrations, charts, graphs, and design elements, to inform and persuade readers, as well as to add visual interest to their documents. Visual content presents information and arguments itself, and it includes design elements that convey relationships between images and surrounding text.

The visual presentation of content shapes how people perceive it—how they evaluate it, what relationships they perceive among its parts, and what verbal content they remember most. **Design content** refers to how and what the visual information in a document communicates to readers. Design content includes the arrangement of content on the page or screen, as well as the spatial and logical relationships between verbal text and visual content. Design content communicates attitudes toward the verbal content, and it sometimes makes arguments about the relative importance of information—in the form of visual hierarchies, for example. (For this reason, it is sometimes referred to as *information architecture.*) Design content also reveals the writer's assumptions about what an audience might be looking for in a document. (See Chapter 19 for more on design content.)

Visuals should be chosen with consideration of how they will help you accomplish your rhetorical goals in a given context, and they should serve a specific purpose. You will need to decide whether to include visuals at all and, if you do include them, which kind of visuals you need and how to present them.

Visual content typically plays one of two roles in a text:

1. **Illustration and explanation.** Visual content may complement description or may help explain complex information.
2. **Content for analysis.** Information graphics and images serve as the source material for analysis and elaboration in the text. They are the primary content, in other words, with the verbal content meant to inform readers about what they see. In an essay on a painting, for example, the image of the painting serves as the subject for analysis. In an essay on a film, screenshots serve as content for analysis and also help readers remember important scenes.

See Chapter 6 for detailed information on reading images critically.

Project Checklist

Tips for Integrating Images and Tables into a Text

1. Every image should serve a specific function, as either illustration or content for analysis. When you use an image to bolster an argument or provide information, take the time to explain in your text how you want your readers to interpret the visual content of the image. Don't presume that everyone will see what you see or that the information graphic's point is self-evident.
2. Images and information graphics should be placed in the text after they are first mentioned and as near as possible to the point of reference. They should be referred to with labels such as *Figure 1* and *Table 2*.
3. Every photograph and illustration in a text should have a caption beneath it. In most cases, the caption begins with *Figure #* and a title or description. Captions are numbered consecutively throughout the text. Images that function only as design elements or visual cues (such as arrows) do not need captions.
4. Every chart, graph, and table needs a caption that summarizes its content. If it is a table of information, the caption should be placed above the table and begin with *Table #*.
5. All images should be accompanied by copyright or permission information and should be properly cited in the document's caption. (See Chapters 13–16 for information on documenting images and screenshots from films.)
6. Double-check your math to make sure that the information in charts, graphs, and tables makes sense. For example, the slices in a pie chart need to add up to a full pie (100%). Use clear and concise labels on the axes of a graph. Clearly identify what each portion of a chart indicates.
7. Leave enough padding (white space) around the image so that text doesn't run up against it.

Permission to Republish Visual Content

Most images that you find are copyrighted, so not only do you need to cite their sources—you also need to request permission of the copyright holder before you republish them publicly, such as on your own website or in a student magazine.

In some cases, you may be able to claim "fair use," allowable under U.S. copyright law. Whether fair use applies in a particular case depends greatly on the nature of your use of the content and the nature of the source itself. Even if your use falls under fair use guidelines, you still must identify the copyright holder and cite your source. Generally speaking, it is allowable to

1. Use a small portion of a larger work in your own review or critical analysis of the original work.
2. Use visual content that has been substantially changed and thus bears little relation to the source.
3. Use or alter visual content for the purposes of satire.
4. Use a screenshot of a website for the purposes of analysis and demonstration, as long as you don't include the software shell in the image.
5. Use a screenshot from a film or television show in the context of a review.

In all of these cases, you still need to name the copyright holder and cite the source in your text. List this information in a caption under the image. For the content of a caption in MLA style, see citation model 19 on page 192. For APA style, see citation model 16 on page 254. For information on how to place an image and add a caption using Word, see page 228.

Requesting Permission to Reprint

If you do need to request permission, you can write to the copyright holder. Let this person or organization know how you want to use the image, why, and where. In many cases, copyright holders will let you use the visual content if you agree to identify the copyright holder in your work.

Any visual content from outside sources needs to be cited in your text. While the Internet has made finding images much faster with tools like Google Images (http://www.google.com/images), image repositories, and clip art collections, it still remains the responsibility of the writer to provide documentation for visual content. Whenever you use visual content, you should keep records so that you have the information you will need later.

Record This Information

1. Name of the person who created the work
2. Title of the work
3. Publication date or date of creation of the work
4. Publication information, including URL (if the image was originally published on the Internet), name of the archive or print publication, and copyright holder and information (if available)

Parts 4 and 5 provide specific details on formatting sources.

Check the Library of Congress's database of copyright records at http://www.copyright.gov if you are having trouble locating the copyright owner.

18c Using Visual Content to Inform

Visual content can be useful as information in a variety of situations that you're likely to come across as you create documents for your courses, including websites, magazines, photographic essays, and multimedia presentations. In any of these situations, be sure that the visual content pulls its weight; it should add and clarify information and not be used purely for decorative purposes.

Visual Content: Purposes, Situations, and Examples

Purpose	Situations and Examples
Provide readers with concise visual evidence of something referred to in the text	▪ You explain or analyze a painting, photograph, or other work of visual art in an essay and need to give readers an image so that they can see what you are referring to. ▪ You observe or participate in an event and need to show your readers what you witnessed or experienced. ▪ You write a critique of a scene in a film or TV show and want to help readers who may not recall the scene. ▪ In your archival research on a historical subject, you discover images that may help your readers understand the subject more clearly. ▪ In a magazine article, you report on a trend or event in the news.
Illustrate complex processes or sequences	▪ In a paper describing a process or series of steps, you want to show readers concisely what the steps look like when performed. ▪ In a science report, you need to illustrate the relationship between objects or the constitution of an object. ▪ In an engineering report, you want to provide a diagram of an instrument and how it works.
Summarize, explain, or interpret data	▪ You have collected data on people's attitudes toward a subject in your field of research and want to show how these attitudes are different now than they were previously. ▪ You find data on demographic variables at a data repository like the U.S. Census and want to show that they are related. ▪ You collect data over time indicating that a significant change has occurred, and you want to show this trend in a graph.

Inserting Graphs and Charts into a Document

Charts and graphs that have been constructed from data in a spreadsheet program can be inserted directly into a word-processing document. Some word processors, such as Microsoft Word 2007, allow you to construct the chart or graph in the program. The following steps describe the process of inserting a chart in Word 2007, but the process is similar in WordPerfect and in OpenOffice.org.

1. In Word 2007, place the cursor where you want to insert the chart.
2. Choose the Insert tab and then select the Chart icon on the Insert ribbon.
3. Choose the chart type that will best represent your data, then click OK. (See Figure 18.1.)

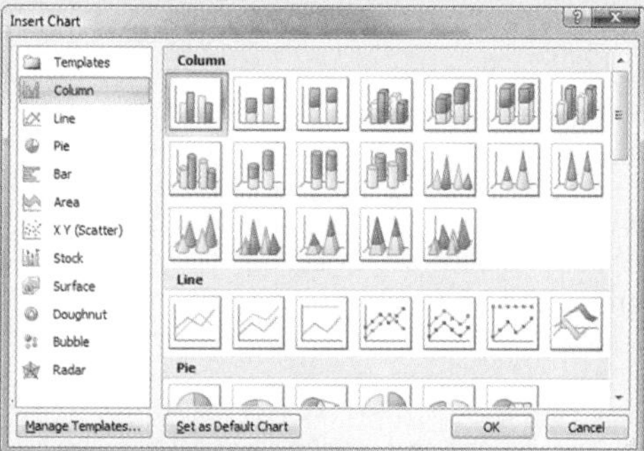

Figure 18.1

4. Microsoft Excel 2007 will open, allowing you to prepare your data. When finished, close the Excel document. Your generated chart will appear in your Word 2007 document. (See Figure 18.2.)

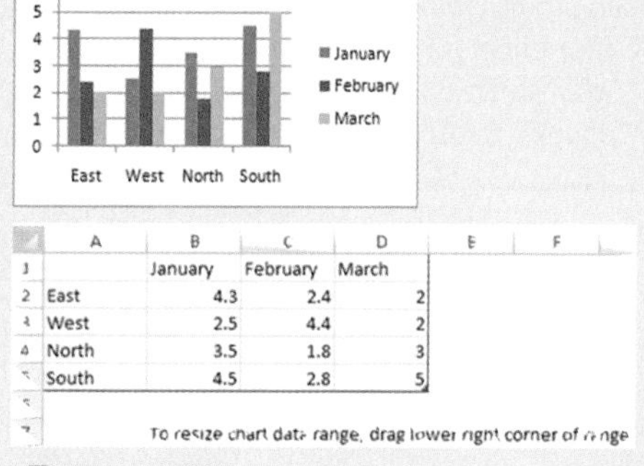

	A	B	C	D	E	F
1		January	February	March		
2	East	4.3	2.4	2		
3	West	2.5	4.4	2		
4	North	3.5	1.8	3		
5	South	4.5	2.8	5		
6						
7		To resize chart data range, drag lower right corner of range				

Figure 18.2

(continued)

Types of Information Graphics

Line graphs show relationships among types of data, such as the change in a quantity (e.g., revenue) over time. Data are divided into logical units on the vertical and horizontal axes. A line graph showing revenue growth over time might have time units (e.g., months) placed horizontally and revenue units (e.g., dollars) vertically. You can graph several sets of data horizontally if they share a common reference (e.g., time).

Bar graphs show comparative relationships across a data set, correlated with a common reference point. For example, a bar graph could show how much time people in different fields spent writing at their jobs. Each bar's height would be correlated with a certain amount of time, mapped on the vertical axis. A label for each bar would be placed on the horizontal axis, as in the example to the left.

Pie charts show the relative quantities of the components of something. You could use a pie chart to show the makeup of a group of people, with each slice of the pie having a size corresponding to the percentage of people in that group. The slices in any pie chart must add up to 100 percent.

Flowcharts include visual illustrations and arrows to show how a process unfolds over time or how one idea or action leads to another. See page 88 for an example.

Diagrams are illustrations of something that consists of parts (such as an engine). They provide readers with orientation and perspective.

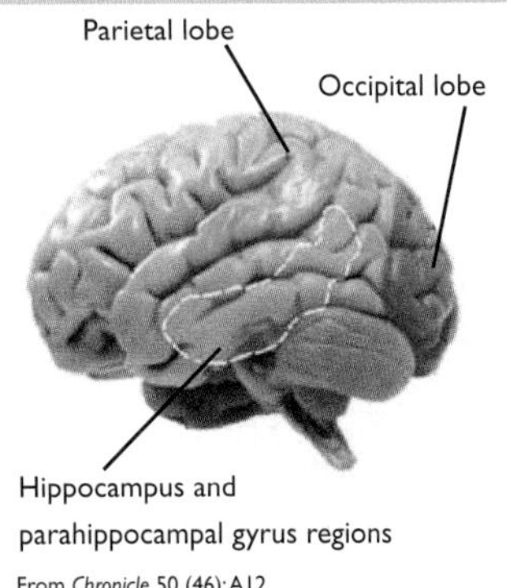

From *Chronicle* 50 (46):A12 <http://chronicle.com>.

Venn diagrams use circles or arcs to show how one thing intersects or overlaps with something else. The "Margin of Overlap" (page 72) is an example of a Venn diagram.

Maps are visual illustrations of a physical space (such as a city). Maps are also used to associate a region or idea with an event, action, or other phenomenon.

5. Adjust the appearance of the chart by double-clicking on any of its components.
6. Add a number and descriptive caption to the chart so that you can refer to it in your document. For tables and charts, the caption is placed above the object, as shown in Figure 18.3.

Table 1: Cost of Hiring Website Consultant for Nonprofit Organizations

	Cost per Hour	Total Hours	Total Cost
Option 1: Part-time employee, working in store and on website	\$8 to \$10	20 hours per week	\$8320 to \$10,400 per year
Option 2: Temporary skilled employee, contracted to reformat website	\$20 to \$30	40 hours	\$800 to \$1200 (one time)

Figure 18.3

The process of inserting tables, charts, and graphs is similar when you have already made them using a spreadsheet program. In cases where you want to publish the object in a printed document so a high-quality image is important, you can convert the object into an image (such as a JPG or TIF file) directly from the spreadsheet program.

For instructions that apply to Microsoft® Word® 2003, visit the handbook's website: **cengage.com/english/blakesley**

Images as Arguments

Visual content can stand on its own as information and as argument, without depending on its relationship with written text. In the image below, there is no verbal argument, but the action depicted makes an explicit argument nevertheless. The stack of books is being sawed in half. The books look like leather-bound volumes. It is hard to read the spine text, so we don't know what kind of books they are. The saw blade—with its shiny glint and the refracted rainbows—looks like a CD. The title of the image, *Computer Age Ending Literature,* makes the argument even more clear. Literature (represented by books) is being destroyed by the advent of the digital age (represented by the CD). Whether or not we agree with the argument, we can see how the image makes its point.

Computer Age Ending Literature by Chuck Savage.

Writers use visual content in their work to persuade people to take action or to change their attitudes. As a writer and a reader, you should be aware of how people use visual content to persuade—effectively or not, ethically or not.

Visual and Verbal Content as Argument

Visual content can make an argument on its own, without supporting text. Often, however, visual content works in conjunction with printed text to inform and persuade readers.

Visual Content as Evidence in an Argument

Writers often use visual content as an example in an argument, to prove a point and to persuade a reader that a particular interpretation of an image (or of something the image represents) has merit. Visual content may serve as documentary evidence that something has happened or has happened as is argued in the text. It may also—as information—bolster an argument for changing course or for adopting new policies. Data from research are represented visually in charts, graphs, and tables for clarity but also to give the reader a snapshot that can be taken in at a glance and thus also function persuasively.

College writing still includes research papers printed on 8½" × 11" paper. But teachers also regularly encourage students to try their hand at new ways of expressing ideas. Today, software tools for word processing, design and layout, and digital imaging are readily available. Because of these technological developments, the opportunity to manage all aspects of publishing, from the writing through the design, layout, and typesetting of printed documents, has shifted to writers and designers.

In college, you may find yourself participating in service learning projects that involve working with community organizations to help them produce documents like brochures and flyers. You may want to promote a student club or advertise a special event. You might start your own ezine in a creative writing class or create a poster board for display at a local conference.

After you graduate, you may be involved in preparing documents for an organization—either by contributing content or by managing the production and collaboration processes. These documents might communicate inside the organization or reach out to the general public. In any of these contexts, it will be useful to know how to represent your and others' work in print.

Project Checklist

Formatting an Essay or Research Report for Submission

The style manuals described in Parts 4 and 5 set standards for formatting essays and research reports for submission to an instructor or to a journal for possible publication. Instructors often require that you follow other formatting guidelines also. Take the time early in your projects to review these guidelines so that you can plan ahead to follow them. Then be sure to adhere to them when you print and submit your work. The guidelines make it easier for instructors and editors to process large quantities of information and to respond effectively. Your instructors will judge your ability to format a document as one sign that you have paid careful attention to all aspects of your work.

1. **Format.** Follow the formatting guidelines in the discipline's style manual or provided by your instructor, including those for placement of title, author, date, course, page numbers, and headers; size of margins; placement and use of visual content; footnotes or endnotes; and Works Cited or References.
2. **Legibility.** Use a font size that is legible. In most cases, 12-point Times New Roman is a good choice for printed essays and research projects.
3. **Printing.** Print your work using a good-quality printer on standard white paper, unless the situation calls for a specialty paper (for a flyer, for example). Double-check to make sure that all pages have printed and that the printer used sufficient ink.
4. **Submission requirements.** Instructors may ask you to submit your work in a folder with a title page, or they may have other requirements. The style guides for each discipline recommend how to submit work when no other guidelines are available. Many essays and research projects are bound with a paperclip, which allows the reader to separate pages and thus review the Works Cited or Bibliography while reading the paper.

Creating Proximity to Convey Meaningful Relationships

Visual Argument in the Digital Age:

Political Advertising as Propaganda in the

2004 Presidential Campaign

Andrea Wilson and Joe Malinger

April 1, 2006

No clear relationships exist among pieces of information.

Visual Argument in the Digital Age:
Political Advertising as Propaganda in the
2004 Presidential Campaign

Andrea Wilson and Joe Malinger
April 1, 2006

Relationships are created between the title and subtitle and between the authors and the date.

Brown 2

Alfred Hitchcock films are sometimes as famous for their openings as they are for their contents. Critics have noted how the themes of voyeurism and spectatorship have been illustrated by acts of spying, shown most directly in films like *Rear Window, Vertigo,* and *Psycho.*

They have also focused on how male characters often presume to speak for women, most memorably in *Psycho* when Norman Bates voices his mother. These themes work their way into the opening credit sequences. For example, the theme of voyeurism is expressed in the opening of *Vertigo* as the viewer seems to be spying on the woman, who seems fearful as the camera moves in. The Saul Bass/John Whitney credit sequence unfolds with an extreme close-up

Brown 3

of a woman's face, slightly off-center to the left. The viewer crosses the proxemic space of the familiar into the intimate. Then we see "James Stewart" appear above the woman's lips, with the implication that he (or his character) will speak for her, like a ventriloquist. (See Illustration 1.)

Illustration 1. Opening credits, *Vertigo.* © 1986 Universal City Studios, Inc. Restored version © 1996 Leland H. Faust, Patricia Hitchcock O'Connell, and Kathleen O'Connell Fiala.

The text that refers to the image precedes it, and the image is close to its description. Readers will understand the connection.

A primary goal of graphic design is to present content so that visual, design, and textual content work in harmony to convey information and create the desired effect. That goal is one to work for, whether your material is a brochure for a student club or program, a poster for a special event, a business card, or a research report that uses the visual representation of data to reinforce or extend an argument.

The principles of proximity, alignment, repetition, and contrast can be followed to make sure that your visual and design content works in concert with your verbal content so that you communicate efficiently or argue effectively.

Proximity

Proximity means closeness. Proximity is a familiar way to convey meaning, and as readers in a visual culture, we're so used to making judgments about meaning based on proximity that we often don't notice we're doing it. Readers expect images and text that are close to each other to have a meaningful relationship. As a writer/designer, try to put closely related images and text close to each other on the page.

Alignment

Alignment refers to the spatial layout of elements on a page in discernible patterns. Generally speaking, it is good practice to align every object on a page with the edges of other elements to establish a pattern and a relationship. Alignment helps create consistency and express relationships between pieces of information. Good page design often exhibits consistent alignment (in margins, for example) and sometimes draws attention to important information by deliberately misaligning it. Misaligned elements attract attention because of the effects of contrast, covered on page 317.

Repetition

Repetition of design elements conveys important structural information to a reader and thus can assist the writer in communicating information unobtrusively. When you repeat a design element—a typeface, an alignment, or a visual metaphor—you create meaningful connections among types of content, pages, or regions of a page. In a report, for example, it is common practice to use a consistent style for headers. A-level headers (like chapter titles or major sections) might be centered in 14-point type. B-level headers might be flush left in 12-point type.

Creating Alignment to Convey Meaningful Patterns

Here is information for an exhibit arranged in a logical order but without any design principles applied to its alignment:

Jennifer Sterling Design Exhibit
San Francisco, California
March 30 to June 24, 2001
San Francisco Museum of Modern Art

Below is a poster on which the designer, Jennifer Sterling, has realigned (and highly stylized) the information. On the left, you see the title and dates of the exhibit in a visual pattern that reflects the playfulness of her work. The eye leaps to the word *Exhibit* in the right column because of the large font, and then the artist's name is only partly revealed. People who know her work (professional designers) will complete the name. Those who don't may be curious. The bottom of the poster, where the eye moves last, repeats key information in a more familiar pattern so that there's no doubt about what the poster has announced.

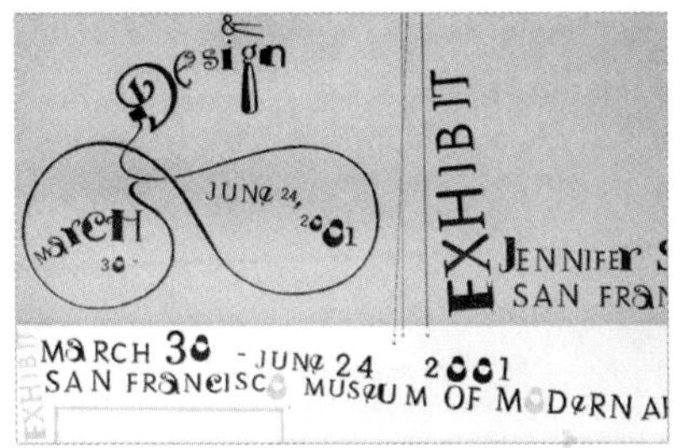

Final poster for the San Francisco Museum of Modern Art's exhibition of Jennifer Sterling's work.

Using Repetition to Convey Structural Information

A cover from a recording company's annual report, using repetition in the pattern to suggest the relationship between recordings and their musical sources.

Contrast Used to Suggest a Close Relationship

This poster for the sociology department at Temple University uses an extremely large font size, with people cut-outs in a contrasting color, to suggest an equation between sociology and the study of group life.

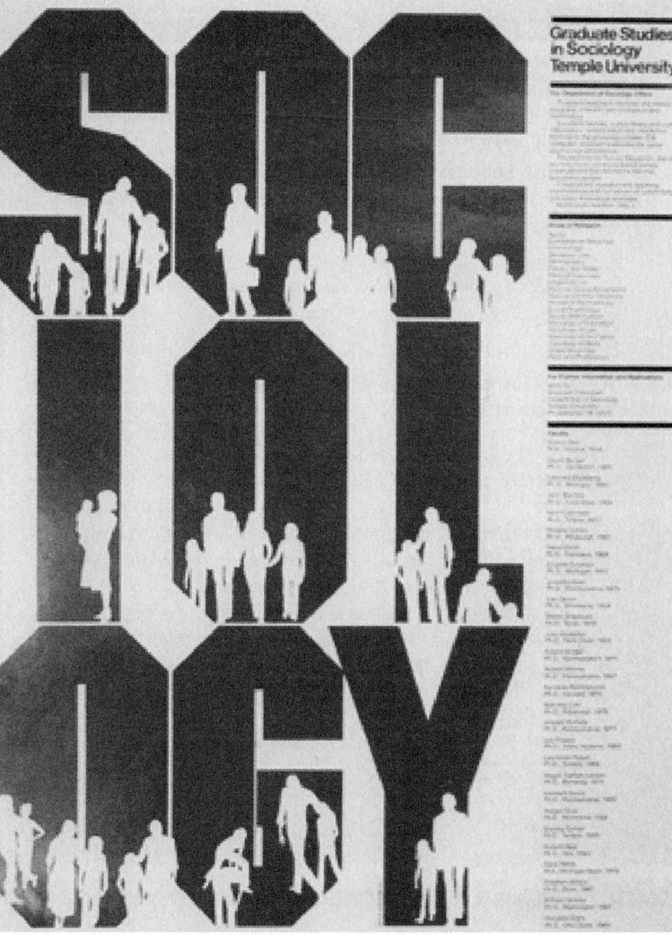

The large font size used for "Sociology" contrasts sharply with the people cut-outs and the smaller text on the right, which provides information about the department. Image reproduced with permission of the copyright owner, Temple University.

Readers use this consistency to identify how sections of a document are related.

Repetition may involve more than the use of a consistent style for like elements. It may also involve modest variation on a design theme throughout a document.

In a tri-fold brochure, you might include a separator bar between columns (▶ page 323). Or in a newspaper, you might consistently place visual data in the right column on the same page every day so readers know where to find it. On a website, you might provide a consistent visual cue such as an up-arrow (▲) to indicate where a reader should click to go to the top of the page.

Contrast

Contrast—sharp differences in color, typography, or other design elements—is used to highlight or prioritize information, and it adds visual interest. You can use contrast to direct your reader's eye where you want it to move first or to draw attention to some especially important elements on a page.

Typography refers to the overall balance and interplay of the letters on the page or screen. You can use typography to enhance the readability of information and to direct the flow of an argument by following design principles to establish a unified theme and style.

Attributes of Type

Type can be described by font family, typeface, and point size.

Fonts

Fonts are classified as serif and sans serif. Serif fonts have small strokes at the ends of some lines. Times New Roman is a serif font. Sans serif fonts do not have these additional strokes. For example, Arial does not. These two basic font styles (serif and sans serif) each include thousands of specific font families.

Typefaces

Use a normal typeface for most body text, and reserve special typefaces (bold, italics) for headings, titles, and other special elements.

Point Size

Most writers use 10-, 11-, or 12-point fonts for body text on paper documents, but for headings you can vary the point size modestly. For posters and other display documents, choose point sizes that will make the information stand out at the distance from which readers are likely to be viewing the piece.

Project Checklist

Choosing Type

- ❑ Distinguish body text from headings by using contrasting fonts. Serif fonts are useful for body text on a printed page, and sans serif fonts are often used for headers.

Serif Fonts	Sans Serif Fonts
Times New Roman	Arial
Bookman Old Style	Century Gothic
Garamond	Tahoma
Book Antiqua	Verdana

- ❑ Check to be sure the font is legible.
  Not very legible, even at 12-point Quite legible at 12-point
- ❑ Make sure the tone and style of the type reinforce the message of your content. A script font like *Lucida Handwriting* would look odd in a formal research paper, but it might work well for a short header on a poster or a Web page.
- ❑ Use bold and italic for special purposes, such as to emphasize headings or words used in special senses (▶ section 44h).
- ❑ Consider your audience when deciding on point size. In a newsletter for elders, for example, you might use 14-point instead of 10-point.

Line Length in Two 5" x 8" Books

Notice how the line length in the following two excerpts affects your perception. The first is actually from the novel *The Kite Runner,* by Khaled Hosseini. The second shows how the book would look with a shorter line length.

24-pica line

What was I doing on this road in the middle of the night? I should have been in bed, under my blanket, a book with dog-eared pages at my side. This had to be a dream. Had to be. Tomorrow

22.5-pica line

What was I doing on this road in the middle of the night? I should have been in bed, under my blanket, a book with dog-eared pages at my side. This had to be a dream. Had to

Leading

14.4-point leading

This setting usually makes for comfortable reading, but in cases where you want to create contrast or make the text especially easy to read (on the screen, for example, or on a flyer viewed at a distance), increase the leading.

18-point leading

This setting usually makes for comfortable reading on the screen or at a distance. Greater leading provides more white space when you need to create contrast or provide eye relief.

Page Layout Issues

Line length, leading, margins and alleys, and justification all affect page appearance.

Line Length

Depending on the nature of the document (brochure, report, flyer, book, and so on) and the size of the paper, choose a line length for maximum readability. The upper limit for easy reading is 75 characters on a line, so keep your line length shorter than that.

Leading

Leading refers to the distance between successive lines of text. A double-spaced page of text has twice the leading of a single-spaced page of text, for example. Most word processors and desktop publishing programs use automatic leading. A typical leading value for body text on a printed document is related to the point size of the typeface. So, for example, if you are using 12-point Times New Roman, the leading will likely be about 14.4 points.

Margins and Alleys

Establish a consistent pattern with margins and alleys. A margin is the distance between the outer edge of text and the edge of the page. An alley is the distance between columns on a multi-column page. Typical margins on a typed essay are 1".

19b

Justification

Word processors allow you to set margins so that they are either aligned or jagged. For most informal writing, it's best to use a jagged right margin. For more formal documents, full justification (alignment) of the left and right margins improves visual appeal. However, most word processors do not create fully justified lines very well.

Justification

Fully justified text

This is fully justified text in a column with a short line length. Notice how there are rivers of white space that you can see traveling down the page. At a typical reading distance, these rivers can be very noticeable.

Left-justified text

This is left-justified text in a column with a short line length. Notice that here the letters are equally spaced across the line so that there are no discernible variations in distances between letters and words.

19c Managing Color Effectively

Color adds life to display documents like flyers, posters, and brochures. Unfortunately, while graphics editors increase the range of options for incorporating color into designs, they also grant opportunities for designers to create awful color combinations. Furthermore, designers need to pay careful attention to ensure that color choices will be translated accurately by the printer that will run the job. Professional designers use color guides and palettes (collections of complementary colors). Color wheels show the spectrum of color and help designers choose analogous and complementary colors. **Analogous colors** are next to each other on the color wheel. They usually go well together, both in print and in digital documents. **Complementary colors** lie on opposite sides of the color wheel. They usually contrast well and print effectively.

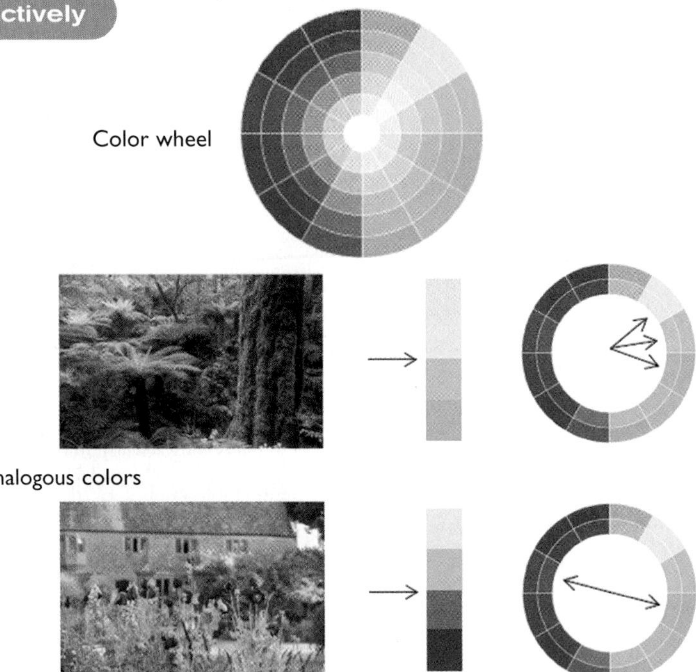

Complementary colors

Resources on Color

For links to resources, visit **cengage.com/English/Blakesley**

Project Checklist

Tips for Creating Flyers and Posters

1. **Do your research.** Make sure that all the factual information you have about time, date, and location is accurate, that days and dates correspond, that you have identified the exact location (e.g., room number) of the event, and that people's names are spelled correctly. Also find out where and under what circumstances you are allowed to display your flyers or posters.
2. **Storyboard.** Create a mock-up of your flyer or poster, sketching out where you plan to place headers, images, and text. Tape your mock-up to a wall, and then stand back from it. Is anything about it unusual or striking? Will it grab your attention? If not, what can you do so it will?
3. **Grab attention.** Since a major goal is to catch someone's eye, you can be more assertive with your design than you might be in a handheld document. Grab attention with striking (but relevant) and larger-than-usual images, large headers or titles, and bold colors.
4. **Hold attention.** Once you have interested your audience, you need to give them useful and precise information. This information need not be presented as boldly as your header or title, but it should be legible from a short distance. Use subheads (fonts in larger point sizes) to make information stand out.
5. **Use graphic design principles to structure images and information.** Put related information close together on the page; align your edges; use sharp contrasts among white space, content, and images to add visual interest; and establish a color scheme that complements your images and content.
6. **Leave time to revise and edit text and design.** Ask at least one other person to read your flyer before you say "print it." Encourage reviewers to comment on your selection of images; sometimes the pictures we use suggest more than we intend or notice, and another reader can help you identify unintended connotations.
7. **Print your flyer on durable paper.** A coated, matte finish on card stock will help your flyer stand out from the rest and last.

Flyers, posters, poster display boards, and brochures are all documents that should be visually appealing, include ample white space, have highly readable typefaces, and be printed on (or mounted on) durable paper.

Flyers and Posters

Flyers and posters, two kinds of signs, share a common rhetorical goal. They need to catch the reader's eye—often from a distance—and make key information readily discernible closer up. The Sociology poster on page 317 effectively captures the eye from a distance and then provides detailed information once the viewer moves closer. Posters are typically large (at least 11" × 17"). They may be used for displaying information and images at an exhibit or other special event, such as a poster session. Flyers are used to announce events. Flyers are sometimes handed out, but more often they are posted in public places.

Flyers and posters can be used to announce events. Such announcements should include the following information:

- Title and nature of the event
- Time, date, and location
- Contact information for the organizers (people often have questions) and associated URL, if any
- Sponsorship information

Poster Display Boards

Like flyers, poster display boards at exhibits or special events need to be easily readable from a distance. However, the information they provide is usually more detailed—for example, summarizing the key findings of a research or lab project. Project display boards "tell the story" of a project and provide the audience with a snapshot or synopsis of the project's key points or features. Your local bookstore or art supply store may sell specially designed and foldable project display boards on which you can mount printed images and text.

Poster display boards are large, complex documents composed of images and text. In some respects, they function like a large page and thus need to guide the reader's eyes carefully to critical information. Plan your poster board in such a way that your reader will know how to read in sequence (if sequence matters). Don't be afraid to use numbers or other navigational cues to help people along. Some poster sessions or exhibits may have guidelines for the layout of posters, perhaps in the interest of keeping an audience moving along in a crowded space or in a competition.

Sample Poster Display Board in APA Style

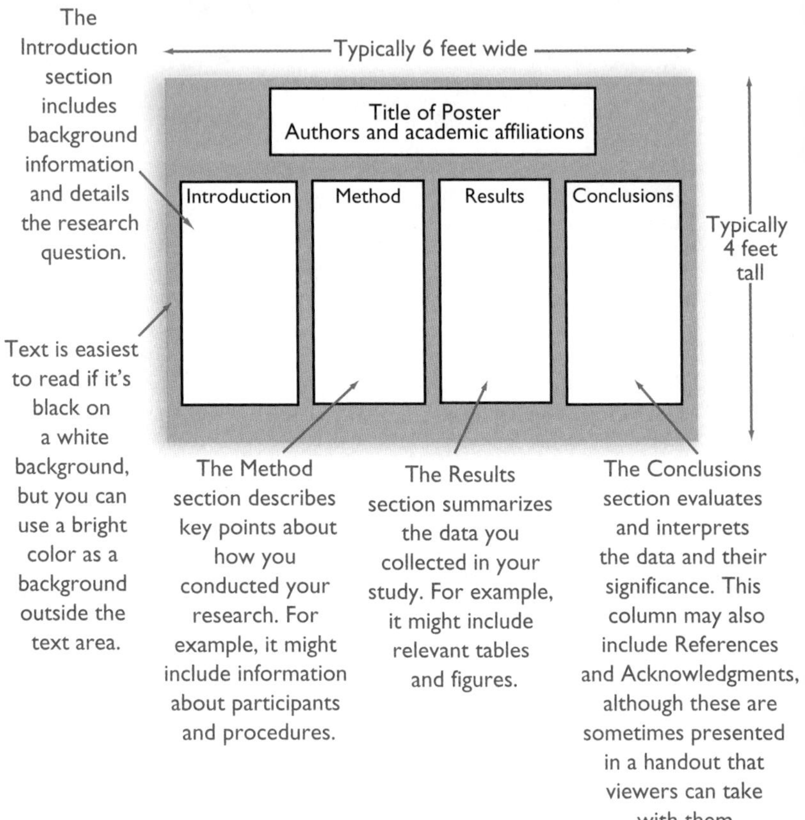
The Introduction section includes background information and details the research question.
Typically 6 feet wide
Title of Poster
Authors and academic affiliations
Introduction
Method
Results
Conclusions
Typically 4 feet tall
Text is easiest to read if it's black on a white background, but you can use a bright color as a background outside the text area.
The Method section describes key points about how you conducted your research. For example, it might include information about participants and procedures.
The Results section summarizes the data you collected in your study. For example, it might include relevant tables and figures.
The Conclusions section evaluates and interprets the data and their significance. This column may also include References and Acknowledgments, although these are sometimes presented in a handout that viewers can take with them.

Conference posters generally follow the same pattern as research papers formatted in APA style. (See section 14c for a sample APA paper.) They are prepared so that they can be read from the top of the left column down, from the top of the next column down, and so on.

This example shows the layout for a 6' x 4' poster, the recommended size in APA style. Another popular size for posters is 4' x 3'. They are designed as tri-fold display boards using three columns, with the center column measuring 2' and each side panel 1'. Presenters typically place the primary content in the center column and use the outer columns for related information or examples.

Sample Template for a Tri-Fold Brochure

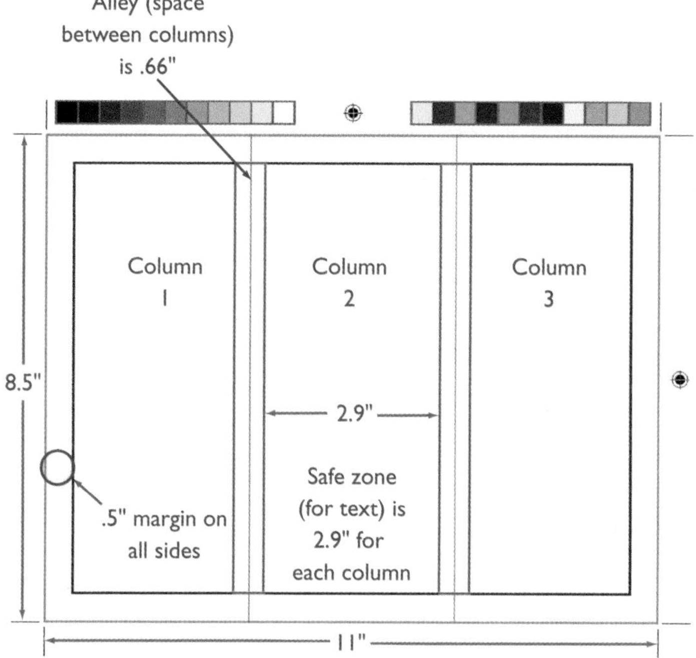

Sample layout specifications for a tri-fold brochure, with printer's marks.

Brochures

Brochures are pamphlets that contain only a few pages. They are often created by folding a single piece of paper into sections and having columns of text that correspond to the folded sections. Brochures can be informational, such as a brochure found in a hospital waiting room that describes the symptoms of a particular disease, or persuasive, such as a brochure that advertises a manufacturer's line of swimming pools.

One of the best methods of planning for a successful printing project is to prepare a prototype of what you hope to accomplish. That's especially true when you are working with unusual paper sizes or will be folding paper into its final form, such as when creating a brochure. Consider how you want the brochure to open and be read—in what sequence should the panels be read? Then fold a piece of paper and start blocking out sections of text and visuals. Note that it may be awkward for text to cross from one folded section to another, but photographs and illustrations can do so to good effect.

College students have many occasions for making oral presentations, in communication courses especially. Other courses may offer the opportunity to provide progress or research reports to peers, introduce ideas to the wider community at poster sessions, or convey information about a complex process or a series of events. Oral presentations often come at the tail end of a careful research process and might be thought of as "repurposing" printed or multimedia content for a dynamic, interactive context.

An effective presentation is the result of careful planning, invention and analysis of the context and content, and rehearsal of the delivery. Even though you will deliver your talk "live" instead of delivering it in written form, the same basic rhetorical principles govern the oral situation as the written one. What do you need to say, to whom, and where? To the right is the rhetorical triangle for an oral presentation, with just a few of the questions that might come to mind when you use this visual representation as a heuristic for thinking about a talk you have to give.

The Rhetorical Triangle for an Oral Presentation

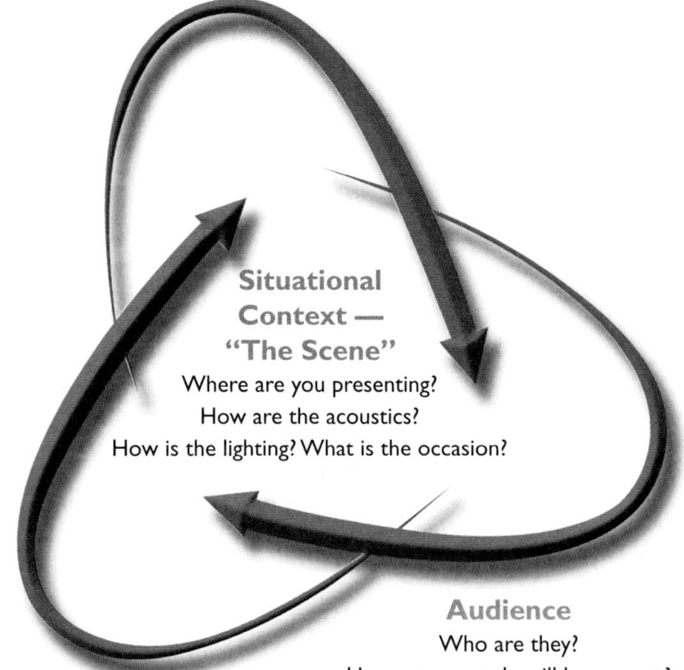
Presentation Content
What are the most important aspects of your topic?
What should your audience remember about it?
What visual information can you provide to enhance verbal content?
Situational Context — "The Scene"
Where are you presenting?
How are the acoustics?
How is the lighting? What is the occasion?
Audience
Who are they?
How many people will be present?
What do people already know about your topic?
What feelings do they have about it?
What expectations will they have about your talk?
Speaker
What can you do to help the audience trust you and what you are saying (ethos)?
What do you already know about your topic?
What have others said about it?
How do you feel about it?

Project Checklist

Considering the Context for an Oral Presentation

1. Know your subject matter, and reduce it to a few major points. Oral presentations usually emphasize the results of a process of research and analysis.
2. Understand your audience, including the interests they share with you and their reasons for attending your presentation.
3. Plan (and rehearse) well in advance. Know how much time you have for your presentation, and time yourself as you rehearse.
4. Double-check the availability and functionality of technology resources (projector, screen, computers and software, easels, pointer, lighting, and so on).
5. Develop a feel for the ambience of the space in which you'll present. Go there in advance if you've never been there before. Find out how your voice carries in the room. Consider:
   - ❑ How large is the room?
   - ❑ Are there air conditioners or other ambient noises that will muffle your voice? If so, is there a microphone you can use?
   - ❑ Will you have the freedom to move around the room, or will you be anchored to a podium?
   - ❑ What will the lighting be like when you present?
   - ❑ What will be behind you while you hold center stage?
   - ❑ Will audience members be able to move around during the presentation, in the event you want to encourage small group discussion?
   - ❑ How far are wall outlets from the podium, in the event you need to project your presentation?
   - ❑ Will late-arriving audience members be potentially distracting?
   - ❑ If you need to place any props (posters, easels, etc.), where can you put them?
   - ❑ If you have presentation slides, will you be able to position yourself in a triangular relationship with the audience so that you can avoid turning your back on the audience when you look at what is projected?

The steps for planning the content of an oral presentation are much the same as those for any complex project and include invention, research, and outlining. Once you have collected your content, you need to consider delivery: How will you present the content to an audience?

Outline the Presentation in Detail

Break the content into its major parts. Consider following the structure of what is known as the "classical oration."

Introduction. Introduce yourself and the focus of your presentation.

Narration of background information. Help the audience understand the issue and the basis for the key points that you will present next.

Key points. Bear in mind that you will likely have time to make only a few key points. Choose the most interesting and important ones.

Contrasting points. Consider whether you need to address any positions that differ from your own. If you decide to refute the most important one, treat it fairly.

Conclusion. Briefly review key points and/or discuss the importance of what you have just presented. If you want to encourage action on the part of the audience, say so here.

20a

Convert Your Outline into Notes

Use notes during the presentation to keep yourself on track. If you are doing a slide presentation, you can print out the content of your slides with accompanying notes, as shown in the illustration on page 329 from Kristofer Whited and Lauren Armenta's presentation on "The Hidden Persuaders."

Rehearse Your Presentation until It Seems Natural

Visualize yourself in the presentation context, as though looking out at your audience, and then deliver the content orally. If you are nervous, present your talk to someone whom you trust to give you constructive feedback—at least several times. Also practice the presentation on your own. Some people like to rehearse before a mirror. The more you practice, the easier you will find the actual presentation.

If you are complementing your presentation with slides, presentation software allows you to time when slides change, so you can synchronize your talk with the visual presentation, using your notes (on index cards or printed from the presentation software).

A Set of Keynote Slides Printed for the Presenter's Reference

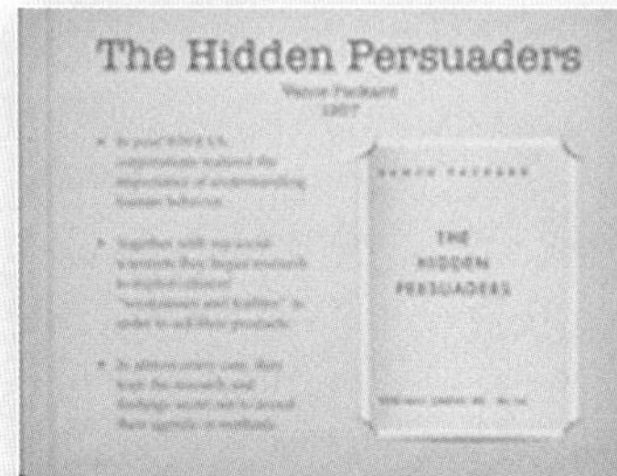

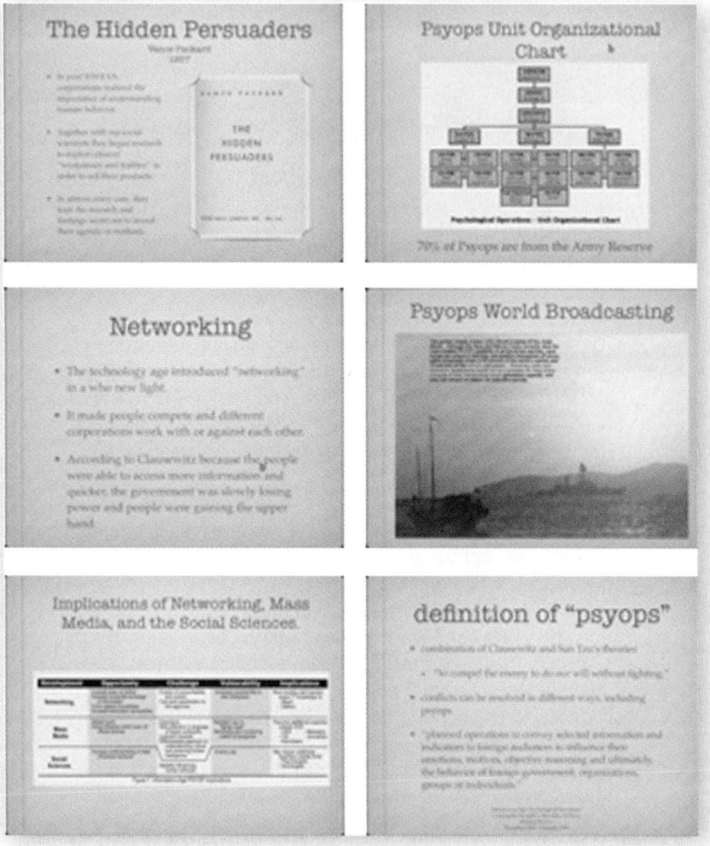

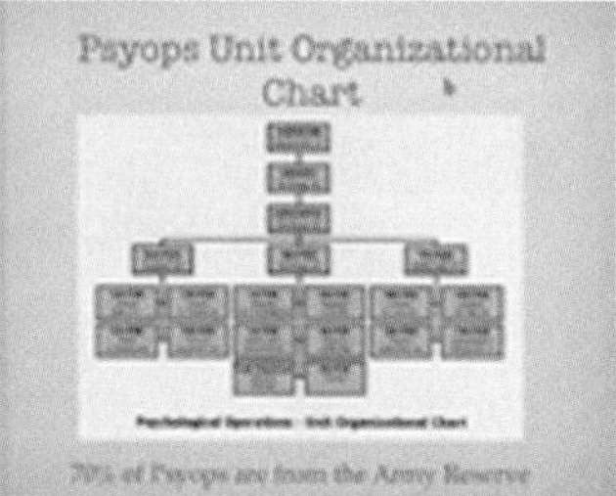

Networking

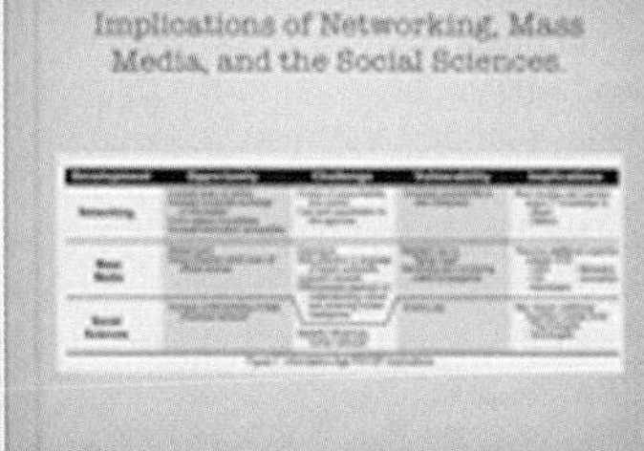

definition of "psyops"

From Kristofer Whited and Lauren Armenta's "The Hidden Persuaders."

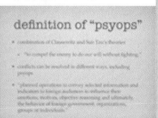

Using Visual Aids: Advantages and Disadvantages

Advantages	Disadvantages
Add interest or even excitement to your presentation.	Can be distracting if they aren't obviously related to your content.
Illustrate and/or summarize key points in a way the audience is likely to remember.	Can be frustrating if they are hard to see.
Focus the audience's attention.	Can be boring if they contain only the text of your presentation.
Help the audience grasp your points more quickly if you are interpreting, analyzing, or otherwise discussing a projected visual such as a photo, a piece of art, a graph, or a chart.	Can be obscure if in your talk you fail to indicate clearly which part or aspect of the visual you are discussing.

Information to Include in a Presentation Summary

A one-page presentation summary would include the following information:

- Title of presentation
- Name of speaker
- Date and location
- Abstract or summary of the presentation (with key points listed)
- Resource list (including URLs of websites)
- Citations (complete documentation of verbal and visual sources cited in the presentation)

Note that even when you don't offer a summary, your list of verbal and visual sources should be made available in handout form. The list should be formatted according to the documentation style appropriate to the subject matter and field (◀ Parts 4 and 5).

Resources on Visual Aids

For links to resources, visit **cengage.com/English/Blakesley**

Slide Shows

Use visual aids to help you achieve your rhetorical purpose. Carefully plan what you want to present and decide which points are most important to your presentation.

Two popular software programs for designing slide shows are Microsoft PowerPoint and Apple Keynote™. Adobe Acrobat® Professional can also be used for a full-screen slide show.

Posters and Flip Charts

Display posters are useful when presentations take place in spaces where audience members can clearly see the posters and can congregate around the speaker. Flip charts give you a writing surface that others can see in smaller presentation rooms.

Printed Documents

Audience members like to have some printed material to remind them of the presentation and to use for follow-up in the event they want to contact the speaker or conduct further research on their own. Make handouts, such as a presentation summary, available *after* your presentation for those who want them—not beforehand—because otherwise people may read your paper to themselves without paying attention to your presentation.

If you use more than one presentation technology (overhead transparences, a dry-erase board, and video, for example), the choreography of your presentation will be more challenging to manage, but not insurmountably so.

Video

If you want to include video (film clips, for instance), you can embed clips directly into a slide presentation and project them on a screen, rather than relying on a videotape and a TV. You will need to convert the video to digital format, however, if it is from a videotape. Digital content from DVDs or camcorders will be easier to handle with programs like Apple iMovie® or Windows Producer®, both of which come with the newest operating system of each platform.

Audio

If you decide to play music or the soundtrack from a video, for example, you should test whether it will be audible all over the room. If you refer to what is said on the audio in your presentation, you must ensure that everyone in the room will be able to hear the audio.

"Demo or Die": What Do You Do When Technologies Fail?

Create a Plan B in the event you have problems with your presentation because of a failure in technology or insufficient hardware or software. Anticipate that such failures will happen—because they sometimes do, and when they do, you don't want to be frazzled. If you have a backup plan, all will not be lost.

Interestingly, major software companies plan for presentation disasters to occur as part of the process of demonstrating new products. They have programmers nearby to help them fix any problems with the software on the spot, which always captures the interest of the audience. In his book *Snap to Grid,* Peter Lunenfeld sees this process of intentional failure as an ironic and crafty response to the dictum "Demo or die" (your technology had better work or you're doomed). This is coordinated and well-planned disaster management. It is a good idea for converting one's liabilities into assets and a smart rhetorical move.

In case the worst-case scenario happens—your carefully planned PowerPoint presentation can't be projected, for instance—consider bringing the following:

- Overhead transparencies that you can project, assuming there is a transparency projector in the room. (With most inkjet or laser printers, you can print slides individually on transparencies.)
- Handouts, either to give to each individual or for the audience to pass around
- Printed copies of the major points and slides in your presentation for your own reference

If your presentation is a team effort, put one person in charge of the technology during the presentation so that any technical glitches receive attention without distracting the speakers. Also arrange for two people to bring copies of the presentation.

PowerPoint and Keynote both offer convenient "packaging" options on the File menu that allow you to save your presentation on disk in multiple formats, along with a stand-alone Viewer program that allows you to present the information using a computer that does not have PowerPoint or Keynote on it. If you use Adobe Acrobat to create your slides, you can usually count on Adobe Reader to be available on the presentation machine (but have a Plan B in case it's not).

A Notes Slide

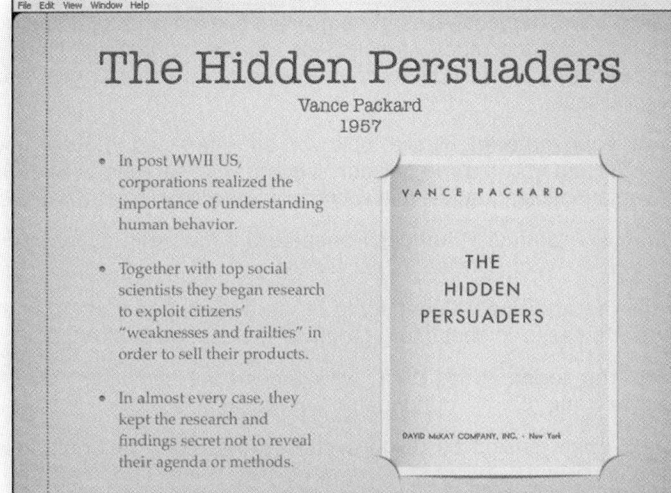

File Edit View Window Help
The Hidden Persuaders
Vance Packard
1957
In post WWII US, corporations realized the importance of understanding human behavior.
Together with top social scientists they began research to exploit citizens' "weaknesses and frailties" in order to sell their products.
In almost every case, they kept the research and findings secret not to reveal their agenda or methods.
VANCE PACKARD
THE HIDDEN PERSUADERS
DAVID McKAY COMPANY, INC. · New York

•*The Hidden Persuaders* by Vance Packard was a very popular book at the height of the Cold War, when psychological operations (or PsyOps) were in full gear. **Question: How many of you have read this book?**

•The possibilities of adapting principles of PsyOps were not lost on major advertisers who sponsored research studies on human behavior and responses to images. **Question: Has anyone participated in a consumer survey? One that asked you to view images?**

•These studies—often conducted by social scientists—examined the tendencies people had to be fooled by what they saw and heard. Sometimes people mistakenly associate a pleasing image, for example, with the truth value of the ad. Or they believe that a good endorsement by a celebrity must mean that the product is good or the message naturally truthful. **Question: Do you think you can be fooled into liking something?**

•It was very important that this research remain secret so that consumers would not understand the strategies being used against them. **Question: Why is it important to be visually literate?**

These notes from Kristofer Whited and Lauren Armenta's presentation on psychological techniques used in advertising suggest ways of involving the audience in discussing these questions.

Software or Process Demonstrations

You may need to present information in its native format, such as Web pages in a browser or images in Adobe Photoshop® or Macromedia Flash®. In many cases, it is useful to collect all these images and Web pages in static PDF files, which you can make with Adobe Acrobat and then present using only Adobe Reader®. If you have Adobe Acrobat, you can convert any document from any software program on your computer to PDF format. Acrobat allows you to combine and rearrange PDF files into an order that will suit your presentation.

Using Technologies to Enhance Audience Interaction

People may be reluctant to ask questions or contribute to the dialogue until they've had a chance to hear your presentation, but you can consult them along the way if time allows. Use a white board to write their responses to your questions, or type them into a word processor so that they're projected on screen.

It's also all right to step into the audience now and then. As with any technique, you should have a good reason for doing what you do—and a back-up plan in case something that you thought would be creative turns out not to go over as well as you had expected.

Toastmasters International is a nonprofit organization founded in 1924 to address the widespread anxiety about delivering speeches common among businesspeople and other professionals—even those with considerable experience. The group shares the 10 tips shown to the right.

10 Tips for Successful Public Speaking

Feeling some nervousness before giving a speech is natural and even beneficial. But too much nervousness can be detrimental. Here are some proven tips on how to control your butterflies and give better presentations:

Know your material. Pick a topic you are interested in. Know more about it than you include in your speech. Use personal stories and conversational language—that way you won't easily forget what to say.

Practice. Practice. Practice! Rehearse out loud with all equipment you plan on using. Revise as necessary.

Know the audience. Greet some of the audience members as they arrive. It's easier to speak to a group of friends than to strangers.

Know the room. Arrive early, walk around the speaking area, and practice using the microphone and any visual aids.

Relax. Ease tension by doing exercises. Transform nervous energy into enthusiasm.

Visualize yourself giving your speech. Imagine yourself speaking, your voice loud, clear, and confident. Visualize the audience clapping—it will boost your confidence.

Realize that people want you to succeed. Audiences want you to be interesting, stimulating, informative, and entertaining. They don't want you to fail.

Don't apologize for any nervousness or problem—the audience probably never noticed it.

Concentrate on the message—not the medium. Focus your attention away from your own anxieties and concentrate on your message and your audience.

Gain experience. Experience builds confidence, which is the key to effective speaking. A Toastmasters club can provide the experience you need in a safe and friendly environment.

From Toastmasters International, http://www.toastmasters.org.

Writing in Digital Spaces

PART 7

New Contexts for Writing: Civic Action

There are more ways of expressing your rights as a citizen than voting, though that responsibility is not to be taken lightly. The networking capacity of the Internet has mobilized people around the world to organize civic and political action, express their views, conduct research on social issues and politicians, educate the wider public, coordinate protests, and serve philanthropies, both online and in public.

Music for America (http://www.musicforamerica.org) is an online community of music fans who have banded together to express their views, share ideas about political events, and find the political and cultural value in music. Their site uses Drupal, open source software that enables networked blogging, RSS feeds, and much more. The Music for America site was built on a particular configuration of the Drupal software by CivicSpaceLabs, which customizes Drupal for groups that want to create social networks, conduct polls and surveys, maintain contacts, share news and photographs, organize smart mob events, and much more (see http://www.civicspacelabs.org). Groups with access to a server or site hosting service can get the CivicSpaceLabs configuration of Drupal for free.

Civic action is a form of nonviolent action carried out for political purposes to induce social change or foster social awareness of important issues. It is not limited to public protests but may also be carried out online, in the rapid give-and-take of writing.

Social and political networks are groups of people connected by communication technologies that push news (and new writing) to others quickly, making it possible to rally others to an important social cause. **Smart mobs,** a concept described by Howard Rheingold in his book with that title, are groups of protesters who take advantage of communication and Internet technologies (cell phones, GPS trackers, blogs) to organize their activities quickly and efficiently. As a site of civic action, the Internet can also become an instrument of **propaganda,** which is rhetoric that deliberately advocates a position while suppressing alternative perspectives.

Get Involved!
Google Directory > Society > Activism
http://www.google.com/top/society/activism/

Find a Yahoo! Group or create your own
http://groups.yahoo.com

Create a civic action website with CivicSpace
http://www.civicspacelabs.org

Only Connect . . .

Ten Habits of Successful Emailers

1. Reply promptly to email that requires a response, ideally within 24 hours, as you would to a phone message.
2. Be slightly more formal than you think you need to be.
3. Take some time to edit and revise your message before sending it.
4. Include an informative subject line, appropriate greeting, and purposeful message.
5. Avoid replying too quickly to a message that provokes strong emotions.
6. Realize that sarcasm and irony may be interpreted as condescension, and that subtle shifts in intonation are easily missed. Using all capital letters will make your reader feel as though you are SHOUTING. Using too many exclamation marks in an email message can diminish their effectiveness in conveying your enthusiasm or surprise.
7. Don't feel that you need to respond to every email posted to a discussion list or newsgroup (pick your moments, in other words), and stay on the topic thread when you do respond.
8. Quote the relevant material in previous messages to establish the context, but delete unnecessarily long quotations and indicate *<snip>* if appropriate.
9. When sending an attachment, identify what you've sent and the nature of the file. If you need to send a large attachment (over 1 MB, for example), you should check with your recipient to ensure that she or he can receive a large file.
10. Identify yourself by signing your name to your message.

The Public Nature of Email

Keep in mind that email is public. It can be forwarded or printed and thus be read by anyone else. Consider the conseqences when composing messages.

Throughout *Writing: A Manual for the Digital Age, Brief Edition* we have emphasized the importance of making writing decisions based on your analysis of the rhetorical context—your audience, the situation, your purpose, and your content. Not surprisingly, the rhetorical context of email still involves these components, so careful consideration of your audience, your reason and purpose for writing, and your content will help you write messages that effectively communicate information, share knowledge, solicit answers, and foster collaboration on projects and other writing activities.

Writing Effective Email 21a

You will have many occasions to exchange email with other students and instructors as you move through college. Some classes will depend heavily on your ability to read, respond to, and archive email effectively. Each rhetorical situation will have its own characteristics related to your primary and subsidiary audiences and how effectively you need to address them, the specific purpose of your email, and *kairos*—the time and occasion for your writing. Because email between instructors and students conducting class business is a professional situation, you also need to consider some conventions of email in professional contexts.

Here's a sample situation, with associated considerations. One student's choices are reflected in the email shown to the right.

Situation
You have been asked by an instructor to conduct field research—to interview another professor by email and in the process find answers to questions you have about your project.

Purpose
You want answers to your questions, but you also want to make sure your recipient is willing to provide them, understands your reasons for asking, and has enough time to respond.

Kairos
You want to contact the professor at a convenient time and allow the opportunity for reflective responses. You want to set the ambience for the occasion by using a professional but friendly and eager tone.

Conventions
Emoticons are generally not used in professional communication, especially with strangers. You should find out the professor's title (whether he or she should be addressed as *Dr.,* for example). If you can't find out how to address the recipient, you can use "Dear Professor ___________."

Note that the email message is in plain text. In academic or professional contexts, it is good practice to avoid heavily stylized (HTML) text, fancy backgrounds, and other ornaments.

Annette probably should have copied her peer group members with this message.

Kairos: The email message was sent in the morning on a work day, which is good timing since it will likely be responded to fairly quickly.

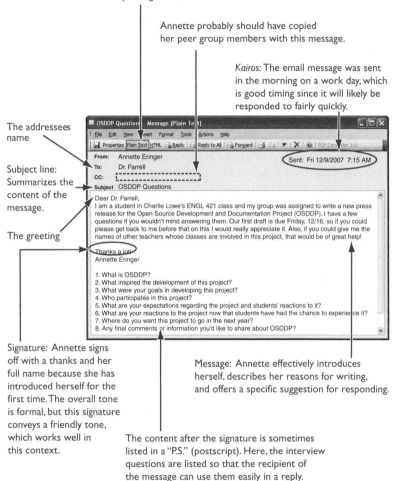

The addressees name

Subject line: Summarizes the content of the message.

The greeting

OSDDP Questions - Message (Plain Text)

File Edit View Insert Format Tools Actions Help

Properties Plain Text HTML Reply Reply to All Forward PDF Converter 3.0

From: Annette Eringer
To: Dr. Farrell
CC:
Subject OSDDP Questions
Sent: Fri 12/9/2007 7:15 AM

Dear Dr. Farrell,
I am a student in Charlie Lowe's ENGL 421 class and my group was assigned to write a new press release for the Open Source Development and Documentation Project (OSDDP). I have a few questions if you wouldn't mind answering them. Our first draft is due Friday, 12/16, so if you could please get back to me before that on this I would really appreciate it. Also, if you could give me the names of other teachers whose classes are involved in this project, that would be of great help!

Thanks a lot!
Annette Eringer

1. What is OSDDP?
2. What inspired the development of this project?
3. What were your goals in developing this project?
4. Who participates in this project?
5. What are your expectations regarding the project and students' reactions to it?
6. What are your reactions to the project now that students have had the chance to experience it?
7. Where do you want this project to go in the next year?
8. Any final comments or information you'd like to share about OSDDP?

Signature: Annette signs off with a thanks and her full name because she has introduced herself for the first time. The overall tone is formal, but this signature conveys a friendly tone, which works well in this context.

Message: Annette effectively introduces herself, describes her reasons for writing, and offers a specific suggestion for responding.

The content after the signature is sometimes listed in a "P.S." (postscript). Here, the interview questions are listed so that the recipient of the message can use them easily in a reply.

Annette's email message, annotated to show the parts of an email message. Is the message well suited to the rhetorical context? Why or why not?

Addressing an Email Message: Audience Considerations

Address Field	Type of Audience	Purpose or Effect
To: This field is visible to recipients.	The primary audience for the message, whether one or more persons, a discussion list, or a newsgroup	Readers presume that the message has been written directly to them and that they may need to respond or take some other action.
Cc: (carbon copy) This field is visible to recipients.	The subsidiary audience—readers you want to receive the message but usually just for informative reasons	People who are copied need to know the content of the email message but may not need to respond or act.
Bcc: (blind carbon copy) This field is *not* visible to all recipients.	Subsidiary audiences to whom you want to send copies without revealing that you have done so and without revealing their addresses (used to send messages to large groups; otherwise, used infrequently)	This field is sometimes used to copy sensitive information to another person or to establish a record that the email exchange has taken place.

Subject Lines: Providing Context and Previewing Content

Notice the level of generality or specificity in these subject lines:

Ineffective	**Subject:**	Important Attachment
Effective	**Subject:**	Project I Submission for English 309
Ineffective	**Subject:**	Help!
Effective	**Subject:**	Problems performing screen captures in Mac lab

Every email message has to have an **addressee** (or addressees) and a **message.** An email message sent in a professional context usually includes three other components: a **subject line,** a **greeting,** and a **signature.** Many email messages also include **attachments** containing files meant to be shared, such as documents, images, or other email messages.

The Addressee

The addressee of an email message is its audience. All email programs and services offer users *To:*, *Cc:*, and *Bcc:* fields for email addresses.

The Subject Line

The subject line announces or summarizes the content of the email message or preserves the thread of a prior discussion. It establishes *context,* in other words.

Subject lines should be informative, specifically related to the content of the message or to a previous thread, and composed carefully in light of the subject lines commonly associated with spam and computer viruses. For example, avoid asking a question or including strange punctuation.

The Greeting

The greeting is an important component of an email message because it sets the tone for the message, shows recipients that the message is intended for them, and confirms (importantly) that the message was not randomly generated by a spammer. Use a greeting that is well suited to your familiarity with the recipient and the formality of the occasion.

In some situations, such as when you exchange multiple email messages with a person in a short time span, you don't need to use a greeting because the subject line will provide the recipient with the context immediately.

The Message Body

What you say in the body of an email message will vary greatly with purpose and context. In all but the most informal situations, you should begin by establishing the purpose of your message and explaining the nature of any file attachments. Because active emailers read and write a lot of email, you should make sure that your message makes its point, asks its question(s), or shares information as clearly and concisely as possible.

Email Greetings

Notice that in the examples of messages addressed to specific people, we always use the person's name. Doing so conveys a positive tone. It also assures the recipient that the email message is not spam or a virus. Although viruses sometimes include the first part of the person's email address in the subject line, usually the person's name is not in the message greeting.

Greeting	Context
Dear _______ :	More formal situations, when you have never corresponded with or met the recipient and want to set a serious or professional tone
Dear _______ ,	Informal situations, when you have a close relationship with the person (as in "Dear Mom")
Hi, ______ — or *Hi, ______ :* or *Hi ______ ,*	More familiar situations, when it's appropriate to set an informal tone. Consider using a dash (or double hyphen) after the person's name to avoid the awkwardness of a double comma, as in "Hi, Ann," or simply omit the first comma.
To Everyone: or *Dear Everyone,* or *Hi, Everyone—*	Messages sent to a discussion list or a group of people
Firstname,	Informal situations, when the recipient knows you and (probably) expects messages from you
Dear Firstname (if I may),	When you have begun a formal correspondence with someone and feel the need to be more informal. If a person doesn't know you, asking permission to use his or her first name helps break the ice.

Plain Text Formatting Conventions

- **Italics.** Indicate italics by using an underscore (_) to show where the italics should begin and end:

> I am reading Erik Larson's nonfiction book _The Devil in the White City_ for my Books and Coffee seminar.

- **Line length.** Email programs vary in how they handle line length. It's customary to set your line length at about 70 characters, which is the length of a typical line in a well-designed book (usually under Tools/Options/Mail Format or Preferences/Formatting, but consult Help if you're not sure where to find it). The reader's eye has trouble tracking back to the next line when lines are longer than that.
- **Headers.** Use headers in an email message to indicate new sections of text or to provide a list or other information that needs to be separated from the rest of the text.

Quoting Previous Messages

Most email programs give you several options for handling quoted material in responses (see Figure 21.1). You can usually find these settings under Options > Preferences > Email Options (or something similar).

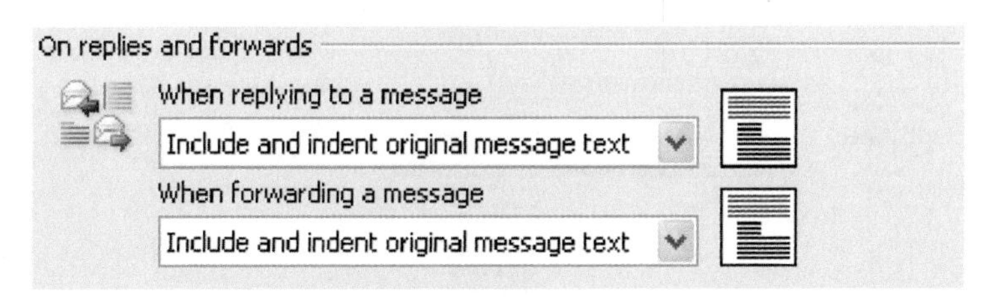

Figure 21.1 Sample Settings for Reply and Forwarding Options

Formatting
Most email programs give you the option of sending email in plain text or HTML format. Formatting in HTML allows you to use alternative fonts, font styles (such as boldface and italics), and font sizes. Because plain text formatting won't allow you to change font styles (from normal to italic, for example), there are a few conventions that you should know about.

Length
Keep your email messages to under 500 words for most situations, especially when you want a quick response. For purely informative purposes, such as announcements, it's okay to write a longer message because you don't expect the recipient to respond.

Quoting Previous Messages
When responding to an email, include the previous message as quoted material, usually at the end of your response after your signature. Unless there's a need to keep a precise trail of the exchange, trim quoted material to highlight the parts to which you're responding. When you trim quoted material, let your reader know you have done so by typing <*snip*> where you delete words.

Attachments

Email makes sending file attachments, such as documents, images, and other email messages, easy. Thus it enables collaboration on complex projects at a distance. However, as the sender, you need to consider how your audience will receive attachments, whether they will be able to open them, and how they will file them away for later review. In addition, because of the spread of computer viruses through email attachments, you need to be careful that you don't send such viruses yourself (in an infected file, for example) and that you take into account how difficult it can be for recipients to judge whether an email attachment is legitimate or some kind of hoax.

Preparing Attachments

Effective document sharing requires attention to the format of the files you plan to send to others. If you are writing an essay in a word processor such as WordPerfect, OpenOffice.org's Writer, or Word, you have the option to save your file in Rich Text Format, or RTF. These files will have the .rtf extension at the ends of their names. Here's how to make an RTF file in a word processor:

1. From the File menu, choose "Save As."
2. In the pop-up dialogue box, select "Rich Text Format," "RTF," or the equivalent from the

Attaching a File to an Email Message

After you have addressed your message and informed your correspondent what type of file you're sending and why, attach your file. In desktop email programs and "stand-alone" email clients (such as Eudora, Outlook, Thunderbird, Outlook Express, Mac Mail, or Entourage), files are attached in a similar way:

1. Click on "Attach" on the top menu bar or, in some cases, choose File > Attach File (see Figure 21.2).

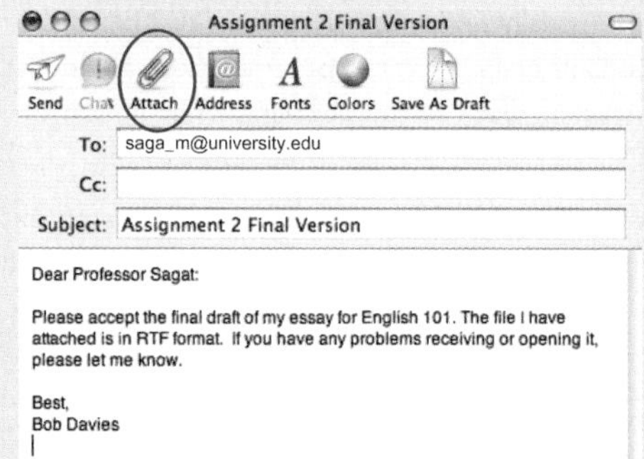

Figure 21.2 In Mac Mail, like many other email clients, you add attachments by clicking on a paperclip icon.

2. In the folder navigation dialogue box that pops up, navigate to the file you want to attach, select the file (see Figure 21.3), and then click on "Choose File" (Mac) or "Open" (Windows).

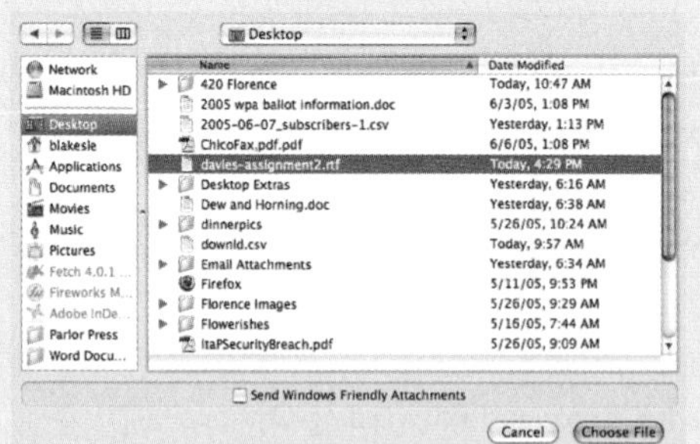

Figure 21.3 Find the file you want to attach to your email message.

3. Your file name will appear either in an attachment line near your address bar or in the body of your message (as shown in Figure 21.4).

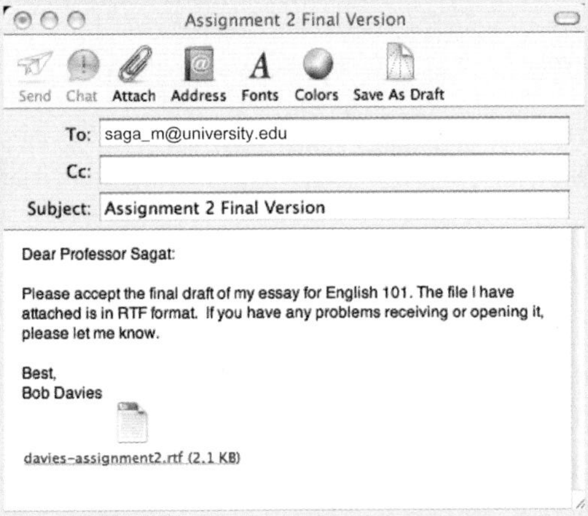

Figure 21.4
Check to see that the file has been attached to your message.

When using Web-based mailing services (like Yahoo! Mail or Google Mail), attach your file as follows:

1. Browse to and select the file you want to attach: In the Attach File box, click on "Browse" and then navigate to the file on your computer, select it, and click "Choose File" (Mac) or "Open" (Windows).
2. Upload the file by clicking on "Attach." Some Web-based mail services then require that you click on the Attach button right beneath the browser window. If yours does, click on it to upload your file, and then send your message when you're ready.

drop-down menu box called "File Type" or "Type."

3. Name your file and then navigate to the folder where you'd like to save it.
4. Choose "Save."

Sending Attachments

- *Let your recipients know that you have attached a file to your email, why, and what they can do to view it.* Identify (a) the reason you're sending the attachment and what it contains; (b) the file name and format; and (c) in cases where it isn't obvious, the program the recipients will need to use to open it.
- *Give the file attachment a name that accurately identifies its contents and allows the recipient to save it easily.* Name your file with identifying information that distinguishes it from other file attachments that may be received. For example, if your instructor asks all students to submit "Project 1" by email, you could name your file *lastname_project1.pdf.* If your instructor receives 20 file attachments all named *project1.pdf,* he or she will need to rename each file before saving it and may even accidentally replace another file named *project1.pdf* when saving a new one.
- *Add the attachment!* Right after you write the recipient about the nature of the attachment, pause for a moment to attach it to your message.

Signature

The signature line(s) for an email message should include your name so that the recipient knows who is writing. In most situations, you'll also want to include a closing sentiment, depending on the level of familiarity you have established with your correspondent.

In professional contexts, it's customary to provide additional information under your name: contact information, job title, URL of your website, and such. Limit your signature to five or six lines, however, because such information is usually not critical in routine correspondence with colleagues or peers. When writing to people you don't know, use an informative signature so that they know more about you and how to reach you by means other than email.

Quotations

After their signature information, some email authors like to include witty, smart, or philosophical quotations from their favorite authors, in part to add some personality to their messages. It's understandable that this would become common practice. But quotations like these grow stale quickly, particularly for readers. In all but the most informal email or groups that encourage swapping witty quotations, avoid using quotations in your signature, especially ones that are more than a few words.

Closing Sentiments: Degrees of Formality

Formal	**Familiar**	**Casual**
Sincerely yours,	Best,	Thanks,
Sincerely,	Yours,	Cheers,
Best regards,	Regards,	Later,
Best wishes,	Take care,	TTFN, CYA, etc.
	Thank you,	

Signature Information

Here is a template for the kinds of information people include in signature lines, along with an example.

Template	**Example**
Title Firstname Lastname	Ms. Maryan Liban
Job title/Major/Course	Coordinator of Special Services
Company/University	The University of Manitoba
Email address	Maryan.Liban@umanitoba.ca
URL	http://www.services.umanitoba.ca

Emailing on a PDA or a Cell Phone

Increasingly, people are reading and even writing email and instant messages on PDAs and cell phones. Because of the smaller screen size, most messages sent from PDAs and cell phones will be short, so use them when a short message is enough to accomplish your purpose and use a laptop or desktop when you need to send longer messages or attachments. When sending messages to someone who is using a PDA or cell phone, you should realize that some of these same restrictions apply. It's likely that long messages will be hard for the recipient to read, and attachments sent to cell phones may not even be received. PDAs and cell phones can be especially useful for participating in chat and instant messaging, where all messages tend to be short and where it has become common practice for people to use abbreviations and acronyms for common sayings. (See section 21g for more on participating in synchronous, real-time online conversations.)

Guidelines for Participating on an Email Discussion List

1. **Research the list.** Before you join, take the time to find out as much about the list as you can to see if it matches your interests.
2. **Read the list FAQs.** After joining the list, you will receive instructions, often in the form of a set of FAQs, that you should read and save. They usually explain important details, such as how to adjust your subscription settings, how to unsubscribe, and how to receive the list email in digest form. Save this message for later reference.
3. **Introduce yourself.** After joining a list, it's a good idea to observe for a while (called *lurking*) before you put in your oar. Your first message to the list can be in response to another message that has been posted, but it's also accepted practice on most lists for your first posted message to be one that introduces yourself. Your message might go something like this:

> Hi, Everyone—
>
> I wanted to introduce myself to let you know that I've joined the list and look forward to listening to and joining the discussion. I'm especially interested in ______________.

4. **Preserve threads.** When you respond to what others have said, be sure that you use the same subject line (beginning with *Re:*) and that you quote the message thread you're responding to.
5. **Don't respond to every new post.** Give others a chance, too.
6. **It's fine to lurk.** You don't need to feel guilty about not posting your own messages. Lurking is fun.
7. **Don't post throwaway lines.** It's inappropriate to post a message like "How true!" or "Me, too!" or "Well said!" If you feel compelled to say so, take the time to explain why you feel the way you do.
8. **Take the time to prune quoted material.** You'll save bandwidth, and the people who subscribe to the list in digest form will like you, if you prune the amount of material you quote. (Digests of a discussion list are daily messages that contain all the messages posted in a given day. It can be very difficult to

(continued)

Email discussion lists or newsgroups may be formed by people with similar interests or may be attached to college classes. Thousands of public lists revolve around topics ranging from hobbies to bands to scholarly and professional interests. Some discussion lists have been running for ten years or more, almost back to the days when people first started using email for social and professional communication. Discussion lists have endured because they are convenient ways to socialize and professionalize—to stay in touch with friends and network with others with similar personal or professional interests.

List members have adopted certain common practices to ensure that list discussion is (mostly) on topic and that list members enjoy the time they spend communicating with each other. Like any social group, networked communities have well-developed guidelines for interacting that you should understand and follow. Even if your discussion list is not a public one but, for example, attached to a course you're taking, you'll find that these guidelines can help you gain the most from your list participation as well as enrich the experience of others.

Participation on email discussion lists can be immensely rewarding, whether the members are all enrolled in a single small class or writing from all around the world. Public discussion lists in professional fields offer newcomers a chance to learn the ins and outs of specialized work from more experienced colleagues, whom they formerly would have encountered only at annual conferences or other meetings. Discussion lists also give people the opportunity to join a discourse community—to learn the "lingo" and ways of making meaning that can help them understand their subject more deeply and in the context of the concerns that others share.

To find out more about discussion lists that might interest you, try some of these clearinghouses:

Yahoo! Groups: http://groups.yahoo.com
Topica: http://www.topica.com
Hotmail Groups: http://groups.msn.com
AOL Groups: http://groups.aol.com
L-Soft (Listserv): http://www.lsoft.com/lists/listref.html

find new contributions to a discussion when reading a digest because people don't prune quoted material. A typical digest might contain 90 percent quoted material and only 10 percent new material.)

9. **Don't post personal messages to the list, forward list messages to others not on it, or forward messages to the list from others not on it.**
10. **Ask the moderator if it's okay to post announcements.** Moderators appreciate such requests because announcements, even when well focused, are spam.
11. **Try to avoid being a hit-and-run commentator.** If you plan to participate on a list, read the messages in the thread carefully. It kills a discussion when people who haven't been paying attention post messages that repeat what has already been said or asked. If others can tell that you haven't been paying attention, they may resent you for it.
12. **Let the list moderator answer questions about the conduct of the list.**
13. **Read the most recent messages before responding to older ones.** When a person asks a question that is fairly easy for others to answer, someone may answer right away. And then 18 others may answer, too, in a short time. Do the best you can to stay current before posting the 19th message providing exactly the same answer.
14. **If a message to a list asks for data, provide the information off list (in a message to the requester of the data only) unless it's clear that others will want to read it.**
15. **Before posting open-ended research questions or surveys to academic lists, be sure to check with the list moderator and consult with others who may be able to advise you about how your request will be received.** Sometimes people will see a list as a perfect opportunity to tap a research pool, which can be fine, but do your homework first. Your research should be well advanced before you ask other people for new data.

The terms *synchronous* and *asynchronous* refer to how communication online takes place in time.

synchronous communication Communication that happens simultaneously, in real time. When you talk to someone on a cell phone, your communication is synchronous because each party can hear the other at the moment words are spoken. On the Internet, technologies used in chat rooms (such as Instant Messenger) are called "synchronous" because they produce an exchange that takes place in real time. You type a message and click Send, and your message is received instantly.

asynchronous communication Communication that takes place over an extended period of time. When you write a letter to a friend and send it via snail mail, you're communicating asynchronously. Likewise, when you post a message to an online bulletin board or a weblog, that's asynchronous communication.

The difference between synchronous and asynchronous communication matters because what we write and how we write it should be shaped by our understanding of how our readers receive our messages. Are they reading quickly? Are they composing their own responses even as they read ours? Are they holding multiple conversations simultaneously? Are they waiting and reflecting, then posting a response? How does the urgency of the synchronous context shape intention and message? What shortcuts (e.g., "TTFN!") do people use in synchronous situations to communicate more efficiently? Do you need to use them, too?

Over time, communities of users have come together online on the basis of shared interest or need. Because these communities have unique interests and goals, they use a wide variety of communication technologies, each of which offers a different experience for writers and readers. You can find online bulletin boards and forums on thousands of subjects, from home improvement and politics to desktop publishing and software. Blogger, the major service provider for weblogs on the Internet, lists 1.1 million users and over 200,000 active weblogs. There are also now millions of users worldwide of synchronous communication technologies, such as ICQ®, Instant Messenger™, and MSN® Chat. MUDs (Multi-User Domains) and MOOs (MUDs, Object-Oriented) have been popular for more than ten years. Many of these software technologies are in use on college campuses.

Writing in online communities sometimes requires learning new software applications (or *clients*) and interfaces, and each tool may be used in particular rhetorical situations and sometimes for very specific purposes. Writers need to be careful judges of the rhetorical situation—audience, message, and purpose—and to adapt the capabilities of the technologies in ways that help them write effectively in each situation.

Online Communication: Uses, Tools, and Examples

Communication	Uses	Tools and Examples
SYNCHRONOUS		
Audio conference	Spoken conversation, meetings	Phones, conference calls, Skype
Chat	Real-time written conversation, planning meetings, interviews, group discussion	ICQ, iChat, Instant Messenger, NetMeeting
MOOs, MUDs	Chat, real-time writing conversation, group meetings, group analysis (using Web Projector), archiving documents, quick feedback	Telnet, Pueblo, enCore
Video conferencing	Spoken dialogue with a live visual feed, meetings, distance education	iSight, NetMeeting, ViaVideo, PicTel, Breeze
Whiteboard	Sharing screen space for collaborative writing, brainstorming, sharing desktops and applications	MOO (Projector), ClearBoard, WebCT, GRCLive
Web-based conference	Interactive presentations, meetings	Breeze, NetMeeting
ASYNCHRONOUS		
Email discussion lists, newsgroups	Group discussion, resource sharing, collaboration and planning, community-building	Listserv, Mailman, Majordomo, Topic, Google Groups, Usenet Newsgroups, Yahoo! Groups
Bulletin boards, forums, threaded discussion lists	Focused group discussion, reading responses and discussion, project logs, information-sharing	Ultimate Bulletin Board, Ceilidh, Blackboard, WebCT, FirstClass, Sakai
Content management systems (CMSs)	Managing diverse content, documents, and discussion; weblogs, chat, peer review of documents, archiving; journals and ezines; digital portfolios	Drupal, CivicSpace, Mambo, Manila, Moodle
Weblogs and social networking services	Personal journaling and reflection, project logs, research notes, public discussion, dissemination of research, political action, information filtering, establishing a reputation	Blogger, b2Evolution, Drupal, FaceBook, Movable Type, LiveJournal, WordPress, ElGG, Orkut, MySpace, Friendster
Wikis	Collaborative authoring, resource-building, archiving, polling	Wikipedia, EServer TC Library, Wikibooks

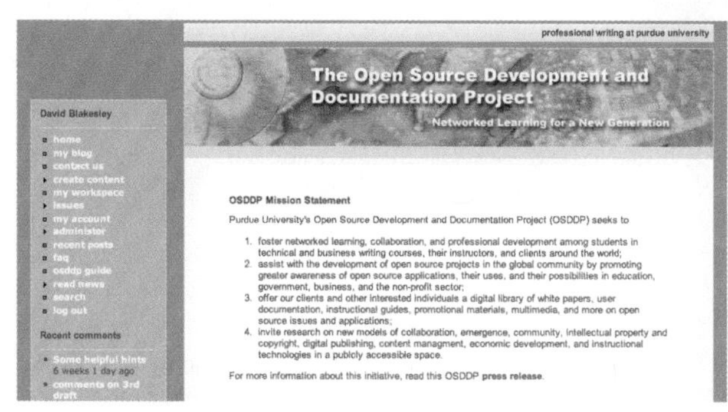

Asynchronous communication: This site is run by Drupal, a content management system and weblog. Drupal helps students manage their collaborative projects and link to each other's work and outward to the Internet, enhancing communication across classes and to the wider world. See **http://www.osddp.org**.

Resources on Discussion Boards and Forums

Here are starting points for exploring discussion boards and forums. In addition, many software and hardware makers provide forums where people can ask technology questions and search for answers offered previously. We highly recommend that you visit such forums when you have technical questions about the technologies you use in your courses:

Sample Discussion Boards

Motley Fool: **http://boards.fool.com/?ref=topnav**
Slashdot: **http://slashdot.org**

Directories

Google's Directory:
http://www.google.com/Top/Computers/Internet/On_the_Web/Message_Boards/
Big Boards: **http://www.big-boards.com**

See section 21b for a description of email discussion groups.

Bulletin Boards, Forums, and Threaded Discussion Lists

Bulletin boards, forums, and threaded discussion lists allow users to post messages in threaded discussions, using a standard Web browser like Mozilla Firefox®, Netscape®, Internet Explorer, Opera, or Safari® as an interface.

Discussion boards and forums tend to be most useful for sustained discussion in close communities, as you find in class situations, when writers share ideas, responses, and feedback on work in progress. However, for these lists to work well, participants need to follow their user guidelines and return regularly enough to keep the discussion fresh.

Rhetorical Considerations in Discussion Networks

One of the main goals of a discussion board is to carry out sustained discussion on specific topics. So users are encouraged to "stay on topic" and "keep the discussion relevant." If, as a writer, you violate these conventions, it is likely that your messages will be skipped over and your opportunities to contribute to the conversation seriously reduced.

Weblogs

Weblogs (blogs for short) have become popular as a form of publishing topical commentary unmediated by conventional media outlets, a kind of unfiltered civic discourse. Blogs differ from discussion boards in several ways:

- They are usually authored by one individual or a small group of people.
- Community networks such as MySpace—run by what's known as *social networking software*—collect multiple individual blogs together under one umbrella.
- Readers are given permission (or not) to post comments that respond to the blog author(s).
- The software typically allows bloggers to share topics and RSS feeds (Rich Site Summary feeds), making content more dynamic and accessible.

A blog can "syndicate" the content from other blogs—the software will automatically scan for updated content on other websites that the blog can link to. For a good example, see the news aggregator in action at Kairosnews: http://kairosnews.org/aggregator.

Project Checklist

Networking in Online Forums

The following recommendations come from careful consideration of the typical rhetorical situation of discussion forums—public spaces where people with shared interests or values and special expertise gather to discuss the topics that interest them.

1. Read the user guidelines and be sure to follow them.
2. Read through all the messages in a particular thread before posting a response.
3. Provide enough context in your message (by quoting from a previous post, for example) so that all readers understand what you're responding to or what you're proposing.
4. If you can't stay on topic, begin a new thread and give it a subject line that conveys the topic clearly.
5. If you want to reply to someone but your message seems somewhat personal or off topic, consider sending a personal message instead (through email or, if possible, the board's internal message server).
6. Preview and edit your messages before you post them.
7. When your message is posted to the forum, open it and read it to see if it says what you intended. If it doesn't, re-edit it.
8. Return frequently to the forum to see how others have responded to your post or how the thread has continued. If the system has a "notifications" option that will send you an email when someone responds to your posts, turn it on.
9. If people respond to your post, keep the discussion going with another message (if appropriate).
10. Give other people opportunity and time to reply.

For links to online resources, visit
cengage.com/English/Blakesley

Effective and Ineffective Blog Entries

An overly contentious entry?

> Subject: Blog Losers
> I heard a ridiculous story on NPR this morning that weblogs were having a significant impact on how Americans perceive the war in Iraq, in part because blog authors were writing from the scene and didn't have to run their commentary through media outlets or others who might censor their writing (see http://discover.npr.org/rundowns/segment.jhtml?wfId=1212461). How do we know who these goofballs are and where they're writing from? Isn't it the case that journalists are journalists because they verify sources and aren't free to write anything, true or not? Who cares what Joe Schmoe thinks? We see the pictures and know what's going on.

An entry people might respond to:

> Subject: Blogs in Wartime
> NPR reported this morning that weblogs were having a significant impact on how Americans perceive the war in Iraq. I see this as a good thing because it's important for us to weigh multiple perspectives on such weighty issues. It can be difficult to judge the integrity of the sources of information, but we should ask the same questions of media coverage also. It seems to me that one of the great benefits of a blog perspective is that it's personal and (somewhat) unscripted. We should know enough not to accept what we hear as "fact," but we can still begin to understand how one person experiences a significant event. That in itself is useful. What do you think? Should we trust bloggers from the war zone? What if they are soldiers? Should we care if they are biased? Could they NOT be biased?
> Link: http://discover.npr.org/rundowns/segment.jhtml?wfId=1212461

Notice how the writer goes out of her way to invite readers to respond. As a writer, don't be afraid to let your readers know how you'd like them to respond.

Rhetorical Considerations in Weblogs

If you are the author of a blog, consider the contexts in which others will read and (possibly) respond to your writing. As the author, it is likely that you can restrict who can respond to your entries and, if the blogging software allows for multiple user-roles, who gets to see your entries. These factors will help you decide how much to say, on what kinds of topics.

A blog author who wants interesting comments from users walks a delicate line between being overly contentious and being too timid. No one will want to respond if it's clear that you will leap on anyone who argues for a different view. Also, don't simply make observations—reflect on them in a bit of detail so that people who come to your blog have something to ponder.

As a reader making comments, you have some obligation to preserve the thread because readers typically read the author's posts and then the comments. If you do make comments, be sure to explain yourself rather than simply making an observation and then quitting.

Many students participate in online communities associated with classes or group projects. Because each communication technology has some unique features that shape how discussion unfolds online, student writers should take the time to establish guidelines for participation, including the expected frequency of posts, length, level of engagement, and more. These guidelines should be posted to the site so that people can refer to them later. Such guidelines create conventions for lively and interesting discussions; they ensure that everyone understands how online conversations can develop fruitfully for all involved.

The screen capture to the right shows a list of seven guidelines that a group of students came up with and everyone in the class agreed to follow. Your class (or community) may generate guidelines of its own.

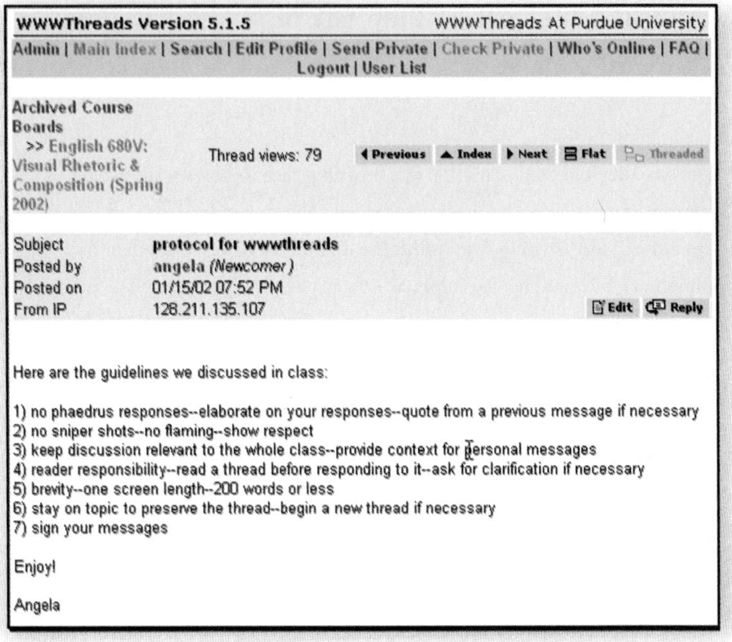

WWWThreads Version 5.1.5 WWWThreads At Purdue University

Admin | Main Index | Search | Edit Profile | Send Private | Check Private | Who's Online | FAQ | Logout | User List

Archived Course Boards
>> English 680V: Visual Rhetoric & Composition (Spring 2002)

Thread views: 79 Previous Index Next Flat Threaded

Subject **protocol for wwwthreads**
Posted by angela *(Newcomer)*
Posted on 01/15/02 07:52 PM
From IP 128.211.135.107 Edit Reply

Here are the guidelines we discussed in class:

1) no phaedrus responses--elaborate on your responses--quote from a previous message if necessary
2) no sniper shots--no flaming--show respect
3) keep discussion relevant to the whole class--provide context for personal messages
4) reader responsibility--read a thread before responding to it--ask for clarification if necessary
5) brevity--one screen length--200 words or less
6) stay on topic to preserve the thread--begin a new thread if necessary
7) sign your messages

Enjoy!

Angela

Class guidelines developed by students for interaction in WWWThreads, a Web-based discussion board.

Documenting Sources in Your Online Posting

Title of post

Authors are cited indirectly and a link to the source is provided.

Money can't buy happiness

A new scientific study reveals that (shocker!) a nation's economic fortitude is not as tied tc the well-being of its citizens as previous believed. The results of the study--prepared by researchers at the University of Illinois and University of Pennsylvania--appeared in the latest issue of Psychological Science in the Public Interest.

> "It has been assumed that money increases well-being and, although money can be measured with exactitude, it is an inexact surrogate to the actual well-being of a nation. In a 1985 survey, respondents from the Forbes list of the 400 richest Americans and the Maasai of East Africa were almost equally satisfied and ranked relatively high in well-being. The Maasai are a traditional herding people who have no electricity or running water and live in huts made of dung. It follows, that economic development and personal income must not account for the happiness that they are so often linked to."

Instead, the authors propose that a population's "engagement, purpose and meaning, optimism and trust, and positive and negative emotions in specific areas such as work life and social relationships" should be considered when measuring the strength of a nation. Link

posted by David Pescovitz at 05:20:14 AM permalink | Other blogs commenting on this post

Author of post

Block quotation: Although quotation marks are used here, they are not needed because the material has already been formatted as a quotation.

Sample blog posting at Boing Boing (**http://boingboing.net**). This is a good example of how a weblog posts reports on an issue, provides a link for users to track, and quotes from the source.

In asynchronous communication contexts, such as blogs and discussion boards, citation practices are governed by context and purpose, as well as by the community's understanding of what qualifies as common knowledge. For example, in a weblog posting that refers to a news event, it is common practice to provide a link to the source in the form of a URL that readers can track if they want to learn more.

Direct quotations are indicated by quotation marks or block quotations. Weblog posts do not typically include parenthetical documentation (such as page numbers) or bibliographies. They do, however, name the authors and titles of the works they cite in their text. Information and terms that are common knowledge in a particular blogging network are not cited because the authors presume that the audience already shares that knowledge. On discussion boards, the practice is similar.

Synchronous reading and writing take place quickly in unmoderated chat rooms, MUDs, and MOOs, so the rhetorical context that shapes these written conversations is very different from that in asynchronous environments. People don't have much time to think through topics, write or read extended responses, or revise their writing.

Like discussion boards, chat or MOO communities develop explicit or implicit guidelines for decorum that you should learn, either by reading them or by sitting in on the conversation a bit (lurking) until you feel confident that you understand what people expect from your participation.

Chat

In writing courses, chat rooms allow for continued discussion of course content, brainstorming activities, group management, and live interaction when F2F (face-to-face) meetings may not be possible. Students who aren't comfortable expressing themselves in F2F meetings sometimes find chat a comfortable way to express themselves. At the same time, however, chat rooms typically don't offer much space for entering responses, require good typing skills, and favor frequent users who know the tricks of fast give-and-take, such as how to take turns.

Project Checklist

Participating in Online Synchronous Communication

1. Read the user guidelines for the community, or develop some with your group.
2. When you enter a live discussion, announce your presence with a short greeting to the list, when it seems appropriate to do so. (Example: "Hi, everyone. It's nice to be here.")
3. As messages are posted, try to read them all, but pay special attention to messages that are directed specifically to you or to something you've mentioned.
4. Try to stay on topic and preserve threads, but recognize that multiple threads may go on simultaneously.
5. If you can't stay on topic, begin a new thread and make sure that you announce how you'd like to shift the discussion.
6. If your post is meant for a particular person, preface it with that person's user name (e.g., "To MaryD:").
7. If you want to reply to someone but your message seems somewhat personal or off topic, consider sending a personal message instead (through email or, if possible, the board's internal message server). Many chat rooms and MOOs, for example, will also allow you to send private (backchannel) messages to other participants.
8. "Emoting" is a common practice that allows users to emulate physical gestures (e.g., "Joe waves to Dan") and helps establish group congeniality.
9. Take a moment to read over your messages before you post them.
10. Watch to see if others respond to you. If they do—or ask questions—follow up. It's frustrating when people post messages and then leave the space or don't pay attention to the responses of others.
11. When you leave a synchronous conversation, it's customary to announce your exit. (Example: "Bye, everyone. Gotta run! TTFN.")
12. Don't be so eager to reply to every post that you overwhelm everyone else. Give other people opportunity and time to reply. Learn to take turns.

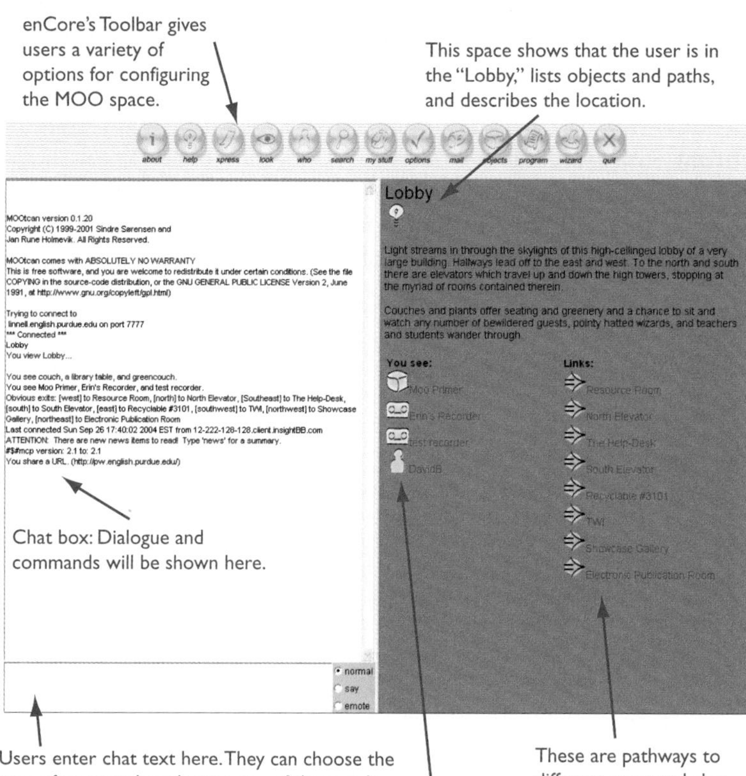
enCore's Toolbar gives users a variety of options for configuring the MOO space.
This space shows that the user is in the "Lobby," lists objects and paths, and describes the location.
about
help
xpress
look
who
search
my stuff
options
mail
objects
program
wizard
quit
Lobby
You see:
Links:
Chat box: Dialogue and commands will be shown here.
normal
say
emote
Users enter chat text here. They can choose the type of message by selecting one of three radio buttons: normal = a command, say = dialogue, emote = a physical gesture.
These are pathways to different areas and chat rooms, such as instructor "offices" or other meeting places.
These are objects and people in the current room. You can click on an object to see its description.

enCore MOO allows users to interact in a wide variety of ways. On the left are a chat box (bottom) and a chat transcript (top). On the right are tools (such as recorders, for "taping" chats; notebooks, for keeping journals and logs; and even projectors, for sharing images and websites with other users). Users can navigate to different spaces in the MOO where people gather to chat, share documents, archive material, and work collaboratively on ongoing projects.

MOO Resources

See the Resources Guide at the enCore Open Source MOO Project (by Jan Rune Holmevik and Cynthia Haynes): **http://lingua.utdallas.edu/encore/**

MOOs

MOO stands for "Multi-User Domain, Object Oriented." MOOs provide a virtual space for chats, often situating them in "rooms" and "parlors" that give users the feeling that they're visiting a material space. The MOO uses virtual objects (such as rooms, recorders, and projectors) to help users navigate to chat rooms where they can meet privately, keep a transcript of their discussions, and discuss readings or websites.

To use a MOO, users need a MOO client such as enCore, which structures the interface through a Web browser or an IRC (Internet Relay Chat) client, like Telnet.

ICQ

ICQ, which stands for "I Seek You," is the most popular software for synchronous communication on the Internet. The software can be used as a portal to other forms of communication as well, such as email and audio or video messaging. Thousands of ICQ groups are organized around shared interests. (See http://web.icq.com/groups/ for a full listing.)

In writing classes and other courses, synchronous chat such as that enabled by ICQ may be used to facilitate group discussion, brainstorm, plan projects, and meet at a distance. It is common practice to arrange ICQ meetings in advance.

22 WRITING AND RHETORIC ON THE WEB

The World Wide Web is the new global marketplace for sharing information, buying and selling property, and influencing opinion. It is a public space much like the *agora* of ancient Greece, where people gathered to exchange goods, discuss ideas and politics, and form bonds with others in the wider community. (*Agora* is the Greek term for "gathering place.") As a social space, the Web naturally creates the conditions for persuasion to occur.

As you learn to write for the Web and to design websites, you should not forget that the Web is inherently a public space. While it may be the case that only your primary audience—peers, teachers, co-workers, friends, family—will likely read your work, you should keep your subsidiary audiences in sight as you shape information for publication on the Web.

Information Literacy

Here are some questions that attentive writers and readers ask about information. You will notice that these are by now familiar questions about the rhetorical situation, couched here in the context of information literacy.

What Writers Should Ask

1. Is the information accurate?
2. Is the information useful?
3. What information is most important to readers?
4. What should readers understand most deeply after reading?
5. What can readers reference later, as the need arises?
6. How can I make information stick in the reader's mind?
7. What do I want my readers to do with the information?
8. What do my readers want to do with the information?

Information literacy is the ability to evaluate, synthesize, and "repurpose" information. *Repurposing* refers to the process of revising material for one particular purpose and audience so that it will become better suited to a new rhetorical situation. How we convey and organize information is at least as important as the information we convey. Information architect Richard Saul Wurman, author of *Information Anxiety* and *Information Anxiety 2,* makes this point frequently: unorganized and unprocessed information is virtually useless. It is, rather, the power to convey and transform information that is valuable. Information needs to be made manageable and useful by sorting, synthesizing, and assigning relative value to the content.

What Readers Want to Know

1. Is the information accurate?
2. Is the information useful?
3. What information is most important to me?
4. What do I need to remember most deeply?
5. What can I refer to later, as the need arises, and how can I find it again?
6. How can I remember so much information?
7. What does the writer want me to do with the information?
8. What do I need to do with the information?

Virtually any purpose that you can invent for print-based writing can also be applied to writing on the Web, and you can find examples of genres that have emerged in the digital age. Because they emerged as a result of a social process of sharing information and ideas, many of these genres resemble their counterparts in print, but with some important variations.

Scenarios for Web Writing

Consider composing for the Web from the very start if you want your writing to

- be accessible to a wide and public audience
- network with what others have said on the Web
- offer readers choices about how and in what order to read
- evolve as you discover new ideas
- be accessible over time
- integrate multimedia components like video, audio, and animation

If *any* of these scenarios fit your circumstances, consider making a decision to publish your work on the Web at the point of invention and planning rather than later. You will find it easier to include Web-based components if you plan for them at the start.

Web Publishing

Publishing on the Web would be a good choice in these situations:

1. Your assignment for a class is to compose an annotated bibliography on your topic and to include entries that can be accessed on the Web. You want your bibliography to be accessible to your classmates and others interested in the topic, and you think they will benefit from reading some of the works youve listed.
2. You want others (including people you may not know) to respond to and offer feedback on your writing, so you decide to create a weblog that will allow comments.
3. You want to develop a digital portfolio of your writing so that prospective employers will notice your work.
4. You have some special expertise on a subject and want to share your knowledge and establish your reputation as someone well informed on the subject.
5. You want to advertise and sell a product.
6. You want to create a journal or ezine of your own that collects articles and hypertexts submitted by others, but you don't have a budget to pay for printing and mailing copies.
7. You plan to present your work to a live audience at a poster session or conference and want people to have access to your work later.
8. You want to enlist the help of other people at a distance in creating a community website that provides up-to-date information.
9. You have created an ebook that includes multimedia components, such as video and audio, and have put it on a CD. You want readers to have access to it from anywhere.
10. You want to demonstrate a complex process to others, such as how to perform a task or make something, and can do so efficiently with video or other animation.
11. Your writing is about content easily accessible on the Web—at a museum website, for instance—and it would help readers to visit that website as they read your essay or hypertext.

Comparison of Print-Based and Digital Content on the Web

General Characteristics of Print-Based Content	General Characteristics of Digital Content
Longer units of text with fewer breaks	Shorter units of text with more breaks
No links or multimedia content	Frequent use of links and multimedia content
Minimal design elements	Design elements a critical component
Linear and sequential form; readers start at the beginning and read left to right down the page to the end, in serial fashion	Nonlinear and nonsequential form; readers enter the text at different points, choose from multiple pathways, access content through an interlinked series of nodes
Content is fixed	Content may change

Printed content and digital content may each exhibit some characteristics of the other. Printed content may sometimes resemble a node (location) on the Web, and digital content may deliberately simulate characteristics normally found only in printed forms. For example, TK3 ebooks allow the reader, by clicking on the right corner of the screen, to "dog-ear" pages, creating bookmarks.

Genres on the Web

Any writing that has a characteristic form and function in print can find its way to the Web. Google search results, for example, will often list websites and files in various formats that indicate how they were created: HTML—hypertext markup language; PDF—portable document format; RTF—rich text format; and so on. Many such documents were composed for print publication. Others were repurposed from print for the Web or were composed for the Web from the start. The difference between print-based and Web-based writing may seem subtle at first, but as a careful reader and writer of online content, you can learn to discern and appreciate content that has been composed specifically for the Web.

The writing style you choose for the Web depends on your purpose for writing, the nature of your content, and the motivation of your readers in reading and responding to it. On the Web, style—sometimes called "Web style"— refers to design content as well. Your decisions about composing, sorting, and presenting your writing will be informed by your knowledge of your audience: what they expect when reading on the Web, what they already know about your topic, and what others have said about it elsewhere. You also need to consider accessibility and usability in addition to writing style. (For more on accessibility and usability, see pages 360–361.)

Generally speaking, your writing should be composed so that it is well suited to the rhetorical context, which includes the interface and media through which your readers access your work. When you create content specifically for the Web, you can follow some guidelines that will help you keep the attention and interest of a wide audience. Websites that serve as navigation portals (such as the top-level node in a larger website or the first node of a hypertext) should include clearly written text presented in a logical arrangement, which will help site visitors easily find what you want them to find and what they are looking for.

W3C Guide to Writing Style

Consider the W3C (World Wide Web Consortium) recommendations for Web style, which reflect in many respects advice you'll find throughout the handbook.

1. Strive for clear and accurate headings and link descriptions. Use link phrases that are terse and that make sense when read out of context or as part of a series of links. (Some users browse by jumping from link to link and reading or listening to only link text.) Use informative headings so that users can scan a page quickly for information rather than having to read it in detail. Links should be integrated into the content and not simply be pointers. The destination should be implicit in the way the link is phrased so that readers understand (a) that it's a link and (b) where it is headed. (See section 25d on informative headings; see below for an example of an effective link.)

Sample link:

> At the Internet Movie Database, you will find useful information on the films of David Cronenberg.

2. State the topic of the sentence or paragraph at the beginning of the sentence or paragraph. Called *front-loading,* this will help not only people who are skimming visually but also people who use speech synthesizers. Users who "skim" with speech jump from heading to heading or paragraph to paragraph and listen to just enough words to determine whether the current chunk of information (heading, paragraph, link, etc.) interests them. If the main idea of the paragraph is in the middle or at the end, speech users may have to listen to most of the document before finding what they want (2d). Depending on what users are looking for and how much they know about the topic, search features may also help them locate content more quickly.
3. Limit each paragraph to one main idea (2d).
4. Avoid slang, jargon, and specialized meanings of familiar words, unless defined within your document (28e).
5. Favor words that are commonly used.
6. Use active rather than passive verbs (34f).
7. Avoid complex sentence structures (Chapter 24).

From W3C, "Core Techniques for Web Content Accessibility Guidelines 1.0," 2000 <http://www.w3.org/TR/WCAG10-CORE-TECHS/#writing-style>.

copyrights A collection of legal rights, conferred by governments, that relate to the reproduction, distribution, and performance of original literary, visual, artistic, or dramatic work.

intellectual property Copyrighted content as well as the more intangible property of trademarks, inventions and patents, ideas, and designs.

In many contexts—business and academia, for example—ideas are considered commodities to be distributed, bought, and sold. People have certain rights over their work when it is published and may claim ownership of ideas and other content by establishing copyright. Copyrights are simply "rights to copy" content that is intellectual property. An essay or Web text is the intellectual property of the person or group who created it or who hired someone to create it.

Textual Content

If you are the author of textual content, you own the copyright to your work even if you haven't officially registered the work with the U.S. Copyright Office. To reaffirm your rights to the work and your authorship, however, identify yourself as the author and include a copyright notice.

If you use source material, provide proper citation information for anything that is not common knowledge. (See section 12f for a definition and examples of common knowledge.) Provided you give complete bibliographic information, it is acceptable to cite from previously published textual sources in critical reviews, scholarship, or information research.

Sample Copyright Notice for Your Work Online

Here is a sample copyright notice for textual, visual, or audio content. You can include it in the footer area of each node or—when used with an image—immediately beneath the image.

"Title of Work" © Year by Author Name

Creative Commons License

This Creative Commons license icon indicates that others are allowed to use the content if the original author is credited or to adapt the work as long as the revision is also published under such license. For more information, see **http://www.creativecommons.org**.

When reproducing significant portions of a poem or a song, provide copyright information and, if you have asked for and received permission from the copyright holder to use the work, a formal acknowledgment somewhere in your text (in a caption or endnote, for example) that thanks the copyright holder. You will also need to provide the usual citation information in your Works Cited or References list. If you want to simply republish portions of poems or song lyrics outside of a formal review or critique, you will need to ask for permission from the copyright owner before you post them on the Web.

Visual Content

You are almost always required to secure permission to publish on your own website any images that you have not created yourself.

The exception is when the copyright holder has published the work under a Creative Commons license, which allows others to use the work if the original author is credited.

Many Internet sites and software programs offer free stock photography that is copyright-free. Creative Commons provides a comprehensive directory of quality work that you might find useful in developing your own content for the Web.

Sample of Formal Acknowledgment

Here is a sample of an acknowledgment that thanks a copyright holder for permission to reprint lyrics:

> The author gratefully acknowledges Warner Records for allowing use of these lyrics on this website.

Images: Do You Need Copyright Permission to Use Them Online?

Note that even when copyright permission is not required, **citation is required.** Provide full source information for every use. Normally, give source information right beneath the image. (For captions in MLA style, ◀ page 192; for APA style, ◀ page 254.) When many images are used on a site, it is acceptable to identify the source in an acknowledgments section of your website, next to the image, or in the footer on a given node—unless the copyright holder specifies the placement of the notice.

Type of Image	Do You Need Copyright Permission?
Photographs someone else has taken	Yes, unless they are copyright-free, Creative Commons licensed, or provided with your software
Clip art someone else has drawn	Varies; check for copyright notices, usually prominent at clip-art sites
Illustrations someone else has drawn	Yes
Company logos	Yes
Screenshots from films or television shows	Not usually; see "Fair Usage Publication of Film Stills," an article in *Cinema Journal* that offers guidelines many publishers abide by: **http://www.cmstudies.org/cinema_journal_reports.html**
Screenshots of websites for the purposes of illustration and information	Not usually

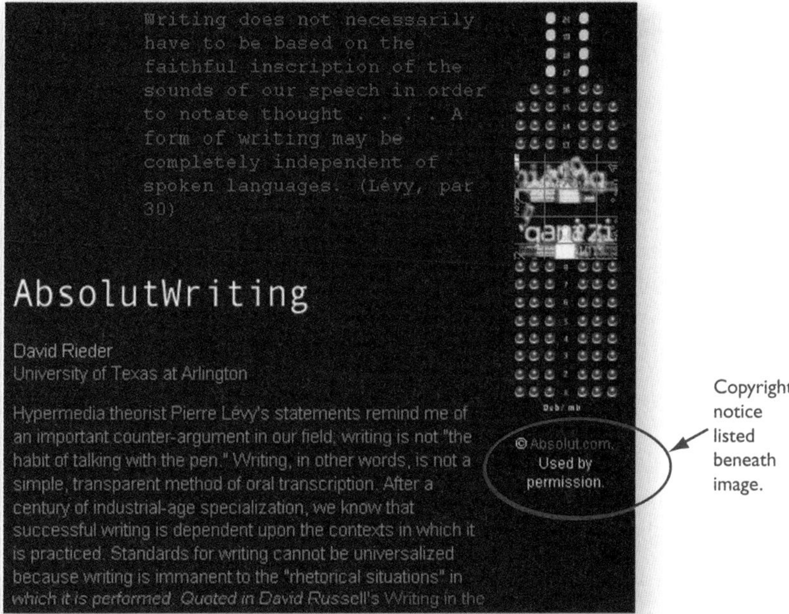

Writing does not necessarily have to be based on the faithful inscription of the sounds of our speech in order to notate thought . . . . A form of writing may be completely independent of spoken languages. (Lévy, par 30)
AbsolutWriting
David Rieder
University of Texas at Arlington
Hypermedia theorist Pierre Lévy's statements remind me of an important counter-argument in our field: writing is not "the habit of talking with the pen." Writing, in other words, is not a simple, transparent method of oral transcription. After a century of industrial-age specialization, we know that successful writing is dependent upon the contexts in which it is practiced. Standards for writing cannot be universalized because writing is immanent to the "rhetorical situations" in which it is performed. Quoted in David Russell's Writing in the
© Absolut.com. Used by permission.
Copyright notice listed beneath image.

A screenshot from David Rieder's online article "AbsolutWriting" showing the use of a copyrighted image and the proper citation method. Rieder asked for and received permission to use this image from Absolut.com. From *The Writing Instructor*, Sept. 2001, 20 Oct. 2004 <http://www.writinginstructor.com/absolutwriting>.

Resources on Copyright and Intellectual Property

The U.S. Copyright Office: **http://www.copyright.gov**
- Copyright Basics: **http://www.copyright.gov/circs/circ1.html**
- Copyright FAQs: **http://www.copyright.gov/help/faq/**
- Digital Millennium Copyright Act: **http://www.copyright.gov/legislation/dmca.pdf** (PDF format)
- Copyright Searches: **http://www.copyright.gov/records/**

Stanford University Copyright and Fair Use Center: **http://fairuse.stanford.edu**

Copyright Clearance Center: **http://www.copyright.com**

Musical and Audio Content

With the rise and fall of Napster—the peer-to-peer music sharing network that caused such a stir in 1999—the rights to use and share copyrighted music became more strictly limited by copyright law and fair use guidelines. If you want to use music or audio content on your website, be sure to find sources whose use is unrestricted or is governed by a Creative Commons license or to gain permission to use them. If you want to use preexisting music in the soundtrack of a multimedia project, for example, you will need to get permission from the copyright holder and provide proper credit.

Adapting and Modifying Content

For the purposes of parody, a form of critique that sometimes falls under fair use guidelines, copyrighted content may be adapted and then republished. It is also possible to use image and audio editing software to substantially re-engineer source material—as in the technique of audio "remixing" or image filtering. However, it is ethical practice to cite your sources in every case.

The accessibility of your Web content will be affected by material conditions (hardware and software) and by the nature of your audience. The contexts for reading and writing online vary dramatically. Hardware and software will shape the context, for example, because they define the interface—the lens through which you view Web content.

- The nature, size, and screen resolution of your monitor affect how you see the content.
- The particular way your browser renders Web content may not be consistent with that of other browsers.
- The platform and operating system of your computer—Mac, Windows, or Linux, for example—also affect the interface context.

As a producer of Web content, you need to be aware of the effects of these different contexts on how your work is received. If your goal is to make your work public on the Web, you should not unnecessarily restrict your audience to, for example, users of Internet Explorer 6, as you will see some sites do. Instead, you should make your content accessible through usability testing, by following guidelines for accessibility, and by accepting peer feedback.

accessibility The degree to which Web content can be navigated and read by everyone, regardless of location, experience, physical ability, cultural background, or the type of computer technology used to access the content.

usability testing Systematic testing of the ease with which users can access and learn to use information. It involves checking to see whether usability guidelines have been followed, measuring how readers use a website, and testing that all elements of a website function as the authors intend and users expect.

Diverse Contexts for Visiting a Website

Many Web users will be coming to your website in contexts different from your own and from those in which usability testing was performed:

- They may not be able to see, hear, or move or may not be able to process some types of information easily or at all.
- They may have difficulty reading or comprehending text.
- They may not have or be able to use a keyboard or mouse.
- They may have a text-only screen, a small screen, or a slow Internet connection.
- They may not speak or understand fluently the language in which the document is written.
- They may be in a situation where their eyes, ears, or hands are busy or interfered with (e.g., driving to work or working in a loud environment).
- They may have an early version of a browser, a different browser entirely, a voice browser, or a different operating system.

From http://www.w3.org/TR/WAI-WEBCONTENT/.

W3C Priority 1 Principles of Accessibility

1. Provide equivalent alternatives to auditory and visual content.
2. Don't rely on color alone.
3. Use markup and style sheets and do so properly.
4. Clarify natural language usage.
5. Create tables that transform gracefully.*
6. Ensure that pages featuring new technologies transform gracefully.*
7. Ensure user control of time-sensitive content changes.
8. Ensure direct accessibility of embedded user interfaces.
9. Design for device-independence.
10. Use interim solutions.
11. Use W3C technologies and guidelines.
12. Provide context and orientation information.
13. Provide clear navigation mechanisms.
14. Ensure that documents are clear and simple.

* Tables and pages that "transform gracefully" resize without drastically altering the display of text or images when the browser window is resized or when the page is viewed on monitors of varying resolution and size.

Resources on Accessibility and Usability
For links to accessibility and usability resources, visit **cengage.com/English/Blakesley**

Take into account the challenges that persons with physical disabilities face in accessing Web content. People with impaired vision, for example, may use screen readers to access Web content. To make the site accessible, all images on a website should be tagged with an <alt> HTML tag, which displays the writer's textual description of the image, either when the user has set the browser to not load images or when the reader mouses over the image itself. Screen readers read the content of these <alt> tags. Web designers who take advantage of cascading style sheets (CSS) can make it possible for users to change how their websites appear; users can choose to apply alternative style sheets of their own for viewing content.

The governing organization of the Internet—the World Wide Web Consortium, or W3C—has published a wide variety of readability guidelines for ensuring that Web content is accessible across hardware and software platforms and to a wide variety of users. Following such guidelines—which include suggestions for arranging information and using design content to reinforce the message—will help you create effective websites for the widest possible audience.

23 DESIGNING WEBSITES AND MULTIMEDIA PROJECTS

An effective Web design process consists of six steps:

1. **Planning** involves determining what you want to write about, deciding how you want to present the information to your primary and subsidiary audiences, and shaping your content and design so that you accomplish your purpose.
2. **Composing** involves crafting your textual, visual, and even aural content so that it suits your purpose, context, and audience. The composing process encompasses all the steps of the writing process described in Chapters 1–3, particularly regarding drafting, revising, and editing your writing so that it represents you well to a public audience, as well as to a narrower audience of peers.
3. **Designing** involves shaping your content for presentation on the Web.
4. **Testing** involves making sure that your website functions as it should and that your readers can access and interact with it.
5. **Publishing** involves finding a server to host your website and uploading the files to it.
6. **Updating** involves periodically checking to make sure that your website (or individual page) has the latest information and that all hyperlinks still work.

The Web Design Process, Expanded

Planning, composing, designing, and publishing a website are creative processes that involve making numerous decisions based on how you want viewers to use your site and on the reasons they may have for visiting it.

Planning: What assets do you have (text, images, design elements)? Which navigational and page layout schemes will help you and your audience achieve your respective purposes?
Composing: Should you compose in a Web design and development program or Web authoring software? Or use HTML programming in a text editor? Or write with a word processor and then import the text into an HTML document? If your site has images, audio, or video content, what software can you use to prepare such content for easy access?
Designing: How can you make the site inviting and helpful? How will visual and design content complement and amplify the textual content to achieve your purpose? (See Chapter 19 for design principles to consider.)
Testing: Does your site display properly on different browsers and operating systems (Mac, Windows, Linux)? At different screen resolutions? Do all links work? Do all pages meet standard accessibility guidelines? How do your intended users interact with the site?
Publishing: What server should host your site? Which FTP program do you want to use to upload your files?
Updating: How often do you need to update your site? (The answer to this question will depend on how current the content needs to be.) How often should you check for broken links?

Questions to Ask When Planning and Analyzing a Site

An important step in developing a website is general planning with regard to purpose and audience. The *Web Style Guide,* 2nd edition (see **http://www.webstyleguide.com**) recommends taking the key steps listed here. Use the questions listed below each step as prompts when planning or analyzing a site for content and design (or form).

Identify Your Goals (and Roles)

1. What textual, visual, and design content do you want to provide?
2. What is your timeline, from development through user testing?
3. How will you evaluate the success of your website?
4. What roles will there be for the Web development team (writers, designers, user-testers, etc.)?

Identify the Target Audience

5. Who is the site's primary audience? Subsidiary audience(s)?
6. Is that audience explicitly named or not? If not, how do you know who it is?
7. Based on its navigational design and use of browser technology, will the site be targeted to novices or "power users"?
8. Will the site make any appeals to casual visitors? If so, how? If not, why not?

Use Design Models

9. What successful models might help guide you in site development?
10. What does the design look like from the site user's point of view?

Define Your Purpose

11. Will the purposes of the site be explicitly stated? If so, what are they? If not, will they be evident from the textual, visual, and design content?
12. Will the primary purpose of the site be to teach (provide reference, training, or educational content)? Persuade (advertise and sell, move to action, promote)? Delight (entertain with content, including literature, games, images, video)? Network?
13. What other purposes might there be for the website (entertainment, business, promotion, news, reputation enhancement, etc.)?

Take Inventory of Your Content

14. Briefly, what is the nature of the information you plan to present on the website?
15. How will this information help achieve the website's purposes?
16. Will this information be presented in the form of a site map or set of FAQs?
17. Will the site offer links that take the user to other websites? If so, will these links be separate from the site content or will they be integrated?

The content on a typical Web page (node) consists of written information, images, and hyperlinks. Good nodes have four components:

1. **Textual content** that is interesting, entertaining, or informative (including verbal and visual material)
2. **Visual and design content** that (a) is well suited to the textual content, (b) guides the reader's eyes to the most important information and keeps attention focused where it should be, (c) makes text legible, and (d) appeals in its own right as interesting content
3. A clear **navigation system** and, for complex sites, search tools that help people quickly find what they're looking for and what you want them to find
4. **Provenance information** that identifies copyright, dates published and modified, and authorship. Provenance establishes both the ownership and the value of the work and will be needed by others who want to refer to or cite it.

Textual Content 23b

You develop textual content for a website in much the same way that you generate content for an essay or research paper. You think hard about what you want to say, whom you need to say it to, and what consequence you hope will result, and then you write and plan. As with any complex project, it's likely that you will need to conduct research to verify facts and to support arguments.

Organize Interesting Textual Content with Readers in Mind
Make content relevant and sufficient. Give readers what they need to know and what you want them to know. Don't overwhelm them with information so unorganized that nothing stands out. On websites with long documents, for example, it's customary to give readers the choice of reading a long article all on one page or in chunks. A working rule among Web designers is that you should make your readers scroll down the page only when you have to or when they will want to. If your content is engaging, readers will scroll down.

Provide Sufficient Information for Click-Through
Click-throughs, a measure of how many mouse clicks it takes to get to information from the parent page of a site, should be kept to a reasonable number—usually five or six at most. Your written information should be sufficient to warrant clicking through to the next page.

Converting Content from Word Processor to HTML Editor

You can take any content created in a word processor and convert it to HTML format so that you can import it into a Web design and development program like Adobe Dreamweaver® or NVu, a free Web authoring system (http://www.net2.com/nvu/).

To save your file in HTML (short for "Hypertext Markup Language") format, use the "Save as" command, available in most word processors. The following example uses Microsoft Word 2007 and Mac Word 2008.

1. Open your document in your word processor and then in Word 2007 choose the Office button > Save as > Other formats. In Mac Word 2008, choose File > Save as and choose the Save as Web Page button.
2. In the "Save As" dialogue box, first navigate to the folder where you want to save the file.
3. Name your file by typing its name in the "File name:" field. We recommend using the .html extension, which is the most common file name extension on the Web. Be sure not to use any spaces in the file name. The file name will ultimately appear as the last part of your Web page's URL.
4. In Word 2007, give your Web page a title by clicking on the "Title" field beneath the file name box.
5. In Word 2007, from the drop-down menu in the "Save as type:" field, choose "Web Page, Filtered (*.htm; *.html)." In Mac Word 2008, make sure that you select the radio button "Save only display information into HTML."
6. Word will save your file in HTML format. You can then open it in a Web authoring program, make adjustments as needed, and upload your file (along with any associated image files) to the Web.

Note: When saving in HTML, most word processors include style and formatting code that you won't need in your HTML file. Sometimes it causes Web pages to display improperly. Web editors like Dreamweaver have tools for cleaning up Word coding. (In Dreamweaver, choose Commands > Clean Up Word HTML to remove most of the extraneous HTML code.)

For instructions that apply to Microsoft® Word® 2003, visit the handbook's website: **cengage.com/english/blakesley**

Fifteen HTML Tags to Remember

HTML Tag	Function
<html></html>	Used to create a Web page. The <html> tag always starts and ends an HTML document.
<head></head>	Sets off the title and "head content," which doesn't display in the browser, from the body of the document, which does
<body></body>	Sets off the visible portion of the document that will display in the browser
<h1></h1>	Creates the largest headline. Related tags include <h2> (second largest headline), <h3> (third largest headline), etc.
<a href="URL"></a>	Defines a hyperlink. For example, <a href="http://www.wikipedia.com"> Wikipedia</a> tells the browser that what follows the equals sign is the URL for the text between the <a> and </a> tags. The URL is put in quotation marks.
<p></p>	Creates a new paragraph
<img></img>	Inserts an image. Parameters may be added, including size and border. For example, <img src= "http://www.mysite.com/myphoto.jpg"> tells the browser where to find the image file; *src* is short for "source."
<blockquote></blockquote>	Indents text from both sides and puts space above and below the text
 	Inserts a line break

(continued)

The Basics of HTML Coding

Hypertext Markup Language is programming code that helps browser programs interpret the information in an HTML file so that it can be displayed in the browser window. Knowing how such coding works will help you fine-tune your design, check for errors when a page doesn't display properly, and even examine the HTML code of Web pages that you want to use as models. HTML consists of *tags* that mark text and images and function as commands. For example, the HTML tag for creating italicized text is <em> (short for "emphasis").

WYSIWYG Web authoring programs, such as Nvu, work much like word processors because they allow you to open an HTML file and view an approximation of how the Web page will appear in a browser. (WYSIWYG stands for "What you see is what you get.") They also allow you to use command buttons to apply tags to your document, rather than entering HTML tags manually. Even though this simplifies the process of tagging an HTML document, you should understand how these tags work. Some people prefer to compose their HTML documents in "Code View" (in Dreamweaver, for example) or directly in a text editor like Notepad (in Windows) or SimpleText (on a Mac).

All HTML tags have what amounts to an "on" switch such as <em>, which tells the browser when to start italicizing text, and an "off" switch such as </em>, which tells the browser to stop italicizing. The tag is enclosed in angled brackets. The closing tag includes a forward slash, /, to indicate a stop. To create italicized text in an HTML document, you can have the Web design and development program enclose the text in an <em> tag, or you can add the tag yourself directly in the code. Either way you choose to do it, here's what the code for *italicized text* looks like:

<em>italicized text</em>

Here's what it will look like in an HTML file viewed in a Web browser:

italicized text

Fifteen HTML Tags to Remember (continued)

HTML Tag	Function
<strong></strong>	Creates bold text: <strong>boldface text</strong>
<em></em>	Creates italicized text: <em>italicized text</em>
<hr>	Creates a horizontal rule (or bar). Parameters may be added. For example, <hr width="200" size="1" noshade>
<table></table>	Creates a table. Parameters for size, border, background color, and more may be added in the start tag. For example, <table width="700" border="0" cellpadding="10" cellspacing="0" align="left">
<tr></tr>	Creates a row in a table. Parameters may be added. For example, <tr color="#999999">
<td></td>	Creates a column in a table. Parameters may be added. For example, <td width="200" height="400">

For a complete list of HTML tags, attributes, and parameters, see the HTML Reference Guide on the handbook's website:

cengage.com/English/Blakesley

Resources for Web Development Tools

You can get free Web developer tools for the Firefox browser (also free) that will help you test your Web pages for usability, accessibility, and more.

Firefox: **http://www.mozilla.org/products/firefox/**

Web Developer Extension:

http://www.chrispederick.com/work/firefox/webdeveloper/

Making an Absolute Link

1. Go to the website you want to link to and copy the Web address (URL) from the location bar in your browser, using the Copy command (Ctrl + C on a Windows-based computer or Apple + C on a Mac).
2. Go back to your Web editor.
3. Highlight the text you want to make into a hyperlink.
4. In Dreamweaver, paste the URL you copied in step 1 (Ctrl + V on a PC or Apple + V on a Mac) into the link box in the Properties window.

   In FrontPage, choose Insert > Link and then paste the URL into the link box. (Other Web editors use a similar process.)
5. Click Enter.
6. Save the file.
7. Test the link by previewing the HTML file in a browser.

Making a Relative Link

In Dreamweaver:

1. Highlight the text you want to make into a link.
2. Click on the Properties window and then select the Folder icon, , next to the Link window. Browse to the file you want to link to and select it.
3. Hit Enter. Dreamweaver will automatically create the HTML code.
4. Save your file.
5. Test the link in your browser.

In Composer:

1. Highlight the text you want to make into a link.
2. From the top menu bar, choose Insert > Link.
3. In the "Link Properties" dialogue box, check the "URL is relative to page location" box and then click on the "Choose File" button.
4. Navigate to and then select the file you want to link to. Click on Open.
5. The relative path to the file and the file name should now appear in the Link Location window.
6. Click on OK or select "Advanced Edit" to add attributes, classes, or events (see Web resources in section 23h).

Making Hyperlinks

Hyperlinks—or links for short—are used on websites to help people navigate to different pages within the site (relative links) or to pages elsewhere on the Internet (absolute links). A hyperlink consists of a URL and some HTML code that tells browser software what to look for and where and how to display it. Web design and development editors such as Composer, Dreamweaver, and FrontPage offer automated "link checkers" to help you test whether your links are still working properly. You should also do some manual usability testing of your hyperlinks.

Absolute Links to Other Sites on the Internet

An absolute link contains the full URL (protocol, domain name, and folder hierarchy (or path)—see page 134) for the file you want to link to.

Relative Links to Other Pages on Your Website

A relative link includes only path information because the files being linked to are located within the same domain. Such links are called "relative" because the actual URL depends on the location of the linked file relative to the page that contains the link (called the "referrer" page).

Email Links so Visitors Can Contact You
Email links are useful when you want visitors to be able to click on a hyperlink and have their default email program load automatically, with a message pre-addressed to you. The process of creating an email link is similar to that for making absolute and relative links. In this case, though, the URL uses the "mailto:" protocol.

Making an Email Link

1. Highlight the text you want to make into an email link.
2. In Dreamweaver, click in the Properties window and then click inside the link box.

   In Composer, choose Insert > Link and then click inside the link box.

   In FrontPage, click on the hyperlink button on the toolbar, .
3. Type the word mailto: and then the email address in the link box (for example, mailto:user@somewhere.edu).
4. Click OK.
5. Test the link in your browser.

23c Visual Content

The visual content of a Web page consists of images and colors used for a variety of purposes, including the following:

1. to complement and extend the textual content
2. to direct the reader's attention with visual cues
3. to add information
4. to create visual interest
5. to establish a visual theme

During the planning stage, create or collect the images you plan to use. You may use a graphics editor to create images and drawings, take photographs of your own, or look for visual content that suits your purpose in repositories of ready-made images. Keep in mind that any image on a Web page should bear a clear relationship to textual content.

Inserting an Image on a Web Page

Inserting an image on a Web page involves establishing a link to it, in much the same way that you create a hyperlink to another document or website. In the case of images, the <img> tag tells the browser to "go get the image and put it here and make it this big." The browser will get the image from a folder within the current website or from another site.

Example of a relative link to a local image:

```
<img src="images/steenthumb.gif" width="30" height="39">
```

Example of an absolute link to an image at another website:

```
<img src="http://www.writinginstructor.com/images/epubcollage.jpg"
width="30" height="39">
```

(continued)

Inserting an Image on a Web Page (continued)

- In the relative link, the path, which is in quotation marks, points to the file "steenthumb.gif" in the images subfolder.
- In the absolute link, the path is to an image on another website, so the full URL is used: http://www.writinginstructor.com/images/epubcollage.jpg.
- The HTML tag is <img>.
- The first attribute is *src* for "source." The two other attributes used are *width* and *height*. You can use these attributes to specify the size at which the image should be displayed (the width and height will be in pixels, which is a unit of measure relative to the screen resolution on your monitor), but if you leave them blank, the image will appear at its original size. Dreamweaver, FrontPage, and other Web editors will create the HTML code for you.

To make a link to an image in a Web authoring program:

1. Place your cursor where you want the image to appear.
2. Click on the Insert menu and choose Image.
3. Navigate to the folder where your image is stored and then select it.
4. Click on the Open or OK button (depending on which editor you're using).
5. If you want the image to display at its normal size, leave the image dimensions unchanged. To make it smaller or larger, adjust the dimensions in the Properties toolbox. However, be aware that your original image may not appear as intended because the browser will resize it on the fly, which will also increase the time it takes for the page to load. Consider using dimension resizing to enrich the experience for visitors. For example, you might use thumbnails—small image links that take users to a larger image file for better viewing.
6. Test the link in your browser by opening the page to see if the image displays as you intended.

When placing images on a Web page, keep in mind the principles of proximity, alignment, repetition, and contrast, covered more extensively in section 19a.

Proximity: Place images close to the textual content that refers to them or that the images complement.

Alignment: Align images on the Web page with the edges of text, and leave enough space between the images and the surrounding text. To place images precisely, use tables to manage your layout.

Repetition: Use images to create a visual theme that gives your Web page or website an identifiable character, one that reinforces its purpose.

Contrast: Use images to create visual contrast with the text—to provide eye relief and break up the monotony of lines of text running across the screen.

In addition, keep text and images in proportion. Be careful not to overwhelm your text by making images excessively large or using lots of images just to "spice things up." Avoid distracting animated graphics and elaborate background images that make textual content unreadable. Colors should likewise be chosen to highlight, not overwhelm, the content.

Technology Toolbox

Optimizing Images for the Web

Images are usually larger in size than HTML files, so to make sure that your Web page loads quickly—especially for users with slow Internet connections—optimize your images for Web delivery. For most file types, you can reduce file size substantially without loss of image quality by using the graphics editor's "Save for Web" or "Export" command, usually found on the File menu.

Web browsers are capable of displaying JPG, GIF, PNG, and TIF images. JPG and GIF files are used most often because they offer a smaller file size.

JPG files. The JPG format works best with photographs. Images with the JPG extension ("Joint Photographic Experts Group") can usually be optimized at 80 percent without any degradation in quality. If your file is originally in another format, such as PSD (Photoshop), CDR (CorelDRAW®), or PNG (Fireworks®), you can save a copy in JPG format that will be viewable in a browser and have a smaller file size. The original image below has a file size of 901 KB, but when optimized at 80 percent it has a file size of only 133 KB. In many cases, you should compress your images as much as possible, so use the Preview windows in your graphics program to evaluate the results at different compression percentages.

GIF files. The GIF format works best with text, color, line art, and other images that have been generated on a computer. GIF files can be given a transparent background so that the image will display well against any colored or patterned background (the transparent background of the image allows the background of the Web page to come through). GIF files can't be compressed like JPG files, but their file size will be naturally small.

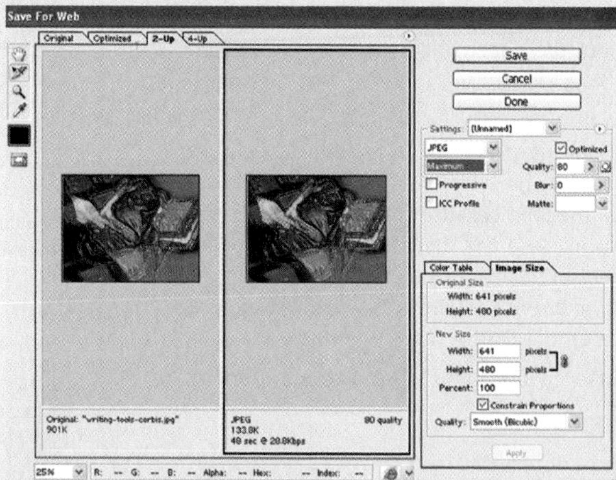

This Photoshop "Save For Web" dialogue box allows the user to adjust optimization level (here set at 80 percent), image size, and more.

Image placement balances the page. Edges are aligned with other elements of the design.

The header for this site uses large type for the main title, with the subtitle of the exhibition placed beneath in a smaller font size and complementary color.

The search box is placed discreetly in the upper right.

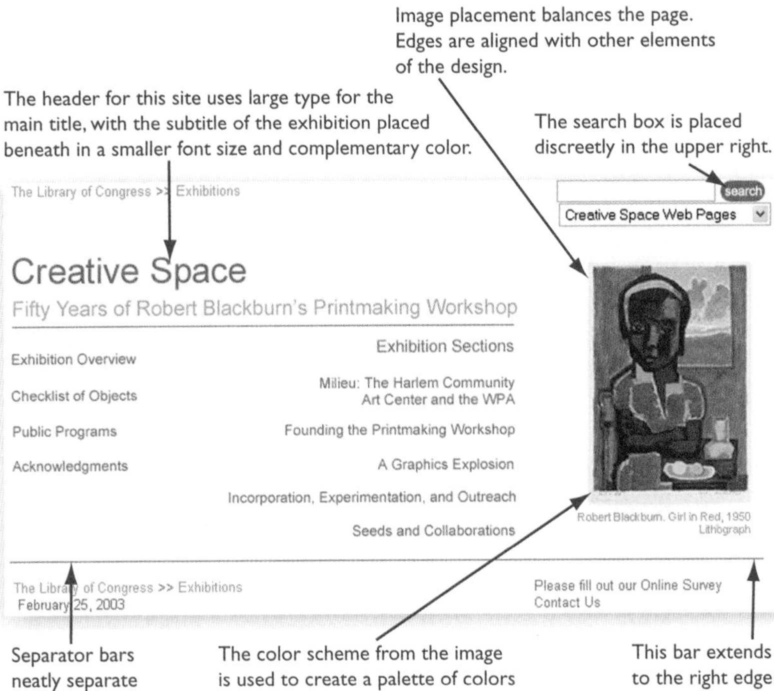

Separator bars neatly separate the links from header and footer information.

The color scheme from the image is used to create a palette of colors for fonts and links.

This bar extends to the right edge to align with the image.

This Web page uses design elements, such as title headers, colors, and separator bars, to effectively arrange visual and verbal content.

From http://www.loc.gov/exhibits/blackburn/.

For links to resource websites for design models and tips, visit **cengage.com/English/Blakesley**

When you're creating a website from scratch, rely on your own design sensibilities and experience as a reader to arrange visual elements, white space, and layout so as to structure information, guide the reader's eye to key components of the page, and add visual interest.

Banners and Headers

Web designers use banners and headers at the top of their Web pages to

- announce the title of the page or site
- establish a visual theme that gives the site a unique identity
- orient readers so they know what site they are viewing

Like the cover of a book, a banner draws the reader in and may also contain navigational elements, a search box, and (on commercial sites) advertising.

Borders, Separator Bars, Bullets, and Arrows

Decorative text elements can help structure information on a Web page and provide visual cues to readers about navigation.

Footers

Provenance and navigational links are typically included in footers, often with a separator bar above this information so that it isn't confused with body text.

Designing the navigational elements of a website seems simple, but it can get complex quickly as the website grows and the range of content widens. On a simple website consisting of only a few nodes, navigational elements are usually included in a side column or in the header and footer. They appear on every page in the site to help the reader navigate. In many cases, you should make it possible for readers to go directly from any node in a site to any other node.

To develop a navigational system, you need to organize the information that your site will contain. Here are four steps to follow in organizing information. It's helpful to sketch out this hierarchy using a grid, or template, like the one shown to the right.

1. Divide your information into logical categories.
2. Establish a hierarchy of importance and generality, moving from the most general to the most specific.
3. Use the hierarchy to create relationships or links across chunks of information.
4. Analyze your structure to see whether it will make sense to others. Move chunks of information to other branches if necessary.

Scenario for Developing a Navigational System

Susan is majoring in Art History and is hoping to someday be a museum curator. She wants to develop a Web portfolio to show to prospective employers. She has collected the best examples of her work from her courses and previous jobs, a resume (including lists of relevant courses and skills), and some links to favorite sites that have influenced her work. Her primary audience will be people in her field who may be in a position to judge whether or not she would be a suitable job candidate.

Here is her initial draft of a website structure.

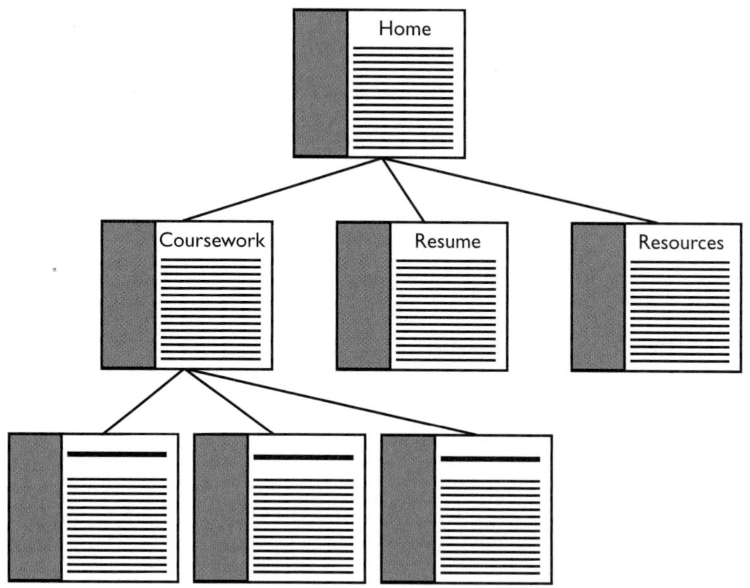

A tree diagram showing the site map for Susan's digital portfolio.

Susan's Navigational Decisions

Susan has a number of samples of her work that she would like to feature, so in the Coursework branch she has subcategories, with new pages devoted to major projects she has completed. She doesn't want visitors to go directly to the samples of her work because she would like them to first get a sense of the range and quantity of her work. So she settles on including three major links at the top level of her website, each to a B-level node. She will include these three links on each node of the website so that anyone can get back to the second level of the hierarchy. She also needs to have a "Home" link that will take readers back to the top level. So she needs a navigational system that has four links but also allows room for expansion later:

Home
Coursework
  Sample 1
  Sample 2
  Sample 3
Resume
Resources

On a navigation bar on each node of the site, she will create links to the four main nodes:

Home | Coursework | Resume | Resources

On her Coursework node, she will arrange thumbnail images of the samples, placing a brief description next to each to let readers know the nature of the sample.

Sample of Node Navigation

Node navigation is useful for long documents that should be broken into smaller chunks.

properties we want students to learn about print literacy. Specifically it is important to explore television's qualities as a medium of popular response, distraction and simulation, and emotion.

continued
1 | 2 | 3 | 4 | 5 | Works Cited | >>Next

Sample Footer

Provenance information is typically included in the footer of every page. Sometimes it is included with footer navigation, as in this example.

Site content © 2004 - 2006 by *KB Journal*. Comments and forum messages © the individual author. Article content is published under a Creative Commons license attached to each article. *KB Journal* is sponsored by the Kenneth Burke Society and hosted at Purdue University by the Professional Writing Program. CMS theme design by David Blakesley. *KB Journal* is powerered by Drupal.

Readers sometimes resist reading a node that scrolls down for more than a screen or two, so you may want to lure them along in a longer document by breaking it up into pieces and providing navigational links at the bottom of each page. You can create a brief link to each node in the longer document and include a "continued" cue for the reader. Use the same list of links on each node, but disable (remove) the link for the active node.

Provenance 23f

Provenance establishes the ownership and authorship of a website. It is used not only by the author but also by others, and for multiple reasons.

- When people need to evaluate the nature, reliability, and timeliness of the content, they look to the provenance to see who authored the page and decide whether it's someone they can trust.
- When people have questions, they look for contact information so that they can write to website authors.
- When people want to cite the work in their own scholarship, they look for provenance information.

23g Managing Folders and Files

It is helpful to match your folder structure to the major categories of information you have devised and to also include a folder (or more) for storing images, banners, navigational aids, and other design elements that will be used across a range of pages on your site.

Sample Website Folder Structure

This folder structure is for a small professional portfolio site:

images
  imagetemplates
  banner.jpg .jpg
stylesheets
templates
index.html .html
portfolio.html .html
resume.html .html

23h Using Cascading Style Sheets

The principle behind a cascading style sheet (CSS) is that it is efficient to separate textual content from design content. Once a design is defined by CSS codes, content can be added without recreating design. It's now possible to change the look of a website dramatically (even one with thousands of pages) by changing just a few style definitions in a CSS file.

A CSS file is a collection of programming codes that tells a browser how to display aspects of an HTML or other dynamically created page. For example, suppose a CSS file says that all text inside the <p> tag (paragraph tag) should be displayed in Verdana font with a pixel size of 13 and a leading (distance between lines) of 17 pixels. All nodes on a website that contain text inside <p> tags and that use the CSS file definitions will display at 13-pixel Verdana with 17-pixel leading. You can achieve this same level of precision with almost any element of a Web page.

Resources for Cascading Style Sheets

W3C's Guide to Cascading Style Sheets: **http://www.w3.org/Style/**

W3C's CSS Tips and Tricks: **http://www.w3.org/Style/Examples/007/**

Web Design Group's Cascading Style Sheets: **http://www.htmlhelp.com/reference/css/**

Web Developer's Virtual Library: **http://www.wdvl.com/Authoring/Style/Sheets/**

Max Design (for creating stylized lists): **http://css.maxdesign.com.au**

Zen Garden: The Beauty of CSS Design: **http://www.csszengarden.com**

Cascading Style Sheets: The Definitive Guide, 2nd edition, by Eric Meyer (Sebastapol, CA: O'Reilly & Associates, 2004)

Information You Need in Order to FTP Your Files to a Remote Server

Host: ______________________ For example, twi.english.purdue.edu

User Name: ______________________

Password: ______________________ For example, /var/www/twi-html/upload

Initial Remote Host Directory: ______________________

Sample Screen from an SFTP Program

You can drag and drop files from your local computer to the server, or you can use the download button to transfer files from the server to your local machine.

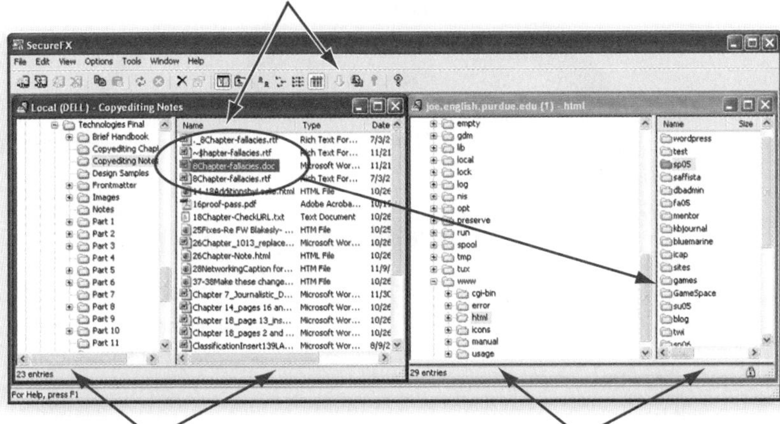

These panes show the folders, subfolders, and files on **your computer**.

These panes show the folders, subfolders, and files on **the server.**

SecureFX is an SFTP program that allows users to transfer files from their computer to a server securely, without risk of having their files intercepted by hackers enroute. Folders on the left are on the local computer. The server files are in the right pane. The user uploads files by selecting them in the left pane and dragging and dropping them into the proper folder on the right.

For links to resources for finding server space for your site, visit **cengage.com/English/Blakesley**

To publish your website to the Internet, you'll need to upload your files to a computer set up to serve Web pages, called a server. Web editors such as Dreamweaver and FrontPage have built-in functionality that allows you to "define a site" and then upload your files to the server after you've entered the information needed to make a connection.

To pass your files to another computer, you use FTP (File Transfer Protocol) or SFTP (Secure File Transfer Protocol). Standalone programs allow you to easily upload your files to other computers. Following are the most popular of these programs.

For PCs:

WS_FTP (see http://www.download.com)

SecureFX (see http://www.vandyke.com/download/securefx)

For Macs:

Fetch (see http://fetchsoftworks.com)

Fugu (see http://rsug.itd.umich.edu/software/fugu)

All come in fully functional versions that are free or available at low cost to college students. Windows XP and Mac OS 10.4 (Tiger™) come with FTP functionality built into their own file management systems.

In the most general sense, *multimedia* means "multiple media." *Multimedia composing* refers to putting together several media elements to create a presentation, project, or performance. *Media* include printed text, of course, but also images and graphics (photographs, drawings, video) and audio (spoken words, music, sound effects). Multimedia composing may also involve communicating with tactile elements (things that you can touch and feel or that you interact with through bodily movements, called haptics). Taken together, these forms are sometimes called "the new media."

Like authors of many familiar forms of printed text, effective multimedia composers take into account the rhetorical situation and audience—the circumstances of writing and communicating to others—as well as all the means (ethos, logos, pathos, delivery, style, arrangement, memory) of accomplishing the purpose (to inform, delight, or persuade).

The Multimedia Rhetorical Triangle

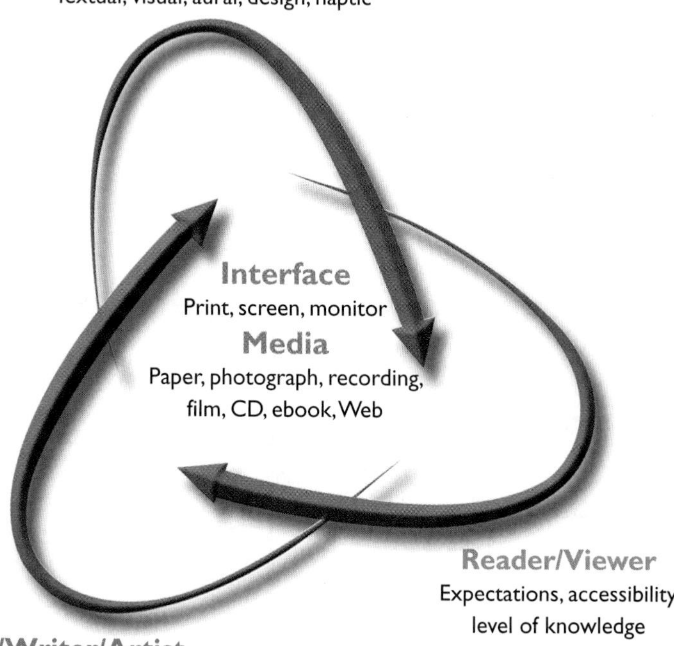

Media and interface balance relationships among authors, readers, and content.

1

Project Checklist

30 Questions for Planning Multimedia Projects

Purpose

1. Is your primary purpose to teach or inform, delight or entertain, persuade or move, or some combination of these?
2. What specifically do you want your project to do?

Textual Content

3. What do you want to say? (Logos)
4. What content do you want to show? (Logos)
5. What tone do you want to take in relation to the content? (Ethos)
6. Is there any emotional content that you want to express? If so, what is it? (Pathos)

Design Content

7. How do you want to display your textual content? (Logos)
8. How do you want to show visual content? (Logos)
9. What relationships do you want to express between textual and visual content?
10. How would you describe the "look" or tone you're after—simple elegance, contemporary, urban chic, grunge, fanciful, or what? (Ethos)
11. What feelings do you want your design to invoke—happiness, sadness, wonder, anger, curiosity, desire? (Pathos)
12. What color schemes will you use to help you capture the look and feel you want? (See questions 10 and 11.)

Audience

13. Who is your primary audience—peers in your class or at your college or university, your instructor, people in your community, people with a contrary viewpoint, or like-minded citizens? What knowledge and experience will readers and viewers

(continued)

You should choose media to suit the occasion and your purpose, audience, and content, rather than letting the media dictate your rhetorical choices.

For example, if you want to share information about what students in your major or club do and their possible career paths, you might choose to make a QuickTime movie on the Web (reaching a broad audience and helping to recruit new students) or hold a special screening for current majors on a "movie night." You could even take screenshots from your video and surround them with text about your club—thus turning the video into a multimedia profile.

If you want to create a permanent record of student life on your campus, you will probably choose a print medium—a magazine or journal, for instance. If your goal is to reach out to students off campus, you might choose the Web as your medium—using an ezine or weblog, for example—and then repurpose the material as a printed document that can be archived in the library.

If you are looking for a job, you could prepare a printed resume to send to employers who request one and to take to job fairs. You could make an electronic version to email or fax to employers, presenting your experience as neatly as possible given the medium. Or you could integrate your resume into a larger portfolio that includes printed samples of your work and a CD with more complex sample projects.

In the Project Checklist, notice that we have used the phrases *textual content* and *design content* to emphasize that both the textual and the visual elements of your multimedia projects convey messages. Contrary to some opinions, design or visual content is every bit as important as its textual counterpart. In other words, design content is not just ornamentation, but, as Marshall McLuhan suggested, part of the overall message itself. Design content conveys meaning by juxtaposing textual and visual information, by moving the eyes of the reader or viewer in strategic ways, and even by appealing to the emotions with color. For more on visual rhetoric, see Chapters 6 and 19.

Ask the questions in the Project Checklist not only as you start your projects but also as you come to key stages in production. In multimedia projects, for example, there may be instances when you need to provide background information—with a hyperlink, for example—for readers unfamiliar with a concept, so you will need to consider purpose, textual and visual content, audience, media, delivery, arrangement, and collaboration at many points in the project's development. The point is to use your answers to shape your decisions as you compose.

2

bring to the work? (Recall that the primary audience is the group of readers or viewers most likely to interact with and respond to your work. You shape your textual, visual, and design content to appeal to your primary audience.)

14. Who are your subsidiary audiences? What knowledge and experience might they bring to the work? (Recall that the subsidiary audiences are the groups of readers or viewers who may also find your work appealing or at least be interested in your work. Very often, for example, an ezine will have as its primary audience peers in the same class, but its subsidiary audiences in the Internet community will include people from around the world.)

Media and Delivery

15. What media or interfaces will best convey your meaning under the circumstances? (*Kairos*)

16. What balance between print and other media do you want to achieve? (Proportion)

17. If your project is digital, what technologies will people need to read or view it? What directions will you need to provide for opening and viewing files, for example? If you're presenting your project orally, how will you project it? Will your project look different when projected than it does on your monitor?

18. If your project is in print, what kind of paper or other material do you want to use? How will you print visual material? Will you package or present your project in any way? If you're preparing a poster, for example, what material can you use? Does your bookstore or art supply store sell posterboard for live presentations?

19. If your project is print and digital, how will you package the two pieces together? Be sure also to address questions 17 and 18 if yours is a hybrid print-digital project.

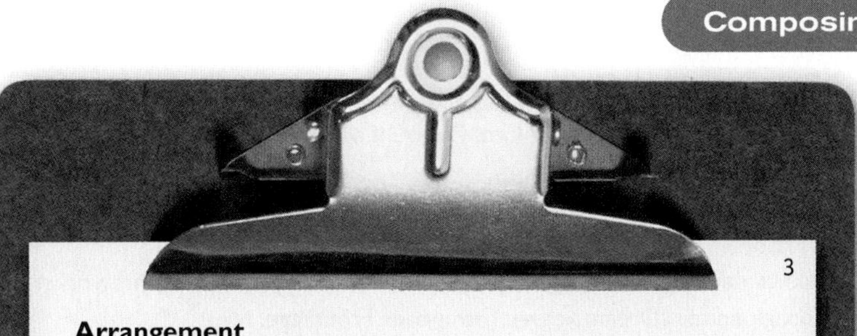

3

Arrangement

20. How can you arrange your textual and visual information in meaningful patterns or hierarchies? What do viewers need to notice first? What next?
21. What headings and subheadings can you use to help readers or viewers navigate through your project? Can you think of some headings and subheadings that will give readers or viewers a quick sense of the gist of your project?
22. Have you used print or screen space in ways that highlight the most important information?
23. Does your project have a clear beginning, middle, and end, with graceful transitions between parts?

Collaboration and Project Management

24. What are the steps you need to take to complete your project?
25. How much time will it take to complete each aspect of your project?
26. What information do you need to know (about technologies, for instance) before you get too far along in your project?
27. Does anyone on your team have particularly strong skills with certain technologies or media, such as Web design, video or audio production, photography, digital copyediting, file management?
28. What kinds of records should you keep of your collaboration—meeting notes, calendars, project plans?
29. If your project is a collaborative one, have you done all you can to complete the work you agreed to do on time and well, be a clear and responsive communicator, allow others opportunities to be as much involved as you are, and offer constructive feedback to team members?
30. How do you plan to evaluate your collaboration?

A multimedia essay integrates text and other media to accomplish its purpose, which may be to teach or inform, delight or entertain, or persuade and move an audience. You can write multimedia essays in any genre; you just need to adapt the form to the genre and the particular requirements of the assignment.

Multimedia essays can be constructed as a website. Alternatively, they may be packaged on a CD-ROM, a DVD, or, if the file sizes are small, a floppy disk. They can also be presented in printed format, with photographs, tape recordings, CDs, or podcasts used to supplement the textual content. We have also seen multimedia essays packaged in boxes or as well-designed posters that include printed text, visual and design content, and music. (At very low cost, you can buy nicely designed or blank cigar boxes for this purpose at Thompson Cigar: http://www.thompsoncigar.com. Search for item 994000: "Premium Empty Cigar Bxs-10.")

23l

Technology Resources

Multimedia essays can be challenging to compose, but if you have some experience incorporating visual content into your projects (Chapter 19) or designing websites, then you already have the computer literacy you will need. The tools you choose make it possible to shape and render content, so you should have some idea from the outset about what form your writing will take.

Useful Software Tools for Composing Multimedia Essays

- Word processor (Microsoft Word, OpenOffice, WordPerfect, Notepad, SimpleText)
- Presentation software (PowerPoint, Apple Keynote, OpenOffice, Adobe Acrobat, Flash)
- Graphics editor (Photoshop, CorelDRAW, Photoshop Elements, Fireworks)
- Webpage editor (Dreamweaver, Composer, FrontPage, Nvu)
- Video editor (Adobe® Premiere®, Apple Final Cut Pro®, iMovie)
- Digital audio editor (Audacity, SoundEdit™, GarageBand, Pinnacle Studio)
- Comic book editor (Comic Life)
- Software for making CDs and DVDs (Roxio Easy CD Creator, Nero®, Toast®)
- Ebook authoring software (Sophie, TK3)

23m Designing a Multimedia Portfolio

Multimedia or digital portfolios are quickly becoming an important means of featuring the work of students, artists, graphic designers, engineers—anyone who has samples to share with peers, potential employers, or the general public. A professional portfolio can serve as a repository where students archive class projects, essays, and any other work that illustrates the scope of their endeavors. In some courses, you may be asked to keep a portfolio of your work to demonstrate your accomplishments over the course of a semester.

Elements That Might Be Included in a Professional Portfolio

- **Background information:** a short narrative about who you are and what you do. In professional portfolios, it's often best not to share too much specific and sensitive information about yourself unless you don't mind being contacted by random visitors to your site.
- **Resume or vita:** a printable document stored as a PDF file, created with Adobe Acrobat or a PDF conversion plug-in such as PDF Maker for Microsoft Word or the stand-alone freeware CutePDF™ Writer
- **Sample publications and projects:** PDF versions of your printed work, screenshots of websites, video projects, scanned artwork, links to your work on the Web
- **Weblog:** your running commentary on current events in your field of interest, discussions of the work of others, etc. (◀ Chapter 21)
- **Links and resources:** a storehouse of links to websites that you find useful in your own work and that others might benefit from, a collection of documents that you have authored and that you can share with others, or a news aggregate

For links to multimedia sites on the web, visit **cengage.com/English/Blakesley**

Making Choices about Style

PART 8

New Contexts for Writing: 826 Valencia

826
VALENCIA
Tutoring
Workshops
826 Valencia helps students, ages 8–
their writing skills, in the realm of
writing, expository writing, or Engl
second language.
Field Trips

826 Valencia is the name of a public literacy project in San Francisco that focuses on helping students from 8 to 18 develop their writing ability by providing free tutoring, workshops, storytelling sessions, field trips, and facilities. It has become much more than that, however. It has become the catalyst for launching similar sites across the nation, with 826s now in Ann Arbor, Chicago, Los Angeles, New York City, and Seattle. Tutors, even some famous writers now and then, volunteer their time to help the young writers. Workshop topics include writing for the Web, filmmaking, bookmaking, and more.

The idea for 826 Valencia was originally hatched and supported by Nínive Calegari and Dave Eggers, the author of *A Heartbreaking Work of Staggering Genius* and the co-founder of McSweeney's, which now publishes a literary and DVD magazine, books, a website, 826 Valencia student projects, and more. Eggers and Calegari, as well as many generous volunteers, have inspired others to join in, so plans to develop more 826 sites are in the works. College students can volunteer their time as tutors, writers, Web designers, and hardware specialists at 826 sites, and they might even organize efforts to start an 826 site in their own community.

Service learning projects in college involve students in working with clients, nonprofit agencies, and other community organizations on real projects that make a difference in people's lives.

Engagement is a movement among those in higher education to become partners in the wider community's cultural and social life. When you learn to apply your talents as a writer in contexts outside of the classroom, the rhetorical situation takes on added urgency. You are no longer writing merely for a grade (an important goal, of course); you are writing to and with people whose lives may change because of what you say. When you help others learn to write, you become a better writer yourself and have the satisfaction of knowing that you might have made someone else's life a little better.

What Can *You* Do?

Organize a student group project that helps a nonprofit organization build a website or weblog; make a brochure for a community organization; find out how you can volunteer in a local literacy campaign; ask your instructor what opportunities exist for you to tutor and mentor others; or even help launch a new 826 site.

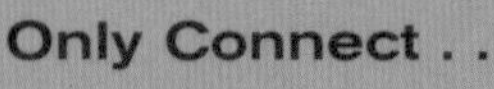

826 and Related Sites on the Web

826 Valencia: http://www.826valencia.org

826NYC: http://www.826nyc.org

826LA: http://www.826la.com

826 Chicago: http://www.826chicago.org

826 Michigan: http://www.826michigan.org

826 Seattle: http://www.826seattle.org

The Pirate Supply Store: http://www.826valencia.org/store

McSweeney's Internet Tendency: http://www.mcsweeneys.net

The Five Principles of Readability

Good sentences are readable. Readability is the general ease with which readers can understand and remember sentences. The words we choose affect readability, and so do our sentence structures, or style. Following the five principles of readability may help you communicate more effectively. These principles are not "rules" but general guidelines to follow unless circumstances demand some alternative. You should have a good reason for deviating from these principles.

1. Use an agent/action style.
2. Keep agent and action close together.
3. Put modifiers close to the words they modify.
4. When possible, put people in the agent position in a sentence.
5. Put old information first and new or most important information last.

Each principle is discussed in the following pages of this chapter. Chapters 25–27 then discuss these and related matters in detail.

Good sentences take many forms, but they share these qualities:

- They are purposeful and timely—they are well suited to the rhetorical occasion.
- They are well suited to the ideas they represent. Simple ideas often require simple sentences; complex ideas may require more complex sentences.
- They express meaning that affects readers in ways the writer intended.
- Taken together, good sentences accomplish rhetorical goals such as teaching, persuading, delighting, cajoling, reporting, moving, and so on.

Using an Agent/Action Style 24a

Sentences that follow the natural word order of English (subject-verb-object, or S-V-O) can be understood more readily than can transformations of that order. In addition, readers understand sentences better when the verb is an action and the agent performing the action precedes it.

Here is a sentence using the natural word order of English:

Agent/action — John (S) hit (V) the ball (O).
[This order is called the active voice.]

And here is a transformation of the natural order:

Action/agent — The ball (O) was hit (V) by John (S). or The ball (O) was hit (V).
[This order is called the passive voice.]

The sentence with the O-V-S word order is a transformation of the natural word order that English grammar allows, but it makes more demands on readers, who must translate it into something like "John performed a hitting action on the ball." In the brief moment it takes the reader to gain clarity, some readability is lost. As the number of passive sentences in a passage increases, readability declines.

24b Keeping Agent and Action Close Together

Sentences are easy to understand when the reader doesn't have to hold important information suspended while reading other words that come between the subject and the verb.

Easier to understand	Knowing that her team depended on her, **Joan hit** the ball.
Harder to understand	**Joan,** knowing that her team depended on her, **hit** the ball.

The subject and verb are the two most important words in an English sentence. In the first sentence, they are close together, and the sentence is easy to understand. In the second sentence, the reader has to hold the thought of "Joan" suspended while awaiting the verb. This decreases readability.

24c Putting Modifiers Close to the Words They Modify

Group the information in your sentences into logical chunks so that readers can take in the whole chunk at once. For example, a noun may have some words that modify it: *the slightly balding, stooped* ***man.*** A verb may collect some modifiers: ***saw*** *quickly out of the corner of his eye.* Be sure to keep all the related words together.

Here, the modifier is in italics and the word that it modifies is in bold:

Easiest to understand	*Feeling satisfaction for the first time in his miserable life,* **Fred** caught the ball that was hit.
Harder to understand	**Fred** caught the ball that was hit, *feeling satisfaction for the first time in his miserable life.*
Hardest to understand	Fred caught **the ball,** feeling satisfaction for the first time in his miserable life, *that was hit.*

Can you see how readability declines with each move away from keeping all the related words together as one chunk?

24d When Possible, Putting People in the Agent Position

It's easier to understand a sentence when a person or a character is performing an action than when the agent is an abstraction: ***Alexander*** *likes tennis* versus ***Socialism*** *is losing ground.*

Easier to understand	Hitchcock implicates the viewer in Norman's Oedipal guilt.
Harder to understand	Hitchcock's implication is that the viewer shares Norman's Oedipal guilt.

Note here that the second sentence needs *is that* because the subject of the sentence is a noun phrase—*Hitchcock's implication* rather than *Hitchcock.* In the first sentence, not only is a person the agent, but the verb *implicates* conveys both that an implication is being made and that the implication involves some kind of sharing.

Easier to understand:

> The Cassini spacecraft has beamed images back to NASA and ESA scientists, who now ask some astonishing questions about *the nature of Saturn's rings.* Once believed to be heated gases, Saturn's rings are composed of *dust, rocks, and crystalline ice that give clues to the nature of planetary formation.* If scientists can understand how frozen water became suspended in orbit around Saturn, they may be able to solve the *mystery of the migration of water through the solar system and thus the origins of life itself.*

Notice in the paragraph above how the new information (italicized) begins subsequent sentences as old information (underlined).

Harder to understand:

> The Cassini spacecraft has beamed images back to NASA and ESA scientists, who now ask some astonishing questions about *the nature of Saturn's rings. Dust, rocks, and crystalline ice give clues to the nature of planetary formation* and compose Saturn's rings, not heated gases. *The mystery of the migration of water through the solar system and thus the origins of life itself can be solved by understanding how* frozen water became suspended in orbit around Saturn.

The second and third sentences begin with new information, which makes the passage read awkwardly and taxes short-term memory.

Suppose you are reading along and a woman's name, *Marcie,* appears. In the next sentence, you read the word *she,* and you understand that the writer is talking about *Marcie.* On first mention, *Marcie* was new information. By the next sentence, *Marcie* is old information, and thus the writer can refer to her as *she* with confidence. The same pattern holds true in general when people are reading. As they read each sentence, they build up a body of knowledge about the topic. What used to be new information becomes old information. A sentence that refers first to old information (as in the use of *she*) creates a bridge for readers to the new information.

PARALLELISM 25

You can improve the clarity of your sentences by putting similar content into grammatically equal form. Parallelism draws the reader's attention, relates ideas to one another, and gives sentences a pleasing rhythm.

Example 1 Parallelism

To highlight contrasts	**Injustice anywhere** is a threat to **justice everywhere.** —Martin Luther King Jr.
For emphasis	. . . and that this government **of the people, by the people, for the people** shall not perish from the earth. —Abraham Lincoln

25a Using Parallelism with Conjunctions

Coordinating conjunctions—*and, or, not, for, but, yet, so*—signal a need for parallelism. One way to improve your sentence style is to look at sentence elements joined by a coordinating conjunction to see whether you've put them into parallel form.

Correlative conjunctions also signal a need for parallelism. When revising, check sentences that use *both . . . and, either . . . or, neither . . . nor, not . . . but, not only . . . but also, just as . . . so, whether . . . or,* and similar constructions to see that parallel elements are treated in a parallel fashion.

Example 2 Parallelism with conjunctions

Cow power dairies **produce** milk and **generate** electricity. [parallel verbs]

Marathon runners use **intensive training, precise strategy,** and **balanced nutrition** to help them finish races. [parallel adjectives and nouns]

Credit for saving [the cowboy song "Goodbye Old Paint"] from obscurity must be given to three Texans: **a cowboy who sang on trail drives, a cowboy who remembered it,** and **a college professor who put it down on paper.** [parallel noun clauses]

From Jim Bob Tinsley, *He Was Singin' This Song.*

Neither **exercising** nor **dieting** appealed to him.

Whether it's **baseball players who take steriods to boost Major League performance** or **students who take Ritalin to improve SAT scores,** America has a drug problem.

25b Using Parallelism with *than* or *as*

Constructions using *than* or *as* to make comparisons require parallel treatment of the ideas being compared.

Example 3 Parallelism in comparisons

Roger is as interested in **studying philosophy** as in **working.**

In an ideal world, elected leaders would find **governing wisely** more important than **getting reelected.**

In an ideal world, elected leaders would find **good government** more important than **reelection.**

25c Repeating Function Words in Parallel Constructions

Be consistent in deciding whether to repeat function words, such as prepositions (*by, for, in, near, of, with*), articles (*a, an, the*), and the infinitive *to* in parallel constructions. At times a function word must be repeated for clarity.

Example 4 Repeating function words

While visiting temples in India, you will be expected **to remove** shoes and any leather items before entering, **to dress** conservatively (women should ideally cover their heads), **to stay out** of unauthorized areas, and **to ask** permission before photographing buildings, symbols of deities, or people.

Headings in a paper

The Gothic Novel Mocked

Elements of the Gothic in *Northanger Abbey*

Catherine Morland as Gothic Heroine

Catherine Morland as Herself

Items in a list

Guidelines for Participating in Email Discussion Lists

1. **Send** private messages to the individual, not to the list.
2. **Keep** on topic to preserve the message thread.
3. **Use** a signature to identify yourself.
4. **Respond** promptly to keep the discussion lively.

The items in formal lists and outlines and the headings in a paper should be parallel in structure. See section 2g for sample outlines.

COORDINATION AND SUBORDINATION 26

Coordination and subordination clarify the relationships between ideas.

- Coordination emphasizes that the clauses, phrases, or words joined are rhetorically and logically equivalent. To join two independent clauses into a compound sentence, use a comma and a coordinating conjunction or use a semicolon.
- Subordination highlights one clause and suppresses another. To join an independent clause and a dependent clause to create a complex sentence, use a subordinating conjunction or a relative pronoun.

Example 1 Coordination and subordination

Coordinated words	The work was **hot** and **slow.** [adjective + adjective]
Coordinated phrases	A cowboy **might find** himself out of work in the winter and **would go** from ranch to ranch looking for a job or a meal. [verb phrase + verb phrase]
Coordinated independent clauses	**The Royal Governor recalled Randolph,** so **Jefferson went in his place.** [Each independent clause has its own subject-verb pair.]
One clause subordinated to the other	When the Royal Governor recalled Randolph, Jefferson went in his place. [No longer grammatically parallel because the word *when* changes the first clause from independent to dependent]

26a Forming Compound Sentences

The most common way to form compound sentences is to link two independent clauses with a comma and a coordinating conjunction.

and suggests addition or sequence
but and *yet* suggest contrast
or and *nor* suggest choice or alternatives
for suggests causes
so suggests effects or consequences

You can also create compound sentences by using a semicolon to join the independent clauses. This option works best to balance two short, direct statements that are closely parallel.

Example 2 Creating compound sentences by using coordinating conjunctions

The comma always precedes the coordinating conjunction in a compound sentence.

Some dogs like to swim, and some dogs like to race in the snow.

Some dogs like to race in the snow, but others prefer to snooze by the fire.

Either a large dog is trained to be a happy and obedient member of the family, or it is left untrained and becomes a nuisance and a danger.

Border collies have a zealous drive to run, work, and herd, so it's better to keep them as working dogs than as family pets.

Example 3 Creating compound sentences by using a semicolon

Payton Randolph was recalled by the Royal Governor; the 33-year-old Jefferson went in his place.

As responsible custodians of the land, we must consume less fossil fuel; as responsible citizens of our country, we're told, we must use more plastic.

26b Revising Faulty Coordination

Two common problems arise in creating compound sentences:

- excessive coordination
- illogical coordination

Excessive coordination occurs when you string too many independent clauses together, thus obscuring the logical relationships between thoughts. Faced with a muddle of loosely connected clauses, the reader doesn't see any formal relationship among ideas. The ideas simply pile up.

Example 4 Revising excessive coordination

Excessive coordination:
What most cowboys' lives were really like is captured in such songs as "The Dreary, Dreary Life" and "The Old Chisholm Trail" and that life was mostly hard work and poor pay. For most cowboys earned on average a dollar a day and the work was seasonal and jobs were scarce.

Revised:
What most cowboys' lives were really like is captured in such songs as "The Dreary, Dreary Life" and "The Old Chisholm Trail": hard work and poor pay. Most cowboys earned on average a dollar a day. The work was seasonal; jobs were scarce.

Illogical coordination occurs when you either choose the wrong conjunction to support your meaning or yoke together two independent clauses that have no logical relationship.

Example 5 Revising illogical coordination

Vague The big cattle drives were seasonal, and cowboys were often out of work in the winter.

Revised The big cattle drives were seasonal, so cowboys were often out of work in the winter.

Forming Complex Sentences 26c

Use a complex sentence to show that one idea is more important than another. Place the more important idea in the independent clause and the less important idea in the dependent clause.

Be careful to choose the subordinating conjunction that best conveys the relationship you want to establish between the two ideas. Subordinating conjunctions include *although, because, since, while,* and *as.* (See page 418 for a more extensive list.)

You can also create complex sentences by using one of the relative pronouns, such as *that, which,* or *who.*

Example 6 Combining two sentences with subordination

Jefferson was **an awkward public speaker.**
Jefferson was acknowledged as **an eloquent and forceful writer.**

Revision emphasizing Jefferson's skill as a writer:

DEPENDENT CLAUSE — INDEPENDENT CLAUSE

Although he was an awkward public speaker, Jefferson was acknowledged as an eloquent and forceful writer. [Notice the comma that follows the dependent clause when it precedes the independent clause. If the independent clause comes first, no comma is needed.]

Revision emphasizing Jefferson's awkwardness as a public speaker:

DEPENDENT CLAUSE — INDEPENDENT CLAUSE

Although he was acknowledged as an eloquent and forceful writer, Jefferson was an awkward public speaker.

Revision more strongly de-emphasizing Jefferson's awkwardness as a speaker:

APPOSITIVE (A PHRASE, NOT A CLAUSE)

Jefferson, **an awkward public speaker,** was acknowledged as an eloquent and forceful writer. [This sentence is not a complex sentence because it has only one subject-verb pair.]

Example 7 Subordinating with relative clauses

Bert never met a squirrel **that** he didn't like.

Chasing squirrels, **which** is Bert's favorite hobby, keeps him occupied.

Champ is the dog **who** is in the lead position.

Two common problems arise in creating complex sentences:

- excessive subordination
- illogical subordination

Excessive subordination occurs when you jumble so many ideas into a sentence that the reader can no longer follow your meaning. Illogical subordination can occur when you choose the wrong subordinating conjunction or relative pronoun to support your meaning.

In many sentences, choosing which clause to make more important (the independent clause) and which to make less important (the dependent clause) is a matter of personal preference. But some sentences become illogical if you place the less important information in the independent clause—that is, if you mistakenly emphasize what needs to be de-emphasized or vice versa.

Example 8 Revising excessive subordination

Excessive:

The Iditarod Trail Sled Dog Race, which officially began in 1973, honors the heroism of the some 20-odd mushers and their teams of dogs who crossed almost 700 miles in 127 hours (about six days) when the trip normally took around three weeks or more, to bring the serum needed to stop a diphtheria epidemic.

Revised:

The Iditarod Trail Sled Dog Race, which officially began in 1973, honors the heroism of the teams of dogs and mushers who in 1925 brought the serum needed to stop a diphtheria epidemic threatening isolated Nome. Some 20-odd mushers and their teams of dogs crossed almost 700 miles in 127 hours (about six days)—a trip that normally took at least three weeks.

Example 9 Revising illogical subordination

Illogical: **Because** the great cattle drives lasted only a few decades, the mythology of the cowboy remains one of the most compelling in American life.

Revised: **Even though** the great cattle drives lasted only a few decades, the mythology of the cowboy remains one of the most compelling in American life.

Example 10 Shifting the emphasis for logic's sake

Illogical: Buck was a greenhorn, **although** he surprised everyone with his skill in breaking broncos.

Revised: **Although** Buck was a greenhorn, he surprised everyone with his skill in breaking broncos.

When you strive for conciseness, variety, and emphasis, *kairos* should be your guiding principle. Make sure that your sentences are well timed and suited to the context, taking into account the subject matter, the interests of your audience, and your goals.

Writing Concise Sentences 27a

Writing concisely means making every word count. Some sentences need to be longer than others, as some thoughts take more words to express. But often sentences are weighed down by words and phrases that take up space without conveying meaning.

Cut Empty Words and Phrases

Cut these kinds of empty words and phrases:

- overused intensifiers, such as *very, really, definitely, actually*
- vague nouns, such as *factor, kind of, type of, thing*
- puffy connector phrases, such as *in the nature of, as a matter of fact, for all intents and purposes*
- phrases that unnecessarily draw attention to the writer, such as *the point I am making is, I think that, what I'm trying to say is*

Example 1 Revising to make your prose concise

Wordy — **Generally—though definitely not always the case—** students' happiness is determined by the friends they make and the social lives they develop.

Concise — Students' happiness is determined by the friends they make and the social lives they develop.

Cut these phrases

all things considered
as a matter of fact
for all intents and purposes
for the most part
in a manner of speaking
in a very real sense
in the case of
in the final analysis
in the process of
it is a fact that
it is clear/obvious that
it seems that
last but not least
more or less
that exists

Revise these phrases

Revise ...	To become ...
at a certain point in time, at that time	then
at the present time, at this time	now
because of the fact that	because
despite the fact that	although
due to the fact that	because
have a tendency to	tend to
in case	if
in connection with	with
in most instances	usually
in spite of the fact that	although
in the event that	if
in this day and age	today
in those days	then

27a

Eliminate Redundancy

Redundant phrases and word pairs, such as *circle around, final and conclusive, period of time, personal friend,* and *repeat again,* clog up prose. Once is enough.

Common Redundancies
blue [red, etc.] in color: blue
large [small, etc.] in size: large
square [round, etc.] in shape: square
few [many] in number: few
seventeen [eighteen, etc.] years of age: seventeen

Combine Sentences

Use the revision technique of sentence combining to tighten your prose and to clarify what you want to say. Sometimes, two short sentences that share the same grammatical subject or some other element can be better and more economically phrased as one sentence. Two wordy, vague, or overly circular sentences can be condensed into one pithy sentence. Other sentences can be eliminated entirely, either because the information they deliver isn't important or because they are so vague as to deliver no information at all.

Example 2 Say it once!

Original	the **financial cost** to taxpayers
Revised	the cost to taxpayers
Original	**the low self-esteem** that young men **possess about themselves**
Revised	young men's low self-esteem

Revise these redundant phrases

Revise . . .	**To become . . .**
advance notice [planning]	notice [planning]
consensus of opinion	consensus
each and every	each, every [use either but not both]
final completion	completion
important [basic] essentials	essentials
reason . . . is because	because

Example 3 Combining sentences for conciseness

Original	An antidote for arsenite poisoning in humans is British Anti-Lewisite (BAL) (Oehme, 1972). This drug was developed during World War I in response to gas warfare with arsenical compounds.
Revised	One antidote for arsenite poisoning is British Anti-Lewisite (BAL), developed during World War I in response to gas warfare with arsenical compounds (Oehme, 1972).
Original	A learning environment such as this does not promote good learning. It may only cause the intellectual ship to sink in a sea of ignorance.
Revised	Rather than promote good learning, such an environment causes the intellectual ship to sink in a sea of ignorance.

Example 4 Cutting unnecessary expletives

Original For as long as I can remember, **there was** a striving in the Roth household to be better than everyone else.

Revised For as long as I can remember, the Roths strove to be better than everyone else.

Original **It is true that** each teen birth costs taxpayers an estimated $37,000 over the lifetime of mother and child.

Revised Each teen birth costs taxpayers $37,000 over the lifetime of mother and child.

Original In Mamet's play *Oleanna,* **there exists** a rift between John the instructor and Carol the student.

Revised In Mamet's play *Oleanna,* communication breaks down between the instructor, John, and the student, Carol.

Example 5 Changing passive to active voice

Original Poverty **has been looked at** in plays and short stories such as *A Raisin in the Sun* by Lorraine Hansberry, "Sonny's Blues" by James Baldwin, and "Everyday Use" by Alice Walker.

Revised Lorraine Hansberry's *Raisin in the Sun,* James Baldwin's "Sonny's Blues," and Alice Walker's "Everyday Use" all portray poverty.

Original It **was believed** that Atkins's heart problems **were caused** by his ingestion of steaks and cheese cubes, but his family maintained that his heart **had been damaged** by a viral infection.

Revised Many believed that Atkins's fondness for steaks and cheese cubes caused his heart problems, but his family maintained that a viral infection disrupted his heart's rhythm.

Original My room **was so cluttered** with piles of mail and applications that eventually my mother bought me one of those rolling filing cabinets so that I could create a separate file for each prospective school.

Revised So many college applications and piles of mail cluttered my room that eventually my mother bought me a rolling filing cabinet.

Use Strong Verbs

The three verbs *be, do,* and *have* are weaker than verbs that portray action. If you find yourself using these verbs again and again, revise with stronger, more active verbs.

Cut Expletive Constructions

Expletive constructions begin with *it* or *there,* followed by a form of the verb *to be.* An occasional *it is* phrase can help slow the reader down and emphasize an important point. But in general, expletives unnecessarily clog your prose.

Choose the Active Voice

The sentence *I questioned him* is in the active voice. *He was questioned* and *He was questioned by me* are in the passive voice. The active voice is direct, uses vivid verbs, and clearly states who does what to whom; the passive voice is indirect, uses the weak *is* and *have* verbs (in all their grammatical forms), and often leaves the question of who initiated the action unanswered. Choose the active voice unless you have good rhetorical reasons to do otherwise (▶ section 34f).

Revise Nominalizations

A nominalization is a verb turned noun, often ending in *-ance, -ment,* or *-tion*, such as *tolerance* (from *tolerate*) and *deviance* (from *deviate*).

Nominalizations cause prose to be wordy because they lead to sentences with linking verbs. If you nominalize, you will have to use linking verbs to make your sentences grammatical, and these verbs often function like an equal sign, requiring both subject and object to be in noun (or noun phrase) form. Even more important, readers prefer to hear about a world of action where people do things rather than a world of inanimate or abstract concepts. So, if you find a verb hiding in a nominalization in one of your sentences, use it to recast the sentence. Your prose will become more dynamic and readable.

Revise Verb Phrases

Revise wordy verb phrases when a simple verb will do: use *support* rather than *be supportive of, envy* rather than *be envious of, appreciate* rather than *be appreciative of,* and so on.

Example 6 Recasting nominalizations as verbs

Original — With the family's **declination** to have an autopsy done to prove critics wrong and **the cremation** of Atkins's body, suspicions were raised about whether the Atkins diet was indeed a healthy diet.

Revised — The Atkins family **declined** to have an autopsy and then **cremated** Atkins's body, which raised suspicions about whether the Atkins diet was indeed healthy.

When the Atkins family **declined** to have an autopsy and then **cremated** Atkins's body, many became suspicious about whether the Atkins diet was indeed healthy.

Original — My **assumption** was that the ceremony suffered a deliberate **disruption** at the hands of Malefoy.

Revised — I **assumed** that Malefoy deliberately **disrupted** the ceremony.

Example 7 Revising wordy verb phrases

Original — The candidate **is supportive of** health-care reforms.

Revised — The candidate **supports** health-care reforms.

Original — He **is capable of** much.

Revised — He **can do** much.

Original — The children **were appreciative of** the new backpacks.

Revised — The children **appreciated** the new backpacks.

Original — Many scientists think that the decline in amphibians **is indicative of** an overall breakdown in the environment.

Revised — Many scientists think that the decline in amphibians **indicates** an overall breakdown in the environment.

Example 8 The four basic English sentence types

Simple	Few indigenous languages in North America are being taught to the next generation.
Compound	Numerous tongues—perhaps one-third of the total—are on the verge of disappearing along with their last elderly speakers, and many others are not far behind.
Complex	Even though the Navajos have been more successful than some other groups in keeping their language alive, the percentage of Navajos speaking only English more than doubled from 1980 to 1990 (Crawford).
Compound-complex	Some linguists mourn the loss of data implied by these languages becoming extinct, and others believe that this loss entails losing "intellectual diversity," while Crawford himself finds the most important issue to be "the human costs to those most directly affected."

Example 9 Sentence length

Be aware of your reaction to each sentence as you read this paragraph. Which idea is emphasized the most?

Scarlett, the Brooklyn stray who saved her five kittens from a raging fire, is perhaps the most famous cat of the twentieth century. As firemen battled the flames engulfing an abandoned Brooklyn garage and alleged crack house, Scarlett ran back into the fire repeatedly and each time ran back out carrying a tiny kitten. Scarlett's heroism cost her dearly. She emerged from the fire more dead than alive—eyes blistered shut, ears burned to ragged nubs, fur scorched from most of her body—but when Fireman David Gianelli placed her with her kittens, she purred and gently touched each one by the nose as if counting to make sure all were there. Gianelli took Scarlett and her kittens to an animal shelter, and within three months all but one of the animals had recovered and were well enough to be adopted. Once a castoff, an alley cat, a stray, brave Scarlett became a national hero.

Sentence variety keeps writing lively and helps readers sort the more important ideas from the less important. Using emphasis to focus the reader's attention will also help you achieve your broader rhetorical goal of informing, persuading, or entertaining.

Vary Sentence Structure

Lively writing contains a mix of sentence structures:

- A *simple sentence* is made up of one independent clause.
- A *compound sentence* is made up of two independent clauses.
- A *complex sentence* is made up of one independent and at least one dependent clause.
- A *compound-complex sentence* is made up of at least two independent clauses and one dependent clause.

Too many simple and compound sentences make writing choppy. Too many complex and compound-complex sentences make writing hard to follow.

Vary Sentence Length

A change in sentence length acts as a signal to the reader to sit up and pay attention. For example, writers often use a very short sentence as a means of placing emphasis on a key thought or theme.

Emphasize Key Ideas by Making Them the Topics of Sentences

Readers focus on the grammatical subject, so one way to place emphasis in a sentence is through your choice of grammatical subject.

The examples to the right contain the same information, but emphasize different aspects of it by putting different words in the subject position. When the topic of the sentence—the focus of attention—changes, so does the rhetorical emphasis.

Vary Sentence Openings

Although most sentences begin with the grammatical subject, writing in which *all* sentences begin with the subject soon becomes tedious. To aid readability, vary your sentence openings by beginning with phrases, with dependent clauses, or with connecting words such as transitional expressions, coordinating conjunctions, or conjunctive adverbs. Introductory phrases should generally be fairly short so that the delay in getting to the core of the sentence—the subject-verb pair or the agent and action—does not suspend the reader's closure for too long. Readers look for that closure and depend on it to make sense of what they read.

Example 10 Focusing attention by putting information in the subject

SUBJECT — VERB

<u>The Bureau of Labor Statistics</u> found that employed women spend an hour per day more than employed men in doing household tasks and child care.

SUBJECT — VERB

<u>Employed women</u> spend an hour per day more than employed men in doing household tasks and child care, according to the BLS survey.

SUBJECT — VERB

<u>One hour per day more</u> is devoted to household tasks and children by employed women than by employed men, according to the BLS survey.

Example 11 Varying sentence openings to allow for smooth reading

[PHRASE] In *Magnolia,* filmmaker P.T. Anderson looks at betrayal and forgiveness—especially that between parent and child. [SUBJECT] The film intertwines the stories of multiple characters: a day-in-the-life that becomes a day like no other. [SUBJECT] Frank T. J. Mackey is the self-made star of a men's how-to workshop called "Seduce and Destroy." [PHRASE] Prowling the stage as he instructs men in how to cheat and lie their way to seduction, Mackey displays a public persona constructed on a lie. [PHRASE] Behind the character's rage and cockiness lies a 14-year-old boy, abandoned by his father and left to care for his mother as she dies an agonizing death from cancer. [CONJUNCTIVE ADVERB] Now the father, TV producer Earl Partridge, is also dying. [COORDINATING CONJUNCTION] And Earl—through the pain and the morphine and the regret—wants one thing only: to see his son. [SUBJECT] Whether Earl's nurse can find his long-lost son before Earl dies and whether Jack/Frank can or should forgive the father who abandoned him are key plot elements that drive the story forward. [TRANSITIONAL EXPRESSION] Without a doubt, the scene of their reunion is one of the film's highlights.

Example 12 Using verb-subject order to emphasize the end of the sentence

Subject-verb: The sad collection (S) of hovels stood (V)—or rather leaned, drooped, and sagged—at the end of that dusty winding path.

Verb-subject: At the end of that dusty winding path stood (V)—or rather leaned, drooped, and sagged—the sad collection of hovels (S).

Example 13 Changing from a cumulative to a periodic sentence

Cumulative: Earl (S) asks (V) to see his son, even though he is barely able to speak as he struggles against the pain and against the numbing effects of morphine.

Periodic: Struggling against the pain, through a morphine-induced fog, Earl (S) asks (V) to see his son.

Example 14 Using climactic order

My father, when drunk, was neither funny nor honest; he was pathetic, frightening, deceitful.

From Scott Russell Sanders, "Under the Influence," in *The Art of the Personal Essay: An Anthology from the Classical Era to the Present* (New York: Anchor Books/Doubleday, 1994), 735.

Homosexual survival lay in artifice, in plumage, in lampshades, sonnets, musical comedy, couture, syntax, religious ceremony, opera, lacquer, irony.

From Richard Rodrigues, "Late Victorians," in *The Art of the Personal Essay: An Anthology from the Classical Era to the Present* (New York: Anchor Books/Doubleday, 1994), 760.

Reverse Subject-Verb Order

Reversing the strongly ingrained subject-verb pattern packs a strong punch. So, on occasion, you might want to try adding variation or shifting emphasis by using the sentence pattern verb-subject.

Take care when deciding to reverse the sentence pattern, however. Verb-subject reversal is not a technique to use arbitrarily, since many constructions won't yield gracefully to this shift. As Yoda of *Star Wars* might put it, "Confuse you it will."

Use Periodic Sentences

Most sentences are cumulative; that is, the main subject-verb pair comes first, and the rest of the information follows. In contrast, periodic sentences withhold the subject-verb pair until the end. Although a periodic sentence maintains the expected subject-verb order, it places emphasis by making the reader wait until the end for the main information.

Use Climactic Order for Items in a Series

Readers expect that ideas listed in a series will be arranged in climactic order—that is, that the ideas will progress from least important to most important. If you vary from this pattern, you should have a clear reason for doing so.

Use Questions, Commands, or Exclamations

Most sentences make statements; they are declarative. Occasionally, it's effective to use questions, commands, or exclamations to enhance variety.

Questions (interrogative sentences) can be an effective way to initiate a shift in thought, often at the beginning or end of a paragraph, or to emphasize an important point.

Commands (imperative sentences) tend to belong to how-to manuals, cookbooks, and advice columns, all challenging and often artful forms of nonfiction in their own right. Occasionally, imperative sentences can be useful in other types of nonfiction.

Exclamatory sentences get a lot of use in grocery store tabloids, but on rare occasions an exclamation can add the right bit of oomph to more serene or serious nonfiction.

Example 15 Using questions, commands, or exclamations

Question:

"You ask girls here what they want to do and they'll tell you—'to be a Miss Venezuela.'"

But is the pressure too much?

Giselle Reyes, 38, who runs a beauty school and was once a beauty queen, thinks not. . . .

From Juan Forero, "A Bevy of Teeny Beauties, Minds Set on Being Queens," *New York Times*, April 15, 2005.

Commands:

No, I can't see how it's a good idea. I would suggest that what's done is done, that you gave it a shot and it didn't work out and the best thing to do is let it go. Let him find someone else. And you find someone else as well. Don't fall for it. File for divorce. Get the papers signed. Forget about him.

From Cary Tennis, "Since You Asked . . ." column, *Salon*, April 14, 2005.

Exclamation:

Well, when I had reached this period of silence, I was forced into a measure that no one ever adopts voluntarily: I was impelled to think. God, was it difficult! The moving about of great secret trunks. I wondered whether I had ever thought.

From F. Scott Fitzgerald, "The Crack-Up," in *The Art of the Personal Essay: An Anthology from the Classical Era to the Present* (New York: Anchor Books/Doubleday, 1994), 527.

Use Repetition to Emphasize Key Ideas

The skillful, deliberate repetition of a word or phrase is an effective way to emphasize a key idea.

Example 16 Using repetition

We shall go on to the end, **we shall fight** in France, **we shall fight** on the seas and oceans, **we shall fight** with growing confidence and growing strength in the air, we shall defend our Island, whatever the cost may be, **we shall fight** on the beaches, **we shall fight** on the landing grounds, **we shall fight** in the fields and in the streets, **we shall fight** in the hills; we shall never surrender . . . .

From Winston Churchill.

Regionalisms

As you move across the United States, you'll find that people use different words for the same thing. So, for example, a soft drink might be called a *soda* in one place and *pop* in another; the evening meal might be *dinner* in one place and *supper* somewhere else. In addition, groups of people—different socioeconomic classes or ethnic groups, for example—may also share speech patterns because of a shared cultural background. Along with variations in word usage, dialects may also exhibit grammatical variations. It is critical to note that these variations are each worthy of our respect. All dialects bind a people together, have a long and interesting history, and show regular and consistent grammatical principles at work.

Language varies from place to place and from group to group—there is no one and only "correct" English; rather, there are *varieties* of English. Standard Written English, Southern States English, Boston Brahmin English, American Indian English, Appalachian English, Spanish-influenced English, and African American Vernacular English, among others, are all equally valid varieties.

Using Standard Written English in Most College Writing 28a

Standard Written English (SWE) is the English of newspapers, books, and magazines; the English of government publications; the English of business and professional life and of academia.

As its name suggests, Standard Written English conforms to certain standards of grammar and usage (themselves the topic of this handbook). Although the idea of a standard has been wrongly used to treat other varieties of English as inferior, a mastery of Standard Written English is imperative for having one's point of view or one's presentation of self given serious consideration in public contexts.

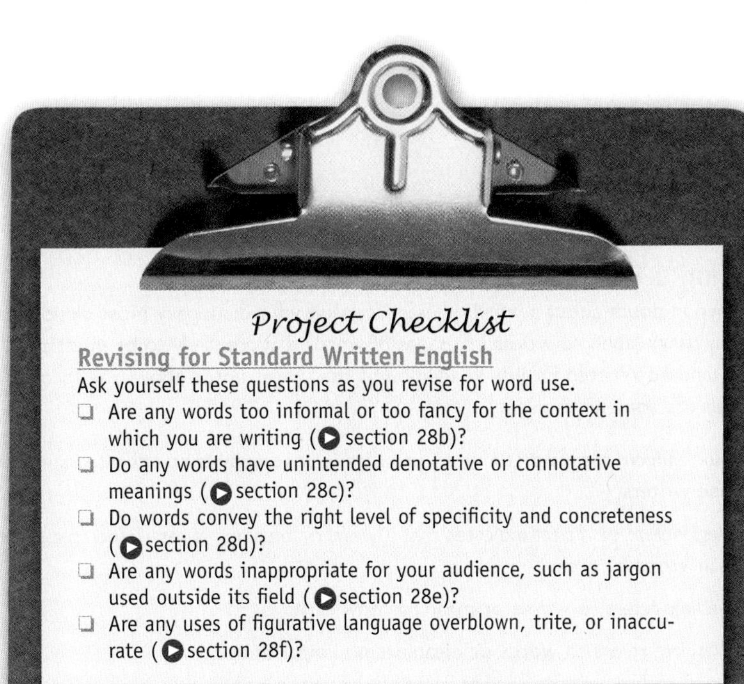

Project Checklist

Revising for Standard Written English

Ask yourself these questions as you revise for word use.

- ❑ Are any words too informal or too fancy for the context in which you are writing (▶ section 28b)?
- ❑ Do any words have unintended denotative or connotative meanings (▶ section 28c)?
- ❑ Do words convey the right level of specificity and concreteness (▶ section 28d)?
- ❑ Are any words inappropriate for your audience, such as jargon used outside its field (▶ section 28e)?
- ❑ Are any uses of figurative language overblown, trite, or inaccurate (▶ section 28f)?

28b Understanding the Levels of Diction

Most academic writing calls for the use of Standard Written English and a more formal level of diction than that found in everyday speech. *Diction* is just a fancy word for word choice, and *level of diction* refers to where your language sits on a continuum of least to most formal. Students writing in college should typically strive for a level of diction more formal than "What's up, dude?" but not so stuffy or overblown as to make them sound like pompous windbags. Readers of academic writing value above all clarity, simplicity, and intelligibility.

Diction on a Continuum from Informal to Formal

Least formal

Slang	Informal or Colloquial Diction
Street talk, a word of recent coinage, often the specialized vocabulary of a particular group, "lingo"	Language appropriate to everyday speech but unlikely to be appropriate to the more formal demands of college writing
"The Pit and the Pendulum" **creeps me out.** It gives me **the willies.**	"The Pit and the Pendulum" **scares me.** It gives me **goosebumps.**
Lots of companies treat the acid rain issue like a big **pain in the butt.**	Lots of companies treat the acid rain issue **as too big a hassle or too small to deal with.**
Jane's future **sucks.**	Jane is **doomed.**

Using a Dictionary

When in doubt about a word or usage, consult your dictionary. Most dictionaries apply usage labels to words or usages of words that are likely to be questionable in Standard Written English. In addition to the usages noted above, the following labels are sometimes used.

- *Nonstandard* means that a word or usage is unacceptable to educated speakers and writers.
- *Regionalism* or *dialect* indicates that a word or meaning is restricted to a particular group or area.
- *Archaic* refers to words or meanings now rare.
- *Obsolete* refers to words or meanings no longer in use.

Even when you are writing in college, certain rhetorical situations may call for using diction other than Standard Written English. For example, if you are writing dialogue, you may want to represent a particular way of speaking in order to get across a speaker's tone, style, or background. In other rhetorical situations, you'll also vary the level of diction: if you are writing a survey for teenagers that will appear in a music magazine, your diction may well be slang. The point is not to restrict yourself to one level, but to become aware of which level of diction is most appropriate for a given context.

Most formal →

Formal Diction	Pompous Language
Language characterized by precise word choice, minimal use of contractions, formal but not pompous tone, terminology of a field	Language that uses long words where short ones will do, obscure ones where direct ones exist, old forms where new ones have become common, hyphenated words, nominalizations, and passive voice
In "The Pit and the Pendulum," Poe creates an atmosphere of **terrifying claustrophobia, torture, and suspense.**	"The Pit and the Pendulum" arouses **physiologically** a fight-or-flight reaction, **indicative of anxiety.**
Many polluting industries try either to **minimize the seriousness** of acid rain's devastating effect on the environment or to **overplay the costs of implementing environmental regulations.**	**Pollution-incognizant** companies overestimate their **inculpability** and exhibit reluctance to accept responsibility for the **infraction** of acid-rain build-up.
Jane's future **looks bleak.**	The **prognostication** for Jane's future was beset by **darkening clouds.**

Sample Dictionary Entries with Usage Labels

tummy (tŭm′ē) *n.pl.* -**mies** *Informal* The human stomach or belly. [Baby-talk alteration of STOMACH.]
tummy tuck *n.Informal* Abdominoplasty.

From *American Heritage Dictionary of the English Language,* 4th edition.

Denotation is the meaning of a word. **Connotation** is an emotional association a word implies. To choose and use a word effectively, you must know what a word means and be aware of what it implies.

Denotation

Find a word's denotative meanings in a good college-level dictionary, such as the *American Heritage Dictionary of the English Language, Merriam-Webster's Collegiate Dictionary,* or the *Random House Webster's College Dictionary.*

Connotation

Many words share a basic meaning but imply shades or differences of meaning that are distinctly important. Consider this quotation from the British journalist Katherine Whitehorn:

> I am firm. You are obstinate. He is a pig-headed fool.

Firm, obstinate, and *pig-headed* all mean "strong willed," but the connotation of *pig-headed* is that one is stupidly obstinate; the connotation of *firm* is that one is admirably resolute. You can use a thesaurus to find synonyms (words that are alike in meaning), but to clarify differences in connotation, use a dictionary.

Decide Which Synonym to Use by Checking Your Dictionary's Usage Notes

Consider a word's connotations when deciding which of several synonyms to use. They help set the emotional context of your ideas for readers. Here are some of the definitions and a list of synonyms for *easy* from the *American Heritage Dictionary of the English Language,* 4th edition.

eas•y (ē′zē) *adj.* **-i•er, -i•est 1.** Capable of being accomplished or acquired with ease; posing no difficulty; *an easy victory; an easy problem.* **2.** Requiring or exhibiting little effort or endeavor; undemanding: *took the easy way out of her problems; wasn't satisfied with easy answers.* **3.** Free from worry, anxiety, trouble, or pain: *My mind was easy, knowing that I had done my best.* **4a.** Affording comfort or relief; soothing: *soft light that was easy on the eyes.* **b.** Prosperous; well-off: *easy living; easy circumstances. . . .*

Synonyms *easy, simple, facile, effortless* These adjectives mean requiring little effort or posing little if any difficulty. *Easy* applies to tasks that require little effort: "*The diagnosis of disease is often easy, often difficult, and often impossible*" (Peter M. Latham). *Simple* implies a lack of complexity that facilitates understanding or performance: "*the faculty … of reducing his thought on any subject to the simplest and plainest terms possible*" (Baron Charnwood). *Facile* stresses readiness and fluency: *a facile speaker.* Often, though, the word implies glibness or insincerity, superficiality, or lack of care: *explanations too facile for complex events. Effortless* refers to performance in which the application of great strength or skill makes the execution seem easy: *wrote effortless prose.*

The Dangers of Using Biased Language

Be deliberate in your use of connotation, taking care not to undermine your own argument by sloppily using words with negative connotations to smear a person or position with which you disagree. Some words are especially loaded and, if used unthinkingly, can make your work seem biased. If, for example, all women politicians are *shrill* in your vocabulary or all union organizers are *bullheaded,* you might want to examine your writing for gender or class bias overall. The challenge here is not to censor your criticisms but to be aware that your argument will be undermined if you use emotionally loaded language or promote biased stereotypes rather than presenting your position objectively and reasonably. (For more on eliminating biased language, see Chapter 29.)

Sample Paragraph from Judith Ortiz Cofer

Color

In the animal world it indicates danger: the most colorful creatures are often the most poisonous. Color is also a way to attract and seduce a mate. In the human world color triggers many more complex and often deadly reactions. As a Puerto Rican girl born of "white" parents, I spent the first years of my life hearing people refer to me as *blanca,* white. My mother insisted that I protect myself from the intense island sun because I was more prone to sunburn than some of my darker, trigueño playmates. People were always commenting within my hearing about how my black hair contrasted so nicely with my "pale" skin. I did not think of the color of my skin consciously except when I heard the adults talking about complexion. It seems to me that the subject is much more common in the conversation of mixed-race peoples than in mainstream United States society, where it is a touchy and sometimes even embarrassing topic to discuss, except in a political context.

From Judith Ortiz Cofer, "The Story of My Body," in *The Latin Deli: Prose and Poetry* (Athens: University of Georgia Press, 1993).

The first three sentences are mostly general and abstract. The author makes generalizations about the significance and effects of skin color. Sentences 4–7 become more specific and concrete; the author shares her personal experiences with readers. The last sentence zooms out to abstraction again to compare the frequency of conversation about skin color in two cultures.

Good writing requires the deft balancing of the specific and the general, the concrete and the abstract.

- General words are used to define a category of thing: *vertebrates, American literature, undergraduates.* Specific words locate an item within that category: *aardvark; Toni Morrison's novel* Beloved; *Jane Smith, first-year student at Seattle Central Community College.*
- Abstract words identify concepts: *truth, justice, freedom, equality.* Concrete words create impressions based on our five senses (seeing, hearing, smelling, tasting, and touching): *yellow, loud, rank, sweet, soft.*

Specific and concrete words put readers in actual contexts, helping them identify people, actions, scenes, and the particularities of a moment. General and abstract terms stand above the immediacy of context, making it possible for readers to think about what many contexts have in common. We need all kinds of words to capture experience and reflect upon it.

Don't confuse or mislead your reader with language that is overly specialized, obscure, pretentious, or archaic.

Cut Buzzwords

Buzzwords are trendy words often chosen to signify that their users are in the know. In academic writing, use words to convey your thoughts rather than to signify your membership in the club.

Rewrite Bureaucratese

Bureaucratese is language that includes a high proportion of nouns and *to be* verbs; these make writing seem weighty and consequential, but that impression is false. This kind of writing obscures meaning rather than revealing it. Impress your readers instead with clear, direct, and vivid language.

Use the Jargon of Fields of Study with Care

Specialized language has a place in writing, depending on the context, including audience and purpose. Rock climbers know the difference between *scumming, smedging,* and *smearing,* but the ordinary person might not. Specialists need specialized language to talk to one another with clarity and precision. To reach a general audience, you'll want to use a more accessible vocabulary.

Some Contemporary Buzzwords to Avoid

Nouns and Adjectives

action plan buy-in
centers of excellence
core competencies
mission-critical
pushback
thought leadership
trend rifts
turnkey solution
value added
value proposition

Verbs Created from Nouns

to actualize
to dialogue
to gift
to disincent
to incentivize
to monetize
to operationalize
to productize
solutioning (a problem)

Bureaucratese, Revised

Bureaucratese	The experience of sudden hood fly-up may restrict the field of vision such that unfortunate circumstances result for the operator.
Revision	If the hood of your car opens while you're driving, you might not see where you're going and crash.

Jargon in the Disciplines: An Example from Psychology

Every field of study uses a specialized vocabulary. If you were writing a paper on learning for a psychology class, for example, you might well need to use some of the following terms:

associative learning
classical conditioning
operant conditioning
conditioned stimulus
conditioned response
backward conditioning
extinction
reinforcement
avoidance conditioning
partial reinforcement schedule
shaping
modeling

Because these terms are jargon, you should refer to the glossary of your textbook for exact definitions when using any of them in your project. If your audience is only your instructor, you may not need to define these specialized terms, but if your audience includes others outside of the field, you may have to provide definitions for your readers.

Using Euphemisms to Cover Up Embarrassment, Fear, and Disgust

At times euphemisms are appropriate—writing a note to a bereaved mother, you might well use the phrase *passed on* instead of *died*. In academic writing, however, it's best to be more direct. Each time you use a euphemism, consider what you are hiding from readers or yourself. Also, although the euphemisms listed below are at approximately the same level of diction as the words they are covering up, many euphemisms lower the level and thus become unsuitable in Standard Written English:

the facilities (the toilet)
know [someone] in the Biblical sense (have sex with)
passed on, passed away (died)
sanitary landfill (garbage dump)

Recognize Euphemisms

A **euphemism** is a word that is substituted for another in an attempt to make things "nice": *toilet* becomes *bathroom* becomes *washroom* becomes *restroom; undertaker* becomes *mortician* becomes *funeral director.*

Using Figurative Language Effectively 28f

Mixed Metaphors

A mixed metaphor creates an awkward combination of images:

Mixed — The **burning anger** of the colonists **rained down** over Taxation without Representation. [Mixes metaphors of fire and rain]

Revised — The **burning anger** of the colonists **blazed** over Taxation without Representation.

Clichés

A cliché is a metaphor that has worn out its welcome through overuse:

bent out of shape
between a rock and a hard place
grasping at straws

Similes

Similes make explicit comparisons between one thing and another using the word *like* or *as:*

> The man . . . had to walk half a mile to water, the weasel dangling from his palm, and **soak him off like a stubborn label.**

From Annie Dillard, "Living like Weasels," in *Teaching a Stone to Talk* (New York: HarperCollins, 1982).

Figures of speech can help the reader see what you mean by creating word pictures.

Metaphor and simile both compare one thing to another. **Metaphors** imply a comparison: *His mind is a steel trap.* **Similes** spell out a comparison using the word *like* or *as: His mind works like a steel trap.*

An **allusion** refers to a familiar phrase or other part of a literary work, such as a character, storyline, or title. If you call something a "Sisyphean task," you're making an allusion to the myth of Sisyphus, who was condemned to endlessly roll a giant boulder up a hill only to have it fall down again each time he reached the top.

Hyperbole is the use of deliberate exaggeration to make a point: *This book weighs a ton.*

All **biased language** is based on unstated assumptions that position one group as dominant and normative and give that group the right to speak and to name others, while denying equal voice or dignity to those others.

Inclusive language respects differences and seeks to present them in nonjudgmental terms.

Biased language harms your credibility with potential readers. Inclusive language widens your audience.

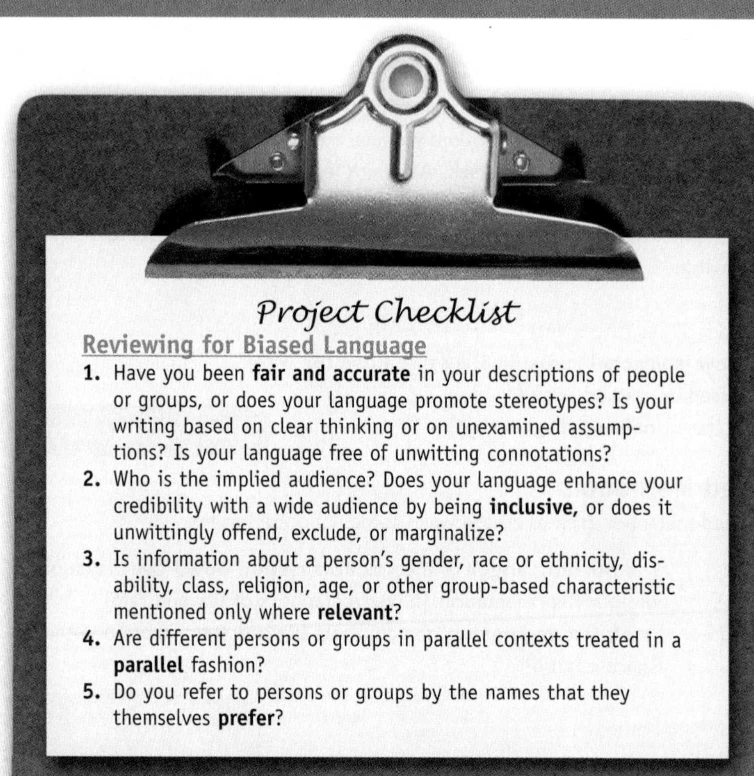

Project Checklist

Reviewing for Biased Language

1. Have you been **fair and accurate** in your descriptions of people or groups, or does your language promote stereotypes? Is your writing based on clear thinking or on unexamined assumptions? Is your language free of unwitting connotations?
2. Who is the implied audience? Does your language enhance your credibility with a wide audience by being **inclusive,** or does it unwittingly offend, exclude, or marginalize?
3. Is information about a person's gender, race or ethnicity, disability, class, religion, age, or other group-based characteristic mentioned only where **relevant**?
4. Are different persons or groups in parallel contexts treated in a **parallel** fashion?
5. Do you refer to persons or groups by the names that they themselves **prefer**?

29a Eliminating Gender Bias

Avoid using the pronoun *he* to refer to a person whose gender is unknown. Strategies to consider are listed to the right.

Approaches to Eliminating the Generic *he*

1. Eliminate the pronoun altogether.

a. Delete it.

b. Replace it with an article.

Original	Every citizen should cast **his** vote on November 2.
Deleted	Every citizen should vote on November 2.
Replaced	Every citizen should cast **a** vote on November 2.

2. Change the person or number of antecedent and pronoun.

a. Use *we, one,* or *you.*

b. Make the antecedent itself plural.

Original	The savvy traveler packs **his** suitcase lightly.
Revised	Savvy travelers pack **their** suitcases lightly.
Revised	Savvy travelers pack lightly.

3. Recast the sentence altogether.

a. Use the imperative mood.

b. Use the passive voice.

c. Use entirely different wording.

Original	A zookeeper observes several precautions when **he** feeds the lions.
Imperative	**Observe** these precautions when feeding the lions.
Recast	Without proper precautions, feeding the lions can be dangerous.

Original	Every citizen must pay **his** taxes by April 15.
Passive	Taxes **must be paid** by April 15.
Recast	April 15 is the deadline for paying federal taxes.

4. Use the phrase *his or her* sparingly.

While too-frequent use of the combination pronoun *his or her* can result in unwieldy or awkward prose, sometimes it's the right choice for a particular context.

Original	Each child paid for his ice cream.
Revised	Each child paid for his or her own ice cream.

Occupational Titles: Men and Women at Work

Instead of . . .	Consider using . . .
businessman	businessman or businesswoman, businessperson
chairman	chair, chairman or chairwoman, chairperson, convener, coordinator, presiding officer
congressman	congressional representative, congressman or congresswoman, legislator, member of Congress, representative
fireman	firefighter
housewife	homemaker, householder
mailman, postman	letter carrier, mail carrier, postal worker

Another linguistic trouble spot is the word *man* used to represent all of humanity. Other *man* words, such as *manpower* or the verb *to man,* also require careful scrutiny, as do historical and cultural references to figurative *fathers* when what is meant is the more-inclusive *founders, innovators, pioneers,* or *ancestors.*

Many job titles that used to be gender specific have been revised for inclusivity. Equally important is not labeling occupations as male or female, as in *male nurse, male secretary, female engineer,* or *female executive.* Refer to gender only when gender is relevant, and try to word your sentences to put the emphasis on accomplishment, not gender.

In scientific circles, the notion of race is an increasingly contested one, with current research showing that so profound are genetic interconnections around the globe that variation between individuals is more significant than variation among groups. A more current way of discussing our differences is by referring to the idea of *ethnicity,* which looks beyond skin color to ancestry, language, and custom. Nevertheless, discussions about race and ethnicity remain among the most difficult in contemporary America. And group differences remain a source of pride as well as prejudice.

Eliminating language bias in regard to race or ethnicity is a matter of applying the five guidelines—to be fair and accurate, inclusive, relevant, parallel, and respectful of preferences—and then stepping back to consider how your language might sound to another.

Writing about Ethnicity: Which Do You Prefer?

African American	Preferred by some groups and individuals
Afro-American	Considered dated
Black, black	Preferred by some groups and individuals; may be either lowercased or capitalized; consult a style guide
colored, Negro	Use only as part of the name of an organization (e.g., the National Association for the Advancement of Colored People, founded in 1909)
American Indian	Most widely used term; use a more specific description when appropriate; does not refer to Inuits or Aleuts
Eskimo, Inuit, Native Alaskan	Though still widely used and most recognizable, *Eskimo* is considered offensive by many; *Inuit* is preferred; some groups and individuals use *Native Alaskan*
Indian	Preferred by some groups and individuals; use a more specific description when appropriate
native, indigenous, aboriginal	As nouns, *native* and *aboriginal* can be considered offensive; as an adjective, *indigenous* is more widely preferred, but *native* (as in *Native American, Native Hawaiian*) and *aboriginal* are still widely used
Native American	Preferred by some groups and individuals; use a more specific description when appropriate
nation, people	Preferred to *tribe*
Chicana, Chicano	Derived from the Spanish term *mexicano;* preferred by some Mexican Americans but considered objectionable by others—use with care; *Chicano* refers to a man, *Chicana* to a woman, though specific English usage varies
Hispanic	Refers to persons descended from residents of Spanish-speaking countries or cultures, including Spain (cf. *Latino, Latina*); preferred by some groups and individuals; does not mean the person speaks Spanish; does not refer to race; use a more specific description when appropriate, such as *Mexican American, Puerto Rican,* or *Cuban American*
Latina, Latino	Refers to persons of Latin American origin; preferred by some groups and individuals; does not refer to race; *Latino* refers to a man, *Latina* to a woman, though specific English usage varies; use more specific description when appropriate, such as *Mexican American, Puerto Rican,* or *Cuban American*

Caucasian, Caucasoid	Derives from nineteenth-century pseudo-anthropological system of racial classification and refers to peoples from Europe, western Asia, northern Africa, and parts of India; has been misused as a synonym for European or white
Amerasian	Refers largely to children fathered by American servicemen during Korean and Vietnam wars
Asian	Preferred term to refer to residents of Asian countries (China, Japan, Korea, Vietnam, etc.) and to things relating to Asia; use more specific national descriptions when appropriate
Asian American	Preferred term; use more specific description when appropriate, such as *Korean American, Chinese American,* or *Filipino American*
Asiatic	Considered offensive; do not use
Oriental	Considered dated or offensive; do not use
hyphenated American	Disparaging; do not use
hyphen as punctuation	Open compounds are more widely preferred; but usage varies (e.g., the *New York Times* still hyphenates such terms as *Vietnamese-American*)
ethnicity	A group definition based on culture, geography, language, country of origin
race	A contested term, so use with consideration; avoid nineteenth-century pseudo-anthropological terms, such as *Negroid, Mongoloid, Caucasoid* (or *Caucasian*), and *Australoid*
minority	Considered offensive by some but appropriate and useful by others; use with consideration
nonwhite	Considered offensive by some but appropriate and useful by others; use with consideration
persons of color	Preferred by some groups and individuals as an alternative to *minorities* for referring to people other than whites
brown, yellow, red, white	Use with consideration; can be considered offensive

Using Preferred Terms

One issue that demands special attention is the importance of using preferred terms. Preferences aren't static; they change as the social landscape itself changes. As Harvard professor Henry Louis Gates Jr. wrote in his 1969 application to college, "My grandfather was colored, my father was a Negro, and I am black." Some Native Americans prefer to be called American Indians; some persons of Latin American origin call themselves Hispanic, some Latino, some Chicano, and others something else entirely, depending on gender, cultural identification, and country of ancestry. Do your homework: if you're writing about a particular group of people, know what they call themselves and prefer for others to call them, and use terms accurately.

It is also important to use more specific designations as appropriate. There are over three hundred American Indian nations currently identified in the United States alone. A Hispanic person might be from Spain, Paraguay, Cuba, Mexico, or any point in between. Asian Americans come from countries as diverse as India, China, and the Philippines.

A final usage note: Don't use hyphens in terms like Chinese American or Cuban American. The use of hyphens in such compounds, as well as the term *hyphenated American* itself, has increasingly come under criticism.

One of the most useful guidelines for eliminating bias in all writing has come out of the disability movement: the People First rule, which says to put the person first, not the disability (or any other qualifier, such as gender, ethnicity, age, or class). Rather than calling someone an *AIDS patient,* use *person living with AIDS;* rather than referring to an entire group of persons as *the learning disabled,* use *persons with learning disabilities* or, more specifically, *children with dyslexia.* Calling someone *a diabetic* equates the person with the disease; calling someone *a person with diabetes* requires more words, but it more fully recognizes that person's humanity.

In writing about disabilities, be specific and accurate. For example, *deaf* means that a person cannot hear; *Deaf* means that the person is self-identified as belonging to a community that uses American Sign Language as the primary form of communication. *Blind* refers to someone without sight; someone with *limited sight* might also be referred to as *visually impaired* or *partly blind.*

In writing about a particular group, do your homework: be informed enough to be current and accurate. Avoid terms that are unnecessarily emotional or negative, such as *victim of* or *cripple,* as well as euphemisms such as *challenged.*

Writing about Disability

Words to use

Preferred terms for talking about disability are *disability* (noun) and *disabled* (adjective); they are considered to be the most straightforward and hence respectful. Their English usage dates back to 1557.

Follow the People First rule: put the person first, then the disability.

Yes persons with disability
No the disabled, disabled persons

Yes person with paraplegia
No paraplegic

Yes person with cancer
No cancer patient

Yes person with bipolar disorder
No manic-depressive

Words to avoid

Though still widely used in law and in everyday speech, *handicapped*—as in *handicapped parking* or *handicapped accessible*—is considered by many to be offensive or euphemistic. For many disabled persons, the handicap is not the disability itself but the physical, legal, and social barriers they may encounter.

Challenged, differently abled, and *handicapable* should be avoided as condescending, awkward, or euphemistic.

Yes She uses a wheelchair.
No She is mobility challenged.

Afflicted with, crippled by, cripple, suffers from, sufferer, victim of, victim, and *deformed* should be avoided as unnecessarily negative or emotional.

Yes . . . the study found that those with arthritis . . .
No . . . the study found that arthritis sufferers . . .

Confined to a wheelchair should be avoided; wheelchairs are not necessarily confining to those who need them.

Yes . . . student Tom Baker, who uses a wheelchair . . .
No . . . student Tom Baker, who is confined to a wheelchair . . .

Understanding and Revising Sentences

PART 9

New Contexts for Writing: Bumper Stickers, T-Shirts, CDs, and DVDs

You might not normally think of the writing and visual content on bumper stickers, T-shirts, CDs, and DVDs as requiring very sophisticated composing processes or rhetorical awareness. But, for example, the rhetorical situation of a bumper sticker, as a claim frozen in time, poses all the usual problems for its creator, while also making unreasonable demands. The work must be concise and visually effective while also fostering identification between the speaker and the audience, presenting a trustworthy ethos, and appealing to the emotions and good sense of the audience.

A bumper sticker that says "A woman needs a man like a fish needs a bicycle" or "My honor student beat up your honor student" makes a political point (in the first case, about gender equity and feminism; in the second, about the proliferation of "honor student" bumper stickers, which may function as social-class markers). The person who owns this old Volkswagen van (itself a statement) has a lot to say. The sheer number of the bumper stickers, in fact, now makes the cumulative point that people should speak out and exercise their right to free speech, an American ideal.

Presentation or **display text** is a kind of advertising meant to catch the attention and hold visual interest. It has to be to the point (i.e., concise), catchy or witty without being too obscure (like a good metaphor), and able to be taken in at a glance. **Identification,** a primary aim of rhetoric, is the process of asserting identity between people or between people and ideas.

Genre Knowledge

Bumper stickers (and T-shirts) express identity, so while you have to worry about what to say and how to say it, you also need to realize that you will be identified with your words and images. In a nutshell, these are the same rhetorical challenges faced by any writer, no matter the genre and circumstances.

With CD and DVD packaging, you face similar challenges: to be concise while capturing visual interest, to represent the content of the CD or DVD accurately while also expressing its character visually, and to write and design within tightly controlled dimensions. CD and DVD packaging has become a genre all its own, with sleeve books and jackets telling more of the story, whether the content is music, movies, photographs, or other multimedia content.

Each of these genres may serve social and political purposes also. Bumper stickers announce political allegiances. T-shirts define identity and show solidarity with causes, groups, or products. CD and DVD packaging conveys the essence of content in ways that extend meaning. In writing in each of these contexts, you exercise rhetorical abilities that can serve you well in others.

Make Your Own!

- Buy blank bumper sticker labels for your printer.
- Create your own T-shirt design in a graphics editor and print it on fabric transfer paper.
- Design CD or DVD labels and write the content for the sleeve book using a free program like Avery's Design Pro Limited (http://www.avery.com).

The context of grammar is the sentence. The grammatical functions of some words in the following sentence are labeled.

> In a corporate [ADJECTIVE] jet flying 37,000 feet above [PREPOSITION] the Amazon rainforest [NOUN], I heard [VERB] the three words I [PRONOUN] will never [ADVERB] forget: "We've been hit."
>
> From Joe Sharkey, "Colliding with Death at 37,000 Feet, and Living," *New York Times*, Oct. 3, 2006.

Examples of Nouns

Proper	**Common**	**Concrete**	**Abstract**
Linda Chavez	woman	bed	comfort
Vancouver	city	wind	anger
Hyundai	car	bells	belief

Collective	**Countable**	**Uncountable**
team	players	team spirit
faculty	classmates	homework
army	soldiers	equipment

Multilingual writers: Most errors in noun form result from problems in distinguishing between countable and uncountable nouns; see Chapter 48.

A Noun?

The following questions can help you decide whether a word is acting as a noun.

1. Can the form of the word be changed to indicate singular or plural (▶ section 48a)?
2. Can you make the word possessive (▶ section 41a)?
3. Can you insert *a, an, the,* or *some* directly before the word?
4. Does the word end with one of these suffixes, which usually indicate nouns: *-ance, -ence, -ment, -ness,* or *-ty*?

Knowing how words function within a sentence and how sentences are structured will increase your options as a writer.

Nouns 30a

A **noun** refers to a person, place, thing, quality, state, action, or concept. Anything that can be pointed to or singled out can be named with a noun.

- **Proper nouns** name a specific person, place, or thing. The first letter of a proper noun is capitalized. **Common nouns** name the types of things that a proper noun represents.
- **Concrete nouns** name things or objects that you can see, hear, taste, smell, touch, or experience in the world. **Abstract nouns** name things that cannot be known through the senses.
- **Collective nouns** name a collection or group. **Countable nouns** name things that may exist as distinct units and that may be counted. Most count nouns can be made plural by adding *s: voters.* **Uncountable nouns** name things that are usually considered wholes or abstract ideas and can't be counted: *mud, confusion, enthusiasm.* They normally can't be made plural.

A **pronoun** usually substitutes for a noun in a sentence. The noun that the pronoun refers back to or replaces is called the **antecedent.**

- **Personal pronouns** refer to people or things: *I, you, he, she, it, we, they, me, him, her, it, us, them.*
- **Indefinite pronouns**, such as *all, anyone, each, everybody,* and *some,* refer to unnamed or indefinite antecedents.
- **Relative pronouns,** including *which, that, who,* and *whom,* introduce a noun clause or an adjective clause.
- **Interrogative pronouns,** including *who, whom,* and *which,* introduce questions.
- **Demonstrative pronouns**—*this, that, these,* and *those*—refer to a noun or pronoun antecedent.
- **Reflexive pronouns** such as *myself* and *yourselves* refer back to nouns or personal pronouns when the subject of an action and the object of that action are the same.
- Pronoun forms such as *myself* can also be used to intensify an antecedent. When they are used this way, they are called **intensive pronouns.**
- **Reciprocal pronouns**—*each other* and *one another*—refer to an action that two antecedents perform mutually.

See Chapter 33 for more on pronouns.

Example 1 Pronouns

Personal pronouns:

Grace opened her book, but **she** couldn't find **her** place.

Indefinite pronouns:

All it takes to succeed in this course is a little hard work.

Relative pronouns:

NOUN CLAUSE

She is the girl ***who*** **earned straight As in high school.**

ADJECTIVE CLAUSE

Go up the trail ***that*** **starts at the beach.**

Interrogative pronouns:

Which book will you read tonight?

Demonstrative pronouns:

This is the best book I have ever read. [A book the speaker is holding]

That one makes me fall asleep. [A book that is farther away]

Reflexive pronouns:

He hit **himself** in the foot with the puck.

Intensive pronouns:

The author **herself** signed the book for me.

Reciprocal pronouns:

When two people are talking to **each other** at the same time, it's doubtful either one is listening.

Indefinite Pronouns

all	each	more	one
another	either	most	several
any	everybody	neither	some
anybody	everyone	nobody	somebody
anyone	everything	no one	someone
anything	few	none	something
both	many	nothing	

Example 2 Verbs

Active sentence with action verb:

He *sat* quietly in front of the monitor.

Passive sentence with auxiliary and action verbs:

Mistakes *were made*.

Sentence describing state of being:

She *is* happy.

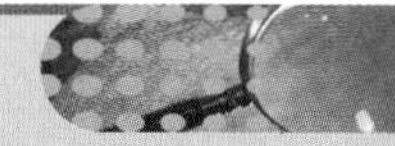

How Can You Identify...

A Verb?

The following questions can help you decide whether a word is acting as a verb in a sentence.

1. Can you change the tense to indicate past time? Most verbs add *-ed* or *-d* to the plain form to indicate past tense: *played* (play + ed), *hiked* (hike + d). Some verbs form the past tense irregularly: *ride/rode, run/ran, eat/ate* (▶ pages 447–448).
2. If you put the word after a singular noun subject, would it change form in the present tense? *The child [swim]* ⟶ *The child swim***s**. Nearly all present tense verbs add *-s* or *-es* to the base form of the verb: *hugs* (hug + s), *kisses* (kiss + es). The two exceptions are *be,* which becomes *is,* and *have,* which becomes *has.*
3. Is the word one of two forms that can never be the verb in a sentence unless other verbs are helping them: infinitives (*to hug, to hit*) and *-ing* forms (*pleasing, writing*) (▶ section 31a)?

A verb is the central unit of any sentence or clause, and all the other words in a sentence take grammatical form based on how they relate to it. A **verb** can express action (*run, live, change*), states of being (*is, are*), or occurrences (*happen, become*). Sentences can have more than one verb. A clause is a sub-unit of a sentence that has one verb.

Action verbs express action by an agent in a sentence or clause. The agent needn't be present in the sentence, however. For example, in passive sentences agents may be deliberately omitted (▶ 34f).

***To be* verbs** express states of being; they are sometimes referred to as *stative* verbs. *To be* verbs are *am, is, are, was,* and *were.*

See Chapter 34 for more on verbs.

Adjectives 30d

Adjectives describe nouns and pronouns. Some adjectives limit or specify the noun or pronoun by showing its quantity, location, ownership, or other qualities.

Example 3 Adjectives modifying nouns

The **Lippit** *Morgans* are **beautiful** *horses*.

- **Articles** are used before nouns. The articles are *a, an,* and *the*. The definite article *the* is used before a noun to indicate a specific item or items. The indefinite articles *a* and *an* indicate that a noun is used in a more general way.
- **Demonstrative adjectives**—*this, that, these, those*—emphasize a noun or pronoun.
- **Indefinite adjectives** are indefinite pronouns used to modify nouns and work much the same way as demonstrative adjectives.
- **Interrogative adjectives** go before a noun in a question.
- **Possessive adjectives** describe who possesses or owns the object named by a noun.
- **Proper adjectives** are proper nouns used to modify a noun.
- **Relative adjectives** are like relative pronouns, except they modify nouns instead of standing in for them.

Example 4 Adjectives

Articles:

The *teacher* used **a** laser *pointer.*

Demonstrative adjectives:

I'll carry **these** *boxes* if you take **that** *one.*

Indefinite adjectives:

Other *people* like these apples.

Each *kid* ran away from that school bus.

Interrogative adjectives:

What *kind* of motorcycle is that?

Whose *machine* broke first?

In **which** *tree* did you build a fort?

Possessive adjectives:

She hit **her** first *homerun* on the last day of the season.

Our *apartment* is too small for all of **your** *magazines.*

Proper adjectives:

Swedish *meatballs* are less popular with children than **Turkish** *taffy.*

Relative adjective:

If you would ask for directions, we would know **which** *road* to take.

Multilingual writers: Adjectives before a noun often need to be in a certain order; see section 50c.

30e Adverbs

Adverbs modify verbs, but they also modify adjectives, other adverbs, and whole clauses. They answer the questions "When?" "Where?" "How?" "To what degree or extent?"

Example 5 Adverbs

I *ran* **yesterday**. [Modifies verb]

It was **really** *dark.* [Modifies adjective]

Hibiscus blooms **very** *profusely.* [Modifies adverb]

Quickly, the tourists *snapped* dozens of photos. [Modifies verb]

Adverbs of degree

Positive degree	I run **quickly.**
Comparative degree	I run **more quickly** than he does.
Superlative degree	I run the **most quickly** of all the competitors.

Conjunctive adverbs and their meanings

	Conjunctive Adverbs
Comparing and contrasting	conversely, however, instead of, likewise, nevertheless, nonetheless, similarly, still
Adding information	additionally, also, besides, furthermore
Suggesting implications and results	accordingly, consequently, then, therefore, thus
Expressing time order	finally, first, meanwhile, next, second, subsequently, then
Making or emphasizing a point	always, certainly, definitely

- **Adverbs of degree** answer the question "To what degree or extent?" Some adverbs of degree compare one item with a second; these are called **comparative adverbs.** Others compare an item with two or more other items; these are called **superlative adverbs** (▶ Chapter 36).
- **Conjunctive adverbs** indicate specific relationships between sentences and ideas. Conjunctive adverbs create lexical ties, which are direct relationships of meaning across sentences (◀ Chapter 2).

Prepositions 30f

Prepositions indicate relationships, often of space or time, between the nouns or pronouns that follow them and the other words in a sentence. Prepositions do not change form. English has many prepositions, but you can recall some of the most familiar ones if you imagine all the places you can be in relation to, for example, a house: *in, on, above, below, beside, around, between, over, under, at,* and so on. Some prepositions consist of more than one word.

Example 6 Prepositions

I ran **into** the *woods* and **across** the *stream* to escape my little brother.

Common Prepositions

about	below	in spite of	past
above	beneath	inside	since
according to	beside	instead of	through
across	between	into	to
after	beyond	near	toward
against	by	of	under
along	despite	off	underneath
among	down	on	until
around	during	onto	upon
aside from	except	out	with
at	for	outside	within
before	from	over	without
behind	in		

Conjunctions connect clauses, phrases, and individual words. Three types of conjunctions are coordinating, subordinating, and correlative.

- **Coordinating conjunctions** place words in a sentence in coordinate (that is, parallel) relationships. The seven coordinating conjunctions are *and, but, so, yet, for, or,* and *nor.* Notice that when the conjunction joins independent clauses, a comma must precede the conjunction.
- **Subordinating conjunctions** express a logical or temporal relationship among elements in a sentence or between ideas across sentence boundaries. If the subordinate clause precedes the independent clause to which it is attached, separate the clauses with a comma.
- **Correlative conjunctions** express relationships of contrast or similarity between different elements in a sentence. They come in pairs: *both . . . and, either . . . or, neither . . . nor,* and *not only . . . but also.*

Example 7 Conjunctions

Coordinating conjunctions:

He studies every afternoon, **but** he rarely passes his exams. [*But* joins two independent clauses. Notice the comma.]

I like to run marathons **and** lift weights. [*And* joins two phrases.]

Subordinating conjunctions:

Although he was quick on his feet, the attack surprised him.

You'd better have lots of money with you **when** you go shopping for a plasma TV.

Correlative conjunctions:

She **not only** *rose* to the top of her class **but also** *became* an ambassador for the school.

Notice that the words following each part of the correlative conjunction are of the same grammatical form (*rose* and *became* are both past-tense verbs). When you use correlative conjunctions, take care to preserve this parallel structure.

Subordinating Conjunctions

after	if	till
although	if only	unless
as	in order that	until
as if	now that	when
as long as	once	whenever
as soon as	provided (that)	where
as though	rather than	whereas
because (of)	since	wherever
before	so that	whether
due to	such that	which
even if	than	while
even though	that	why
how	though	

Interjections 30h

Interjections begin or interrupt sentences and express strong or sudden emotion, as well as attitude or tone, such as surprise, resignation, or irony. Interjections can also be words used to address someone, such as *hi, hello,* or *hey.*

Example 8 Interjections

Wow! That McDonald's coffee is hot.

Oh, how disappointing!

Subject and Predicate 30i

The grammatical terms for the noun-verb pair that is the core of every sentence are *simple subject* and *simple predicate.* Every sentence can be broken into these two parts.

- The **simple subject** is whomever or whatever the sentence is about; it and all the words that go with it are called the **complete subject.** In the complete subjects to the left, the simple subjects are in bold.
- The **simple predicate** is the verb that relays the subject's action or state of being. The verb and all the words that go with it are called the **complete predicate.** In the complete predicates to the left, the verbs are in bold.

Sentences can also have compound subjects and compound predicates. **Compound subjects** consist of two or more nouns linked by *and.* **Compound predicates** include two or more verbs joined by *and.*

Subjects	Predicates
Bao	**is** funny.
The beautiful **boat**	**sails** in the harbor.
Throwing pottery on a wheel	**takes** practice.
She	**has been thinking** about her family.
Suki and **Eriko**	**laughed** loudly.
Tomas's **car**	**skidded** and **flipped** over.

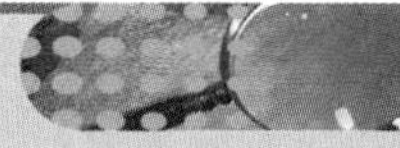

How Can You Identify...

The Subject of a Sentence?

1. Find the verb.

   The peacock **runs.** [Active voice]

   The research study **was conducted** by first-year students. [Passive voice]

2. Ask "Who or what . . .?"

   Who or what runs? [*The peacock* is the subject of the first sentence.]

   Who or what was conducted? [*The research study* is the subject of the second sentence.]

30j Five Basic Patterns of English Sentences

Most English sentences conform to one of five standard patterns.

Sentence Pattern 1

Subject + Verb

The predicate in the subject + verb pattern consists of the intransitive verb only. **Intransitive verbs** do not take objects or complements; their meaning is complete. You can add descriptive details, however.

Sentence Pattern 2

Subject + Verb + Direct Object

Transitive verbs require a direct object to complete the thought. Transitive verbs can be in the active voice or the passive voice. In the active voice, the subject of the sentence performs the action. In the passive voice, the subject receives the action (▶ section 34f).

In a sentence in the active voice, the **direct object** receives the action and is usually a noun, pronoun, or noun phrase.

Sentence Pattern 3

Subject + Verb + Indirect Object + Direct Object

Indirect objects indicate *to whom* or *to what* or *for whom* or *for what* an action is performed.

Pattern 1: Intransitive verbs don't need objects or complements

Subject	**Verb**
Lightning	**flashed.**
The clock	**ticks.**
The library	**will open** at 10 a.m. [*At 10 a.m.* is a prepositional phrase, not an object or a complement.]
Visitors	**should leave** now. [*Now* is an adverb, not an object or a complement.]

Pattern 2: Transitive verbs require direct objects

Subject	**Verb**	**Direct Object**
Alexander Selcraig	navigated [what?]	a British ship.
The sailors	ate [what?]	dried peas and salt meat. [Compound object]

Many verbs have both transitive and intransitive meanings. Consult a dictionary if you need to.

Intransitive	**Transitive**
The water **runs.**	Luca **runs** the drill press.

Pattern 3: The indirect object usually receives or benefits from the action of the verb on the direct object

Subject	**Verb**	**Indirect Object**	**Direct Object**
David	sent	Angelina	*Silent Snow.*
This book	tells	readers	a frightening story.

Multilingual writers: See section 50b on the order of direct and indirect objects following different verbs.

Pattern 4: The object complement renames or describes the direct object

Subject	Verb	Direct Object	Object Complement
The voters	elected	Hawley	mayor.
Environmentalists	found	McKibben's argument	compelling.

Pattern 5: The subject complement renames or describes the subject

Subject	Verb	Subject Complement
This forest	feels	lonely. [forest = lonely]
The conference	was	a disaster. [conference = disaster]

Example 9 Word order shifts

Forming a yes/no question:

Statement Taxes are high.

Question Are taxes high?

Multilingual writers: See section 50d.

Inverting a declarative sentence:

VERB SUBJECT

At the end of the elf's nose grew a large wart.

For more on reversing subject-verb order, see page 397.

Expletive construction:

VERB SUBJECT

There are one hundred violinists in that orchestra. [One hundred violinists are in that orchestra.]

Sentence Pattern 4

Subject + Verb + Direct Object + Object Complement

Object complements add to, describe, identify, or rename the direct object. Complements can be nouns, noun phrases, or adjectives. Object complements help complete the meaning of transitive verbs such as *call, elect, make,* and *name.*

Sentence Pattern 5

Subject + Verb + Subject Complement

The **linking verbs** used in the subject + verb + subject complement pattern require a complement to complete the thought. The complement renames, identifies, adds to, or describes the subject. Complements can be nouns, noun phrases, or adjectives. The most common linking verb is *be* (in all its forms, such as *is, are, was, were, was being*). Other linking verbs include *appear, become, feel, grow, look, make, seem, smell, sound,* and *taste.*

Word Order Shifts

Three kinds of sentences call for inverting subject and verb. See Example 9.

30k Phrases

Phrases are word groups that do *not* contain the subject-verb pair needed for a complete sentence. Phrases function as a single part of speech: as a noun, verb, adjective, or adverb.

Noun Phrases

Noun phrases function as nouns and are made up of the main noun and its accompanying modifiers (adjectives and adverbs).

Verb Phrases

Verb phrases function as verbs and are made up of the main verb and any accompanying auxiliaries, including *be, can, could, do, have, may, might, must, shall, should, will,* and *would,* in all their forms.

Verbal Phrases

Verbal phrases are made up of a verbal—an infinitive, gerund, or participle—and its accompanying modifiers, objects, or complements.

- **Infinitive phrases** can act as nouns, adjectives, or adverbs. The infinitive is made up of *to* plus the root form of the verb.
- **Gerund phrases** act as nouns. A gerund is formed from the *-ing* form of the verb.

Example 10 Phrases

S V

In summer she likes **getting chocolate ice cream cones from the vendor at the beach.**

Example 11 Noun phrases

NOUN PHRASE

Nineteenth-century author Charlotte Bronte lived

NOUN PHRASE

a very restricted life.

Example 12 Verb phrases

VERB PHRASE

His many illnesses **might have been caused** by the approaching final exams.

Example 13 Infinitive phrases

To err is human; **to forgive,** divine. [As nouns]

The *cakes* in the window were **only to look at.** [As adjective]

They were *afraid* **to speak.** [As adverb]

Example 14 Gerund phrases

Going to school is part of **growing up.**

Example 15 Participial phrases

Present participle phrase:
Swinging with all his might, *he* struck a homer into the bleachers.

Past participle phrase:
Chosen in a competition that included 1,421 submissions, Maya Ling Lin's *design* for the Vietnam Memorial was a V-shaped black granite wall etched with the names of the war's 58,000 American casualties.

Example 16 Prepositional phrases

PREP OBJ PREP PREP OBJ PREP
On NASA Road in Houston, Texas, is the Lyndon B. Johnson Space Center.

As adjective	The *quest* **for greater knowledge** continues.
As adverb	Everyone in the area *was evacuated* **to higher ground.**
As adverb	The game *was canceled* **because of the rain.**

Example 17 Absolute phrases

The gold hidden, the pirates sailed away.

Example 18 Appositive phrases

Nonrestrictive (nonessential) appositive phrase with commas:

NOUN APPOSITIVE
Charlotte Bronte's *Jane Eyre,* **a novel that shocked Victorian England,** made her both famous and infamous.

Restrictive (essential) appositive phrase with NO commas:

NOUN APPOSITIVE
The novels ***Jane Eyre* and *Wuthering Heights*** shocked Victorian England with their portrayals of passionate, strong-willed women.

- **Participial phrases** function as adjectives. A present participle is formed from the *-ing* form of the verb. A past participle is formed from the *-ed* form for regular verbs and variously for irregular verbs (the past participle of *to choose* is *chosen*). Irregular verbs are listed in section 34a.

Prepositional Phrases

Prepositional phrases consist of a preposition followed by a noun, pronoun, or noun phrase known as the **object of the preposition**. The prepositional phrase also includes any modifiers of the object of the preposition. For a list of prepositions, see page 417.

Prepositional phrases can function as adjectives and adverbs.

Absolute Phrases

Absolute phrases function as adverbs for an entire independent clause. An absolute phrase is usually made up of a noun and a present or past participle. (Sometimes the participle is understood but omitted.) Absolute phrases are set off by a comma.

Appositive Phrases

Appositive phrases function as noun equivalents and restate, rename, or more fully define the noun immediately preceding.

See section 38f.

Clauses are word groups that contain both a subject and a verb. An **independent clause**—as the name implies—can function independently as a simple sentence. It is grammatically *independent*. An independent clause can also combine with other clauses to form a larger, more complex sentence.

A **dependent clause**—as the name implies—cannot function independently as a simple sentence. It is grammatically *dependent*. All dependent clauses begin with a subordinating word, usually a subordinating conjunction or relative pronoun, that renders them unable to stand on their own as an independent sentence. Subordinating conjunctions are words like *because, as if, wherever,* and *even though*. A list of subordinating conjunctions appears on page 418.

Dependent clauses, like phrases, function as a single part of speech. They can be nouns, adjectives, or adverbs.

Noun Clauses

A **noun clause** begins with a relative pronoun (listed to the right) or a subordinating conjunction (usually *when, where, whether, why,* or *how*). Like all nouns, noun clauses answer the question "Who?" or "What?" in relation to the verb.

Like all nouns, noun clauses can function within a sentence as subjects, objects, or complements.

Example 19 Clauses

Independent clause as simple sentence:

I like chocolate ice cream.

Independent clauses as part of larger sentence:

Although I'm allergic to chocolate, **I like chocolate ice cream**.

I like chocolate ice cream because it is delicious.

Dependent clauses	although I'm allergic to chocolate because it is delicious
Noun clause	**What I love best about summer** is eating chocolate ice cream cones at the beach.
Adjective clause	The *ice cream* **that I love best** is chocolate.
Adverb clause	I *like* chocolate ice cream **because it is delicious.**

Relative Pronouns

that	which	whoever	whomever
what	whichever	whom	whose
whatever	who		

Example 20 Noun clauses

Noun clauses introduced by relative pronoun:

***That* men still make more money** is a fact. ***That* they deserve it** is not.

Noun clauses introduced by subordinating conjunction:

We can never know ***whether* he committed the crime or lied to the jury about his innocence**.

***How* we live** matters.

Noun clause as subject:

How wood frogs restart their hearts when unfreezing from hibernation is still a mystery.

Noun clause as direct object:

Scientists still don't understand **how wood frogs restart their hearts when unfreezing from hibernation.**

Noun clause as subject complement:

For scientists studying amphibians, one of the most intriguing questions is **how wood frogs restart their hearts when unfreezing from hibernation.**

Example 30l.1 Adjective clauses

According to a recent study, *athletes* **who wear red** win more often.

Revenge of the Sith, **which completes the *Star Wars* saga**, tells the story of how Anakin Skywalker becomes Darth Vader.

Manhattan's Lower East Side is a *place* **where many immigrants first began life in the United States.**

Elliptical adjective clause:

This is a *movie* [that] **everyone should see!**

Example 30l.2 Adverb clauses

They finally *left* the party **after eating all the food, drinking all the drinks, and monopolizing every conversation.**

At that moment, my father looked *older* **than he ever had before.**

The hair tonic never worked as *well* **as the advertisement promised.**

When the tornado sirens sound, *seek shelter.*

Elliptical adverb clauses:

George is just as *boring* **as Henry** [is].

Illogical While mowing the lawn, a frog jumped in my way. [Here, readers may try to imagine just how frogs look while mowing the lawn, when you really intended one of the following.]

Logical While I was mowing the lawn, a frog jumped in my way.

or

While [I was] mowing the lawn, I tripped over a frog.

Adjective Clauses

Adjective clauses are usually introduced by relative pronouns and occasionally by *when, where,* or *why.* Like all adjectives, they modify nouns and pronouns and answer the question "Which one?" or "What kind of?" An adjective clause usually comes immediately after the noun it modifies.

Some adjective clauses are *elliptical*—that is, some part of the wording is understood rather than stated.

Adverb Clauses

Adverb clauses are always introduced by subordinating conjunctions. Like all adverbs, adverbial dependent clauses modify verbs, adjectives, other adverbs, or even entire clauses. They answer the questions "How?" "When?" "Where?" "Why?" "In what manner?" "Under what conditions?" "With what result?" "To what degree?"

Some adverb clauses are *elliptical*—that is, some part of the wording is understood rather than explicit. In elliptical constructions in which both subject and verb are omitted from the adverb clause, watch out for illogical phrasings.

Sentences can be classified by grammatical structure—that is, by the kinds of clauses they are built out of—as simple, compound, complex, or compound-complex.

Simple Sentences

A **simple sentence** consists of one independent clause. The essence of the simple sentence is the subject-verb pair. Although built on a single subject-verb pair, simple sentences can vary in length and complexity.

Compound Sentences

A **compound sentence** is made up of at least two independent clauses. In a compound sentence, the two independent clauses are usually joined by a comma and a coordinating conjunction (*and, but, or, nor, for, so, yet*). The two clauses can also be joined by a semicolon (sections 26a–26b).

Complex Sentences

A **complex sentence** consists of one independent clause and at least one dependent clause (sections 26c–26d).

Example 23 Simple sentences: one independent clause

S V
Snow is cold.

We saw the Grand Canyon.

Madame C. J. (Sarah Breedlove) Walker is considered to be America's first African American woman millionaire.

Example 24 Compound sentences

INDEPENDENT CLAUSE / INDEPENDENT CLAUSE
We saw the Grand Canyon / , and / they saw the ocean.

INDEPENDENT CLAUSE / INDEPENDENT CLAUSE
Madeleine is our calico cat / ; / she hates to catch mice.

INDEPENDENT CLAUSE / INDEPENDENT CLAUSE
Walker made millions / , and / she donated generously to African American causes, becoming one of the early twentieth century's most notable philanthropists.

Example 25 Complex sentences

DEPENDENT CLAUSE / INDEPENDENT CLAUSE
While we saw the Grand Canyon, / they saw the ocean.

INDEPENDENT CLAUSE / DEPENDENT CLAUSE
In visiting the rain forest, we at last saw the landscape / that we had imagined so vividly.

DEPENDENT CLAUSE / INDEPENDENT CLAUSE
Although she was born to sharecroppers, orphaned at age seven, and widowed at twenty, / Walker made an independent fortune by developing and selling her own line of beauty products.

Example 26 Compound-complex sentences

INDEPENDENT CLAUSE

Walker used her wealth to support the preservation of African American history and the advancement of black culture / : /

INDEPENDENT CLAUSE

she helped to purchase the home of Frederick Douglass / , /

DEPEPENDENT CLAUSE

which is today a National Historic Site under the National Park Service /

INDEPENDENT CLAUSE

; and / the townhouse she built in New York City became an important gathering place for black artists during the Harlem Renaissance.

In the final independent clause, a dependent clause comes between subject and verb: [*that*] *she built in New York City.*

Compound-Complex Sentences

A compound-complex sentence is made up of two or more independent clauses and at least one dependent clause. To learn more about creating compound, complex, and compound-complex sentences, see Chapter 26.

Classifying Sentences by Discourse Function 30n

Sentences can also be classified by discourse function—that is, by considering one's purpose in writing or speaking.

Sentences Classified by Discourse Function

Declarative sentences give information:
Charlie found a worm in his apple.

Interrogative sentences ask questions:
Did he eat it?

Rhetorical questions, rather than being literal requests for information, are intended to engage or focus the reader's attention:
What is freedom? Freedom is a right and a privilege . . .

Imperative sentences issue commands; the subject, *you,* is usually implied:
Spit out that worm!

Exclamatory sentences express strong feelings or judgments; they usually begin with *what* or *how,* and they may be fragments rather than complete sentences:
How could he have done it! How disgusting!

31 SENTENCE FRAGMENTS

A sentence is a grammatically and rhetorically complete unit that contains a subject and a verb. Whether a sentence is two words long or two hundred, the core of each sentence is someone or something (the subject) carrying out some action or expressing a state of being (the verb).

Sentence fragments are grammatically and rhetorically incomplete constructions, masquerading as sentences. Fragments lack a verb, a subject, or both. Or they have a subject and verb, but these appear in a subordinate clause that renders the clause dependent on another sentence for meaning. Even though fragments may be punctuated as if they were complete sentences, they are not.

Eliminate fragments by attaching them to complete sentences or by changing the fragment itself to a complete sentence.

Example 1 Revising fragments

Fragment—no verb:

The hidden diamond.

Revised by adding a verb:

S V

The hidden diamond gleamed.

Fragment—no subject or verb:

After hiding the diamond.

Revised by adding an independent clause:

S V

After hiding the diamond, Jane ran away.

Fragment—subordinate clause:

Because the diamond had been hidden for centuries. No one expected to find it that day.

Revised by attaching to a nearby independent clause:

S V

Because the diamond had been hidden for centuries, no one expected to find it that day.

Fragment—two parts of a compound predicate separated:

Jane hid the diamond. And ran away.

Revised by joining them:

S V V

Jane hid the diamond and ran away.

Example 2 Revising a fragment caused by an infinitive

Fragment The students to run in the halls.

Revised by adding a verb before the infinitive:

The students ^want to run in the halls.

Revised by making the infinitive phrase into the subject:

~~The students to~~ ^To run in the halls ^is fun.

Example 3 Revising a fragment caused by an *-ing* verb

Fragment The python swallowing its prey whole.

Revised by adding a helping verb before the *-ing* verb:

The python ^was swallowing its prey whole.

Revised by changing the *-ing* verb to a simple past tense verb:

The python ^swallowed ~~swallowing~~ its prey whole.

Revised by making the verbal phrase into the subject and adding information:

The python swallowing its prey whole ^is an amazing example of nature's adaptability.

Example 4 Revising a fragment caused by a past participle

Fragment The blankets washed.

Revised by adding a helping verb to make it a complete verb:

The blankets ^were washed.

Revised by making the past participle into a simple past tense verb:

^She washed the ~~The~~ blankets ~~washed~~.

Revised by changing the past participle into an adjective and then adding a new verb:

The ^washed blankets ^smelled clean ~~washed~~.

A complete sentence requires a subject and a complete verb. Some verb forms (called *verbals*) cannot function independently as verbs. Watch for these verb forms when revising to eliminate sentence fragments.

- **Infinitives**, such as *to run, to laugh,* or *to hit,* cannot act as verbs.
- **-ing verbs,** such as *running, laughing,* and *swallowing,* cannot act as verbs unless paired with helping (auxiliary) verbs like *am* and *have.*
- **Past participles,** such as *washed* and *hidden,* can act as verbs only if paired with helping (auxiliary) verbs like *am* and *have.*

While past participles are usually created by adding *-ed* to the base verb, some common verbs form the past participle irregularly—for example, *bitten, slept,* and *blown.* (For a list of irregular verbs, see section 34a.)

31b Missing Subjects

All sentences require a subject: a noun or pronoun that defines who or what the sentence is about.

Compound predicates are a common source of sentence fragments. A compound predicate consists of two verbs that belong to one subject: *She ate and drank*. The second verb sometimes gets cut adrift in its own sentence. To revise, either put the verbs back together again in one sentence or repeat the subject for one of the verbs.

Example 5 Revising a fragment caused by a compound predicate

The second word group is a fragment:

He broke her heart. And took her money.

Revised by putting the verbs back together in the same sentence:

He broke her heart, ~~And~~ *and* took her money.

Revised by repeating the subject:

He broke her heart. ~~And~~ *He* took her money.

31c Subject-Verb Pairs That Can't Act as Sentences: Dependent Clauses

A dependent (or *subordinate*) clause begins with a subordinating word. Common subordinating words include subordinate conjunctions (listed on page 418) and relative pronouns (listed on page 424).

A dependent clause on its own is a sentence fragment. To revise a dependent-clause fragment, either attach it to an independent clause, eliminate the subordinating words and make it into a complete sentence, or recast it entirely.

Example 6 Revising a fragment caused by a subordinating word

The first word group is a fragment:

Because deforestation and pesticide use threaten the monarch butterfly. Its future is uncertain.

Revised by attaching the dependent clause to the complete sentence with a comma:

Because deforestation and pesticide use threaten the monarch butterfly, ~~Its~~ *its* future is uncertain.

Revised by eliminating the subordinating word *because:*

~~Because deforestation~~ *Deforestation* and pesticide use threaten the monarch butterfly. Its future is uncertain.

Revised by recasting the sentence:

Deforestation and pesticide use have made the monarch butterfly's future uncertain.

Example 7 Revising phrase fragments

Prepositional phrase fragment:

After walking down the street a little ways. She turned into the library.

Complete sentence:

After walking down the street a little ways, ~~She~~ she turned into the library.

Infinitive phrase fragment:

To walk down the street unhindered. It was a luxury she could scarcely imagine.

Complete sentence:

To walk down the street unhindered ~~It was~~ was a luxury she could scarcely imagine.

Participial phrase fragment:

People walking down the street. No one noticed the fire.

Complete sentence:

People walking down the street ~~No one noticed~~ didn't notice the fire.

Gerund phrase fragment:

What's my favorite pastime? Walking down the street and looking in the shop windows.

Complete sentence:

Walking down the street and looking in the shop windows is my favorite pastime.

The second word group is an appositive fragment:

To add a reddish cast to gold, medieval artists used dragon's blood. A darkish red paint made from palm tree resin.

Complete sentence:

To add a reddish cast to gold, medieval artists used dragon's blood, ~~A~~ a darkish red paint made from palm tree resin.

The second word group is a list fragment:

For my birthday I want four kinds of cake. Lemon, German chocolate, coconut with custard filling, and Boston cream pie.

Complete sentence:

For my birthday I want four kinds of cake: ~~Lemon~~ lemon, German chocolate, coconut with custard filling, and Boston cream pie.

A phrase is a group of words that lacks a subject-verb combination and that functions as a single part of speech. A phrase can be (and usually is) *part* of a sentence, but a phrase cannot *be* a sentence. An orphaned phrase is a sentence fragment.

For a review of phrases, see section 30k.

In general, it is best to avoid sentence fragments in formal and college writing. However, it's important to be aware that good writers do use fragments, sparingly.

Example 8 A deliberate fragment in fiction

[The peacock] shook itself, and the sound was like a deck of cards being shuffled in the other room. It moved forward a step. Then another step.

From Raymond Carver, "Feathers," in *Where I'm Calling From: New and Selected Stories* (New York: Vintage Contemporaries, 1988), 351.

32 RUN-ON SENTENCES AND COMMA SPLICES

Run-on sentences and comma splices are the result of problems in punctuating compound sentences. To find run-on sentences and comma splices, look for subject-verb pairs. When you find a sentence that includes more than one subject-verb pair, make sure that it is punctuated correctly.

A run-on sentence occurs when two independent clauses are joined without punctuation and without an appropriate conjunction. Like a grammatical train wreck, the first sentence *runs* right *on* into the second.

A comma splice occurs when two independent clauses are joined by a comma only; like a "splice" in a length of rope, this joining creates a weak spot.

Correct run-ons or comma splices using one of the strategies in sections 32a–32e.

Example 1 A compound sentence: two independent clauses

Each independent clause has a subject-verb pair and can stand alone as a complete sentence.

S V S V
Rover is our dog; / she loves to chase cats.

S V CONJ S V
Carlise sells software to businesses, / and / her friend Marcos installs it.

Example 2 Run-on sentence

Two sentences with no punctuation separating them:
No one would be more surprised than Mary Shelley at the idea most immediately evoked by the name *Frankenstein* she intended her novel as a meditation on creativity, not creepy monsters.

Example 3 Comma splice

Two sentences with only a comma between them:
No one would be more surprised than Mary Shelley at the idea most immediately evoked by the name *Frankenstein,* she intended her novel as a meditation on creativity, not creepy monsters.

Revising by Separating into Two Distinct Sentences 32a

Example 4 Forming two distinct sentences

Comma splice:

Ready-mixed paints weren't commercially available until the 1880s, before that time, artists had to mix their own colors.

Revised to become two distinct sentences by using a period and a capital letter:

Ready-mixed paints weren't commercially available until the 1880s. Before that time, artists had to mix their own colors.

To emphasize the distinction between the ideas in the independent clauses, make each of the independent clauses into a separate sentence. (See section 30i for more about sentences.)

Revising by Using a Comma and Then a Coordinating Conjunction 32b

Example 5 Using a comma and coordinating conjunction

Run-on sentence:

Galileo recanted his confirmation that the Earth revolves around the Sun in return the Pope commuted his sentence to house arrest.

Revised with comma and coordinating conjunction:

Galileo recanted his confirmation that the Earth revolves around the Sun, and in return the Pope commuted his sentence to house arrest.

Comma splice:

Galileo knew that the Earth revolved around the Sun, he recanted to escape Giordano Bruno's fate of being burned at the stake.

Revised with comma and coordinating conjunction:

Galileo knew that the Earth revolved around the Sun, yet he recanted to escape Giordano Bruno's fate of being burned at the stake.

Using a comma and a coordinating conjunction to join the independent clauses is a good strategy when

- you want to give the ideas in each of the clauses equal weight
- you want to emphasize the parallel relationship between the two clauses
- the logic communicated by a particular conjunction (for example, addition, contrast, choice, or causality) is the most effective way to emphasize this relationship

The coordinating conjunctions are *and, but, yet, or, nor, for,* and *so.* To make a compound sentence, use the appropriate conjunction plus a comma. (See section 26a for more about using coordinating conjunctions to form compound sentences.)

32c Revising by Using a Semicolon or Colon

Use a semicolon when you want to emphasize the continuity of thought between two closely related independent clauses.

Use a colon between independent clauses when the first sentence formally introduces the second. Colons are also used to introduce lists of related items (see Chapter 40 for more about punctuating sentences with colons).

Example 6 Using a semicolon

Run-on sentence:

Although Galileo never married, he had three children, Virginia, Livia, and Vincenzio he placed his two daughters in a convent and had his son legitimized and brought to live with him.

Revised with semicolon:

Although Galileo never married, he had three children, Virginia, Livia, and Vincenzio; he placed his two daughters in a convent and had his son legitimized and brought to live with him.

Example 7 Using a colon

Comma splice:

Phyllis Wheatley's life story is an astounding one, born in West Africa, kidnapped, and sold into slavery, she distinguished herself as an internationally celebrated poet and as the first African American to be published.

Revised with colon:

Phyllis Wheatley's life story is an astounding one: born in West Africa, kidnapped, and sold into slavery, she distinguished herself as an internationally celebrated poet and as the first African American to be published.

32d Punctuation with Transitional Expressions

When two independent clauses are joined by a transitional expression (see section 2d), a semicolon or a period—not a comma—separates them. Common transitional expressions include *however, indeed, likewise, notwithstanding, for instance, subsequently, all in all,* and *consequently.* After the transitional expression, use a comma to separate it from the rest of the second independent clause.

Example 8 Punctuation with transitional expressions

Run-on sentence:

Time has reversed the fame and status of Mary and Percy Bysshe Shelley indeed today *Frankenstein* is a household word, while such works as "Epipsychidion" have faded into relative obscurity.

Revised with semicolon between the clauses and a comma after the transition:

Time has reversed the fame and status of Mary and Percy Bysshe Shelley; indeed, today *Frankenstein* is a household word, while such works as "Epipsychidion" have faded into relative obscurity.

Example 9 Revising by recasting the sentence

Comma splice:

Reality TV draws on our collective desire for instant status and celebrity, it puts ordinary people in the spotlight.

Revised by changing the second clause into a phrase, thus de-emphasizing it:

Reality TV draws on our collective desire for instant status and celebrity by putting ordinary people in the spotlight.

Revised by making the second clause subordinate and changing the order of the two clauses:

Because it puts ordinary people in the spotlight, reality TV draws on our collective desire for instant status and celebrity.

Revised by removing *it* and using a compound predicate (i.e., having two verbs but one subject):

Reality TV draws on our collective desire for instant status and celebrity and puts ordinary people in the spotlight.

Depending on your purpose, sometimes the best strategy is to rewrite the sentence by making one clause subordinate, by making one clause a phrase, or by recasting in some other manner.

PRONOUNS 33

Example 1 Pronouns

A pronoun replaces or refers back to an antecedent:

ANTECEDENT PRONOUN PRONOUN

Bruno was thrilled when **he** received **his** acceptance letter.

A pronoun may come before its antecedent:

PRONOUN ANTECEDENT

Unlike **their** grandmothers' grandmothers, today's *women* can vote.

In general, a **pronoun** replaces a noun in a sentence. The noun the pronoun replaces is called the **antecedent.**

Most antecedents come before their pronouns (indeed, as an adjective *antecedent* means "going before"), but occasionally an antecedent can follow its pronoun.

The personal pronouns *I, we, you, he, she, it,* and *they* and the relative and interrogative pronoun *who* change their form, or **case,** to indicate how they function in a sentence.

Subjective Case

I	we
you	you
he/she/it	they
who	

Objective Case

me	us
you	you
him/her/it	them
whom	

Possessive Case

my/mine	our/ours
your/yours	your/yours
his/her/hers/its	their/theirs
whose	

The possessive pronouns *its* and *whose* are commonly confused with contractions. If the pronoun in question modifies a noun, then *its* or *whose* should not have an apostrophe: *its color; Whose cell is this?* If you can substitute *it is* for *it's* or *who is* for *who's,* then *it's* and *who's* should have an apostrophe: *It's raining; Who's calling?*

Pronouns in the subjective case

Subject	**He** flew through the air.
Subject complement	The leading trapeze artist is **he**.
Appositive that renames a subject	The leading trapeze artists—Beaufort, Beaumont, and **he**—will be touring in the upcoming production.

Pronouns in the objective case

Direct object	She couldn't avoid **him**.
Indirect object	She gave **him** back his love notes.
Object of the preposition	She had seen enough *of* **him**.
Appositive that renames an object	Beaufort mistimed his somersault and dropped the *other two artists,* Beaumont and **him**, as the crowd gasped in horror.
Subject of an infinitive	She wanted **him** *to go* away.
Object of an infinitive	She wanted *to snub* **him** in front of everyone.

Pronouns in the possessive case

His tardiness was **our** undoing.
We made good use of **their** survival skills on **our** camping trip.

Possessives used as adjectives and nouns

Some possessive pronouns have one form when used as an adjective and another when used as a noun.

my/mine	It's **my** *fault.*
	The fault is **mine.**
your/yours	**Your** *cat* just ate my canary.
	That bad animal is **yours.**
her/hers	**Her** *persistence* paid off.
	The victory was **hers.**
their/theirs	**Their** *house* was painted.
	Theirs is the unpainted house.

Pronoun Case in Compounds 33b

Pronouns that function as part of a compound word group are a common source of confusion. But fortunately, the rule is clear: a pronoun that is part of a compound word group takes the same case as it would take if it were standing alone.

A pronoun that is part of a compound subject takes the subjective case.

A pronoun that is part of a compound object takes the objective case.

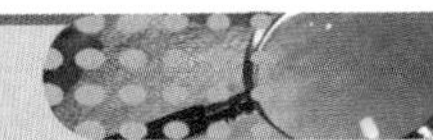

How Can You Identify...

Which Case to Use in a Compound?

1. Identify the compound:

   Josef and [*I* or *me*] danced.

   He visited my friends and [*I* or *me*] every Friday afternoon.

2. Make a sentence using only the pronoun part of the compound.

   [*I* or *me*] danced.

   He visited [*I* or *me*] every Friday afternoon.

3. Select the case that's right when the pronoun stands alone.

   I danced. He visited me.

4. Put the compound back together.

   Josef and I danced.

   He visited my friends and me every Friday afternoon.

Example 3 Pronoun case in compounds

Subjective case in a compound subject:

Scotty and **he** worked on the warp drive engines.

Objective case in a compound object:

Eyes narrowed, Spock considered Captain Kirk and **her**.

Pronoun Case after *than* or *as* 33c

Which pronoun form should you use in a comparison after *than* or *as*? It depends on what you want to compare. Often such constructions are elliptical—that is, words are understood but left out. So to supply the correct case of the pronoun, you must decide what meaning you want to communicate.

Example 4 Pronoun case when subjects or objects are being compared

Paulo likes Zack de la Rocha better than [*I* or *me*].

Revision if the comparison is between subjects *Paulo* and *I:*

Paulo likes Zack de la Rocha better than **I** [like Zack de la Rocha].

Revision if the comparison is between objects *Zack de la Rocha* and *me:*

Paulo likes **Zack de la Rocha** better than [Paulo likes] **me**.

33d Pronoun Case and Appositives

Pronouns can function as part of an appositive that renames a noun or as the noun that an appositive renames.

When you use a pronoun in an appositive, first identify whether the word it renames is a subject or an object. If the appositive renames a subject, use the subjective case. If the appositive renames an object, use the objective case.

When *we* or *us* is followed by a noun appositive—*we students, us students*—the correct case is determined by the pronoun's function within the sentence. If the pronoun functions as a subject, use the subjective case; if the pronoun functions as an object, use the objective case.

To decide which pronoun to use, remove the noun that follows. Select the pronoun that best fits the sentence without the noun.

Example 5 Pronouns in appositives

Appositive that renames a subject:

SUBJECT — SUBJECTIVE CASE

The class officers, Tamika and **he,** get together at least once a week.

Appositive that renames an object:

DIRECT OBJECT — OBJECTIVE CASE

The class officers chose my two friends, Raoul and **him,** for the faculty relations committee.

Example 6 Pronouns followed by a noun appositive

SUBJECT

We students asked for changes in the cafeteria food.

OBJECT

The cafeteria food's lack of variety prompted **us** students to ask for changes.

33e Pronoun Case with Infinitives

The base or root form of a verb is called the infinitive: *to steal, to laugh, to run*. Infinitives can have both subjects and objects. The subject of the infinitive is the noun that does the infinitive's action. The subject of the infinitive usually comes after the main verb and directly before the infinitive.

The object of the infinitive receives the action of the infinitive.

Pronouns take the objective case when used as either the subject or the object of an infinitive.

Example 7 Pronouns as the subject or object of an infinitive

SUBJECT OF THE INFINITIVE

Zelda wanted **Scott** *to leave* that den of iniquity.

OBJECT OF THE INFINITIVE

Scott wanted *to leave* **Zelda.**

SUBJECT OF THE INFINITIVE

The reporters kept asking **her** *to comment* on the president's odd statement.

OBJECT OF THE INFINITIVE

But the secretary of state refused *to contradict* **him.**

The words *who* and *whoever* are subjective; *whom* and *whomever* are objective

Subject	**Who** is he?
Subject complement	Madonna is **who** she is—no excuses.
Direct object	They brought **whomever** they wanted.
Object of the preposition	[A]nd therefore never send to know for **whom** the bell tolls; it tolls for thee. From John Donne, "XVII Meditation."

Example 8 *Who* as subject of clause serving as direct object

CLAUSE AS OBJECT
SUBJECT VERB

I know **who did it.**

Example 9 *Who* as subject of clause serving as object of preposition

CLAUSE AS OBJECT OF THE PREPOSITION
SUBJECT VERB

[You] Give the apples to **whoever** wants them most.

How Can You Identify...

Whether the Pronoun Is a Subject or an Object in Its Clause?

Sample sentence:
She was the star [*who* or *whom*] all the fans adored.

1. Identify the clause that the pronoun is in.
   [*who* or *whom*] all the fans adored
2. Change the order, if needed, to subject-verb-object.
   All the fans adored [*who* or *whom*].
3. Substitute in the appropriate personal pronoun (*he* or *him, she* or *her*).
   All the fans adored *her* (or *him*). [In other words, an object]
4. If the pronoun is an objective form, reassemble the sentence using *whom;* if the pronoun is a subjective form, use *who.*
   She was the star *whom* all the fans adored.

The pronoun *who* functions both as an interrogative pronoun and as a relative pronoun. Like the personal pronouns (*I, we, you, he, she, it, they*), *who* has both a subjective and an objective form.

Use the subjective case *who* for subjects and the objective case *whom* for objects.

Keep in mind that (as with all other pronouns) **case is determined by the pronoun's function within its clause,** *not* by that clause's function within the sentence.

In Example 8, although the clause *who did it* is the object of the verb *know,* the pronoun *who* functions as the subject of the clause *who did it.* So the correct form is *who.*

In Example 9, although the clause *whoever wants them most* is the object of the preposition *to,* the pronoun *whoever* functions as the subject of the clause *whoever wants them most.* So the correct form is *whoever.*

33g Pronoun Case with Gerunds and Participles

A gerund is a noun made from the *-ing* form of a verb. Pronouns used to modify a gerund or a gerund phrase should be in the possessive.

A pronoun used with a present participle (a modifier made from the *-ing* form of a verb) does *not* take the possessive. If it is used as a subject, it takes the subjective case, and if it is used as an object, the objective case.

Use the possessive case for pronouns that modify gerunds . . .

POSSESSIVE PRONOUN — GERUND

His comings and goings mystified everyone.

The pronoun *his* acts as an adjective modifying the noun phrase *comings and goings*.

. . . but not for pronouns with present participles

PRESENT PARTICIPLE — SUBJECTIVE PRONOUN

Coming and going, **he** mystified everyone.

OBJECTIVE PRONOUN — PRESENT PARTICIPLE

We watched **him** coming and going.

33h Understanding Pronoun Agreement

A pronoun must match its antecedent in gender, number, and person. (The antecedent is the noun that the pronoun replaces or refers back to.) This matching is called **pronoun agreement**.

The personal pronouns *he, she,* and *it* must take the same gender as their antecedents.

A singular antecedent requires a singular pronoun; a plural antecedent requires a plural pronoun.

A first-person antecedent requires a first-person pronoun; a second-person antecedent requires a second-person pronoun; a third-person antecedent requires a third-person pronoun.

First-person pronouns: *I* and *we*
Second-person pronoun: *you*
Third-person pronouns: *he, she, it,* and *they*

Example 10 Agreement in gender

Feminine	Rosa washed **her** hair.
Masculine	Raymond shaved off **his** beard.
Neutral	The cat washed **its** paws.

Example 11 Agreement in number

Singular	Billy shouted as **he** raced onto the playground.
Plural	The children shouted as **they** raced onto the playground.

Example 12 Agreement in person

First person	We like washing **our** dishes the old-fashioned way.
Second person	How do you prefer to wash **your** dishes?
Third person	They would rather wash **their** dishes in a dishwasher.

Agreement with Antecedents Joined by *and, or,* or *nor* 33i

Use a plural pronoun with antecedents joined by *and*

As young boys, Wilbur and Orville Wright first became interested in flight when **their** father brought home a toy helicopter.

Unless the antecedents are preceded by *each* or *every*

Each cup and saucer was carefully dried and put back in **its** place.

Match the closer antecedent if antecedents are joined by *or* or *nor*

Neither Lucy nor Felipa brought **her** toothbrush to the campout.

Awkward	Neither the hens nor the rooster liked **its** new pen.
Revised	Neither the rooster nor the hens like **their** new pen.
Awkward	Neither Mario nor Melissa got back to **her** work after the earthquake.
Revised	After the earthquake, both Mario and Melissa left work for the day.

Compound antecedents joined by *and* require a plural pronoun.

An exception is when the antecedents are preceded by *each* or *every.*

With compound antecedents joined by *or* or *nor,* the pronoun matches the antecedent nearest to it.

If one antecedent is singular and another plural, put the plural antecedent nearest to the pronoun. Doing so will make the sentence sound more natural. If the antecedents differ in gender or person, it's often best to recast the sentence.

Agreement with Collective Nouns 33j

Example 13 Emphasizing the individuals or the group with the pronoun used with a collective noun

The flock resumed **its** journey north. [Singular; emphasis is on the flock as a unit.]

The lightning flashed, and the herd stampeded in all directions, **their** eyes wide with fright. [Plural; emphasis is on the individual animals within the herd.]

The committee brought **its** proposal to the larger assembly. [Singular; emphasis is on the committee as a unit.]

The committee found that **their** competing loyalties and ideologies kept **them** from working together effectively. [Plural; emphasis is on the individuals on the committee.]

A collective noun refers to a group.

Collective Nouns

audience	family
band	flock
bunch	group
choir	herd
class	jury
club	litter
committee	number
couple	pride
corps	public
crowd	team
faculty	

When used as an antecedent, a collective noun can take either a singular or a plural pronoun. When the emphasis is on the group as a unit, use a singular pronoun. When it is on the individuals within the group, use a plural pronoun.

33k Agreement with Indefinite Pronouns and Generic Nouns

Indefinite pronouns (such as *anybody, each, none, someone*) refer to nonspecific persons or things. (For a list of indefinite pronouns, see section 30b.) Most indefinite pronouns are singular in formal written English.

However, the indefinite pronouns *both, few, many,* and *several* are always plural.

The indefinite pronouns *all, any, more, most,* and *some* can be singular or plural, depending on their meaning in a particular sentence.

Generic nouns (such as *dancer, lawyer, refugee, student*) refer to types or categories of persons or things and behave much the same way as indefinite pronouns. A singular generic noun requires a singular pronoun. A plural generic noun requires a plural pronoun.

Treating singular generic nouns as plural is a common mistake.

See section 29a on revising pronouns to eliminate gender bias.

Most indefinite pronouns are singular

Everyone has **his** or **her** favorite food.

Each of the ballerinas bowed after **she** completed **her** solo.

Each sumo wrestler bowed to **his** competitor at the start of the match.

But *both, few, many,* and *several* are always plural

Both strategies have **their** own merits.

Few thought that the president's proposal served **their** best interest.

Many thought **they** could have solved the problem better.

Several felt that **their** ideas had been overlooked.

And some vary depending on meaning

Most of the runway was impassable, **its** surface covered in several inches of ice.

When the flights were canceled, most of the passengers found **themselves** stranded in the airport overnight.

Nouns used generically can be singular or plural, and pronouns match them

Singular	A person needs a goal if **he or she** wants to accomplish something meaningful.
Plural	People need goals if **they** want to accomplish something meaningful.
Incorrect	A person depends on **their** wits.
Revised	A person depends on **his or her** wits.
	People depend on **their** wits.

33l Using Inclusive Language with Pronouns

Three strategies for avoiding sexist use of the pronoun *he* are to use *he or she,* recast the sentence as plural, and recast the sentence entirely to omit the pronoun.

For more on this topic, including detailed strategies for recasting sentences, see section 29a.

Example 14 Revising for inclusiveness

Original	A zookeeper observes several precautions when **he** feeds the lions.
Revised	Zookeepers observe several precautions when **they** feed the lions.

Understanding Pronoun Reference 33m

Example 15 Problems of pronoun reference

Two possible antecedents:

Charlotte brought Anne to the seashore to recuperate, but there **she** died. [Who died? Anne or Charlotte?]

Distant antecedent:

The different theories drew many questions from people **that** had evidence to support them. [Who or what had evidence to support them? The theories or the people?]

Vague antecedent:

In this week's episode, the doctors tell Shereen her illness is terminal, **which** upsets her family. [Is the family upset because Shereen's illness is terminal or because the doctors tell her?]

The reader must be able to easily identify which person, place, or thing a pronoun refers to.

Unclear pronoun reference usually results from there being

- more than one possible antecedent,
- an antecedent that is too far away, or
- an antecedent that is implied, vague, or missing.

Revise unclear pronoun reference by repeating the noun or recasting the sentence.

Reference to More Than One Possible Antecedent 33n

Each pronoun can refer to only a single antecedent

Confusing — Frank (?) told Morris (?) that **he** didn't care. [Who didn't care? Frank or Morris?]

Revised — Frank told Morris that Morris didn't care.
Frank told Morris, "You don't care."

Make sure that the pronoun clearly refers to one antecedent and only one.

Reference to a Distant Antecedent 33o

An antecedent must not be too far away

Confusing — Charlotte Bronte wrote *Jane Eyre* while still surrounded by her close-knit family circle. Then less than a year after *Jane Eyre* was published, Branwell died. Emily followed soon after. And within six months, Anne too was dead. **She** was alone.

Revised — Charlotte Bronte wrote *Jane Eyre* while still surrounded by her close-knit family circle. Then less than a year after *Jane Eyre* was published, Branwell died. Emily followed soon after. And within six months, Anne too was dead. **Charlotte** was alone.

If antecedent and pronoun are too far apart, the reference is likely to be unclear.

33o

To avoid confusion, it's generally necessary to place the pronouns *who, which,* and *that* directly after the word to which they refer.

The words *who, which,* and *that* need to follow directly after the antecedent

Confusing — Warren fed the cat some milk **that** followed him home. [The milk followed Warren home?]

Revised — Warren fed some milk to the cat **that** followed him home.

Confusing — The athlete won the pole vault **who** also won the high jump. [The pole vault won the high jump?]

Revised — The athlete **who** won the pole vault also won the high jump.

33p Antecedent Implied, Vague, or Missing

In many cases, pronoun reference is unclear because the antecedent is implied, vague, or missing.

Do not use possessives as implied antecedents. Technically, the possessive form of a noun cannot serve as an antecedent, unless both pronoun and antecedent are in the possessive case. But of course a noun in the subjective case can function as the antecedent to a possessive pronoun.

Avoid using the pronouns *it, this, that,* and *which* to make broad references to an entire idea, phrase, statement, sentence, or paragraph. To ensure clarity, make sure that each pronoun has a clear and specific antecedent.

Possessives can't be antecedents unless the pronoun is also possessive

ANT ? — PRONOUN

Confusing — Smith's appointment to the federal bench brought **him** to national attention. [*Smith's* cannot function as the antecedent to *him*—you couldn't write *brought Smith's to national attention.*]

Revised — Smith's appointment to the federal bench brought **his** judicial record and **his** personal history to national attention. [Both *Smith's* and *his* are in the possessive case: *brought Smith's judicial record and Smith's personal history.*]

or

Smith came to national attention when **he** was appointed to the federal bench. [Both *Smith* and *he* are in the subjective case: *when Smith was appointed.*]

Example 16 Making broad references specific

Confusing — I told Grover that I had voted for Smith, **which** shocked Sanders to no end. [Is Sanders shocked that you voted for Smith or shocked that you told Grover about it?]

Revised — Sanders was shocked when he learned I'd voted for Smith.

or

Sanders was shocked when he learned I'd been brave enough to tell Grover how I'd voted.

Do not use *it, they,* or *you* as an indefinite pronoun. Only indefinite pronouns—such as *anybody, all, both, each, everybody, nobody, neither, none, somebody, something*—can be used without antecedents. But in informal speech, the pronouns *it, they,* and *you* are commonly left dangling, with no antecedent to be found. This misuse in writing is confusing and ungrammatical; it often makes sentences weak and wordy. The misuse can also reveal a poorly supported argument.

However, in all but the most formal writing, the pronoun *you* can legitimately be used in direct addresses to the reader.

Do not use *it* in multiple ways in one sentence. The pronoun *it* can perform many functions. To avoid confusion, use *it* in only one way in a given sentence.

Example 17 Revising uses of *it, they,* or *you* as indefinite pronouns

Weak — In the news **it** says that more and more bike messengers are now entering the world of bike racing. [Use of the phrase *in the news it says* indicates a weak argument without proper citation. Grammatically, *the news* cannot function as the antecedent to *it* when it is the object of the preposition *in*.]

Revised — A recent *New York Times* article describes how more and more bike messengers are entering the world of bike racing (Corder A5).

Example 18 Addressing the reader as *you*

To make meringues, **you** will need good weather. Dampness defeats them utterly.

Example 19 Revising sentences in which *it* is used in multiple ways

Confusing — **It** was not surprising that when the thunder cracked **it** made us jump right out of our beds last night when **it** rained so heavily.

Revised — The <u>thunder</u> cracked so loudly last night **it** made us jump right out of our beds.

Using *who, which,* and *that* 33q

Use *who* for people and named animals and *which* or *that* for objects, unnamed animals, and abstract concepts. Occasionally, you may need to use *whose* for animals and things to avoid an awkward *of which*.

That is restrictive: it introduces a clause, phrase, or word that tells you something essential to defining the noun it modifies.

Which is nonrestrictive: it introduces a clause, phrase, or word providing information *non*essential to defining the noun it modifies.

Example 20 Using *who, which,* and *that*

In the Bonampak murals, the ruler is the <u>man</u> **who** is wearing jaguar skin sandals.

The <u>helmet</u> **that** the queen is handing to him is made from the head of an actual jaguar.

The <u>dogs</u> **that** I saw performed magnificently.

Foxes, **whose call** is an eerie guttural bark, prey on small mammals.

The <u>book</u> **that I returned** is the one your records still show as missing. [The book that I returned, and no other, is the one still shown as missing.]

This <u>book</u>, **which I just returned,** was outstanding. [The book was outstanding. The fact that I just returned the book is parenthetical and nonessential to its being outstanding.]

34 VERBS

All verbs except *to be* have five basic forms. Some forms can stand alone as the main verb of a sentence, but others need the help of auxiliary verbs. See section 34b for information about auxiliary, or helping, verbs.

The **plain form**, or *base form,* of verbs is used to express actions, occurrences, or states of being in the present tense.

The **-*s* form** is created by adding *s* or *es* to the plain form: *swim / swims, classify / classifies.* Use the *-s* form with subjects that are singular nouns *(child, Margaret);* the pronouns *he, she,* and *it;* and indefinite pronouns such as *anybody.* The *-s* ending on a verb indicates the present tense.

Present participle verbs indicate action happening now. The present participle is formed by adding *-ing* to the plain form: *singing.*

The **past-tense form** indicates actions that happened before now. Normally, you form the past tense by adding a *-d* or an *-ed* to the plain form, but some verbs form the past tense irregularly (▶ section 34a).

The **past participle form** is the same as the past form except in some irregular verbs (▶ section 34a).

The Five Forms of Regular Verbs

The first three forms are called the principal parts.

Plain (base) Form	-*s* Form (used with *he, she,* and *it* in the present tense)	Present Participle (*-ing* form)	Past Tense	Past Participle
walk	walks	walking	walked	walked
hope	hopes	hoping	hoped	hoped
classify	classifies	classifying	classified	classified

Example 1 Verb forms

The plain form can be used alone as a main verb:

I **want** to shop for shoes today.

You always **tell** me you **love** me after your dogs **do** something wrong.

The -s form can be used alone as a main verb:

He always **walks** the same route, and then he **eats** lunch down at the diner.

Delivering the mail **makes** his arm hurt after an hour or so.

The present participle form needs a form of *to be* to be a main verb:

I ***am*** **running** for help.

We ***are*** **hoping** that your leg will heal before our ski vacation starts.

The past-tense form can be used alone as a main verb:

My car **died** on the Los Angeles freeway.

He **wrestled** the big masked man called the Undertaker.

The past participle form needs a form of *to be* or *to have* to be a main verb:

I ***was*** **fascinated** and **repelled** by the Michael Jackson documentary.

We ***have*** **operated** the heavy machinery for a month.

Jillian and DeShawn ***had*** **stopped** by the time we arrived.

The Principal Parts of Common Irregular Verbs

Plain Form	Past Tense	Past Participle
be	was/were	been
beat	beat	beaten
become	became	become
begin	began	begun
bend	bent	bent
bite	bit	bitten
blow	blew	blown
break	broke	broken
bring	brought	brought
build	built	built
burn	burned/burnt	burned/burnt
buy	bought	bought
catch	caught	caught
choose	chose	chosen
come	came	come
cost	cost	cost
cut	cut	cut
do	did	done
draw	drew	drawn
drink	drank	drunk
drive	drove	driven
eat	ate	eaten
fall	fell	fallen
fight	fought	fought
find	found	found
fly	flew	flown
get	got	got (preferred)/gotten (informal)
give	gave	given
go	went	gone
grow	grew	grown
hang	hung/hanged (if a person)	hung/hanged (if a person)
hear	heard	heard
hide	hid	hidden
hit	hit	hit
hurt	hurt	hurt

You can tell the difference between regular and irregular verbs by how they are formed in the past tense and past participle. Almost all verbs are regular, which means that you form the past and past participle by adding *-d* or *-ed: laugh/laughed, arrive/arrived*. With irregular verbs, however, there is no general pattern to show you how to make the past and past participle forms. When you aren't sure whether a verb is regular or irregular, consult a dictionary. If the verb is irregular, the different tense constructions will be listed, often with a brief sample sentence to clarify the usage.

The Irregular Verb *to be*

***Forms of* to be**

Plain (base) form: *be*

Be ready at noon.

Past-tense form: *was* (singular); *were* (plural)

Was Jose unhappy yesterday?
Were Grant and Devon home?

Past participle: *been*

They have **been** friends since they were little kids.

-s form: *is*

That lifeguard **is** not paying attention.

Present participle: *being*

She is **being** a good sport.

The Irregular Verbs *to have* and *to do*

Forms of the verbs *to have* and *to do* can be used as main verbs or, as discussed in section 34b, as auxiliary verbs.

Forms of to have

Plain (base) form: *have*
Past-tense form: *had*
Past participle: *had*
-s form: *has*
Present participle: *having*

Forms of to do

Plain (base) form: *do*
Past-tense form: *did*
Past participle: *done*
-s form: *does*
Present participle: *doing*

Plain Form	Past Tense	Past Participle
keep	kept	kept
know	knew	known
lay	laid	lain
lead	led	led
leave	left	left
let	let	let
lie	lay	lain
light	lit (preferred)/lighted	lit (preferred)/lighted
lose	lost	lost
make	made	made
pay	paid	paid
put	put	put
ride	rode	ridden
ring	rang	rung
rise	rose	risen
run	ran	run
say	said	said
see	saw	seen
send	sent	sent
shut	shut	shut
sing	sang/sung	sung
sink	sank/sunk	sunk
sit	sat	sat
speak	spoke	spoken
spend	spent	spent
steal	stole	stolen
swear	swore	sworn
swim	swam	swum
take	took	taken
tell	told	told
think	thought	thought
throw	threw	thrown
wake	woke/waked	woken/waked
wear	wore	worn
win	won	won
write	wrote	written

Example 2 Auxiliary verbs

	AUX.	MAIN (PRESENT PARTICIPLE)
Tense	She **was**	**running** for president.

	AUX.	MAIN (PAST PARTICIPLE)
Voice	He **was**	**influenced** by his colleagues.

	AUX.	AUX.	MAIN (PLAIN FORM)		AUX.	MAIN (IMPLIED)
Mood	She **might**	**have**	**run**	for president if her friend	**hadn't**	[run].

Example 3 Progressive tenses: A form of *be* + present participle

Present progressive	Lidia ***is*** **writing** her essay on the East African city-states.
Past progressive	She ***was*** **smiling** at the camera.
Future progressive	I ***will be*** **enjoying** my lunch for the next hour.

Example 4 Modal + *be*

	MODAL	THE WORD *BE*
You	must	**be** waiting at the bus stop in the morning.
She	had better	**be** going home now.

Auxiliary verbs are often referred to as helping verbs. Auxiliary verbs help main verbs indicate shades of meaning, tense, voice, or mood. The main verb carries the basic meaning of the verb and can be in the plain form, the present participle form (the *-ing* form), or the past participle form (the *-ed* form for regular verbs). Together, the main verb and any auxiliary verbs are called the **verb phrase.**

Forms of *be, have,* and *do* are the most common helping verbs. They can be used as auxiliaries to other verbs, but in other cases they are used as main verbs. See pages 447 and 448 for a list of the forms of these verbs.

Progressive Tenses

When you use a form of the auxiliary verb *to be* and the present participle *(-ing)* form of a main verb, you create a progressive tense, which shows that an action is, was, or will be progressing over a period of time.

If you use the word *be* as an auxiliary verb, one of the modal auxiliaries needs to come before it.

The modal auxiliaries communicate various shades of meaning, only a few of which are shown in the examples to the right.

Multilingual writers: See section 49e.

If you use the word *been* as an auxiliary verb, a form of the auxiliary verb *to have* (*has, had,* or *have*) is needed before it.

Any time you use a form of *to be* as a helping verb, you must use an additional auxiliary verb.

Passive Voice

When you use a form of the verb *to be* with the past participle of a verb, you create the passive voice, which shows that the subject of your sentence is receiving the action of the sentence. Only transitive verbs (verbs that take an object) can be used in the passive voice (▶ section 34f). See Example 6.

Uses of *to do* as an Auxiliary Verb

The auxiliary verb *to do (do, does,* and *did*) functions in three ways to aid the main verb. (See Example 7.)

Modal Auxiliary Verb	**Example**
be able to*	Soon you **will be able to run** ten miles.
can, could	My dog **can find** his way home.
had better	She **had better wear** sandals while walking across the hot beach sand.
had to, has to, have to*	We **have to swim** quickly to catch the wave.
may, might, must	**May** I **get** you a drink? No, I **must leave** now.
shall, should	I **should pick up** my brother at school.
be supposed to*	You **are supposed to drink** water with that aspirin. [Note the *-d:* suppose<u>d</u>.]
used to	He **used to take** his baby to the park every Monday. [Note the *-d:* use<u>d</u>.]
will, would	You **will meet** our manager soon.

*These modals change form to indicate singular and plural subjects. For example, use *I (you/we/they)* ***have to*** *ask permission,* but *He (she)* ***has to*** *find out why. It* ***has to*** *be that way.*

Example 5 Form of *have* + *been*

	FORM OF *HAVE*	THE WORD *BEEN*
Ali	had	**been** experiencing problems with his computer.
Farhiya	has	**been** tired from all her studying.

Example 6 Passive voice: A form of *be* + past participle

Jackie **was taken** to the hospital. [Jackie is the recipient of the *taking* action.]

She **was given** an examination. [Someone gave her an exam.]

Example 7 Functions of *do* as an auxiliary verb

To ask a question	How **do** you **change** the car's oil?
To create emphasis	That dog **did bite** my neighbor!
With *not,* to negate the main verb	He **did** not **ask** for your help.

Multilingual writers: In the first sentence, notice how the subject, *you,* is located after the auxiliary verb *do* and before the main verb *change*. See section 50d for more information on forming questions.

Transitive verbs perform an action on an object

VERB OBJECT

I **uploaded** the files via FTP.

Intransitive verbs do not take direct objects—the action they express ends or is modified somehow

VERB

I **wonder** about that advice. [No direct object]

VERB

He **spoke** passionately about freedom. [*Spoke* is modified by the adverb *passionately.*]

Some transitive verbs can function intransitively in some contexts, especially when paired with an adverb or prepositional phrase

Transitive, with direct object	She **studies** calculus.
Intransitive, with adverb	She **studies** daily.
Intransitive, with prepositional phrase	She **studies** in the afternoon.

Here is the standard written usage for each pair

lay To place, as in to put down. Does take an object.

He **laid** the newspaper on the table.

lie To recline. Does not take an object.

The dog **lies** by the door whenever Sergio says "Go **lie** down."

raise To lift up. Does take an object.

She **raised** the standards for everyone in the class.

rise To go higher. Does not take an object.

Her test scores **rose** all semester.

set To place (synonym of *lay*) or to configure. Does take an object.

Please **set** your bookbags in the hallway.
Please **set** the clock back an hour.

sit To sit down, to be seated. Does not take an object.

Will you **sit** at the table and eat?

Transitive verbs take direct objects; intransitive verbs do not (◀ section 30j). Many verbs can be used both ways, and context determines whether they are working with an object or not.

The Pairs *lie* and *lay, sit* and *set, rise* and *raise*

The most common mistakes made with transitive and intransitive verbs occur with these pairs of irregular verbs: *lay/lie, raise/rise,* and *set/sit.*

34d Verb Tenses

Tense is the form of a verb that communicates time. For example, time can be expressed in the past, present, and future tenses: *talked, talk, will talk*. These forms are the simple tenses. The perfect tenses usually indicate time completed before another time or action: *The farmer* ***had plowed*** *the field before she planted*. The progressive tenses indicate continuing action: *The council members* ***were considering*** *the zoning plan*.

Verb Tenses of a Regular Verb (in Active Voice)

Name of Tense	Time of Action	Example
PAST TENSE		
Simple past	Action happened before now.	She *ran*.
Past progressive	Action continued during a time period in the past.	She *was running*.
Past perfect	Action was completed in the past before another past action.	She *had run*.
Past perfect progressive	Continuing action was completed before another past action.	She *had been running*.
PRESENT TENSE		
Simple present	Action happens now or habitually.	She *runs*.
Present progressive	Action continues during a time period in the present.	She *is running*.
Present perfect	Action happened in the past and may be continuing in the present.	She *has run*.
Present perfect progressive	Action happened in the past and is still continuing.	She *has been running*.
FUTURE TENSE		
Simple future	Action may happen in the future.	She *will run*.
Future progressive	Action will be happening during a period of time in the future.	She *will be running*.
Future perfect	Action will occur and end at some point in the future.	She *will have run*.
Future perfect progressive	Future action will have been completed before another future action.	She *will have been running*.

Past Tenses

The Simple Past Tense

Use the simple past tense to express an action or state of being that began and ended in the past.

Past tense: plain form + *-d* or *-ed*

A spider **crawled** across my fork just a minute ago.

The plane **landed** and **burst** into flames. [*Burst* is irregular; see section 34a.]

The Past Progressive Tense

Use the past progressive tense to express actions that occurred in the past and were ongoing. The actions normally started at one point and finished later.

Past progressive: *was* or *were* + *-ing* form of main verb

Those men **were running** along the beach this morning.

One of them **was carrying** a backpack full of rocks.

The Past Perfect Tense

Use the past perfect tense to express actions or states of being that occurred in the past and were finished before another past event.

Past perfect: *had* + *-ed* form of main verb

I arrived at school ten minutes late for class, and my instructor **had** already **marked** me absent.

Since the dog **had eaten** the entire turkey, we went out and ate duck at a Chinese restaurant. [*Eaten* is irregular; see section 34a.]

The Past Perfect Progressive Tense

Use the past perfect progressive tense to express ongoing actions that were completed before another past action.

Past perfect progressive: *had been* + *-ing* form of main verb

Those kids **had been running** around the cafeteria for twenty minutes before I stopped them.

Clark **had been meaning** to fix his CD player until someone stole it.

Present Tenses

The Simple Present Tense

The simple present tense describes actions or states of being that happen now. It is also used to describe

- regular or recurring (habitual) action
- with an adverb, actions in the near future
- general truths
- observations and judgments about conditions

The present tense is also used when referring to a literary text, a painting, or the like (section 5d).

Present tense: plain form or *-s* form

Action happening now	The boat's sail **whips** in the wind.
With adverb, for the near future	The club **opens** at nine o'clock tonight.
Habitual action	Every morning he **takes** his medicine.
General truth	Water **freezes** at 32 degrees Fahrenheit.
	This temperature **is** its freezing point.
Observations	The five-year-old girl **picks** up a red balloon and **waves** it over her head.
Judgments	The waves **appear** to be about sixteen feet high.
Reference to a text	Bilbo Baggins **sets off** from his cozy hobbit hole on a great quest.

The Present Progressive Tense
Much like the simple present tense, the present progressive expresses the ongoing nature of an action or state of being. You can also use the present progressive with an adverb or adverb phrase to indicate action in a future situation.

Present progressive: *am, is,* or *are* + *-ing* form of main verb

I **am running** a fever.

Holly **is thinking** about it right now.

They **are drawing** the winning ticket in the lottery drawing at noon.

The Present Perfect Tense
Use the present perfect tense to express action that

- started in the past and continues in the present
- has just stopped when you are describing it

Present perfect: *have* or *has* + past participle (with *-d* or *-ed*)

I **have received** those CDs from home that I want you to hear.

Jacques **has forgotten** what he is supposed to take to the picnic.

The Present Perfect Progressive Tense
The present perfect progressive tense expresses an action that has happened in the past and is affecting the present. The present perfect progressive emphasizes the ongoing nature of the action or state of being.

Present perfect progressive: *have* or *has* + *been* + *-ing* form

Those neighbors **have been stealing** our mail for years.

Carmella **has been feeling** depressed since she found out she wouldn't get the promotion.

Future Tenses

The Simple Future Tense
Use the simple future tense to express actions or states of being that will occur in the future.

Future tense: *will* + plain form of main verb

She **will discover** your secret if you aren't careful.

Will you **drive** me to the movies tonight?

The Future Progressive Tense
Use the future progressive tense to express actions or states of being that will continue for a period of time in the future.

Future progressive: *will be* + *-ing* form of main verb

Trent Reznor **will be performing** with Saul Williams tonight from 8:00 to 11:00.

Will they **be discussing** the proposed teen center designs at the meeting?

Future perfect: *will have* + past participle (with *-d* or *-ed*)
Chris Rock **will have made** a couple of formulaic movies before the studios allow him to make something really funny.

Future perfect progressive: *will have been* + *-ing* form of main verb
If he keeps this up until tomorrow, Kevin **will have been ignoring** me for a full month.

Example 8 Verb tense shifts

Appropriate shifts:

Several African artists **have donated** [PRESENT PERFECT] paintings to benefit the American Anti-Slavery Group. The organization **is hosting** [PRESENT PROGRESSIVE] an art auction on eBay. Proceeds **will go** [FUTURE] to their anti-slavery efforts in Africa.

Confusing shifts:

Andrej Mucic **is going to bicycle** [FUTURE] 7,000 miles across Siberia to raise $10,000 to support the American Anti-Slavery Group. Mucic **takes off** [PRESENT] 100 days of work from Home Depot, where he **worked.** [PAST] He **spends** [PRESENT] his whole summer biking.

Revised for clarity:

Andrej Mucic **is going to bicycle** [FUTURE] 7,000 miles across Siberia to raise $10,000 to support the American Anti-Slavery Group. Mucic **will take off** [FUTURE] 100 days of work from Home Depot, where he **works.** [PRESENT] He **will spend** [FUTURE] his whole summer biking.

The Future Perfect Tense
Use the future perfect tense to express actions or states of being that will end before another action occurs.

The Future Perfect Progressive Tense
Use the future perfect progressive tense to express an ongoing action or state of being that will be finished at some point in the future.

Avoiding Unnecessary Shifts in Verb Tense

You will often vary verb tenses in your writing to indicate different times. But when you shift verb tenses for no good reason, readers become confused. Your first sentence sets up an expectation about the time of the action; the time frame becomes known information. Each verb shift after that is new information that readers have to assimilate.

Understanding the Sequence of Verb Tenses

Every clause has a verb. Verbs in nearby clauses that relate actions occurring at about the same time should be expressed in the same tense. If clauses within the same sentence or in nearby sentences include actions happening at different times, then verb tenses, used precisely, can help readers sort out what happened when.

When one past event occurs before another past event, use the past perfect for the one that happened first.

When one future event happens before another future event, use the future perfect for the one that will happen first and the present tense (or the present perfect) for the one that will happen after it.

If you use the future tense in the independent clause, then use the simple present tense in the dependent clause to indicate an event happening at about the same time or the past perfect tense to indicate an earlier action.

Infinitives (such as *to walk, to look*) are used after verbs to indicate a sequence of time. Use the present infinitive to show an action happening at the same time as or later than the action expressed by the main verb.

Use the perfect infinitive if the action is earlier than the action of the main verb. The perfect infini-

Example 9 Using verb tenses to convey time sequence

Both verbs in present tense:
Joel **takes** avalanche gear when he **skis.** [Simple present tense for both verbs indicates habitual actions.]

Past perfect tense with past tense:
The last time he **went** telemarking, he **used** his probe to locate another skier who **had been buried** in a sudden snow slide. [The general time frame is the past. The past perfect tense in *had been buried* indicates that the skier was buried before being located. This phrase is also in the passive voice.]

Future perfect tense with present tense:
Joel **will have bought** a new DSP beacon by the time he **goes** into the backcountry again. [First he will buy the beacon; later, he will go.]

Future tense with simple present tense and present perfect tense:
On the anniversary of Martin Luther King's assassination, I **will walk** to Washington because I **want** to demonstrate that civil rights still **need** attention. I **will speak** to any groups I **have managed** to find.

Example 10 Infinitives

Present infinitive:
She <u>wants</u> **to perform** well tonight.

Perfect infinitive:
Rene <u>would like</u> **to have noticed** the rare bird first.

tive is composed of *to have* + the past participle.

The present participle is used to express action that happens at the same time as the action of the main verb.

The past participle is used to express action that happens earlier than the action of the main verb.

Example 11 Participles

Present participle:

Taking photos in the Arctic, Cherry Alexander had shot a closeup of a penguin family that won her the 1995 BBC Wildlife Photographer of the Year award.

Past participle:

Adopted by a Siberian woman, the orphaned baby reindeer lived a long and pampered life.

Mood 34e

Verb mood conveys a writer's attitude toward the subject.

The indicative mood is used to state facts, opinions, and questions.

Example 12 Indicative mood

Vietnamese writer Duong Thu Huong **was imprisoned** for nine months in 1991.

Use the imperative mood to request something or to make a command.

Example 13 Imperative mood

Please **enjoy** yourselves.

Use the subjunctive mood to indicate conditions that are contrary to fact, desires, suggestions, and recommendations.

Use the subjunctive in subordinate clauses beginning with *if, as though,* or *as if* when the clause expresses speculation or a condition contrary to fact.

Use the subjunctive to make requests, demands, or suggestions in dependent clauses starting with *that*. Verbs that introduce such clauses include *request, invite, suggest, demand, insist,* and *require*.

Example 14 Subjunctive mood

Condition contrary to fact	The car seat seemed as if it **were** safer than a regular seat belt for children aged two to eight, but the FARS data indicate that this is not true.
Speculation	If the results **were** to become well known, children over two might not have to use car seats anymore.
Request	I ask that we **be** given the option of buying booster seats.
Demand	Parents are demanding that the agency **prove** the expensive car seats are needed.
Suggestion	In 2001, the Insurance Institute for Highway Safety was suggesting that the National Highway Traffic Safety Administration **reconsider** its call for booster seats.

34e Forming the Subjunctive Mood

To form the **present subjunctive,** always use the plain form of the verb: *carry, be, do.*

To form the **past subjunctive,** use the simple past tense, except for the verb *to be,* which in the past subjunctive is always *were* (even for singular subjects).

Example 15 Present subjunctive

It is crucial that the bear **be** quarantined when it reenters the country.

Example 16 Past subjunctive

Stephanie Allen wished she **had** a way to get families to eat dinner together again. She and Tina Kuna thought that if it **were** possible, they would like to be the ones to make it happen.

34f Active and Passive Voice

When a sentence is in the active voice, the subject performs the action. In passive voice, the subject is acted upon, and the performer of the action (called the *agent*) either is stated in a prepositional phrase or is missing from the sentence.

Active voice emphasizes the agent of the action, whereas passive voice emphasizes the action. Active voice sentences are written in the normal word order of English: subject-verb-object. They are easier to read and take fewer words than passive voice sentences. Sentences in the active voice are stronger and more direct than sentences in the passive. Unless you have a specific reason to use the passive, write in the active voice.

Passive verbs: a form of *to be* + past participle of transitive verb (with *-d* or *-ed*)

Other helping verbs may also be used, as in these examples:

was conducted
was being conducted
have been conducted
will be conducted

Example 17 Active vs. passive voice

	AGENT IS SUBJECT · ACTIVE VERB · DIRECT OBJECT
Active voice	Sara **hurled** the iron pot at the intruder.
	OBJECT IS NOW SUBJECT · PASSIVE VERB · AGENT IN PREP. PHRASE
Passive voice	The iron pot **was hurled** at the intruder by Sara.
Agent omitted	The iron pot **was hurled** at the intruder.

Example 18 Revising from passive to active voice

	PASSIVE VERB / AGENT IN PREP. PHRASE
Passive voice	Creative works **are protected** by copyright laws.

	NEW SUBJECT / ACTIVE VERB / NEW OBJECT
Active voice	Copyright laws **protect** creative works.

Uses of the Active and Passive Voices

- The active voice is strong and direct:

  The door **slammed** shut, and we **avoided** each other's eyes.
  Gil Scott Heron **recorded** the first rap album.

- The passive can be used to avoid responsibility by removing the agent:

  Active voice — I **stole** your chocolate chip cookies.
  Passive voice — Your chocolate chip cookies **were stolen.**

- The passive is used when the agents are less important than what they accomplished:

  Active voice — Legislative assistants **wrote** the civil union laws.
  Passive voice — The civil union laws **were written** by legislative assistants.
  or
  The civil union laws **were written.**

- The passive is used when giving "how to" directions:

  When the screw **has been tightened,** the guitar string should be in tune.

Social Science Writing Sample

Sets of data from surveys and interviews of American, Canadian, Japanese, Mayan, North African, Navajo, and Indonesian women **were compared** (Beyene, 1986; Flint & Samil, 1990; Lock, 1994; Walfish, Antonovksy, & Maoz, 1984; A. L. Wright, 1983).

Revising Passive Voice to Active Voice

To convert a sentence from passive to active, make the agent into the subject of the new sentence, change the verb form to active voice, and use the subject of the original sentence as the object of the new one.

Passive voice is useful when the person who performed an action is less important than the action. For example, observations made in the social sciences and reports of experiments in the sciences often use the passive more frequently than writing in the humanities, which tends to emphasize the individual agent.

Actions are emphasized; agents are listed in the in-text citation.

35 SUBJECT-VERB AGREEMENT

In every sentence, the subject and its verb must agree. **Subject-verb agreement** means that the noun and verb forms match in person and in number. A first-, second-, or third-person noun requires a first-, second-, or third-person verb, respectively. A singular noun requires a singular verb; a plural noun requires a plural verb.

In general, the first- and second-person singular forms of the verb and all plural forms of the verb are the plain form—for example, *run*. Variation appears in the third-person singular (as in *runs*)—the verb form that matches the pronouns *he, she,* and *it* and other third-person subjects, such as *the boy, the dog,* and *the car.* For regular verbs, the third-person singular is formed by adding *-s* (or *-es*) to the base verb form.

The verbs *to be, to have,* and *to do* are irregular. Unlike other verbs, the verb *to be* also varies in person and number in the past tense.

Subject-verb agreement remains one of the thorniest problems in English usage. Problems in subject-verb agreement arise when the subject is hard to identify, when the subject appears after the verb, when modifiers or prepositional phrases separate the subject from the verb, or when the subject is hard to identify as singular or plural.

Example 1 Third-person singular subjects and verbs

She **loves** you, yeah, yeah, yeah.

From John Lennon and Paul McCartney, "She Loves You."

My cat **catches** many mice.

The courthouse **stands** on the village green.

Three Irregular Verbs

The verb *to be*

First-person singular	I **am**	First-person plural	we **are**
Second-person singular	you **are**	Second-person plural	you **are**
Third-person singular	he/she/it **is**	Third-person plural	they **are**

The verb *to have*

First-person singular	I **have**	First-person plural	we **have**
Second-person singular	you **have**	Second-person plural	you **have**
Third-person singular	he/she/it **has**	Third-person plural	they **have**

The verb *to do*

First-person singular	I **do**	First-person plural	we **do**
Second-person singular	you **do**	Second-person plural	you **do**
Third-person singular	he/she/it **does**	Third-person plural	they **do**

Past tense forms of the verb *to be*

First-person singular	I **was**	First-person plural	we **were**
Second-person singular	you **were**	Second-person plural	you **were**
Third-person singular	he/she/it **was**	Third-person plural	they **were**

Example 2 Subjects joined by *and*

Plural subject takes plural verb:

The bride and groom **cut** the cake together.

Singular subject takes singular verb:

Rock and roll **is** here to stay.

From David White, "Rock 'n' Roll Is Here to Stay."

Each or *every* + subject takes singular verb:

Every hedge and tree **is** pruned carefully.

Each knife, fork, and spoon **is** cleaned until it shines.

Plural subject + *each* or *every* takes plural verb:

Knives, forks, and spoons each **have** their own uses.

Example 3 Expressions that do not affect the number of the subject

The teacher, as well as her students, **enjoys** the field trip.

The proposed development, together with the added noise, pollution, and traffic it would bring, **dismays** many residents.

Example 4 Revising to a compound subject using *and* + plural verb

Original Lead, together with air pollution, pesticides, environmental tobacco smoke, and drinking water contamination, **is** one of the top five environmental threats to children's health.

Revision Lead, air pollution, pesticides, environmental tobacco smoke, and drinking water contamination **are** the top five environmental threats to children's health.

Compound subjects can be either singular or plural, depending on the conjunction or conjunctions that join them. Some phrases appear to create compound subjects but do not.

Subjects Joined by *and*

Compound subjects joined by *and* are plural and take a plural verb.

The exception is two nouns joined by *and* that refer to a single person, place, or thing. Such a compound takes a singular verb.

Compound subjects joined by *and* take a singular verb if they are preceded by *each* or *every.*

However, if *each* or *every* follows a plural subject, the subject takes a plural verb.

Unlike compound subjects linked by conjunctions such as *and,* words or phrases introduced by *accompanied by* and similar expressions do not affect the number of the subject.

alongside	including
along with	no less than
as well as	plus
besides	together with
in addition to	with

When using such phrases, consider carefully whether a simple *and* would reflect your meaning more closely.

35a

Subjects Joined by *or*

Compound subjects joined by *or* or *nor* can be singular or plural. If both nouns are singular, the sentence takes a singular verb.

If one noun is plural and one singular, the verb agrees with the noun closest to it.

Likewise, if the nouns are in different persons, the verb agrees with the noun closest to it.

Example 5 Subjects joined by *or*

Two singular subjects take singular verb:
The judge or her clerk **writes** the decision.

When one noun is singular and the other is plural, verb agrees with closer noun:
Neither the Pony Express nor the wagon trains **cross** Buzzard Pass during blizzards.

Neither the juvenile male gorillas nor the ranking adult male gorilla **likes** the new zookeeper.

When one noun is second person and the other is third, verb agrees with closer noun:
Either you or Ravi **is** going to drive the van.
Either Ravi or you **are** going to drive the van.

35b Words Intervening between Subject and Verb

Prepositional phrases and other kinds of word groups that intervene between subject and verb can mislead you into making an incorrect verb choice. But subject-verb agreement is not altered by these intervening words or word phrases. The basic rule remains unchanged: identify the subject and choose the verb form that agrees in person and in number. In Example 6, subjects are underlined, words that intervene between subject and verb are in italics, and verbs are in boldface.

Example 6 Ignoring intervening words

The list *of requirements* **is** daunting to many prospective majors.

Trophy hunting *of elephants for their tusks* still **claims** too many animals.

The child *of alcoholic parents* sometimes **overachieves** as a way of winning self-confidence.

The trees, *acknowledging the power of the protector,* **bow** in unison as she passes.

You may be interested to learn that multimedia books—*whether or not you like the feel of a printed book*—**are** here to stay.

Each *of the teams, including the Padres,* **plays** 162 games.

Linking Verbs Agree with Subjects, Not Subject Complements 35c

Example 7 Agreement of linking verbs

Singular subject takes singular linking verb:

SUBJECT / LINKING VERB / SUBJECT COMPLEMENT

Her main research interest **is** ants.

Plural subject takes plural verb:

SUBJECT / LINKING VERB / SUBJECT COMPLEMENT

Ants **are** her main research interest.

In sentences in the subject–linking verb–subject complement pattern, the verb agrees with the subject, not the subject complement (◀ section 30j, pattern 5).

Common Linking Verbs

to appear	to remain
to be	to seem
to become	to smell
to feel	to sound
to get	to stay
to grow	to taste
to look	to turn
to prove	

Agreement When Subject Follows Verb 35d

Example 8 Agreement when sentences are inverted

For effect:

V S

At the end of the hall **looms** the vampire.

At the end of the hall **loom** the vampires.

In questions:

AUX V S V

Does the train **stop** here?

Do the trains **stop** here?

In expletive constructions:

V S

There **are** few who know.

There **is** one who knows.

There **is** food to be cooked and beds to be made. [In this expletive construction, the first item in the compound subject is a singular noun.]

Although the subject comes before the verb in most English sentences, occasionally the subject comes after the verb. In such cases, the general rule still applies: the verb agrees with the subject in person and number. Inverted word order is used for emphasis or effect, in questions, and in expletive constructions (that is, constructions that begin with *there is, there are,* or *it is*).

In expletive constructions that have a compound subject, you may use a singular verb if the first element in the subject is singular.

Indefinite pronouns (*all, everybody, few, many, none, several,* and so on) pose problems for many writers, because some are singular, others are plural, and still others vary depending on context.

Most indefinite pronouns are singular and always take a singular verb.

Singular Indefinite Pronouns

anybody	everyone	nothing
anyone	everything	one
anything	much	somebody
each	neither	someone
either	nobody	something
everybody	no one	

Example 9 Singular indefinite pronoun

Each **has** to take the exam.

A few indefinite pronouns are always plural and thus take a plural verb.

Plural Indefinite Pronouns

both many few several

Example 10 Plural indefinite pronouns

Both **are** wrong.
Many **run** for office, but few **get** enough votes to win.
Several of the lamps **use** 40-watt bulbs.

A few indefinite pronouns can be either singular or plural, depending on the context.

Indefinite Pronouns That May Take Singular or Plural Verbs, Depending on Context

all	more	some	any
most	half	none	

Example 11 Indefinite pronouns whose number depends on context

Half of the children **were** overweight.
Half a loaf **is** better than none.
None of their new songs **are** any good.
None of the music **is** any good.
All **are** welcome.
All **is** well.

Examples of Collective Nouns

audience	corps	herd
band	couple	jury
bunch	crowd	litter
choir	faculty	number
class	family	pride
club	flock	public
committee	group	team

Example 12 Agreement with collective nouns

If the faculty **decides** to change the student handbook, students will be appointed to the revisions committee.

The faculty **are** divided on this issue.

Based on the DNA evidence, the jury **finds** the accused innocent.

The jury **are** sequestered in various hotels throughout the city.

Example 13 Agreement with *a number* and *the number*

A number of pedestrians **are** jaywalking.
The number of pedestrians who jaywalk **is** shocking.

Example 14 Agreement with *media* and *data*

Emphasizes the multiple types of media—print news, television and radio news, magazines:
The media **are** accountable to the public good.
Emphasizes that there are pieces of information:
The data **show** a warming trend.
Emphasizes information as one entity:
Very little data **was** provided.

Collective nouns, such as *audience,* name a group of things or individuals and can be either singular or plural, depending on the context. A sentence that emphasizes the group's actions as a unit takes a singular noun. A sentence that emphasizes the actions of the individual members within the group takes a plural noun.

The collective noun *number* can be either singular or plural. Used in the phrase *the number,* it is treated as singular; used in the phrase *a number,* it is treated as plural.

The words *data* and *media* have caused grammatical controversy since they first entered English as the plurals of the Latin words *datum* and *medium,* respectively. Until recently, both were always treated as plurals in formal and academic writing, although they were used widely as singular in both spoken and written communication. Current usage guides like *The New York Times Manual of Style and Usage* call for treating *data* as a singular noun when it is a synonym for *information* and a collective plural noun when it refers to "a collection of facts and figures." *Media* is still considered plural, but its widespread use in spoken language as singular suggests that its usage will change fairly soon as well.

35g Measurement Words as Subjects

Most measurement words used as subjects can be either singular or plural, depending on the context.

For indefinite pronouns that describe amounts (such as *each, both, half, all*), see section 35e. For phrases of the type *a number of* and *the number of,* see section 35f. For phrases of the type *one of* and *only one of,* see section 35j.

Example 15 Agreement with measurement words

After the sold-out concert was abruptly canceled, fully three-fourths of all ticket holders **were** demanding their money back.

Three-fourths of the fund **is** missing, and yet no one has been held accountable.

One hundred pounds **is** a lot to lose.

One hundred pounds of meat **were** consumed at the company barbeque.

35h Singular Words Ending in *-s* as Subjects

Words that end in *-s* but are singular in meaning, such as *physics, economics, politics, news, measles,* and *United States,* take a singular verb.

A few of these words can be construed as either singular or plural, depending on the context.

Example 16 Agreement with singular words ending in *-s*

Physics **is** required of all science majors.
The news **is** promising.
Statistics **is** a challenging field.

but

The infant mortality statistics **reveal** a region in crisis.

35i Titles, Names, Words Used as Words, and Gerunds as Subjects

Titles of works, names of businesses and institutions, and words used as words are all singular and take singular verbs.

Example 17 Singular verbs with titles, names, and words used as words

"The Snows of Kilimanjaro" **is** one of Hemingway's best known short stories.
Doctors without Borders **provides** volunteer medical assistance around the world.
The word *data* **comes** from Latin as the plural form of *datum.*

Gerund phrases (the *-ing* form of the verb plus any accompanying complements or modifiers) function as singular subjects.

Example 18 Singular verbs with gerunds

Making homemade bread **is** a challenging and rewarding activity.
Training your new puppy **requires** patience and persistence.

Example 19 Agreement with *who*

ANTECEDENT RELATIVE CLAUSE

The student who **is** giving tonight's address comes from Africa.

ANTECEDENT RELATIVE CLAUSE

The students who **attend** this school come from many countries.

ANTECEDENT RELATIVE CLAUSE

She is one of those legislators who **have** integrity. [In this sentence, the antecedent of *who* is *legislators,* so *who* takes a plural verb.]

ANTECEDENT RELATIVE CLAUSE

She is the only one of those legislators who **has** integrity. [In this sentence, the antecedent of *who* is *one,* so *who* takes a singular verb.]

Example 20 Singular verb with subject clause starting with *what*

What the committee recommended **is** at odds with what the students want.

In dependent clauses beginning with the relative pronoun *who, whom, whose, which,* or *that,* the relative pronoun requires the same verb form as its antecedent. A singular antecedent causes the relative pronoun to require a singular verb. A plural antecedent causes the relative pronoun to require a plural verb.

Constructions such as *one of the things that* or *one of the people who* require careful scrutiny to decide which noun is the antecedent of the relative pronoun.

In relative clauses introduced by the words *only one of,* the antecedent is almost always the word *one.*

In general, subject clauses beginning with *what* are singular.

36 ADJECTIVES, ADVERBS, AND MODIFYING PHRASES

Modifiers bring sentences to life by providing concrete detail about things and actions. All modifiers function as either adjectives or adverbs.

- Adjectives modify nouns and pronouns. In the phrase *a* ***lucky*** *man,* the adjective *lucky* modifies the noun *man.* In the sentence *He is* ***lucky,*** the adjective *lucky* is the subject complement to the pronoun *he.*
- Adverbs modify verbs, adjectives, other adverbs, and whole clauses. For example, the adverb *fast* modifies the verb *ran* in *He ran* ***fast,*** the adverb *very* modifies the adjective *fast* in *He was a* ***very*** *fast runner,* and the adverbial phrase *as the wind* modifies the adverb *fast* in *He ran fast* ***as the wind.***

Adjectives answer these questions

Which one?	The *black* cat runs faster than the white cat.
What kind of?	I like *tortoise shell* cats best.
How many?	She called, and *several* cats meowed in answer.

Adverbs answer these questions

How?	The cat crept up *slowly.*
When?	Cats hunt *at night.*
Where?	Our cats sleep *on the beds, the sofas, the floor, the tables—everywhere.*
Why?	Cats sometimes hunt mice *because they enjoy hunting for its own sake.*
How often?	My cats ask for food *continually.*
In what manner?	The cat batted the mouse *playfully.*
Under what conditions?	Cats will purr *if you scratch them behind the ears.*
With what result?	The cat ate *until it was so full it could barely walk.*
To what degree?	The cat stalked the mouse *very* stealthily.

36a After Linking Verbs

Use adjectives, not adverbs, as subject complements after linking verbs. Subject complements follow linking verbs and add to, rename, or otherwise complement the meaning of the subject. (See pattern 5 on page 421.)

Some Linking Verbs		
appear	look	sound
be	prove	stay
become	remain	taste
feel	seem	turn
grow	smell	

Adjectives, not adverbs, act as subject complements

SUBJECT SUBJECT COMPLEMENT

The audience remained **silent** until one person broke out in wild applause.
Lata is **happy** that she is home again.
He looks **older** now.
The detective's hunch proved to be **true.**

Should you use an adjective or an adverb?

To describe a noun, use an adjective. To modify a verb, use an adverb.

Adjective	Suki felt **awful** after eating ten chocolate bars.
Adverb	Roger felt **cautiously** for the edge of the cliff. [The adjective *awful* describes *Suki;* the adverb *cautiously* modifies the verb *felt.*]

After Direct Objects 36b

Should you use an adjective or an adverb after direct objects?

Use an adjective to modify the direct object itself; use an adverb to modify the verb.

Adjective Brennan called the hawk **magnificent.**
Adverb Brennan called the hawk **repeatedly.**

Adjective Nora considered the project **completed.**
Adverb Nora considered the project **carefully.**

A direct object can be followed by either an adjective or an adverb. Which you choose depends on the meaning you intend. To modify the direct object itself, use an adjective, but to modify the verb, use an adverb.

Commonly Misused Adjectives and Adverbs 36c

Should you use *bad* or *badly*?

Adjective I felt **bad** when the pitcher sprained his ankle.
Adjective Lefty pitched a **bad** game after he sprained his ankle.
Adverb The pitcher played **badly** after he sprained his ankle.

Should you use *good* or *well*?

Adjective I feel **good.**
Adverb Though Katya's hands were numb with cold, she could feel just **well** enough to slip the key into the lock.

Adjective This year the Yankees have an exceptionally **good** pitcher.
Adverb This year the pitcher played exceptionally **well.**

Adjective **Good** education for our children is our top priority.
Adverb Educating children **well** is our top priority.

As an adjective, *well* means "healthy"

Adjective They are **well.**
Adjective After a year of battling a series of mysterious diseases, Fernando felt **well** at last.
Adjective He seems **well,** but doctors fear a relapse.

Should you use *real* or *really*?

Adjective Gregor drinks coffee only with **real** milk.
Adverb Gregor **really** detests nondairy creamer.

Although standard usage clearly dictates that only adjectives can modify nouns and pronouns and that only adverbs can modify verbs, adjectives, and adverbs, each is commonly misused for the other, especially in everyday speech.

Among the most commonly misused adjective-adverb pairs are *bad/badly, good/well,* and *real/really.*

Use the adjective *bad* as a subject complement or to modify nouns or pronouns. Use the adverb *badly* to modify verbs, adjectives, or other adverbs.

Use the adjective *good* as a subject complement or to modify nouns or pronouns. Use the adverb *well* to modify verbs, adjectives, or other adverbs.

Use *well* as an adjective when you mean *healthy.*

Use the adjective *real* as a subject complement or to modify nouns or pronouns. Use the adverb *really* to modify verbs, adjectives, or other adverbs.

36d Understanding Comparatives and Superlatives

Most adjectives and adverbs have three forms—positive, comparative, and superlative—used to compare degrees or amounts of a particular quality.

In general, use the comparative ending *-er* and the superlative ending *-est* with adjectives of one to two syllables and with one-syllable adverbs.

Use *more/most* and *less/least* with longer adjectives and with most adverbs.

The modifiers *good, bad, far, many, much, little, well,* and *badly* are irregular in the comparative and superlative forms.

Some adjectives can form the comparative and superlative either with *-er* and *-est* or with *more/less* and *most/least*. These include *able, angry, clever, common, cruel, friendly, gentle, handsome, happy, narrow, pleasant, polite, quiet, simple, tender,* and *yellow.* But don't use both methods together—for instance, don't write *more commoner.*

Because English is a language as notable for its exceptions as its rules, always check a dictionary if in doubt about the correct form of a comparative or superlative.

Positive	**Comparative**	**Superlative**
Adjectives		
fast	faster	fastest
brilliant	more brilliant	most brilliant
awkward	less awkward	least awkward
Adverbs		
steadily	more steadily	most steadily
carefully	less carefully	least carefully

Positive	**Comparative**	**Superlative**
Adjectives		
old	older	oldest
pretty	prettier	prettiest
Adverbs		
fast	faster	fastest
slow	slower	slowest

Positive	**Comparative**	**Superlative**
Adjectives		
terrible	more terrible	most terrible
palatable	less palatable	least palatable
Adverbs		
easily	more easily	most easily
accurately	less accurately	least accurately

Positive	**Comparative**	**Superlative**
Adjectives		
good	better	best
bad	worse	worst
far	farther/further	farthest/furthest
many	more	most
much	more	most
little (quantity)	less	least
Adverbs		
badly	worse	worst
far	farther/further	farthest/furthest
well	better	best

In formal writing, use the comparative for comparing two things or categories of things; use the superlative for comparing three or more things or for comparisons that imply that all items in a given category are being compared.

A comparative can be preceded by the article *a, an,* or *the,* but use *the* before a superlative.

Use the comparative for comparing two items, the superlative for more than two

She is the **older** of the two sisters.
She is the **oldest** child in her family.

An **older** dog is harder to train than a **younger** one.
The bristlecone pine is Earth's **oldest** living organism.

Use *a, an,* or *the* with comparatives, *the* with superlatives

A **younger** bristlecone can be about 1,500 years old; an **older** bristlecone can be upwards of 4,000 years old. The **oldest** bristlecone, known as Methuselah, is dated at 4,767 years.

Do Not Use Double Comparatives or Superlatives 36e

Do not combine the *-er* or *-est* form with the *more/less* or *most/least* form in a single comparison. Such double comparatives and superlatives are ungrammatical.

Ungrammatical comparisons: Don't use *more* and *-er* (or *most* and *-est*) forms together

Faulty The pistachio is the more better flavor.
Revised The pistachio is the better flavor.

Faulty This must be the most hottest day of the year.
Revised This must be the hottest day of the year.

Using Absolute Adjectives 36f

Some adjectives cannot logically be compared. A *fatal* blow is just that, *fatal,* and can never be *more fatal* or *less fatal, the most fatal* or *the least fatal.* Other such **absolute adjectives** include *eternal, impossible,* and *unique.* Controversy exists over some usages, as in the United States Constitution's "more perfect union," but in formal writing it is best to avoid using absolute adjectives in comparative or superlative forms.

Illogical comparisons: Don't use absolutes in the comparative or superlative

absolute	fatal	possible	unanimous
adequate	final	priceless	unavoidable
chief	ideal	principal	uniform
complete	impossible	round	universal
dead	incessant	simultaneous	unique
entire	inevitable	stationary	utter
equal	infinite	straight	whole
eternal	main	sufficient	
excellent	minor	supreme	
false	perfect	total	

36g Do Not Use Double Negatives

While it's okay for Mick Jagger to sing "I **can't** get **no** satisfaction," such double negatives are considered ungrammatical in standard written English.

Examples of Negative Modifiers	
no	never
none	neither
not	barely
nothing	hardly
nowhere	scarcely
nobody	the contraction
no one	*-n't (not)*

In other languages, the double negative is used for emphasis; in contemporary English, a double negative is logically construed to give a positive meaning. The only admissible double negative construction is *neither . . . nor.*

Ungrammatical *no*'s: Use only a single negative modifier

Faulty We **can't** find **no** publisher for these magnificent poems.
Revised We **can't** find **a** publisher for these magnificent poems.

Faulty The citizens of this county will **never** vote for **no** new taxes.
Revised The citizens of this county will **never** vote for new taxes.

Faulty They **can't** give **no** reasons for their decision.
Revised They **can't** give **any** reasons for their decision.

Only *neither . . . nor* is acceptable

Faulty I **didn't** say yes **nor** no to their suggestion.
Revised I said **neither** yes **nor** no to their suggestion.
I **didn't** say yes **or** no to their suggestion.

36h Understanding the Placement of Modifiers

Modifiers should be placed near the word or words they modify. Adjectives almost always come directly before the word they modify. The exceptions are subject complements and adjective clauses introduced by relative pronouns. Adjectives functioning as subject complements come after the linking verb. (Yoda, from *Star Wars,* speaks distinctively in part because he places his adjectives functioning as subject complements *before* the linking verb, as in "Sad he is, today.")

Where do adjectives go?

Before nouns:

I like the **blue** dress, not the **pink** one.

After linking verbs as subject complements:

He is **sad** today.

Bibi considers herself **lucky.**

Adjective clauses usually follow the word they modify

The pianist **who is now playing** is known for her technique.

The house **that I grew up in** has been demolished.

Where do adverbs go?

Before or after the verbs they modify:

The car **quickly** sped down the road.

The car sped **quickly** down the road.

At the beginning or end of a sentence:

Quickly, the car sped down the road.

The car sped down the road **quickly.**

But ***not*** between a verb and its direct object:

Faulty	The snail crossed **slowly** the path.
Revised	The snail **slowly** crossed the path.
	The snail crossed the path **slowly.**
	Slowly, the snail crossed the path.

Adverbial clauses can go before or after the word they modify

When the music stopped, the children scrambled for the chairs.

The children scrambled for the chairs **when the music stopped.**

Conjunctive adverbs can be moved around

However, it is true that whales are not fish.

It is true, **however**, that whales are not fish.

It is true that whales are not fish, **however**.

Adverbs are considerably more flexible in their placement than adjectives. Although they usually go directly before or after the word they modify, adverbs can also go at the beginning or end of sentences.

Like single-word adverbs, adverbial clauses can go before or after the word they modify.

And like adverbs that modify verbs, adjectives, or other adverbs, conjunctive adverbs can often go several places in a given sentence.

Placing Modifiers Near the Words They Modify 36i

Confusing	The duchess pointed out the many pictures of her ancestors who had performed great and noble deeds **in the gallery.** [What had they been doing in the gallery?]
Clear	**In the gallery,** the duchess pointed out the many pictures of her ancestors who had performed great and noble deeds.
Confusing	Nala returned to the home in which she had experienced such poverty **in a private jet.**
Clear	**Traveling in her private jet,** Nala returned to the home in which she had experienced such poverty.
Confusing	**Roaring from a tremendous height,** Muir saw Yosemite Falls.
Clear	Muir looked at Yosemite Falls, **roaring above him from a tremendous height**.

Adjectives or adverbs placed too far away from the words they modify account for a fair number of unintentional gaffes. (A *gaffe* is a clumsy error.)

36j Revising Squinting Modifiers

Sometimes a modifier is positioned so that it appears to modify two different words or phrases. Such misplaced modifiers are called **squinting modifiers.** Reposition the adverb so that it clearly modifies one word or phrase only.

Example 1 Revising squinting modifiers

Does the following sentence mean that you sometimes fed the cat or that the cat sometimes asked to be let in?

Squinting The little stray cat we fed sometimes asked to be let in.

Notice the difference in the following revisions:

Revised The little stray cat we **sometimes** fed asked to be let in.
The little stray cat we fed asked to be let in **sometimes.**

36k Revising Dangling Modifiers

Modifiers are said to dangle when the word they are intended to modify is missing altogether. Dangling modifiers modify the wrong word, often with rather surrealistic results.

Among the constructions most likely to cause dangling modifiers are participial phrases, infinitive phrases, prepositions followed by gerund phrases, and elliptical clauses.

Example 2 Revising dangling modifiers

Dangling As a little girl, my father liked to tell me stories about mermaids.

Literally, the sentence means that when your father was a young girl he told you stories about mermaids. Not too likely. The intended subject *I* is missing. To revise, supply the correct subject and place the modifier and the word it modifies in correct proximity, as below.

Revised When I was a little girl, my father liked to tell me stories about mermaids.
As a little girl, I loved listening to my father's stories about mermaids.

Dangling Driving out of the Channel Tunnel, France beckoned ahead. [France drove out of the Channel Tunnel?]
Revised As we drove out of the Channel Tunnel, France beckoned ahead.
Driving out of the Channel Tunnel, we saw France beckoning ahead.

Dangling To make a perfect soufflé, the eggs must be fresh. [The eggs are making a soufflé?]
Revised To make a perfect soufflé, you must use fresh eggs.

Punctuating with Purpose

PART 10

New Contexts for Writing: Scripting and Directing Digital Video

Budding filmmakers can now write, produce, and distribute their videos with relative ease. The basic tools for making movies on a personal computer already exist, and now new software, including video games, and new distribution services, like Google™ Video, IndieFlix, and YouTube, give filmmakers all they need to make videos or films. You can create and edit your own digital video or adapt and remix digital content produced by others.

Now you can create original movies in video game environments. In this screenshot from *The Movies* (Lionhead Productions), you see the crew and cast on a movie set, in this case a graveyard. The cast lineup is on the left. Directors can place actors, script dialogue, add a film score, and add scenes, transitions, and credits to create a feature film that can then be uploaded to the Web, where it will be viewed and rated by other filmmakers on *The Movies*'s community website. See http://movies.lionhead.com

Digital video is film footage that has been converted to digital format, meaning it can be edited, reassembled, stored, and distributed electronically. You can shoot digital video with a camera and capture it on a computer using video editing software, which helps you add, delete, and rearrange scenes, add music and sound effects, edit dialogue, create special effects, and export video for others to view.

A **script** (or **screenplay**) is a detailed written account of the video's content. Scripting involves writing dialogue, describing settings, and providing stage (or scene) directions. **Storyboarding** involves sketching out events in a scene, showing how they will be filmed (camera angles, distance, and movement), and describing how sound, music, and special effects should be included. You can use screenwriting software like Movie Magic, Screenwriter, or Final Draft. Storyboard your video using printed templates or software designed to make storyboarding simpler, such as FrameForge 3D Studio. Try the free trial versions first.

Write a Screenplay and Storyboard Your Video

If you want to make a film that earns more than one star from reviewers and the audience, you'll want to write a good script and create storyboards that describe how each scene, and even each individual shot, in your film should be handled. To learn this process, most filmmakers start by making short videos (five to ten minutes) that show an interesting incident, provide information, or sell a product or service.

You'll want to start with a story concept—the gist of what you want to show or teach with your video. Even short videos will have a clear beginning, middle, and end.

END PUNCTUATION 37

Periods (.), question marks (?), and exclamation points (!), known as *end punctuation,* show the reader where statements, questions, and emphatic declarations end.

Example 1 Using periods at the end of sentences

Claire's results should help resolve her controversial hypothesis.
Juan's research asks why the Dodo bird is extinct.
Be careful around that burner.

Using Periods 37a

Use a period at the end of sentences that are statements, indirect questions, or mild commands.

Periods to Punctuate Initials and Some Abbreviations

Periods are always used with initials and often used with abbreviations.

When a sentence ends with an abbreviation, the period that follows the abbreviation also serves as the end punctuation for the sentence.

Example 2 Using periods with initials and abbreviations

Use periods with . . .

- **initials:**

  George W. Bush Carolyn B. Maloney William J. Clinton

- **many common abbreviations:**

Mr.	Ms.	Dr.	Rev.
St.	Ave.	Sun.	Jan.
6:30 p.m.	etc.	9:15 a.m.	

But do not use periods with . . .

- **abbreviations indicating academic degrees:**

  PhD MA MS BA MD

- **postal abbreviations for states:**

  MA NC WA TX FL NY IL MN

- **abbreviations that appear in all uppercase letters (such as names of organizations, corporations, and government agencies):**

  NBA AFL-CIO PBS IBM FBI PDF ASAP

- **acronyms (pronounced as words, these abbreviations are formed from the first letters of the major words in longer names or phrases):**

  AIDS (Acquired Immune Deficiency Syndrome)
  OPEC NAFTA OSHA radar laser scuba

- **commonly shortened words and technical terms:**

  dorm math lab

37a Periods to Mark Divisions in Numbers, URLs, and Email Addresses

A period is used to separate the decimal portion of a number from the integer portion, as well as to separate parts of URLs and email addresses.

Example 3 Using periods to mark divisions

Use periods with . . .

- **numbers with decimal places:**

  2.5 m $20.00   7.5 cm

- **URLs:**

  http://www.parlorpress.com
  (For an explanation of the parts of a URL, see page 134.)

- **email addresses:**

  Firstname.Lastname@anywhere.com

37b Using Question Marks

A direct question states someone's exact words. (Use a period after an indirect question in which the writer reports that someone else asked a question.) Note that a single word can be used as a question.

Example 4 Using a question mark with a direct question

Do you think it's the heat or the humidity that makes it so uncomfortable?

She's running for reelection. Why?

Use a question mark to indicate the end of a direct question within a sentence. Such a question will typically be set off by quotation marks, dashes, or parentheses.

Example 5 Using a question mark with a direct question within a sentence

She kept asking, "Who wrote that book?" even when it was clear nobody knew the answer.

Exams are early tomorrow morning—why are they always scheduled at eight o'clock?—and I need to study and sleep.

Question marks are also used to indicate the ends of questions in a series, even if the questions are not complete sentences.

Example 6 Using question marks with a series of questions

Who wrote that article? When? Was it a reprint?

Use a question mark to indicate the end of a question in a compound sentence that begins with a statement and ends with a question.

Example 7 Using a question mark in a compound sentence that ends with a question

Our professor would really like to know something: Why did you miss class yesterday? When she asks you, what will you say?

Example 8 Using exclamation points for emphasis

STRONG EMOTION:

Grow up! Get over it! How dare you!

DRAMATIC EMPHASIS:

The governor was not even aware that his name was used for advertising face cream!

SHOCKING OR SURPRISING STATEMENT:

I like your parents!

In David Mamet's *Oleanna,* Carol exclaims, "I'm bad!"

DIRECT ORDER:

Don't yell at me!

Example 9 Avoiding overuse of exclamation points

OVERUSE:

Casual clothing at work is a relic of the 1980s! Only an idiot would think that he or she could get ahead by wearing torn jeans in Corporate America!!! These people need to be brought into today's world!

EMPHASIS CONVEYED BY DICTION:

Some workers still cling to the notion that Casual Friday exists. Casual Friday was a philosophy derived from business schools in the 1980s. The idea was that workers would increase productivity and engage one another more socially and more productively if they were comfortable in their clothing. Unfortunately, even though this philosophy seems archaic, some workers still abide by the idea of wearing clothing that is simply too casual for today's workplace.

Exclamation points may be used to indicate a strong emotion, to emphasize a point dramatically, to make a surprising or shocking statement, or to give a direct order.

Overuse of Exclamation Points

Use exclamation points sparingly. Overuse of the exclamation point diminishes its impact. Rely instead on choosing words carefully to add emphasis. Especially in business and academic writing, exclamation points are rarely used. The exception is when an exclamation point is part of a direct quotation. Never use more than one exclamation point at the end of a sentence.

38 COMMAS

Commas (,) are used to define boundaries within a sentence. They help readers understand how the writer has grouped ideas together or kept them apart. Commas are also used in other situations to clarify meaning—for example, to make numerals easier to grasp at first glance.

Example 1 Commas

The proposed four towers of the new World Trade Center are huge, and they will dramatically change the New York skyline.

Rising to 1,776 feet, the Freedom Tower was the first new skyscraper to be planned for ground zero.

Towers 2, 3, and 4, as they are known for now, were each designed by a famous architect: Norman Foster, Richard Rogers, and Fumihiko Maki.

38a Use a Comma between Independent Clauses

Use a comma *before* a coordinating conjunction (*and, but, or, for, so, nor,* or *yet)* when you join two or more independent clauses. An independent clause is one that can stand alone as a complete sentence. It has a subject and a complete verb (not an *-ing* verb or a *to* verb standing alone—see section 31a), and it does not begin with a subordinating conjunction (*because, since, while, even though,* and so on).

Note: Do not place the comma after the coordinating conjunction. The comma goes first:

My lab partner is late today, and she has our lab notes.

Example 2 Link independent clauses

INDEPENDENT CLAUSE **, [and, but, or, for, so, nor, yet]** INDEPENDENT CLAUSE

This new style of music was unique, **and** it impacted music and culture for years after its creation.

From Nicole M. Walsh, Purdue University, "George Gershwin."

The pope did not mention the eccentricities of his predecessor, Urban VIII, **nor** did he directly criticize the behavior of the Inquisition.

From James B. Reston Jr., *Galileo: A Life* (New York: HarperCollins, 1994).

Multilingual writers: Note that in the example above, in the second independent clause after *nor,* the helping verb comes before the subject, just as in a question.

INDEPENDENT CLAUSE **,** INDEPENDENT CLAUSE **, and** INDEPENDENT CLAUSE

Paleobiologists study plant and animal fossils, paleoanthropologists study ancient humans, **and** paleoecologists study the interactions between ancient organisms and their environments.

Example 3 Use semicolons when commas are used within the clauses

We oppose the proposed power lines, factory, and apartment building; we favor regulations to help our community maintain the feel of a traditional village.

To link two independent clauses that already contain commas, use a semicolon instead of a comma. This usage is preferred in academic writing since it makes the grouping of ideas in the sentence clear.

Example 4 Omit the comma or coordinating conjunction in certain contexts

NO COMMA:

Feed the cat and walk the dog.

NO COORDINATING CONJUNCTION:

Very short, contrasting clauses	She lied, I did not.
Reported speech	Margaret says only a few students stayed in touch: "Some went back to their native country, some stayed here, some just lost contact." From Zhumei Meng, Purdue University, "Day in the Life."

Some writers omit the comma when the two independent clauses joined by a coordinating conjunction are very brief.

Depending on the context, some writers use a comma without a coordinating conjunction to join two very short contrasting independent clauses. In formal nonfiction writing, such as much academic writing, use a period or semicolon to separate the clauses. If you are quoting someone who is speaking informally, you can sometimes omit the coordinating conjunctions. But see Chapter 32 on comma splices.

Avoid Creating Comma Splices 38b

Example 5 Correct comma splices by adding coordinating conjunctions after commas

NO INDEPENDENT CLAUSE , INDEPENDENT CLAUSE

Maryam liked the look of the Liberty, ^but they decided to buy a Mini Cooper.

Do not use a comma alone to join two independent clauses. (See exceptions in Example 4.) A major sentence error called a comma splice results. See Chapter 32 for various ways to correct comma splices.

38c Use Commas after Introductory Elements

Use a comma after an introductory word, phrase, or clause that comes before the subject to help readers identify the subject. If the introductory element is very short, some writers omit the comma as long as the meaning remains clear, but in college writing you can always use the comma.

Example 6 Use commas to set off introductory elements from independent clauses

INTRODUCTORY ELEMENT , INDEPENDENT CLAUSE

Sometimes the martial arts are taught as a form of combat. However, tai chi is used for self-defense and meditation. [Conjunctive adverb]

To receive the best grades, you will need to take notes and stay organized. [Infinitive phrase]

Crying pathetically, the starving calico cat got our attention. [Participial phrase]

On the way to the Winter Carnival in Saint Paul, Silvio and Christopher could not resist taking some photos. [Prepositional phrase]

When we run in the morning, we like to warm up and stretch briefly. [Dependent clause]

38d Use Commas between Items in a Series

Use commas to separate the items in a series of three or more words, phrases, or clauses of equal weight and grammatical structure. The last item in the list typically follows a comma and a coordinating conjunction, but in cases where the coordinating conjunction is omitted, the comma is still used.

The comma before the last item in a series is sometimes omitted in popular writing—for example, in newspapers and magazines—but in academic writing, the final comma is preferred.

Example 7 Use commas to separate items in a series

FIRST ITEM IN A SERIES , SECOND ITEM , [and, or] THIRD ITEM

You can watch any of the following shows on MTV: *The Osbournes, Pimp My Ride, Punk'd,* or *Real World.*

The police ticketed him for speeding, driving to endanger, and obstructing justice.

Sleepless, cornered, and fighting mad, the soldiers hurled down the hill with muskets raised to their shoulders.

It didn't take me too long to figure out that Curly was the crazy one, Larry was the comic foil, and Moe was the ringleader.

When the items in a list or series include commas, use semicolons to separate the items.

Example 8 Use semicolons with series within series

Get me a beach sticker, good for the whole season; two inflatable rafts, preferably ones large enough for two kids; an umbrella, bright blue is best; and six beach towels.

Use Commas between Coordinate Adjectives 38e

Example 9 Use commas between coordinate adjectives

COORDINATE ADJECTIVE **,** COORDINATE ADJECTIVE NOUN

That decrepit**,** unpainted house may be haunted.

Multilingual writers: For more on adjective order, see section 50c.

Commas are used between coordinate adjectives. Coordinate adjectives in a series modify a single noun; they each add separate meaning: *honest, hardworking carpenter.* You can identify coordinate adjectives by changing their order. If the sentence still makes sense, the adjectives are coordinate. When adjectives are cumulative, however—that is, when the details accumulate or build toward a particular meaning—no comma separates them: *vivid blue eyes.*

Use Commas to Set Off Nonrestrictive (Nonessential) Elements 38f

Example 10 Use commas with nonrestrictive elements

INDEPENDENT CLAUSE **,** NONRESTRICTIVE ELEMENT

I love to go camping**,** which I do every year with my family and friends. [You could remove everything after the comma and the core meaning of the sentence would remain intact: the writer loves camping.]

NONRESTRICTIVE ELEMENT **,** INDEPENDENT CLAUSE

An enthusiastic speaker**,** Reverend Jones spoke during freshman orientation.

PART OF INDEPENDENT CLAUSE **,** NONRESTRICTIVE ELEMENT **,** REST OF INDEPENDENT CLAUSE

The west side of the city**,** which receives far fewer city services than the east side**,** has had a crime problem for over twenty years.

Lucia Hernandez**,** who is a good friend from college**,** just arrived.

Lucia Hernandez**,** a good friend from college**,** just flew in from Miami. [Without *who is,* this nonrestrictive element is an appositive, a noun or noun equivalent that follows a noun and describes it.]

What Is a Nonrestrictive Element?

A **nonrestrictive element** is a word group that is not essential to the core meaning of the sentence. You can omit a nonrestrictive element from a sentence without changing its main idea. Nonrestrictive elements are often (but not always) signaled by the words *which* and *who.*

Remember: When the nonrestrictive element is in the middle of the sentence, two commas are needed to enclose it.

38f

What Is a Restrictive Element?

Restrictive elements provide information that is crucial to understanding the sentence. Removing this information would make the sentence confusing or even nonsensical. Restrictive clauses literally restrict, or make more specific, the meaning of the sentence element they modify. Do not use commas with restrictive elements.

Example 11 Do not use commas with restrictive elements

PART OF INDEPENDENT CLAUSE RESTRICTIVE ELEMENT REST OF INDEPENDENT CLAUSE

A dog that bites children does not make a good family pet. [The meaning of this sentence changes dramatically if the restrictive clause is removed.]

My good friend Lucia Hernandez just flew in from Miami. [The name restricts the meaning of *my good friend.* It is not set off with commas, since it is essential information.]

Joyce Carol Oates's book *The Falls: A Novel* is set in Niagara Falls. [Oates has written many books; without the title, the sentence would not make sense. No commas are needed.]

38g Use Commas to Set Off Parenthetical and Transitional Expressions

Parenthetical expressions offer extra information that isn't needed to understand the main idea of a sentence. (Unlike nonrestrictive elements, parenthetical elements are typically words or phrases rather than clauses or appositives.) This information can be enclosed within commas or parentheses, depending on the degree of separation you want between the sentence and the extra information; commas suggest less separation than parentheses.

Transitional expressions move the reader from one idea to the next and show the reader how the ideas are related. (See page 22 for a list of transitions.) Conjunctive adverbs are one kind of transitional expression (◀ section 30e).

Example 12 Use commas to set off parenthetical expressions

PARENTHETICAL EXPRESSION , SENTENCE

Understandably, she is happy about getting that promotion.

PART OF SENTENCE , PARENTHETICAL EXPRESSION , REST OF SENTENCE

For me, at least, chocolate is as valuable as gold.
That geology professor, of course, knows where granite is most prevalent.

Example 13 Use commas to set off transitional expressions

Jill, as a matter of fact, is returning to school next semester.

Braun's work validated many of Solms's findings; however, Hobson still maintained that those findings did not support a Freudian interpretation.

Use Commas to Set Off Contrasts, Interjections, Direct Address, and Tag Sentences 38h

Example 14 Use commas to set off contrasts, interjections, and the like

TO SET OFF CONTRASTS:

We must address environmental issues now, not wait until there is a disaster later.

TO SET OFF INTERJECTIONS:

Whoa, you're running too fast for me to keep up.

TO SET OFF WORDS IN DIRECT ADDRESS:

Stop, that flooring is likely to give way under your weight.

TO SET OFF TAG SENTENCES:

You have written your survey for Sociology 101, haven't you?

When the later part of a sentence offers information that contrasts with the information in the first part, use a comma to emphasize the contrast.

Use a comma to set off an interjection—a word that expresses emotion, such as amazement or surprise, and that is not grammatically a part of the sentence.

Use a comma in direct address, when you the writer speak directly to the reader.

Use a comma to set off tag sentences and questions at the end of a sentence. If the tag is a question, the entire sentence ends with a question mark.

Use Commas to Set Off Quotations 38i

Example 15 Use commas to set off quotations

"I am starving," Pauline complained.

Maggie said, "Come back at noon and we'll have lunch."

"Get the sandwiches," Pauline yelled as she drove by, "and I'll meet you at the park."

When Representative Harold Velde writes, "Educating Americans through the means of the library service could bring about a change of the political attitude more quickly than any other method," he is referring to a change of politics more than a change in education.

Exceptions:

I believe that "the life well lived is the only one worth living."

(continued)

Commas separate quoted words from the words you use to introduce or explain them.

Several exceptions exist:

- When a quotation blends smoothly into the grammar of your sentence, omit the comma.

- When an exclamation point or question mark ends the quotation, do not use a comma.
- Use a colon, not a comma, to introduce a quotation when the introduction is a complete sentence, especially if the quotation is long.

"Did you remember to lock the door?" Jonathan asked.

"I don't want to leave!" she sobbed.

Faulkner's style is considered experimental: "Faulkner always strove to open new ground so his readers would experience his text as a world in a world."

38j Use Commas with Dates, Places, Addresses, and Numbers

Use commas in dates . . .

- between date and year.
- between day and date.
- after the year in a full date within a sentence.

Do not use a comma in dates when . . .

- only the month and year are shown.
- only the month and day are given.
- only the season and year are given.
- the date is inverted.

Use commas in places and addresses . . .

- to separate city and state.
- after the state within a sentence.
- to separate elements of an address from the rest of the sentence.

Use commas in large numbers after each group of three digits (moving from right to left). Commas are optional in most four-digit numbers, but be consistent.

Use commas in dates like these

January 1, 2006
Monday, February 14, 2005
Einstein was born on March 14, 1879, in Ulm, Germany.

Don't use commas in dates like these

November 2007
September 17
fall 2008
24 July 2006

Use commas in place names and addresses like these

Tulsa, Oklahoma
American Forests' Historic Tree Nursery is a company located in Jacksonville, Florida, from which you can order a tree with historic significance.
Send donations to the Heifer Project International, P.O. Box 8058, Little Rock, Arkansas 72203, to aid in the fight against hunger worldwide.

Use commas in large numbers

3,456,789
Of the 3,500 families served by the program, 2,899 live below the poverty level.

Use Commas with Names and Titles 38k

Use a comma before a title or degree

Rene Sommers, PhD John O'Hara, MD

Don't use a comma before a family designation

Martin Luther King Jr. Ramses II

Use a comma with a title or degree following a person's name. When a name is inverted so that the last name is given first, use a comma to separate the names.

You do not need to use a comma when a person's name is followed by *Jr.*, *Sr.*, *II, III,* and so on.

Avoid Misusing Commas 38l

Don't use commas in situations like these

Don't use a comma . . .

That man, allows his dogs to roam without supervision.

- to separate a subject from a verb.

Neither a young person, nor an older person can join that organization.
Speeders will be ticketed, and will receive points on their licenses.
Shanice had trouble distinguishing blue, from green.

- to separate compound subjects, predicates, or objects.

Will you remember to buy, soap, detergent, and bathroom cleaner?

- at the beginning of a series.

Carol likes to read the *LA Times*, travel magazines, and short stories, before bed.

- after the last item of a series.

Jackie brought the names of applicants, who are eligible for interviews.

- with essential (restrictive) modifiers.

Philip Foner was an excellent historian and, he worked on political justice for his whole life.

- after a coordinating conjunction between independent clauses.

She did well on the history exam because, I helped her study.

- after a subordinating conjunction.

I recall the lyrics that, "the best things in life are free."

- with quotations that fit into the structure of your sentence.

I love, "Dolan's Cadillac" by Stephen King.

- with quotation marks that enclose titles.

39 SEMICOLONS

The semicolon (;) is used to show that the phrases or clauses on either side of it are closely related and equally important. When a comma is too weak to separate the word groups and a period is too strong, the semicolon is used.

Example 1 Semicolons

Genuine tradition is not for sale, because no one needs to buy it; it's moored in the customs of one's own family (remember them?).

From Caitlin Flanagan, *To Hell with All That* (New York: Little, Brown, 2006).

39a Use a Semicolon between Closely Related Independent Clauses

When you want to show readers that independent clauses are closely related, you have a couple of choices. You can separate the clauses with a comma and a coordinating conjunction, or you can use a semicolon. The semicolon is a particularly good choice when the two independent clauses provide either parallel or contrasting information.

Example 2 Using semicolons to link independent clauses

Parallel information:

INDEPENDENT CLAUSE

Horses frequently serve as ideals of human independence in works of art;

INDEPENDENT CLAUSE

the film *Spirit* is a good example.

Contrasting information:

Casual readers accept facts; critical readers evaluate them.

39b Use a Semicolon between Independent Clauses Connected with Words Such as *however, then,* and *for example*

To clarify how independent clauses are related, you can use conjunctive adverbs such as *however, consequently,* and *furthermore* (page 417) or transitional expressions such as *for example, in addition,* and *as a result* (page 22).

A semicolon is used between independent clauses. A comma follows a conjunctive adverb or transitional expression when it begins the second independent clause.

Example 3 Using semicolons with conjunctive adverbs and transitional expressions to clarify the relationship between independent clauses

INDEPENDENT CLAUSE ; CONJUNCTIVE ADVERB OR TRANSITIONAL EXPRESSION , INDEPENDENT CLAUSE

Napoleon was exiled to the island of Elba to remove him from world politics; nevertheless, he proceeded to make this small island in the Italian Riviera a kingdom all his own.

Jack the Ripper terrorized Whitechapel while never revealing his identity; therefore, many Ripperologists, as they are known, falsely believe that he must have either drowned in the Thames or been protected by royal connections.

Use a Semicolon between Items in a Series Containing Other Punctuation 39c

Items in a series of three or more are usually separated by commas. However, if an item in the series already includes a comma or other punctuation, use semicolons to separate the items.

Example 4 Separating items in a series with semicolons

Lewis and Clark ventured into the Western wilderness fully loaded with all of the modern weapons technologies they could muster: military rifles, service muskets, and personal firearms; scalping knives and pipe tomahawks, which would be traded along the way for other supplies; and bullet molds, gun worms, ball screws, and other supplies that would help the expedition repair arms during its trip.

Avoid Misusing Semicolons 39d

Do **not** use semicolons in the following situations:

1. **To join unequal sentence parts.** For example, do not use a semicolon to separate an introductory phrase from the rest of a sentence, and do not use a semicolon to separate a dependent clause from an independent clause. Either use creates a sentence fragment. Similarly, do not use a semicolon between a phrase and a clause.
2. **To introduce lists or quotations.** When an independent clause introduces a list, a colon—not a semicolon—separates the introduction from the list (section 40b). Quotations are typically introduced with a comma (section 38i). If a complete sentence introduces the quotation, a colon is used (section 40c). Never use a semicolon to introduce a quotation.

Don't use a semicolon . . .

- **after an introductory phrase:**

  INTRODUCTORY PHRASE — INDEPENDENT CLAUSE

  With wide aperture lenses on binoculars and a steady hand, amateur scientists can observe Jupiter's moons.

- **between a dependent clause and an independent clause:**

  DEPENDENT CLAUSE — INDEPENDENT CLAUSE

  Since our classes ended at two o'clock, we shopped for the party.

- **to introduce a list:**

  Live 8 focused the world's attention for a brief spell on three kinds of poverty on the continent of Africa: excessive foreign debt, failing national economies, and widespread famine.

- **to introduce a quotation:**

  Fitzgerald concluded *The Great Gatsby* with the suggestion that the fight against vanity in a world of moral and spiritual decay never ends: "So we beat on, boats against the current, borne back ceaselessly into the past" (189).

40 COLONS

Colons (:) introduce information. A colon usually comes at the end of an independent clause (complete sentence) and draws attention to the example, explanation, quotation, or list that follows.

Example 1 Colons

Levitt and Dubner share a risk analysis that is likely to be surprising: a child under ten "is roughly 100 times more likely to die in a swimming accident . . . than in gunplay . . ." (149–50).

40a Use Colons after Independent Clauses to Introduce Appositives

An appositive is a word or group of words that modifies or describes a noun, a noun phrase, or a pronoun. Colons introduce explanatory information, so it is natural to use one before an appositive phrase that modifies the independent clause that precedes it.

Example 2 Use a colon after an independent clause to introduce an appositive

INDEPENDENT CLAUSE : APPOSITIVE

Throughout my entire life, I have loved only one person: my mother. [Appositive: *one person I have loved* = *my mother*]

40b Use Colons after Independent Clauses to Introduce Lists

If an independent clause introduces a list, you can use a colon to keep the introduction and the list separate. The independent clause may include a phrase such as *as follows, the following, such as the following*, or *including the following*.

But do **not** use a colon after expressions such as *for example, that is, namely*, or *such as*. The colon has the same function as these phrases: to point to and emphasize what comes next. It would be redundant to use them both.

Example 3 Use a colon after an independent clause to introduce a list

INDEPENDENT CLAUSE : LIST

Yes — Three moisture-retaining media can be used to keep root crops crisp over the winter: sawdust, sand, or chipped leaves.

No — Three moisture-retaining media can be used to keep root crops crisp over the winter, namely: sawdust, sand, or chipped leaves.

Use Colons after Independent Clauses to Introduce Quotations 40c

Example 4 Use a colon after an independent clause to introduce a quotation

The opening paragraph of the 67-page essay is a model of reason and composition, repeatedly disrupted by that single obscenity:

> One of the most salient features of our culture is that there is so much [bull]. Everyone knows this. Each of us contributes his share. But we tend to take the situation for granted. Most people are rather confident of their ability to recognize [bull] and to avoid being taken in by it. So the phenomenon has not aroused much deliberate concern, nor attracted much sustained inquiry.

From Peter Edidin, "Between Truth and Lies, an Unprintable Ubiquity" [Review of *On [Bull]* by Harry G. Frankfurt], *New York Times,* Feb. 14, 2005, p. E1.

A colon is used at the end of an independent clause that introduces a long quotation. If the introduction is not a complete sentence, a comma is typically used instead of a colon (◀ section 38i).

Use a Colon to Introduce a Second Independent Clause 40d

Example 5 Use a colon to introduce a second clause that illustrates the first

Kate was the worst kind of neighbor: she once stole my lawnmower and used the engine for her go-cart.

ABC News took more than ideas from MTV: it hired one of the youth network's talented young producers, David Berrent.

From Mitchell Stephens, *The Rise of the Image, The Fall of the Word* (New York: Oxford University Press, 1998).

Men have to register with the Selective Service, but that doesn't mean they will be drafted if the draft is reinstated: clergy, conscientious objectors, men who are disabled, and others may be exempt from service.

The FBI has not yet managed to put into operation a modern computerized case management system: Why?

A colon is used between two independent clauses only when the second one illustrates or explains the first.

If the second independent clause is a question, you should capitalize its first letter. Otherwise, you can use a lowercase or a capital letter after a colon in such cases, but use one or the other consistently throughout your project.

- **In correspondence.** Use a colon after the salutation in a formal letter or email. In an informal letter or email to a person you know well, use a comma rather than a colon. In memos, use a colon after each element in the memo header.

Dear Doctor Williard:
I am sorry to report that I could not attend your October 20 symposium on rat behavior in the East Science Building. . . .

- **In titles.** Use a colon to separate a title and subtitle. If the documentation style you are using requires titles to be italicized, italicize the colon as well as the words.

Example 6 Use a colon to separate a title and subtitle

Zambelli: The First Family of Fireworks
"Figure and Place: A Context for Five Post-War Artists"

- **In expressions of time**

Example 7 Use colons to separate hours, minutes, and seconds

She gets up at 7:30 every morning.
Paula Radcliffe ran the London marathon in 2:15:25 in April 2003.

- **To indicate a ratio**

Example 8 Use a colon in a ratio

1:10 means "1 to 10" or "1/10."

41 APOSTROPHES

An apostrophe ('), usually with an *s* following it, indicates the possessive case. Apostrophes also form contractions: they show where letters have been omitted from a word. Apostrophes create the plurals of numbers, letters, symbols, and words used as words.

Example 1 Using apostrophes

Possessive case	Sally's business
Contractions	can't (can + not)
Special plurals	three *m*'s

Example 2 Using 's to form the possessive case

SINGULAR NOUNS:

Her mother's shawl was wrapped around the child's shoulders.

Alice Smith's vocal range spans four octaves.

INDEFINITE PRONOUNS THAT END IN *-BODY* OR *-ONE*:

I would like everyone's vacation requests on my desk by Friday.

IRREGULAR PLURAL NOUNS THAT DON'T END IN *-S*:

The women's voting coalition meets Tuesdays at 7:00.

Example 3 Using only an apostrophe to form the possessive case

PLURAL NOUNS THAT ALREADY END IN *-S*

The pilots' complaints about the airline have not been resolved.

The Joneses' house got an environmental award for its passive solar heating and wind-powered generator. [The house is owned by more than one person—perhaps a whole family—named Jones.]

SINGULAR PROPER NOUNS THAT END IN *-S* BUT SOUND LIKE *Z*:

Socrates' ideas come to us via Plato.

Example 4 Forming the possessive case of inanimate objects

Yes	The **door of the car** was left open all night.
Yes	The **car door** was left open all night.
No	The car's door was left open all night.

The possessive case indicates ownership or possession: *Vikram's photograph of his sister.*

Apostrophe + *s*

Use an apostrophe and the letter *s* to form the possessive case of certain nouns and pronouns:

- singular nouns
- indefinite pronouns that end in *-body* or *-one*
- irregular plural nouns (irregular because they don't end in *-s,* such as *children, women, men, people, sheep, fish, deer)*

When a plural noun does end in *-s,* as most of them do, add only the apostrophe.

Apostrophe Only

Use only an apostrophe to make plural nouns ending in *-s* possessive. If a singular proper noun ends in *-s* but has a *z* sound, use an apostrophe only.

Multilingual writers: In conventional usage, the possessive case of an inanimate object, such as a car, often does not take *'s.* Instead, a noun phrase is employed. Though there are exceptions, you won't be wrong if you use a noun phrase.

41a

Individual and Joint Ownership

When you want to indicate that items are owned or possessed individually, each noun gets its own apostrophe and *s*. When items are owned or possessed jointly, use an apostrophe and *s* only after the last noun. The same goes for compound words: to make them possessive, put the apostrophe and *s* on the last word.

Some Examples of Compound Words
in-laws' visit (plural)
sister-in-law's invitation
attorney general's indictment
anybody else's opinion

Example 5 Showing individual and joint ownership

INDIVIDUAL OWNERSHIP:

Tamora Pierce's and Garth Nix's young adult novels feature heroines who are intelligent and resourceful.

JOINT OWNERSHIP:

Ben and Jerry's first ice cream store opened in Burlington, Vermont.

Example 6 Making compound words possessive

My mother-in-law's brisket recipe is a family heirloom.

41b Use Apostrophes to Form Contractions

Apostrophes are used in contractions to take the place of one or more letters that have been omitted. Contractions are combination words that include a pronoun and a verb (like *she's* for *she is*) or the elements of a verb phrase (*aren't* for *are not*).

Contractions are a sign of informal writing; they are commonly used in emails, personal letters, and blogs, as well as in reported speech. Contractions are too informal for some types of college writing, such as research essays, but may be acceptable in others, depending on your audience's expectations about the rhetorical context and the genre in which you are writing.

Example 7 Making contractions

"It's a beautiful day in this neighborhood," Mr. Rogers used to sing at the beginning of his TV show for children.

Painter Roy Lichtenstein's cartoonish work *Drowning Girl* shows a woman in water exclaiming, "I don't care! I'd rather sink—than call Brad for help."

Some Common Contractions

I am = I'm
I will = I'll (similarly: you'll, he'll, she'll, we'll, they'll)
I have = I've (you've, we've, they've)
I would, I had = I'd (he'd, she'd, we'd, you'd, they'd)
you are = you're (we're, they're)
it is, it has = it's (he's, she's)
let us = let's
who is = who's
there is = there's
is not = isn't (aren't, don't, didn't, wasn't, weren't)
can not = can't
will not = won't

Use Apostrophes to Form Plurals of Letters, Symbols, Words Used as Words, and Abbreviations 41c

Example 8 Forming plurals

WITH APOSTROPHE AND *S:*

In England and Canada, z's are called zeds.

According to a concordance of *Death of a Salesman* compiled by Potter and Struss at Iowa State, there are 23,140 unique words in the play, which has 909 *you*'s and 816 *I*'s.

WITH *S* ONLY:

The Online Film Critics Society lists the top 100 overlooked films of the 1990s, including *Miller's Crossing* as number 1.

Since I am 19, I always get lottery tickets that have *1*s and 9s in them, but so far, I haven't had any luck.

Do you kids have proper IDs?

Letters, symbols (for example, &, #, and @), words used as words, and abbreviations can be made plural either by adding an apostrophe and *s* or by adding only an *s.* (The decision may be dictated by the style you are following—for example, MLA style—or it may depend on your personal preferences.) The letter, word, or symbol should be placed in italics (or underlined), but the apostrophe and the *s* (or just the *s*) should be in roman (regular) type. Abbreviations do not need to be in italics.

Make sure that your usage is consistent throughout your project.

Avoid Misusing Apostrophes 41d

Example 9 Avoiding apostrophe errors

USE ONLY *S* TO MAKE MOST NOUNS PLURAL:

No Dog's are great company for kid's.
Yes Dogs are great company for kids.

ITS, YOURS, HIS, HERS, OURS, THEIRS ARE ALREADY POSSESSIVE:

Robert Frost begins the first two lines of his poem "Stopping by Woods on a Snowy Evening" with possessive personal pronouns: "Whose woods these are I think I know. / His house is in the village though."

USE ONLY *S* OR *ES* TO MAKE MOST PRESENT-TENSE VERBS AGREE WITH *HE, SHE,* OR *IT:*

No Codi say's she is carsick. She want's to go home.
Yes Codi says she is carsick. She wants to go home.

An apostrophe is **not** used

- to make most nouns plural.
- to make personal pronouns possessive. (They are already possessive.)

Possessive Personal Pronouns

mine	ours
yours	yours
hers	theirs
his	
its	

- to make present-tense verbs agree with *he, she,* or *it.*

42 QUOTATION MARKS

Quotation marks signal to readers that the exact words between them come from someone other than the writer or the narrator. They also enclose the titles of short works such as essays, songs, and short stories.

Example 1 Quotation marks

Bill Bryson is a master at helping readers understand geologic time: "If you could fly backwards into the past at the rate of one year per second, it would take you . . . a little over three weeks to get back to the beginnings of human life. But it would take you twenty years to reach the dawn of the Cambrian period" (325–26).

42a Use Quotation Marks to Enclose Short Direct Quotations

In MLA style, a prose quotation is considered "short" if it is four or fewer lines long (page 183). If you are quoting from a poem, three or fewer lines is considered short. In APA style, a short prose quotation is up to forty words (page 246). In either style, when you quote the exact words of a source, use double quotation marks at the beginning and end of the quotation.

For handling long quotations in MLA style, see page 184; for APA style, see page 247.

Example 2 Short quotations

MLA STYLE:

Lourie says, "It is to Pop I owe my love of wilderness" (34).

APA STYLE:

By Bazerman et al.'s account (2005), "Writing across the Curriculum, like any academic program, arises out of a complex of institutional, intellectual, and social events and forces" (p. 5).

42b Use Single Quotation Marks for Quotations within Quotations

Material that you want to quote may itself include a quotation. In this case, use double quotation marks to indicate the beginning and end of the entire quotation and replace any quotation marks within the material with single quotation marks. (As described in section 13a, long quotations are set off from the text by indentation rather

Example 3 A quotation within a quotation

ORIGINAL SOURCE:

NEA chairman Dana Gioia, himself a poet, called the findings shocking and a reason for grave concern. "We have a lot of functionally literate people who are no longer engaged readers," Gioia said in an interview with The Associated Press.

From The Associated Press, "Report Shows Big Drop in Reading," *MSNBC*, 8 July 2004 <http://www.msnbc.msn.com/id/5389382>.

CHANGE TO SINGLE QUOTATION MARKS:

Each generation proclaims a literacy crisis, almost as a rite of passage. These days, the Internet is blamed, for example, for a whole host of declines both moral and intellectual. According to an anonymously written Associated Press article, "NEA chairman Dana Gioia, himself a poet, called the findings shocking and a reason for grave concern. 'We have a lot of functionally literate people who are no longer engaged readers'" ("Report").

than by quotation marks. Thus, any quotations within the material should be reprinted exactly as they are printed in the original.)

Example 3 shows double quotation marks being used around the entire direct quotation, and single quotation marks enclosing Gioia's words. Notice that Gioia's words and the entire quotation end at the same time; the single quotation mark ends Gioia's words and the double quotation mark follows immediately.

Use Quotation Marks in Dialogue 42c

Enclose each speaker's words in a pair of quotation marks. When the speaker changes, start a new paragraph. If one speaker's words take more than a single paragraph, start each paragraph with a double quotation mark, but use an ending quotation mark only at the end of the entire speech, not after each paragraph.

If you report a speaker's words but do not quote them, do not use quotation marks. Such reported speech is known as **indirect discourse** (section 50e).

Example 4 Using quotation marks in dialogue

In this passage from Edgar Allan Poe's story of revenge, "The Cask of Amontillado" (1846), each line of dialogue by a new speaker is treated as a new paragraph.

> "Drink," I said, presenting him the wine.
>
> He raised it to his lips with a leer. He paused and nodded to me familiarly, while his bells jingled.
>
> "I drink," he said, "to the buried that repose around us."
>
> "And I to your long life."

Example 5 Direct vs. indirect discourse

DIRECT DISCOURSE:

Sheila said, "I want to help you decorate your new house." [Exact quotation]

INDIRECT DISCOURSE:

Sheila said *that she wanted* to help *me* decorate *my* new house. [Reported but not quoted exactly]

42d Use Quotation Marks to Set Off the Titles of Short Works

The titles of short works and works that are part of larger works, such as chapters of books, are placed inside quotation marks.

Important exception: Do not use quotation marks, italics, or underlining with the title of your essay. However, if the title of another work appears within your title, mark it appropriately. If it's a long work, italicize it; if it's a short work, put quotation marks around it.

Example 6 Quotation marks in your title

DO NOT USE QUOTATION MARKS AROUND THE TITLE OF YOUR PAPER:

The Unveiling of the Ultra-Chic South Beach Diet

BUT IF THE TITLE OF A SHORT WORK IS PART OF YOUR TITLE, ENCLOSE THAT TITLE IN QUOTATION MARKS:

Selective Point of View in Hemingway's "A Clean, Well-Lighted Place"

Use quotation marks around titles of these types of short works

- Short story
- Short poem
- Song
- Essay (other than your own)
- Article in newspaper, magazine, or journal
- Chapter or section of book
- Photograph
- Unpublished speech
- Individual episode of television or radio series
- Page or document on a website

Titles of longer works should be italicized (▶ section 44g).

42e Use Quotation Marks to Set Off Words Used in Special Senses

When a word is used as a word, either italicize it or enclose it in quotation marks.

Quotation marks can also be used to indicate the English translation of a word or phrase.

Quotation marks are sometimes used to indicate irony or sarcasm, although this is not a preferred usage in college writing and other somewhat formal situations. Very often, the effect is different from the one the writer intended.

Don't use quotation marks around clichés, either. Instead, omit the cliché and use your own fresh language to say what you mean.

Example 7 Word used as a word

What kind of "science" denies global warming?

Example 8 Quotation marks with English translations

Nemo me impune lacessit. ("No one injures or attacks me with impunity.")

Project Checklist

Proofreading for Quotation Marks with Other Punctuation Marks

- ❑ Commas and periods should be inside the closing quotation mark unless a citation in parentheses follows the closing quotation mark.
  Comma: She worried that we would "undervalue return investments," but I assured her we had high hopes.
  Period: Walter Mitty was overheard saying "puppy biscuits."
  But: Yeats describes "the great wings beating still" (1).

- ❑ Colons and semicolons should be outside the closing quotation mark.
  Colon: Renoir delighted in the peaceful moments of "companionship": people in a park, a mother and daughter, two friends.
  Semicolon: Hemingway bragged about "A Clean, Well-Lighted Place"; he felt it was one of his finer technical achievements.

- ❑ Question marks, exclamation points, and dashes should be inside the quotation marks if they are part of the quotation and outside if they are part of the larger sentence.
  Inside: Ophelia asks, "How does your Honor for this many a day?"
  "Watch your head!" she yelled, right after I'd bumped it on the cupboard.
  "Remember to flip the switch—the one for the lights—" was the last thing I heard her say.
  Outside: What does he mean when he warns about her "quaint honor"?
  If you want to be heard, "Take it to the streets"!
  Near the beginning of DeLillo's *White Noise,* the flight attendant—consulting the "Manual of Disasters"—has a complete breakdown of command presence.

Commas and periods are placed inside closing quotation marks. One important exception is when a citation in parentheses follows a quotation. In that case, the period is placed after the citation.

Colons and semicolons are usually placed outside closing quotation marks, but if they are part of the original material being quoted, they go inside.

Question marks, exclamation points, and dashes are placed inside closing quotation marks if they are part of the original quoted material; otherwise, they are outside.

43 OTHER PUNCTUATION MARKS

43a Using Dashes for Emphasis

A dash looks like this: —. It is keyed using two hyphens. (The use of hyphens is covered in Chapter 46.)

Dashes allow you to interrupt a sentence to provide and emphasize additional information. When you use dashes, place the interrupting information as close as possible to the material it relates to. Dashes point backward in a text, modifying or clarifying information that has come before.

Dashes should be used sparingly—normally you should limit yourself to one set in a paragraph. Commas, which are less emphatic than dashes, are used more frequently.

Dashes with Other Punctuation Marks

If the material enclosed in dashes is a question or an exclamation, it can end with a question mark or exclamation point.

You can use quotation marks around material within dashes if the context calls for them.

Other than in the situations described above, do not use the dash next to other punctuation marks, including commas, periods, semicolons, or colons.

Functions of Dashes

- **To set off material that interrupts the flow of a sentence:**

  Photographer Ansel Adams built on the traditions of painted landscapes but showed that the camera—even when dependent on black-and-white film—could reveal mysterious beauties that painting never had.

  From Philip Yenawine, *How to Look at Modern Art* (New York: Abrams, 1991), 69.

- **To emphasize appositives and examples:**

  Not even cities that are growing—southern and western boom cities—are keeping pace with their suburbs.

  From Bruce Katz and Jennifer Bradley, "Urban Affairs," *Atlantic Monthly* 284.6 (December 1999) <http://www.theatlantic.com/issues/99dec/9912katz.htm>.

  Giving you some money—five hundred dollars!—is not high on my list of priorities.

  I've read that essay—"Have Typewriter, Will Travel"—and it was lively.

- **To set off a term's definition:**

  SIM, like one version of TPF, is an interferometer—a set of small telescopes.

  From Tim Appenzeller, "Search for Other Earths," *National Geographic,* December 2004, p. 92.

- **To emphasize statements that summarize or describe a list of items:**

  Other fish, birds, even small mammals—the tigerfish of the Okavango Delta eats them all.

- **To mark a shift in tone:**

  So many things have been produced and accumulated that they can never possibly all be put to use—certainly not a bad thing when it comes to nuclear weapons.

  From Jean Baudrillard, *The Transparency of Evil,* trans. James Benedict (London: Verso, 1993), 32.

- **To indicate a hesitation or a break in dialogue:**

  In the old man's obituary—cancer!—seven years later, Mary is listed as Executive Vice President and sole heir.

  From Katherine Dunn, *Geek Love* (New York: Warner Books, 1989), 150.

Functions of Parentheses

- **To enclose interrupting words:**

Significantly, their intermediary in this was Jim Hickman of the Russian Exchange Program of the Esalen Institute in California (more on this later).

From Lynn Picknett and Clive Prince, *The Stargate Conspiracy* (New York: Berkley, 1999), 149.

- **To enclose examples and explanations:**

It is virtually impossible to determine the exact number of journalists on the CIA payroll—much less those who are informally slipped information (but in 1977 Carl Bernstein, in an article for *Rolling Stone,* estimated the number at that time to be about 400).

From Jim Keith, *Mass Control: Engineering Human Consciousness* (Lilburn, GA: IllumiNet Press, 2002), 38.

- **To enclose citation information:**

Slavery was described as "torturous, barbaric, counterproductive, and completely inhumane" (Smith 119).

Notice that the parentheses are after the closing quotation mark and before the final end punctuation. In longer quotations (MLA, more than four lines; APA, more than forty words), the quotation is indented and the closing period comes before the parenthetical citation.

- **To enclose numbers or letters of items in a list:**

The situational elements that may shape a writer's purpose include (a) the textual context, (b) the immediate context, and (c) the social and historical context.

- **To enclose numbers, dates, and cross-references:**

During World War I (1914–1918), Australian solider Francis James Mack wrote a series of letters home that are collected at "Trenches on the Web."

Gardner used eight criteria of "intelligence" as he reviewed the literature (see pp. 62–69).

- **To enclose examples, phone numbers, directions, and the like:**

In addition, the bank would never use a cell phone number (514-588-5569) on their checks.

From Wayne Madsen, "Texas to Florida: White House-Linked Clandestine Operation Paid for 'Vote Switching' Software," *Online Journal,* 12 Jan. 2004 <http://www.onlinejournal.org/Special_Reports/120604Madsen/120604madsen.html>.

Parentheses are used to enclose material that interrupts the flow of a sentence or paragraph. Only material that is not essential to a sentence's meaning—that illustrates, supplements, clarifies, or expands on the main point being made—should be placed in parentheses. Parentheses can enclose a word, phrase, list, or sentence. Parentheses are also used to enclose citation information.

Compared to information enclosed by dashes or commas, material in parentheses is less necessary for understanding the sentence. Parentheses should be used sparingly. If you have many pairs of parentheses, you should reconsider how your information fits together and rewrite your sentences, either to integrate the information into the sentences or to omit some of it.

In legal and business writing, parentheses are used to enclose spelled-out versions of numbers so that there can be no mistake with figures: *Your contract states that you must work seven (7) hours daily.*

In technological and scientific writing that includes frequent references to measurements, parentheses are used to enclose comparative forms of numbers: *6 inches (152.4 millimeters).*

Parentheses with Other Punctuation Marks

When you insert a complete parenthetical sentence within another sentence, do not capitalize the first letter of the enclosed sentence or end it with a period.

Example 1 Parenthetical sentence within a sentence

Educators worry about a growing gender imbalance in colleges (in 2000, women outnumbered men 128:100; by 2010, the proportion will be 138:100).

Adapted from Barrett Seaman, *Binge* (New York: Wiley, 2005), 50.

However, you can use an exclamation point or a question mark at the end of a parenthetical sentence placed within another sentence, even though the first word of the parenthetical sentence is not capitalized.

Example 2 Parenthetical question within a sentence

Repeated studies have shown that conflicts over gender (should the wife work? who should do what?) are leading causes of divorce.

From S. L. Nock, "The Consequences of Premarital Fatherhood," *American Sociological Review 63* (1998): 250–262.

When you insert a complete sentence enclosed in parentheses *between* two other sentences, capitalize the first word of the enclosed sentence and end it with a period inside the right parenthesis.

Example 3 Parenthetical sentence between sentences

More than once during World War II, Jack Kennedy courageously rescued enlisted men under his command. (Many officers were beloved by their subordinates and committed unrecognized heroic actions.) Kennedy was an example of the best that can emerge during war.

Do not use any punctuation before a parenthetical remark. A comma can follow the parentheses if the material before it would have required one.

Example 4 Punctuation with parentheticals

No — Whatever the experiment's outcome, (and the boiling point must be reached before final analysis) the goal is the same.

Yes — Whatever the experiment's outcome (and the boiling point must be reached before final analysis), the goal is the same.

Functions of Brackets within Quotations

- **To indicate that the words they enclose are yours and not those of the original author:**

  As Terry Eagleton aptly points out, "An advertisement for a daily newspaper announces [as though we still believed in killing off unborn infants or putting the mentally ill on show], 'Times change, Values don't'" (11).

- **To indicate that you have changed a direct quotation:**

  In *The Book Club Companion,* Diana Loevy shares advice on running book clubs: which books to read, which thematic snacks to serve with different novels, and which pets to allow at meetings. On whether to give up a seat to a pet, she quotes Dr. Merry Crimi, a veterinarian, who says "Humans need to assert their rightful alpha position and seating is no different"; Crimi "tell[s] [her] dog occasionally, 'sometimes you just have to be the dog'" (27).

- **To distinguish ellipsis points you have used to replace omitted material from ellipses present in the original source, when using MLA style:**

  The introduction concludes with a quotation from Weinberger's multi-layered and richly textured pastiche of the beautiful city of Vienna: "The Vienna of popular imagination [. . .] does indeed exist, but no one really lives there . . . except the most willfully sentimental of foreign visitors" (xi–xii).

- **To point out or correct errors in source material:**

  In an attempt to gain the sympathy of the voters, the school board candidate spoke of the averse [sic] conditions under which he had been working for the past two years.

Function of Brackets within Parentheses

- **To add very brief additional information about the material in parentheses:**

  Three former members of the Black Panther Party famous today for their political activism are Danny Glover, board chair of TransAfrica Forum (also well known as a director and actor in more than 25 films, including the *Lethal Weapon* movies [1987–1998]); Malik Rahim, co-founder of the hurricane relief organization Common Ground Collective; and Aaron Dixon, candidate for U.S. Senate on the Green Party ticket in 2006.

Brackets are squared parentheses: [ ]. They are used less frequently than parentheses and only for specialized purposes.

A pair of brackets is used *within quotations* to show that you are making minor additions or changes to a source's words. Be careful that your changes don't alter the meaning of the original material. Use brackets to

- indicate that the words they enclose are yours and not those of the original author. For example, you might need to add a word or change a verb tense so the quotation will fit smoothly into the grammar of your sentence.
- indicate that you have changed a direct quotation. If you add italics to the quotation, for example, you should note in brackets that you did so.
- distinguish ellipsis points you have used to replace omitted material from ellipses already present in the original source (see also section 43d).
- point out or correct errors in source material (e.g., an incorrect date, fact, etc.). The word *sic* (Latin for "so" or "thus") in brackets indicates that the error (in spelling, grammar, or usage) is in the source.

Brackets are also used *within parentheses.* When one pair of parentheses falls inside another, change the inner set to brackets.

Ellipsis points (also known as *an ellipsis*) are three spaced periods (. . .) that indicate omissions from quoted material or unfinished statements in dialogue.

Omission of Material from Quotations

Ellipsis points indicate the intentional omission of some amount of text from a quotation, whether a single word or whole paragraphs. An ellipsis is preceded and followed by a space. No matter how much material is removed, the omission should never change the fundamental meaning of the material being quoted.

In MLA documentation style, an ellipsis may be enclosed in brackets in order to differentiate it from ellipses in the original. The brackets make clear that the omission is the choice of the person quoting, not the person being quoted. In other documentation styles, brackets are not typically used to enclose ellipses used in quotations.

Prose Quotations

When you quote only a few words from another source, you don't need to use an ellipsis. Similarly, you don't usually need an ellipsis at the beginning of a sentence. If the quotation starts with a capital letter, readers assume that you are starting with a full sentence; if the

Example 5 No ellipsis needed when it's obvious that only a few words are quoted

Describing custodial involvement in human activities, Robert Temple writes, "No doubt we are under routine monitoring" (313).

Example 6 Ellipsis to show an omission in the middle of a sentence

Investigative researcher Jim Marrs writes, "Various discrepancies in Oswald's military records . . . support the idea that Oswald was given secret intelligence training" (112).

Example 7 Ellipsis to show an omission at the end of a sentence

Roman Polanski recalls, "Although I was never questioned about the tape, I should no doubt be accused of concealing a significant aspect of our lifestyle . . ." (298).

IF CITATION INFORMATION HAS ALREADY BEEN GIVEN, THE PERIOD FOLLOWS DIRECTLY AFTER THE ELLIPSIS AND BEFORE THE CLOSING QUOTATION MARK:

On page one of *V.*, Pynchon writes, "Christmas Eve, 1955, Benny Profane, wearing black levis, suede jacket, sneakers, and a big cowboy hat, happened to pass through . . . ."

IF ANOTHER SENTENCE THEN APPEARS IN FULL, THE NEXT SENTENCE BEGINS DIRECTLY AFTER THE ELLIPSIS AND PERIOD:

That is what is meant here by "mythical knowledge . . . . It was only understood by a very few" (de Santillana, Giorgio, and Von Dechend 53).

Example 8 Ellipsis to show that an entire sentence has been omitted

As Pfaff points out, "But the meaning of class is dangerous ground for an American. . . . There is an identifiable upper class in Britain with an aristocratic ethos and a hereditary base" (39).

Example 9 Ellipsis to show omission from the middle of one sentence to the middle of another

Hancock concludes, "As at Giza, therefore, a real correlation exists between sky and ground . . . and this correlation only 'locks' perfectly at a very remote date" (133).

Example 10 Ellipsis points in quotations from poetry

ORIGINAL SOURCE:

Miss Nancy Ellicott smoked
And danced all the modern dances;
And her aunts were not quite sure how they felt about it,
But they knew that it was modern.

From T. S. Eliot, "Cousin Nancy," in *Prufrock and Other Observations* (London: The Egoist, 1917), lines 7–10.

ELLIPSIS TO SHOW OMISSION OF A LINE:

T. S. Eliot puts Nancy Ellicott under a microscope to show the difference between performance and authenticity: "Miss Nancy Ellicott smoked / And danced all the modern dances; / . . . / But [her aunts] knew that it was modern" (7–10).

Example 11 Ellipsis points in dialogue

Eric looked across the gorge and, with an air unequal to the gravity of the question, asked, "It is . . . safe?"

Example 12 Ellipsis points with other punctuation

ORIGINAL SOURCE:

However, it soon becomes apparent that fashion embraces more than the need to be seen in the right places, doing the right things with the right people, and wearing the right clothes.

From Neil Sammells, *Wilde Style: The Plays and Prose of Oscar Wilde* (New York: Longman, 2000), 100.

COMMAS IN THE SERIES DROPPED:

Sammells goes on to say, "However, it soon becomes apparent that fashion embraces more than the need to be seen in the right places . . . and wearing the right clothes" (100).

quotation begins with a lowercase letter, readers will know you have started mid-sentence. Using brackets around the initial capital letter on the first word of a quoted sentence indicates that the word did not start a sentence in the original. The examples show various situations in which you do and do not need to use ellipses.

Poetry Quotations

When you omit words from within a line of poetry, the rules are the same as those for prose. When you omit an entire line of poetry and have indented the lines to preserve their original layout, show the omission with a row of spaced periods equal in length to the missing line or the one above it.

Unfinished Statements in Dialogue

An ellipsis can be used to indicate that a speaker's words are trailing off or that a speaker is hesitating.

Ellipsis Points with Other Punctuation

When you omit words from a quotation, you also omit any related punctuation, unless it is important to the structure of the sentence.

43e Using Slashes to Separate Parts or Indicate Options

Slashes are diagonal lines that look like this: /. They are used to separate the parts of a whole. Slashes are also used to indicate options.

Slashes Separate the Parts of a Whole

- Slashes are used between lines of poetry quoted in an essay. When you quote three or fewer lines of poetry, use a slash to indicate the end of each line. Each slash should be preceded and followed by a space. If you quote more than three lines, the poem appears as a block quotation and is printed without slashes (◀ section 13a).
- Slashes are used to separate the numerator and denominator in a fraction written in numerals. No space separates the slash from the numerals on either side.
- Slashes are used in Web addresses (URLs). If a Web address runs onto a second or subsequent line, break it right after a slash.

Slashes Separate Options

Slashes are used to separate words that indicate a choice of options: *win/lose, pass/fail.* One such construction, *he/she,* should not be used in college writing; see section 29a for a detailed discussion of the nonsexist use of language.

Functions of Slashes

- **To separate lines of poetry quoted in an essay:**

  In lines 39 through 41 from "Mending Wall," Robert Frost writes, "Bringing a stone grasped firmly by the top / In each hand, like an old-stone savage armed / He moves in darkness as it seems to me" (46).

- **To separate numerator and denominator in fractions:**

  3/5

- **To separate parts of a Web address:**

  Roald Dahl's *Charlie and the Chocolate Factory* is popular with children and adults, but if you want to know why, read this *New Yorker* piece: <http://www.newyorker.com/critics/atlarge/articles/050711crat_atlarge>.

- **To separate options:**

  The questionnaire was composed of ten yes/no questions.

Note: Current MLA guidelines recommend not using URLs in Works Cited entries unless they are needed for the reader to find the source or your instructor requires them.

Understanding Mechanics

PART 11

New Contexts for Writing: Machinima

Writers these days have so many new contexts for writing that the choices are sometimes bewildering. Now, not only must you choose what to write and how to write it, but also you must choose how to present your writing—on paper or computer screen, animated, aurally, next to photographs or video, and, yes, even inside the world of a video game. Fear not! The auteurs are here.

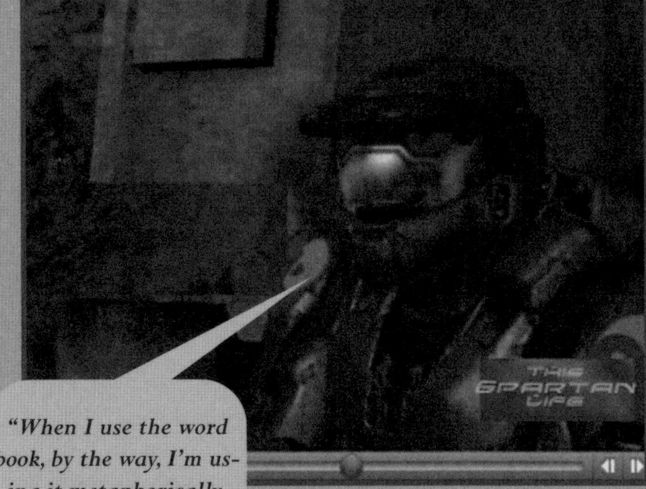

"When I use the word book, by the way, I'm using it metaphorically. Not the objects, but the vehicle that humans use to move heavy ideas around, big ideas around, and that vehicle is shifting from page to screen."
— Bob Stein

At **This Spartan Life: A Talk Show in Game Space** (http://www.thisspartanlife.com), Chris Burke interviewed Bob Stein, maker of the first multimedia CD ever, founder of the Voyager Company with its 300 films and 75 CD companion titles, creator of the TK3 multimedia ebook authoring software, and now director of the Institute for the Future of the Book, which has developed Sophie, the next generation of multimedia authoring tools. The setting is the video game *Halo 2*.

Auteur, the French term for "author," was once used to describe a film director who had total control over a film's style, content, and delivery. In many respects, today's writers are auteurs, with more options now for controlling the reception of their work. Auteurs understand genres and conventions, but they know as well how to manipulate them, make games work to their purposes, and add some fun and even irony to their writing.

Machinima is a new form of auteurism that uses video game systems to produce animated movies. (*Machinima* is pronounced "machine-i-ma.") Writers script dialogue or record interviews, game players perform actions to suit the dialogue, and a sound person records and syncs the game play with the audio to produce a movie. With a video game machine and a computer, you can record it all, then publish it to the Web. Amateur machinima artists now make films for MTV, Spike TV, and other cable channels. *Red vs. Blue* (or RvB), made by RoosterTeeth, is the most popular machinima on the Web. Its website http://rvb.roosterteeth.com/home.php has 444,000 registered users who write more than 6 million forum messages per year. There are already 79 episodes of RvB.

So, You Want to Be a Director?

Invent and **create** stories for machinima films:
Read Paul Marino's *3D Game-Based Filmmaking: The Art of Machinima* (2004)

Connect with machinimists
http://www.machinima.com

Read *Machinimag*
http://www.machinimag.com

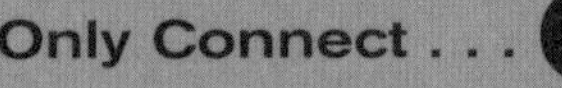

Using a Capital Letter at the Beginning of a Sentence 44a

Complete Sentences

- **After a colon, capitalize or do not capitalize a sentence, as you choose; do not capitalize a phrase.**

  Hammurabi's Code seems harsh today: **It** [or **it**] called, quite literally, for "an eye for an eye."

  The material after the colon has a subject, *It,* and a verb, *called,* but no subordinating word; it is an independent clause. Compare the clause with the material after the colon in this sentence, which has no subject or verb:

  My department manager has one major concern: **overspending** in my department.

- **After a colon, capitalize a question.**

  Darius III came to his throne by way of a string of murders: **Didn't** his own later murder mark the end of the Persian Empire?

- **In free-standing parentheses, capitalize.**

  Most full-time jobs offer some form of health insurance. (**If** health insurance costs keep rising at this rate, only employers from the largest corporations will be able to offer any kind of insurance.)

- **In parentheses within another sentence, do not capitalize.**

  Helen wished that she could afford to buy a new car (**this** car, she thought, is a real wreck!), but she knew she was lucky to own even her old Ford Escort.

- **Between dashes within another sentence, do not capitalize.**

  Cellular bonding—the process has been a common laboratory procedure for generations—is normally taught in the second semester.

Intentional Sentence Fragments

Hey, you! Whatever. Honest? Yikes!

The first word of a sentence always begins with a capital letter:

> **H**ammurabi was the king of Babylonia. **H**e is known for his far-reaching code of laws. **H**ave you heard of it?

If you write a complete sentence *after* a colon, you can choose either to capitalize the first word of that sentence or to use a lowercase letter. Choose the style you prefer and use it consistently in a document. When the information after a colon is not a complete sentence, use a lowercase letter to begin the phrase.

If a question follows a colon, capitalize the first word of the question.

When you write a complete sentence in parentheses, capitalize the first word of the sentence. However, if the parenthetical comment is *within* another sentence, do not capitalize the first word.

It is customary *not* to capitalize the first word of a sentence enclosed by dashes.

Capitalize the first word of intentional sentence fragments.

44b Capitalizing Proper Nouns and Proper Adjectives

Proper nouns are used to designate specific people, places, and things. They are capitalized except in rare cases in which a person has managed to establish (legally or otherwise) unconventional usage. Sometimes a phrase with a proper noun includes a common noun that is capitalized as part of the phrase—the word *mountains* in *Rocky Mountains,* for example.

Proper adjectives are adjectives formed from proper nouns: *Marxist* is formed from *Karl Marx*. They are always capitalized. If you use a hyphen to combine a proper noun with another word in order to form an adjective, capitalize only the proper noun: ***French**-speaking.* Don't capitalize prefixes used with proper adjectives—for example, ***pre**-Columbian*—except when they appear in titles or begin a sentence.

Proper Nouns and Adjectives

	Capitalize	But don't capitalize
Names of people and characters and adjectives formed from their names	Emma Goldman; Charles Darwin, Darwinian; Mother Jones; Mom, Mother, Dad [emphasizes the named individual]. Some people, such as writer *bell hooks* and poet *e. e. cummings,* do not capitalize their names. Follow their lead, but use capitalization if the name begins the sentence (e.g., E. E. Cummings).	my mom, my mother, my dad [emphasizes relationship]. Some names include elements such as *van, ten, de,* and *der,* which should not be capitalized unless the individual traditionally does so.
	Aunt Helen	your aunt
	Grandpa Joe	Robert's grandfather Joe
	Harry Potter	
Titles	Senator Rick Santorum	the senator
	President Clinton, the President of the United States	the president, a president, a former president
	Condoleezza Rice, National Security Advisor	a new national security advisor
	the Vice President for Academic Affairs	the vice president
Academic degrees	Harold K. Oates, PhD	a doctor of philosophy
	Dr. Atkins	the doctor
National, political, and ethnic groups	South African, Mexican; Republican, Democrat, Maoist; Latina, Hispanic, African American, Black, White	upper middle class [a socioeconomic group], black, white
	Note that the words *black* and *white* used to refer to race can be either capitalized or spelled lowercase, depending on your preference. Whichever you choose, be consistent throughout your text.	

	Capitalize	But don't capitalize
Names for God, religious leaders, religious groups, and sacred books	God, Allah, Zeus, Diana; the Buddha, the Dalai Lama, the Pope; Baptists, Islam, Islamic, Jews, Jewish; the Qur'an, Koranic, the Bible, the Torah, Scripture	gods and goddesses; a priest, rabbi, or pastor; a religion; religious people or group; a holy book, biblical times; scriptural interpretation
Languages	French, Kiswahili, Arabic	
Organizations, companies, clubs	National Organization for Women, Bard College, Halliburton, Fox Network, WiFi Communications, Lions Club	the company, the club
Trademarked products and brand names	Rice-a-Roni, Big Mac, Subaru Legacy, BCBG Max Azria	
Place names and geographic regions and features	Las Vegas, Nevada; the Northeast, the Badlands [regions]; the Snake River; the Pyrenees Mountains	to the north, south of Baghdad, east of Eden [directions]
Buildings, monuments, and bridges	Empire State Building, the Washington Monument, the Golden Gate Bridge	
Academic courses	English 103, Psychology of Women, Introduction to Chemistry	introductory chemistry course
Specific time periods, historical events, and significant historical documents	Mesozoic Era, the Ming Dynasty, the Renaissance; the Civil Rights Movement, World War Two, the American Revolution; the Declaration of Independence, the Magna Carta	medieval, renaissance, a declaration of independence
Literary, artistic, and cultural movements	Formalism, Dadaism, the Beat Generation	
Days, months, holidays	Sunday, New Year's Day, February, St. Patrick's Day, Hanukkah	spring, summer, fall, winter
Scientific and technical terms	Mars, Jupiter, Earth [when discussed as a planet]; Milky Way	
Acronyms and initialisms	DNA, OPEC, UN, NATO	

44c Using Capital Letters in Titles

In MLA style, all significant words in the titles of books, articles in journals and magazines, movies, television shows, plays, newspaper stories, and works of art are capitalized.

In APA reference lists, capitalize the first word of a title, proper nouns and proper adjectives, and the first word after a colon: *Blink: The power of thinking without thinking.* However, capitalize all important words in journal names: *Journal of Family Psychology.*

In CMS style, capitalize every major word of the title and the first and last words of both title and subtitle. Use lowercase for articles *a, an,* and *the;* conjunctions *and, but, for, or,* and *nor;* the words *to* and *as;* and most prepositions, except when they are emphasized: *The Devil in the White City: Murder, Magic, and Madness at the Fair That Changed America.*

Capitalization in Titles, MLA Style

Book	*The Mind at Night: The New Science of How and Why We Dream*
	Harry Potter and the Half-Blood Prince
Essay	"Eight Simple Rules for Dating My Daughter"
Movie	*Star Wars: Revenge of the Sith*
Painting	*Water Lilies*

In MLA style, capitalize . . .

- the first and last word of the title
- the first and last word of a subtitle that follows a colon
- all other major words, including those that follow hyphens

Certain words are not capitalized, unless they appear at the beginning or end of the title or subtitle:

- prepositions (such as *on, in, at*)
- coordinating conjunctions (*and, but, or, nor, for, so, yet*)
- articles (*a, an, the*)
- the word *to* in infinitives

44d Using Capital Letters in Quotations

Whether you capitalize the first word in a quotation depends on the material you are quoting and where you place it in your sentence. If you are quoting a complete sentence of prose or starting a sentence with a quotation, capitalize the first word. However, if you are quoting directly from another work using a verb such as *said* or *stated,* capitalize the first word of the quoted material only if it is capitalized in the original work.

Capitalization When Quoting Prose

Capitalize the first word of a quotation . . .

- **when quoting a complete sentence:**

  George told me, "Don't recycle that kind of plastic anymore."

  Walker writes, "Womanism is the fullest expression of life." [Capital letter used in original work]

  Gladwell said Levi's had found that "baby boomer men felt that the chief thing missing from their lives was male friendship." [No capital letter in original]

- **when beginning your sentence with a quotation:**

  "Of the many ways to fail on a dating website, not posting a photo of yourself is perhaps the most certain," claim Levitt and Dubner (82).

Do not capitalize the first word of a quotation . . .

- **if the quotation is not a complete sentence:**

Walker describes a "system wherein slave labor is turned into capital."

The best way to investigate a story is "to follow the money."

- **if the quotation follows an interruption created by your own words:**

"When my sister eats popcorn," he explained, "she loves to watch a movie."

Do not capitalize a quotation if it is not a complete sentence.

When you interrupt a quoted sentence with your own words, don't capitalize the first word after your interruption.

Capitalize the first word in each line of quoted poetry if the poet has done so. If the poet has not used capitals, neither should you.

Capitalization When Quoting Poetry

- **First word of line capitalized in original:**

When Donne wrote "That thou may'st know me" (42), he was admitting that full disclosure was critical to salvation. . . .

- **First word of line not capitalized in original:**

In "anyone lived in a pretty how town," e. e. cummings writes, "she laughed his joy she cried his grief" (14).

Using Capital Letters in Lists 44e

When list items are complete sentences, use a capital letter to start each item in the following kinds of lists:

- lists within a paragraph (called run-in lists)
- lists displayed vertically
- formal outlines
- series of questions

When the list items are not complete sentences but are arranged vertically or are in the form of questions, you may capitalize or not as you choose, but be consistent throughout a writing project.

Example 1 Capitalization in run-in lists in which list items are complete sentences

A job candidate may be asked a number of painful questions in a job interview: (1) What is your most obvious character weakness? (2) What would your current co-workers say they like least about you? (3) How well would you say you handle stressful situations?

Example 2 Capitalization in formal outlines

START EACH LINE WITH A CAPITAL LETTER AND END FULL SENTENCES WITH A PERIOD:

I. Communicating-to-Learn Activities
 a. Follow the principles in informal writing.
  i. Put the principles into practice daily.
  ii. Focus on elaborating content, not on correctness. . . .

44f Using Capital Letters in Email Addresses and URLs

Although most of what you encounter on the Internet is not case sensitive, all parts of a URL that appear after the domain name are case sensitive. So when tracking down a website, listing a URL in your citations or text, or sending someone a URL, make sure that you don't deviate from the capitalization used in the original URL. Email addresses are not case sensitive, so it doesn't matter whether you capitalize them or not.

Example 3 Capitalization in URLs and email addresses

THESE TWO URLS ARE THE SAME:

http://www.POWELLS.com   http://www.powells.com

THESE TWO ARE *NOT* THE SAME:

http://www.virtualparlor.org/Rhetoric   http://www.virtualparlor.org/rhetoric

THESE TWO EMAIL ADDRESSES ARE THE SAME:

joe.schmoe@google.com   Joe.Schmoe@google.com

44g Using Italics for the Titles of Long Works

Use italics (or underlining) to indicate the titles of long works or of works that are subdivided into parts. (For short works, see section 42d.)

Note: Italicize or underline an article (*A, An,* or *The*) only if it is part of the title. The definite article can be left off newspaper titles: *New York Times* instead of *The New York Times.*

Don't italicize (or underline) names of major religious works, books of the Bible, or legal documents.

Please note, however, that current MLA guidelines recommend italics in place of underlining.

Use italics for titles of long works

Book	*The Eyre Affair*
Newspaper	*New York Times, Washington Post*
Journal	*A Cancer Journal for Clinicians*
Magazine	*People*
Ezine	*Y3K Software News*
Weblog	*Shadow of the Hegemon*
Film	*Wizard of Oz*
Television show	*The Sopranos*
Radio program	*Morning Sedition*
Play	*Hamlet*
Long poem	*In Memoriam*
Long musical work, CD, record album	*And All That Might Have Been*
Painting, drawing, sculpture, dance	*Ground Level Overlay*
Cartoon or comic strip that appears regularly	*Doonesbury*
Computer game	*Battlefield: Vietnam*
Pamphlet	*Men 18–25 Years*

Do not use any italics, underlines, or quotation marks for major religious works, books of the Bible, or legal documents

Major religious work	Bible, Qur'an, Torah
Book of the Bible	Leviticus, Nehemiah, James
Public, legal, or classic document	Declaration of Independence

Using Italics for Words and Letters Referred to as Such 44h

Example 4 Using italics to refer to words, letters, and numbers

The word *weird* is derived from Old English.

Spell out *5* as *five* unless exact quantities are critical or you're reporting data.

Speakers of Maay-Maay from Somalia may have trouble distinguishing the English sound *b* from the sound for *p*.

Italicize words, letters, and numbers when they are used to refer to themselves or when they are being defined.

Using Italics for the Names of Spacecraft, Aircraft, Ships, and Trains 44i

Use italics for names of specific individual crafts

The *Columbia* disaster *Air Force One*

H.M.S. *Queen Elizabeth II*

But do not italicize names of categories of vehicles or types of crafts

the Ford Mustang a Baycraft sailboat United Airlines DC-10

Use italics for the names of specific trains and other crafts, but not for kinds of vehicles or craft.

Using Italics for Some Foreign Words and Phrases 44j

Example 5 Using italics with foreign words and phrases

FOREIGN WORD IN COMMON USE—NO ITALICS:

When he missed the piñata, he struck me in the face with the stick.

FOREIGN PHRASE NOT IN COMMON USE—USE ITALICS:

He spoke *ad nauseam* about the state of his liver, so I wanted to bolt from the table.

LATIN NAME IN NONSCIENTIFIC WRITING—USE ITALICS:

While searching for rare birds, we saw a *Pterocles coronatus* alight nearby.

Italicize foreign words and phrases only if they are not in common use. If you don't know whether a term is in common use, consult a dictionary.

Italicize Latin names of plants and animals, except in scientific/technical contexts where they are more commonly used.

Using Substitutes for Italics in Email Messages 44k

Example 6 Substituting for italics in email

I want to read that book _The Monuments of Mars: A City on the Edge of Forever_ by Richard Hoagland.

Email programs that require plain text and thus limit text styling do not allow you to use italics or underlining, so use a pair of underscores to set off words or terms you would normally italicize.

45 ABBREVIATIONS AND NUMBERS

45a Abbreviations in Academic Writing

Abbreviations are shortened versions of words or brief phrases. Use abbreviations sparingly in nontechnical academic writing. For example, spell out the names of disciplines (*sociology,* not *soc.*), and use the phrase *and so forth* or *and so on* instead of *etc.*

The first time you use an abbreviation, write the term out in full and put the abbreviation immediately after it in parentheses. After doing so, you can use just the abbreviation.

Example 1 Writing out most words in formal academic writing

No Angela Davis taught philosophy at the **Univ.** of **Calif., L.A.,** from 1969–1970.

Yes Angela Davis taught philosophy at the **University** of **California, Los Angeles,** from 1969 to 1970.

Example 2 Defining abbreviations on first mention

Many users expect that their Local Area Network **(LAN)** will function without fail; however, **LAN** administrators often experience daily troubles with their hardware.

45b Abbreviating Titles, Ranks, and Degrees

Titles commonly used either before (*Mr., Mrs., Ms., Rev.*) or after names (*Jr., MD, MA, PhD*) are regularly abbreviated.

Certain titles can be preceded by the article *The*. When they are, the title is spelled out.

Other titles are usually given in full, although they can be abbreviated if they are placed before a first name or initial.

Academic degrees are indicated either by an abbreviation before the name or by an abbreviation after it, but not both together. First letters are capitalized. Abbreviations for academic degrees can stand alone.

Example 3 Abbreviating titles, ranks, and degrees

- **Abbreviated:**

Rev. stands for *Reverend*   *PhD* stands for *Doctor of Philosophy*
MA stands for *Master of Arts*   *JD* stands for *Juris Doctor* (doctor of law)

- **Preceded by *The*:**

Rev. Howard	but	The Reverend Howard
Hon. Gov. Rendell	but	The Honorable Governor Edward Rendell

- **Spelled out unless followed by a first name or initial:**

Senator	Senator Kennedy	Sen. Edward Kennedy
President	President Bush	Pres. George W. Bush
Professor	Professor Hatashi	Prof. K. Hatashi

Abbreviating Names of Agencies and Organizations 45c

Write out the names of organizations, companies, and government agencies in full, unless they are commonly referred to by abbreviations.

Example 4 Writing names of agencies and organizations

WRITE OUT THE NAMES OF ORGANIZATIONS:

Royal Geographic Society   The Allstate Corporation
Pennsylvania Coalition Against Domestic Violence   Avon Products

BUT USE ABBREVIATIONS FOR ORGANIZATIONS KNOWN BY THEIR ABBREVIATIONS:

USDA	United States Department of Agriculture
FedEx	Federal Express
NBA	National Basketball Association

Abbreviating Place Names 45d

The names of states, countries, provinces, regions, and continents are not usually abbreviated unless they are part of an address, although some countries are commonly referred to by abbreviations: *UK, USA.* State names should be written out in full in formal writing, unless they are part of a specific address. When a state name appears in a sentence after a city name, it is preceded and followed by a comma.

Example 5 Writing place names

No Sarita Perez lived on Euclid **Ave.** in Pittsburgh, **PA,** for three years.

Yes Sarita Perez lived on Euclid **Avenue** in Pittsburgh, **Pennsylvania,** for three years.

Yes Sarita Perez lived at 345 Euclid Avenue, Pittsburgh, PA, 15120, for three years.

When state names are part of a specific address, they are abbreviated using the United States postal codes. For a list of postal codes, go to the United States Postal Service website:
http://www.usps.com/ncsc/lookups/usps_abbreviations.html#suffix

Abbreviating Units of Measure 45e

You can use abbreviations for units of measure that accompany numbers, but it is generally better to write both the number and the unit of measure out in full in nontechnical academic writing. However, in technical writing that

Example 6 Writing out numbers and units of measure in nontechnical academic writing

It took her **fifteen minutes** to complete the task.
He traveled over **fifteen thousand miles** during the **six-**month period.
The new wall was **twenty feet** taller than the old one.

includes numerous units of measure (*cm, mm*), periods of time (*yr*), and acronyms (*URL, LAN*), abbreviations are expected.

In scientific and technical writing, periods are usually omitted unless doing so would cause confusion (*in* versus *in.* for *inch*). Periods are not typically used with metric measurements.

When the unit of measure is not well known to readers, offer an equivalent, in familiar units, within parentheses immediately after the abbreviation.

Typical Abbreviations for Units of Measure

1 qt.	15 oz.	7½ in.	12° F (Fahrenheit)
3 yd.	3 tsp.	10 kg	–6 K (Kelvin)
750 lb.	30 mpg	15 km	33° C (Celsius)

Example 7 Providing a familiar equivalent for an unfamiliar unit

The first Olympic marathon was 40 km (24.85 **miles**). Today, the word *marathon* refers to a running event of 42.195 km (26 **miles** and 385 **yards**).

45f Using Signs and Symbols

Use the dollar sign ($) as an abbreviation for the word *dollar* only when you are referring to a specific sum of money. Similarly, when you are reporting percentages in a nontechnical document in the humanities, spell out % as *percent*. In a document that reports data, use the percent symbol: %.

Use symbols such as +, –, =, and # only in tables, charts, and graphs or in technical writing. An exception is the @ sign, which you should use when you include an email address in your text.

Example 8 Using $ only with specific amounts

You had to pay **$7.50** for a movie ticket?

The Defense Department asked for an additional **$5 billion** for the war on terrorism.

How many **dollars** do you have in your wallet right now?

Example 9 Using % only in documents that report data

The news media report that fewer than **50 percent** of registered voters actually vote in the November elections. [Nontechnical source]

I think you will find that the **percentage** is far higher this year. [The % sign is never a proper replacement for *percentage*.]

In our survey of self-described "Internet junkies," **43%** of the respondents reported that they frequently google their last names, while another **32%** admitted that they compare numbers of hits with their friends. [Document that reports data]

Abbreviation	Latin Term	English Equivalent
i.e.	id est	that is
N.B.	nota bene	note well
cf.	confer	compare
viz.	videlicet	namely
e.g.	exempli gratia	for example
et al.	et alia	and others
etc.	et cetera	and so on

Use Latin abbreviations sparingly in your academic writing. Most can be easily translated into their English equivalents.

Note: You can use the abbreviations to the left when documenting sources or in parenthetical citations.

Writing Numbers 45h

Writers in scientific disciplines frequently use numerals in their texts; those in the humanities tend to use a combination of spelled-out numbers and numerals.

In both the MLA style and the APA style, spell out numbers that start sentences. To avoid the awkwardness of writing out large numbers, you may need to recast the sentence so that the number comes later.

Example 10 MLA style for numbers

one	two hundred	three-quarters	55,372
fifteen hundred	thirty-five thousand	five-eighths	1,300,541
thirty-five	three million	six billion	1,095

- Spell out all numbers that are one or two words long and use numerals for those that are longer.
- Hyphenate spelled-out numbers from 21 to 99: *twenty-one, eighty-eight, ninety-nine*. Hyphenated numbers count as one word, so you would still spell out *thirty-five thousand.*

Example 11 APA style for numbers

one	11	99	300	1,200	13,466

- Spell out the numbers from one to nine.
- Use numerals for all numbers 10 and above.

Example 12 Writing numbers

No	**3,705** people voted for the incumbent.
Awkward	**Three thousand seven hundred five** people voted for the incumbent.
Yes	The incumbent received 3,705 votes.

45i Combining Words and Numerals

When you use specific numbers frequently—for example, statistics, temperatures, or percentages—it is acceptable to use numerals. Otherwise, combine words and numbers in order to make your writing as clear as possible to the reader.

Within a sentence or a longer passage when you are using numbers to refer to items that belong in the same category or to express a range, use numerals and be consistent. This allows the reader to more easily identify the numbers and make comparisons.

When numbers follow each other in a sentence, use a numeral for one and words for the other, for the sake of clarity.

In a sentence where one number stands alone and the others form a series of related numbers, it makes sense to spell out the single number and provide the rest as numerals.

Combine words and numerals to express large round numbers.

Example 13 Using numerals in comparisons

In April, the company produced **15** new models; in June, **2,000;** and by December, it was turning out **2,500** models per week.

Between **1,000** and **3,500** pedestrians cross that street every weekday.

Example 14 Combining words and numerals

Sixteen 18-wheeler trucks just drove by the house.
I'd like **one hundred 3⁄4-**inch nails, please.

Example 15 Distinguishing between types of numbers

Over the course of a month, the **three** friends each increased the distance they ran from **2,** to **5,** to **8** miles per day.

Example 16 Writing large round numbers

New statistics reveal that **1.7 million** jobs were lost last year.
The meteorite hit Earth approximately **300 million** years ago.

45j Using Numerals for Exact Measurements

Numerals are typically used with abbreviations for units of measure and with exact measurements.

Note: For nontechnical writing, most style guides allow the use of either numerals or words for percentages and even amounts of money. If you use a symbol (%, $, ¢) for the unit, however, you must use a numeral for the quantity.

Numerals for Exact Measurements

Decimals	1.07		
Measured amounts	17° Celsius	3.5 gallons	12 feet
	32° F	25% (or 25 percent)	
Statistics, scores, ratios,	8–5 (score)	a 3-to-1 ratio; 3:1	
surveys	9 out of 10	a mean of 12	
Rates of speed	120 mph	4,500 rpm	25 kmh
Large or non-even amounts	$25,000	$1.5 million	
of money	$7.99		

For clarity, use numerals to express fractions, unless they are common fractions used in a nontechnical context.

Example 17 Writing fractions

Nontechnical	I will be home in half an hour. Make that a quarter of an hour.
Technical	Ground water indirectly contributes 1/4 of the water input to Calliope River.

Using Numerals for Dates and Times 45k

Dates and times should generally be written in numerals. But in nontechnical writing, spell out dates written in ordinal numbers and spell out times incorporating words like *past, after, to,* and *o'clock.*

Numerals for Most Dates and Times

Dates	35 BCE AD 1666 350 CE the 1960s the twenty-first century April 15, 1955 or 15 April 1955 November fifth from 1914 to 1918 between 1860 and 1923
Time of day	11:15 2315 hrs 9 a.m. 3 p.m. (not three p.m.) three o'clock in the morning (not 3 o'clock) half past seven

Note: When specifying a range of numbers in text, use the word *to* instead of a dash.

Example 18 Specifying a range of numbers

No	From **1954–1972,** Cold War fears found expression in science fiction films like *Them* and *Night of the Lepus.*
Yes	From **1954 to 1972,** Cold War fears found expression in science fiction films like *Them* and *Night of the Lepus.*

Other Uses of Numerals 45l

Use numerals for addresses, routes, phone numbers, television channels, radio stations, and social security numbers.

Numerals for Various Types of Numbers

Addresses	1600 Pennsylvania Avenue Washington, DC 20500	P.O. Box 312 Interstate 91
Telephone numbers	202-456-1111 (comments line for White House)	
Television and radio stations	Channel 22	WAMC FM 90.3
Social security numbers	101-01-1000	

Commas

Use commas in numerals with four or more digits (five or more digits in CSE style). Starting from where the decimal point would be, place a comma after each group of three digits, to indicate thousands, millions, and so on. Don't use the comma in numbers used to express calendar years.

Example 19 Using commas with numbers

4,000 100,534 50,000 1,546,378

But 1066 CE

Hyphens

Don't use a hyphen to link a number or a fraction to the word it modifies if that word stands alone, but do use a hyphen to link a number and a word that together modify a following noun.

Example 20 Using hyphens with numbers

2.5 gigabytes 2.5-gigabyte memory disk

3⁄4 mile 3⁄4-mile road race

Example 21 Using hyphens to help distinguish numbers

She asked me to buy 3 six-packs of diet cola, 1 two-liter bottle of ginger ale, and 5 gallons of milk.

Spaces

Put a space between a number and the word it modifies, unless they are connected by a hyphen. If you are formatting your fractions as full-size numbers arranged horizontally, insert a space between the whole number and the fraction.

Example 22 Using spaces with numbers

There are four 1/8-inch drill bits missing from my toolbox.

The spider spun 14 1/2 feet of web in under a day. [Otherwise, the number could be read as $^{141}\!/_{2}$.]

Plurals

You can make a number plural by adding the letter *s*. When referring to decades, be sure to include the century.

Example 23 Making numbers plural

No I loved the 80's.

No I loved the eighties.

Yes I loved the 1980s.

My wallet is full of 10s and 20s.

Developing Good Spelling Habits 46a

A Practical Proofreading Strategy

frenzy antibeef an promted States United the in disease mad-cow of case single a after 2004 early in point this made Jersey, New Princeton, in consultant" comunications "risk self-discribed a Sandman, Peter assesors. Risk terrible parent, Molly's like are, us of most But

From Steven D. Levitt and Stephen J. Dubner, *Freakonomics* (New York: William Morrow, 2005), 150. Reordered, with spelling and punctuation mistakes added.

Project Checklist

Developing Good Spelling Habits

- ❑ Reach for the dictionary whenever in doubt.
- ❑ Check words as you go for spelling, meaning, and usage—or save that step for after you've completed a draft. If you like to write first and think about spelling later, you can still flag words you're not sure about as you go. Simply write *(sp?)* after a word you're unsure about.
- ❑ Once your draft is complete, run the spell checker and find as many errors as you can. Then print out your document, grab a pen and your dictionary, and check your spelling.
- ❑ When all revisions are complete, repeat the previous step and then proofread one last time.

Try Proofreading Backward

One proofreading strategy is to start with the last word in a document and read backward. To show you the effectiveness of this strategy, the words to the left have been arranged from last to first. Notice how your eye lingers on each word when you can't make sense of surrounding word groups, as you would naturally do when reading. What spelling errors do you find? Which words would you need to look up in a dictionary to see if they were spelled correctly?

Use a Spell Checker, but Beware!

The spell check feature in most word-processing programs can be a big help, but beware: your computer will never be as smart as you are. Spell check won't recognize when you use *it's* incorrectly for *its, who's* for *whose,* and a host of other spelling errors that depend on context as well as on the word itself.

46b Checking for Commonly Misspelled Words

Use this list of commonly misspelled words as a starting point.

225 Commonly Misspelled Words, Spelled Correctly

absence
accidentally
accommodate
accumulate
achievement
acquaintance
acquire
acquitted
advice
advise
affidavit
amateur
analysis
analyze
apparatus
apparent
appearance
arctic
arguing
argument
arithmetic
ascend
athletic
attendance
balance
battalion
beautiful
beginning
belief
believe
beneficial
benefited
boundaries
business
calendar
candidate
category
cemetery
changeable
choose
chose
commission
committee
comparative
compelled
complexion
conceivable
conceive
conferred
conscience
conscientious
conscious
controversial
controversy
criticize
deferred
definitely
definition
describe
description
desperate
dictionary
dining
diphtheria
disappearance
disappoint
disastrous
discipline
dissatisfied
dormitory
effect
eighth
eligible
eliminate
embarrass
eminent
encouragement
encouraging
environment
equipped
especially
exaggerate
excellence
exhilarate
existence
existent
experience
explanation
familiar
fascinate
February
fiery
fitting
foreign
formerly
forty
fourth
frantically
generally
government
grammar
grandeur
grievous
harass
height
heroes
hindrance
humorous
hypocrisy
hypocrite
immediately
incidentally
incredible
independence
inevitable
inoculate
intellectual
intelligence
interesting
irresistible
knowledge
laboratory
laid
led
lightning
loneliness
lose
maintenance
maneuver
manufacture
marriage
maybe
miniature
mischievous
misspell
mysterious
necessary
noticeable
occasionally
occurred
occurrence
omitted
opinion
opportunity
optimistic
paid
parallel
paralysis
paralyze
particular
pastime
performance
permissible
perseverance
personal
personnel
perspiration
physical
picnicking
possession
possibility
possible
practically
precede
precedence
preference
preferred
prejudice
preparation
prevalent
principal
principle
privilege
probably
procedure
proceed
profession
professor
prominent
pronunciation
pursue
quantity
quizzes
recede
receive
receiving
recommend
reference
referring
repetition
restaurant
rhyme
rhythm
ridiculous
roommate
sacrifice
sacrilegious
schedule
seize
separate
separation
sergeant
severely
siege
similar
sincerely
sophomore
specifically
specimen
succeed
succession
supersede
surprise
technique
temperamental
tendency
tragedy
transferring
truly
tyranny
unanimous
undoubtedly
unnecessary
villain
weather
weird

Example 1 Using *it's/its, you're/your,* and *who's/whose*

It's a wonder that our cat left **its** food untouched.

You're so possessive about **your** cat that no one else can pet her.

Who's going to drive **whose** car when we shuttle back from our bike trip?

Homonyms are words that sound alike but have different meanings: *pair / pear; bare / bear; to / too / two.* Homonyms and near-homonyms, such as *accept / except, affect / effect,* and *conscience / conscious,* are a common source of misspellings. You will find many of these words in the Glossary of Usage that begins on page G-6 at the end of the book.

Following Spelling Rules 46d

Forming Plurals

The plurals of most nouns are formed by adding *s* to the end of the word.

Nouns ending in *-s, -sh , -ch,* or *-x* require the addition of *es* to form the plural.

Nouns ending in *-o* require *s* or *es,* depending on whether the *o* is preceded by a vowel or a consonant.

For nouns ending in *-y,* change *y* to *i* and add *es.*

Nouns ending in *-f* or *-fe* vary. Some form plurals by adding *s.* For others, change *f* to *v,* and add *es* or *s.*

Examples of Making Nouns Plural

elephant + *s* = elephant*s*
muffin, muffin***s***
prize, prize***s***
table, table***s***

process + *es* = process*es*
dish, dish***es***
church, church***es***
fox, fox***es***

Vowel: patio + *s* = patio*s*
radio, radio***s***
taboo, taboo***s***
zoo, zoo***s***

Consonant: potato + *es* = potato*es*
tomato, tomato***es***
veto, veto***es***
Exceptions:
memo, memo***s***
piano, piano***s***

party ⟶ parti + *es* = parti*es*
responsibility, responsibilit***ies***
forty, fort***ies***

belief + *s* = belief*s*
fife, fife***s***

cal*f* ⟶ cal*v* + *es* = cal*ves*
half, hal***ves***
leaf, lea***ves***
life, li***ves***
wife, wi***ves***

Closed compound nouns (compounds written as one word) take *s* or *es* at the end of the last word.

For hyphenated and open compounds (that is, compounds that are two separate words), add *s* or *es* to the more significant word, usually the noun that can be counted.

Some words form plurals irregularly.

Other Changes in Word Form

Along with the formation of plurals, spelling rules govern other changes in word form.

Doubling Consonants to Retain Short Vowel Sounds

In changing word forms, the general rule is to use double consonants to retain a short vowel sound.

In words of more than one syllable in which the stress in pronunciation shifts from one syllable to another when the word changes form, do not double the consonant.

Exceptions to the doubling rules are words like *travel* and *cancel,* which can acceptably become *traveled, traveling, travels, traveler* or *travelled, travelling, travels, traveller* and *canceled, canceling* or *cancelled, cancelling,* respectively.

Closed Compounds

breakthrough**s** cupful**s** handful**s**

Hyphenated Compounds

city-state**s**
sister**s**-in-law

Open Compounds

civil right**s**
history major**s**

Irregular Plurals

child, children
foot, feet
man, men
mouse, mice
ox, oxen
tooth, teeth
woman, women

deer, deer
elk, elk
fish, fish
moose, moose
series, series
sheep, sheep
species, species

Short Vowel Sound and Long Vowel Sound Pairs

hop, hopped, hopping
hope, hoped, hoping

slop, sloppy, sloppier, sloppiest
slope, sloping

Rule: Double the consonant when a one-syllable stem ends in one vowel and one consonant

sla***p***, sla***pp***ed, sla***pp***ing
big, bi**gg**er, bi**gg**est

slo***p***, slo***pp***y, slo***pp***ier, slo***pp***iest
sho***p***, sho***pp***ed, sho***pp***ing, sho***pp***er

Rule: Double the consonant when a stem of more than one syllable ends in one vowel and one consonant and the stress remains on that syllable

Stress remains on the short-vowel syllable—consonant doubles

refer´, referred´, refer´ring, refer´ral
prefer´, preferred´, prefer´ring, prefer´rer

Stress shifts to another place—consonant does not double

in´ference, inferen´tial, inferen´tially
ref´erence, referee´, referen´tial

Rule: Keep the final silent *e* with a suffix beginning with a consonant; drop the final silent *e* with a suffix beginning with a vowel

+ consonant: state, state*ment*
+ vowel: state, stat*ing*

+ consonant: force, force*ful*
+ vowel: force, forc*ible*

+ consonant: like, like*ly*
+ vowel: like, lik*ing*

+ consonant: require, require*ment*
+ vowel: require, requir*ing*

Exceptions:

dye, dyeing
shoe, shoeing
courage, courageous
outrage, outrageous
change, changeable
embrace, embraceable
manage, manageable
notice, noticeable
marriage, marriageable
argue, argument
due, duly
true, truly

Vowel + *y*—keep the *y*

cloy, cloying
joy, joyous
play, playful

Exceptions:

day, daily
gay, gaily

Consonant + *y*—omit the *y*

city, cities
deputy, deputize
lively, livelier

Exceptions:

dry, drying, dryly
try, trying
reply, replying

i before *e* except after *c*

achieve, retrieve, sieve, aerie, friend, pier, town crier, pliers, diet, hierarchy; ceiling, receive, inconceivable

or when pronounced "ay" as in *neighbor* or *weigh*

lei, sleigh, weight, freight, beige, dreidel, eight, rein, veil, vein

Exceptions:

-ei: weird, seize, caffeine, protein, either, neither, deity
-ie: fallacies, frequencies, species, science, society

Keeping or Dropping the Final e
Suffixes are word endings such as *-ed, -ing, -er, -est, -ance, -ment,* and *-or.* Keep a word's final silent *e* when adding a suffix that begins with a consonant. Drop a word's final silent *e* when adding a suffix that begins with a vowel.

Note that with the suffix *-ment,* the word *judge* can become either *judgment* or *judgement* (but not both in the same paper). The preferred American spelling is *judgment;* the preferred British spelling is *judgement.*

Keeping or Dropping the Final y
When adding a suffix to a word ending in *-y,* keep the final *y* when the *y* is preceded by a vowel. Change the word's final *y* to *i* when the *y* is preceded by a consonant, unless the suffix itself also begins with an *i.*

With some proper nouns, you retain the *y* (*Kennedy, Kennedyesque*); with others, you do not (*Kentucky, Kentuckian*). Check a dictionary.

The *ie* Rule

Remembering the familiar rhyme will help you use *-ie* and *-ei* properly.

i before *e* except after *c*
or when pronounced "ay"
as in *neighbor* or *weigh*

46e Using Hyphens in Compound Words

Compound words—that is, words made up of two or more words—can be open, closed, or hyphenated: *water ski, waterskiing,* and *water-skier*. Because our language is in flux, hyphens come into play as new words are coined. Some words start out open, then become hyphenated, and finally enter the dictionary as closed compounds: *on line* becomes *on-line* becomes *online.* When in doubt, use your dictionary.

Contrasting Examples

Open	Closed	Hyphenated
water ski	waterskiing	water-skier
water buffalo	waterfowl	water-resistant
water hole	waterfall	water-repellent

46e Using Hyphens with Prefixes and Suffixes

Prefixes are word parts added to the beginning of words to form new words; some examples are *re-, de-, anti-, mini-,* and *in-*. Suffixes are word parts added to the ends of words—for example *-ism, -ian, -er, -ent,* and *-ion*. Words formed with prefixes and suffixes—*cyberspace, interfaith, minivan, postmodern, socioeconomic, underemployed*—are almost always closed. But there are some exceptions.

In general, use a hyphen . . .

- **to form words with the prefix *all-, ex-* (used to mean "former"), or *self-***

  all-purpose, all-star ex-president, ex-husband, ex-marine self-expression

- **to form words with the suffix *-elect* or *-odd***

  president-elect, mayor-elect hundred-odd, 350-odd

- **to join a prefix to a capitalized word**

  anti-Semitism non-Euclidian sub-Saharan
  pre-Columbian post-Victorian un-American
  mid-Atlantic post-Vietnam

- **to join a capitalized initial to a word**

  T-shirt I-beam X-ray

- **to join a prefix to a number**

  pre-1950 post-2004

- **to clarify potentially ambiguous meaning**

  re-creation vs. recreation re-dress (dress again) vs. redress (set right)
  re-ally vs. really re-sort vs. resort

- **to enhance readability**

  anti-intellectual wall-less
  de-ice sub-subentry

Grammar for Multilingual Writers

PART 12

New Contexts for Writing: Wikipedia

Wikipedia (http://www.wikipedia.org) is the world's largest encyclopedia, with more free content about more topics than any other encyclopedia ever published. It has grown so large so fast because it has become a new context for writing, a place on the Internet where anyone with an Internet connection and a Web browser can create, revise, and improve the sum of human knowledge, at least as that knowledge is represented at Wikipedia.

A **wiki** (pronounced "wick-ee") is software that enables authors to collaborate on a common text on the Internet using only a Web browser (such as Internet Explorer or Firefox). People also use the term to refer to websites built by this method of collaborative authorship. Wikis allow users to add, delete, move, and revise the content on a website. A **version tracking system** keeps a record of these changes and previous drafts so that—when mistakes are made, for example—site administrators can use the wiki's **rollback** feature to restore a previous version.

What Should You Use an Encyclopedia to Do?

Good encyclopedias sum up general knowledge about a wide range of subjects. Ideally, encyclopedic information should be **reliable, accurate, timely, accessible,** and **comprehensive.** Even the best encyclopedias, however, are not meant to be the final word on a subject. Think of encyclopedias as starting points for further research, the touchstones that can stimulate your deeper consideration of complex subjects.

For Internet researchers, Wikipedia is a good place to begin research because it offers rich linking to other sources on the Internet (and within Wikipedia itself), it is free and easily accessible, and it covers a huge range of topics.

Make the World a Better Place Right Now . . .

- Read Wikipedia's "Policies and Guidelines" so that you understand how (and why) a publicly authored encyclopedia works: **http://en.wikipedia.org/wiki/Wikipedia:Policies_and_guidelines**
- Click on the "History" tab at a Wikipedia article to see how it has changed over time.
- The next time you come across a Wikipedia article that contains inaccurate or incomplete information, click on the [edit] link next to each section. You'll find good directions for contributing.

Preferred Patterns of Organization 47a

Typical Organizational Pattern of the Academic Essay in English

INTRODUCTORY PARAGRAPH	▪ Grab readers' attention ▪ Introduce topic and place it in context ▪ Present main idea of entire essay (the thesis)
BODY PARAGRAPH 1 First idea in support of thesis	▪ State main idea of paragraph 1 (topic sentence 1) ▪ Explain main idea 1 ▪ Provide facts, quotations, statistics, and so on, to support main idea 1
BODY PARAGRAPH 2 Second idea in support of thesis	▪ State main idea of paragraph 2 (topic sentence 2) ▪ Explain main idea 2 ▪ Provide facts, quotations, statistics, and so on, to support main idea 2
THIRD AND SUBSEQUENT PARAGRAPHS Third and subsequent body ideas in support of thesis	▪ State main idea of each paragraph (topic sentences) ▪ Explain main idea ▪ Provide facts, quotations, statistics, and so on, to support main idea
CONCLUDING PARAGRAPH	▪ Present concluding ideas ▪ Sometimes restate main point of paper (thesis)

Following the general pattern shown here can help you organize your writing for English-speaking audiences, but keep in mind that readers have different expectations for the organization of different types of writing, so it is always a good idea to inquire about the organizational requirements of the writing task you are being asked to complete. Your instructors and writing tutors are good sources of guidance.

Readers of academic English share some general preferences. Broadly speaking, readers of English expect the main idea of an academic text, referred to as its thesis, to be explicitly stated early on (usually somewhere in the first few paragraphs) and then developed throughout the remainder of the paper. This preference is not a hard-and-fast rule, but it is common among readers of academic discourse, particularly writing for college courses. Delaying your main point until the end of an academic paper or expecting readers to infer it will generally be seen as ineffective.

Readers also expect writers to remain closely focused on their main point (thesis) throughout the body of a paper and to avoid digressions.

A common way for writers to show that they are remaining on topic is by beginning each paragraph in the body of a paper with an explicit statement of its main point. These paragraph introductory sentences are referred to as *topic sentences,* and they generally announce the subtopics or subpoints that a writer is going to discuss to support the thesis.

The best way to learn to meet the expectations for academic writing in English is to write a first draft, get feedback from readers on that draft, and then revise in response to their feedback. Feedback from your teachers can not only help you identify your strengths and weaknesses in a given piece of writing but also provide direction concerning areas you should work on in future writing.

To get an idea of how you can make use of teacher feedback, consider this sample student draft. The assignment required students, working in pairs, to conduct a survey on a topic of interest to them and then write a report presenting their findings.

1

Youjin Song and MeeSook Wang

Survey Report, First Draft

English 101: Cross Cultural Composition

American and International Students' Perceptions of Studying Abroad

This survey was done to find out what students think about studying abroad. As we all may realize, studying abroad means having to make several changes in our lifestyles. People living in different parts of the world have different cultures. We decided to pursue this topic because we would [verb tense] like to know if students ever considered [verb tense] to further their studies in a different place. There are many possible reasons that could affect their decisions to either study or not study abroad. The reason that we are most interested in is the cultural differences. We would [verb tense] like to find out how far the cultural differences affect their decisions. Do students find cultural differences as a positive or negative factor in deciding to study abroad?

We developed a questionnaire to gather information from the students in the campus. The first segment of the questionnaire asked questions regarding to the respondents' demographic factors such as sex, age, and nationality. The second segment of the questionnaire asks [verb tense] eight questions that are directly related to our topic. We distributed 20 questionnaires to the students on campus. The students were surveyed at different places that included dorms, classes, apartments, library, and sidewalks. This was done to ensure that we gathered information from a variety of students. We surveyed the students at convenient times such as during our breaks in between classes. All of the students were cooperative and did not hesitate to fill out the questionnaire. They seemed comfortable with the questions asked on the questionnaire and that made our tasks run smoothly.

Not needed; repeats info from previous ¶. Topic sentence of this ¶ should reflect its focus, which = who your participants included.

2

20 questionnaires were distributed to the students on campus in order to get the relevant information for our topic. We surveyed 12 American students that consisted of six females and six males, and eight international students that consisted of five females and three males. The students consisted of 11 freshmen, three sophomores, and six juniors. We did not get any senior or graduate student respondents, although we were hoping to get respondents from all categories of students. Out of the 20 students, 12 were from the School of Management while the rest were from other schools such as Engineering, Mathematics, and Computer Science. All of the American students that filled out the questionnaire have never studied abroad. Amazingly, 92% of them have considered to study. However, only 42% of them actually have plans to study abroad in the future. Most of the students who are thinking of studying abroad in the future would want to start their education in the foreign country in the junior year for a duration of two to three years. In our opinion, most of the students chose the junior as the starting point of their studies abroad because a majority of them are freshmen. They might not get any information about the opportunities of studying abroad until they have entered college. Therefore, they could only make plans after their freshmen year.

verb tense

After analyzing the questionnaires, we found that the three major reasons that affected the American students' decisions to study abroad are to gain more knowledge about the world, to escape from the usual environment, and to learn new culture. These findings showed that cultural differences affected their decisions in a positive way. They would want to go to another country knowing that it is a perfect opportunity for them to learn about other people's culture.

When all of the members of a group have not done something, make the quantity word negative rather than the verb: "None of the American students have studied abroad."

Don't Edit Yet

While it may be tempting to go through your first draft, correcting all of the errors marked in the margins, and then deal with the suggestions in the end comment, this would not be the best strategy to adopt. In fact, there are a number of good reasons for postponing editing until after you have had a chance to make meaningful revisions. For one thing, this approach allows you to focus your attention on the larger and usually more complex task of revising your writing for content and organization issues. For another, it is more efficient: as you revise, you may end up correcting some of your errors and/or deleting portions of text that contain errors, so there is really no point in attending to these errors before revising. The teacher's feedback on the sample draft (shown on pages 535 and 536) explicitly advises the writers to delay editing until after they have revised for focus and development.

Revise for Content and Organization

A better strategy for responding to your teacher's feedback, then, is to start by addressing comments related to issues of content and organization. Notice that three-fourths of the teacher's comments at the end of the sample draft (pages 535 and 536) focus on content and organization. These comments not only give the writers insight into how well their current draft meets the rhetorical expectations for survey reports but also provide direction for revision. If you need help understanding your teacher's suggestions for revision, you should speak to the teacher and/or consult a writing center tutor, who can help you put revision strategies into action.

3

On the other hand, financial difficulties, no application to majors, and language differences are the three major reasons that are stopping them from studying abroad. Language differences might be the main reasons why students chose countries such as England and Australia where English is used widely. We think that students are concerned about the differences in *noun number* language spoken in a country because it could cause some communication problems.

As for the international students who are currently studying in the United States, their reasons to *verb form* study abroad are exactly the same as the American students. However, compared to the American students, the international students planned to stay longer in the foreign country, which is four to five years. This might be due to the fact that they are starting their education in the foreign country from the freshman year.

As we had expected, cultural differences as well as language differences have a great effect on students' decisions to study abroad. Most of the students that were surveyed listed the opportunity to learn a new culture as one of the strongest reasons that affected them to study abroad. They are willing to live in another country with different lifestyles. However, the American students are more interested *verb form* to go to countries that are similar to their own country. This might be because they *verb tense* have to learn many aspects of life that may not be common in the Western countries. On the other hand, language differences *verb form* affected them not to study abroad. They are more inclined to go to English-speaking countries to avoid any problems in communication. However, most of the students see the point of studying abroad is to know more about the world as a whole.

Verb form: when the object of the verb affect is human, it can be either (1) a noun/pronoun that refers to the humans (x affected them) or (2) a noun referring to the humans' thoughts or actions plus an infinitive complement (x affected their decision to study . . .).

Youjin and MeeSook:

All of the hard work you put into designing your questionnaire clearly paid off. Your report is interesting and includes good information about the administration of the survey and the demographics of your participants. I can see that you have worked on developing generalizations based on your findings, which is very good. The main weakness in the current draft is the lack of a comprehensive thesis statement (stating your overall finding) and insufficient support for the generalizations/main points you make. Below, I offer suggestions for improving these aspects of your report.

(1) Focus/Thesis Statement: Overall, what did you learn about international and American students' attitudes toward study abroad? Your answer to this question will be your thesis statement. One of the main goals of the survey report assignment is to help you learn to develop and support a thesis statement, so you will want to work on this first. Keep in mind that your thesis should be included early in the report (a good place would be at the end of your introduction). Review what you've written in the conclusion of your report, as this may help you develop your thesis. You can refer to section 2b in your handbook if you need help.

(2) Content: When reporting research, it is crucial that your generalizations (the thesis and main points of individual paragraphs) accurately reflect your findings. In the current draft, you say that one of the top three reasons American students gave for wanting to study abroad is to learn new cultures, but you also found that they would prefer to study in English-speaking countries that are similar

Learn a Few Things at a Time

As the sample draft illustrates, teacher feedback is generally selective. Rather than addressing everything at once, it focuses on specific aspects of writing that your teacher thinks you should work on at a given point. This is because our capacity to learn complex processes like writing is limited—we can learn only a few things at one time. With this fact in mind, the teacher who responded to the sample draft limited her comments to three major (related) content issues.

The language issues the teacher chose to mark in Youjin and MeeSook's draft paper include two types of errors (verb tense and verb form errors). These errors form a pattern in the draft, are considered serious by English-speaking readers, and are governed by rules that can be fairly readily taught and learned. The teacher's goal in marking these errors is to help the writers learn to edit for these errors themselves.

Learning a second language is a complex and gradual process, and errors are a natural—and unavoidable—part of this process. Generally speaking, grammatical errors will disappear on their own as your skill in using a second language develops. But the process takes time—and both the rate at which your accuracy improves and the skill level you ultimately attain will depend on a number of factors, including your motivation to learn the language, your need to write in the language, and the amount of reading and writing you do in the language, to name a few. Unfortunately, second language writers rarely find themselves in situations where grammatical accuracy is not important. Usually, readers expect academic writing to conform to standard rules for English grammar, regardless of the amount of time students have had to develop their English proficiency. Thus, multilingual students generally cannot wait for their grammar to improve slowly.

to the US. What can you conclude from the conflicting data? What do these two findings (together) show about American students' attitudes toward cultural differences? You may need to revise your thesis and the main points of specific paragraphs to reflect this contrast. You can refer to section 3a in your handbook if you need help with this.

(3) Development: The generalizations you make (based on your analysis of participants' responses) need to be supported with evidence from the data to convince readers of the credibility of your report. When you report that "most" American students would prefer to study abroad in their junior year, you need to follow up with a sentence reporting the details. How many Americans chose junior year? How many chose other years? Similarly, after you report Americans' major reasons for studying abroad, you need to report the specifics. What reasons were given and by how many students? Look through your draft to be sure that you support main points with details from the results. You can refer to section 7h in your handbook for help with this.

(4) Editing for Grammar: After you have revised your draft for focus and development, you can edit for errors. I have selected two patterns of errors to mark in this draft: verb tense and verb form errors. I recommend editing for all verb tense errors first, then editing for all verb form errors. Sections 34d and 34a in your handbook can help you with these issues.

Decoding Your Teachers' Comments

Your teachers may comment on the following aspects of your writing.

Content and organization issues

Content: the ideas and information in a paper. Comments on content may refer to the accuracy of ideas; the appropriateness and relevance of the topic to the assignment; and/or specific ideas, facts, arguments, and other evidence used to support your thesis.

Focus: the extent to which your writing establishes a main point (thesis) and sticks to it

Development: the extent to which your main points are supported with relevant facts, data, ideas, research, statistics, experiences, and the like

Organization: the order in which your ideas are presented and linked together in the paper and in individual paragraphs. The organization is expected to reflect typical preferred patterns for writing in English. (If it does not, some readers will deem the writing illogical—though logic, of course, is culture-specific.)

Audience awareness: the extent to which your writing takes into account your readers' knowledge of and attitudes toward your topic

Language issues

Sentence structure: the extent to which your sentences meet accepted standards for construction (word order, punctuation) and readers' expectations for complexity

Grammar: the extent to which your writing follows grammatical rules regarding verb tense, verb form, modals, noun number, subject/verb agreement, and the like

Vocabulary (or style): the extent to which the words you use accurately express your intended meaning and are appropriate to the rhetorical situation

Convention use (or mechanics): the extent to which your writing follows rules regarding punctuation, spelling, capitalization, style for citing sources, margin size, spacing, pagination, and the like

Understand Teachers' Comments

Teachers' comments generally fall into two broad categories: comments on *content and organization issues* and comments on *language issues.*

48 NOUNS AND ARTICLES

This chapter focuses on specific aspects of noun formation and determiner use that have proven to be difficult for multilingual writers.

48a Understanding Three Main Distinctions in the English Noun System

English speakers differentiate among nouns in three ways. Every noun is either

- proper or common
- countable or uncountable
- singular or plural

Nouns Are Either Proper or Common

Proper nouns name specific people, places, time periods, events, groups, or things. They must be capitalized. They usually do not take determiners.

Common nouns name people, places, things, processes, and the like that are *not* specific or unique. They are not capitalized.

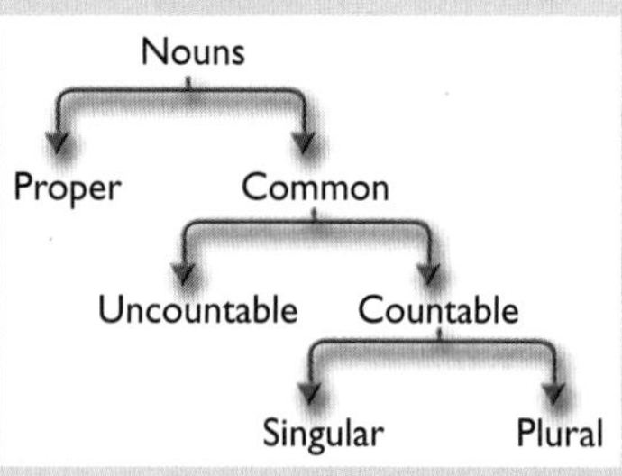

Example 1 Capitalization of proper nouns

TITLES ARE CAPITALIZED WHEN THEY APPEAR WITH PROPER NOUNS:

President Clinton visited **Prime Minister Blair** in May.

Example 2 Capitalization of common nouns

COMMON NOUNS ARE NOT CAPITALIZED:

No My **Aunt** encouraged me to major in **Chemistry** in college.
Yes My **aunt** encouraged me to major in **chemistry** in college.

A NOUN THAT IDENTIFIES AN ACADEMIC SUBJECT IS CAPITALIZED WHEN A SPECIFIC COURSE IS NAMED:

I want to be an **accountant,** so I am taking **Accounting 101** this semester.

A NOUN THAT REFERS TO A RELATIVE IS CAPITALIZED WHEN IT IDENTIFIES A SPECIFIC PERSON:

Clearly, **Aunt** Donna likes to dance.

Four Categories of Common Nouns

	Singular	Plural
Uncountable	advice	—
	information	—
Countable	day	days
	jury	juries [if preceded by consonant, *y* → *ie* before *s*]
	foot	feet
	child	children

Example 3 Uncountable nouns are always singular (never add plural marker -*s*)

No I have increased my **knowledges** of the topic through **researches.**

Yes I have increased my **knowledge** of the topic through **research.**

Example 4 An uncountable noun takes a singular verb

The **homework** *is* due tomorrow.

Example 5 An indefinite article is never used with an uncountable noun

No She gave me *an* **advice** about buying a used car.

Yes She gave me **advice** about buying a used car.

If the noun is . . .	Choose one of these quantity terms:		
uncountable	a great deal of a large/small amount of a little a piece/pair/liter of one or more pieces/pairs/cups of less little much		a lot of all all of the any enough more most no
plural and countable	a few few many	both fewer several	not any other some
singular and countable	another either	each every	

Common Nouns Can Be Uncountable or Countable

Uncountable nouns name things that cannot be counted because they are abstractions or substances or processes that cannot be divided into individual parts. Uncountable nouns often have a collective or mass meaning. They do not have a plural form.

Uncountable nouns require singular verbs. They are not typically used with numbers or the indefinite article (*a/an*).

Common Uncountable Nouns

Masses: advice, art, clothing, environment, equipment, experience, fuel, furniture, glue, hair, homework, information, knowledge, labor, luggage, medicine, money, news, paint, plastic, progress, research, technology, time, trade, traffic, training, water, wealth, work

Abstract concepts: existence, failure, faith, freedom, independence, intelligence, justice, mercy, patience, peace, poverty, respect, safety, security, status, trust

Fields of study: agriculture, biology, chemistry, education, history, political science

Natural phenomena and substances: electricity, metal, nature, oil, soil, weather, wood

Food: milk, spaghetti

A number of uncountable nouns are tricky because they end in *-s,* which makes them look like plural countable nouns. Keep in mind that these are uncountable nouns and should be treated as singular.

Nouns Ending in s *That Are Uncountable*
Diseases: arthritis, bronchitis, diabetes, herpes, multiple sclerosis, rabies
Fields of study: aeronautics, classics, economics, genetics, linguistics, mathematics, physics, politics, statistics
Games: billiards, cards, checkers, chess, darts, dominoes, tennis

Nouns with Both Uncountable and Countable Forms

Some nouns may be uncountable *or* countable, depending on their meaning and the context in which they are used. They are uncountable when they refer to something in general or as a mass and countable when they refer to a specific instance of something or different types of something.

Nouns That Are Both Uncountable and Countable
audience, cast, committee, conflict, family, light, opposition, victory, work

Indicating Quantity with Uncountable Nouns

To refer to a quantity of an uncountable noun, you need to use an

Example 6 Some nouns can be either uncountable or countable

AUDIENCE IS REFERRED TO AS A MASS, SO THE NOUN IS UNCOUNTABLE:

The magician searched *the* **audience** for a volunteer.

DIFFERENT TYPES OF *AUDIENCES* ARE REFERRED TO, SO THE NOUN IS COUNTABLE (AND PLURAL):

Television shows have to appeal to the tastes of different **audiences.**

Example 7 Indicating quantity with uncountable nouns

AN APPROPRIATE QUANTITY TERM IS USED TO INDICATE THE QUANTITY OF AN UNCOUNTABLE NOUN:

No *Every* **furniture** was delivered today.
Yes *All of the* **furniture** was delivered today.

THE VERB AGREES IN NUMBER WITH THE QUANTITY TERM, NOT THE UNCOUNTABLE NOUN:

A piece of **luggage** *was* lost by the airline.
Two pieces of **luggage** *were* lost by the airline.

Countable Nouns

Example 8 Verb agreement with countable nouns

A SINGULAR VERB FORM IS USED WHEN A COUNTABLE NOUN IS SINGULAR:

My **friend** *loves* to go hiking.

A PLURAL VERB FORM IS USED WHEN A COUNTABLE NOUN IS PLURAL:

My **friends** *love* to travel.

Example 9 Nouns modified by numbers

WHEN A SPECIFIC QUANTITY (OTHER THAN ONE) IS INDICATED, A COUNTABLE NOUN IS MADE PLURAL:

Three **cats** live in that house.

Example 10 Adjective form with plural nouns

AN ADJECTIVE THAT MODIFIES A PLURAL NOUN IS NOT MADE PLURAL:

No Discount stores sell *inexpensives* **products.**

Yes Discount stores sell *inexpensive* **products.**

Special Plurals

Special plurals for things people wear:

glasses (spectacles)	gloves	jeans
	overalls	pajamas
pants	shorts	slacks

Special plurals for tools:

binoculars	pliers	scissors
shears	skis	tongs

To refer to one of these items, use *a pair of* before the noun. To refer to a quantity (more than one) of these items, use a quantity term with *pairs of*:

I packed *two pairs of* **pajamas** for my trip.

To refer to an unspecified number or to make a generalization about a special plural, use the noun alone (without a determiner):

The children used **scissors** to cut out paper snowflakes.

appropriate quantity term. Refer to the chart on page 539 for a selection of quantity terms that may be used with uncountable nouns.

Countable nouns name things that can be counted. You can put numbers (*one, two,* etc.) in front of them.

Countable Nouns
accident, chapter, college, effect, group, hour, job, library, method, model, product, project, thought

Countable Nouns Have Singular and Plural Forms

Singular countable nouns take singular verbs. They require determiners (▶ section 48b).

The plural form of a regular countable noun is created by adding *s* or *es* to the singular form. However, there are some irregular plurals that do not follow this rule (for example, *woman/women*). These plurals must be memorized. Nouns must be marked for plurality *even when a number is used with them.* Plural nouns take plural verbs. Adjectives that modify nouns are *never* made plural in English.

Special Plurals

Some nouns refer to tools and clothing composed of two identical parts. The nouns that refer to such items are always plural.

48b Using Definite Articles with Proper Nouns

Most proper nouns do not take definite articles. However, certain categories of proper nouns require the definite article:

- *Specific bodies of land and water:* deserts, oceans, lakes, rivers, regions of a country
- *Specific physical structures:* museums, monuments, buildings, bridges
- *Specific time periods and events:* historical eras, wars

Example 11 Definite articles are not used with most proper nouns

No We celebrated *the* **Halloween** by dressing in costumes.

Yes We celebrated **Halloween** by dressing in costumes.

Example 12 Using the definite article with proper nouns

THE DEFINITE ARTICLE IS NOT CAPITALIZED WITH PROPER NOUNS:

No We studied *The* Great Lakes in environmental science.

Yes English has changed a great deal since *the* Middle Ages.

AN ARTICLE IS CAPITALIZED WHEN IT IS PART OF A TITLE:

I read *The Catcher in the Rye* last week.

48c Using Determiners with Common Nouns

Determiners indicate whether the things being referred to are general or specific. The table to the right summarizes the use of determiners with common nouns.

Determiners for Different Types of Common Nouns

	Uncountable	Countable	
		Singular	**Plural**
General	—	a, an	—
Specific	the, this, that	the, this, that	the, these, those
	my, our, your, his, her, its, their		

Example 13 Using determiners with common nouns that have a general reference

NO DETERMINER IS USED WITH A PLURAL NOUN THAT HAS A GENERAL REFERENCE:

Cats and **dogs** are the most common house pets.

AN INDEFINITE ARTICLE IS USED WITH A SINGULAR NOUN THAT HAS A GENERAL REFERENCE:

We went to the humane society today to adopt *a* **cat.**

Example 14 Using determiners with common nouns that have a specific reference

A DEFINITE ARTICLE IS USED WHEN THE COMMON NOUN HAS ALREADY BEEN REFERRED TO:

The deans will make *a* **recommendation** to the board. The board can accept or reject *the* (or *their*) **recommendation.**

Example 15 Using the definite article to refer back to known information

AN INDEFINITE ARTICLE IS USED TO INTRODUCE A GENERAL COUNTABLE NOUN; A DEFINITE ARTICLE IS USED TO REFER BACK TO THE NOUN:

My doctor gave me *a* **prescription** for antibiotics. *The* **prescription** seemed illegible to me, but the pharmacist was able to read it.

Example 16 Using the definite article with uncountable nouns that are qualified

THE DEFINITE ARTICLE IS USED WHEN THE UNCOUNTABLE NOUN IS QUALIFIED IN A PREPOSITIONAL PHRASE:

No Social workers are concerned about **welfare** <u>of foster children</u>.

Yes Social workers are concerned about *the* **welfare** <u>of foster children</u>.

Example 17 Using the definite article with superlative or sequential adjectives

THE DEFINITE ARTICLE IS REQUIRED BEFORE NOUNS MODIFIED BY ADJECTIVES:

No I had **best** ice cream **last** time we ate at this restaurant.

Yes I had *the* **best** ice cream *the* **last** time we ate at this restaurant.

Example 18 Using the definite article to refer to an entire group or human body part

The fastest animal on land is *the* **cheetah.**

The **Andersons** have a big family reunion each August.

Excessive consumption of alcohol can severely damage *the* **liver.**

The definite article *the* is the most common specific determiner. It is used in a number of ways:

- with a noun that refers to a unique thing that everyone knows (shared knowledge): *the Web, the Moon*
- with common time expressions: *in the past, in the evening*
- with a noun that refers back to something that has already been mentioned or that is clear from the context or from what you have already written
- with an uncountable noun that is followed by a qualifier that relates it to a particular group or makes it specific: *The kindergarten teacher has the* **patience** <u>*of a saint*</u>.
- before a superlative or sequential adjective (*best, fastest, next*)
- to make a comment about all members of a group or species or about a human body part

49 VERBS AND VERBALS

This chapter is designed to help you learn the rules for using different types of verbs and verb phrases in your writing.

49a Phrasal Verbs

A phrasal verb consists of a verb followed by one or more words (particles) that help specify the verb's meaning. The verb and particle(s) function together as a single verb whose meaning is rarely the same as the meaning of its component parts. Most phrasal verbs are idiomatic.

Like other verbs, when used in clauses, phrasal verbs must be inflected for tense, person, and number. Some phrasal verbs can be used both transitively (with a direct object) and intransitively (without a direct object); others are exclusively transitive (they require a direct object). Be aware of the three types of phrasal verbs.

Separable Phrasal Verbs

Separable phrasal verbs allow a direct object to be inserted between the verb and the particle. If the direct object is a pronoun, separation is *required*.

Common Separable Phrasal Verbs

The phrases with asterisks (*) can be used transitively and intransitively.

add up	hold on*	point out	tell apart
bring up	keep up*	push over	tell off
buy out	kick out	put off	think over
clean up*	knock out*	put on	think through
draw up	lay down	rip off	tie down
drop off	lay off*	scale down*	tip off
fill in	let down*	seal off	tire out
filter out	let up*	seek out	try on
find out*	look up	set aside	try out
finish up*	make up	set off	turn in
follow up*	mess up	settle down	turn up*
give away	pay back	settle in*	use up
give up*	phase out	show off	waste away*
hand down	pin down	start out*	wrap up
hand out	plug in	take off*	

Example 1 The separable phrasal verb *call off* (meaning "to cancel")

THE DIRECT OBJECT CAN FOLLOW THE PARTICLE OR BE INSERTED BETWEEN VERB AND PARTICLE:

Yes The couple decided to **call off** *the wedding.*

Yes The couple decided to **call** *the wedding* **off.**

IF THE DIRECT OBJECT IS A PRONOUN, IT MUST SEPARATE VERB AND PARTICLE:

No The couple decided to **call off** *it.*

Yes The couple decided to **call** *it* **off.**

IF THE DIRECT OBJECT IS A LONG PHRASE, IT SHOULD FOLLOW THE PARTICLE (*NOT* SEPARATE THE PHRASAL VERB):

No The couple decided to **call** *the wedding they had been planning for the last two years* **off.**

Yes The couple decided to **call off** *the wedding they had been planning for the last two years.*

Inseparable Phrasal Verbs

Inseparable phrasal verbs do not allow the verb and particle to be separated.

Common Inseparable Phrasal Verbs

The phrases with asterisks (*) can be used transitively and intransitively.

account for	drop by*	look into	reason with
back down	expand on	look like	settle on
back off*	fall apart*	miss out	speak up*
bow out*	fall behind*	move over*	stand back*
chip in*	fall out*	opt out*	stay up*
come across	flare up*	own up	step down*
come out	get ahead*	make for	stop by*
crop up*	get by*	meet with	tamper with
dawn on	get over	pay up*	wait on
die down*	go ahead	pick on	wait up*
double back*	go over	pitch in*	watch out*
draw on	lay into	provide for	

Example 2 The inseparable phrasal verb *reason with* (meaning "to persuade through logic")

THE DIRECT OBJECT CANNOT BE INSERTED BETWEEN VERB AND PARTICLE:

No I tried to **reason** *my opponent* **with,** but she refused to listen.

Yes I tried to **reason with** *my opponent,* but she refused to listen.

Example 3 Agreement in person and number with the phrasal verb *fall behind* (meaning "to be late in doing something")

THIRD PERSON SINGULAR VERB IS REQUIRED TO MATCH SUBJECT IN PERSON AND NUMBER:

No Every year during football season, *Pat* **fall behind** in his studies.

Yes Every year during football season, *Pat* **falls behind** in his studies.

Three-Word Phrasal Verbs

Three-word phrasal verbs must be used with specific prepositions in order to convey the intended meaning. In these cases, the preposition can be considered part of the phrasal verb (verb + particle + preposition). Three-word phrasal verbs are inseparable. It would be a good idea to learn these verbs as units; you will notice that they have their own entries in most dictionaries.

Common Inseparable Three-Word Phrasal Verbs

back away from	cut back on	keep up with	run up against
back down from	cut down on	lay off of	shy away from
be on to	drop in on	live up to	sit in on
bear down on	ease up on	look forward to	stand up for
bow out of	end up with	look in on	stick up for
break out of	get along with	look out for	stock up on
break up with	get away with	look up to	talk down to
brush up on	get back to	make off with	walk away with
catch up with	get by with	make up for	watch out for
check out of	get down to	miss out on	zero in on
check up on	give in to	pick up on	
clean up after	give up on	play along with	
crack down on	go in for	put up with	

Example 4 Forming three-word phrasal verbs with *look down*

ON IS REQUIRED TO CONVEY THE MEANING "VIEW AS INFERIOR":

My boss **looks down on** applicants who have not graduated from high school.

AT CONVEYS A DIFFERENT MEANING—THAT THE DIRECT OBJECT IS PHYSICALLY LOWER THAN THE SUBJECT:

My boss **looks down at** the workers on the floor below.

Example 5 Using an *-ing* form following a three-word phrasal verb

AFTER A THREE-WORD PHRASAL VERB, THE *-ING* FORM OF A VERB (NOT THE PLAIN FORM) IS REQUIRED:

No I **look forward to** *hear* from you soon.
Yes I **look forward to** *hearing* from you soon.

Verbs That Take Only Infinitive Complements, Not *-ing* Forms

The phrases with asterisks (*) can take a noun or pronoun before the infinitive complement.

afford	deserve	long	resolve
agree	desire*	manage	seek
aim	endeavor	mean	seem
appear	expect*	need*	survive
arrange	fail	neglect	swear
ask*	fight*	offer*	tend
attempt	grow	opt	threaten*
beg*	happen	pay*	volunteer*
care	have	plan	vote
choose*	help*	pledge	vow
claim	hesitate	prepare*	wait
consent	hope	pretend	want*
dare*	intend*	promise*	wish*
decide	learn	prove	
demand	live	refuse	

Example 6 Using the plain form of the verb in an infinitive verbal complement

THE VERB USED IN AN INFINITIVE IS NEVER MARKED FOR TENSE OR NUMBER:

No Xiao *decided* **to helped** raise money for the school

No Xiao *decided* **to helps** raise money for the school.

Yes Xiao *decided* **to help** raise money for the school.

Example 7 Using the infinitive complement to describe events that have not taken place

ACTIVITY OF PAYING BILLS FAILED TO TAKE PLACE AND SUBJECT *I* IS RELATED TO ITS OCCURRENCE, SO INFINITIVE IS REQUIRED:

No I *neglected* **paying** my bills last month.

Yes I *neglected* **to pay** my bills last month.

ACTIVITY OF FINISHING HOMEWORK HAS NOT YET TAKEN PLACE AND SUBJECT *SHE* HAS AN INTEREST IN ITS COMPLETION, SO INFINITIVE IS REQUIRED:

She *wanted* me **to finish** my homework.

Infinitives (*to* + verb) and *-ing* forms (verb + *ing*) are two of the most troublesome structures in English for multilingual writers to master. These forms share some functions, but they also perform distinct functions and differ in the grammatical structures in which they can be used. The following guidelines can help you determine when to use each form.

When and How Infinitives Are Used

An **infinitive** consists of *to* plus the uninflected (plain) form of a verb: *to dance, to read.* Infinitives perform a variety of functions in English.

1. **Infinitives may be subjects.** Infinitives can be used as subjects when you want to highlight the activity they refer to. They require a third person singular verb: ***To lose*** *ten pounds by summer is Yu's goal.*
2. **Infinitives may be verbal complements.** Infinitives are used following main clause verbs—in complement clauses—to convey activities that are hypothetical, that failed to take place, or that will take place in the future: *The witness swore* ***to tell*** *the truth in the courtroom.* Verbs that take infinitive complements tend to have subjects that are somehow related to or interested in the real or hypothetical occurrence of

the event depicted in the infinitive clause.

Some verbs *allow* a noun or a pronoun before an infinitive complement. Verbs that can function either transitively or intransitively take an object (noun or pronoun) before the infinitive complement when used transitively.

Transitive verbs *require* a noun or pronoun before an infinitive complement.

3. **Infinitives may express a purpose.** When an infinitive is used to express a purpose, a noun or pronoun is *required* between the main clause verb and the infinitive. You can replace *to* in the infinitive with *in order to,* and the sentence will still convey the same meaning.
4. **Infinitives follow some nouns.** Infinitives are used following certain nouns that express ability, desirability, possibility, necessity, or circumstance (place or time). These nouns are limited in number, and many of them are used idiomatically. Examples include *ability, choice, decision, desire, duty, job, necessity, need, obligation, option, place, possibility, time.*

Verbs That Require a Noun or Pronoun before an Infinitive Complement in Active Voice

advise	command	force	lead	recruit	tempt
allow	convince	hire	move	remind	train
appoint	defy	induce	order	require	trust
authorize	enable	inspire	permit	select	urge
buy	encourage	instruct	persuade	teach	use
cause	forbid	invite	program	tell	warn
challenge					

Example 8 A noun or pronoun may appear before the infinitive complement *to leave*

I *asked* **to leave** the room. I *asked* my friend **to leave** the room.

Example 9 A noun or pronoun is required before the infinitive complement *to pursue* in active voice

No A former teacher *convinced* **to pursue** my master's degree.

Yes A former teacher *convinced* me **to pursue** my master's degree.

Example 10 The infinitive *to take* used to express a purpose

BOTH VERSIONS CONVEY THE SAME MEANING; THE REQUIRED DIRECT OBJECT IS THE INSTRUMENT USED TO ACHIEVE THE GOAL EXPRESSED IN THE INFINITIVE CLAUSE:

I *bought* a camera **to take** photographs on our trip.

I *bought* a camera **in order to take** photographs on our trip.

FOR IS NEVER USED BEFORE AN INFINITIVE COMPLEMENT:

No I *bought* a camera for **to take** photographs on our trip.

Example 11 Infinitives are used following certain nouns

AN INFINITIVE IS USED FOLLOWING A NOUN THAT EXPRESSES ABILITY OR CIRCUMSTANCE:

The mayor has the *ability* **to improve** the budget.

The junior executive chose the right *time* **to ask** for a promotion.

AN INFINITIVE IS USED FOLLOWING A NOUN THAT IS THE DIRECT OBJECT OF A CAUSATIVE VERB:

I finally made the *decision* **to fire** my real estate agent.

Adjectives That Take Infinitive Complements When They Function as Predicates

annoying	delighted	happy	nice
anxious	difficult	hard	safe
boring	eager	important	sorry
challenging	easy	impossible	
dangerous	fun	interesting	

Example 12 Infinitives are used following certain adjectives

AN INFINITIVE (NOT A PLAIN FORM OR *-ING* FORM) IS USED AFTER AN ADJECTIVE THAT IS A PREDICATE:

No I am *eager* **graduate** from school.

Yes I am *eager* **to graduate** from school.

Example 13 Tricky adjective + infinitive combinations

Yes I am *easy* **to please.** [Meaning "It is easy (for anyone in general) to please me."]

Yes I am *delighted* **to meet** you. [Meaning "I am very happy to meet you."]

No I am *easy* **to learn** math. [Meaning "It is easy for me to learn math."]

The reason the third sentence above is *not* grammatical is complicated. To avoid making this type of error, ask yourself the following question: Does the adjective I'm using describe (a) the subject's *attitude toward* or (b) the subject's *ability to perform* the activity in the infinitive? If the answer is (b), you probably *cannot* use the structure subject + *be* verb + adjective + infinitive + object. Instead, use one of these:

- *It* + *be* verb + adjective + *for* + subject of infinitive + infinitive + object

  It is *easy* for me **to learn** math.

- subject + *find[s] it* + adjective + infinitive + object

  I find it *easy* **to learn** math.

5. **Infinitives follow some adjectives.** Infinitives are used following adjectives that function as main clause predicates and that convey either (1) the subject's attitude toward *or* (2) the writer's or a general/conventional evaluation of the event or behavior described in the infinitive complement. The latter often occurs in sentences that have *it* as empty subject: *It is wrong* **to steal**. This type of sentence can be rewritten as a single clause with the infinitive as subject and still convey the same meaning: **To steal** *is wrong.*

Multilingual writers of English often make errors when using adjective + infinitive sequences in sentences. This is because these sequences are used in sentences that look alike but have quite different underlying structures.

When and How *-ing* Forms Are Used

The **-ing form** of a verb has a variety of functions.

1. ***-ing* form as subject:** *-ing* forms frequently function as subjects (see section 30k). They require the third person singular form of the verb in the predicate: ***Sleeping** eight hours a night refreshes most people.*
2. ***-ing* form as object:** *-ing* forms act as objects in prepositional phrases that describe actions instrumental in bringing about the event in the main clause: *I learned to write by **writing.***
3. ***-ing* form as verbal complement:** *-ing* forms are used following certain verbs and phrasal verbs—in complement clauses—to add information to sentences that describe activities that are real and ongoing or that have taken place. In such instances, the *-ing* form represents the subject's success in accomplishing some outcome.
4. ***-ing* form as nonfinite participial clause***: -ing* forms are used in nonfinite clauses to add information to the main clause: *The defendant walked out of the courtroom **crying.***
5. ***-ing* form in progressive tense:** *-ing* forms are used with forms of *be* to form progressive tenses: *I am **walking** to school tomorrow.*

Verbs That Take Only *-ing* Form Complements, Not Infinitive Complements

admit	contemplate	dread	go	postpone	risk
appreciate	delay	endure	imagine	practice	sit
avoid	deny	enjoy	keep	recall	stand
celebrate	describe	fancy	mention	report	start out
commence	discontinue	finish	mind	resent	suggest
consider	dislike	give up	miss	resist	

Example 14 The *-ing* form as subject takes a third person singular verb

No **Reading** novels *are* my favorite leisure activity.
Yes **Reading** novels *is* my favorite leisure activity.

Example 15 The *-ing* form is used as the object in certain prepositional phrases

I stay in shape *by* **exercising** three times every week.

Example 16 An *-ing* form must be used as the object of a preposition following a three-word phrasal verb

No How can I **make up for** *forget* your birthday?
Yes How can I **make up for** *forgetting* your birthday?

USE OF *HAVING* + PAST PARTICIPLE, WHICH IS MORE FORMAL AND MORE COMMON IN WRITING THAN IN SPEECH, EMPHASIZES THAT THE ACTION OCCURRED IN THE PAST:

How can I **make up for** *having forgotten* your birthday?

Example 17 The *-ing* form is used as the complement of certain verbs

THE EVENT IN THE COMPLEMENT IS REAL AND ONGOING, SO THE *-ING* FORM IS USED:

No I *enjoy* **to cook** for my friends.
Yes I *enjoy* **cooking** for my friends.

THE EVENT IN THE COMPLEMENT IS REAL AND HAS TAKEN PLACE, SO THE *-ING* FORM IS USED:

The defendant *denied* **shooting** the victim.

Verbs That Can Take Infinitive and -*ing* Complements

The asterisk (*) indicates that the meanings of the infinitive and -*ing* forms are different.

begin	hate	prefer	stop*
continue	like	remember*	try
forget*	love	start	

Example 18 Verbs that have the same meaning with infinitive and -*ing* complements

Lassie *began* **to act** when he was just a puppy.

Lassie *began* **acting** when he was just a puppy.

Example 19 Verbs that have different meanings with infinitive and -*ing* complements

I will *forget* **to take** this medicine. [Medicine has not been taken—prediction about future behavior.]

I will *forget* **taking** this medicine. [Medicine is being taken or has just been taken—prediction that in the future I will not remember that I have done so.]

We *stopped* **to eat** lunch at noon. [We ceased some activity in order to eat lunch—lunch has been eaten.]

We *stopped* **eating** lunch at noon. [We no longer eat lunch at noon, as was our ongoing habit.]

Example 20 Verbs that take plain form infinitives

THE CAUSATIVE VERBS *MAKE* AND *LET* REQUIRE PLAIN FORM INFINITIVES (NOT FULL INFINITIVES):

No Their parents *made* them **to wash** the family car every weekend.
Yes Their parents *made* them **wash** the family car every weekend.
Yes The professor *let* us **leave** class early.
But The professor *allowed* us **to leave** class early.

THE SENSORY VERB *HEARD* REQUIRES A PLAIN FORM INFINITIVE (NOT A FULL INFINITIVE):

No The witness said she *heard* a woman **to scream** that night.
Yes The witness said she *heard* a woman **scream** that night.

Some verbs can take both infinitive complements and -*ing* complements. For some of these verbs, it makes no difference which complement type you use. For other verbs, however, the meaning changes when you change the complement type. Be careful when using these verbs to ensure that you convey the meaning you want.

When and How to Use Plain Form Infinitives

Some verbs take **plain form infinitives,** which consist of the verb without the word *to.* These include causative verbs (*have, help, let, make*) and sensory/perception verbs (*feel, hear, notice, perceive, see*). **Causative verbs** depict situations in which the subject of one clause *causes* the subject of the other clause to perform some action.

- The causative verb ***have*** is used when the subject of the main clause causes the infinitive-clause subject to perform an activity based on authority or a business relationship between them.
- The causative verb ***make*** is used when the subject of the main clause uses its power (coercive or otherwise) to cause the infinitive-clause subject to perform an activity: *The devil made me* ***do*** *it.*
- Three causative verbs (*help, let, make*) take *only* plain form infinitive complements.

49c

Verbs That Can Take Both Plain Form and *-ing* Complements

Some verbs allow both plain form and *-ing* complements. These include most sensory/perception verbs and the causative verb *have*. When a verb can take either type of complement, the plain form is used for discrete events whereas the *-ing* form is used for ongoing or repeated events without a specific beginning or ending.

Example 21 Sensory verbs that take both plain form and *-ing* complements

PLAIN FORM IS USED FOR DISCRETE OR COMPLETED EVENTS:

They *saw* Chris **steal** the candy.

-ING FORM IS USED FOR ONGOING EVENTS:

I *smelled* the cookies **baking** in the oven.

49d Present (*-ing*) and Past (*-ed*) Participles as Adjectives

The *-ing* and *-ed* forms of some transitive verbs can function as adjectives. The two forms have different meanings:

- ***-ing* adjectives** report someone's perceptions of the subject of the sentence: they describe enduring aspects of the subject (not something that changes over time).
- ***-ed* adjectives** report the perceptions of the subject of the sentence: they describe the subject's thoughts or feelings. They refer to living beings almost exclusively. The characteristics that *-ed* adjectives attribute to humans and animals are usually temporary and related to a particular context or circumstance.

Verbs That Can Be Used as *-ing* Adjectives or *-ed* Adjectives, with Different Meanings

alarm	charm	disturb	humiliate	overwhelm	surprise
amaze	confuse	embarrass	inspire	please	thrill
amuse	convince	encourage	interest	satisfy	tire
annoy	depress	excite	intimidate	shock	touch
bore	disappoint	frighten	intrigue		

Example 22 Differences between *-ing* and *-ed* forms of the same adjective

I am **boring.** [I and/or other people find *me* (the subject) to be *dull and uninteresting* in general.]

I am **bored.** [I (subject) feel that *my current situation or activity* is *dull and uninteresting.*]

-ING FORM IS USED TO DESCRIBE SOMEONE ELSE'S PERCEPTIONS OF THE SUBJECT OF THE SENTENCE:

No Mosquitoes are quite **annoyed** in Minnesota in late summer.
Yes Mosquitoes are quite **annoying** in Minnesota in late summer.

-ED FORM IS USED TO REPORT PERCEPTIONS/FEELINGS ABOUT SOMETHING ON THE PART OF THE SUBJECT OF THE SENTENCE:

No I am **exciting** about my trip to the city this weekend.
Yes I am **excited** about my trip to the city this weekend.

Example 23 Using modal verbs

MODALS ARE NOT USED ALONE IN WRITING; THEY PRECEDE VERBS:

No We have decided against pursuing a lawsuit at this time; however, we **may** later.

Yes We have decided against pursuing a lawsuit at this time; however, we **may** *pursue* one later.

Yes We have decided against pursuing a lawsuit at this time; however, we **may** *do so* later.

MODALS ARE NOT MARKED FOR SUBJECT-VERB AGREEMENT OR TENSE:

No He **musts** *exercise* twice a week.

Yes He **must** *exercise* twice a week.

THE PLAIN FORM OF THE VERB IS REQUIRED FOLLOWING A MODAL (NO SUBJECT-VERB AGREEMENT):

No My flight **should** *departs* at 9:00 a.m.

Yes My flight **should** *depart* at 9:00 a.m.

Example 24 Forming present, future, and past tenses with modals

PRESENT ONGOING IS MODAL + *BE* VERB + *-ING* FORM:

They **could** *be taking* the final now.

PRESENT HABITUAL IS MODAL + PLAIN FORM:

My cat **can** *fetch* toy mice.

FUTURE IS MODAL + PLAIN FORM:

Miss Kitty **might** *play* fetch with you tonight.

PAST IS MODAL + *HAVE* + *-ED/-EN* FORM OF VERB:

We **should** *have washed* the dishes.

PAST ONGOING IS MODAL + *HAVE* + *BEEN* + *-ING* FORM OF VERB:

We **must** *have been working* for hours.

Keep in mind that certain modals cannot be used with certain time frames (*will*, for example, cannot be used for past time), so you need to attend to meaning when selecting modals to insert into these patterns.

Modals are a special type of auxiliary (helping) verb in English. Like other auxiliaries, they are never used alone. Unlike other auxiliaries, however, they are not marked for tense, person, or number, and they do not combine with full infinitives. They directly precede the plain form of the main verb (the verb without *to*).

Modals	
can	ought to
could	shall
may	should
might	will
must	would

The modal *ought to* is used in casual speech but rarely in writing; *shall* is used primarily in speech, but infrequently. The remainder of the chapter focuses on modals that are used in academic writing, excluding forms that are primarily or exclusively spoken.

Expressing Present, Future, and Past Time Frames with Modals

Because modals do not indicate the time frame referred to in writing, time is marked in other ways, such as through context and through the addition of an auxiliary + present or past participle structures.

Using Phrasal Modals

In addition to true modals, English speakers regularly make use of phrasal modals. Phrasal modals are multi-word sequences that end with the infinitive marker *to* and carry modal-like meanings. Unlike true modals, phrasal modals *are* marked for tense and subject-verb agreement, and the full infinitive form is required for verbs following them.

Phrasal modals are more casual than true modals, but they also carry an added element of meaning: because they are inflected for tense, they allow writers to indicate aspects of time, duration, and modality. In fact, they developed because true modals—which started out as regular, tensed verbs—lost their tense distinctions over time.

The only time phrasal modals are *not* marked for tense is when they follow a true modal.

True Modal	Phrasal Modal with Similar Meaning
can, could	be able to
may, might	be allowed to, be permitted to, be able to
must	have to
should	be supposed to
will	be going to, be about to
would (to refer to a past habit)	used to

Note that *used to* is already in the past tense and is used only in that form.

Example 25 Using phrasal modals

PHRASAL MODALS ARE MARKED FOR SUBJECT-VERB AGREEMENT AND TENSE:

No She **have to** *exercise* twice a week.
Yes She **has to** *exercise* twice a week.
Yes She **used to** *go* to the gym after work. [Past tense]
Yes She **is able to** *work out* in the morning now that she has retired. [Present tense]

THE FULL INFINITIVE VERB FORM IS USED FOLLOWING A PHRASAL MODAL:

Restaurant servers **are** not **permitted** *to wear* jewelry.
They **are going** *to file* a complaint with the labor union.

Example 26 Marking tense with phrasal modals

PHRASAL MODALS MUST BE MARKED FOR TENSE WHEN NOT PRECEDED BY A TRUE MODAL:

No We **are supposed to** study last night.
Yes We **were supposed to** study last night.

THE PHRASAL MODAL IS NOT MARKED FOR TENSE WHEN IT FOLLOWS A TRUE MODAL:

We **may be able to** *buy* pizza at the fair.

Example 27 Combining modals and phrasal modals

TRUE MODAL + TRUE MODAL + VERB IS UNGRAMMATICAL:

No I **should could** *run* five miles without taking a break.

PHRASAL MODAL + TRUE MODAL + VERB IS UNGRAMMATICAL:

No I **used to could** *run* five miles.

TRUE MODAL + PHRASAL MODAL + VERB IS GRAMMATICAL:

Yes I **should be able to** *run* five miles without taking a break.

PHRASAL MODAL + PHRASAL MODAL + VERB IS GRAMMATICAL:

Yes I **am supposed to be allowed to** *swim* in the lake.

Example 28 Forming negatives with modals and phrasal modals

I **will** not *attend* the graduation ceremony.

Inmates **are** not **supposed to be able to** *purchase* drugs inside the prison.

Example 29 Forming questions with modals and phrasal modals

IN PHRASAL MODALS THAT DO NOT START WITH A *BE* VERB, INSERT *DO* BEFORE THE SUBJECT:

I **have to** *serve* on the jury.

No **Have** I **to** *serve* on the jury?

Yes Do I **have to** *serve* on the jury?

He **used to** *smoke* as a teenager.

Did he **used to** *smoke* as a teenager?

IF THE SENTENCE ALREADY CONTAINS A TRUE MODAL, INVERT SUBJECT AND MODAL:

I **can** *go* to the concert.

No Do I **can** *go* to the concert?

Yes **Can** I *go* to the concert?

Combining Modals in Sentences

Modals and phrasal modals can be combined, but only in specific ways. A clause should contain only one true modal, but it can be combined with a phrasal modal. And phrasal modals can be combined. It is not uncommon to see three phrasal modals in succession.

Forming Negatives and Questions with Modals

To form the negative of a sentence that contains one or more modals, insert a negative word (*not, never*) immediately after the modal or, if the sentence does not include a true modal, after the first word of a phrasal modal. In conversation and informal writing, negatives and modals are often combined in contractions: *cannot* → *can't, should not* → *shouldn't, will not* → *won't*. However, contractions are rarely used in formal academic writing.

To form a question, switch the sentence's subject with the true modal or with the first word of the phrasal modal that immediately follows it. In cases where the phrasal modal does not start with a *be* verb (such as *have to* and *used to*), the appropriately tensed form of *do* must be inserted before the subject to create a question.

Expressing Perspective with Modals

Consider these sentences:

She *pays* the bills on time.
She **might** *pay* the bills on time.

The first sentence merely reports a fact, whereas the second sentence includes an assessment of probability—by including *might,* the writer implies that the action expressed by the main verb is not very likely.

Modals perform a variety of functions in discourse, including logical ones, such as expressing degrees of certainty, and social ones, such as making requests politely. Almost all modals can perform both logical and social functions; likewise, the same meaning can be expressed by more than one modal. These multiple meanings are the cause of most difficulties writers encounter. To help you detect and avoid these problems, this section discusses how modals are used to perform three logical functions (expressing probability, necessity, and ability) and two social functions (making requests and giving advice).

Modals Expressing Degrees of Probability

Modals are used to express different degrees of probability or certainty regarding the inferences we make.

must → *will* → *should* → *may* → *could/might*

High Certainty/Probability → Low Certainty/Probability

The same scale applies to expressing degrees of certainty about events in the past, but the past participle (*have* + *-ed* or *-en* form of verb) is added to each modal: **should** *have studied.*

Example 30 Using modals to express present inferences

MUST EXPRESSES A HIGH DEGREE OF CERTAINTY:

I have been coughing all day; I **must** *have* a cold.

WILL EXPRESSES A HIGH DEGREE OF CERTAINTY:

We **will** *present* our findings at the conference.

SHOULD EXPRESSES A MODERATE DEGREE OF CERTAINTY:

The article **should** *appear* in this week's news.

MAY EXPRESSES A LOW DEGREE OF CERTAINTY:

The senator **may** *run* for President.

MIGHT EXPRESSES AN EVEN LOWER DEGREE OF CERTAINTY:

She **might** *win* the election.

Example 31 Using modals to express past inferences

HIGH DEGREE OF CERTAINTY:

The cat **must** *have escaped* when you left for work.

MODERATE DEGREE OF CERTAINTY:

You **should** *have received* your acceptance letter by now.

might not/may not *will not/would not* *cannot/could not*

Low Possibility Impossible

The modals *should* and *must* are not used to express negative present inferences.

Example 32 Using modals to express negative present inferences

MIGHT NOT/MAY NOT EXPRESSES LOW POSSIBILITY:

I liked the offer, but I **might not** *take* the job.

WILL NOT/WOULD NOT EXPRESSES IMPROBABILITY:

I **will not** *move* for my job.

CANNOT/COULD NOT EXPRESSES IMPOSSIBILITY:

I **cannot** *meet* you before noon today.

Example 33 Using modals to express necessity

Students **must** *maintain* a B average in order to qualify for a scholarship.

THE PAST TENSE OF *HAVE TO* IS USED TO EXPRESS PAST NECESSITY; *WERE REQUIRED TO* COULD BE SUBSTITUTED FOR IT HERE:

In the past, international students **had to** *pay* out-of-state tuition.

Example 34 Using modals to express ability or lack of ability

CAN EXPRESSES ABILITY IN THE PRESENT:

I **can** *speak* four languages.

COULD EXPRESSES PAST ABILITY:

When she was young, my cat **could** *jump* onto the refrigerator.

THE PAST PERFECT FORM OF *COULD* EXPRESSES THE IDEA THAT THE SUBJECT HAD THE ABILITY TO COMPLETE THE HOMEWORK IN THE PAST, BUT DID *NOT* DO IT:

You **could** *have finished* your homework last night.

BE ABLE TO EXPRESSES EFFORT OR DIFFICULTY:

After hours of searching, we **were** finally **able to** *find* a hotel room.

CAN CANNOT BE USED IN A PRESENT PERFECT CONSTRUCTION DESCRIBING AN ABILITY THAT STARTED AT SOME POINT AND CONTINUES INTO THE PRESENT:

No She *has* **can** *play* guitar since she was a child.

Yes She *has* **been able to** *play* guitar since she was a child.

Modals can also be used to express present inferences in *negative* terms.

Modals Expressing Degrees of Necessity

The modals most commonly used to express necessity or obligation are *must* and *have to.* A primarily spoken form, *have to* is considerably more informal than its true modal counterpart. *Must* and *be required to* are preferred forms in much academic writing.

Modals Expressing Ability

The modals most commonly used to express ability or potentiality are *can, could,* and *be able to. Can* and *cannot* are used to express ability and lack of ability, respectively, whereas *could* and *could not* are used to express past ability and lack of ability, respectively. *Not be able to* carries the same meaning as *cannot,* but *be able to* and *can* are not exactly synonymous. In contrast to other phrasal modals, *be able to* is more formal than its modal counterpart *can* (which is used more frequently in speech), and it is used primarily to indicate that some effort or difficulty is involved. *Be able to* is also used in structures where a true modal (*can*) cannot be used, such as following another true modal, in perfect forms (*have* + *been able to* + *-ed* or *-en* verb), and with *-ing* and infinitive forms (*being able to; to be able to*).

Modals Used to Make Requests

The modals *will/would, can/could,* and *may/might* are used to make and respond to requests. The forms *would, could,* and *might* are preferred for making requests because they are considered more polite and deferential; they allow for the possibility of a negative reply. In contrast, the forms *will, can,* and *may* are preferred for responding to requests because they are more direct and they do not make the reply sound conditional.

Modals Used to Give Advice

Modals that are used to give advice can be organized on a continuum according to the urgency of the advice and/or the writer's degree of authority.

The present perfect form (*should have* + *-ed* or *-en* verb) is used to express an advisable action that did not occur in the past; the present perfect negative (*should not have* + *-ed* or *-en* verb) is used to indicate a past action that occurred but was not advisable. *Must* is used when the message is very urgent or the writer has great authority. In its negative form (*must not*), it expresses a prohibition (that is, that something is highly unadvisable). *Might/might not* and *could* are used when the writer has a low level of authority or is addressing a person of higher status or when the advice is tentative or not very urgent.

Example 35 Using modals with requests

No **Can** you *write* a letter of recommendation for me?

IN THIS PREFERRED FORM, *WOULD* MAKES IT CLEAR THAT THE PERSON TO WHOM THE QUESTION IS ADDRESSED HAS A CHOICE—THAT THE SPEAKER IS ASKING A FAVOR:

Yes **Would** you *write* a letter of recommendation for me?

COULD INCLUDES A SLIGHT CONNOTATION OF ABILITY, ALLOWING FOR THE POSSIBILITY THAT THE PERSON TO WHOM THE QUESTION IS ADDRESSED MAY BE UNABLE TO PERFORM THE ACTION:

Could you *write* a letter of recommendation for me?

To decide which form to use, consider the facts of the social situation, such as the status of the person to whom you are making a request or responding and the context of the interaction.

might/might not/could *should/should not* *must/must not*

Less Authority/Less Urgent Great Authority/Very Urgent

Should/should not are used most commonly to indicate whether or not something is advisable.

Example 36 Using modals to give advice

You **must not** *plagiarize;* be sure to document all of your outside sources. [Teacher to class]

You **should** *save* ten percent of your earnings each month. [Banker to client]

You **should** *have gone* to the doctor as soon as you started coughing. [Mother to child]

You **should not** *have cheated* on your final exam. [Dean to student]

You **might** *ask* the professor for an extension on the assignment. [Roommate to roommate]

Subjects 50a

The subject should be mentioned only once per clause in a sentence. Do not repeat it within a clause, not even by substituting a pronoun.

Example 1 Subject is named only once per clause in a sentence

No **Ramon,** after **he** graduated from high school, **he** came to the United States.

Yes After **Ramon** graduated from high school, **he** came to the United States.

Order of Direct and Indirect Objects Following Different Verbs 50b

Some verbs allow or require both a direct and an indirect object. A **direct object** denotes the person or thing that is acted upon in a sentence. An **indirect object** denotes the person or thing that receives or benefits from the action expressed by the verb. The order in which direct and indirect objects occur in a sentence is determined by the main verb. Different verbs allow different orders. There are two basic orders you should remember.

Order 1: Verb + Direct Object + *to* or *for* + Indirect Object

Some verbs are never immediately followed by an indirect object; they can take an indirect object only *after* a direct object—and the indirect object must be preceded by a

Verbs That Are Never Followed by an Indirect Object (Order 1)

Introduce indirect object with *to:*	Introduce indirect object with *for:*	Introduce indirect object with either *to* or *for:*
announce	answer	introduce
confess	cash	recommend
donate	close	suggest
explain	narrate	transmit
mention	open	
reveal	repair	

Example 2 Some verbs require order 1

THE INDIRECT OBJECT CANNOT IMMEDIATELY FOLLOW THE VERB:

No Dr. Rodriguez carefully explained **us** *the surgery.*

THE INDIRECT OBJECT FOLLOWS THE DIRECT OBJECT:

Yes Dr. Rodriguez carefully explained *the surgery* (DO) **to us.** (IO)

preposition (*to* or *for*). The preposition used to introduce the indirect object is determined by the verb. Some verbs introduce indirect objects with *to;* other verbs introduce indirect objects with *for.* Still other verbs introduce them with either *to* or *for,* and the preposition that is chosen affects the meaning of the sentence. *To* is used to introduce indirect objects that receive something (concrete or abstract), whereas *for* is used to introduce indirect objects that benefit from the action of the verb.

Order 1 is also commonly used with indirect objects that are lengthy, to aid readability.

Order 2: Verb + Indirect Object + Direct Object

Some verbs are almost always followed by indirect objects; they take indirect objects *before* direct objects. In these cases, no preposition (*to* or *for*) is used before the indirect object. This order is commonly used when the direct object is a pronoun. Because the end of a clause receives emphasis in English, this position is generally reserved for new information. Pronouns, by definition, refer back to things that have already been introduced—old information—so when a pronoun is a direct object it is generally placed in the middle of a clause, where it will not receive emphasis. This allows the indirect object to be emphasized.

Example 3 Preposition use varies with indirect objects that follow direct objects

FOR IS USED TO INTRODUCE INDIRECT OBJECTS OF THE VERB *ANSWER:*

No The explanation answered *many questions* **to both of us.**

Yes The explanation answered *many questions* **for both of us.**

TO IS USED TO INTRODUCE INDIRECT OBJECTS OF THE VERB *ANNOUNCE:*

No Who will announce *the merger* **for the public**?

Yes Who will announce *the merger* **to the public**?

Example 4 Order 1 is used with lengthy indirect objects

The game show offers *a recording contract* **to the singer who receives the most votes.**

Verbs That Are Almost Always Followed by Indirect Objects (Order 2)

allow	cause	deny	promise
ask	charge	envy	refuse
bet	cost	forgive	teach
bill			

Example 5 Some verbs require order 2

No Juan promised *a new bicycle* (DO) **to/for his daughter.** (IO)

Yes Juan promised **his daughter** (IO) *a new bicycle.* (DO)

Example 6 With order 2, no prepositions are used with indirect objects that follow verbs

No The trainer asked **to new clients** *many questions about their general health.*

Yes The trainer asked **new clients** *many questions about their general health.*

Verbs That Allow Objects in Either Order (Order 1 or Order 2)

When using Order 2, introduce indirect object with *to:*	When using Order 2, introduce indirect object with *for:*	When using Order 2, introduce indirect object with either *to* or *for:*
advance	book	bring
award	build	fax
deal	buy	get
forward	cook	leave
give	design	mail
grant	find	pay
hand	guarantee	read
lease	make	send
lend	mix	sing
offer	order	take
owe	paint	write
pass	play	
rent	pour	
sell	prepare	
serve	reserve	
show	save	
tell	secure	
throw	set	
	spare	
	win	

Example 7 When the indirect object is a pronoun, it precedes the direct object

My boss offered **me** *a big raise* to stay with the company.

Example 8 Sentence meaning changes when different prepositions introduce indirect objects

Administrative assistants sometimes *write* letters *for* **their managers.** [Managers do not write letters themselves; assistants write letters on their behalf.]

Administrative assistants sometimes *write* letters *to* **their managers.** [Assistants write letters addressed to their managers.]

Verbs That Allow Either Order

Many verbs can take objects in either order—order 1 *or* order 2. With these verbs, you can switch the order of the objects without altering the meaning of the sentence. The order of the objects determines only what is emphasized in the sentence. The object that is placed second receives emphasis because it is at the end of the clause.

Adjectives are used in two primary ways in English: (1) to add information about nouns (**attributive adjectives**) and (2) to complement *be* and linking verbs (**predicative adjectives**). When used attributively, adjectives are placed immediately before the noun they modify and after any determiners (*a, the, her*): *the* **stunning** *cathedral.* Used predicatively, adjectives are placed after the linking verb.

A third way in which adjectives are used is to modify nouns that function as direct objects of certain transitive verbs, including verbs of causation and verbs indicating a person's opinion of or preference for something. Adjectives used in this way are called **object complements,** and they are placed *after* the noun (direct object) they modify.

Adjective Form

Adjectives have one form; they remain the same regardless of whether the noun they modify is singular or plural or acts as subject or object. Note that many adjectives end in *ing* (most of which are related to the present participles of verbs) or *ed* (most of which are related to the past participles of verbs). Refer to section 49d for more information on the meaning and use of *-ing* and *-ed* adjectives.

Example 9 Placement of attributive adjectives

ATTRIBUTIVE ADJECTIVES PRECEDE THE NOUN THEY MODIFY:

No The *tree* **old** was struck by lightning.

Yes The **old** *tree* was struck by lightning.

Example 10 Placement of predicative adjectives

The attorney's closing argument *was* **convincing.**

Verbs That Take Adjectives as Object Complements

believe	hold	pick	think
consider	keep	prefer	want
drive	leave	render	wipe
eat	like	send	
find	make	serve	
get	paint	show	

Example 11 Placement of object complements

(OBJ = *italic*; OBJ COMP = **bold**)

They keep *their lawn* **immaculate.**

The cab ride made *me* **dizzy.**

I like *my water* **chilled.**

Example 12 Adjectives are never inflected for number or person

No Lee's **musicals** *performances* are **impressives.**

Yes Lee's **musical** *performances* are **impressive.**

Order of Adjectives

NUMBER	EVALUATION	PHYSICAL DESCRIPTION (SIZE, SHAPE, AGE, COLOR)	NATIONALITY	RELIGION	CLASSIFYING ADJECTIVES

The **two, handsome, tall, thin, young, tanned, Greek Orthodox male** *models* smiled at us.

Example 13 Order of adjectives in sequence

EVALUATIVE ADJECTIVES PRECEDE COLOR ADJECTIVES, WHICH PRECEDE CLASSIFYING ADJECTIVES:

No My **leather red beautiful** *briefcase* is from Florence.

Yes My **beautiful red leather** *briefcase* is from Florence.

Order of Adjectives

When a sequence of adjectives is used to modify the same noun, the order of adjectives within that sequence is not completely arbitrary; rules govern the order of certain types of adjectives. In general, qualitative or evaluative adjectives come first, followed by color adjectives, followed by classifying adjectives.

Forming Questions 50d

Yes/No Questions

Example 14 Inverting *were* and subject when main verb is *be*

They **were** happy.

No *Do* they **were** happy?

Yes **Were** they happy?

Example 15 Inverting modal and subject

Corinna **should** adopt a cat.

Should Corinna adopt a cat?

Example 16 Inserting *do* before subject and using plain form of main verb

The virus **affects** your immune system.

No *Does* the virus **affects** your immune system?

Yes *Does* the virus **affect** your immune system?

There are two types of questions in English: *yes/no* questions and *wh-* information questions. Both types end with a question mark. ***Yes/no* questions** can be answered with a simple *yes* or *no* (in practice, answers often include more information and may not contain the word *yes* or *no*).

To form yes/no questions from sentences

- If the predicate is a single *be* verb, reverse the order of the subject and the *be* verb.
- If the predicate contains one or more modals, reverse the order of the subject and the first modal.
- If the predicate is a single main verb (with no modals), insert *do* or *did* before the subject.

Note: *Do* must be marked for tense and must match the subject in person and number. Use the plain form of the main verb.

***Wh-* information questions** begin with a question word (*who, what, when, where, why, how*) and cannot be answered with a simple *yes* or *no.* They are used to request specific information and can refer to any component of a proposition (its subject, objects, verb, etc.).

S DO IO
Who *gave* what to whom?

To form wh- information questions from sentences

Step 1. Express the question you wish to ask in statement form, including the appropriate *wh-* word in place of the information (answer) you seek.
Step 2. Move the *wh-* word to the beginning of the sentence. If the *wh-* word introduces a noun or noun phrase (i.e., *which* + noun), move both the *wh-* word and the noun to the front.
Step 3. Follow the rules for *yes/no* question formation that apply to the predicate of the sentence:

- With a *be* verb, reverse the subject and the *be* verb:

  wh- word + *be* verb + subject + . . . ?

- With a modal, reverse the subject and the first modal:

  wh- word + modal + subject + main verb + . . . ?

- With a main verb, insert *do/did* before the subject:

  wh- word + *do/did* + subject + plain form verb + . . . ?

Choosing the Appropriate *Wh-* Word for Your Question

To ask about . . .	**Use this *wh-* word:**
a person or group of people	*who*
an object or activity	*what* or *which/whose* + noun
time of action	*when*
location	*where*
reason for or cause of action	*why*
manner in which action is performed	*how*

Example 17 Forming *wh-* information questions

STATE QUESTION → MOVE *WH-* TO FRONT → APPLY Y/N QUESTION RULE

Your office *is* **where?** → **Where** your office *is*? → **Where** *is* your office?

Example 18 Word order with *wh-* questions

WITH MODAL, INVERT SUBJECT AND MODAL:

Why *the candidate* **should** resign? → Why **should** *the candidate* resign?

WITH SINGLE MAIN VERB, USE STANDARD WORD ORDER (SVO):

How did **escape** *the inmates* from prison? → How did *the inmates* **escape** from prison?

WHEN *WH-* WORD IS SUBJECT, USE STANDARD ORDER:

Who **wrote** this book?

Example 19 Verb form with *wh-* questions containing single main verb

DO TAKES ON TENSE OF MAIN VERB, SO MAIN VERB CONVERTS TO PLAIN FORM:

Chris supported **who**? → **Who** Chris supported? → **Who** *did* Chris support?

DO IS MARKED FOR THIRD-PERSON SINGULAR, SO *S* IS REMOVED FROM MAIN VERB, LEAVING PLAIN FORM:

Li enjoys **what?** → **What** Li enjoys? → **What** *does* Li enjoy?

DO MATCHES SUBJECT, NOT OBJECT, IN PERSON AND NUMBER:

Jo prefers **which** ones? → **Which** ones Jo prefers? → **Which** ones *does* Jo prefer?

In academic writing, you will frequently need to report what other people have said or written about a topic. You can do this by quoting the exact words of the original source (direct quotation), by reporting the content of the original source using indirect quotation (indirect reported speech), or by rewriting the ideas of the original source entirely in your own words (paraphrase). This section focuses on the second of these three methods. Refer to Chapter 12 for a detailed treatment of direct quotation and paraphrase.

Indirect reported speech, which is used to convey the ideas of a source but not the source's exact words, is far more common in academic writing and everyday conversation than direct quotation. Reporting speech indirectly involves (1) creating a **reporting clause** containing a **reporting verb** and (2) attaching the clause to a **complement clause** containing the information being reported. The type of complement clause you use depends on the type of structure you are reporting (a statement or a question) and the reporting verb you use (different verbs allow different complements).

Example 20 Components of indirect quotation

REPORTING CLAUSE — COMPLEMENT CLAUSE

The author contends **that** the planet is shrinking.

Reporting Verbs That Take Ordinary (Tensed) *that* Clauses as Complements

acknowledge	complain	find	mention	report
admit	conclude	forget	note	reveal
agree	decide	guarantee	observe	say
allege	determine	guess	predict	show
answer	discover	hear	promise	state
argue	doubt	imply	prove	suggest
assume	estimate	know	read	think
believe	expect	learn	realize	understand
claim	explain	maintain	remember	write
comment				

Reporting Verbs That Take an Indirect Object + *that* Clause

assure convince inform persuade remind tell

Reporting Verbs That Take Subjunctive (Uninflected) *that* Clauses as Complements

advise	insist	propose	require
ask	order	recommend	suggest
demand	prefer	request	urge

Example 21 Verb form in *that* complements of reporting verbs

THINK REQUIRES INFLECTED VERB IN *THAT* COMPLEMENT:

I think **that** she *is* treasurer of the organization.

REQUEST REQUIRES PLAIN FORM VERB IN *THAT* COMPLEMENT:

The teacher requested **that** she *arrive* on time for her piano lesson.

Reporting Statements and Thoughts

Using that complements
The most common way to report statements and thoughts is to use a complement clause beginning with *that*. Many reporting verbs take *that*-clause complements, which consist of *that* plus a clause containing a verb that may or may not need to be inflected for tense, person, and number. Some of these verbs require an indirect object; in these cases, the indirect object precedes the *that* clause.

Omitting that
You may have noticed that *that* is sometimes absent from reporting clauses. The decision to omit *that* is based on several factors. In formal contexts and academic writing, *that* is generally included. *That* can be omitted when (1) the subject of the *that* complement is a pronoun (*it, she*), (2) the reporting clause and the *that* clause have the same subject, and/or (3) the writing context is informal.

Infinitive and -ing complements
Some reporting verbs can take infinitive complement clauses (starting with *to* + verb) or *-ing* complement clauses (starting with the *-ing* form).

Example 22 Reporting verbs *say* and *tell*

SAY DOES NOT TAKE AN INDIRECT OBJECT:

The flight attendant said **that** the seat cushions function as flotation devices.

TELL REQUIRES AN INDIRECT OBJECT:

The flight attendant told passengers **that** the seat cushions function as flotation devices.

Example 23 Omitting *that* in complements of reporting verbs

THAT IS FREQUENTLY OMITTED WHEN THE SUBJECT OF THE COMPLEMENT CLAUSE IS A PRONOUN:

The surgeons said (*that*) **he** was doing better.

THAT IS USUALLY OMITTED WHEN THE REPORTING CLAUSE AND COMPLEMENT CLAUSE HAVE THE SAME SUBJECT:

The pilot said (*that*) **she** enjoyed flying.

THAT IS USUALLY RETAINED IN MORE FORMAL AND ACADEMIC TEXTS:

Scientists discovered *that* extensive exposure to ultraviolet light correlates with skin cancer.

Reporting Verbs That Can Take Infinitive Complements

An asterisk (*) indicates that the verb requires an indirect object before the complement.

advise*	instruct*	plan	tell*
ask	intend	promise	urge*
beg	invite*	refuse	want
decide	order*	remind*	warn*
forbid*	persuade*	teach*	

Reporting Verbs That Can Take *-ing* Form Complements

advise	predict	recommend	suggest

Example 24 Infinitive and *-ing* complements of reporting verbs

The test supervisor *instructed* us **to use** a number two pencil to write answers.

Lifeguards *recommend* **waiting** thirty minutes after a meal to swim.

Reporting Verbs That Take *if* and *whether* Clauses as Complements

ask	inquire	remember	see
discover	know	say	wonder

Example 25 Complement clauses with indirect *yes/no* questions

COMPLEMENT CLAUSES IN REPORTED QUESTIONS MUST START WITH *IF* OR *WHETHER:*

No The prosecuting attorney asked me *did I witness* the crime.

Yes The prosecuting attorney asked me **if/whether** *I witnessed* the crime.

INFINITIVE COMPLEMENTS MUST BEGIN WITH *WHETHER; OR NOT* MAY BE INCLUDED BUT IS OPTIONAL:

No I wondered **if** *to bring* an umbrella on my trip.

Yes I wondered **whether (or not)** *to bring* an umbrella on my trip.

TENSED COMPLEMENTS MAY BEGIN WITH *WHETHER* OR *IF:*

I wondered **if/whether** *I should bring* an umbrella on my trip.

Example 26 Word order with indirect *yes/no* questions

REPORTED QUESTIONS FOLLOW STATEMENT ORDER, NOT QUESTION ORDER:

No An accountant would know **whether** *is* the company financially sound.

Yes An accountant would know **whether** the company *is* financially sound.

Reporting Verbs That Take *wh-* Question Complements

ask	forget	realize	suggest
decide	guess	remember	teach
describe	imagine	reveal	tell
discover	inquire	say	think
discuss	know	see	understand
explain	learn	show	wonder
find out			

Example 27 Form of complement clauses with indirect *wh-* questions

REPORTED *WH-* QUESTIONS CAN HAVE TENSED OR INFINITIVE CLAUSES AS COMPLEMENTS:

He explained **where** we *should go* in the event of a tornado. [*wh* word + tensed clause]

He explained **where** *to go* in the event of a tornado. [*wh* word + infinitive clause]

Reporting Questions

In addition to reporting statements in your writing, you may wish to report questions that people ask. These are referred to as **indirect questions,** since you are reporting—not actually asking—the questions.

Indirect yes/no questions

The complement clause of an indirect *yes/no* question consists of *whether* or *if* followed by a tensed or infinitive clause. If the complement clause contains a modal or tensed verb (that is, if it is a tensed clause), it may begin with *whether* or *if.* If the complement contains an infinitive, it must begin with *whether.* Unlike direct questions, indirect questions follow standard statement word order (SVO)—subjects are not inverted with verbs, *do* is not inserted, and question marks are not used.

Indirect* wh- *questions

Indirect *wh-* information questions contain complement clauses that consist of a *wh-* word followed by a tensed or infinitive clause in standard statement word order (SVO). Do not invert subjects and verbs, insert *do,* or use a question mark as end punctuation with indirect questions.

Tense Shifts in Indirect Quotations

Verb tense is one of the most confusing aspects of indirect reporting for multilingual writers of English. Usually when you use indirect speech, you are reporting something that another person said, thought, wrote, or asked in the past. Thus, the reporting verb and the verb in the complement clause are often in past tense. However, if you are reporting something that is still (currently) true or something that is said frequently, you may use either a present tense or a past tense verb in the reporting clause. When you are reporting published statements, it is common to use present tense reporting verbs because what the author wrote remains the same eternally.

Whatever the tense of the verb in the reporting clause, you should put the verb in the complement clause in the tense that is appropriate at the time you are writing (or speaking). See section 34d for more detail on verb tense.

Example 28 Word order with indirect *wh-* questions

REPORTED QUESTIONS FOLLOW STATEMENT ORDER, NOT QUESTION ORDER:

No The researcher asked participants **how** *did* they *exercise* each week.

Yes The researcher asked participants **how** they *exercised* each week.

Example 29 Punctuating indirect questions

USE A PERIOD, NOT A QUESTION MARK, AT THE END OF A REPORTED QUESTION:

No The officers wondered **what** we were doing**?**

Yes The officers wondered **what** we were doing.

INCLUDE A QUESTION MARK WHEN A QUESTION IS REPORTED IN A DIRECT QUOTATION:

The officers asked, "**What** are you doing**?**"

Example 30 Verb tense with indirect quotations

SENTENCES DESCRIBING SITUATIONS THAT ARE STILL TRUE CAN TAKE A PAST OR PRESENT TENSE VERB IN THE COMPLEMENT:

Mary *said* (that) she *was* an associate professor of history.

Mary *said* (that) she *is* an associate professor of history.

TO SHOW THAT A SITUATION IS NO LONGER TRUE, A PHRASAL VERB IS OFTEN USED IN THE COMPLEMENT:

Mary *said* (that) she *used to be* an associate professor of history.

FREQUENTLY REPORTED OR PUBLISHED STATEMENTS CAN TAKE PRESENT TENSE REPORTING VERBS:

Doctors *say* (that) drinking a glass of wine each day *can reduce* the risk of heart disease.

Example 31 Pronoun and verb changes required in indirect speech

DIRECT QUOTATION:

Steve agreed: "You should take the trip alone."

IN INDIRECT REPORTING, SECOND PERSON (*YOU*) CHANGES TO FIRST PERSON OBJECT CASE (*ME*); TENSED VERB CHANGES TO INFINITIVE BECAUSE *ADVISE* TAKES INDIRECT OBJECT + INFINITIVE COMPLEMENT:

No Steve advised **I** *should* take the trip alone.

Yes Steve advised **me** *to take* the trip alone.

Example 32 Modal changes required in indirect speech

DIRECT QUOTATION:

"I will observe the class for one year," said Jane Doe.

IN INDIRECT REPORTING, MODAL *WILL* (PRESENT) CHANGES TO *WOULD* (PAST):

No Doe reported that she **will** observe the class for one year.

Yes Doe reported that she **would** observe the class for one year.

Example 33 Choosing reporting verbs that convey your interpretation of reported information

The researchers _______ that their discovery represents a significant advance in science.

say	neutral
suggest	implies doubt or tentativeness on the part of the researchers
claim	implies that the researchers' statement is nonobvious or unproven
argue	implies that the researchers are making a claim and can support it with reasons
assume	implies that the researchers believe the statement but do not offer reasons for their belief

Other Changes with Indirect Quotations

In addition to modifying the tense of the verb in the reporting clause and/or the complement clause, converting direct to indirect speech may require you to change other expressions, including pronouns, modals, and words for time and place.

Common Changes in Pronouns

I → *she* or *he*
we → *they*
me → *her* or *him*
my → *her* or *his*
you → *me*

Common Changes in Modals

can → *could*
may → *might*
will → *would*
must → *had to*

Common Changes in Expressions of Time and Place

this → *that*
these → *those*
here → *there*

Varying Reporting Verbs

When reporting information in your writing, try to vary the reporting verbs and, where appropriate, incorporate verbs that convey your attitude toward the information you are reporting. Avoid overusing *say, report,* and *state.*

A

absolute phrase A phrase, composed of a noun or pronoun and a participle, that functions as an adverb for an entire clause. An absolute phrase is set off from the clause it modifies by a comma: ***The horse cared for,*** *the veterinarian left.* See 30k.

abstract noun A noun that names something that cannot be known through the five senses, but only sensed internally as a feeling or thought: *poverty, triumph, spirituality.* See also **concrete noun.**

action verb A verb that expresses action by an agent: *The circus performer* ***leaped.*** The agent needn't be present in the sentence, however; in passive sentences (see 34f), action verbs are accompanied by auxiliary verbs (*am, are, is, was, were*): *The old playground equipment* ***was bulldozed.***

active voice The form of a sentence in which the action described by the verb is performed by the subject of the sentence: *The baseball commission* ***instituted*** *a tough new drug policy for players.* See also **passive voice.** See 34f.

adjective A word that describes, limits, or specifies a noun or pronoun by showing its quantity, location, ownership, or other qualities: *tall, green, four.* See 30d and Chapter 36.

adjective clause A dependent clause, introduced by a relative pronoun such as *who, which,* or *that* (or occasionally *when, where,* or *why*), that answers the question "Which one?" or "What kind of?" about the noun or pronoun it follows. See 30l, esp. p. 425.

adverb A word that modifies a verb, adjective, other adverb, or whole clause. An adverb answers the question "When?" "Where?" "How?" or "To what degree or extent?": *ran* ***yesterday, deceptively*** *simple,* ***very*** *loudly.* See 30e and Chapter 36.

adverb clause A dependent clause, introduced by a subordinating conjunction, that modifies a verb, adjective, other adverb, or entire clause. An adverb clause answers the question "How?" "When?" "Where?" "Why?" "In what manner?" "Under what conditions?" "With what result?" or "To what degree?" See 30l, esp. p. 425.

agreement Match in number and person between a subject and its verb: *The* ***plumber fixes*** *the pipes* (see Chapter 35); match in number, person, and sometimes gender between a pronoun and its antecedent: *The* ***woman*** *loves* ***her*** *job* (see 33h–l); and match in number between a demonstrative adjective and its noun: ***These shoes*** *are tight* (see 48c).

antecedent The noun or pronoun that a pronoun refers to or replaces: *The* ***nurses*** *taught first aid to* ***their*** *students.* See 33m–q.

appositive A word or phrase that functions as a noun equivalent. It restates, renames, or otherwise more fully defines the noun immediately preceding it: *Candace,* ***an avid golfer,*** *started playing at 7 a.m.* See 30k, esp. p. 423, and 33d.

article The word *a, an,* or *the.* Articles are used with nouns: *a crisis, an ordeal, the solution.* See Chapter 48.

auxiliary verb Also known as a *helping verb,* a verb that works with other verbs to indicate mood, voice, and tense: *Her son* ***did*** *graduate; he* ***will be*** *working soon.* See 34b and 49e.

C

case The form of a noun or pronoun that indicates whether it is acting as subject *(**I** enjoyed his quick wit),* object (*He laughed with* ***me***), or possessive *(**His** face glowed).* See 33a–g.

clause A word group that contains both a subject and a verb. An independent clause—as the name implies—can function independently as a simple sentence: *Americans typically have less vacation time than Europeans.* (See 30i–j.) A dependent clause (also called a *subordinate clause*) cannot stand alone as a sentence: *although top managers often have four-week vacation packages.* (See 30l.)

collective noun A noun that names a collection or group: *police, faculty, team, family, army, class.* See 30a, 33j, and 35f.

comma splice The error caused by joining two independent clauses with a comma but no coordinating conjunction. See Chapter 32.

common noun A noun that names a generic member of a group: *school, woman, river.* See also **proper noun.** See 30a and Chapter 48.

complement A word or word group that completes (renames, identifies, or describes) the subject, verb, or object. See sentence patterns 4 and 5 in 30j.

complete predicate See **predicate.**

complete subject See **subject.**

complex sentence A sentence that consists of one independent clause and at least one dependent clause. See 26c–d and 30m.

compound sentence A sentence that consists of at least two independent clauses, joined by a comma and a coordinating conjunction (*and, but, or, nor, for, so, yet*) or by a semicolon. See 26a–b and 30m.

compound-complex sentence A sentence that consists of two or more independent clauses and at least one dependent clause. See 30m.

concrete noun A noun that names things that can be sensed—seen, heard, tasted, smelled, touched, or experienced in the world: *computer, woodlands, pockets.* See 30a.

conjunction A word that connects two or more clauses, phrases, or words. See also **coordinating conjunction, subordinating conjunction, correlative conjunction.**

coordinating conjunction A conjunction that joins two or more elements (words, phrases, clauses) of equal grammatical rank: *and, but, so, yet, for, or, nor.* See 26a–b and 30g.

coordination The joining of two or more grammatical elements of equal weight, typically with a coordinating conjunction—for example, adjectives (*stormy* ***and*** *dark*) and clauses (*Brian was accepted into the Marines,* ***but*** *Justin was rejected*). See 26a–b.

correlative conjunction A conjunction that works in a pair (*both . . . and, either . . . or, neither . . . nor, not only . . . but also*) to express a relationship of contrast or similarity between different elements. See 25a and 30g.

countable noun A noun that names something that can be counted: *voter, tree, shoe, byte.* See 30a and Chapter 48.

D

dangling modifier A modifier that refers to a word or phrase that is either not obviously connected to it or not in the sentence at all. See 36k.

demonstrative adjective An adjective that limits or emphasizes a noun: ***this*** *pencil,* ***that*** *night,* ***these*** *ideas,* ***those*** *people.*

demonstrative pronoun A pronoun that points to the antecedent: ***This*** *is the case,* ***These*** *are the ones.*

dependent clause Also known as a *subordinate clause,* a clause that begins with a subordinating word and cannot function independently as a sentence. Dependent clauses function as a single part of speech: they can be nouns, adjectives, or adverbs. See 30l.

determiner An adjective that precedes and limits a noun: a definite article *(the),* indefinite article *(a, an),* quantifier (such as *a little, many, every*), possessive pronoun (such as *her*), or demonstrative pronoun (*this, that, these, those*). See Chapter 48.

direct object A word or word group that receives the action of a transitive verb: *He mailed* ***the letter***. See sentence patterns 2–4 in 30j.

E

expletive A sentence that begins with *it* or *there* and a form of the verb *to be* instead of the subject: ***There were*** *horses in the pasture.* See 27a and 35d.

F

finite verb A verb that is used as the main verb of a sentence and thus is marked for tense, voice, mood, person, and number: *She* ***insisted*** *on it.*

fragment See **sentence fragment.**

G

gerund An *-ing* form of a verb (present participle) acting as a noun: ***Crying*** *helps.* See 33g.

gerund phrase A gerund and its modifiers and objects acting as the subject or object: ***Going home*** *is comforting.* See 30k, esp. p. 422.

I

imperative mood A command, with *you* as the understood subject: *Don't walk on the grass.* See 30n and 34e.

indefinite pronoun A pronoun, such as *all, anyone, each, everybody,* or *some,* that refers to an unnamed or indefinite antecedent. See 30b, 33k, and 35e.

independent clause A group of words with a subject and a verb that can stand alone as a sentence. See 30i–j.

indicative mood The mood of sentences that make statements or ask questions: *That dog is barking.* See 34e.

indirect object A noun, pronoun, or word group that indicates to whom, to what, for whom, or for what an action is performed: *He mailed the letter to* ***Sheila.*** See sentence pattern 3 in 30j.

infinitive A verbal made of the plain form of a verb and often the word *to: to dance.* See 33e, 33f, and 34b.

infinitive phrase An infinitive and its modifiers and object functioning as a noun, adjective, or adverb. See 30k, esp. p. 422, 49b–c, and 49e.

intensive pronoun A pronoun that ends in *-self* or *-selves* and emphasizes the antecedent: *Shelley* ***herself*** *said it was fine.*

interjection A word, standing alone as a sentence or interrupting a sentence, that expresses strong or sudden emotion: ***Hey! Oh, no,*** *that guy hit my car!* See 30h.

interrogative pronoun A pronoun, such as *who, whom, which, what, whoever, whomever, whichever,* or *whatever,* that introduces a question: ***What*** *happened?* For *who* versus *whom,* see 33f.

intransitive verb A verb that does not take a direct object: *The child* ***panicked***. See sentence pattern 1 in 30j and 34c.

irregular verb A verb that forms its past tense and past participle in some way other than by adding *d* or *ed.* See 34a.

M

main verb The verb in a sentence that expresses the main meaning: *She may have been* ***walking*** *to the store.*

misplaced modifier A descriptive word or phrase that is located too far away from the word it modifies, creating confusion about the intended meaning. See 36i.

modal auxiliary verb A helping verb (*can, could, may, might, must, shall, should,* or *will*) that adds shades of meaning to another verb. See 34b and 49e.

modifier A word or word group that limits the meaning of another word or phrase. A modifier functions as an adjective or adverb. See Chapter 36.

mood The attitude that is expressed by a writer or speaker in a sentence. See also **indicative mood, imperative mood, subjunctive mood.** See 34e.

N

noncountable noun See **uncountable noun.**

nonfinite verb See **verbal.**

nonrestrictive (nonessential) element A word or word group that does not provide information essential to understanding the meaning of the element it modifies (and typically follows) and thus is set off from the sentence with punctuation, usually a pair of commas: *Her only brother,* ***Lee,*** *lives in Michigan.* See 38f.

noun A word that names a person, place, thing, quality, or concept. Anything that can be discretely isolated or referred to—pointed to or singled out—can be named with a noun. A noun can function as a subject, object, or complement. See 30a.

noun clause A dependent clause that functions as a subject, object, or complement. See 30m.

noun phrase A noun and its modifiers functioning as a subject, object, or complement. See 30l.

number The form of a word that indicates whether it refers to one (singular number) or more than one (plural): *toy/toys, I/we, swims/swim, this/these.*

O

object A noun, pronoun, or group of words functioning as a noun that receives the action of a verb (direct object), tells to or for whom an action is done (indirect object), or follows a preposition (object of a preposition). See also **direct object, indirect object, prepositional phrase.** See sentence patterns 2–4 in 30j.

object complement A noun or adjective that describes or renames a direct object that follows a verb such as *call, elect, make,* or *name: They named him* ***chief****. I'll make you* ***sorry***. See sentence pattern 4 in 30j.

objective case The case of a noun or pronoun functioning as the object of a verb, verbal, or preposition: *He loves* ***me****. I care about* ***him***. See 33a.

P

parallelism The use of repeated grammatical elements in coordinated sentence structures: *an acute attack or a lingering disease.* See Chapter 25.

participial phrase A phrase that consists of a present or past participle and any objects or modifiers. A participial phrase functions as an adjective. See 30k, esp. p. 423, and 49d.

participle See **present participle, past participle.**

parts of speech The eight categories into which words in a sentence are placed based on function, meaning, form, and placement. See also **noun, pronoun, adjective, verb, adverb, interjection, conjunction, preposition.** See 30a–h.

passive voice The form of a sentence in which the subject receives (rather than performs) the action of a transitive verb: *The train* ***was wrecked***. See also **active voice.** See 34f.

past participle A verbal formed by adding *d* or *ed* to a regular verb (*liked, wanted*) or by transforming an irregular verb (*been, hidden, rode;* see 34a). The past participle functions as an adjective (see 49d) or part of a verb phrase: ***Delighted,*** *I winked. We had* ***been*** *playing for hours.* See also 33g.

personal pronoun A pronoun that refers to particular people or things: *I, you, he, she, it, we, they.* See 30b and Chapter 33.

phrasal verb A verb followed by one or more words (particles) that help specify its meaning. Together, the verb and particle(s) function as a single verb whose meaning is rarely the same as the meaning of its component parts: *add up, phase out, get ahead.* See 49a.

phrase A word group that does not contain a subject, a predicate, or both. Phrases function as a single part of speech: as a noun, verb, adjective, or adverb. See also **absolute phrase, noun phrase, prepositional phrase, verb phrase, verbal phrase.** See 30k.

possessive case The case of a noun and pronoun showing ownership or possession. See 33a.

predicate The part of a sentence that expresses the subject's action or state of being: *Alternative energies* ***should be explored more carefully.*** The complete predicate includes the verb and any modifiers or objects. The simple predicate includes only the main verb and any auxiliary verbs: *should be explored.* See 30i.

preposition A word, such as *in, on, above, below, beside,* or *between,* that indicates a certain relationship between the nouns or pronouns that follow it and the other words in a sentence: *The patient rested* ***in*** *bed.* See 30f.

prepositional phrase A phrase that consists of a preposition followed by a noun, pronoun, or noun phrase known as the *object of the preposition.* The prepositional phrase also includes any modifiers of the object of the preposition: *among the tall yellowed grasses of autumn.* See 30k, esp. p. 423.

present participle A verbal formed by adding *ing* to the plain form of a verb: *caring.* The present participle functions as an adjective (*The couple exchanged a* ***knowing*** *look;* see 49d) or as part of a verb phrase (*The company is* ***dumping*** *chemicals into the river*). See also 33g.

pronoun A word used in place of a noun. See **personal pronoun, indefinite pronoun, relative pronoun, interrogative pronoun, demonstrative pronoun, reflexive pronoun, intensive pronoun, reciprocal pronoun.** See 30b and Chapter 33.

proper adjective An adjective formed from a proper noun: *the* ***British*** *empire.* See 44b.

proper noun A noun that names a specific person, place, or thing. The first letter of a proper noun is capitalized: *The* ***Vatican*** *is the administrative headquarters of the* ***Roman Catholic Church.*** See 44b.

R

reciprocal pronoun The pronoun *each other* or *one another.* A reciprocal pronoun acts as a direct object to a verb describing an action that members of a plural antecedent perform mutually: *The board members trust* ***one another***.

reflexive pronoun The pronoun *myself, yourself, himself, herself, itself, ourselves, yourselves,* or *themselves.* A reflexive pronoun refers back to a noun or personal pronoun when the subject of an action and the object of that action are the same: *She had only* ***herself*** *to blame.*

regular verb A verb that forms its past tense and past participle by adding *d* or *ed* to the plain form: *typed, slipped, regarded.* See Chapter 34.

relative pronoun A pronoun, such as *who, whom, whose, that, which,* or *whoever,* that introduces a subordinate (dependent) clause: *The hurricane,* ***which*** *hit land on August 29, devastated New Orleans.* See 33g; for *who* versus *whom,* see 33f.

restrictive (essential) element A word or word group that provides information essential to understanding the meaning of the sentence: *I'm going to buy the car* ***that I saw advertised in the Sunday paper***. No commas set off a restrictive element. See 38f.

run-on sentence A group of words that is grammatically incorrect because it does not include the punctuation necessary between independent clauses in a sentence. See Chapter 32.

S

sentence A string of words that obeys the grammatical rules of a language. Sentences are the basic units of language for expressing ideas. See Chapter 24.

sentence fragment A part of a sentence incorrectly punctuated as a complete sentence. Either a subject or a verb may be missing, or if both are present, they appear in a subordinate clause that must be attached to another complete sentence. See Chapter 31.

simple predicate The verb that relays the subject's action or state of being. See **predicate.** See 30i.

simple sentence A sentence that consists of a single independent clause. See 30j.

simple subject The noun or pronoun in the subject; whoever or whatever the sentence is about: *His fuzzy* ***earmuffs*** *covered more of his head than his Mohawk.* See also **subject.** See 30i.

split infinitive A phrase in which a word or words are placed between the two parts of an infinitive (*to* + plain form of verb): *to* ***boldly*** *go.*

squinting modifier A modifier placed in a sentence in such a way that it could modify two different words, causing confusion. See 36j.

subject The word or phrase that names the topic of the sentence, including any modifiers: ***His fuzzy earmuffs*** *covered more of his head than his Mohawk.* See also **simple subject.** See 30i.

subject complement A noun, pronoun, or adjective that follows a linking verb and renames or describes the subject: *Their pourable yogurt is* ***a drink***. See sentence pattern 5 in 30j.

subjective case The case of a noun or pronoun that functions as a subject or subject complement (***She*** *loves chocolate; It is* ***I***). See 33a.

subjunctive mood The mood of a verb that indicates speculation, a condition contrary to fact, a request, a demand, or a suggestion. See 34e.

subordinate clause See **dependent clause.**

subordinating conjunction A word or words that express a logical or temporal relationship among elements in a sentence or between ideas across sentence boundaries. When a subordinate clause precedes an independent clause to which it is attached, it is followed by a comma. See 26c–d and 31c.

subordination De-emphasizing one grammatical element by making it dependent on another independent element (for example, beginning it with a subordinating conjunction): ***Although*** *the fan was working, the air felt heavy and inert.* See also **coordination.** See Chapter 26.

T

tense The form of a verb that expresses the time of its action (past, present, or future) and the relationships among events: *He* ***had left*** *before Chloe* ***arrived***. Changes in verb form and endings show tense (*came, come, coming*), and so do combinations of auxiliary verbs and main verbs (*will come, was coming, has come*). See 34d.

transitive verb A verb that requires a direct object to complete the thought. See 34c.

U

uncountable noun Also called a *noncountable* or *noncount noun,* a noun that names something that can't be counted: *mud, confusion, water.* See 30a and Chapter 48.

V

verb A word that indicates the action or state of being of a subject. Verbs can change form and be combined with auxiliary verbs to indicate tense (time of action), voice (whether the subject performs the action or receives it), mood (attitude), number (singular or plural), and sometimes person (the *-s* ending with a subject like *she, he,* or *it eats*). See 30c and Chapters 34 and 49.

verbal Also known as a *nonfinite verb,* a verb form that functions as a noun, adjective, or adverb and so cannot be the complete verb of a sentence. The three types of verbals are infinitives (***To love*** *is divine*), gerunds (***Saluting*** *the flag is a form of respect*), and participles (*The dog* ***burying*** *its bone didn't respond to a whistle*). See 30k and 49b.

verbal phrase A phrase that consists of a verbal and its accompanying modifiers, objects, or complements. See 30k.

verb phrase A verb that consists of a main verb and any accompanying auxiliaries, including *be, do, have, can, could, may, might, must, shall, should, will,* and *would,* in all their forms: *We* ***could have danced*** *all night.* See Chapters 34 and 49.

voice A quality of transitive verbs that indicates whether the subject is acting (active voice: *I* ***lost*** *my homework*) or being acted upon (passive voice: *My homework* ***was lost***) by the verb. See 34f.

A

a, an The article *a* is used before consonant sounds (*a piano, a ukulele, a harmonica, a one-man band*); the article *an* is used before vowel sounds (*an apple, an umpire, an hourglass, an ox*).

accept, except The verb *accept* means "to receive"; the verb *except* means "to exclude." The preposition *except* means "other than."

> She **accepted** all his love tokens **except** the live boa constrictor.
>
> **Excepting** rum raisin, I love all flavors of ice cream.

advice, advise *Advice* is a noun that means "counsel," "recommendation," or "opinion"; to *advise* is to give advice.

> Professor Jones **advised** him to read *The Odyssey* out loud.
>
> Sometime past midnight, he remembered Professor Jones's **advice:** to read *The Odyssey* out loud.

affect, effect The verb *affect* means "to influence"; the verb *effect* means "to accomplish" or "to bring about." An *effect* (noun) is a result or outcome.

> Her binge drinking began to **affect** her health.
>
> The drastic new policy sought to **effect** campus-wide sobriety.
>
> Slurred speech is a common **effect** of heavy drinking.

ain't Nonstandard; do not use. Use *am not, are not, is not,* or the appropriate contraction.

all ready, already In the phrase *all ready,* meaning "completely prepared," the adverb *all* modifies the adjective *ready.*

> By Tuesday the care packages were **all ready** for distribution.

Already is an adverb that means "before," "prior to a specified time," or "so soon."

> By the time we arrived at the station, he had **already** departed.
>
> Are you leaving **already**?

all together, altogether The phrase *all together* is used to mean that all the members of a group perform or receive an action together.

> As the lightning crashed, the cowboys worked desperately to herd the cows **all together.**

In all such sentences, you can reword to separate *all* and *together.*

> As the lightning crashed, the cowboys worked desperately to herd **all** the cows **together.**

Altogether is an adverb that means "wholly," "utterly," "with all counted," or "all things considered."

> After the storm, the cowboys were **altogether** exhausted.
>
> After the storm, there were **altogether** 36 cows missing.
>
> **Altogether**, the cowboys performed bravely during the storm.

a lot of Informal for *many, much, a great deal of.* Do not misspell as *alot.*

alright Nonstandard; use *all right.*

a.m., p.m. *a.m.* stands for *ante meridiem* (the period between midnight and noon), and *p.m.* stands for *post meridiem* (the period from noon to midnight). Both are always lowercase, with each letter followed by a period.

among, between *Between* denotes a one-on-one relationship of individuals; *among* denotes an unspecified relationship of a group or collective entities. While only *between* can be used for two items, which to use when describing a relationship between or among three or more items depends on your intended meaning. For example, describing a bull as charging madly *between* festival goers suggests that no one is being gored, trampled, or otherwise injured. However, describing a bull as charging madly *among* festival goers suggests that someone is likely to get injured any minute.

amount, number See **number, amount.**

an, a See **a, an.**

and etc. See **etc.**

and/or Although suitable in some legal and business communications, avoid in formal prose as awkward and imprecise.

anymore, now, nowadays In formal prose use *anymore* in negative constructions and questions only; in positive constructions use *now* or *nowadays.*

> Most people do not travel by horse and buggy **anymore.**
>
> **Nowadays** we travel by car.
>
> Do they travel by horse and buggy **anymore**?

anyways Nonstandard; do not use. Use *anyway.*

apt to, liable to, likely to Although all three adjectives refer to probability, each has a different shade of meaning. *Apt* connotes a natural talent or tendency (as in *aptitude*); *liable* is most often used with undesirable outcomes (as in *liability*); *likely* conveys a more general sense of probability.

> My three-year-old is **apt** to cry when she falls off the jungle gym.
>
> If she doesn't stop jumping on the jungle gym, that child is **liable to** fall.
>
> Most children are **likely to** prefer chocolate ice cream to pistachio.

assure, ensure, insure See **ensure, insure, assure.**

as to whether Redundant; use *whether.*

awful, awfully Do not use for *very* in formal prose.

B

bad, badly *Bad* is an adjective; *badly* is an adverb.

Sparky is a **bad** dog.

I feel **bad** about her injury.

She limps **badly.**

being as, being that Nonstandard; do not use in formal prose. Use *because.*

beside, besides Use *beside* to mean "by the side of"; use *besides* to mean "in addition to" or "except for."

My cat likes to sit **beside** me.

Besides my cat, I have three parrots and a gerbil.

best, had best; better, had better The idioms *had best* and *had better* are often shortened in everyday speech to *best* and *better,* respectively (*You best stay. We better go*). In formal prose, use *had best* or *had better.*

between, among See **among, between.**

bias, biased *Bias* is generally a noun (the adjective *bias* refers to cloth or clothing only); *biased* is an adjective.

bring, take In general, *bring* means "to convey *toward* you" (or toward the governing point of view of the statement); *take* means "to convey *away from* you" (or away from the governing point of view of the statement).

The senator vowed to **bring** home our troops.

Don't **take** jobs out of the country.

C

calculate, figure, reckon Colloquial when used to mean "consider," "predict," or "suppose"; do not use in formal prose.

can, could *Can* expresses ability; *could* is used to make a conditional statement.

He **can** run fast.

He **could** run faster if he would work out more often.

can't hardly, couldn't hardly; can't scarcely, couldn't scarcely Double negatives; do not use.

The room was so crowded we **could scarcely** move.

can't help but Double negative; do not use in formal prose. Instead of *I can't help but ask why,* use *I cannot help asking why,* or *I can but ask why.*

capital, capitol A *capital* is a city that serves as the seat of government to a state, nation, or other political entity; a *capitol* is the specific building in which a government's legislature meets.

censor, censure *Censor* means "to remove or suppress material deemed unsuitable"; *censure* means "to strongly criticize or reprimand."

center about, center around Use *center on;* do not use *center about* or *center around.*

chair, chairperson, chairman, chairwoman When referring to a specific chairperson, be gender specific. See also p. 407.

cite, sight, site Similar sounding words with unrelated meanings. *Cite* is a verb meaning "to refer to or quote as an authority or example"; *sight* is the sense of seeing or a specific image; a *site* is a specific place.

Once again, our director **cited** Hamlet's advice to the players, and we all groaned.

The fever affected his hearing but not his **sight.**

We beheld a terrible **sight.**

The archeological **site** was damaged in the bombing.

compare to, compare with Use *compare to* when describing similarities between unlike things; use *compare with* when evaluating similarities and differences between like things.

"Shall I **compare** thee **to** a summer's day?" (Shakespeare, sonnet 18)

The committee is **comparing** the House's bill **with** the Senate's.

complement, compliment A *complement* is something that completes or makes perfect; a *compliment* is a remark of praise or admiration. Similarly, *complement* (verb) is to complete or enhance; *compliment* (verb) is to offer a remark of praise or admiration.

comprise, compose Use with care. *Comprise* means "to contain" or "to be made up of"; *compose* means "to form the substance of." Do not use *comprised of;* use *is composed of* or *consists of* instead.

The whole **comprises** the parts.

The parts **compose** the whole.

The wrestling league **comprises** ten counties throughout the state.

The wrestling league **is composed of [consists of, is made up of]** ten counties throughout the state.

conscience, conscious *Conscience* (noun) is one's inner moral compass; *conscious* (adjective) refers to the state of being awake and aware. The adjective form of *conscience* is *conscientious;* the noun form of *conscious* is *consciousness.*

continual, continually; continuous, continuously Related but distinct meanings. *Continuous* refers to something that is constantly ongoing or never stops; *continual* means "recurring regularly or frequently."

> The **continuous** roar of traffic outside my window drove me mad.
>
> Every day I make my **continual** round from home to office and back again.

could care less Illogical and nonstandard; use *couldn't care less.*

could of, should of, would of; may of, might of, must of Nonstandard; do not use. Use *could have, should have, may have, might have, must have;* or the contraction, if appropriate to your rhetorical situation.

council, counsel; councilor, counselor Similar sounding words with related but not interchangeable meanings. A *council* is a governing body. *Counsel* (noun) is advice or guidance; *counsel* (verb) is to give advice. A *councilor* is someone who is part of a council. A *counselor* is someone who gives advice.

couple of Colloquial; do not use in formal prose to mean "a few" or "several."

D

datum, data Although *data* entered English from Latin and traditional usage calls for *datum* to be used as singular and *data* as plural, most dictionaries now consider *data* a collective noun that can take a singular or plural verb depending on one's meaning.

different from, different than In general, use *different from* when the object of comparison is a noun or noun phrase. Use *different than* when the object of comparison is a clause.

> Although we look alike, my twin sister is **different from** me in interests and abilities.
>
> He remembered the incident **differently than** did his siblings.

discreet, discrete Distinguish carefully between these homonyms. *Discreet* (adjective) means "marked by prudence or self-restraint" or "unobtrusive"; *discrete* (adjective) means "separate" or "distinct."

disinterested, uninterested Use *disinterested* to mean "impartial"; use *uninterested* to mean "bored" or "not interested in."

due to the fact that Wordy; use *because.*

E

each and every Wordy and clichéd; do not use.

effect See **affect, effect.**

e.g. Abbreviation of *exemplia gratia,* which means "for instance." Avoid in formal prose; instead use *for example* or *for instance.*

elicit, illicit Similar sounding words with different meanings. The verb *elicit* means "to bring forth" or "to draw out"; the adjective *illicit* means "unlawful" or "immoral."

emigrate, immigrate, migrate *To emigrate* is to leave one's home country to settle elsewhere; to *immigrate* is to enter a new country to settle.

> After much thought, Igor decided to **immigrate** to Canada rather than to France or to the United States.
>
> Her grandmother **emigrated** from Romania in the early 1920s and came to Canada.

To *migrate* is to move from one place to another, especially in a way that is seasonal or periodic.

ensure, insure, assure While all three verbs share a general meaning of "to make sure or certain," each has a different shade of meaning. *Ensure* is the most general of the three. *Assure* refers specifically to setting someone's mind at rest, and *insure* refers specifically to taking out insurance.

> The agent **assured** us that we were **insured** against floods but suggested we build a dam to **ensure** that our home remained safe.

enthuse In formal prose, do not use as a verb (*to enthuse*) or adjectivally as a past participle (I was *enthused* about my new classes). For the adjective form, use *enthusiastic.*

et al. Abbreviation for *et alii,* which means "and others" and is used in reference to people only. Note the period after *al.* Used in source citations.

etc. Abbreviation for *et cetera,* which means "and other things." Avoid in formal prose, as it is often an indication of sloppy writing or thinking. Do not use the redundant *and etc.* Do not use *etc.* in a list introduced by *for example.*

everyday, every day *Everyday* (adjective) means "ordinary"; *every day* is an adjective-noun pair meaning "each day in a series or succession."

except See **accept, except.**

except for the fact that Wordy; do not use.

explicit, implicit *Explicit* means "fully and clearly spelled out"; *implicit* means "implied."

F

farther, further Although the traditional distinction is that *farther* is used for literal distances and *further* is used for metaphorical distances, many dictionaries note that the terms have long been used interchangeably. However, only *further* is used to mean "additional" or "moreover."

> We couldn't go any **farther** until we consulted a map.

> **Further** discussion is clearly needed.
>
> **Further,** before we can decide on this issue, more discussion is clearly needed.

fewer, less Use *fewer* with nouns that can be counted (*fewer students, fewer complaints*); use *less* with nouns that cannot be counted (*less learning, less creativity*).

figure See **calculate, figure, reckon.**

fixing to Regionalism; do not use in formal prose.

flunk Informal; do not use in formal prose. Use *fail.*

former, latter Traditionally in formal prose, *former* and *latter* are used only in referring to pairs; the first item is referred to as *the former* and the second item as *the latter.*

further See **farther, further.**

G

good, well *Good* is an adjective; *well* is an adverb.

> She has a **good** voice. She sings **well.**

H

had better See **best, had best; better, had better.**

had ought to; hadn't ought to Nonstandard; do not use in formal prose.

> He ~~had ought to~~ [ought] to apologize.
>
> He ~~hadn't ought to~~ [should not] apologize.

half Use *half a* or *a half;* do not use *a half a.*

> We bought **half a** gallon of milk.
>
> We bought **a half** gallon of milk.

hardly, scarcely Both are negatives. Do not use as part of a double negative, as in *couldn't hardly move* or *without scarcely a sound.* When used to mean "no sooner," *hardly* is accompanied by *when.*

> I could **hardly** speak.
>
> One can **scarcely** believe that this is true.
>
> I had **hardly** boarded the bus **when** it zoomed back into traffic.

he, he/she, s/he, his/her Avoid using the masculine pronoun to refer to someone whose gender remains unspecified; also avoid such awkward construction as *he/she, s/he,* or *his/her.* For alternative strategies, see pp. 406–407.

himself, herself See **myself, ourselves, yourself, yourselves, himself, herself, itself, themselves.**

hisself Regionalism; do not use in formal prose.

hopefully Standard when used to mean "in a hopeful manner," as in *We waited hopefully for signs of spring.* Controversial when used as a sentence adverb, as in *Hopefully, the bill will pass.* Avoid the latter usage in formal prose.

I

i.e. Abbreviation for *id est,* which means "that is." Avoid in formal prose. Instead, use *that is* or a similar English equivalent.

if, whether Although in informal prose *if* and *whether* are often used interchangeably, formal prose requires greater clarity and precision. For example, the statement *We'll tell you **if** you pass the test* could mean either *We'll tell you **whether** you pass the test* (i.e., we'll let you know **whether** you've passed or failed) or ***If** you pass the test, we'll tell you* (which implies that **if** you don't pass the test, we won't). In formal prose, use *if* to mean "in the event that" or "on the condition that"; use *whether* to express alternatives.

> **If** we exit now, I'm not sure **whether** we'll be going north or south.

illicit See **elicit, illicit.**

immigrate See **emigrate, immigrate, migrate.**

impact In formal prose, do not use as a verb to mean "to affect or influence."

implicit See **explicit, implicit.**

imply, infer To *imply* is to suggest without stating outright; to *infer* is to deduce or figure out.

individual, party, person In formal prose, avoid using *individual* or *party* as a general substitute for *person.* Use *individual* to contrast a single person to a group or to emphasize a person's specialness or distinction. *Party* is often used in legal contexts; *party* can also be used to mean a "participant in or accessory to an enterprise."

> Each **individual** must make his or her own choice.
>
> The ~~individual~~ [person] indicted in the cover-up pleaded not guilty.
>
> The school board will hold a hearing for ~~all individuals~~ [anyone] wanting to respond to the proposed changes.
>
> Stanwich refused to be a **party** to the governor's scheme.

infer See **imply, infer.**

insure See **ensure, insure, assure.**

irregardless Nonstandard; use *regardless.*

is when, is where, reason . . . is because Avoid in formal prose as illogical and ungrammatical. The verb *is* can be followed by a noun or adjective that renames the subject, but not by an adverbial clause.

> Plagiarism is ~~when you copy~~ copying someone else's work without proper acknowledgment.
>
> Totalitarianism is ~~where~~ the centralization of all power ~~is centralized~~ under a single authority.
>
> ~~The reason we~~ We are changing the menu ~~is~~ because so many students are now vegetarian.

its, it's *Its* (no apostrophe) is the possessive of *it*. *It's* is the contraction of *it is* or *it has*. Never use *its'*.

> **It's** a shame that the airline has canceled all **its** flights for today.

itself See **myself, ourselves, yourself, yourselves, himself, herself, itself, themselves.**

K

kind of, sort of, type of Synonyms for a group or category sharing characteristics. Do not use *kind of* or *sort of* to mean "somewhat" or "rather." Use only as necessary to your meaning, as these phrases can contribute to wordiness. Do not use *kind of a, sort of a, type of a*. Do not use without *of*, as in *This type argument is unacceptable.*

> That **type of** person is dangerous. [*type* necessary to emphasize the category itself]
>
> I enjoy eating in family~~-type~~ restaurants. [*type* unnecessary to meaning]
>
> That **kind of** ~~a~~ book is fun to read.

The plural forms are *kinds of, sorts of, types of.*

L

latter See **former, latter.**

lay, lie To *lay* is to put something down; to *lie* is to be in a lying position. The past tense of *lay* is *laid;* the past participle is *laid*. The past tense of *lie* is *lay;* the past participle is *lain.*

> Whenever I **lay** my glasses down, I lose them.
>
> Yesterday I **laid** my glasses on the table, but today I cannot find them.
>
> My great-grandmother had **laid** her hand-crocheted bedspreads in the trunk.
>
> My glasses now **lie** on my desk.
>
> Yesterday my glasses **lay** on the table, but today I cannot find them.
>
> The hand-crocheted bedspreads had **lain** in the trunk for decades before I found them.

less, fewer See **fewer, less.**

let, leave Not interchangeable. To *let* is to allow; to *leave* is to depart or to go away from. An exception is the phrase *leave me alone* or *let me alone*. Some experts accept only the former in formal prose, others accept either one.

liable to See **apt to, liable to, likely to.**

lie See **lay, lie.**

likely to See **apt to, liable to, likely to.**

literally *Literally* means "in a literal manner"; do not use to mean "really" or "actually" (*Some people are **literally** incapable of washing their own clothes*), as an intensifier before a figurative statement (*Her hair was **literally** standing on end*), or as a general intensifier (*When pressed by reporters, he **literally** said nothing*).

loose, loosen, lose To *loose* is to let loose, release, or detach; to *loosen* is to make looser; to *lose* is to misplace or be deprived of something.

lots, lots of, a lot of Informal; do not use in formal prose.

M

man, mankind When referring to people of both genders, avoid using terms that imply that everyone is male. Try using *humanity, humankind,* or *people.*

may be, maybe Related meanings but different parts of speech. The verb phrase *may be* means "might possibly be" (*The river **may be** flooding soon*). The adverb *maybe* means "perhaps" or "possibly" (***Maybe** the river will flood*).

may of See **could of, should of, would of; may of, might of, must of.**

might of See **could of, should of, would of; may of, might of, must of.**

migrate See **emigrate, immigrate, migrate.**

moral, morale As an adjective, *moral* means "ethical" or "in accord with accepted notions of right and wrong"; as a noun, a *moral* is a lesson or ethical understanding. *Morale* is one's enthusiasm for the job at hand.

> What **moral** can we draw from this example?
>
> When the union failed to win health benefits, **morale** plummeted.

must of See **could of, should of, would of; may of, might of, must of.**

myself, ourselves, yourself, yourselves, himself, herself, itself, themselves Do use correctly as reflexive or intensive pronouns; see 30b.

> Bruce cut **himself** while shaving.
>
> The president **herself** will address this fiasco.

Do not use in place of personal pronouns as either subjects or objects.

> Bonnie and ~~myself~~ I will lead the discussion.
>
> The discussion will be led by Bonnie and ~~myself~~ me.

N

nor, or In general, use *nor* in comparisons following *neither;* otherwise, use *or.*

> This movie is **neither** engaging **nor** funny.
>
> The hero is either cowardly **or** confused, but it is difficult to tell which.

nothing like, nowhere near Avoid in formal prose; use *not nearly.*

number, amount Use *number* with nouns that can be counted (*a* ***number*** *of teaspoons, the* ***number*** *of attempts, the* ***number*** *of books*); use *amount* with nouns that cannot be counted (*a small* ***amount*** *of sugar, the* ***amount*** *of effort, the* ***amount*** *of information*).

O

OK, okay Informal; do not use in formal prose.

on, upon Use *on; upon* is considered stilted in most usages.

on account of, owing to the fact that Wordy; use *because.*

on the one hand, on the other hand When using one of these transitional expressions, you should use the other. However, it's often more succinct to use *but, however, yet,* or *in contrast* instead.

or See **nor, or.**

ourselves See **myself, himself, herself, itself, ourselves, yourself, yourselves.**

owing to the fact that See **on account of, owing to the fact that.**

P

party, individual, person See **individual, party, person.**

people, person See **person, people.**

percent, percentage *Percent* is used with numbers; *percentage* is used with qualifying adjectives or when the word stands alone.

> Today, 70 **percent** of American homes boast computers.
>
> Only a small **percentage** own typewriters.

person, individual, party See **individual, party, person.**

person, people *People* is the plural of *person. Persons* is used in some idioms as the plural, such as in *missing persons.*

plenty Do not use as an adverb meaning "very" (*It's plenty hot*).

plus Standard when used as a conjunction to mean "added to" or "along with" (*Strength* ***plus*** *agility makes for a talented gymnast*). Do not use as a synonym for *and;* do not use to introduce an independent clause; do not use the phrase *plus which.*

p.m. See **a.m., p.m.**

practicable, practical *Practicable* and *practical* come from a common root and overlap in meaning. The distinction is that *practicable* connotes feasible or capable of being done, whereas *practical* connotes useful.

> While it's **practicable** to build a monorail around campus, it's not **practical.**

precede, proceed To *precede* is to go or come before; to *proceed* is to continue or go forward, either literally or figuratively. (A helpful mnemonic device is to remember that *precede* shares root meanings with *precedent* while *proceed* shares root meanings with *procession.*)

> John's interview **preceded** Mary's.
>
> We will **proceed** with these hearings tomorrow.

prejudice, prejudiced *Prejudice* is a noun; *prejudiced* an adjective.

pretty Traditionally considered colloquial when used as an adverb meaning "fairly" or "somewhat" (*pretty difficult*). While this usage is now listed as standard in some dictionaries, be aware that such qualifications as *very, pretty,* or *nearly* tend to weaken your prose.

previous to, prior to Awkward and wordy; use *before.*

principal, principle Similar sounding words that have no meanings in common. *Principal* as both a noun and an adjective is related to *main* (*Brazil's* ***principal*** *exports are its most important exports; the* ***principal*** *is the leading authority in a school*). *Principle* is a noun only and means "an underlying rule or law" (*He couldn't eat meat without violating his* ***principles***). A helpful, if clichéd, mnemonic device is "The principal is your pal."

proceed See **precede, proceed.**

Q

question of whether, question as to whether Wordy; use *whether.*

quote, quotation Use *quote* as a verb and *quotation* as a noun.

> I **quoted** the author three times.
>
> I used three **quotations** in my essay.

R

raise, rise *Raise* is a transitive verb (a verb that takes an object) meaning "to lift."

Rise is an intransitive verb (a verb that does not take an object) meaning "to move upward."

Every spring, the melting snow **raises** the water level in the creek.

The creek **rises** every spring when the snow thaws.

rarely ever Do not use in formal prose; use *rarely.*

real, really *Real* is an adjective; *really* is an adverb. Do not use *real* to mean "very."

reason . . . is because See **is when, is where, reason . . . is because.**

reckon See **calculate, figure, reckon.**

respectful, respective *Respectful* means "full of respect"; *respective* means "particular" or "in the order given."

rise See **raise, rise.**

S

scarcely See **hardly, scarcely.**

shall, will *Shall* is rarely used in American English, except in legal contexts and in phrasing polite questions such as *"Shall I bring you a menu?"* or *"Shall we go?"*

should of See **could of, should of, would of; may of, might of, must of.**

site See **cite, sight, site.**

so Do not use as an intensifier unless it is part of an overall phrase such as a *so . . . that* phrase (*She was so drunk that she couldn't walk*).

someplace Informal; do not use in formal prose. Instead use *somewhere.*

sometime, sometimes, some time *Sometime* is an adverb meaning "at an indefinite time"; *sometimes* is an adverb meaning "now and then." In the phrase *some time, some* is an adjective modifying the noun *time.*

I'll see you **sometime** tomorrow.

She **sometimes** walked in the park.

It will be **some time** before he fully recovers.

sort of, kind of, type of See **kind of, sort of, type of.**

stationary, stationery *Stationary* is an adjective meaning "not moving"; *stationery* is a noun meaning "writing paper."

suppose to, supposed to Do not drop the final consonant; use *supposed to.*

sure, surely *Sure* is an adjective; *surely* is an adverb. Do not use *sure* as an adverb meaning "surely" or "certainly."

T

take, bring See **bring, take.**

than, then *Than* is a conjunction used to make comparisons; *then* is an adverb that expresses time.

that, which, who See **who, which, that.**

their, there, they're Similar sounding words with different meanings. *Their* is a possessive pronoun; *there* is an adverb meaning "in that place"; *they're* is a contraction of *they are.*

They lost **their** house in the storm.

If it's not **there,** look elsewhere.

They're excited to be moving.

theirself, theirselves, themself Nonstandard; use *themselves.*

themselves See **myself, ourselves, yourself, yourselves, himself, herself, itself, themselves.**

then, than See **than, then.**

thru No such word; use *through.*

toward, towards American usage is *toward;* British usage is *towards.*

try and Nonstandard; use *try to.*

type of See **kind of, sort of, type of.**

U

uninterested See **disinterested, uninterested.**

unique *Unique* means "one of a kind," so something that is *unique* cannot be *more unique, less unique, very unique,* or *quite unique.*

upon See **on, upon.**

use to, used to Do not drop the final consonant; use *used to.*

V

very Do not overuse.

W

wait for, wait on To *wait for* someone is to be in expectation of that person's arrival; to *wait on* someone is to serve that person.

ways In formal prose, use *way,* not *ways,* in such contexts as *We're a long way from home.*

weather, whether Similar sounding words with entirely unrelated meanings. *Weather* (noun) is what makes you bring your umbrella or slather on suntan oil; *whether* is a conjunction used to introduce alternatives (*She didn't know* ***whether*** *to order chocolate or vanilla ice cream*).

well See **good, well.**

were, we're *Were* is a past tense form of *to be; we're* is the contraction of *we are.*

where Do not use for *that,* as in *I read in the newspaper where he had been voted out of office.*

whether, if See **if, whether.**

whether or not In general, the *or not* is considered to be superfluous in formal prose. Better to use *whether* unless your meaning is "regardless of whether" (*We'll play soccer this Saturday* ***whether or not*** *it snows*). However, many writers defend the redundancy of *or not* as a legitimate means of creating emphasis.

who, which, that Use *who* for people and named animals; use *which* or *that* for objects, unnamed animals, and abstract concepts. See 33q. Use *that* for restrictive clauses; use *which* for nonrestrictive clauses.

> Books **that** bore me don't get read. [I only read books that I like.]
>
> Books, **which** bore me, don't get read. [I find all books boring and don't read any of them.]

who, whom Use *who* as a subject; use *whom* as an object. Case is governed by the word's grammatical function within its clause, not by that clause's grammatical function in the sentence as a whole. See 33f.

> I was delighted to interview a man **who** had entertained so many.
>
> I was eager to interview a man **whom** so many had vilified.

whose, who's Similar sounding words with different meanings. *Whose* is a possessive pronoun (***Whose*** *dog is this?); who's* is a contraction of *who is* (*my aunt,* ***who's*** *living in Boston now*). *Whose* may be used to refer to things as well as people.

will, shall See **shall, will.**

would of See **could of, should of, would of; may of, might of, must of.**

Y

your, you're *Your* is a possessive pronoun (*Your dog is biting my leg*); *you're* is a contraction of *you are*.

yourself, yourselves See **myself, ourselves, yourself, yourselves, himself, herself, itself, themselves.**

These pages constitute an extension of the copyright page. We have made every effort to trace the ownership of all copyrighted material and to secure permission from copyright holders. In the event of any question arising as to the use of any material, we will be pleased to make the necessary corrections in future printings. Thanks are due to the following authors, publishers, and agents for permission to use the material indicated.

Text Credits

Chapter 3. 43: Angela Garrison, "From Over There to Over Here: War Blogs Get Up Close, Personal, and Profitable." Used with permission.

Chapter 4. 52: Excerpt from Steven Johnson, "Tool for Thought," *New York Times,* January 30, 2005. Copyright © 2005 New York Times Co. Inc. Used with permission.

Chapter 5. 63: William Carlos Williams, from "The Red Wheelbarrow" from COLLECTED POEMS: 1909-1939, VOLUME I. Copyright 1938 by New Directions Publishing Corp. Reprinted by permission of New Directions Publishing Corp.

Chapter 8. 93: Eugene Rhee, Resume. Used with permission.

Chapter 9. 119: Excerpt from Kellie Bartlett, "A Glance at the February 5 Issue of *Neuron:* Seeing but not believing—or not noticing," *The Chronicle of Higher Education,* 2/10/04. Copyright © 2004 The Chronicle of Higher Education. Reprinted with permission. **121:** Lambert, Hogan, and Barton, "Collegiate Academic Dishonesty Revisited" from www.sociology.org, September 2004. **125:** "Ethics and Discussion" overview from www.savingsandclone.com. Copyright © 2005 Genetic Savings & Clone. Used with permission. **127:** Excerpt from Kamil Skawinski, "IT & SETI: The Role of Computer Technology in the Search for Extraterrestrial Intelligence," *California Computer News,* July 2, 2002. Copyright © 2002 by Kamil Z. Skawinski. Used with permission.

Chapter 12. 157: Tim Berners-Lee et al., "The Semantic Web," *Scientific American,* May 2001. Copyright © 2001. Used with permission. **176:** Pamela LiCalzi O'Connell, "Blog Bog and an E-mail Pony Express," 10/23/03. Copyright © 2003 New York Times Co. Inc. Used with permission.

Chapter 13. 231: Molly McClure, "Get a Life! Misconceptions about the Tolkien Fan Fiction Culture." Used with permission.

Chapter 14. 269: Jenny Chow, Mira Zaharopoulos, Nancy Huynh, and Xin Xin Wu, "Constellations of Parental Risk Factors Associated with Child Maltreatment." Used with permission.

Chapter 20. 330: "10 Tips for Successful Public Speaking." Reprinted with permission by Toastmasters International.

Chapter 22. 356: Core techniques for Web Content Accessibility Guidelines 1.0. Copyright © 2000 World Wide Web Consortium (Massachusetts Institute of Technology, European Research Consortium for Informatics and Mathematics, Keio University). All Rights Reserved. **360:** "Diverse Contexts for Visiting a Website" from www.w3.org/TR/WAI-WEBCONTENT. Copyright © 2000 World Wide Web Consortium (Massachusetts Institute of Technology, European Research Consortium for Informatics and Mathematics, Keio University). All Rights Reserved. **361:** "W3C Priority 1 Principles of Accessibility." Copyright © 2000 World Wide Web Consortium (Massachusetts Institute of Technology, European Research Consortium for Informatics and Mathematics, Keio University). All Rights Reserved.

Chapter 25. 398: Cary Tennis, "Since you asked . . .," 4/14/05, *Salon.com.* Copyright © 2005 Salon, Inc. Used with permission.

Chapter 28. 401: Definitions of "tummy" and "tummy tuck" from *The American Heritage Dictionary of the English Language,* Fourth Edition. Copyright © 2000 by Houghton Mifflin Company. Reproduced with permission. **402:** Definition of "easy" from *The American Heritage Dictionary of the English Language,* Fourth Edition. Copyright © 2000 by Houghton Mifflin Company. Reproduced with permission. **403:** Judith Cofer, excerpt from *The Latin Deli: Prose and Poetry.* Copyright © 1993 Judith Cofer. Reprinted by permission of the University of Georgia Press.

Image Credits

Chapter 1. 2: © Images.com/CORBIS **4:** top left, © Jose Luis Pelaez, Inc./CORBIS; top right, © Paul Edmondson/CORBIS; center left, © Ariel Skelley/CORBIS; center right, Lucky Look/Danita Delimont; bottom left, David Young-Wolff/PhotoEdit; bottom right, © Tom Stewart/CORBIS

Chapter 4. 49: © Willie Hill, Jr./ The Image Works

Chapter 6. 65: top, © 1993 Universal City Studios, Inc. and Amblin Entertainment, Inc.; bottom, © Photofest, Inc. **66**: top, National Gallery of Australia, Canberra. © 2005 The Pollock-Krasner Foundation/Artists Rights Society (ARS), New York; bottom, Photograph by Ansel Adams. Collection Center for Creative Photography, University of Arizona. © Trustees of the Ansel Adams Publishing Rights Trust **67**: © AP Photo/Alan Diaz **68**: top left, R.G. Ojeda. Réunion des Musées Nationaux/Art Resource, NY; bottom, © Robert Holmes/CORBIS **69**: top, Web design by Hello Design; © 2003 whiteground Ltd. Site owned by Eyestorm Britart; bottom left, Ambigram copyright © 1985 by John Langdon. www.johnlangdon.net. Used by permission; bottom right, Logo designed by Michael Buchmiller in consultation with Guillermo Nericcio Garcia. Used with permission of Hyperbole Books.

Chapter 7. 73: Gary Conner/PhotoEdit, Inc. **76:** top and center, Bill Aron/ PhotoEdit, Inc.; bottom, Colin Young-Wolff/PhotoEdit, Inc.

Chapter 8. 88: top, © Chuck Savage/ CORBIS; bottom and center left, © Dennis MacDonald/PhotoEdit, Inc.; center right, © Michael A. Keller/zefa/ CORBIS

Chapter 9. 100: del.icio.us and del.icio.us logo are trademarks of Yahoo! Inc. Reproduced with permission of Yahoo! Inc. **103:** © Skjold/The Image Works **110:** top, © Michael St. Maur Sheil/CORBIS; center, akg-images; William Faulkner Collection, Special Collections, University of Virginia Library; bottom, © Deborah Davis/PhotoEdit, Inc. **112:** top, © 1958 Universal City Studios, Inc. for Samuel Taylor and Patricia Hitchcock O'Connell as trustees. Courtesy of Universal Studios Licensing LLLP; center left, © Bettmann/ CORBIS; center right, © CORBIS SYGMA; bottom, © Lightscapes Photography, Inc./CORBIS **114:** top, © Bettmann/ CORBIS; center left, © Ruth Orkin/Getty Images; center right, Courtesy of the Albert Einstein Archives, Jewish National & University Library, Hebrew University of Jerusalem, Israel; bottom, © Gerrit Greve/CORBIS **115:** © Getty Images Entertainment/Getty Images **116:** top, © Philip Gould/CORBIS; center left, © Images.com/CORBIS; center right, © Royalty-Free/CORBIS; bottom, © Michael Keller/CORBIS **118:** top, © Images.com/CORBIS; center left, © LWA-Stephen Walstead/CORBIS; center right, © Royalty-Free/CORBIS; bottom, © CORBIS **119:** Reprinted from *Neuron,* Vol. 41, No. 3, 2004, 'The Neural Fate of Consciously Perceived and Missed Events in the Attentional Blink,' page 467, with permission from Elsevier. **120:** top, © Images.com/CORBIS; center left, © Ed Bock/CORBIS; center right, © 2005 Pew Internet & American Life Project; U.S. Census Bureau; bottom, © Royalty-Free/CORBIS **122:** top, © Museum of the City of New York/CORBIS; © Seth Joel/ CORBIS; center left, © LWA-Stephen Westead/CORBIS; center right, © Roger Ressmeyer/CORBIS; © Andrew Brookes/ CORBIS; bottom left, © Bettmann/ CORBIS; Courtesy Camino Books, Inc. **124:** top, Courtesy NHGRI; center left, © David Pollack/CORBIS; center right, © Charles Gupton/CORBIS; © Andrew Brookes/CORBIS; bottom, Courtesy of Oak Ridge National Laboratory, managed for DOE by UT-Battelle, LLC.**125:** © Kim Kulish/CORBIS **126:** top, NASA; center left, © Thom Lang/CORBIS; center right, © NASA/Roger Ressmeyer/CORBIS; © Roger Ressmeyer/CORBIS; bottom, NASA/HST/ASU/J. Hester et al. **127:** Courtesy SETI@home.

Chapter 10. 128: Reproduced with permission of Yahoo! Inc. © 2005 by Yahoo! Inc. **135:** © Amazon.com, Inc. All Rights Reserved. **140:** top, http://www .martinlutherking.org; bottom, © 2004 - The King Center - Atlanta, GA.

Chapter 11. 148: Copyright © 2005, Endeavor Information Systems Incorporated. All rights reserved. Screen shot of Endeavor's Voyager Product.

Chapter 12. 168: top, NASA/Comstock RF; bottom, © BananaStock RF **169:** top, Linear/Peter Arnold, Inc; bottom, © Dennis di Cicco/CORBIS

Chapter 13. 180: © Copyright 2006 Podcast Networks (TM). All Microsoft product screen shot(s) reprinted with permission from Microsoft Corporation.

Chapter 18. 313: © Chuck Savage/ CORBIS

Chapter 19. 315: © 1958 Universal City Studios, Inc. for Samuel Taylor and Patricia Hitchcock O'Connell as trustees. Courtesy of Universal Studios Licensing LLLP **316:** top, Courtesy of Jennifer Sterling; bottom, Courtesy of EMI **317:** Image reproduced with permission of copyright owner, Temple University. All rights reserved. **320:** top, istockphoto.com; center, © Frans Lanting/CORBIS; bottom, © Mark Bolton/CORBIS

Chapter 21. 332: www.musicforamerica .org **334:** Microsoft product screen shot(s) reprinted with permission from Microsoft Corporation. **338:** top, Mail screenshot reprinted by permission from Apple Computer, Inc.; bottom, Finder screenshot reprinted by permission from Apple Computer, Inc. **339:** Mail screenshot reprinted by permission from Apple Computer, Inc. **345:** Drupal.org **351:** MOO provided by the author. enCore Copyright © Sindre Sarensen and Jan Rune Holmevik

Chapter 22. 352: Dynamic Graphics Group/Creatas/Alamy **353:** Justin Pumfrey/Getty Images **359:** The Writing Instructor, Sept. 2001, www.writinginstructor.com/columns/absolutwriting/index.html

Chapter 23. 362: © David Raymer/CORBIS **371:** Library of Congress

Chapter 24. 382: © 826 Valencia

Chapter 28. 412: © Bob Rowan; Progressive Image/CORBIS

Chapter 37. 476: © Lionhead Studios Limited

Chapter 44. 510: Halo 2 (TM) copyright Bungie Studios, a division of Microsoft Corporation. This Spartan Life copyright Damian Lacedaemion

Chapter 47. 534: Wikipedia.org

Trademarks

Product names may be trademarks of their respective owners and they are used for identification purposes only. All other trademarks contained herein are the property of their respective owners.

A9 is a trademark of A9.com, Inc. or its affiliates in the United States and other countries.

Adaptec Toast and ZIP are registered trademarks of Iomega Corporation.

Adobe Acrobat, Adobe Garamond, GoLive, InDesign, Illustrator, Photoshop, Photoshop Elements, Premiere, Reader, and SoundEdit are registered trademarks or trademarks of Adobe Systems Incorporated in the United States and/or other countries.

Amazon, Amazon.com, and the Amazon.com logo are registered trademarks of Amazon.com, Inc. or its affiliates.

AOL and AIM are registered trademarks of America Online, Inc. The AIM Instant Message design and "look and feel" © 2005 by America Online, Inc. The America Online content, name, icons and trademarks are used with permission.

Apple Mac, Final Cut Pro, iMovie, iTunes, QuickTime, and Safari are registered trademarks of Apple Computer, Inc. Apple Garage Band, iSight, Keynote, Finder, Spotlight, and Geneva are trademarks of Apple Computer, Inc.

Arial, Century Gothic and Times New Roman are trademarks of The Monotype Corporation registered in the US Patent and Trademark Office and elsewhere.

The Ask logo and other Ask logos and product and service names are service marks or trademarks of IAC Search & Media.

Avery Design Pro Limited is a trademark of Avery Dennison Corporation.

Blackboard is a trademark or registered trademark of Blackboard Inc. in the United States and/or other countries.

Boing Boing is a trademark of Happy Mutants LLC in the United States [and other countries].

The Clusty mark belongs to Vivísimo, Inc., and is protected by trademark laws.

Corel WordPerfect and CorelDRAW are registered trademarks of Corel Corporation and/or its subsidiaries in Canada, the United States and/or other countries.

Dogpile is a registered trademark of InfoSpace, Inc.

EarthLink is a registered trademark of EarthLink, Inc.

Eudora is a registered trademark of QUALCOMM Incorporated.

ExpressionEngine is a registered trademark of pMachine, Inc.

Final Draft is a registered trademark of Final Draft, Inc.

FirstClass is a registered trademark of Open Text Corporation.

FrameForge 3D Studio is a registered trademark of FrameForge 3D Studio.

Friendster is a service mark of Friendster, Inc.

Google Desktop Search, Google Directory, Google Glossary, Google Groups, Google Images, Gmail, Google News, Google Print, Google Scholar, Google Toolbar, Google Zeitgeist, Blogger and Orkut online community are trademarks of Google, Inc.

Groupee and the Groupee logo are trademarks of Groupee Systems Incorporated.

Helvetica, Palatino, and Times are registered trademarks of Linotype Corporation.

HyperSnap is a trademark of Hyperionics, Inc.

ICQ is a registered trademark of ICQ, Inc. and America Online, Inc.

ITC Garamond and ITC Zapf Dingbats are registered trademarks of International Typeface Corporation.

The registered trademark Linux® is used pursuant to a license from Linus Torvalds, owner of the mark in the U.S. and other countries.

LISTSERV is a registered trademark licensed to L-Soft International, Inc.

LiveJournal is a trademark of LiveJournal in the United States.

Macromedia, Breeze, Dreamweaver, Fireworks, Flash, and SoundEdit are trademarks or registered trademarks of Macromedia, Inc. in the United States and/or other countries.

Mamma is a registered trademark of Mamma.com, Inc.

Microsoft, Windows, Entourage, Front Page, Hotmail, Internet Explorer, MSN Chat, NetMeeting, Outlook, PowerPoint, MSN Search, and Word are registered trademarks of Microsoft Corporation in the United States and/or other countries. Georgia and Verdana are trademarks of Microsoft Corporation registered in the U.S. Patent & Trademark Office and may be registered in other jurisdictions.

The name Moodle is a trademark and/or registered trademark of The Moodle Trust in the U.S. and other countries.

Moveable Type and TypePad are registered trademarks of Six Apart in the United States.

Movie Magic is a registered trademark of Screenplay Systems, Inc.

Mozilla, Firefox, Thunderbird, Mozilla Mail are trademarks or registered trademarks of the Mozilla Foundation.

Nero is a registered trademark of Nero AG.

Netscape, Netscape Navigator, Netscape Composer, the Netscape N and Ship's Wheel logos are registered trademarks of Netscape Communications Corporation in the United States and other countries.

Nvu is a trademark of Linspire, Inc.

Palm OS and Palm Powered are trademarks or registered trademarks of PalmSource, Inc. or its affiliates, or its licensor, Palm Trademark Holding Company, in the United States, France, Germany, Japan, the United Kingdom, and other countries. All rights reserved.

Pinnacle Studio is a trademark of Pinnacle Systems, Inc. in the United States and/or other countries.

Roxio is a trademark of Roxio, a division of Sonic Solutions which may be registered in some jurisdictions.

SecureFX is a registered trademark of VanDyke Software, Inc.

Skype is a trademark of Skype Technologies SA.

UNIX is a registered trademark of the Open Group.

USB is a trademark of Universal Serial Buss Implementers Forum, Inc.

ViaVideo is a trademark of Polycom, Inc. in the US and various countries.

WebCT is a registered trademark in the U.S. Patent and Trademark Office and in the European Union of WebCT, Inc. in the United States and other jurisdictions.

Wikipedia is a registered trademark of the Wikimedia Foundation, Inc.

WriteNote is a registered trademark of Cengage Learning.

XANGA is a registered trademark of Xanga.com, Inc.

YAHOO!, del.icio.us, and the YAHOO! logo are trademarks of Yahoo! Inc.

URLs

Every effort has been made to verify the authenticity and sources of the URLs listed in this book. All URLs were correctly linked to their websites at the time of publication. Due to the quickly evolving nature of the Internet, it is possible that a link may break or a URL may change or become obsolete.Should you discover any inconsistencies, please contact **academic.cengage.com/support/** and a correction will be made for the next printing.

Section numbers are printed in blue. They correspond to the tabs on the outside top of each page of the handbook. Black numbers are page numbers, which you will find at the bottom of each page. Topics of interest to multilingual writers are followed by the designation (ESL).

C

D

E

G

H

I

N

O

P

Q

R

S

U

Y

Z

iting Symbols

r teacher writes . . .	It means . . .	See . . .
	Change the adjective or its form (degree)	Chapter 36
rder	Change the order of adjectives	Section 50c
	Change the adverb or its form (degree)	Chapter 36
	Problem with subject-verb or pronoun-antecedent agreement	Chapter 35 & sections 33h–33l
r *det*	Add, omit, or change an article (determiner)	Chapter 48
	Awkward phrasing; rewrite	Part 8
bold	Make boldface (use dark letters)	
	Close up the space	
	Add or change the conjunction	Chapter 26
	Two or more independent clauses are joined with only a comma	Chapter 32
	Delete the letters or words	
	Modifier doesn't have anything to modify	Section 36k
	Sentence lacks something it needs to be complete	Chapter 31
	Make italic (use slanted letters)	
	Insert	
	Insert space	
d / through letter	Make the letter lowercase	Chapter 44
	Modifier is in the wrong place	Sections 36h–j
	Problem with a modifier	Chapter 36
al	Add, omit, or change a modal auxiliary verb	Section 49e
	Start a new paragraph	
	Use parallel phrasing	Chapter 25
ive	Use or don't use the passive voice	Section 34f
or *pron*	Error in pronoun usage	Chapter 33
agr	Pronoun and antecedent don't agree in number	Sections 33i–33l
ref or *ref*	Not clear to which other word your pronoun points	Sections 33m–33q
	Two or more independent clauses are joined without punctuation	Chapter 32
t	Language usage excludes one gender	Section 29a
	Incorrect spelling	Chapter 46
gr	Subject and verb don't agree in number	Chapter 35
e or *VT*	Incorrect verb tense	Section 34d
	Switch the order of the letters or words enclosed	
r *cap* or ≡	Capitalize the letter	Chapter 44
ge	Use a more accurate word	Glossary of Usage
or *vary*	Vary the sentence structures	Chapter 27
or *vb*	Problem with verb	Chapters 34 & 49
r *word*	Better word choice needed	Chapters 28 & 29
dy	Make more concise	Chapter 27